Kia Sedona Automotive Repair Manual

by Jeff Killingsworth
and John H Haynes
Member of the Guild of Motoring Writers

Models covered:
All Kia Sedona models - 2002 through 2014

ABCDE
FGHIJ
KLMNO
PQRS

Haynes Publishing Group
Sparkford Nr Yeovil
Somerset BA22 7JJ England

Haynes North America, Inc
859 Lawrence Drive
Newbury Park
California 91320 USA
www.haynes.com

A book in the Haynes Automotive Repair Manual Series

Printed in Malaysia

ISBN-13: 978-1-62092-149-4

ISBN-10: 1-62092-149-9

Library of Congress Control Number: 2016934579

16-288

Contents

Introductory pages

About this manual	0-5
Introduction	0-5
Vehicle identification numbers	0-6
Recall information	0-7
Buying parts	0-9
Maintenance techniques, tools and working facilities	0-9
Jacking and towing	0-16
Booster battery (jump) starting	0-17
Automotive chemicals and lubricants	0-18
Conversion factors	0-19
Fraction/decimal/millimeter equivalents	0-20
Safety first!	0-21
Troubleshooting	0-22

Chapter 1
Tune-up and routine maintenance **1-1**

Chapter 2 Part A
V6 engines **2A-1**

Chapter 2 Part B
General engine overhaul procedures **2B-1**

Chapter 3
Cooling, heating and air conditioning systems **3-1**

Chapter 4
Fuel and exhaust systems **4-1**

Chapter 5
Engine electrical systems **5-1**

Chapter 6
Emissions and engine control systems **6-1**

Chapter 7
Automatic transaxle **7-1**

Chapter 8
Driveaxles **8-1**

Chapter 9
Brakes **9-1**

Chapter 10
Suspension and steering systems **10-1**

Chapter 11
Body **11-1**

Chapter 12
Chassis electrical system **12-1**

Wiring diagrams **12-17**

Index **IND-1**

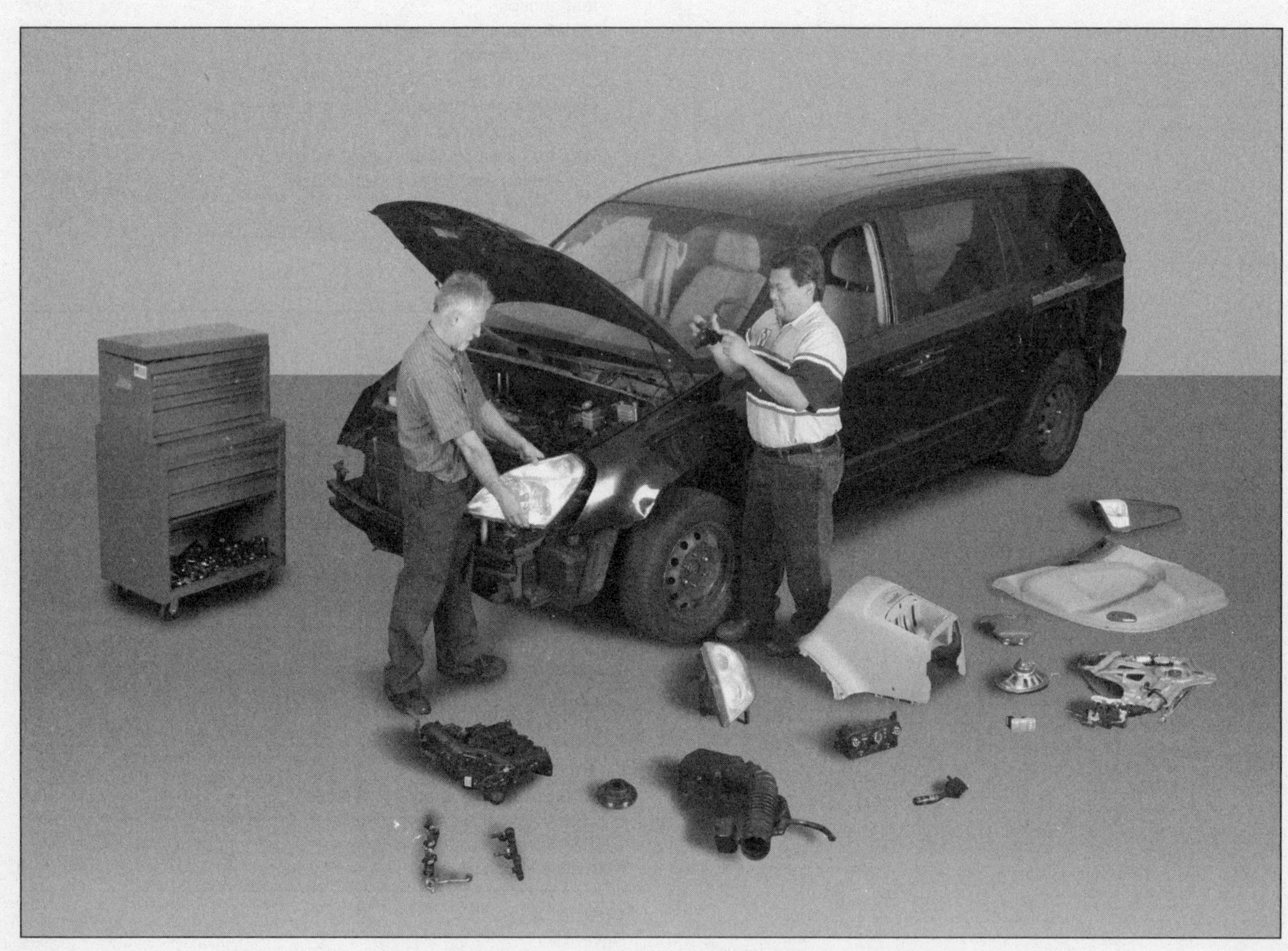

Haynes photographer and mechanic with a 2006 Kia Sedona

About this manual

Its purpose

The purpose of this manual is to help you get the best value from your vehicle. It can do so in several ways. It can help you decide what work must be done, even if you choose to have it done by a dealer service department or a repair shop; it provides information and procedures for routine maintenance and servicing; and it offers diagnostic and repair procedures to follow when trouble occurs.

We hope you use the manual to tackle the work yourself. For many simpler jobs, doing it yourself may be quicker than arranging an appointment to get the vehicle into a shop and making the trips to leave it and pick it up. More importantly, a lot of money can be saved by avoiding the expense the shop must pass on to you to cover its labor and overhead costs. An added benefit is the sense of satisfaction and accomplishment that you feel after doing the job yourself.

Using the manual

The manual is divided into Chapters. Each Chapter is divided into numbered Sections, which are headed in bold type between horizontal lines. Each Section consists of consecutively numbered paragraphs.

The reference numbers used in illustration captions pinpoint the pertinent Section and the Step within that Section. That is, illustration 3.2 means the illustration refers to Section 3 and Step (or paragraph) 2 within that Section.

Procedures, once described in the text, are not normally repeated. When it's necessary to refer to another Chapter, the reference will be given as Chapter and Section number. Cross references given without use of the word "Chapter" apply to Sections and/or paragraphs in the same Chapter. For example, "see Section 8" means in the same Chapter.

References to the left or right side of the vehicle assume you are sitting in the driver's seat, facing forward.

Even though we have prepared this manual with extreme care, neither the publisher nor the author can accept responsibility for any errors in, or omissions from, the information given.

NOTE

A **Note** provides information necessary to properly complete a procedure or information which will make the procedure easier to understand.

CAUTION

A **Caution** provides a special procedure or special steps which must be taken while completing the procedure where the Caution is found. Not heeding a Caution can result in damage to the assembly being worked on.

WARNING

A **Warning** provides a special procedure or special steps which must be taken while completing the procedure where the Warning is found. Not heeding a Warning can result in personal injury.

Introduction

This manual covers 2002 through 2012 and 2014 Kia Sedona models. These vehicles are equipped with either a 3.5L V6 timing belt engine (2005 and earlier), a 3.8L V6 timing chain engine (2006 through 2010) or a 3.5L V6 timing chain engine (2011 and later).

All models are front wheel drive (FWD); the engine drives the front wheels through either a five or six-speed automatic transaxle via independent driveaxles.

The chassis is of unibody construction, with independent suspension on the front end, using strut/coil spring units. On 2005 and earlier models a semi-independent beam-type axle at the rear is used, with individual coil springs and shock absorbers. On 2006 and later models a fully independent multi-link rear suspension is used, with individual coil springs and shock absorbers. A hydraulically assisted rack-and-pinion power steering gear is mounted on the subframe.

The brakes are disc at the front and either drum (2005 and earlier models) or disc (2006 and later models) at the rear. Power assist is standard on all models. An Anti-lock Brake System (ABS) is standard equipment on some models and is available as an option on some others.

Vehicle identification numbers

Modifications are a continuing and unpublicized process in vehicle manufacturing. Since spare parts manuals and lists are compiled on a numerical basis, the individual vehicle numbers are essential to correctly identify the component required.

Vehicle Identification Number (VIN)

This very important identification number is stamped on a plate attached to the dashboard inside the windshield on the driver's side of the vehicle (see illustration). It can also be found on the certification label located on the driver's side door post and on the right (passenger's) side of the firewall. The VIN also appears on the Vehicle Certificate of Title and Registration. It contains information such as where and when the vehicle was manufactured, the model year and the body style.

VIN engine and model year codes

Two particularly important pieces of information found in the VIN are the engine code and the model year code. Counting from the left, the engine code designation is the 8th digit and the model year code designation is the 10th digit.

On the models covered by this manual the engine codes are:

1 3.5L DOHC V6, 2004 and earlier (Sigma)
2 3.5L DOHC V6, 2005 (Sigma)
3 3.8L DOHC V6, 2006-2010 (Lambda)
7 3.5L DOHC V6, 2011 and later (Lambda II)

On the models covered by this manual the model year codes are:

2.......................... 2002
3.......................... 2003
4.......................... 2004
5.......................... 2005
6.......................... 2006
7.......................... 2007
8.......................... 2008
9.......................... 2009
A.......................... 2010
B.......................... 2011
C.......................... 2012
E.......................... 2014

Certification label

The certification label is attached to the driver's door post (see illustration). The plate contains the name of the manufacturer, the month and year of production, the Gross Vehicle Weight Rating (GVWR), the Gross Axle Weight Rating (GAWR) and the certification statement.

Engine identification number

The engine identification number is located on the front left end (driver's side) of the engine block (see illustration).

Transaxle identification number

The transaxle identification number is stamped into a machined pad on the top of the transaxle case (see illustration).

Vehicle Emissions Control Information (VECI) label

The emissions control information label is found on the underside of the hood (see illustration). This label contains information on the emissions control equipment installed on the vehicle, and, in some cases, a vacuum diagram.

3.2 The Vehicle Identification Number (VIN) is located on a plate on top of the dash (visible through the windshield)

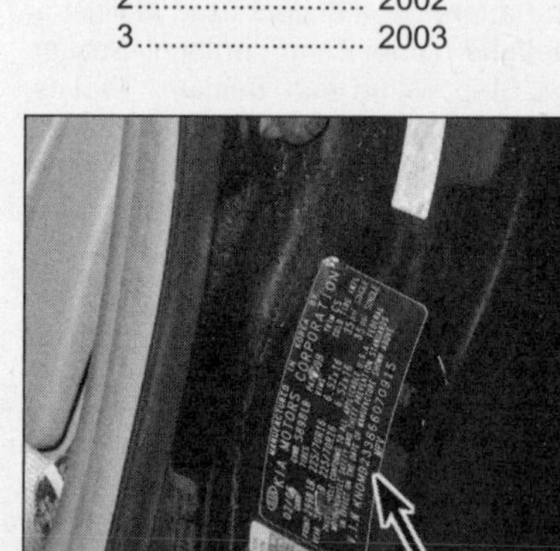

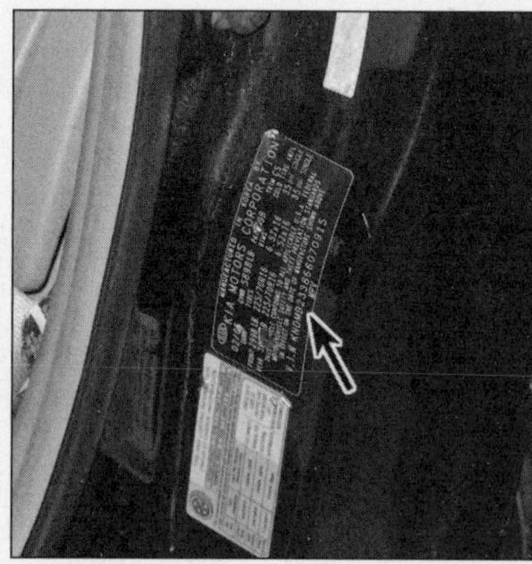

3.6 The vehicle certification label is located on the driver's door post

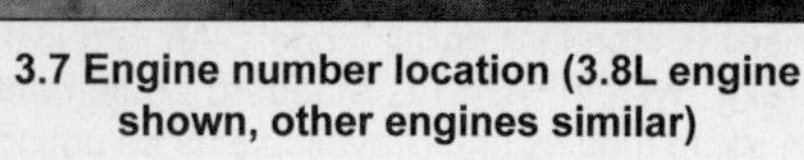

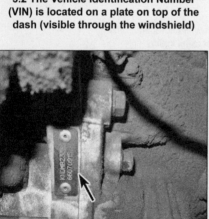

3.7 Engine number location (3.8L engine shown, other engines similar)

3.8 Location of the transaxle identification number

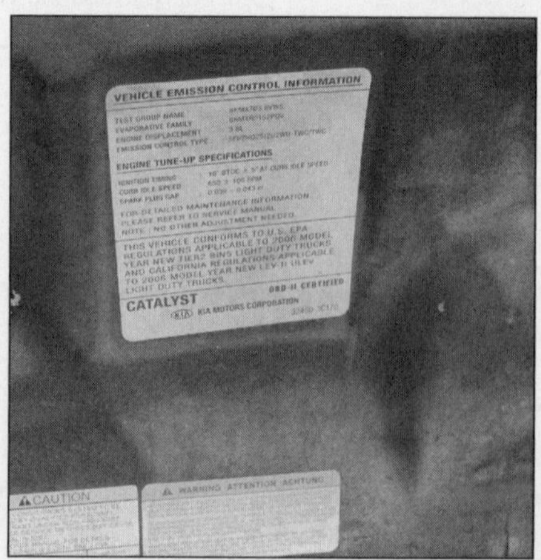

3.9 VECI label

Recall information

Vehicle recalls are carried out by the manufacturer in the rare event of a possible safety-related defect. The vehicle's registered owner is contacted at the address on file at the Department of Motor Vehicles and given the details of the recall. Remedial work is carried out free of charge at a dealer service department.

If you are the new owner of a used vehicle which was subject to a recall and you want to be sure that the work has been carried out, it's best to contact a dealer service department and ask about your individual vehicle - you'll need to furnish them your Vehicle Identification Number (VIN).

The table below is based on information provided by the National Highway Traffic Safety Administration (NHTSA), the body which oversees vehicle recalls in the United States. The recall database is updated constantly. For the latest information on vehicle recalls, check the NHTSA website at www.nhtsa.gov, www.safercar.gov, or call the NHTSA hotline at 1-888-327-4236.

Recall date	Recall campaign number	Model(s) affected	Concern
JAN 22, 2003	03V017000	2002 Sedona	Some models fail to comply with the requirements of FMVSS No. 209, "seat belt assemblies." the second and third seat belt buckle anchor bolts do not comply with the standards. In the event of a vehicle crash, the occupant may not be properly restrained.
APR 03, 2003	03V135000	2002 Sedona	Some of the second and third row seat strikers installed on the vehicle floor pan have been improperly heat treated and could break in a crash. This could result in injuries to occupants of these seats.
APR 25, 2003	03V158000	2003 Sedona	On some vehicles, there was a programming error in the Anti-lock Braking System (ABS) electronic control module logic. The programming error could cause reduced braking force at speeds below 25 mph, which could result in increased stopping distances. Such increased stopping distances could result in a crash.
JAN 19 2005	05V013000	2002, 2003 Sedona	On some models, the throttle cable would twist itself out of position. This can allow the cable to hang up, which could result in a crash.
MAY 19, 2005	05V232000	2003, 2004, 2005 Sedona	On some models equipped with alloy wheels, moisture can accumulate around the rear hub caps causing damage to the outer wheel bearing. Wheel bearing failure may occur without warning which could result in a crash.
JUL 20, 2005	05V329000	2003, 2004, 2005 Sedona	On some models, freezing conditions can cause water on the throttle cable to freeze during normal operation. Resistance to movement of the throttle cable can occur when the driver lifts their foot off of the gas pedal. This can cause the cable to stick, thus preventing the engine from returning to idle and causing the vehicle to maintain speed or accelerate. Such an event can occur without warning and could cause a crash.

Recall date	Recall campaign number	Model(s) affected	Concern
OCT 05, 2005	05V463000	2002, 2003, 2004 Sedona EX	On some vehicles equipped with power seats, the wiring under the front seats could be misrouted, allowing contact with metal seat components. This contact could eventually result in a short circuit condition that may result in a fire in the junction box area of the vehicle.
JUL 19, 2006	06V265000	2006 Sedona	On some vehicles, the rear caliper brake hoses may be out of position. An improperly positioned rear caliper brake hose may contact rear suspension components and over time breach the integrity of the hose. This would result in the loss of brake fluid, which could cause decreased brake function, leading to crash and personal injuries.
SEP 11, 2006	06349000	2006 Sedona	On some vehicles equipped with adjustable brake pedals, the stop lamp switch wiring harness may be out of position. An improperly positioned stop lamp switch wiring harness could make contact with the u-joint assembly of the steering column. Repeated contact may eventually cause the wiring harness insulation to chafe. The chafed insulation could cause a short of the wiring harness resulting in the loss of brake lights, engine stalling, or an inability to start the vehicle increasing the risk of a crash.
APR 17, 2009	09V130000	2006, 2007 Sedona	On some models, the brake light switch might malfunction. This may cause the brake lights to not illuminate when the brake pedal is depressed or may cause the brake lights to remain illuminated when the brake pedal is released. It may also affect the operation of the brake-transmission shift interlock feature so the transmission shifter would not be able to be shifted out of the park position. It may also cause the Electronic Stability Control (ESC) malfunction light to illuminate, and it may not deactivate the cruise control when the brake pedal is depressed. Any of these malfunctions, alone or in combination, may lead to a crash.
APR 01, 2013	13V114000	2007, 2008, 2009, 2010, 2011 Sedona	On some models, the brake light switch may malfunction. This may cause the brake lights to not illuminate when the brake pedal is depressed or may cause an inability to deactivate the cruise control by depressing the brake pedal. Additionally, it may also result in intermittent operation of the push-button start feature, affect the operation of the brake-transmission shift interlock feature preventing the shifter from being moved out of the PARK position and causing the Electronic Stability Control (ESC) malfunction light to illuminate. Failure to illuminate the stop lamps during braking or inability to disengage the cruise control could increase the risk of a crash. Additionally, when the ignition is in the 'ON' position, the transmission shifter may be able to be moved out of PARK without first applying the brake. This may lead to unintentional movement of the car which may increase the risk of a crash.
NOV 05, 2013	13V550000	2006, 2007, 2008, 2009, 2010, 2011, 2012	On some models, the front lower control arms may break due to corrosion resulting from prolonged exposure to salty environments (road salt). A broken control arm can result in the loss of control of the vehicle, increasing the risk of a crash.

Buying parts

Replacement parts are available from many sources, which generally fall into one of two categories - authorized dealer parts departments and independent retail auto parts stores. Our advice concerning these parts is as follows:

Retail auto parts stores: Good auto parts stores will stock frequently needed components which wear out relatively fast, such as clutch components, exhaust systems, brake parts, tune-up parts, etc. These stores often supply new or reconditioned parts on an exchange basis, which can save a considerable amount of money. Discount auto parts stores are often very good places to buy materials and parts needed for general vehicle maintenance such as oil, grease, filters, spark plugs, belts, touch-up paint, bulbs, etc. They also usually sell tools and general accessories, have convenient hours, charge lower prices and can often be found not far from home.

Authorized dealer parts department: This is the best source for parts which are unique to the vehicle and not generally available elsewhere (such as major engine parts, transmission parts, trim pieces, etc.).

Warranty information: If the vehicle is still covered under warranty, be sure that any replacement parts purchased - regardless of the source - do not invalidate the warranty!

To be sure of obtaining the correct parts, have engine and chassis numbers available and, if possible, take the old parts along for positive identification.

Maintenance techniques, tools and working facilities

Maintenance techniques

There are a number of techniques involved in maintenance and repair that will be referred to throughout this manual. Application of these techniques will enable the home mechanic to be more efficient, better organized and capable of performing the various tasks properly, which will ensure that the repair job is thorough and complete.

Fasteners

Fasteners are nuts, bolts, studs and screws used to hold two or more parts together. There are a few things to keep in mind when working with fasteners. Almost all of them use a locking device of some type, either a lockwasher, locknut, locking tab or thread adhesive. All threaded fasteners should be clean and straight, with undamaged threads and undamaged corners on the hex head where the wrench fits. Develop the habit of replacing all damaged nuts and bolts with new ones. Special locknuts with nylon or fiber inserts can only be used once. If they are removed, they lose their locking ability and must be replaced with new ones.

Rusted nuts and bolts should be treated with a penetrating fluid to ease removal and prevent breakage. Some mechanics use turpentine in a spout-type oil can, which works quite well. After applying the rust penetrant, let it work for a few minutes before trying to loosen the nut or bolt. Badly rusted fasteners may have to be chiseled or sawed off or removed with a special nut breaker, available at tool stores.

If a bolt or stud breaks off in an assembly, it can be drilled and removed with a special tool commonly available for this purpose. Most automotive machine shops can perform this task, as well as other repair procedures, such as the repair of threaded holes that have been stripped out.

Flat washers and lockwashers, when removed from an assembly, should always be replaced exactly as removed. Replace any damaged washers with new ones. Never use a lockwasher on any soft metal surface (such as aluminum), thin sheet metal or plastic.

Fastener sizes

For a number of reasons, automobile manufacturers are making wider and wider use of metric fasteners. Therefore, it is important to be able to tell the difference between standard (sometimes called U.S. or SAE) and metric hardware, since they cannot be interchanged.

All bolts, whether standard or metric, are sized according to diameter, thread pitch and length. For example, a standard 1/2 - 13 x 1 bolt is 1/2 inch in diameter, has 13 threads per inch and is 1 inch long. An M12 - 1.75 x 25 metric bolt is 12 mm in diameter, has a thread pitch of 1.75 mm (the distance between threads) and is 25 mm long. The two bolts are nearly identical, and easily confused, but they are not interchangeable.

In addition to the differences in diameter, thread pitch and length, metric and standard bolts can also be distinguished by examining the bolt heads. To begin with, the distance across the flats on a standard bolt head is measured in inches, while the same dimension on a metric bolt is sized in millimeters (the same is true for nuts). As a result, a standard wrench should not be used on a metric bolt and a metric wrench should not be used on a standard bolt. Also, most standard bolts have slashes radiating out from the center of the head to denote the grade or strength of the bolt, which is an indication of the amount of torque that can be applied to it. The greater the number of slashes, the greater the strength of the bolt. Grades 0 through 5 are commonly used on automobiles. Metric bolts have a property class (grade) number, rather than a slash, molded into their heads to indicate bolt strength. In this case, the higher the number, the stronger the bolt. Property class numbers 8.8, 9.8 and 10.9 are commonly used on automobiles.

Strength markings can also be used to distinguish standard hex nuts from metric hex nuts. Many standard nuts have dots stamped into one side, while metric nuts are marked with a number. The greater the number of dots, or the higher the number, the greater the strength of the nut.

Metric studs are also marked on their ends according to property class (grade). Larger studs are numbered (the same as metric bolts), while smaller studs carry a geometric code to denote grade.

It should be noted that many fasteners, especially Grades 0 through 2, have no distinguishing marks on them. When such is the case, the only way to determine whether it is standard or metric is to measure the thread pitch or compare it to a known fastener of the same size.

Standard fasteners are often referred to as SAE, as opposed to metric. However, it should be noted that SAE technically refers to a non-metric fine thread fastener only. Coarse thread non-metric fasteners are referred to as USS sizes.

Since fasteners of the same size (both standard and metric) may have different strength ratings, be sure to reinstall any bolts, studs or nuts removed from your vehicle in their original locations. Also, when replacing a fastener with a new one, make sure that the new one has a strength rating equal to or greater than the original.

Tightening sequences and procedures

Most threaded fasteners should be tightened to a specific torque value (torque is the twisting force applied to a threaded component such as a nut or bolt). Overtightening the fastener can weaken it and cause it to break, while undertightening can cause it to eventually come loose. Bolts, screws and studs, depending on the material they are made of and their thread diameters, have specific torque values, many of which are noted in the Specifications at the beginning of each Chapter. Be sure to follow the torque recommen-

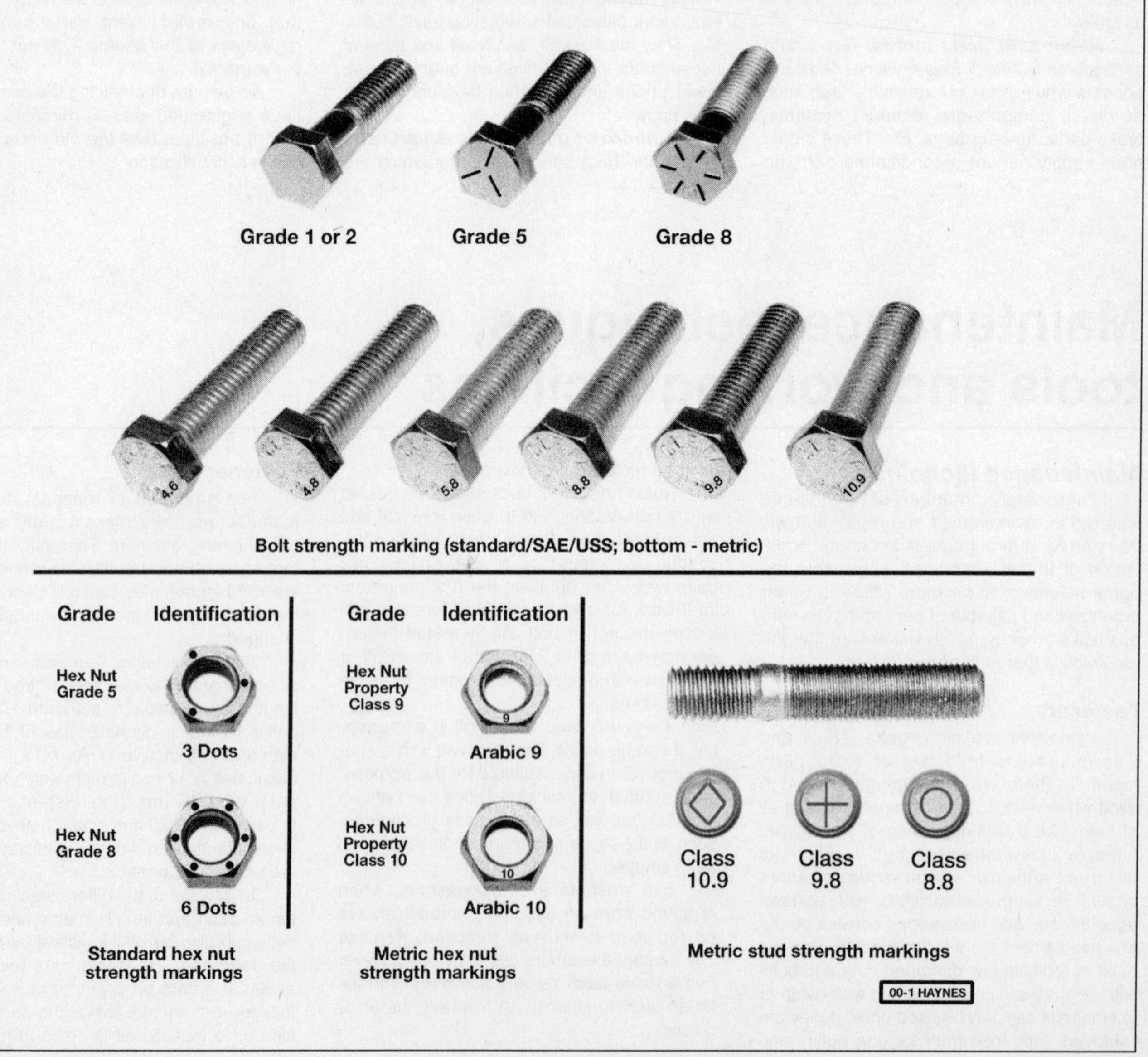

dations closely. For fasteners not assigned a specific torque, a general torque value chart is presented here as a guide. These torque values are for dry (unlubricated) fasteners threaded into steel or cast iron (not aluminum). As was previously mentioned, the size and grade of a fastener determine the amount of torque that can safely be applied to it. The figures listed here are approximate for Grade 2 and Grade 3 fasteners. Higher grades can tolerate higher torque values.

Fasteners laid out in a pattern, such as cylinder head bolts, oil pan bolts, differential cover bolts, etc., must be loosened or tightened in sequence to avoid warping the component. This sequence will normally be shown in the appropriate Chapter. If a specific pattern is not given, the following procedures can be used to prevent warping.

Initially, the bolts or nuts should be assembled finger-tight only. Next, they should be tightened one full turn each, in a criss-cross or diagonal pattern. After each one has been tightened one full turn, return to the first one and tighten them all one-half turn, following the same pattern. Finally, tighten each of them one-quarter turn at a time until each fastener has been tightened to the proper torque. To loosen and remove the fasteners, the procedure would be reversed.

Metric thread sizes	**Ft-lbs**	**Nm**
M-6	6 to 9	9 to 12
M-8	14 to 21	19 to 28
M-10	28 to 40	38 to 54
M-12	50 to 71	68 to 96
M-14	80 to 140	109 to 154
Pipe thread sizes		
1/8	5 to 8	7 to 10
1/4	12 to 18	17 to 24
3/8	22 to 33	30 to 44
1/2	25 to 35	34 to 47
U.S. thread sizes		
1/4 - 20	6 to 9	9 to 12
5/16 - 18	12 to 18	17 to 24
5/16 - 24	14 to 20	19 to 27
3/8 - 16	22 to 32	30 to 43
3/8 - 24	27 to 38	37 to 51
7/16 - 14	40 to 55	55 to 74
7/16 - 20	40 to 60	55 to 81
1/2 - 13	55 to 80	75 to 108

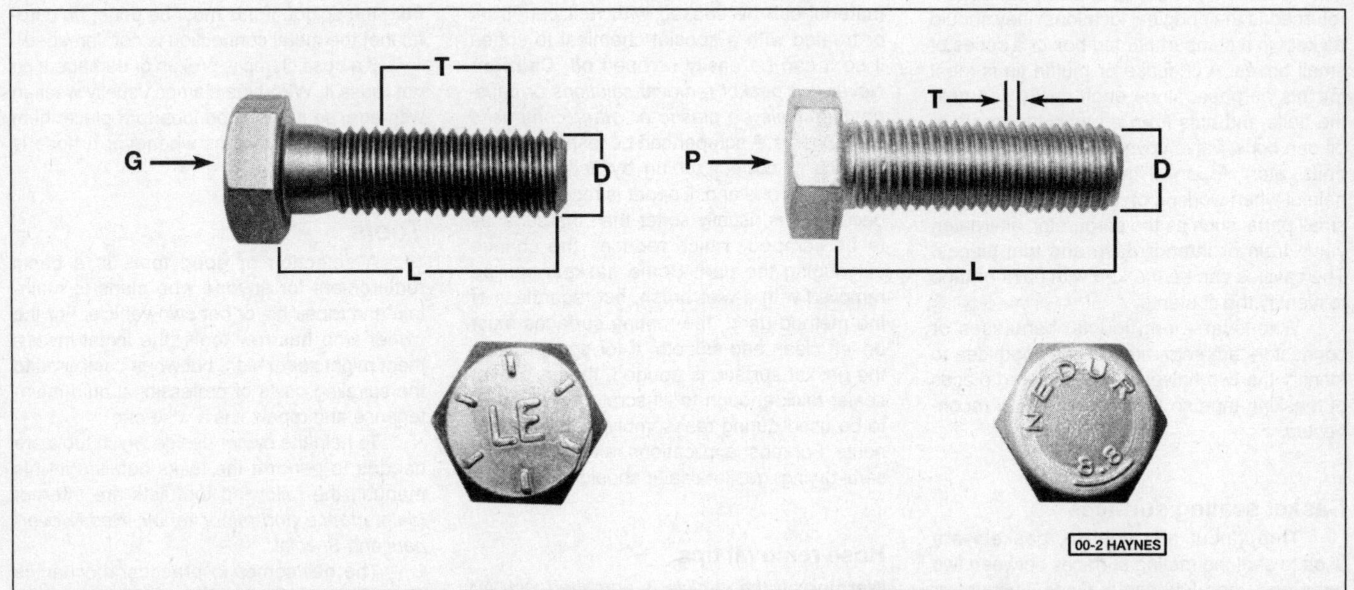

Standard (SAE and USS) bolt dimensions/grade marks

G *Grade marks (bolt strength)*
L *Length (in inches)*
T *Thread pitch (number of threads per inch)*
D *Nominal diameter (in inches)*

Metric bolt dimensions/grade marks

P *Property class (bolt strength)*
L *Length (in millimeters)*
T *Thread pitch (distance between threads in millimeters)*
D *Diameter*

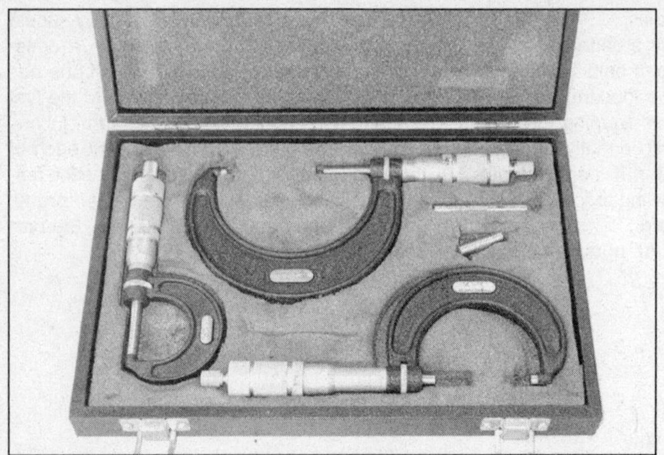
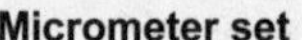

Micrometer set

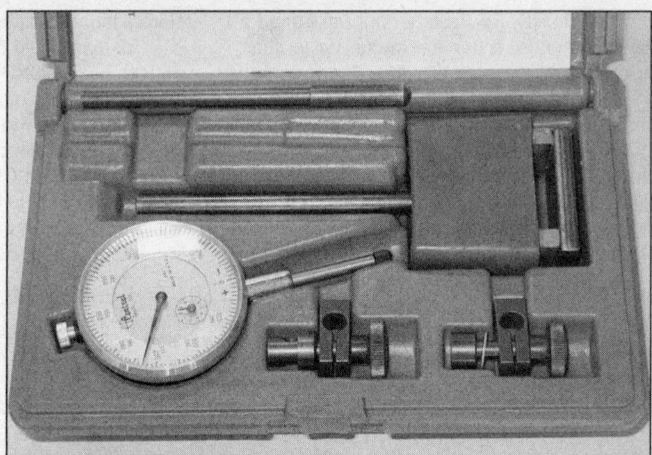

Dial indicator set

Component disassembly

Component disassembly should be done with care and purpose to help ensure that the parts go back together properly. Always keep track of the sequence in which parts are removed. Make note of special characteristics or marks on parts that can be installed more than one way, such as a grooved thrust washer on a shaft. It is a good idea to lay the disassembled parts out on a clean surface in the order that they were removed. It may also be helpful to make sketches or take instant photos of components before removal.

When removing fasteners from a component, keep track of their locations. Sometimes threading a bolt back in a part, or putting the washers and nut back on a stud, can prevent mix-ups later. If nuts and bolts cannot be returned to their original locations, they should be kept in a compartmented box or a series of small boxes. A cupcake or muffin tin is ideal for this purpose, since each cavity can hold the bolts and nuts from a particular area (i.e. oil pan bolts, valve cover bolts, engine mount bolts, etc.). A pan of this type is especially helpful when working on assemblies with very small parts, such as the carburetor, alternator, valve train or interior dash and trim pieces. The cavities can be marked with paint or tape to identify the contents.

Whenever wiring looms, harnesses or connectors are separated, it is a good idea to identify the two halves with numbered pieces of masking tape so they can be easily reconnected.

Gasket sealing surfaces

Throughout any vehicle, gaskets are used to seal the mating surfaces between two parts and keep lubricants, fluids, vacuum or pressure contained in an assembly.

Many times these gaskets are coated with a liquid or paste-type gasket sealing compound before assembly. Age, heat and pressure can sometimes cause the two parts to stick together so tightly that they are very difficult to separate. Often, the assembly can be loosened by striking it with a soft-face hammer near the mating surfaces. A regular hammer can be used if a block of wood is placed between the hammer and the part. Do not hammer on cast parts or parts that could be easily damaged. With any particularly stubborn part, always recheck to make sure that every fastener has been removed.

Avoid using a screwdriver or bar to pry apart an assembly, as they can easily mar the gasket sealing surfaces of the parts, which must remain smooth. If prying is absolutely necessary, use an old broom handle, but keep in mind that extra clean up will be necessary if the wood splinters.

After the parts are separated, the old gasket must be carefully scraped off and the gasket surfaces cleaned. Stubborn gasket material can be soaked with rust penetrant or treated with a special chemical to soften it so it can be easily scraped off. **Caution:** *Never use gasket removal solutions or caustic chemicals on plastic or other composite components.* A scraper can be fashioned from a piece of copper tubing by flattening and sharpening one end. Copper is recommended because it is usually softer than the surfaces to be scraped, which reduces the chance of gouging the part. Some gaskets can be removed with a wire brush, but regardless of the method used, the mating surfaces must be left clean and smooth. If for some reason the gasket surface is gouged, then a gasket sealer thick enough to fill scratches will have to be used during reassembly of the components. For most applications, a non-drying (or semi-drying) gasket sealer should be used.

Hose removal tips

Warning: *If the vehicle is equipped with air conditioning, do not disconnect any of the A/C hoses without first having the system depressurized by a dealer service department or a service station.*

Hose removal precautions closely parallel gasket removal precautions. Avoid scratching or gouging the surface that the hose mates against or the connection may leak. This is especially true for radiator hoses. Because of various chemical reactions, the rubber in hoses can bond itself to the metal spigot that the hose fits over. To remove a hose, first loosen the hose clamps that secure it to the spigot. Then, with slip-joint pliers, grab the hose at the clamp and rotate it around the spigot. Work it back and forth until it is completely free, then pull it off. Silicone or other lubricants will ease removal if they can be applied between the hose and the outside of the spigot. Apply the same lubricant to the inside of the hose and the outside of the spigot to simplify installation.

As a last resort (and if the hose is to be replaced with a new one anyway), the rubber can be slit with a knife and the hose peeled from the spigot. If this must be done, be careful that the metal connection is not damaged.

If a hose clamp is broken or damaged, do not reuse it. Wire-type clamps usually weaken with age, so it is a good idea to replace them with screw-type clamps whenever a hose is removed.

Tools

A selection of good tools is a basic requirement for anyone who plans to maintain and repair his or her own vehicle. For the owner who has few tools, the initial investment might seem high, but when compared to the spiraling costs of professional auto maintenance and repair, it is a wise one.

To help the owner decide which tools are needed to perform the tasks detailed in this manual, the following tool lists are offered: *Maintenance and minor repair, Repair/overhaul* and *Special.*

The newcomer to practical mechanics should start off with the *maintenance and minor repair* tool kit, which is adequate for the simpler jobs performed on a vehicle. Then, as confidence and experience grow, the owner can tackle more difficult tasks, buying additional tools as they are needed. Eventually the basic kit will be expanded into the *repair and overhaul* tool set. Over a period of time, the

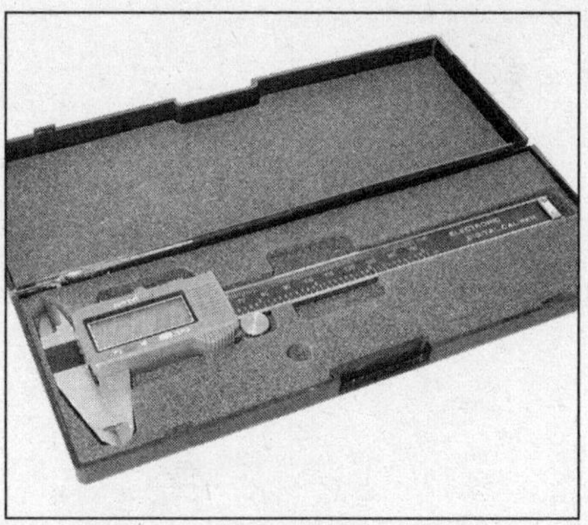

Dial caliper

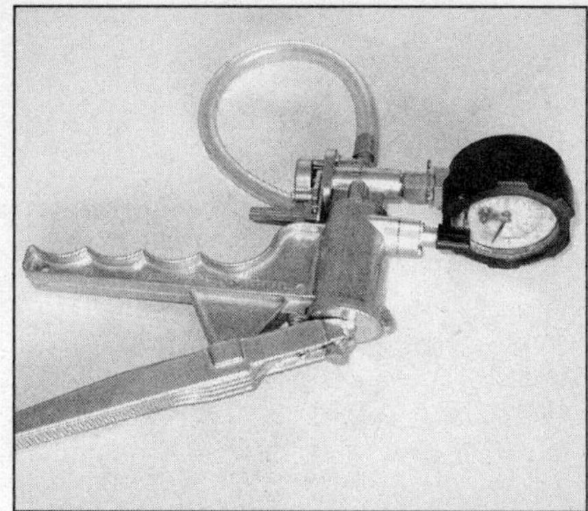

Hand-operated vacuum pump

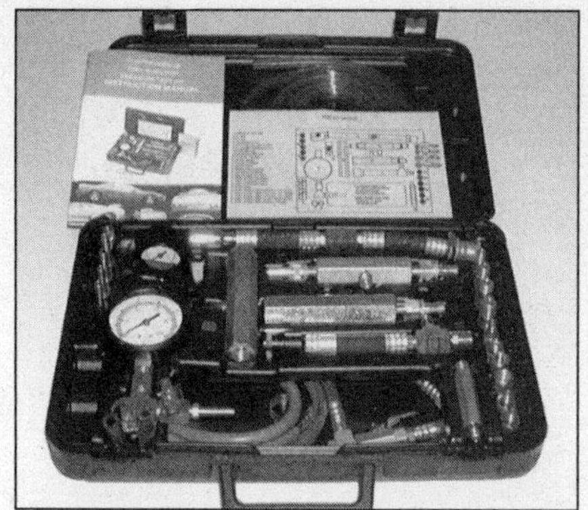

Fuel pressure gauge set

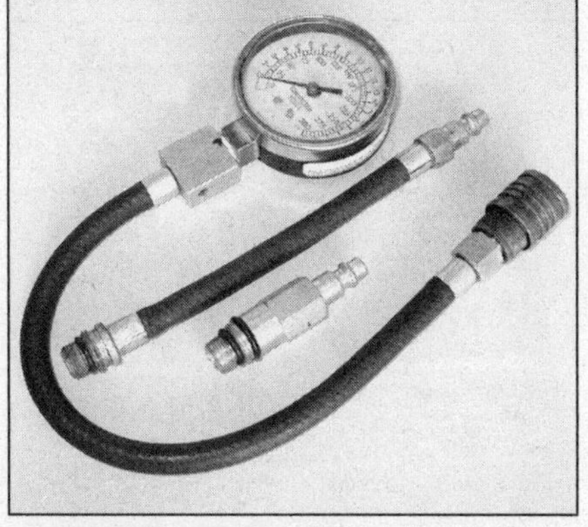

Compression gauge with spark plug hole adapter

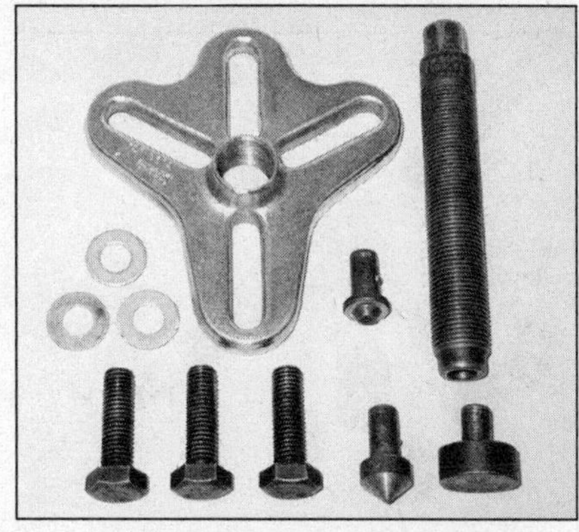

Damper/steering wheel puller

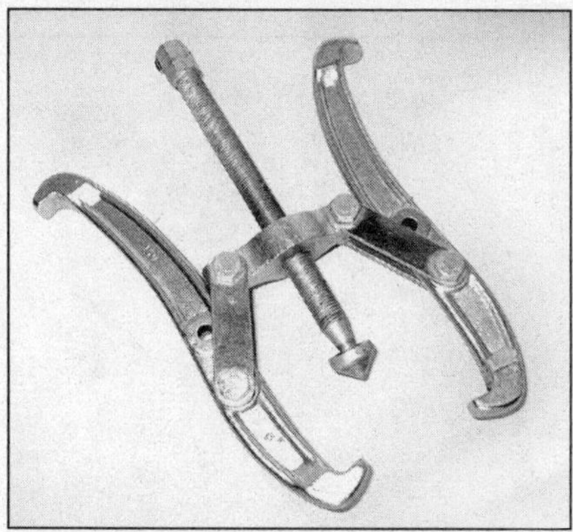

General purpose puller

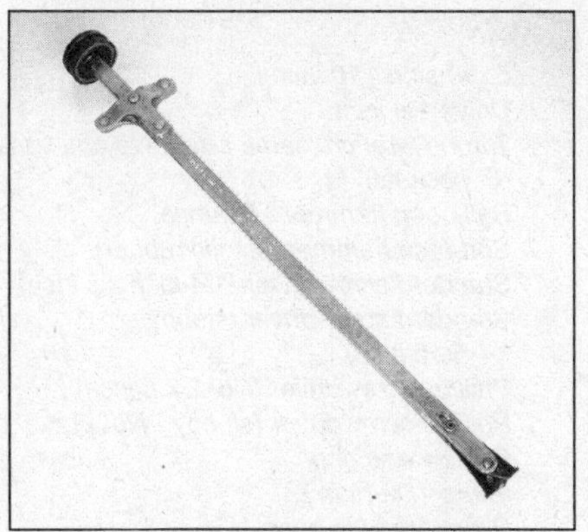

Hydraulic lifter removal tool

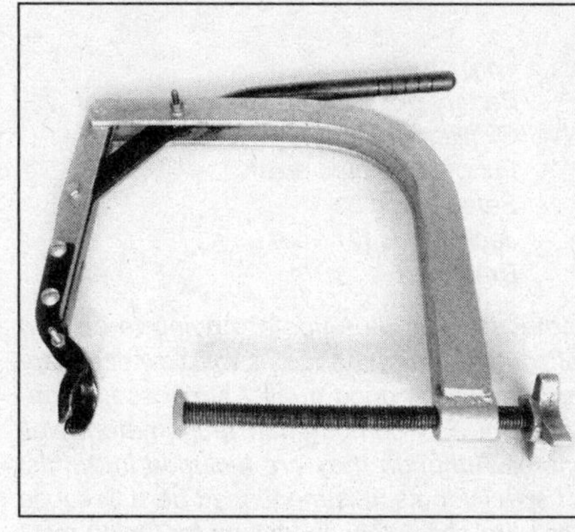

Valve spring compressor

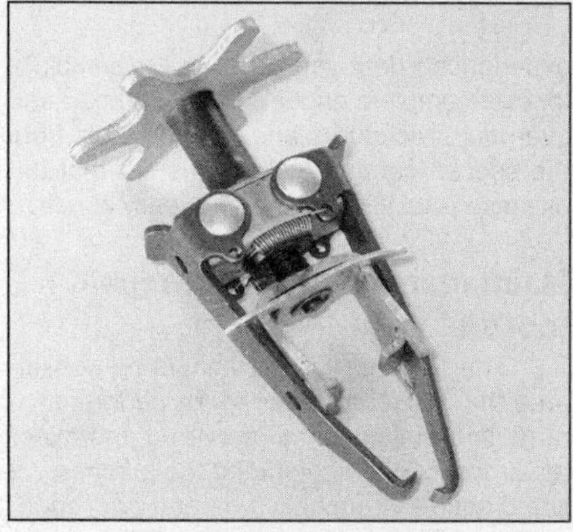

Valve spring compressor

Ridge reamer

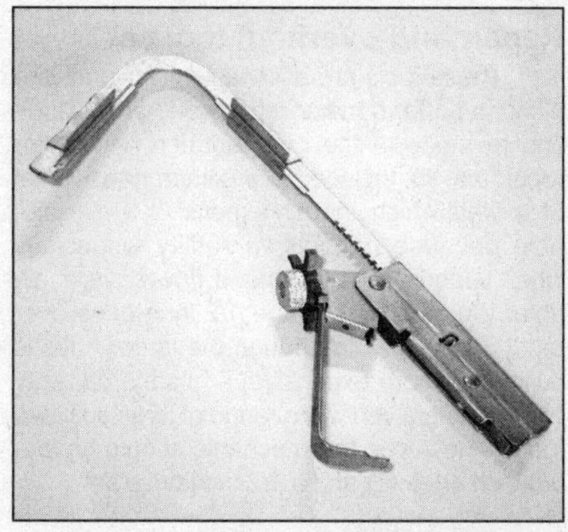

Piston ring groove cleaning tool

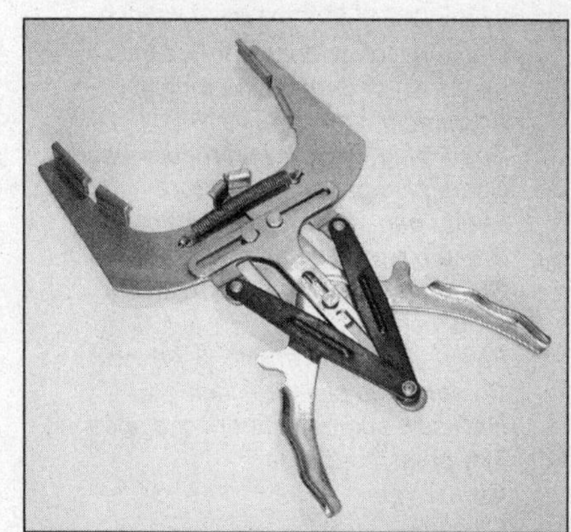

Ring removal/installation tool

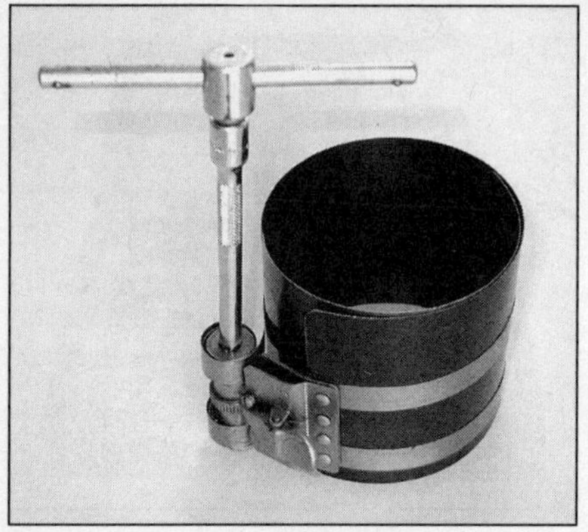
Ring compressor

Cylinder hone

Brake hold-down spring tool

Torque angle gauge

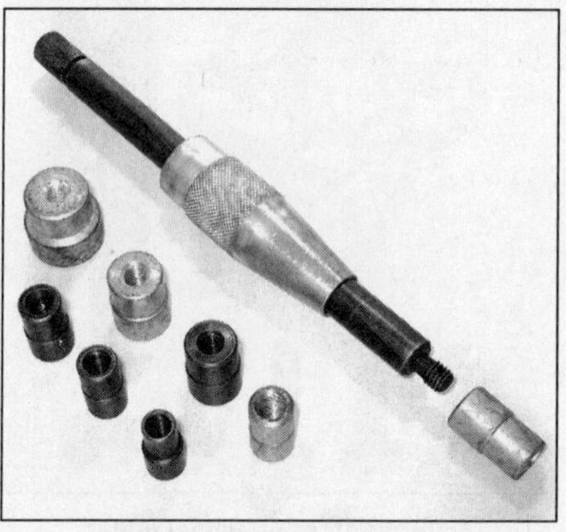
Clutch plate alignment tool

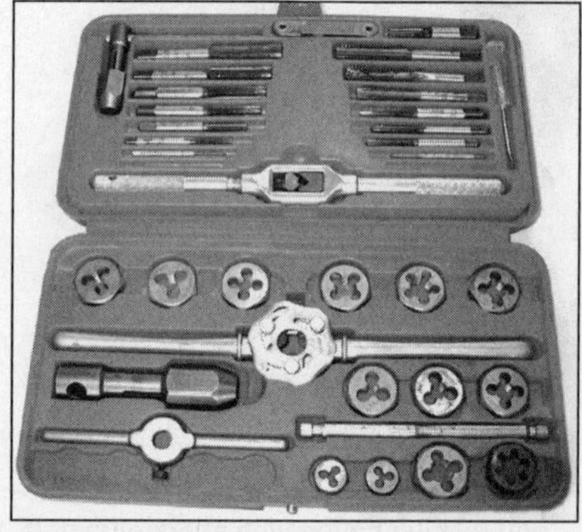
Tap and die set

experienced do-it-yourselfer will assemble a tool set complete enough for most repair and overhaul procedures and will add tools from the special category when it is felt that the expense is justified by the frequency of use.

Maintenance and minor repair tool kit

The tools in this list should be considered the minimum required for performance of routine maintenance, servicing and minor repair work. We recommend the purchase of combination wrenches (box-end and open-end combined in one wrench). While more expensive than open end wrenches, they offer the advantages of both types of wrench.

Combination wrench set (1/4-inch to 1 inch or 6 mm to 19 mm)
Adjustable wrench, 8 inch
Spark plug wrench with rubber insert
Spark plug gap adjusting tool
Feeler gauge set
Brake bleeder wrench
Standard screwdriver (5/16-inch x 6 inch)
Phillips screwdriver (No. 2 x 6 inch)
Combination pliers - 6 inch
Hacksaw and assortment of blades
Tire pressure gauge
Grease gun
Oil can
Fine emery cloth
Wire brush
Battery post and cable cleaning tool
Oil filter wrench
Funnel (medium size)
Safety goggles
Jackstands (2)
Drain pan

Note: *If basic tune-ups are going to be part of routine maintenance, it will be necessary to purchase a good quality stroboscopic timing light and combination tachometer/dwell meter. Although they are included in the list of special tools, it is mentioned here because they are absolutely necessary for tuning most vehicles properly.*

Repair and overhaul tool set

These tools are essential for anyone who plans to perform major repairs and are in addition to those in the maintenance and minor repair tool kit. Included is a comprehensive set of sockets which, though expensive, are invaluable because of their versatility, especially when various extensions and drives are available. We recommend the 1/2-inch drive over the 3/8-inch drive. Although the larger drive is bulky and more expensive, it has the capacity of accepting a very wide range of large sockets. Ideally, however, the mechanic should have a 3/8-inch drive set and a 1/2-inch drive set.

Socket set(s)
Reversible ratchet
Extension - 10 inch
Universal joint
Torque wrench (same size drive as sockets)
Ball peen hammer - 8 ounce
Soft-face hammer (plastic/rubber)
Standard screwdriver (1/4-inch x 6 inch)
Standard screwdriver (stubby - 5/16-inch)
Phillips screwdriver (No. 3 x 8 inch)
Phillips screwdriver (stubby - No. 2)
Pliers - vise grip
Pliers - lineman's
Pliers - needle nose
Pliers - snap-ring (internal and external)
Cold chisel - 1/2-inch
Scribe
Scraper (made from flattened copper tubing)
Centerpunch
Pin punches (1/16, 1/8, 3/16-inch)
Steel rule/straightedge - 12 inch
Allen wrench set (1/8 to 3/8-inch or 4 mm to 10 mm)
A selection of files
Wire brush (large)
Jackstands (second set)
Jack (scissor or hydraulic type)

Note: *Another tool which is often useful is an electric drill with a chuck capacity of 3/8-inch and a set of good quality drill bits.*

Special tools

The tools in this list include those which are not used regularly, are expensive to buy, or which need to be used in accordance with their manufacturer's instructions. Unless these tools will be used frequently, it is not very economical to purchase many of them. A consideration would be to split the cost and use between yourself and a friend or friends. In addition, most of these tools can be obtained from a tool rental shop on a temporary basis.

This list primarily contains only those tools and instruments widely available to the public, and not those special tools produced by the vehicle manufacturer for distribution to dealer service departments. Occasionally, references to the manufacturer's special tools are included in the text of this manual. Generally, an alternative method of doing the job without the special tool is offered. However, sometimes there is no alternative to their use. Where this is the case, and the tool cannot be purchased or borrowed, the work should be turned over to the dealer service department or an automotive repair shop.

Valve spring compressor
Piston ring groove cleaning tool
Piston ring compressor
Piston ring installation tool
Cylinder compression gauge
Cylinder ridge reamer
Cylinder surfacing hone
Cylinder bore gauge
Micrometers and/or dial calipers
Hydraulic lifter removal tool
Balljoint separator
Universal-type puller
Impact screwdriver
Dial indicator set
Stroboscopic timing light (inductive pick-up)
Hand operated vacuum/pressure pump
Tachometer/dwell meter
Universal electrical multimeter
Cable hoist
Brake spring removal and installation tools
Floor jack

Buying tools

For the do-it-yourselfer who is just starting to get involved in vehicle maintenance and repair, there are a number of options available when purchasing tools. If maintenance and minor repair is the extent of the work to be done, the purchase of individual tools is satisfactory. If, on the other hand, extensive work is planned, it would be a good idea to purchase a modest tool set from one of the large retail chain stores. A set can usually be bought at a substantial savings over the individual tool prices, and they often come with a tool box. As additional tools are needed, add-on sets, individual tools and a larger tool box can be purchased to expand the tool selection. Building a tool set gradually allows the cost of the tools to be spread over a longer period of time and gives the mechanic the freedom to choose only those tools that will actually be used.

Tool stores will often be the only source of some of the special tools that are needed, but regardless of where tools are bought, try to avoid cheap ones, especially when buying screwdrivers and sockets, because they won't last very long. The expense involved in replacing cheap tools will eventually be greater than the initial cost of quality tools.

Care and maintenance of tools

Good tools are expensive, so it makes sense to treat them with respect. Keep them clean and in usable condition and store them properly when not in use. Always wipe off any dirt, grease or metal chips before putting them away. Never leave tools lying around in the work area. Upon completion of a job, always check closely under the hood for tools that may have been left there so they won't get lost during a test drive.

Some tools, such as screwdrivers, pliers, wrenches and sockets, can be hung on a panel mounted on the garage or workshop wall, while others should be kept in a tool box or tray. Measuring instruments, gauges, meters, etc. must be carefully stored where they cannot be damaged by weather or impact from other tools.

When tools are used with care and stored properly, they will last a very long time. Even with the best of care, though, tools will wear out if used frequently. When a tool is damaged or worn out, replace it. Subsequent jobs will be safer and more enjoyable if you do.

How to repair damaged threads

Sometimes, the internal threads of a nut or bolt hole can become stripped, usually from overtightening. Stripping threads is an all-too-common occurrence, especially when working with aluminum parts, because aluminum is so soft that it easily strips out.

Usually, external or internal threads are only partially stripped. After they've been cleaned up with a tap or die, they'll still work. Sometimes, however, threads are badly damaged. When this happens, you've got three choices:

1) *Drill and tap the hole to the next suitable oversize and install a larger diameter bolt, screw or stud.*
2) *Drill and tap the hole to accept a threaded plug, then drill and tap the plug to the original screw size. You can also buy a plug already threaded to the original size. Then you simply drill a hole to the specified size, then run the threaded plug into the hole with a bolt and jam nut. Once the plug is fully seated, remove the jam nut and bolt.*
3) *The third method uses a patented thread repair kit like Heli-Coil or Slimsert. These easy-to-use kits are designed to repair damaged threads in straight-through holes and blind holes. Both are available as kits which can handle a variety of sizes and thread patterns. Drill the hole, then tap it with the special included tap. Install the Heli-Coil and the hole is back to its original diameter and thread pitch.*

Regardless of which method you use, be sure to proceed calmly and carefully. A little impatience or carelessness during one of these relatively simple procedures can ruin your whole day's work and cost you a bundle if you wreck an expensive part.

Working facilities

Not to be overlooked when discussing tools is the workshop. If anything more than routine maintenance is to be carried out, some sort of suitable work area is essential.

It is understood, and appreciated, that many home mechanics do not have a good workshop or garage available, and end up removing an engine or doing major repairs outside. It is recommended, however, that the overhaul or repair be completed under the cover of a roof.

A clean, flat workbench or table of comfortable working height is an absolute necessity. The workbench should be equipped with a vise that has a jaw opening of at least four inches.

As mentioned previously, some clean, dry storage space is also required for tools, as well as the lubricants, fluids, cleaning solvents, etc. which soon become necessary.

Sometimes waste oil and fluids, drained from the engine or cooling system during normal maintenance or repairs, present a disposal problem. To avoid pouring them on the ground or into a sewage system, pour the used fluids into large containers, seal them with caps and take them to an authorized disposal site or recycling center. Plastic jugs, such as old antifreeze containers, are ideal for this purpose.

Always keep a supply of old newspapers and clean rags available. Old towels are excellent for mopping up spills. Many mechanics use rolls of paper towels for most work because they are readily available and disposable. To help keep the area under the vehicle clean, a large cardboard box can be cut open and flattened to protect the garage or shop floor.

Whenever working over a painted surface, such as when leaning over a fender to service something under the hood, always cover it with an old blanket or bedspread to protect the finish. Vinyl covered pads, made especially for this purpose, are available at auto parts stores.

Jacking and towing

Jacking

Warning: *Never work under the vehicle or start the engine while this jack is being used as the only means of support.*

1 The jack supplied with the vehicle should only be used for raising the vehicle when changing a tire or placing jackstands under the frame.

2 When jacking the vehicle, the jack should be engaged with the rocker panel seam, between the two notches (see illustration).

3 The vehicle should be on level ground with the wheels blocked and the transmission in Park. Pry off the hub cap (if equipped) using the tapered end of the lug wrench. Loosen the lug nuts one-half turn and leave them in place until the wheel is raised off the ground.

4 Place the jack under the side of the vehicle in the indicated position. Use the supplied wrench to turn the jackscrew clockwise until the wheel is raised off the ground. Remove the lug nuts, pull off the wheel and replace it with the spare.

5 With the beveled side in, reinstall the lug nuts and tighten them until snug. Lower the vehicle by turning the jackscrew counterclockwise. Remove the jack and tighten the nuts in a diagonal pattern to the torque listed in the Chapter 1 Specifications 0. If a torque wrench is not available, have the torque checked by a service station as soon as possible. Install the hubcap by placing it in position and using the heel of your hand or a rubber mallet to seat it.

Towing

6 These vehicle can be towed from the front with the front wheels off the ground, using a wheel-lift type tow truck. If towed from the rear, the front wheels must be placed on a dolly.

7 In an emergency the vehicle can be towed a very short distance with a cable or chain attached to one of the towing eyelets located under the front or rear bumpers. The driver must remain in the vehicle to operate the steering and brakes (remember that power steering and power brakes will not work with the engine off). Make certain that the vehicle is in neutral with the parking brake off.

The jack fits between the notches in the rocker panel pinch-weld (there are two jacking points on each side of the vehicle)

Booster battery (jump) starting

1 Observe these precautions when using a booster battery to start a vehicle:

- *a) Before connecting the booster battery, make sure the ignition switch is in the Off position.*
- *b) Turn off the lights, heater and other electrical loads.*
- *c) Your eyes should be shielded. Safety goggles are a good idea.*
- *d) Make sure the booster battery is the same voltage as the dead one in the vehicle.*
- *e) The two vehicles MUST NOT TOUCH each other!*
- *f) Make sure the transaxle is in Neutral (manual) or Park (automatic).*
- *g) If the booster battery is not a maintenance-free type, remove the vent caps and lay a cloth over the vent holes.*

2 Connect the red-colored jumper cable to the positive (+) terminal of the booster battery and the other end to the positive (+) terminal of the dead battery. Then connect one end of the black jumper cable to the negative (-) terminal of the booster battery, and the other end of the cable to a good ground, such as a bolt or bracket.

3 Start the engine using the booster battery, then run the booster vehicle at a fast idle for a few minutes to instill some charge in the dead battery. Let the engine idle, then disconnect the jumper cables in the reverse order of connection. The vehicle with the dead battery may have to be driven for 20 minutes or more to sufficiently recharge the battery for independent starting.

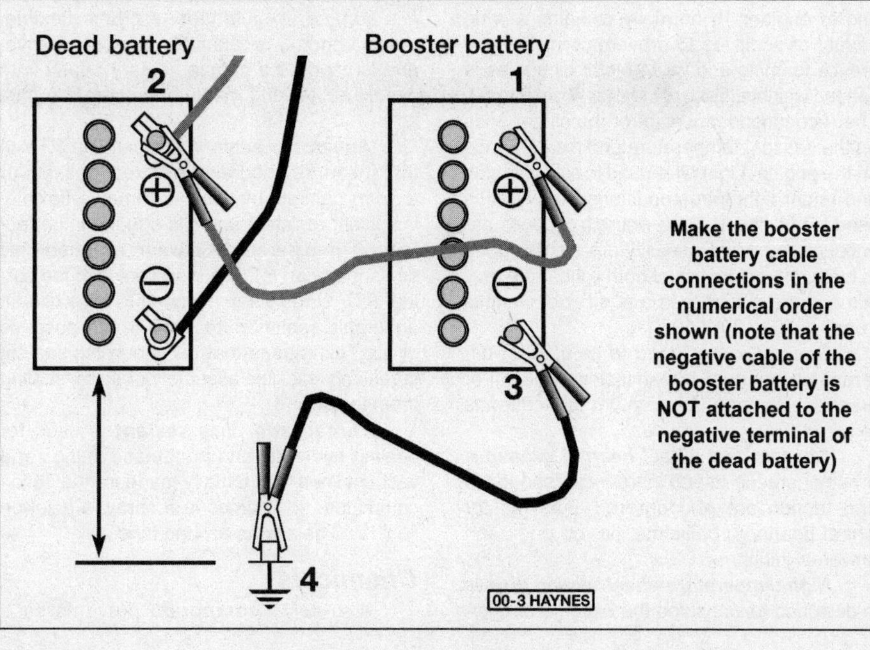
Dead battery
Booster battery
2
1
3
4
Make the booster battery cable connections in the numerical order shown (note that the negative cable of the booster battery is NOT attached to the negative terminal of the dead battery)
00-3 HAYNES

Automotive chemicals and lubricants

A number of automotive chemicals and lubricants are available for use during vehicle maintenance and repair. They include a wide variety of products ranging from cleaning solvents and degreasers to lubricants and protective sprays for rubber, plastic and vinyl.

Cleaners

Carburetor cleaner and choke cleaner is a strong solvent for gum, varnish and carbon. Most carburetor cleaners leave a dry-type lubricant film which will not harden or gum up. Because of this film it is not recommended for use on electrical components.

Brake system cleaner is used to remove brake dust, grease and brake fluid from the brake system, where clean surfaces are absolutely necessary. It leaves no residue and often eliminates brake squeal caused by contaminants.

Electrical cleaner removes oxidation, corrosion and carbon deposits from electrical contacts, restoring full current flow. It can also be used to clean spark plugs, carburetor jets, voltage regulators and other parts where an oil-free surface is desired.

Demoisturants remove water and moisture from electrical components such as alternators, voltage regulators, electrical connectors and fuse blocks. They are non-conductive and non-corrosive.

Degreasers are heavy-duty solvents used to remove grease from the outside of the engine and from chassis components. They can be sprayed or brushed on and, depending on the type, are rinsed off either with water or solvent.

Lubricants

Motor oil is the lubricant formulated for use in engines. It normally contains a wide variety of additives to prevent corrosion and reduce foaming and wear. Motor oil comes in various weights (viscosity ratings) from 0 to 50. The recommended weight of the oil depends on the season, temperature and the demands on the engine. Light oil is used in cold climates and under light load conditions. Heavy oil is used in hot climates and where high loads are encountered. Multi-viscosity oils are designed to have characteristics of both light and heavy oils and are available in a number of weights from 0W-20 to 20W-50.

Gear oil is designed to be used in differentials, manual transmissions and other areas where high-temperature lubrication is required.

Chassis and wheel bearing grease is a heavy grease used where increased loads and friction are encountered, such as for wheel bearings, balljoints, tie-rod ends and universal joints.

High-temperature wheel bearing grease is designed to withstand the extreme temperatures encountered by wheel bearings in disc brake equipped vehicles. It usually contains molybdenum disulfide (moly), which is a dry-type lubricant.

White grease is a heavy grease for metal-to-metal applications where water is a problem. White grease stays soft under both low and high temperatures (usually from -100 to +190-degrees F), and will not wash off or dilute in the presence of water.

Assembly lube is a special extreme pressure lubricant, usually containing moly, used to lubricate high-load parts (such as main and rod bearings and cam lobes) for initial start-up of a new engine. The assembly lube lubricates the parts without being squeezed out or washed away until the engine oiling system begins to function.

Silicone lubricants are used to protect rubber, plastic, vinyl and nylon parts.

Graphite lubricants are used where oils cannot be used due to contamination problems, such as in locks. The dry graphite will lubricate metal parts while remaining uncontaminated by dirt, water, oil or acids. It is electrically conductive and will not foul electrical contacts in locks such as the ignition switch.

Moly penetrants loosen and lubricate frozen, rusted and corroded fasteners and prevent future rusting or freezing.

Heat-sink grease is a special electrically non-conductive grease that is used for mounting electronic ignition modules where it is essential that heat is transferred away from the module.

Sealants

RTV sealant is one of the most widely used gasket compounds. Made from silicone, RTV is air curing, it seals, bonds, waterproofs, fills surface irregularities, remains flexible, doesn't shrink, is relatively easy to remove, and is used as a supplementary sealer with almost all low and medium temperature gaskets.

Anaerobic sealant is much like RTV in that it can be used either to seal gaskets or to form gaskets by itself. It remains flexible, is solvent resistant and fills surface imperfections. The difference between an anaerobic sealant and an RTV-type sealant is in the curing. RTV cures when exposed to air, while an anaerobic sealant cures only in the absence of air. This means that an anaerobic sealant cures only after the assembly of parts, sealing them together.

Thread and pipe sealant is used for sealing hydraulic and pneumatic fittings and vacuum lines. It is usually made from a Teflon compound, and comes in a spray, a paint-on liquid and as a wrap-around tape.

Chemicals

Anti-seize compound prevents seizing, galling, cold welding, rust and corrosion in fasteners. High-temperature ant-seize, usually made with copper and graphite lubricants, is used for exhaust system and exhaust manifold bolts.

Anaerobic locking compounds are used to keep fasteners from vibrating or working loose and cure only after installation, in the absence of air. Medium strength locking compound is used for small nuts, bolts and screws that may be removed later. High-strength locking compound is for large nuts, bolts and studs which aren't removed on a regular basis.

Oil additives range from viscosity index improvers to chemical treatments that claim to reduce internal engine friction. It should be noted that most oil manufacturers caution against using additives with their oils.

Gas additives perform several functions, depending on their chemical makeup. They usually contain solvents that help dissolve gum and varnish that build up on carburetor, fuel injection and intake parts. They also serve to break down carbon deposits that form on the inside surfaces of the combustion chambers. Some additives contain upper cylinder lubricants for valves and piston rings, and others contain chemicals to remove condensation from the gas tank.

Miscellaneous

Brake fluid is specially formulated hydraulic fluid that can withstand the heat and pressure encountered in brake systems. Care must be taken so this fluid does not come in contact with painted surfaces or plastics. An opened container should always be resealed to prevent contamination by water or dirt.

Weatherstrip adhesive is used to bond weatherstripping around doors, windows and trunk lids. It is sometimes used to attach trim pieces.

Undercoating is a petroleum-based, tar-like substance that is designed to protect metal surfaces on the underside of the vehicle from corrosion. It also acts as a sound-deadening agent by insulating the bottom of the vehicle.

Waxes and polishes are used to help protect painted and plated surfaces from the weather. Different types of paint may require the use of different types of wax and polish. Some polishes utilize a chemical or abrasive cleaner to help remove the top layer of oxidized (dull) paint on older vehicles. In recent years many non-wax polishes that contain a wide variety of chemicals such as polymers and silicones have been introduced. These non-wax polishes are usually easier to apply and last longer than conventional waxes and polishes.

Conversion factors

Length (distance)						
Inches (in)	X	25.4	= Millimeters (mm)	X	0.0394	= Inches (in)
Feet (ft)	X	0.305	= Meters (m)	X	3.281	= Feet (ft)
Miles	X	1.609	= Kilometers (km)	X	0.621	= Miles
Volume (capacity)						
Cubic inches (cu in; in^3)	X	16.387	= Cubic centimeters (cc; cm^3)	X	0.061	= Cubic inches (cu in; in^3)
Imperial pints (Imp pt)	X	0.568	= Liters (l)	X	1.76	= Imperial pints (Imp pt)
Imperial quarts (Imp qt)	X	1.137	= Liters (l)	X	0.88	= Imperial quarts (Imp qt)
Imperial quarts (Imp qt)	X	1.201	= US quarts (US qt)	X	0.833	= Imperial quarts (Imp qt)
US quarts (US qt)	X	0.946	= Liters (l)	X	1.057	= US quarts (US qt)
Imperial gallons (Imp gal)	X	4.546	= Liters (l)	X	0.22	= Imperial gallons (Imp gal)
Imperial gallons (Imp gal)	X	1.201	= US gallons (US gal)	X	0.833	= Imperial gallons (Imp gal)
US gallons (US gal)	X	3.785	= Liters (l)	X	0.264	= US gallons (US gal)
Mass (weight)						
Ounces (oz)	X	28.35	= Grams (g)	X	0.035	= Ounces (oz)
Pounds (lb)	X	0.454	= Kilograms (kg)	X	2.205	= Pounds (lb)
Force						
Ounces-force (ozf; oz)	X	0.278	= Newtons (N)	X	3.6	= Ounces-force (ozf; oz)
Pounds-force (lbf; lb)	X	4.448	= Newtons (N)	X	0.225	= Pounds-force (lbf; lb)
Newtons (N)	X	0.1	= Kilograms-force (kgf; kg)	X	9.81	= Newtons (N)
Pressure						
Pounds-force per square inch (psi; lbf/in^2; lb/in^2)	X	0.070	= Kilograms-force per square centimeter (kgf/cm^2; kg/cm^2)	X	14.223	= Pounds-force per square inch (psi; lbf/in^2; lb/in^2)
Pounds-force per square inch (psi; lbf/in^2; lb/in^2)	X	0.068	= Atmospheres (atm)	X	14.696	= Pounds-force per square inch (psi; lbf/in^2; lb/in^2)
Pounds-force per square inch (psi; lbf/in^2; lb/in^2)	X	0.069	= Bars	X	14.5	= Pounds-force per square inch (psi; lbf/in^2; lb/in^2)
Pounds-force per square inch (psi; lbf/in^2; lb/in^2)	X	6.895	= Kilopascals (kPa)	X	0.145	= Pounds-force per square inch (psi; lbf/in^2; lb/in^2)
Kilopascals (kPa)	X	0.01	= Kilograms-force per square centimeter (kgf/cm^2; kg/cm^2)	X	98.1	= Kilopascals (kPa)
Torque (moment of force)						
Pounds-force inches (lbf in; lb in)	X	1.152	= Kilograms-force centimeter (kgf cm; kg cm)	X	0.868	= Pounds-force inches (lbf in; lb in)
Pounds-force inches (lbf in; lb in)	X	0.113	= Newton meters (Nm)	X	8.85	= Pounds-force inches (lbf in; lb in)
Pounds-force inches (lbf in; lb in)	X	0.083	= Pounds-force feet (lbf ft; lb ft)	X	12	= Pounds-force inches (lbf in; lb in)
Pounds-force feet (lbf ft; lb ft)	X	0.138	= Kilograms-force meters (kgf m; kg m)	X	7.233	= Pounds-force feet (lbf ft; lb ft)
Pounds-force feet (lbf ft; lb ft)	X	1.356	= Newton meters (Nm)	X	0.738	= Pounds-force feet (lbf ft; lb ft)
Newton meters (Nm)	X	0.102	= Kilograms-force meters (kgf m; kg m)	X	9.804	= Newton meters (Nm)
Vacuum						
Inches mercury (in. Hg)	X	3.377	= Kilopascals (kPa)	X	0.2961	= Inches mercury
Inches mercury (in. Hg)	X	25.4	= Millimeters mercury (mm Hg)	X	0.0394	= Inches mercury
Power						
Horsepower (hp)	X	745.7	= Watts (W)	X	0.0013	= Horsepower (hp)
Velocity (speed)						
Miles per hour (miles/hr; mph)	X	1.609	= Kilometers per hour (km/hr; kph)	X	0.621	= Miles per hour (miles/hr; mph)
Fuel consumption*						
Miles per gallon, Imperial (mpg)	X	0.354	= Kilometers per liter (km/l)	X	2.825	= Miles per gallon, Imperial (mpg)
Miles per gallon, US (mpg)	X	0.425	= Kilometers per liter (km/l)	X	2.352	= Miles per gallon, US (mpg)

Temperature

Degrees Fahrenheit = (°C x 1.8) + 32

Degrees Celsius (Degrees Centigrade; °C) = (°F - 32) x 0.56

****It is common practice to convert from miles per gallon (mpg) to liters/100 kilometers (l/100km), where mpg (Imperial) x l/100 km = 282 and mpg (US) x l/100 km = 235***

DECIMALS to MILLIMETERS

Decimal	mm	Decimal	mm
0.001	0.0254	0.500	12.7000
0.002	0.0508	0.510	12.9540
0.003	0.0762	0.520	13.2080
0.004	0.1016	0.530	13.4620
0.005	0.1270	0.540	13.7160
0.006	0.1524	0.550	13.9700
0.007	0.1778	0.560	14.2240
0.008	0.2032	0.570	14.4780
0.009	0.2286	0.580	14.7320
0.010	0.2540	0.590	14.9860
0.020	0.5080	0.600	15.2400
0.030	0.7620	0.610	15.4940
0.040	1.0160	0.620	15.7480
0.050	1.2700	0.630	16.0020
0.060	1.5240	0.640	16.2560
0.070	1.7780	0.650	16.5100
0.080	2.0320	0.660	16.7640
0.090	2.2860	0.670	17.0180
0.100	2.5400	0.680	17.2720
0.110	2.7940	0.690	17.5260
0.120	3.0480	0.700	17.7800
0.130	3.3020	0.710	18.0340
0.140	3.5560	0.720	18.2880
0.150	3.8100	0.730	18.5420
0.160	4.0640	0.740	18.7960
0.170	4.3180	0.750	19.0500
0.180	4.5720	0.760	19.3040
0.190	4.8260	0.770	19.5580
0.200	5.0800	0.780	19.8120
0.210	5.3340	0.790	20.0660
0.220	5.5880	0.800	20.3200
0.230	5.8420	0.810	20.5740
0.240	6.0960	0.820	21.8280
0.250	6.3500	0.830	21.0820
0.260	6.6040	0.840	21.3360
0.270	6.8580	0.850	21.5900
0.280	7.1120	0.860	21.8440
0.290	7.3660	0.870	22.0980
0.300	7.6200	0.880	22.3520
0.310	7.8740	0.890	22.6060
0.320	8.1280	0.900	22.8600
0.330	8.3820	0.910	23.1140
0.340	8.6360	0.920	23.3680
0.350	8.8900	0.930	23.6220
0.360	9.1440	0.940	23.8760
0.370	9.3980	0.950	24.1300
0.380	9.6520	0.960	24.3840
0.390	9.9060	0.970	24.6380
0.400	10.1600	0.980	24.8920
0.410	10.4140	0.990	25.1460
0.420	10.6680	1.000	25.4000
0.430	10.9220		
0.440	11.1760		
0.450	11.4300		
0.460	11.6840		
0.470	11.9380		
0.480	12.1920		
0.490	12.4460		

FRACTIONS to DECIMALS to MILLIMETERS

Fraction	Decimal	mm	Fraction	Decimal	mm
1/64	0.0156	0.3969	33/64	0.5156	13.0969
1/32	0.0312	0.7938	17/32	0.5312	13.4938
3/64	0.0469	1.1906	35/64	0.5469	13.8906
1/16	0.0625	1.5875	9/16	0.5625	14.2875
5/64	0.0781	1.9844	37/64	0.5781	14.6844
3/32	0.0938	2.3812	19/32	0.5938	15.0812
7/64	0.1094	2.7781	39/64	0.6094	15.4781
1/8	0.1250	3.1750	5/8	0.6250	15.8750
9/64	0.1406	3.5719	41/64	0.6406	16.2719
5/32	0.1562	3.9688	21/32	0.6562	16.6688
11/64	0.1719	4.3656	43/64	0.6719	17.0656
3/16	0.1875	4.7625	11/16	0.6875	17.4625
13/64	0.2031	5.1594	45/64	0.7031	17.8594
7/32	0.2188	5.5562	23/32	0.7188	18.2562
15/64	0.2344	5.9531	47/64	0.7344	18.6531
1/4	0.2500	6.3500	3/4	0.7500	19.0500
17/64	0.2656	6.7469	49/64	0.7656	19.4469
9/32	0.2812	7.1438	25/32	0.7812	19.8438
19/64	0.2969	7.5406	51/64	0.7969	20.2406
5/16	0.3125	7.9375	13/16	0.8125	20.6375
21/64	0.3281	8.3344	53/64	0.8281	21.0344
11/32	0.3438	8.7312	27/32	0.8438	21.4312
23/64	0.3594	9.1281	55/64	0.8594	21.8281
3/8	0.3750	9.5250	7/8	0.8750	22.2250
25/64	0.3906	9.9219	57/64	0.8906	22.6219
13/32	0.4062	10.3188	29/32	0.9062	23.0188
27/64	0.4219	10.7156	59/64	0.9219	23.4156
7/16	0.4375	11.1125	15/16	0.9375	23.8125
29/64	0.4531	11.5094	61/64	0.9531	24.2094
15/32	0.4688	11.9062	31/32	0.9688	24.6062
31/64	0.4844	12.3031	63/64	0.9844	25.0031
1/2	0.5000	12.7000	1	1.0000	25.4000

Safety first!

Regardless of how enthusiastic you may be about getting on with the job at hand, take the time to ensure that your safety is not jeopardized. A moment's lack of attention can result in an accident, as can failure to observe certain simple safety precautions. The possibility of an accident will always exist, and the following points should not be considered a comprehensive list of all dangers. Rather, they are intended to make you aware of the risks and to encourage a safety conscious approach to all work you carry out on your vehicle.

Essential DOs and DON'Ts

DON'T rely on a jack when working under the vehicle. Always use approved jackstands to support the weight of the vehicle and place them under the recommended lift or support points.

DON'T attempt to loosen extremely tight fasteners (i.e. wheel lug nuts) while the vehicle is on a jack - it may fall.

DON'T start the engine without first making sure that the transmission is in Neutral (or Park where applicable) and the parking brake is set.

DON'T remove the radiator cap from a hot cooling system - let it cool or cover it with a cloth and release the pressure gradually.

DON'T attempt to drain the engine oil until you are sure it has cooled to the point that it will not burn you.

DON'T touch any part of the engine or exhaust system until it has cooled sufficiently to avoid burns.

DON'T siphon toxic liquids such as gasoline, antifreeze and brake fluid by mouth, or allow them to remain on your skin.

DON'T inhale brake lining dust - it is potentially hazardous (see *Asbestos* below).

DON'T allow spilled oil or grease to remain on the floor - wipe it up before someone slips on it.

DON'T use loose fitting wrenches or other tools which may slip and cause injury.

DON'T push on wrenches when loosening or tightening nuts or bolts. Always try to pull the wrench toward you. If the situation calls for pushing the wrench away, push with an open hand to avoid scraped knuckles if the wrench should slip.

DON'T attempt to lift a heavy component alone - get someone to help you.

DON'T rush or take unsafe shortcuts to finish a job.

DON'T allow children or animals in or around the vehicle while you are working on it.

DO wear eye protection when using power tools such as a drill, sander, bench grinder, etc. and when working under a vehicle.

DO keep loose clothing and long hair well out of the way of moving parts.

DO make sure that any hoist used has a safe working load rating adequate for the job.

DO get someone to check on you periodically when working alone on a vehicle.

DO carry out work in a logical sequence and make sure that everything is correctly assembled and tightened.

DO keep chemicals and fluids tightly capped and out of the reach of children and pets.

DO remember that your vehicle's safety affects that of yourself and others. If in doubt on any point, get professional advice.

Steering, suspension and brakes

These systems are essential to driving safety, so make sure you have a qualified shop or individual check your work. Also, compressed suspension springs can cause injury if released suddenly - be sure to use a spring compressor.

Airbags

Airbags are explosive devices that can **CAUSE** injury if they deploy while you're working on the vehicle. Follow the manufacturer's instructions to disable the airbag whenever you're working in the vicinity of airbag components.

Asbestos

Certain friction, insulating, sealing, and other products - such as brake linings, brake bands, clutch linings, torque converters, gaskets, etc. - may contain asbestos or other hazardous friction material. Extreme care must be taken to avoid inhalation of dust from such products, since it is hazardous to health. If in doubt, assume that they do contain asbestos.

Fire

Remember at all times that gasoline is highly flammable. Never smoke or have any kind of open flame around when working on a vehicle. But the risk does not end there. A spark caused by an electrical short circuit, by two metal surfaces contacting each other, or even by static electricity built up in your body under certain conditions, can ignite gasoline vapors, which in a confined space are highly explosive. Do not, under any circumstances, use gasoline for cleaning parts. Use an approved safety solvent.

Always disconnect the battery ground (-) cable at the battery before working on any part of the fuel system or electrical system. Never risk spilling fuel on a hot engine or exhaust component. It is strongly recommended that a fire extinguisher suitable for use on fuel and electrical fires be kept handy in the garage or workshop at all times. Never try to extinguish a fuel or electrical fire with water.

Fumes

Certain fumes are highly toxic and can quickly cause unconsciousness and even death if inhaled to any extent. Gasoline vapor falls into this category, as do the vapors from some cleaning solvents. Any draining or pouring of such volatile fluids should be done in a well ventilated area.

When using cleaning fluids and solvents, read the instructions on the container carefully. Never use materials from unmarked containers.

Never run the engine in an enclosed space, such as a garage. Exhaust fumes contain carbon monoxide, which is extremely poisonous. If you need to run the engine, always do so in the open air, or at least have the rear of the vehicle outside the work area.

The battery

Never create a spark or allow a bare light bulb near a battery. They normally give off a certain amount of hydrogen gas, which is highly explosive.

Always disconnect the battery ground (-) cable at the battery before working on the fuel or electrical systems.

If possible, loosen the filler caps or cover when charging the battery from an external source (this does not apply to sealed or maintenance-free batteries). Do not charge at an excessive rate or the battery may burst.

Take care when adding water to a non maintenance-free battery and when carrying a battery. The electrolyte, even when diluted, is very corrosive and should not be allowed to contact clothing or skin.

Always wear eye protection when cleaning the battery to prevent the caustic deposits from entering your eyes.

Household current

When using an electric power tool, inspection light, etc., which operates on household current, always make sure that the tool is correctly connected to its plug and that, where necessary, it is properly grounded. Do not use such items in damp conditions and, again, do not create a spark or apply excessive heat in the vicinity of fuel or fuel vapor.

Secondary ignition system voltage

A severe electric shock can result from touching certain parts of the ignition system (such as the spark plug wires) when the engine is running or being cranked, particularly if components are damp or the insulation is defective. In the case of an electronic ignition system, the secondary system voltage is much higher and could prove fatal.

Hydrofluoric acid

This extremely corrosive acid is formed when certain types of synthetic rubber, found in some O-rings, oil seals, fuel hoses, etc. are exposed to temperatures above 750-degrees F (400-degrees C). The rubber changes into a charred or sticky substance containing the acid. *Once formed, the acid remains dangerous for years. If it gets onto the skin, it may be necessary to amputate the limb concerned.*

When dealing with a vehicle which has suffered a fire, or with components salvaged from such a vehicle, wear protective gloves and discard them after use.

Troubleshooting

Contents

Symptom — *Section*

Engine and performance
Engine backfires 15
Engine continues to run after switching off 18
Engine hard to start when cold 3
Engine hard to start when hot 4
Engine lacks power 14
Engine lopes while idling or idles erratically 8
Engine misses at idle speed 9
Engine misses throughout driving speed range 10
Engine rotates but will not start 2
Engine runs with oil pressure light on 17
Engine stalls 13
Engine starts but stops immediately 6
Engine stumbles on acceleration 11
Engine surges while holding accelerator steady 12
Engine will not rotate when attempting to start 1
Oil puddle under engine 7
Pinging or knocking engine sounds during acceleration or uphill .. 16
Starter motor noisy or excessively rough in engagement 5

Engine electrical system
Battery will not hold a charge 19
Excessive fuel consumption 22
Fuel leakage and/or fuel odor 23
Voltage warning light fails to come on when key is turned on 21
Voltage warning light fails to go out 20

Cooling system
Coolant loss 28
External coolant leakage 26
Internal coolant leakage 27
Overcooling 25
Overheating 24
Poor coolant circulation 29

Automatic transaxle
Engine will start in gears other than Park or Neutral 33
Fluid leakage 30
General shift mechanism problems 32
Transaxle fluid brown or has a burned smell 31
Transaxle slips, shifts roughly, is noisy or has no drive in forward or reverse gears 34

Driveaxles
Clicking noise in turns 35
Knock or clunk when accelerating after coasting 36
Shudder or vibration during acceleration 37

Brakes
Brake pedal feels spongy when depressed 45
Brake pedal travels to the floor with little resistance 46
Brake roughness or chatter (pedal pulsates) 40
Dragging brakes 43
Excessive pedal effort required to stop vehicle 41
Excessive brake pedal travel 42
Grabbing or uneven braking action 44
Noise (grinding or high-pitched squeal) when the brakes are applied 39
Parking brake does not hold 47
Vehicle pulls to one side during braking 38

Suspension and steering systems
Abnormal noise at the front end 54
Abnormal or excessive tire wear 49
Cupped tires 59
Erratic steering when braking 56
Excessive pitching and/or rolling around corners or during braking 57
Excessive play or looseness in steering system 63
Excessive tire wear on inside edge 61
Excessive tire wear on outside edge 60
Hard steering 52
Rattling or clicking noise in steering gear 64
Shimmy, shake or vibration 51
Steering wheel does not return to center position correctly 53
Suspension bottoms 58
Tire tread worn in one place 62
Vehicle pulls to one side 48
Wander or poor steering stability 55
Wheel makes a "thumping" noise 50

This section provides an easy reference guide to the more common problems which may occur during the operation of your vehicle. These problems and their possible causes are grouped under headings denoting various components or systems, such as Engine, Cooling system, etc. They also refer you to the chapter and/or section which deals with the problem.

Remember that successful troubleshooting is not a mysterious black art practiced only by professional mechanics. It is simply the result of the right knowledge combined with an intelligent, systematic approach to the problem. Always work by a process of elimination, starting with the simplest solution and working through to the most complex - and never overlook the obvious. Anyone can run the gas tank dry or leave the lights on overnight, so don't assume that you are exempt from such oversights.

Finally, always establish a clear idea of why a problem has occurred and take steps to ensure that it doesn't happen again. If the electrical system fails because of a poor connection, check the other connections in the system to make sure that they don't fail as well. If a particular fuse continues to blow, find out why - don't just replace one fuse after another. Remember, failure of a small component can often be indicative of potential failure or incorrect functioning of a more important component or system.

Engine and performance

1 Engine will not rotate when attempting to start

1 Battery terminal connections loose or corroded (see Chapter 1).
2 Battery discharged or faulty (see Chapter 1).
3 Automatic transaxle not completely engaged in Park (see Chapter 7).
4 Broken, loose or disconnected wiring in the starting circuit (see Chapters 5 and 12).
5 Starter motor pinion jammed in flywheel ring gear (see Chapter 5).
6 Starter solenoid faulty (see Chapter 5).
7 Starter motor faulty (see Chapter 5).
8 Ignition switch faulty (see Chapter 12).
9 Transmission Range (TR) sensor faulty (see Chapter 6).
10 Starter pinion or driveplate teeth worn or broken (see Chapter 5).

2 Engine rotates but will not start

1 Fuel tank empty.
2 Battery discharged (engine rotates slowly) (see Chapter 5).
3 Battery terminal connections loose or corroded (see Chapter 1).
4 Leaking fuel injector(s), fuel pump, pressure regulator, etc. (see Chapter 4).
5 Fuel not reaching fuel injection system (see Chapter 4).
6 Broken timing belt or chain (see Chapter 2A or 2B).
7 Ignition system problem (see Chapter 5).
8 Defective crankshaft sensor or camshaft sensor (see Chapter 6).

3 Engine hard to start when cold

1 Battery discharged or low (see Chapter 1).
2 Fuel system malfunctioning (see Chapter 4).
3 Emissions or engine control system malfunctioning (see Chapter 6).

4 Engine hard to start when hot

1 Air filter clogged (see Chapter 1).
2 Fuel not reaching the fuel injection system (see Chapter 4).
3 Corroded battery connections, especially ground (see Chapter 1).
4 Emissions or engine control system malfunctioning (see Chapter 6).

5 Starter motor noisy or excessively rough in engagement

1 Pinion or driveplate gear teeth worn or broken (see Chapter 5).
2 Starter motor mounting bolts loose or missing (see Chapter 5).

6 Engine starts but stops immediately

1 Insufficient fuel reaching the fuel injectors (see Chapter 4).
2 Vacuum leak at the gasket between the intake manifold/plenum and throttle body (see Chapters 1 and 4).
3 Restricted exhaust system (most likely the catalytic converter) (see Chapters 4 and 6).

7 Oil puddle under engine

1 Oil pan gasket and/or oil pan drain bolt seal leaking (see Chapters 1 and).
2 Oil pressure sending unit leaking (see Chapter 2A).
3 Rocker arm cover gaskets leaking (see Chapter 2A).
4 Engine oil seals leaking (see Chapter 2A).

8 Engine lopes while idling or idles erratically

1 Vacuum leakage (see Chapter 4).
2 Leaking EGR valve or plugged PCV valve (see Chapter 6).
3 Air filter clogged (see Chapter 1).
4 Fuel pump not delivering sufficient fuel to the fuel injection system (see Chapter 4).
5 Leaking head gasket (see Chapter 2A).
6 Camshaft lobes worn (see Chapter 2A).

9 Engine misses at idle speed

1 Spark plugs worn or not gapped properly (see Chapter 1).
2 Faulty coil(s) or spark plug wires (see Chapter 5).
3 Vacuum leaks (see Chapters 1 and 4).
4 Uneven or low compression (see Chapter 2B).

10 Engine misses throughout driving speed range

1 Fuel filter clogged and/or impurities in the fuel system (see Chapter 4).
2 Low fuel pressure (see Chapter 4).
3 Faulty or incorrectly gapped spark plugs (see Chapter 1).
4 Leaking spark plug wires (see Chapter 1).
5 Faulty emission system components (see Chapter 6).
6 Low or uneven cylinder compression pressures (see Chapter 2A).
7 Weak or faulty ignition system (see Chapter 5).
8 Vacuum leak (see Chapter 2A).

11 Engine stumbles on acceleration

1 Spark plugs fouled (see Chapter 1).
2 Fuel injection system problem (see Chapter 4).
3 Fuel filter clogged (see Chapter 4).
4 Intake manifold air leak (see Chapter 4).
5 Problem with emissions/engine control system (see Chapter 6).

12 Engine surges while holding accelerator steady

1 Intake air leak (see Chapter 4).
2 Fuel pump faulty (see Chapter 4).
3 Problem with the fuel injection system (see Chapter 4).
4 Problem with the emission or engine control system (see Chapter 6).

13 Engine stalls

1 Fuel filter clogged and/or water and impurities in the fuel system (see Chapter 4).
2 Faulty emissions or engine control system components (see Chapter 6).
3 Faulty or incorrectly gapped spark plugs (see Chapter 1).
4 Faulty spark plug wires (see Chapter 1).
5 Vacuum leak (see Chapter 2A).

14 Engine lacks power

1 Faulty or incorrectly gapped spark plugs (see Chapter 1).
2 Restricted exhaust system (most likely the catalytic converter (see Chapters 4 and 6).
3 Fuel injection system malfunctioning (see Chapter 4).
4 Faulty coil(s) (see Chapter 5).
5 Brakes binding (see Chapter 9).
6 Automatic transaxle fluid level incorrect (see Chapter 1).
7 Fuel filter clogged and/or impurities in the fuel system (see Chapter 1).
8 Emission control system not functioning properly (see Chapter 6).
9 Low or uneven cylinder compression pressures (see Chapter 2A).

15 Engine backfires

1 Emissions system not functioning properly (see Chapter 6).
2 Fuel injection system malfunctioning (see Chapter 4).
3 Vacuum leak at fuel injectors, intake manifold or vacuum hoses (see Chapter 4).
4 Valves sticking (see Chapter 2A).
5 Timing chain worn (see Chapter 2A).

16 Pinging or knocking engine sounds during acceleration or uphill

1 Incorrect grade of fuel.
2 Fuel injection system malfunctioning (see Chapter 4).
3 Improper or damaged spark plugs (see Chapter 1).
4 Worn or damaged ignition components (see Chapter 5).
5 Faulty emissions or engine control system (see Chapter 6).
6 Vacuum leak (see Chapter 2A).

17 Engine runs with oil pressure light on

1 Low oil level (see Chapter 1).
2 Short in wiring circuit (see Chapter 12).
3 Faulty oil pressure sender (see Chapter 2A).
4 Oil viscosity too low or oil diluted.
5 Worn engine bearings and/or oil pump (see Chapter 2A).

18 Engine continues to run after switching off

1 Excessive engine operating temperature (see Chapter 3).
2 Excessive carbon deposits on valves and pistons.
3 Leaking fuel injector(s).

Engine electrical system

19 Battery will not hold a charge

1 Drivebelt or tensioner defective (see Chapter 1).
2 Battery terminals loose or corroded (see Chapter 1).
3 Alternator not charging properly (see Chapter 5).
4 Loose, broken or faulty wiring in the charging circuit (see Chapter 5).
5 Internally defective battery (see Chapters 1 and 5).

20 Voltage warning light fails to go out

1 Faulty alternator or charging circuit (see Chapter 5).
2 Drivebelt or tensioner defective (see Chapter 1).
3 Alternator voltage regulator inoperative (see Chapter 5).

21 Voltage warning light fails to come on when key is turned on

1 Warning light bulb defective (see Chapter 12).
2 Fault in the printed circuit, dash wiring or bulb holder (see Chapter 12).

Fuel system

22 Excessive fuel consumption

1 Dirty or clogged air filter element (see Chapter 1).
2 Emissions or engine control system not functioning properly (see Chapter 6).
3 Fuel injection system malfunctioning (see Chapter 4).
4 Low tire pressure or incorrect tire size (see Chapter 1).

23 Fuel leakage and/or fuel odor

1 Leak in a fuel feed or vent line (see Chapter 4).
2 Tank overfilled.
3 Evaporative emissions control canister defective (see Chapter 6).
4 Fuel injector seals faulty (see Chapter 4).

Cooling system

24 Overheating

1 Insufficient coolant in system (see Chapter 1).
2 Drivebelt or tensioner defective (see Chapter 1).
3 Radiator core blocked or grille restricted (see Chapter 3).
4 Thermostat faulty (see Chapter 3).
5 Electric cooling fan blades broken or cracked (see Chapter 3).
6 Radiator cap not maintaining proper pressure (see Chapter 3).
7 Faulty water pump (see Chapter 3).

25 Overcooling

Incorrect (opening temperature too low) or faulty thermostat (see Chapter 3).

26 External coolant leakage

1 Deteriorated/damaged hoses or loose clamps (see Chapters 1 and 3).
2 Water pump seal defective (see Chapter 3).
3 Leakage from radiator core (see Chapter 3).
4 Engine drain or water jacket core plugs leaking (see Chapter 2A).

27 Internal coolant leakage

1 Leaking cylinder head gasket (see Chapter 2A).
2 Cracked cylinder bore or cylinder head (see Chapter 2A).

28 Coolant loss

1 Too much coolant in system (see Chapter 1).
2 Coolant boiling away because of overheating (see Chapter 3).
3 Internal or external leakage (see Chapter 3).
4 Faulty radiator cap (see Chapter 3).

29 Poor coolant circulation

1 Inoperative water pump (see Chapter 3).
2 Restriction in cooling system (see Chapters 1 and 3).
3 Drivebelt or tensioner defective or out of adjustment (see Chapter 1).
4 Thermostat sticking (see Chapter 3).

Automatic transaxle

30 Fluid leakage

1 Automatic transmission fluid is a deep red color. Fluid leaks should not be confused with engine oil, which can easily be blown by airflow to the transaxle.
2 To pinpoint a leak, first remove all built-up dirt and grime from the transaxle housing with degreasing agents and/or steam cleaning. Drive the vehicle at low speeds so air flow will not blow the leak far from its source. Raise the vehicle and determine where the leak is coming from. Common areas of leakage are:

Fluid pan
Fluid cooler lines (see Chapter 7)
Vehicle Speed Sensor (see Chapter 6)

31 Transaxle fluid brown or has a burned smell

Transaxle overheated. Change fluid (see Chapter 1).

32 General shift mechanism problems

1 Chapter 7 deals with checking and adjusting the shift linkage on automatic transaxles. Common problems which may be attributed to a poorly adjusted linkage are:

Engine starting in gears other than Park or Neutral.
Indicator on shifter pointing to a gear other than the one actually being used.
Vehicle moves when in Park.

2 Refer to Chapter 7 for the shift linkage adjustment procedure.

33 Engine will start in gears other than Park or Neutral

Transmission Range (TR) sensor malfunctioning (see Chapter 6).

34 Transaxle slips, shifts roughly, is noisy or has no drive in forward or reverse gears

1 There are many probable causes for the above problems, but the home mechanic should be concerned with only one possibility - fluid level. Before taking the vehicle to a repair shop, check the level and condition of the fluid as described in Chapter 1.
2 Correct the fluid level as necessary or change the fluid and filter if needed. If the problem persists, have a professional diagnose the probable cause.

Driveaxles

35 Clicking noise in turns

Worn or damaged outer CV joint. Check for cut or damaged boots (see Chapter 1). Repair as necessary (see Chapter 8).

36 Knock or clunk when accelerating after coasting

Worn or damaged CV joint. Check for cut or damaged boots (see Chapter 1). Repair as necessary (see Chapter 8).

37 Shudder or vibration during acceleration

1 Worn or damaged CV joints. Repair or replace as necessary (see Chapter 8).
2 Sticking inner joint assembly. Correct or replace as necessary (see Chapter 8).

Brakes

38 Vehicle pulls to one side during braking

1 Incorrect tire pressures (see Chapter 1).
2 Front end out of alignment (have the front end aligned).
3 Unmatched tires on same axle.
4 Restricted brake lines or hoses (see Chapter 9).
5 Sticking caliper or wheel cylinder piston (see Chapter 9).
6 Loose suspension parts (see Chapter 10).
7 Contaminated brake pad material (see Chapter 9).

39 Noise (grinding or high-pitched squeal) when the brakes are applied

Disc brake pads worn out. Replace pads with new ones immediately (see Chapter 9).

40 Brake roughness or chatter (pedal pulsates)

1 Excessive brake disc lateral runout.
2 Parallelism of disc not within specifications (see Chapter 9).
3 Defective brake disc (see Chapter 9).

41 Excessive pedal effort required to stop vehicle

1 Malfunctioning power brake booster (see Chapter 9).
2 Partial system failure (see Chapter 9).
3 Excessively worn pads (see Chapter 9).
4 One or more caliper or wheel cylinder pistons seized or sticking (see Chapter 9).
5 Brake pads contaminated with oil or grease (see Chapter 9).
6 New pads or shoes installed and not yet seated. It will take a while for the new material to seat.

42 Excessive brake pedal travel

1 Partial brake system failure (see Chapter 9).
2 Insufficient fluid in master cylinder (see Chapters 1 and 9).
3 Air trapped in system (see Chapter 9).
4 Faulty master cylinder (see Chapter 9).

43 Dragging brakes

1 Master cylinder pistons not returning correctly (see Chapter 9).
2 Restricted brake lines or hoses (see Chapters 1 and 9).
3 Incorrect parking brake adjustment (see Chapter 9).
4 Defective brake calipers (see Chapter 9).

44 Grabbing or uneven braking action

Contaminated brake pads (see Chapter 9).

45 Brake pedal feels spongy when depressed

1 Air in hydraulic lines (see Chapter 9).
2 Master cylinder mounting bolts loose (see Chapter 9).
3 Master cylinder defective (see Chapter 9).

46 Brake pedal travels to the floor with little resistance

Little or no fluid in the master cylinder reservoir caused by leaking caliper, or loose, damaged or disconnected brake lines (see Chapter 9).

47 Parking brake does not hold

Parking brake cables improperly adjusted (see Chapter 9).

Suspension and steering systems

48 Vehicle pulls to one side

1 Mismatched or uneven tires (see Chapter 10).
2 Broken or sagging coil springs (see Chapter 10).
3 Wheel alignment incorrect.
4 Front brakes dragging (see Chapter 9).

49 Abnormal or excessive tire wear

1 Front wheel alignment incorrect.
2 Sagging or broken springs (see Chapter 10).
3 Tire out-of-balance (see Chapter 10).
4 Worn strut or shock absorber (see Chapter 10).
5 Overloaded vehicle.
6 Tires not rotated regularly.

50 Wheel makes a "thumping" noise

1 Blister or bump on tire (see Chapter 1).
2 Improper strut or shock absorber action (see Chapter 10).

51 Shimmy, shake or vibration

1 Tire or wheel out-of-balance or out-of-round (see Chapter 10).
2 Worn wheel bearings (see Chapter 10).
3 Worn tie-rod ends (see Chapter 10).
4 Worn balljoints (see Chapter 10).
5 Excessive wheel runout (see Chapter 10).
6 Blister or bump on tire (see Chapter 1.

52 Hard steering

1 Balljoints, tie-rod ends or steering gear worn (see Chapter 10).
2 Front wheel alignment incorrect.
3 Low tire pressure (see Chapter 1).

53 Steering wheel does not return to center position correctly

1 Balljoints or tie-rod ends worn (see Chapters 1 and 10).
2 Defective rack-and-pinion assembly (see Chapter 10).
3 Front wheel alignment problem.

54 Abnormal noise at the front end

1 Balljoints or tie-rod ends worn (Chapter 1).
2 Loose upper strut mount (see Chapter 10).
3 Worn tie-rod ends (see Chapter 10).
4 Loose stabilizer bar (see Chapter 10).
5 Loose wheel lug nuts (see Chapter 1).
6 Loose suspension bolts (see Chapter 10.

55 Wander or poor steering stability

1 Mismatched or uneven tires (see Chapter 10).
2 Balljoints or tie-rod ends worn (see Chapters 1 and 10).
3 Worn struts or shock absorbers (see Chapter 10).
4 Broken or sagging springs (see Chapter 10).
5 Front wheel alignment incorrect.
6 Worn steering gear clamp bushing (see Chapter 10).

56 Erratic steering when braking

1 Wheel bearings worn (Chapter 10).
2 Broken or sagging springs (see Chapter 10).
3 Leaking caliper (see Chapter 9).
4 Warped brake discs (see Chapter 9).
5 Worn steering gear clamp bushing (see Chapter 10).
6 Wheel alignment incorrect.

57 Excessive pitching and/or rolling around corners or during braking

1 Loose stabilizer bar (see Chapter 10).
2 Worn struts/shock absorbers or mounts (see Chapter 10).
3 Broken or sagging coil springs (see Chapter 10).
4 Overloaded vehicle.

58 Suspension bottoms

1 Overloaded vehicle.
2 Worn struts or shock absorbers (see Chapter 10).
3 Incorrect, broken or sagging springs (see Chapter 10).

59 Cupped tires

1 Front wheel alignment incorrect.
2 Worn struts or shock absorbers (see Chapter 10).
3 Wheel bearings worn (see Chapter 10).
4 Excessive tire or wheel runout (see Chapter 10).
5 Worn balljoints (see Chapter 10).

60 Excessive tire wear on outside edge

1 Inflation pressures incorrect (see Chapter 1).
2 Excessive speed in turns.
3 Wheel alignment incorrect (excessive toe-in or positive camber). Have professionally aligned.
4 Suspension arm bent (see Chapter 10).

61 Excessive tire wear on inside edge

1 Inflation pressures incorrect (see Chapter 1).
2 Wheel alignment incorrect (toe-out or excessive negative camber). Have professionally aligned.
3 Loose or damaged steering components (see Chapter 10).

62 Tire tread worn in one place

1 Tires out-of-balance.
2 Damaged wheel.
3 Defective tire (see Chapter 1).

63 Excessive play or looseness in steering system

1 Wheel bearings worn (see Chapter 10).
2 Tie-rod end loose or worn (see Chapter 10).
3 Steering gear loose (see Chapter 10).

64 Rattling or clicking noise in steering gear

1 Steering gear mounting bolts loose (see Chapter 10).
2 Steering gear defective (see Chapter 10).

Notes

Chapter 1
Tune-up and routine maintenance

Contents

	Section
Air filter check and replacement	13
Automatic transaxle fluid change	25
Battery check, maintenance and charging	8
Brake fluid change	20
Brake system check	14
Cabin air filter replacement	18
Cooling system check	12
Cooling system servicing	22
Drivebelt check, adjustment and replacement	19
Engine oil and filter change	6
Exhaust system check	16
Fluid level checks	4
Fuel system check	17
Introduction	2
Maintenance schedule	1
Positive Crankcase Ventilation (PCV) valve check and replacement	21
Seat belt check	10
Spark plug check and replacement	23
Spark plug wire check and replacement	24
Steering, suspension and driveaxle boot check	15
Tire and tire pressure checks	5
Tire rotation	9
Tune-up general information	3
Underhood hose check and replacement	11
Windshield/rear wiper blade inspection and replacement	7

Specifications

Recommended lubricants and fluids

Engine oil	
Type API "Certified for gasoline engines"	
Viscosity	
2005 and earlier models	SAE 10W-30
2006 and later models	SAE 5W-20
Automatic transaxle fluid	
2010 and earlier 5-speed automatic transaxle	Genuine Diamond ATF SP-III automatic transaxle fluid or equivalent
2011 and later 6-speed automatic transaxle	SP-IV automatic transaxle fluid or equivalent
Power steering fluid	Genuine Diamond PSF-III power steering fluid or equivalent
Brake fluid	DOT type 3 brake fluid
Engine coolant	50/50 mixture of ethylene glycol (for use with aluminum) and water
Door and liftgate latch	Multi-purpose grease
Fuel filler door remote control latch mechanism	Multi-purpose grease
Hood, door and liftgate hinge lubricant	Engine oil
Key lock cylinder lubricant	Graphite spray
Parking brake mechanism	Multi-purpose grease

Capacities*

Engine oil (including filter)		
2005 and earlier models	4.55 quarts	4.3 liters
2006 and later models	5.5 quarts	5.2 liters
Automatic transaxle (total)**		
2005 and earlier models	8.9 quarts	8.5 liters
2006 through 2010 models	11.5 quarts	10.9 liters
2011 and later models	8.2 quarts	7.8 liters
Cooling system		
2005 and earlier models	8.61 quarts	8.2 liters
2006 through 2010 models	9.9 quarts	8.6 liters
2011 and later models	8.8 quarts	8.3 liters

**All capacities approximate. Add as necessary to bring to appropriate level.*

***This is a dry-fill specification. The best way to determine the amount of fluid to add during a routine fluid change is to measure the amount drained. It's important to not overfill the transaxle.*

Brakes

Disc brake pad wear limit (minimum thickness)	1/8 inch (3 mm)
Drum brake shoe wear limit (minimum thickness)	1/16 inch (1.5 mm)

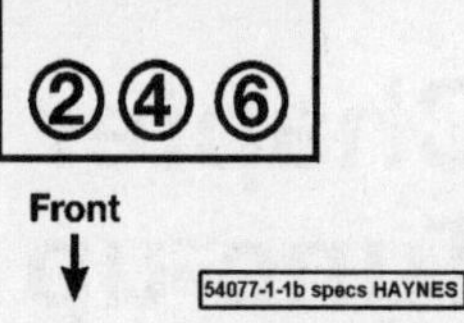

Cylinder location diagram

Ignition system

Spark plug type and gap	
Type	
2005 and earlier models	NGK PFR5N-11 or equivalent
2006 through 2010 models	NGK IFR5G-11 or equivalent
2011 and later models	NGK SILZKR7B11 / Champion
RER8WMPB4 or equivalvent	
Gap	0.039 TO 0.043 inch (1.0 to 1.1 mm)
Firing order	1-2-3-4-5-6

Drivebelt deflection - 2005 and earlier models

Power steering pump belt		
New belt	0.35 to 0.43 inch	8.8 to 11 mm
Used belt	0.49 to 0.56 inch	12.5 to 14.3 mm
Air conditioning compressor/alternator belt		
New belt	0.31 to 0.35 inch	8 to 9 mm
Used belt	0.35 to 0.39 inch	9 to 10 mm

Torque specifications

Note: One foot-pound (ft-lb) of torque is equivalent to 12 inch-pounds (in-lbs) of torque. Torque values below approximately 15 ft-lbs are expressed in inch-pounds, since most foot-pound torque wrenches are not accurate at these smaller values.

Torque specifications	Ft-lbs (unless otherwise indicated)	Nm
Automatic transaxle		
2010 and earlier models		
Drain plug	29 to 36	40 to 50
2011 and later models		
Oil level plug	26 to 32	35 to 44
Banjo bolt*	26 to 32	35 to 44
Drivebelt tensioner mounting bolt		
2005 and earlier models		
Tensioner nut	33 to 36	45 to 50
Pulley bolt	26 to 40	35 to 55
2006 through 2010 models		
8 mm bolt	15 to 16	18 to 21
12 mm bolt	71 to 73	97 to 99
2011 and later models		
8 mm bolt	15 to 16	18 to 21
12 mm bolt	60 to 62	82 to 85
Engine oil drain plug	26 to 32	35 to 45
Engine oil filter cap (2006 and later models)	25	35
Spark plugs	15 to 22	20 to 30
Wheel lug nuts	66 to 79	90 to 108

** Use new bolt/nut(s)*

2.2a Typical engine compartment layout – 3.8L engine shown, other models similar

1. *Air filter housing*
2. *Power steering fluid reservoir*
3. *Brake fluid reservoir*
4. *Battery*
5. *Underhood fuse/relay block*
6. *Coolant reservoir*
7. *Transaxle fluid dipstick*
8. *Engine oil filler cap*
9. *Upper radiator hose*
10. *Engine oil dipstick*
11. *Windshield washer fluid reservoir*
12. *Radiator cap*
13. *Oil filter housing*

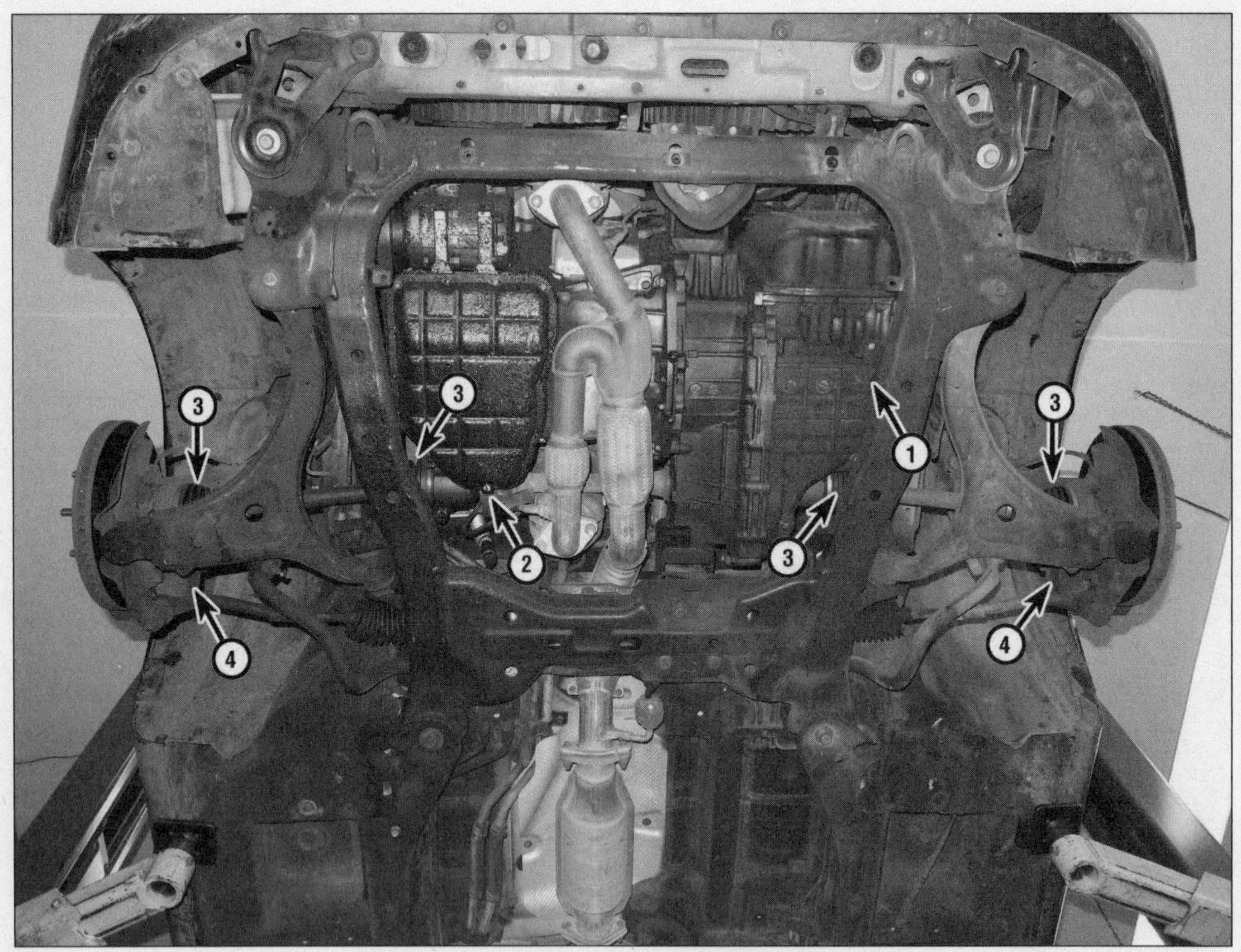

2.2b Typical engine compartment underside components

1. *Automatic transaxle fluid drain plug*
2. *Engine oil drain plug*
3. *Driveaxle boots*
4. *Brake calipers*

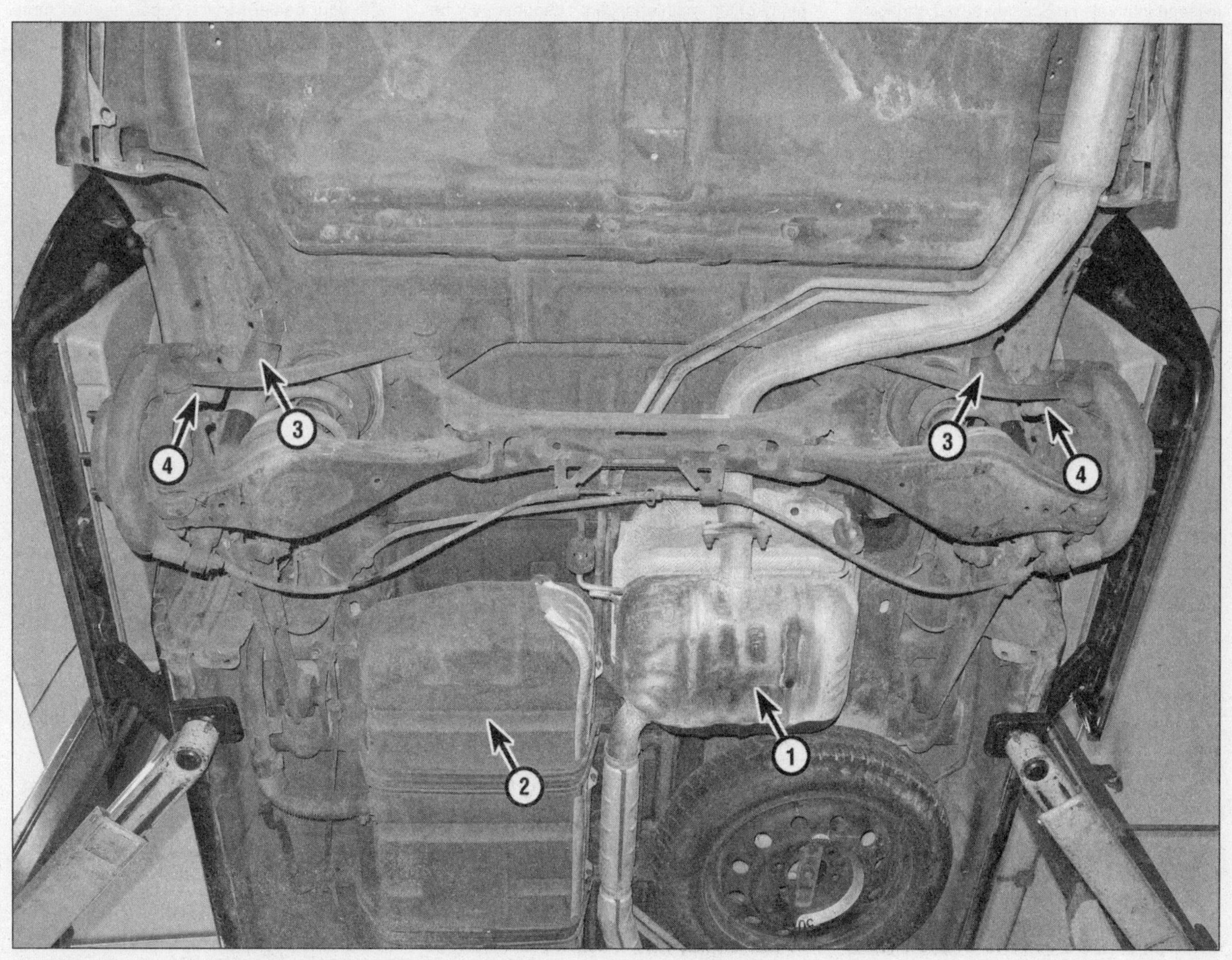

2.2c Typical rear underside components

1 *Muffler*
2 *Fuel tank*
3 *Rear shock absorbers*
4 *Rear brake calipers*

Kia Sedona maintenance schedule

1 The following maintenance intervals are based on the assumption that the vehicle owner will be doing the maintenance or service work, as opposed to having a dealer service department do the work. Although the time/mileage intervals are loosely based on factory recommendations, most have been shortened to ensure, for example, that such items as lubricants and fluids are checked/changed at intervals that promote maximum engine/driveline service life. Also, subject to the preference of the individual owner interested in keeping his or her vehicle in peak condition at all times, and with the vehicle's ultimate resale in mind, many of the maintenance procedures may be performed more often than recommended in the following schedule. We encourage such owner initiative.

2 When the vehicle is new it should be serviced initially by a factory authorized dealer service department to protect the factory warranty. In many cases the initial maintenance check is done at no cost to the owner (check with your dealer service department for more information).

Every 250 miles (400 km) or weekly, whichever comes first

Check the engine oil level (Section 4)
Check the engine coolant level (Section 4)
Check the windshield washer fluid level (Section 4)
Check the brake fluid level (Section 4)
Check the power steering fluid level (Section 4)
Check the tires and tire pressures (Section 5)
Check the operation of all lights
Check the horn operation

Every 3,000 miles (4,800 km) or 3 months, whichever comes first

All items listed above, plus:
Change the engine oil and filter (Section 6)

Every 6,000 miles (9,600 km) or 6 months, whichever comes first

All items listed above, plus:
Check the wiper blade condition (Section 7)
Check and clean the battery and terminals (Section 8)
Rotate the tires (Section 9)
Check the seatbelts (Section 10)
Check the condition of all underhood hoses and connections (Section 11)
Check the cooling system hoses and connections for leaks and damage (Section 12)
Check and replace, if necessary, the air filter element (Section 13)*

Every 12,000 miles (19,200 km) or 12 months, whichever comes first

All items listed above, plus:
Check the automatic transaxle fluid level (Section 4)
Check the brake system (Section 14)
Check the suspension components and driveaxle boots (Section 15)
Check the exhaust pipes and hangers (Section 16)
Check the fuel system hoses and connections for leaks and damage (Section 17)
Replace the cabin air filter (Section 18)*

Every 30,000 miles (48,000 km) or 30 months, whichever comes first

All items listed above, plus:
Check the drivebelts (Section 19)
Replace the air filter element (Section 13)*
Replace the brake fluid (Section 20)
Replace the fuel filter (2006 through 2010 models) (Chapter 4)

Every 45,000 miles (72,400 km) or 45 months, whichever comes first

Replace the fuel filter (2005 and earlier models) (Chapter 4)

Every 60,000 miles (96,000 km) or 60 months, whichever comes first

All items listed above, plus:
Check and replace, if necessary, the PCV valve (Section 21)*
Check and adjust, if necessary, the valve clearance (2005 through 2010 models only) (Chapter 2A)

Every 60 months (regardless of mileage)

Service the cooling system (drain, flush and refill) (Section 22)

Every 100,000 miles (160,000 km)

Replace the spark plugs (Section 23)*
Replace the spark plug wires (2005 and earlier models) (Section 24)
Change the automatic transaxle fluid and filter (2005 and earlier models only) (Section 25)*

Every 120,000 miles (193,000 km) or 120 months, whichever comes first

Replace the timing belt (2005 and earlier models) (Chapter 2A)

** This item is affected by "severe" operating conditions as described below. If the vehicle in question is operated under "severe" conditions, perform all maintenance procedures below, and those procedures above marked with an asterisk (*), at the intervals specified by the mileage headings below.*

Severe operating conditions

Consider the conditions "severe" if most driving is done...

a) In dusty areas
b) Towing a trailer
c) Idling for extended periods and/or low-speed operation
d) When outside temperatures remain below freezing and most trips are less than four miles
e) In heavy city traffic where outside temperatures regularly reach 90-degrees F or higher

Every 3,000 miles (4,800 km)

Check and replace, if necessary, the air filter element (Section 13)

Every 6,000 miles (9,600 km)

Check and replace, if necessary, the cabin air filter (Section 18)

Every 30,000 miles (48,000 km)

Replace the automatic transaxle fluid (2009 and earlier models) (Section 25)

Every 60,000 miles (96,000 km)

Replace the spark plugs (Section 23)
Check and replace, if necessary, the PCV valve (Section 21)
Change the automatic transaxle fluid and filter (2010 and later models) (Section 25)

2 Introduction

1 This Chapter is designed to help the home mechanic maintain the Kia Sedona with the goals of maximum performance, economy, safety and reliability in mind.
2 Included is a master maintenance schedule, followed by procedures dealing specifically with each item on the schedule. Visual checks, adjustments, component replacement and other helpful items are included. Refer to the accompanying illustrations of the engine compartment and the underside of the vehicle for the locations of various components.
3 Adhering to the mileage/time maintenance schedule and following the step-by-step procedures, which is simply a preventive maintenance program, will result in maximum reliability and vehicle service life. Keep in mind that it's not possible for this comprehensive program to produce the same results if you maintain some items at the specified intervals but not others.
4 As you service the vehicle, you'll discover that many of the procedures can - and should - be grouped together because of the nature of the particular procedure you're performing or because of the close proximity of two otherwise unrelated components to one another.
5 For example, if the vehicle is raised, you should inspect the exhaust, suspension, steering and fuel systems while you're under the vehicle. When you're rotating the tires, it makes good sense to check the brakes, since the wheels are already removed. Finally, let's suppose you have to borrow or rent a torque wrench. Even if you only need it to tighten the spark plugs, you might as well check the torque of as many critical fasteners as time allows.
6 The first step in this maintenance program is to prepare before the actual work begins. Read through all the procedures you're planning, then gather together all the parts and tools needed. If it looks like you might run into problems during a particular job, seek advice from a mechanic or an experienced do-it-yourselfer.

Owner's Manual and VECI label information

7 Your vehicle owner's manual was written for your year and model and contains very specific information on component locations, specifications, fuse ratings, part numbers, etc. The Owner's Manual is an important resource for the do-it-yourselfer to have; if one was not supplied with your vehicle, it can generally be ordered from a dealer parts department.
8 Among other important information, the Vehicle Emissions Control Information (VECI) label contains specifications and procedures for applicable tune-up adjustments and, in some instances, spark plugs (see Chapter for more information on the VECI label). The information on this label is the exact maintenance data recommended by the manufacturer. This data often varies by intended operating altitude, local emissions regulations, month of manufacture, etc.
9 This Chapter contains procedural details, safety information and more ambitious maintenance intervals than you might find in manufacturer's literature. However, you may also find procedures or specifications in your Owner's Manual or VECI label that differ with what's printed here. In these cases, the Owner's Manual or VECI label can be considered correct, since it is specific to your particular vehicle.

3 Tune-up general information

1 The term tune-up is used in this manual to represent a combination of individual operations rather than one specific procedure.
2 The engine will be kept in relatively good running condition and the need for additional work will be minimized if the routine maintenance schedule is followed closely and frequent checks are made of fluid levels and high wear items, as suggested throughout this manual from the time the vehicle is new.
3 More likely than not, however, there will be times when the engine is running poorly due to lack of regular maintenance. This is even more likely if a used vehicle, which hasn't received regular and frequent maintenance checks, is purchased. In such cases, an engine tune-up will be needed outside of the regular routine maintenance intervals.
4 The first step in any tune-up or diagnostic procedure to help correct a poor running engine is a cylinder compression check. A compression check (see Chapter 2B) will help determine the condition of internal

4.2 The engine oil dipstick is located at the front of the engine and is clearly marked

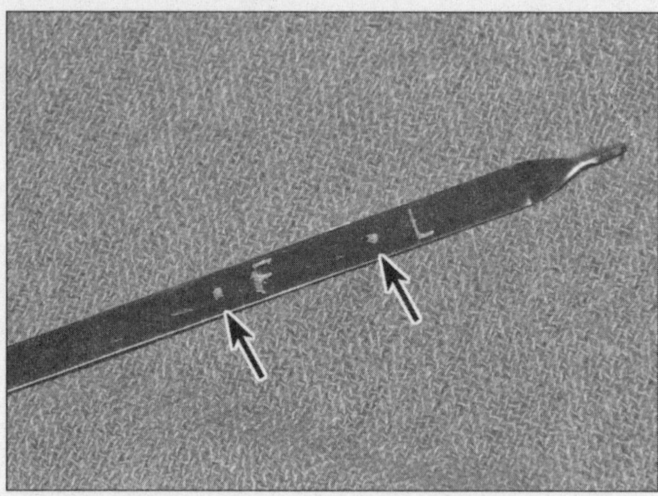

4.4 The oil level should be between the L and F marks on the dipstick - if it isn't, add enough oil to bring the level up to or near the upper mark (do not overfill)

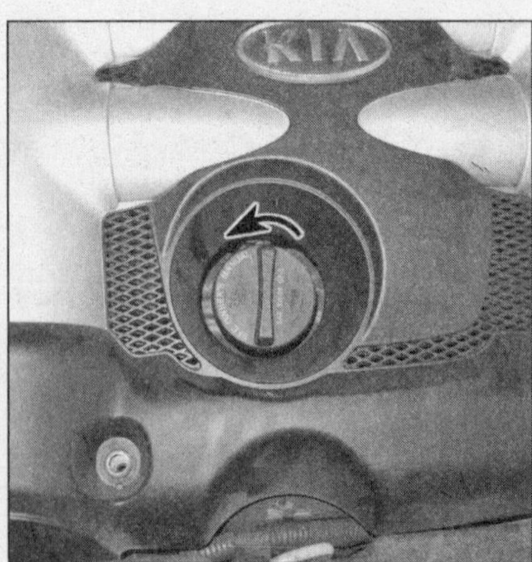

4.5 Turn the oil filler cap counterclockwise to remove it

engine components and should be used as a guide for tune-up and repair procedures. For instance, if a compression check indicates serious internal engine wear, a conventional tune-up will not improve the performance of the engine and would be a waste of time and money. Because of its importance, someone with the right equipment and the knowledge to use it properly should do the compression check.

5 The following procedures are those most often needed to bring a generally poor running engine back into a proper state of tune:

Minor tune-up

Check all engine related fluids (Section 4)
Clean and inspect the battery (Section 8)
Check all underhood hoses (Section 11)
Check and adjust the drivebelt(s) (Section 19)
Check the air filter (Section 13)
Check the PCV valve (Section 21)

Major tune-up

All items listed under Minor tune-up plus...
Check the fuel system (Section 17)
Replace the air filter (Section 13)
Replace the spark plugs (Section 23)
Replace the spark plug wires (2005 and earlier models) (Section 24)
Replace the PCV valve (Section 21)
Service the cooling system (Section 22)
Check the charging system (Chapter 5)

4 Fluid level checks (see Maintenance schedule for service intervals)

Note: *The following are fluid level checks to be done on a 250 mile or weekly basis. Additional fluid level checks can be found in specific maintenance procedures that follow. Regardless of the intervals, develop the habit of checking under the vehicle periodically for evidence of fluid leaks.*

1 Fluids are an essential part of the lubrication, cooling, brake and window washer systems. Because the fluids gradually become depleted and/or contaminated during normal operation of the vehicle, they must be replenished periodically. See Recommended lubricants and fluids in this Chapter's Specifications before adding fluid to any of the following components.

Note: *The vehicle must be on level ground when fluid levels are checked.*

Engine oil

2 Engine oil level is checked with a dipstick that is located on the side of the engine facing the front of the vehicle (see illustration). The dipstick extends through a tube and into the oil pan at the bottom of the engine.

3 The oil level should be checked before the vehicle has been driven, or about 5 minutes after the engine has been shut off. If the oil is checked immediately after driving the vehicle, some of the oil will remain in the upper engine components, resulting in an inaccurate reading on the dipstick.

4 Pull the dipstick out of the tube and wipe all the oil off the end with a clean rag or paper towel. Insert the clean dipstick all the way back into the tube, then pull it out again. Note the oil level at the end of the dipstick. Add oil as necessary to bring the oil level up to the F mark (see illustration).

5 Oil is added to the engine after removing a cap located on the valve cover (see illustration). Use a funnel to prevent spills as the oil is added.

6 Don't allow the level to drop below the L mark on the dipstick or engine damage may occur. On the other hand, don't overfill the engine by adding too much oil - it may result in oil aeration and loss of oil pressure and also could result in oil fouled spark plugs, oil leaks or seal failures.

7 Checking the oil level is an important preventive maintenance step. A consistently low oil level indicates oil leakage through damaged seals, defective gaskets or past worn rings or valve guides. If the oil looks milky in color or has water droplets in it, the block or head may be cracked and leaking coolant is entering the crankcase. The engine should be checked immediately. The condition of the oil should also be checked. Each time you check the oil level, slide your thumb and index finger up the dipstick before wiping off the oil. If you see small dirt or metal particles clinging to the dipstick, the oil should be changed (see Section 6).

Engine coolant

Warning: *Do not allow antifreeze to come in contact with your skin or painted surfaces of the vehicle. Flush contaminated areas immediately with plenty of water. Don't store new coolant or leave old coolant lying around*

4.9 Maintain the coolant level between the LOW and FULL marks on the reservoir

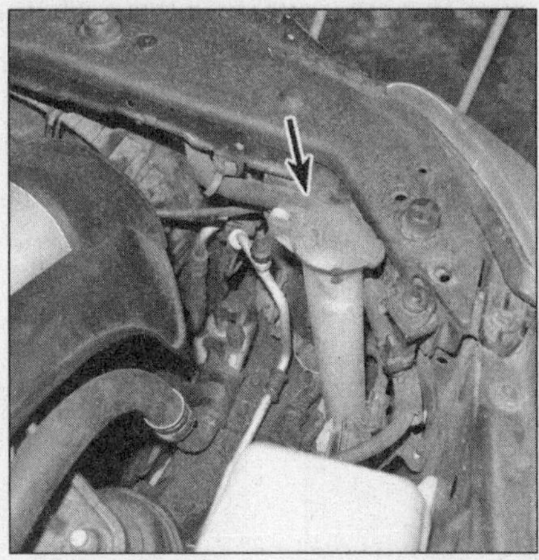
4.14 The windshield washer fluid reservoir is located in the right side of the engine compartment

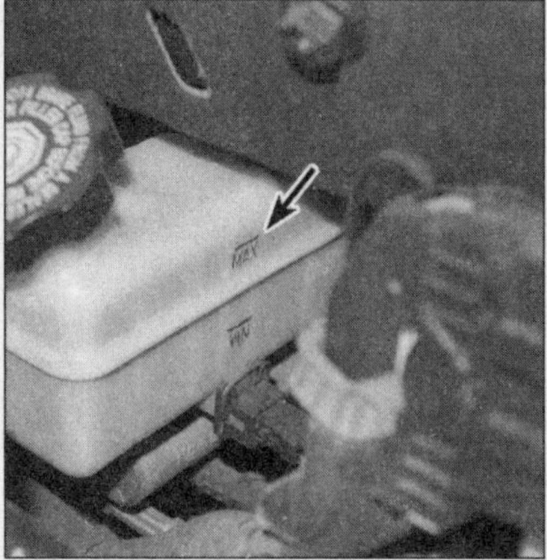

4.17 The brake fluid level should be kept at the upper (MAX) mark

where it's accessible to children or pets – they're attracted by its sweet smell. Ingestion of even a small amount of coolant can be fatal! Wipe up garage floor and drip pan spills immediately. Keep antifreeze containers covered and repair cooling system leaks as soon as they're noticed.

8 All vehicles covered by this manual are equipped with a coolant recovery system. A white plastic coolant reservoir is located at the right side of the engine compartment and is connected by a hose to the radiator filler neck. If the coolant heats up sufficiently during operation, in excess of the radiator cap pressure rating, it can escape past the filler cap and into the reservoir. As the engine cools, the coolant is drawn back into the cooling system to maintain the correct level.

Warning: *Do not remove the radiator cap to check the coolant level when the engine is warm!*

9 The coolant level in the reservoir should be checked regularly. The level in the reservoir varies with the temperature of the engine. When the engine is cold, the coolant level should be mid-way between the LOW and FULL marks on the reservoir. Once the engine has warmed up, the level should be at or near the FULL mark. If it isn't, allow the engine to cool, then remove the cap from the tank and add a 50/50 mixture of ethylene glycol based antifreeze and water (see illustration).

10 Drive the vehicle and recheck the coolant level. If only a small amount of coolant is required to bring the system up to the proper level, water can be used. However, repeated additions of water will dilute the antifreeze and water solution. In order to maintain the proper ratio of antifreeze and water, always top up the coolant level with the correct mixture. Don't use rust inhibitors or additives. An empty plastic milk jug or bleach bottle makes an excellent container for mixing coolant.

11 If the coolant level drops consistently, there may be a leak in the system. Inspect the radiator, hoses, filler cap, drain plugs and water pump (see Section 12). If no leaks are noted, have the pressure cap pressure tested by a service station.

12 If you have to remove the radiator cap, wait until the engine has cooled completely, then wrap a thick cloth around the cap and turn it to the first stop. If coolant or steam escapes, or if you hear a hissing noise, let the engine cool down longer, then remove the cap.

13 Check the condition of the coolant as well. It should be relatively clear. If it's brown or rust colored, the system should be drained, flushed and refilled. Even if the coolant appears to be normal, the corrosion inhibitors wear out, so it must be replaced at the specified intervals.

Windshield and rear window washer fluid

14 The fluid for the windshield washer system is stored in a plastic reservoir located at the right front corner of the engine compartment (see illustration). On 2005 and earlier models, the fluid for the rear wiper/washer system is located in the right rear part of the cargo area, behind a trim panel. On 2006 and later models, the rear wiper washer system uses fluid from the same reservoir as the windshield wiper/washer system.

15 In milder climates, plain water can be used in the reservoir, but it should be kept no more than two-thirds full to allow for expansion if the water freezes. In colder climates, use windshield washer system antifreeze, available at any auto parts store, to lower the freezing point of the fluid. Mix the antifreeze with water in accordance with the manufacturer's directions on the container.

Caution: *DO NOT use cooling system antifreeze - it will damage the vehicle's paint. To help prevent icing in cold weather, warm the windshield with the defroster before using the washer.*

Brake fluid

16 The brake fluid reservoir is located on top of the brake master cylinder on the driver's side of the engine compartment near the firewall.

17 The fluid level should be maintained at the upper (MAX) mark on reservoir (see illustration).

18 If additional fluid is necessary to bring the level up, use a rag to clean all dirt off the top of the reservoir to prevent contamination of the system. Also, make sure all painted surfaces around the reservoir are covered, since brake fluid will ruin paint. Carefully pour new, clean brake fluid obtained from a sealed container into the reservoir. Be sure the specified fluid is used; mixing different types of brake fluid can cause damage to the system. See Recommended lubricants and fluids in this Chapter's Specifications or your owner's manual.

19 At this time the fluid and the master cylinder should be inspected for contamination. Normally the brake hydraulic system won't need periodic draining and refilling, but if rust deposits, dirt particles or water droplets are observed in the fluid, the system should be dismantled, cleaned and refilled with fresh fluid. Over time brake fluid will absorb moisture from the air. Moisture in the fluid lowers the fluid boiling point; if the fluid boils, the brakes will become ineffective. Normal brake fluid is clear in color. If the brake fluid is dark brown in color, it's a good idea to replace it (see Chapter 9).

20 Reinstall the fluid reservoir cap.

21 The brake fluid in the master cylinder will drop slightly as the brake lining material at each wheel wears down during normal operation. If the master cylinder requires repeated replenishing to maintain the correct level, there is a leak in the brake system that should be corrected immediately. Check all brake lines and connections, along with the calipers and power brake booster (see Section and Chapter 9 for more information).

22 If you discover that the reservoir is empty or nearly empty, the system should be thoroughly inspected, refilled and then bled (see Chapter 9 for brake system bleeding).

4.24 The power steering fluid reservoir is located next to the coolant reservoir

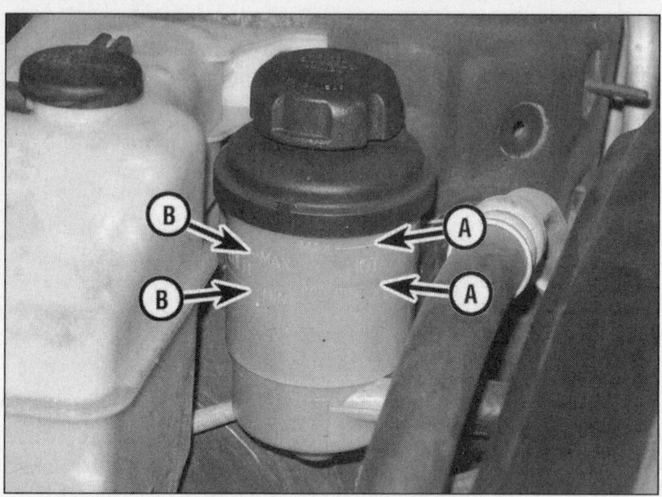

4.26 At normal operating temperature, the power steering fluid level should be between the HOT MIN and MAX marks (A); When cold, it should be between the COLD MIN and MAX marks (B)

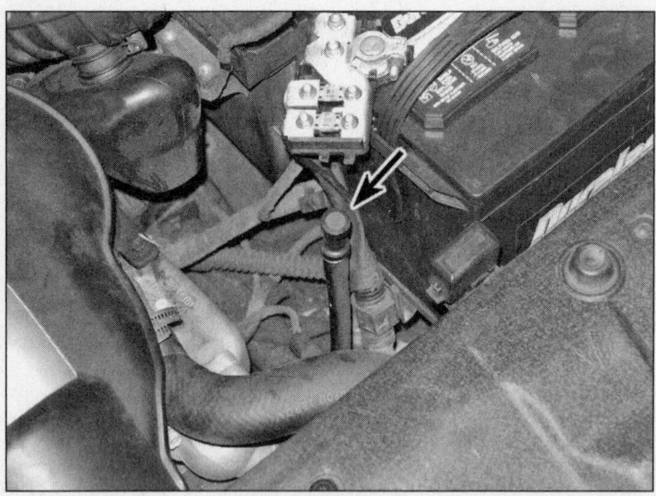
4.31 The automatic transaxle dipstick is located at the left end of the engine

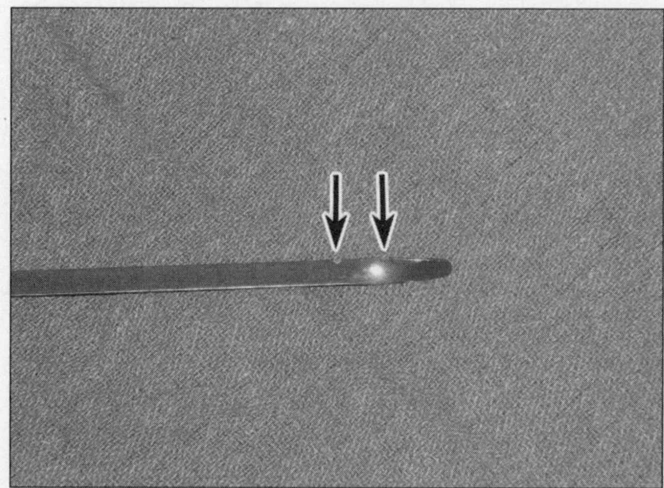
4.34 Check the fluid with the transaxle at normal operating temperature - the level should be kept in the HOT range (between the two marks)

Power steering fluid

23 Check the power steering fluid level periodically to avoid steering system problems, such as damage to the pump.

Caution: *DO NOT hold the steering wheel against either stop (extreme left or right turn) for more than five seconds. If you do, the power steering pump could be damaged.*

24 The power steering reservoir is located in the right side of the engine compartment (see illustration).

25 For the check, the front wheels should be pointed straight ahead and the engine should be off.

26 The reservoir has MIN and MAX fluid level marks on the side for cold and hot levels. The fluid level can be seen without removing the reservoir cap (see illustration).

27 If additional fluid is required, pour the specified type directly into the reservoir, using a funnel to prevent spills.

28 If the reservoir requires frequent fluid additions, all power steering hoses, hose connections, steering gear and the power steering pump should be carefully checked for leaks.

Automatic transaxle

Note: *It isn't necessary to check the transaxle fluid weekly; every 12,000 miles or 12 months will be adequate (unless a fluid leak is noticed).*

Note: *On 2011 and later models, transaxle fluid level check is not a routine maintenance item. Refer Section 25 for the transaxle fluid level check (which would normally only be done if a leak is suspected or when the fluid is replaced).*

2010 and earlier models

29 The automatic transaxle fluid level should be carefully maintained. Low fluid level can lead to slipping or loss of drive, while overfilling can cause foaming and loss of fluid.

30 With the parking brake set, start the engine, then move the shift lever through all the gear ranges, ending in Neutral. The fluid level must be checked with the vehicle level and the engine running at idle.

Note: *Incorrect fluid level readings will result if the vehicle has just been driven at high speeds for an extended period, in hot weather in city traffic, or if it has been pulling a trailer. If any of these conditions apply, wait until the fluid has cooled (about 30 minutes).*

31 With the transaxle at normal operating temperature, remove the dipstick from the filler tube. The dipstick is located between the left end of the engine and the air filter housing (2005 and earlier models) or battery (2006 through 2010 models) (see illustration).

Note: *Normal operating temperature is reached after a few miles of driving.*

32 Wipe the fluid from the dipstick with a clean rag and push it back into the filler tube until the cap seats.
33 Pull the dipstick out again and note the fluid level.
34 At normal operating temperature, the fluid level should be within the HOT range (see illustration). If additional fluid is required, add it directly into the tube using a funnel. Add the fluid a little at a time and keep checking the level until it's correct.
Note: *Wait at least two minutes before re-checking the fluid level to allow the fluid to fully drain into the transaxle.*
35 The condition of the fluid should also be checked along with the level. If the fluid at the end of the dipstick is a dark reddish-brown color, or if it smells burned, it should be changed. If you are in doubt about the condition of the fluid, purchase some new fluid and compare the two for color and smell.

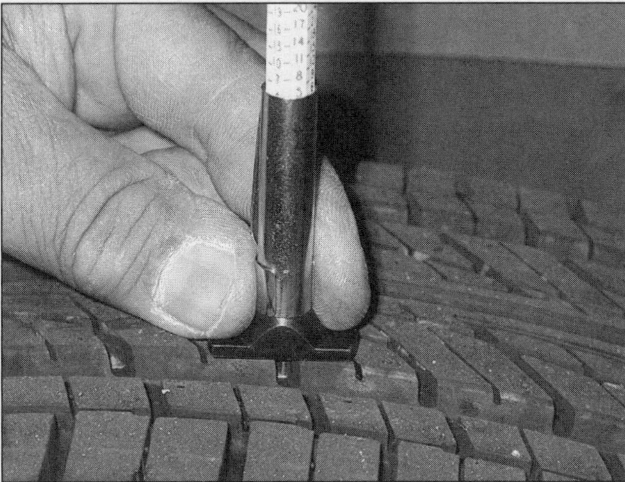
5.2 A tire tread depth indicator should be used to monitor tire wear - they are available at auto parts stores and service stations and cost very little

5 Tire and tire pressure checks (every 250 miles [400 km] or weekly)

1 Periodic inspection of the tires may spare you the inconvenience of being stranded with a flat tire. It can also provide you with vital information regarding possible problems in the steering and suspension systems before major damage occurs.
2 The original tires on this vehicle are equipped with 1/2-inch wide bands that will appear when tread depth reaches 1/16-inch, at which point they can be considered worn out. Tread wear can be monitored with a simple, inexpensive device known as a tread depth indicator (see illustration).
3 Note any abnormal tread wear (see illustration). Tread pattern irregularities such as cupping, flat spots and more wear on one side than the other are indications of front end alignment and/or balance problems. If any of these conditions are noted, take the vehicle to a tire shop or service station to correct the problem.
4 Look closely for cuts, punctures and embedded nails or tacks. Sometimes a tire will hold air pressure for a short time or leak down very slowly after a nail has embedded itself

UNDERINFLATION

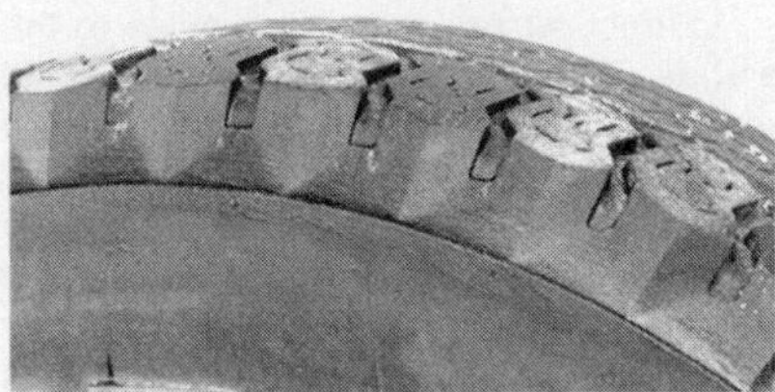
CUPPING

Cupping may be caused by:
- **Underinflation and/or mechanical irregularities such as out-of-balance condition of wheel and/or tire, and bent or damaged wheel.**
- **Loose or worn steering tie-rod or steering idler arm.**
- **Loose, damaged or worn front suspension parts.**

OVERINFLATION

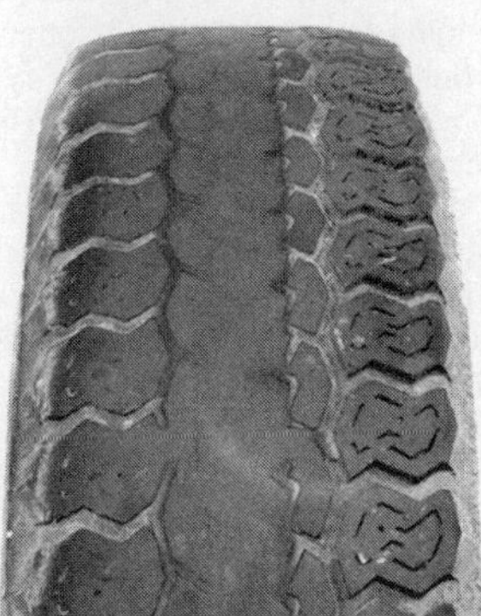
INCORRECT TOE-IN OR EXTREME CAMBER

FEATHERING DUE TO MISALIGNMENT

5.3 This chart will help you determine the condition of your tires, the probable cause(s) of abnormal wear and the corrective action necessary

5.4a If a tire loses air on a steady basis, check the valve core first to make sure it's snug (special inexpensive wrenches are commonly available at auto parts stores)

5.4b If the valve core is tight, raise the corner of the vehicle with the low tire and spray a soapy water solution onto the tread as the tire is turned slowly - slow leaks will cause small bubbles to appear

5.8 To extend the life of your tires, check the air pressure at least once a week with an accurate gauge (don't forget the spare!)

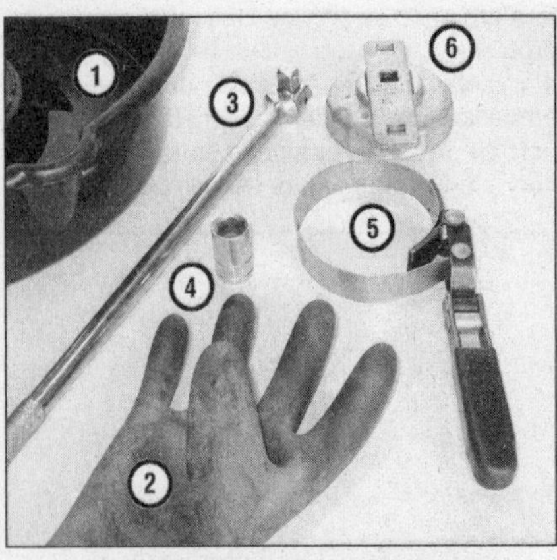

6.2 These tools are required when changing the engine oil and filter

1 **Drain pan** - *It should be fairly shallow in depth, but wide to prevent spills*
2 **Rubber gloves** - *When removing the drain plug and filter, you will get oil on your hands (the gloves will prevent burns)*
3 **Breaker bar** - *Sometimes the oil drain plug is tight, and a long breaker bar is needed to loosen it*
4 **Socket** – *To be used with the breaker bar or a ratchet (must be the correct size to fit the drain plug - six-point preferred)*
5 **Filter wrench** - *This is a metal band-type wrench, which requires clearance around the filter to be effective*
6 **Filter wrench** - *This type fits on the bottom of the filter and can be turned with a ratchet or breaker bar (different-size wrenches are available for different types of filters)*

in the tread. If a slow leak persists, check the valve stem core to make sure it is tight (see illustration). Examine the tread for an object that may have embedded itself in the tire or for a plug that may have begun to leak (radial tire punctures are repaired with a plug that is installed in a puncture). If a puncture is suspected, it can be easily verified by spraying a solution of soapy water onto the puncture area (see illustration). The soapy solution will bubble if there is a leak. Unless the puncture is unusually large, a tire shop or service station can usually repair the tire.

5 Carefully inspect the inner sidewall of each tire for evidence of brake fluid leakage. If you see any, inspect the brakes immediately.

6 Correct air pressure adds miles to the life span of the tires, improves mileage and enhances overall ride quality. Tire pressure cannot be accurately estimated by looking at a tire, especially if it's a radial. A tire pressure gauge is essential. Keep an accurate gauge in the glove compartment. The pressure gauges attached to the nozzles of air hoses at gas stations are often inaccurate.

7 Always check tire pressure when the tires are cold. Cold, in this case, means the vehicle has not been driven over a mile in the three hours preceding a tire pressure check. A pressure rise of four to eight pounds is not uncommon once the tires are warm.

8 Unscrew the valve cap protruding from the wheel or hubcap and push the gauge firmly onto the valve stem (see illustration). Note the reading on the gauge and compare the figure to the recommended tire pressure shown on the tire placard on the driver's side door. Be sure to reinstall the valve cap to keep dirt and moisture out of the valve stem mechanism. Check all four tires and, if necessary, add enough air to bring them up to the recommended pressure.

9 Don't forget to keep the spare tire inflated to the specified pressure (refer to the pressure molded into the tire sidewall).

6 Engine oil and filter change (every 3000 miles [4,800 km] or 3 months)

1 Frequent oil changes are the best preventive maintenance the home mechanic can give the engine, because aging oil becomes diluted and contaminated, which leads to premature engine wear.

2 Make sure you have all the necessary tools before you begin this procedure (see illustration). You should also have plenty of rags or newspapers handy for mopping up any spills.

3 Access to the underside of the vehicle is greatly improved if the vehicle can be lifted on a hoist, driven onto ramps or supported by jackstands.

Warning: *Do not work under a vehicle which is supported only by a bumper, hydraulic or scissors-type jack.*

4 If this is your first oil change, get under the vehicle and familiarize yourself with the locations of the oil drain plug and the oil filter. The engine and exhaust components will be warm during the actual work, so try to anticipate any potential problems before the engine and accessories are hot.

5 Park the vehicle on a level spot. Start the engine and allow it to reach its normal operating temperature. Warm oil and sludge will flow out more easily. Turn off the engine when it's warmed up. Remove the filler cap from the valve cover.

6 Raise the vehicle and support it securely on jackstands.

Warning: *Never get beneath the vehicle when it is supported only by a jack. The jack provided with your vehicle is designed solely for raising the vehicle to remove and replace the wheels. Always use jackstands to support the vehicle when it becomes necessary to place your body underneath the vehicle.*

6.7 Use a proper size box-end wrench or socket to remove the oil drain plug and avoid rounding it off

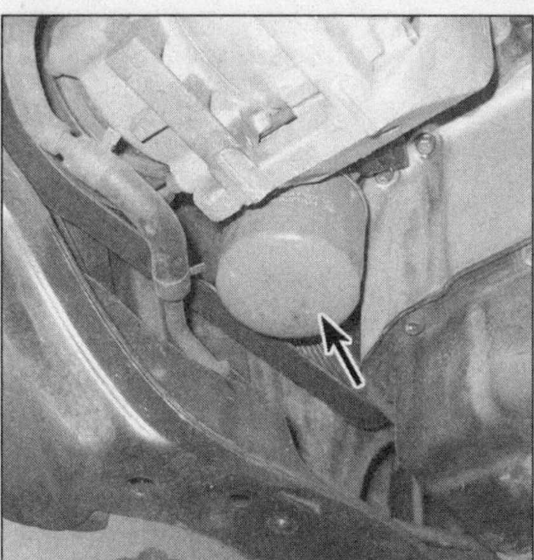

6.12 Use an oil filter wrench to remove the filter (2005 and earlier models)

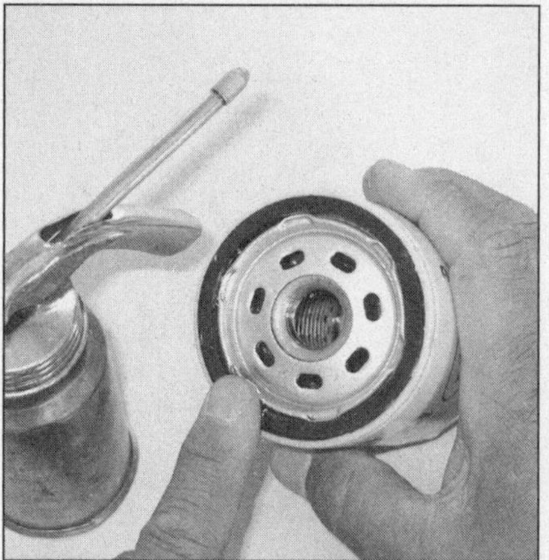

6.14 Lubricate the oil filter gasket with clean engine oil before installing the filter on the engine

6.17a Location of the oil filter housing/filter cap

6.17b Use an oil filter wrench like this to remove the filter cap

6.17c Remove the cap assembly...

7 Being careful not to touch the hot exhaust components, place the drain pan under the drain plug in the bottom of the pan and remove the plug (see illustration). You may want to wear gloves while unscrewing the plug the final few turns if the engine is hot.

8 Allow the old oil to drain into the pan. It may be necessary to move the pan farther under the engine as the oil flow slows to a trickle. Inspect the old oil for the presence of metal shavings and chips.

9 After all the oil has drained, wipe off the drain plug with a clean rag. Even minute metal particles clinging to the plug would immediately contaminate the new oil.

10 Clean the area around the drain plug opening, reinstall the plug and tighten it to the torque listed in this Chapter's Specifications.

2005 and earlier models

11 Move the drain pan into position under the oil filter.

12 Loosen the oil filter by turning it counterclockwise with an oil filter wrench (see illustration). Once the filter is loose, use your hands to unscrew it. Keep the open end pointing up to prevent the oil inside the filter from spilling out.

Warning: *The exhaust system may still be hot, so be careful.*

13 With a clean rag, wipe off the filter mounting surface. Also make sure that none of the old gasket remains stuck to the mounting surface. It can be removed with a scraper if necessary.

14 Compare the old filter with the new one to make sure they are the same type. Smear some clean engine oil on the rubber gasket of the new filter (see illustration).

15 Attach the new filter to the engine, following the tightening directions printed on the filter canister or packing box. Most filter manufacturers recommend against using a filter wrench due to the possibility of overtightening and damaging the seal. Lower the vehicle.

2006 and later models

16 Remove all the tools, rags, etc. from under the vehicle, being careful not to spill the oil in the drain pan, then lower the vehicle.

17 Working in the engine compartment, remove the engine cover, then locate the oil filter/housing on the left end of the engine (see illustration). Place a rag around the housing to absorb any spilled oil, then unscrew the oil filter cap (see illustration). Sometimes the element comes out with the oil filter cap, and can then be separated and discarded. Other times it might stay in the housing (see illustrations).

6.17d... then remove the used element from the housing

6.18a Remove the O-ring from the cap and install a new one...

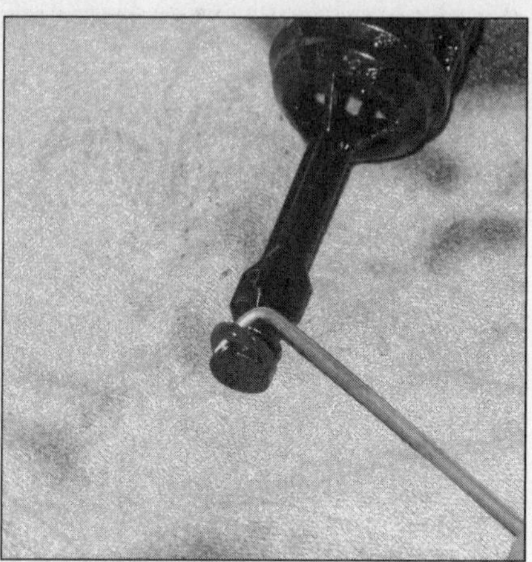

6.18b... and also replace the O-ring on the stem

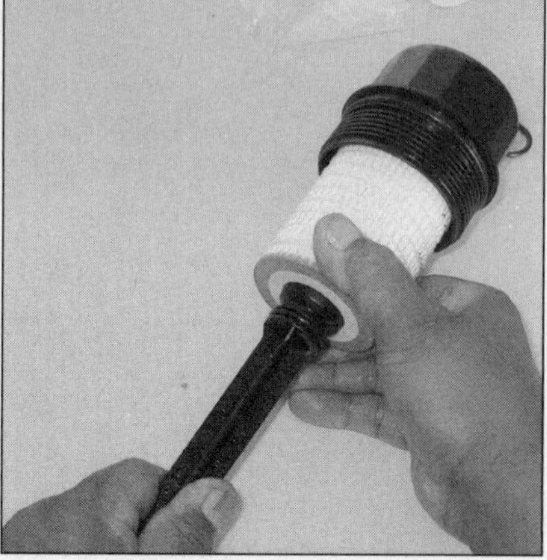

6.19 Install the new filter element

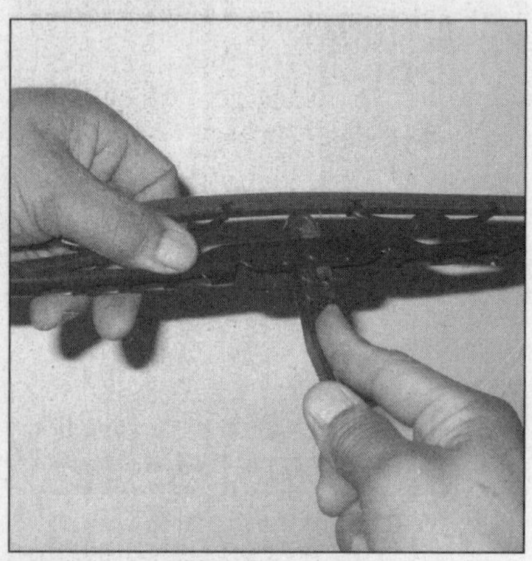

7.5a To release the blade holder, push the release lever...

18 Wipe out the oil filter housing and cap using a clean rag, then install a new O-ring on the cap and stem (see illustrations).

19 Install the filter element onto the cap (see illustration).

20 Lubricate the O-ring on the filter cap with clean engine oil, then install the filter and cap to the filter housing. Tighten the cap to the torque listed in this Chapter's Specifications.

All models

21 Remove the oil filler cap and add new oil to the engine. Use a funnel, if necessary, to prevent oil from spilling onto the top of the engine. Pour four quarts of fresh oil into the engine. Wait a few minutes to allow the oil to drain into the pan, then check the level on the oil dipstick (see Section 4). If the oil level is at or near the FULL mark on the dipstick, install the filler cap, start the engine and allow the new oil to circulate.

22 Allow the engine to run for about a minute. While the engine is running, look under the vehicle and check for leaks at the oil pan drain plug and around the oil filter. If either is leaking, stop the engine and tighten the plug or filter.

23 Wait a few minutes to allow the oil to trickle down into the pan, recheck the level on the dipstick and, if necessary, add enough oil to bring the level to the FULL mark.

24 During the first few trips after an oil change, make it a point to check frequently for leaks and proper oil level.

25 The old oil drained from the engine cannot be reused in its present state and should be disposed of. Check with your local auto parts store, disposal facility or environmental agency to see if they will accept the oil for recycling. After the oil has cooled it can be drained into a container (capped plastic jugs, topped bottles, milk cartons, etc.) for transport to one of these disposal sites. Don't dispose of the oil by pouring it on the ground or down a drain!

7 Windshield/rear wiper blade inspection and replacement (every 6,000 miles [9,600 km] or 6 months)

1 The windshield and rear wiper/blade assembly should be inspected periodically for damage, loose components and cracked or worn blade elements.

2 Road film can build up on the wiper blades and affect their efficiency, so they should be washed regularly with a mild detergent solution.

3 The action of the wiping mechanism can loosen bolts, nuts and fasteners, so they should be checked and tightened, as necessary, at the same time the wiper blades are checked.

4 If the wiper blade elements are cracked, worn or warped, or no longer clean adequately, they should be replaced with new ones.

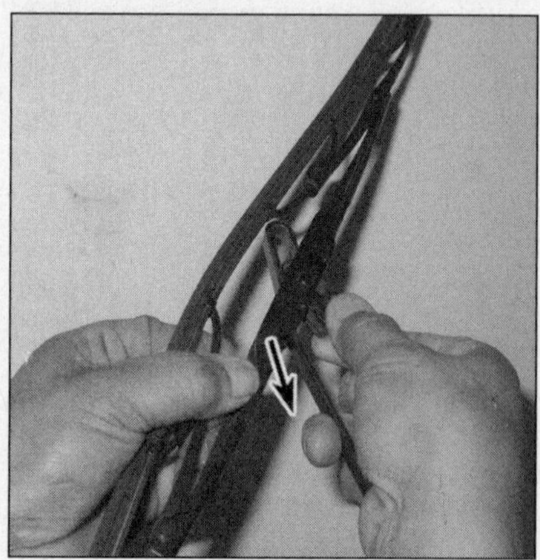

7.5b... and pull the wiper blade in the direction of the arrow to separate it from the arm

Windshield wiper blades (all models) and rear wiper blade (2005 and earlier models)

5 Lift the arm assembly away from the glass for clearance, press the release lever, then slide the wiper blade assembly out of the hook at the end of the arm (see illustrations).

6 Attach the new wiper to the arm. Connection can be confirmed by an audible click.

Rear wiper blade (2006 and later models)

7 Raise the wiper arm, then pivot the wiper blade and pull it away from the arm to disengage the retainer (see illustration).

8 Align the new blade with the arm then push it into place until it clicks.

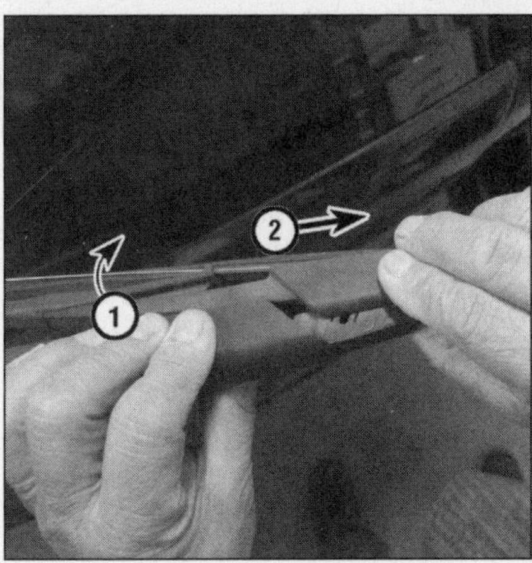

7.7 Angle the blade in relation to the arm (1), then pull the blade sharply away from the arm to disengage it (2)

8 Battery check, maintenance and charging (every 6,000 miles [9,600 km] or 6 months)

Warning: *Certain precautions must be followed when checking and servicing the battery. Hydrogen gas, which is highly flammable, is always present in the battery cells, so keep lighted tobacco and all other open flames and sparks away from the battery. The electrolyte inside the battery is actually diluted sulfuric acid, which will cause injury if splashed on your skin or in your eyes. It will also ruin clothes and painted surfaces. When removing the battery cables, always detach the negative cable first and hook it up last!*

1 A routine preventive maintenance program for the battery in your vehicle is the only way to ensure quick and reliable starts. But before performing any battery maintenance, make sure that you have the proper equipment necessary to work safely around the battery (see illustration).

2 There are also several precautions that should be taken whenever battery maintenance is performed. Before servicing the battery, always turn the engine and all accessories off and disconnect the cable from the negative terminal of the battery (see Chapter 5).

3 The battery produces hydrogen gas, which is both flammable and explosive. Never create a spark, smoke or light a match around the battery. Always charge the battery in a ventilated area.

4 Electrolyte contains poisonous and corrosive sulfuric acid. Do not allow it to get in your eyes, on your skin on your clothes. Never ingest it. Wear protective safety glasses when working near the battery. Keep children away from the battery.

5 Note the external condition of the battery. If the positive terminal and cable clamp on your vehicle's battery is equipped with a rubber protector, make sure that it's not torn or damaged. It should completely cover the terminal. Look for any corroded or loose connections, cracks in the case or cover or loose hold-down clamps. Also check the entire length of each cable for cracks and frayed conductors.

6 If corrosion, which looks like white, fluffy deposits (see illustration) is evident, particularly around the terminals, the battery should be removed for cleaning. Loosen the cable clamp bolts with a wrench, being careful to remove the ground cable first, and slide them off the terminals (see illustration). Then disconnect the hold-down clamp bolt and nut, remove the clamp and lift the battery from the engine compartment.

7 Clean the cable clamps thoroughly with a battery brush or a terminal cleaner and a solution of warm water and baking soda (see illustration). Wash the terminals and the top

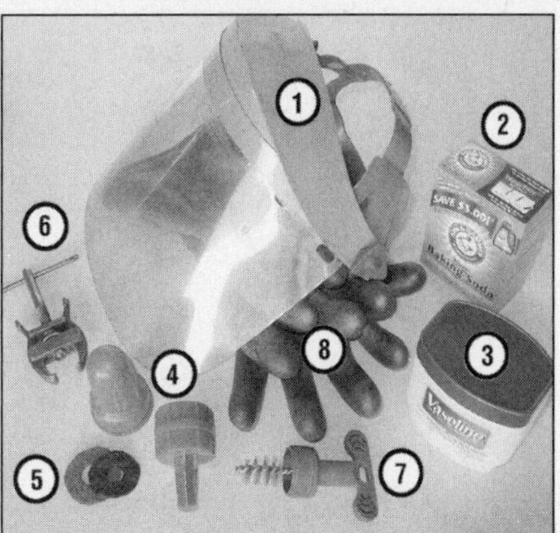

8.2 Tools and materials required for battery maintenance

1 ***Face shield/safety goggles*** *- When removing corrosion with a brush, the acidic particles can easily fly up into your eyes*
2 ***Baking soda*** *- A solution of baking soda and water can be used to neutralize corrosion*
3 ***Petroleum jelly*** *- A layer of this on the battery posts will help prevent corrosion*
4 ***Battery post/cable cleaner*** *- This wire brush cleaning tool will remove all traces of corrosion from the battery posts and cable clamps*
5 ***Treated felt washers*** *- Placing one of these on each post, directly under the cable clamps, will help prevent corrosion*
6 ***Puller*** *- Sometimes the cable clamps are very difficult to pull off the posts, even after the nut/bolt has been completely loosened. This tool pulls the clamp straight up and off the post without damage*
7 ***Battery post/cable cleaner*** *- Here is another cleaning tool that is a slightly different version of Number 4 above, but it does the same thing*
8 ***Rubber gloves*** *- Another safety item to consider when servicing the battery; remember that's acid inside the battery!*

8.6a Battery terminal corrosion usually appears as light, fluffy powder

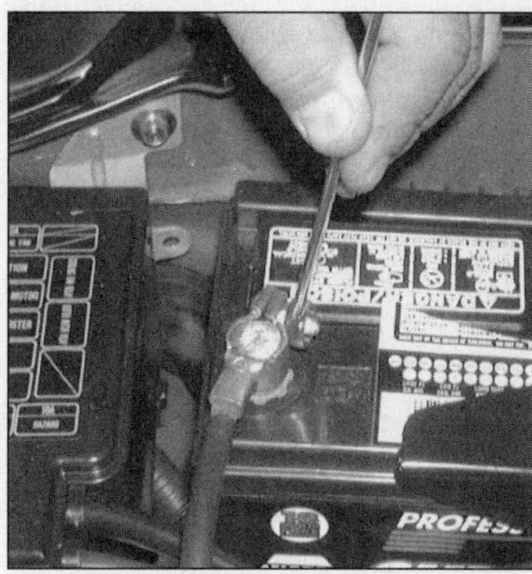

8.6b Removing a cable from the battery post with a wrench - sometimes a pair of special battery pliers are required for this procedure if corrosion has caused deterioration of the nut hex (always remove the ground (-) cable first and hook it up last!)

8.7a When cleaning the cable clamps, all corrosion must be removed

8.7b Regardless of the type of tool used to clean the battery posts, a clean, shiny surface should be the result

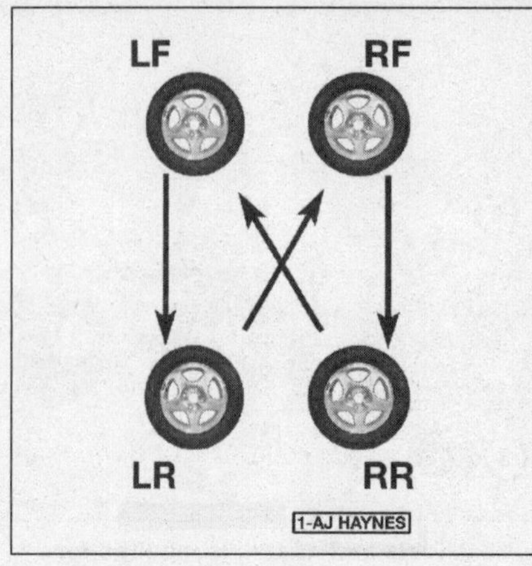

9.2a The recommended four-tire rotation pattern for non-directional tires

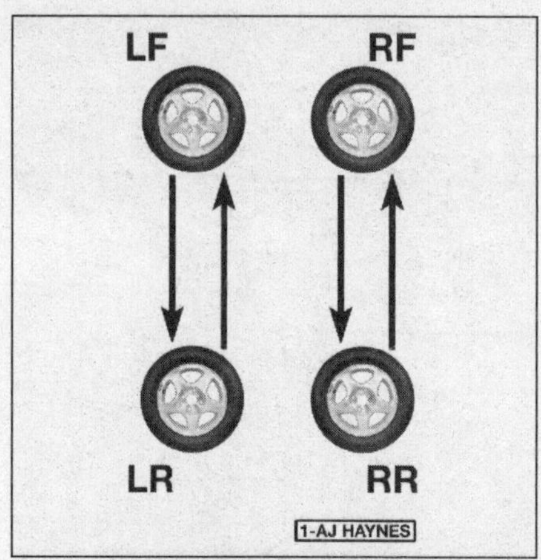

9.2b The recommended four-tire rotation pattern for directional tires

of the battery case with the same solution but make sure that the solution doesn't get into the battery. When cleaning the cables, terminals and battery top, wear safety goggles and rubber gloves to prevent any solution from coming in contact with your eyes or hands. Wear old clothes too - even diluted, sulfuric acid splashed onto clothes will burn holes in them. If the terminals have been extensively corroded, clean them up with a terminal cleaner (see illustration). Thoroughly wash all cleaned areas with plain water.

8 Make sure that the battery tray is in good condition and the hold-down clamp fasteners are tight. If the battery is removed from the tray, make sure no parts remain in the bottom of the tray when the battery is reinstalled. When reinstalling the hold-down clamp bolts, do not overtighten them.

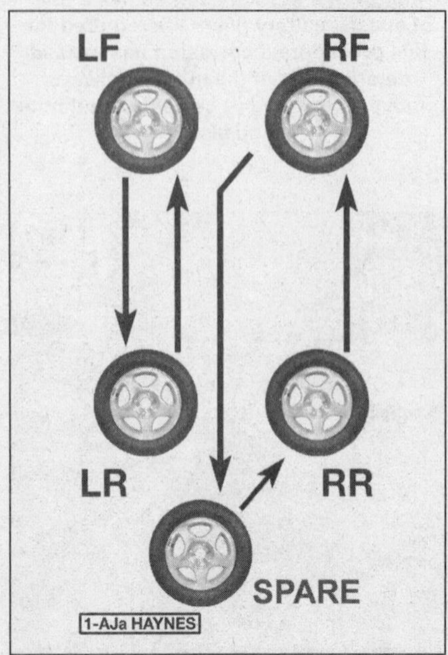

9.2c Five-tire rotation pattern (to be used only if the spare tire is the same as the other four)

9 Information on removing and installing the battery can be found in Chapter. If you disconnected the cable(s) from the negative and/or positive battery terminals, see Chapter. Information on jump starting can be found at the front of this manual. For more detailed battery checking procedures, refer to the Haynes Automotive Electrical Manual.

Cleaning

10 Corrosion on the hold-down components, battery case and surrounding areas can be removed with a solution of water and baking soda. Thoroughly rinse all cleaned areas with plain water.

11 Any metal parts of the vehicle damaged by corrosion should be covered with a zinc-based primer, then painted.

Charging

Warning: *When batteries are being charged, hydrogen gas, which is very explosive and flammable, is produced. Do not smoke or allow open flames near a charging or a recently charged battery. Wear eye protection when near the battery during charging. Also, make sure the charger is unplugged before connecting or disconnecting the battery from the charger.*

12 Slow-rate charging is the best way to restore a battery that's discharged to the point where it will not start the engine. It's also a good way to maintain the battery charge in a vehicle that's only driven a few miles between starts. Maintaining the battery charge is particularly important in the winter when the battery must work harder to start the engine and electrical accessories that drain the battery are in greater use.

13 It's best to use a one or two-amp battery charger (sometimes called a trickle charger). They are the safest and put the least strain on the battery. They are also the least expensive. For a faster charge, you can use a higher amperage charger, but don't use one rated more than 1/10th the amp/hour rating of the battery. Rapid boost charges that claim to restore the power of the battery in one to two hours are hardest on the battery and can damage batteries not in good condition. This type of charging should only be used in emergency situations.

14 The average time necessary to charge a battery should be listed in the instructions that come with the charger. As a general rule, a trickle charger will charge a battery in 12 to 16 hours.

9 Tire rotation (every 6,000 miles [9,600 km] or 6 months)

1 The tires should be rotated at the specified intervals and whenever uneven wear is noticed.

2 Radial tires must be rotated in a specific pattern (see illustrations).

3 Refer to the information in "Jacking and towing" at the front of this manual for the proper procedures to follow when raising the vehicle and changing a tire. If the brakes are to be checked, don't apply the parking brake as stated. Make sure the tires are blocked to prevent the vehicle from rolling as it's raised.

4 Preferably, the entire vehicle should be raised at the same time. This can be done on a hoist or by jacking up each corner and then lowering the vehicle onto jackstands placed under the frame rails. Always use four jackstands and make sure the vehicle is safely supported.

5 After rotation, check and adjust the tire pressures as necessary. Tighten the lug nuts to the torque listed in this Chapter's Specifications.

10 Seat belt check (every 6,000 miles [9,600 km] or 6 months)

1 Check seat belts, buckles, latch plates and guide loops for obvious damage and signs of wear.

2 Where the seat belt receptacle bolts to the floor of the vehicle, check that the bolts are secure.

3 See if the seat belt reminder light comes on when the key is turned to the Run or Start position.

11 Underhood hose check and replacement (every 6,000 miles [9,600 km] or 6 months)

General

Caution: *Never remove air conditioning components or hoses until the system has been depressurized by a licensed air conditioning technician.*

1 High temperatures in the engine compartment can cause the deterioration of the rubber and plastic hoses used for engine, accessory and emission systems operation. Periodic inspection should be made for cracks, loose clamps, material hardening and leaks. Information specific to the cooling system hoses can be found in Section 12.

2 Some, but not all, hoses are secured to their fittings with clamps. Where clamps are used, check to be sure they haven't lost their tension, allowing the hose to leak. If clamps aren't used, make sure the hose has not expanded and/or hardened where it slips over the fitting, allowing it to leak.

Vacuum hoses

3 It's quite common for vacuum hoses, especially those in the emissions system, to be color-coded or identified by colored stripes molded into them. Various systems require hoses with different wall thickness, collapse resistance and temperature resistance. When replacing hoses, be sure the new ones are made of the same material.

4 Often the only effective way to check a hose is to remove it completely from the vehicle. If more than one hose is removed, be sure to label the hoses and fittings to ensure correct installation.

5 When checking vacuum hoses, be sure to include any plastic T-fittings in the check. Inspect the fittings for cracks and the hose where it fits over the fitting for distortion, which could cause leakage.

6 A small piece of vacuum hose (1/4-inch inside diameter) can be used as a stethoscope to detect vacuum leaks. Hold one end of the hose to your ear and probe around vacuum hoses and fittings, listening for the "hissing" sound characteristic of a vacuum leak.

Warning: *When probing with the vacuum hose stethoscope, be very careful not to come into contact with moving engine components such as the drivebelt, cooling fan, etc.*

Fuel hose

Warning: *There are certain precautions that must be taken when inspecting or servicing fuel system components. Work in a well-ventilated area and do not allow open flames (cigarettes, appliances, etc.) or bare light bulbs near the work area. Mop up any spills immediately and do not store fuel soaked rags where they could ignite. The fuel system is under high pressure, so if any fuel lines are to be disconnected, the pressure in the system must be relieved first (see Chapter for more information).*

7 Check all rubber fuel lines for deterioration and chafing. Check especially for cracks in areas where the hose bends and just before fittings, such as where a hose attaches to the fuel filter.

8 High quality fuel line, made specifically for high-pressure fuel injection systems, must be used for fuel line replacement. Never, under any circumstances, use unreinforced vacuum line, clear plastic tubing or water hose for fuel lines.

9 Spring-type clamps are commonly used on fuel lines. These clamps often lose their tension over a period of time, and can be "sprung" during removal. Replace all spring-type clamps with screw clamps whenever a hose is replaced.

Metal lines

10 Sections of metal line are routed along the frame, between the fuel tank and the engine. Check carefully to be sure the line has not been bent or crimped and that cracks have not started in the line.

11 If a section of metal fuel line must be replaced, only seamless steel tubing should be used, since copper and aluminum tubing don't have the strength necessary to withstand normal engine vibration.

12 Check the metal brake lines where they enter the master cylinder and brake proportioning unit for cracks in the lines or loose fittings. Any sign of brake fluid leakage calls for an immediate and thorough inspection of the brake system.

Check for a chafed area that could fail prematurely.

Check for a soft area indicating the hose has deteriorated inside.

Overtightening the clamp on a hardened hose will damage the hose and cause a leak.

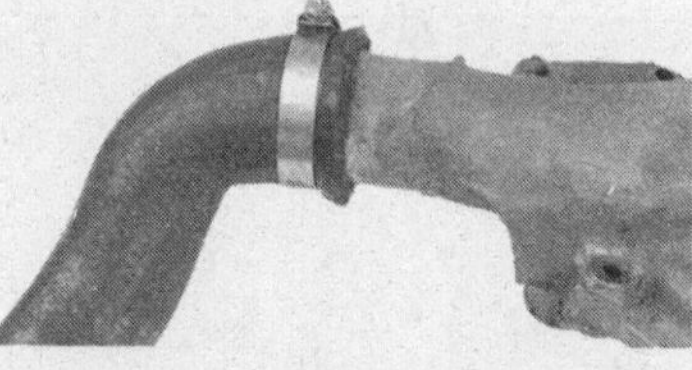

Check each hose for swelling and oil-soaked ends. Cracks and breaks can be located by squeezing the hose.

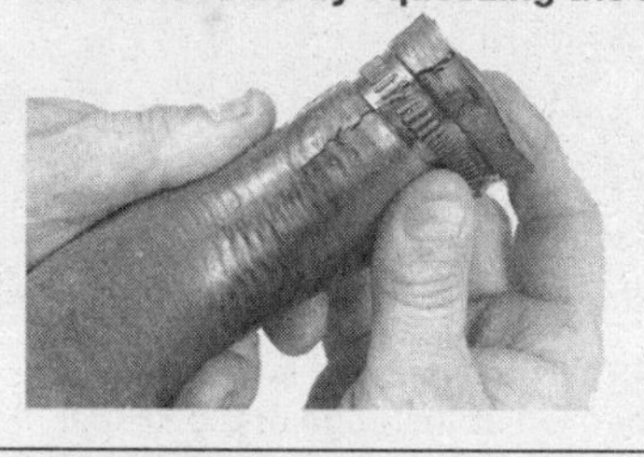

12.4 Hoses, like drivebelts, have a habit of failing at the worst possible time - to prevent the inconvenience of a blown radiator or heater hose, inspect them carefully as shown here

12 Cooling system check (every 6,000 miles [9,600 km] or 6 months)

1 Many major engine failures can be attributed to a faulty cooling system. Since the vehicle is equipped with an automatic transaxle, the cooling system also cools the transaxle fluid and thus plays an important role in prolonging transaxle life.

2 The cooling system should be checked with the engine cold. Do this before the vehicle is driven for the day or after it has been shut off for at least three hours.

3 Remove the radiator pressure cap and thoroughly clean the cap, inside and out, with clean water. Also clean the filler neck on the radiator. All traces of corrosion should be removed. The coolant inside the radiator should be relatively transparent. If it is rust-colored, the system should be drained, flushed and refilled (see Section 22). If the coolant level is not up to the top, add additional antifreeze/coolant mixture (see Section 4).

4 Carefully check the large upper and lower radiator hoses along with the smaller diameter heater hoses that run from the engine to the firewall. Inspect each hose along its entire length, replacing any hose that is cracked, swollen or shows signs of deterioration. Cracks may become more apparent if the hose is squeezed (see illustration). Regardless of condition, it's a good idea to replace hoses with new ones every two years.

5 Make sure all hose connections are tight. A leak in the cooling system will usually show up as white or rust-colored deposits on the areas adjoining the leak. If wire-type clamps are used at the ends of the hoses, it may be a good idea to replace them with more secure screw-type clamps.

6 Use compressed air or a soft brush to remove bugs, leaves, etc. from the front of the radiator or air conditioning condenser. Be careful not to damage the delicate cooling fins or cut yourself on them.

7 Every other inspection, or at the first indication of cooling system problems, have the

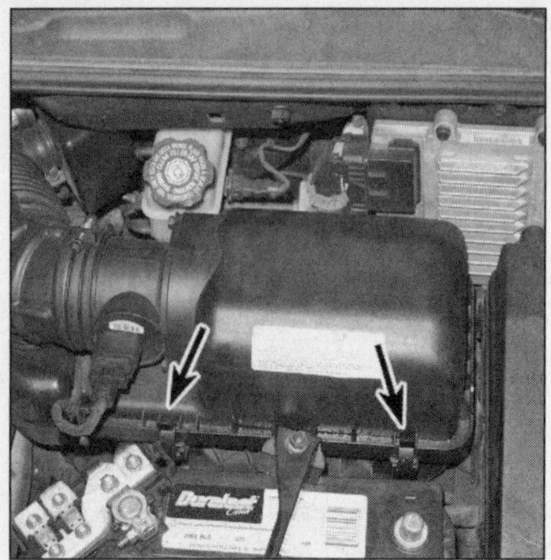

13.3a Remove the screws or release the spring clamps...

13.3b... then lift the air filter housing cover up and remove the air filter element – 3.8L engine shown, other models similar

14.7a Check the thickness of the inner pad through the inspection hole (front brake shown, rear disc brake similar)

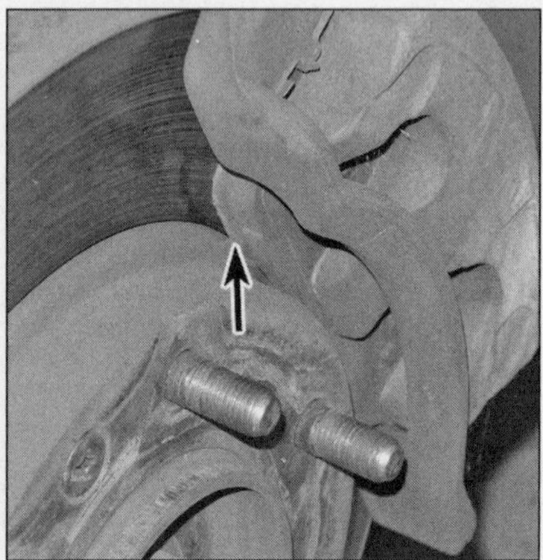

14.7b The outer pad is more easily checked at the edge of the caliper

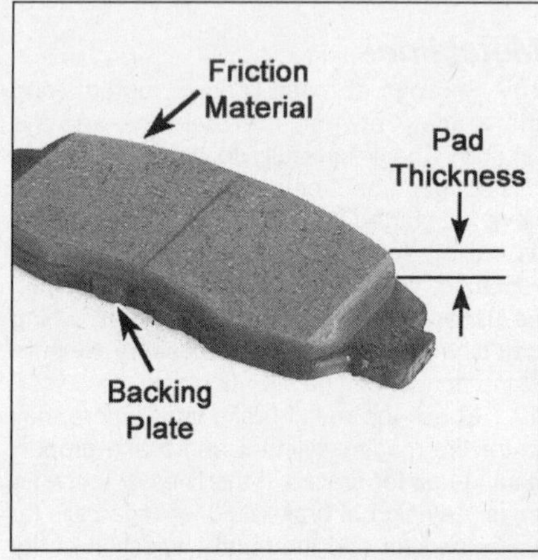

14.9 If a more precise measurement of pad thickness is necessary, remove the pads and measure the remaining friction material

cap and system pressure tested. If you don't have a pressure tester, most repair shops will do this for a minimal charge.

13 Air filter check and replacement (every 6,000 miles [9,600 km] or 6 months)

1 The air filter is located inside a housing at the left (driver's) side of the engine compartment.

2 Disconnect the Mass Air flow (MAF) sensor electrical connector from the sensor on the air filter housing.

3 On 2005 and earlier models, remove the cover mounting screws. On 2006 and later models, release the clamps that secure the two halves of the air filter housing together. Separate the cover halves and remove the air filter element (see illustrations).

4 Inspect the outer surface of the filter element. If it is dirty, replace it. If it is only moderately dusty, it can be reused by blowing it clean from the back to the front surface with compressed air. Because it is a pleated paper type filter, it cannot be washed or oiled. If it cannot be cleaned satisfactorily with compressed air, discard and replace it. While the cover is off, be careful not to drop anything down into the housing.

5 Wipe out the inside of the air filter housing.

6 Place the new filter into the air filter housing, making sure it seats properly.

7 Reinstall the cover and secure it with the screws or clamps. Reconnect the electrical connector.

14 Brake system check (every 12,000 miles [19,200 km] or 12 months)

Warning: *The dust created by the brake system is harmful to your health. Never blow it out with compressed air and don't inhale any of it. An approved filtering mask should be worn when working on the brakes. Do not, under any circumstances, use petroleum-based solvents to clean brake parts. Use brake system cleaner only!*

Note: *For detailed photographs of the brake system, refer to Chapter 9.*

1 In addition to the specified intervals, the brakes should be inspected every time the wheels are removed or whenever a defect is suspected.

2 Any of the following symptoms could indicate a potential brake system defect: The vehicle pulls to one side when the brake pedal is depressed; the brakes make squealing or dragging noises when applied; brake pedal travel is excessive; the pedal pulsates; or brake fluid leaks, usually onto the inside of the tire or wheel.

3 Loosen the wheel lug nuts.

4 Raise the vehicle and support it securely on jackstands.

5 Remove the wheels (refer to your owner's manual, if necessary).

Disc brakes

6 There are two pads (an outer and an inner) in each caliper.

7 Check the pad thickness by looking at each end of the caliper and through the inspection window in the caliper body (see illustrations). If the lining material is less than the thickness listed in this Chapter's Specifications, replace the pads.

Note: *Keep in mind that the lining material is riveted or bonded to a metal backing plate and the metal portion is not included in this measurement.*

8 If it is difficult to determine the exact thickness of the remaining pad material by the above method, or if you are at all concerned about the condition of the pads, remove the caliper(s), then remove the pads from the calipers for further inspection (see Chapter 9).

9 Once the pads are removed from the calipers, clean them with brake cleaner and re-measure them (see illustration).

10 Measure the disc thickness with a

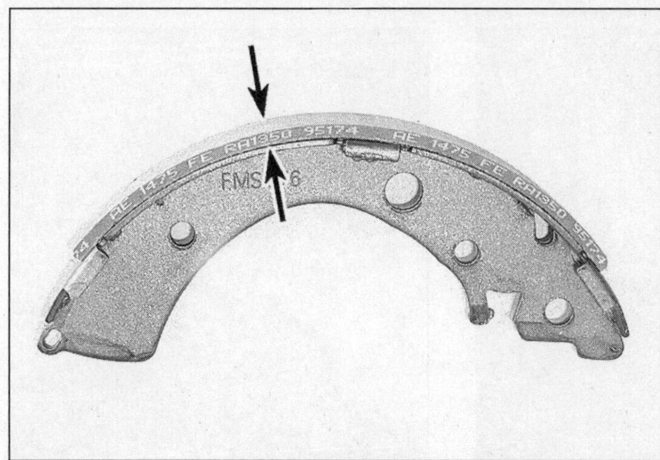

14.15 If the lining is bonded to the brake shoe, measure the lining thickness from the outer surface to the metal shoe. If the lining is riveted, measure from the lining outer surface to the rivet head

15.4 Check the struts and shocks for leakage at the indicated area

micrometer to make sure that it still has service life remaining. Refer to the dimension marked on the disc. If any disc is thinner than the specified minimum thickness, replace it (see Chapter 9). Even if the disc has service life remaining, check its condition. Look for scoring, gouging and burned spots. If these conditions exist, remove the disc and have it resurfaced (see Chapter 9).

11 Before installing the wheels, check all brake lines and hoses for damage, wear, deformation, cracks, corrosion, leakage, bends and twists, particularly in the vicinity of the rubber hoses at the calipers. Check the clamps for tightness and the connections for leakage. Make sure that all hoses and lines are clear of sharp edges, moving parts and the exhaust system. If any of the above conditions are noted, repair, reroute or replace the lines and/or fittings as necessary (see Chapter 9). Make sure the lug nuts are tightened to the torque listed in this Chapter's Specifications.

Drum brakes

12 Make sure the parking brake is off, then tap on the outside of the drum with a rubber mallet to loosen it.

13 Remove the brake drums. If the drum won't come off, refer to Chapter 9.

14 With the drums removed, carefully clean the brake assembly with brake system cleaner.

Warning: *Don't blow the dust out with compressed air and don't inhale any of it (it is harmful to your health).*

15 Note the thickness of the lining material on both front and rear brake shoes (see illustration). Compare the measurement with the limit given in this Chapter's Specifications; if any lining thickness is less than specified, then all of the brake shoes must be replaced (see Chapter 9). The shoes should also be replaced if they're cracked, glazed (shiny areas), or covered with brake fluid.

16 Make sure all the brake assembly springs are connected and in good condition.

17 Check the brake components for signs of fluid leakage. With your finger or a small screwdriver, carefully pry back the rubber cups on the wheel cylinder located at the top of the brake shoes. Any leakage here is an indication that the wheel cylinders should be replaced immediately (see Chapter 9). Also, check all hoses and connections for signs of leakage.

18 Wipe the inside of the drum with a clean rag and brake system cleaner. Again, be careful not to breathe the dangerous brake dust.

19 Check the inside of the drum for cracks, score marks, deep scratches and hard spots which will appear as small discolored areas. If imperfections cannot be removed with fine emery cloth, the drum must be taken to an automotive machine shop for resurfacing.

20 Repeat the procedure for the remaining wheel. If the inspection reveals that all parts are in good condition, reinstall the brake drums, install the wheels and lower the vehicle to the ground.

Power brake booster check

21 Sit in the driver's seat and perform the following sequence of tests.

22 With the brake fully depressed, start the engine - the pedal should move down a little when the engine starts.

23 With the engine running, depress the brake pedal several times - the travel distance should not change.

24 Depress the brake, stop the engine and hold the pedal in for about 30 seconds - the pedal should neither sink nor rise.

25 Restart the engine, run it for about a minute and turn it off. Then firmly depress the brake several times - the pedal travel should decrease with each application.

26 If your brakes do not operate as described, the power brake booster has failed. Refer to Chapter 9 for the replacement procedure.

Parking brake

27 One method of checking the parking brake is to park the vehicle on a steep hill with the parking brake set and the transaxle in Neutral (stay in the vehicle for this check!). If the parking brake cannot prevent the vehicle from rolling, it's in need of adjustment (see Chapter 9).

15 Steering, suspension and driveaxle boot check (every 12,000 miles [19,200 km] or 12 months)

Note: *For detailed illustrations of the steering and suspension components, refer to Chapter 10.*

With the wheels on the ground

1 With the vehicle stopped and the front wheels pointed straight ahead, rock the steering wheel gently back and forth. If freeplay is excessive, a front wheel bearing, steering shaft universal joint, lower arm balljoint or steering gear is worn. Refer to Chapter 10 for the appropriate repair procedure.

2 Other symptoms, such as excessive vehicle body movement over rough roads, swaying (leaning) around corners and binding as the steering wheel is turned, may indicate faulty steering and/or suspension components.

3 Check the shock absorbers by pushing down and releasing the vehicle several times at each corner. If the vehicle does not come back to a level position within one or two bounces, the shocks/struts are worn and must be replaced. When bouncing the vehicle up and down, listen for squeaks and noises from the suspension components.

4 Check the struts and shock absorbers for evidence of fluid leakage (see illustration). A light film of fluid is no cause for concern. Make sure that any fluid noted is from the struts/shocks and not from some other source. If leakage is noted, replace the struts/shocks as a set.

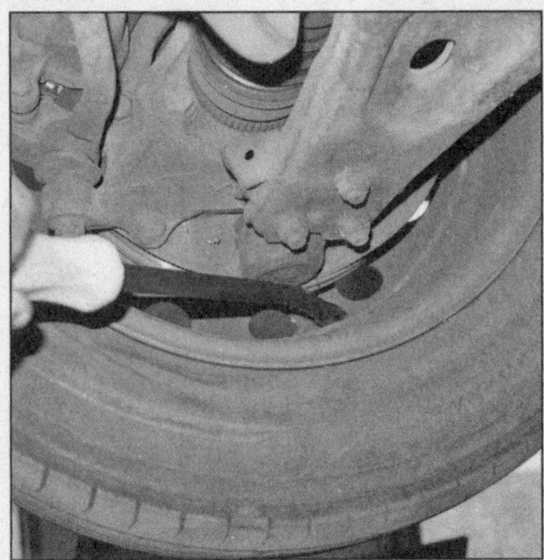

15.10 To check the balljoint for wear, try to pry the control arm up and down to make sure there is no play in the balljoint (if there is, replace it)

15.11 Check the balljoint boot for damage

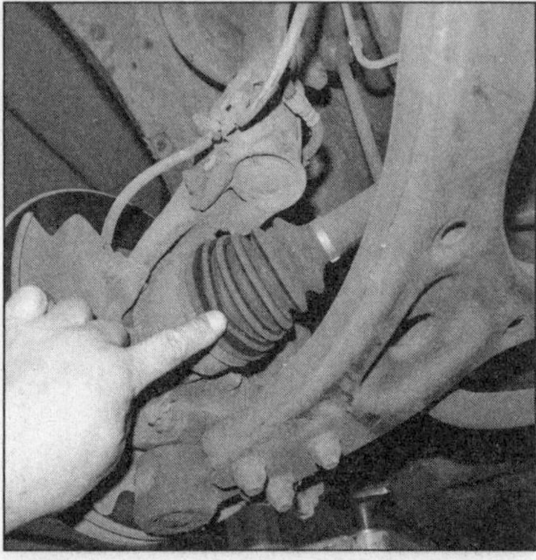

15.14 Flex the driveaxle boots by hand to check for cracks and leaking grease

5 Check the struts and shocks to be sure they are securely mounted and undamaged. Check the upper mounts for damage and wear. If damage or wear is noted, replace the shocks as a set (front and rear).

6 If the struts or shocks must be replaced, refer to Chapter 10 for the procedure.

Under the vehicle

7 Raise the vehicle and support it securely on jackstands.

8 Check the tires for irregular wear patterns and proper inflation. See Section 5 in this Chapter for information regarding tire wear and Chapter 10 for information on wheel bearing replacement.

9 Inspect the universal joint between the steering shaft and the steering gear housing. Check the steering gear housing for lubricant leakage. Make sure that the dust seals and boots are not damaged and that the boot clamps are not loose. Check the steering linkage for looseness or damage. Check the tie-rod ends for excessive play. Look for loose bolts, broken or disconnected parts and deteriorated rubber bushings on all suspension and steering components. While an assistant turns the steering wheel from side to side, check the steering components for free movement, chafing and binding. If the steering components do not seem to be reacting with the movement of the steering wheel, try to determine where the slack is located.

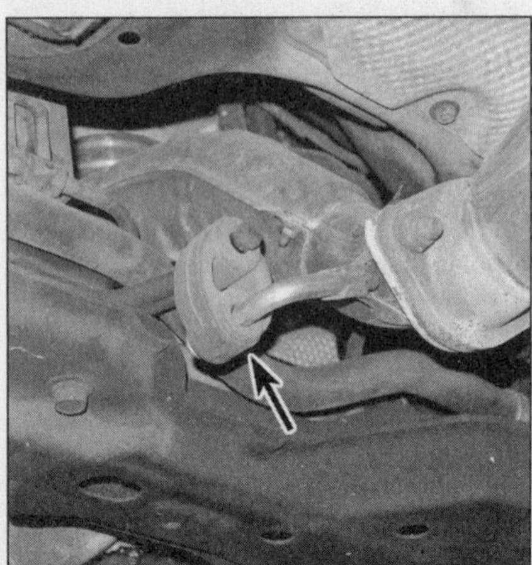

16.2 Check the exhaust system for rust, damage, or broken rubber hangers

10 Check the balljoints for wear by trying to move each control arm up and down with a prybar (see illustration) to ensure that its balljoint has no play. If any balljoint does have play, replace it. Try to turn the balljoint grease fitting with your fingers. If you can move the grease fitting, the balljoint is worn out. See Chapter 10 for the balljoint replacement procedure.

11 Inspect the balljoint boots for damage and leaking grease (see illustration). Replace the balljoints with new ones if they are damaged (see Chapter 10).

12 At the rear of the vehicle, inspect the suspension arm bushings for deterioration. Additional information on suspension components can be found in Chapter 10.

Driveaxle boot check

Note: *For detailed illustrations of the driveaxles, refer to Chapter 8.*

13 The driveaxle boots are very important because they prevent dirt, water and foreign material from entering and damaging the constant velocity (CV) joints. Oil and grease can cause the boot material to deteriorate prematurely, so it's a good idea to wash the boots with soap and water. Because it constantly pivots back and forth following the steering action of the front hub, the outer CV boot wears out sooner and should be inspected regularly.

14 Inspect the boots for tears and cracks as well as loose clamps (see illustration). If there is any evidence of cracks or leaking lubricant, they must be replaced as described in Chapter 8.

16 Exhaust system check (every 12,000 miles [19,200 km] or 12 months)

1 With the engine cold (at least three hours after the vehicle has been driven), check the complete exhaust system from the engine to the end of the tailpipe. Ideally, the inspection should be done with the vehicle on a hoist to permit unrestricted access. If a hoist isn't available, raise the vehicle and support it securely on jackstands.

2 Check the exhaust pipes and connections for evidence of leaks, severe corrosion and damage. Make sure that all brackets and hangers are in good condition and tight (see illustration).

3 At the same time, inspect the underside of the body for holes, corrosion, open seams, etc. which may allow exhaust gases to enter the passenger compartment. Seal all body openings with silicone or body putty.

4 Rattles and other noises can often be traced to the exhaust system, especially the mounts and hangers. Try to move the pipes, muffler and catalytic converter. If the components can come in contact with the body or suspension parts, secure the exhaust system with new mounts.

5 Check the running condition of the engine by inspecting inside the end of the tailpipe. The exhaust deposits here are an indication of engine state-of-tune. If the pipe is black and sooty or coated with white deposits, check for the presence of any stored trouble codes (see Chapter 6).

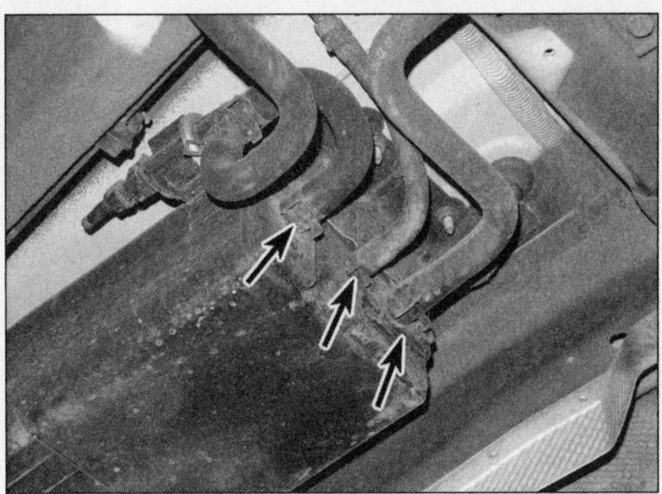
17.6 Check the EVAP system hoses (shown) and fuel system hoses and clamps for damage and deterioration

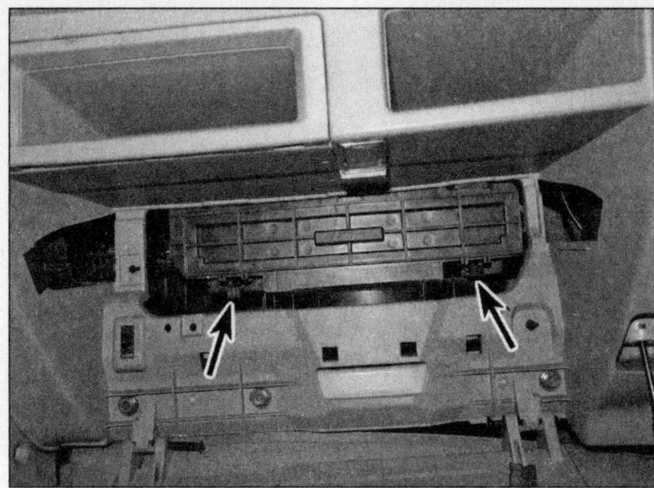
18.2 Lift the tabs upwards to disengage the clips

17 Fuel system check (every 12,000 miles [19,200 km] or 12 months)

Warning: *Gasoline is flammable, so take extra precautions when you work on any part of the fuel system. Don't smoke or allow open flames or bare light bulbs near the work area, and don't work in a garage where a gas-type appliance (such as a water heater or clothes dryer) is present. Since fuel is carcinogenic, wear fuel-resistant gloves when there's a possibility of being exposed to fuel, and, if you spill any fuel on your skin, rinse it off immediately with soap and water. Mop up any spills immediately and do not store fuel-soaked rags where they could ignite. When you perform any kind of work on the fuel system, wear safety glasses and have a Class B type fire extinguisher on hand. The fuel system is under constant pressure, so, before any lines are disconnected, the fuel system pressure must be relieved (see Chapter 4).*

1 If you smell gasoline while driving or after the vehicle has been sitting in the sun, inspect the fuel system immediately.

2 Remove the fuel filler cap and inspect if for damage and corrosion. The gasket should have an unbroken sealing imprint. If the gasket is damaged or corroded, install a new cap.

3 Inspect the fuel feed line for cracks. Make sure that the connections between the fuel lines and the fuel rail are tight.

Warning: *Your vehicle is fuel injected, so you must relieve the fuel system pressure before servicing fuel system components. The fuel system pressure relief procedure is outlined in Chapter 4.*

4 Since some components of the fuel system - the fuel tank and the fuel lines, for example - are underneath the vehicle, they can be inspected more easily with the vehicle raised on a hoist. If that's not possible, raise the vehicle and support it on jackstands.

5 With the vehicle raised and safely supported, inspect the gas tank and filler neck for punctures, cracks and other damage. The connection between the filler neck and the tank is particularly critical. Sometimes a rubber filler neck will leak because of loose clamps or deteriorated rubber. Inspect all fuel tank mounting brackets and straps to be sure that the tank is securely attached to the vehicle.

Warning: *Do not, under any circumstances, try to repair a fuel tank (except rubber components). A welding torch or any open flame can easily cause fuel vapors inside the tank to explode.*

6 Carefully check all hoses and lines leading away from the fuel tank and EVAP canister. Check for loose connections, deteriorated hoses, crimped lines and other damage (see illustration). Repair or replace damaged sections as necessary (see Chapter 4).

18 Cabin air filter replacement (every 12,000 miles [19,200 km] or 12 months)

Warning: *The models covered by this manual are equipped with a Supplemental Restraint System (SRS), more commonly known as airbags. Always disable the airbag system before working in the vicinity of any airbag system component to avoid the possibility of accidental deployment of the airbag, which could cause personal injury (see Chapter 12).*

1 Open the glove box, disengage the stops on each side of the glove box, then lower glove box door (see Chapter 11).

2 Disengage the two clips at the front edge of the cover (see illustration) and remove the cover.

3 Remove the filter from the housing (see illustration).

4 Install the filter, making sure the arrow on the filter is pointing towards the floor.

5 Installation is the reverse of the removal procedure.

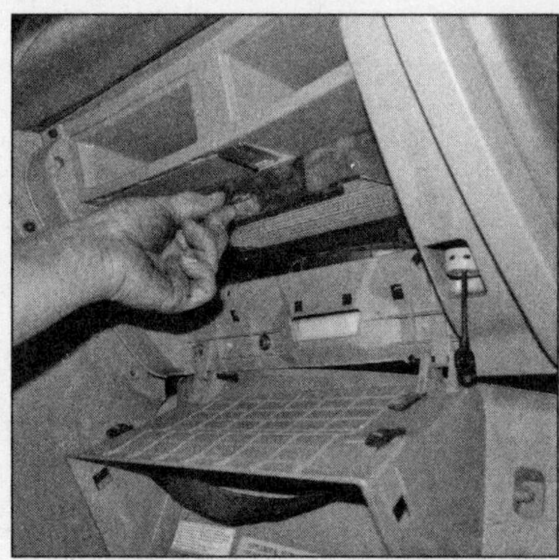
18.3 Remove the filter from the housing, noting the position of the filter as it is removed

19 Drivebelt check, adjustment and replacement (every 30,000 miles [48,00 km] or 30 months)

1 The drivebelt(s) is/are located at the front of the engine. The good condition (and, on 2005 and earlier models, proper adjustment) of the belts is critical to the operation of the engine. Because of their composition and the high stresses to which they are subjected, drivebelts stretch and deteriorate as they get older. They must therefore be periodically inspected.

Check

2 On all except 2005 and earlier models, one belt transmits power to all accessories. On 2005 and earlier models, the inner belt drives the power steering pump and the outer belt drives the air conditioning compressor and alternator.

3 With the engine off, open the hood and use your fingers (and a flashlight, if neces-

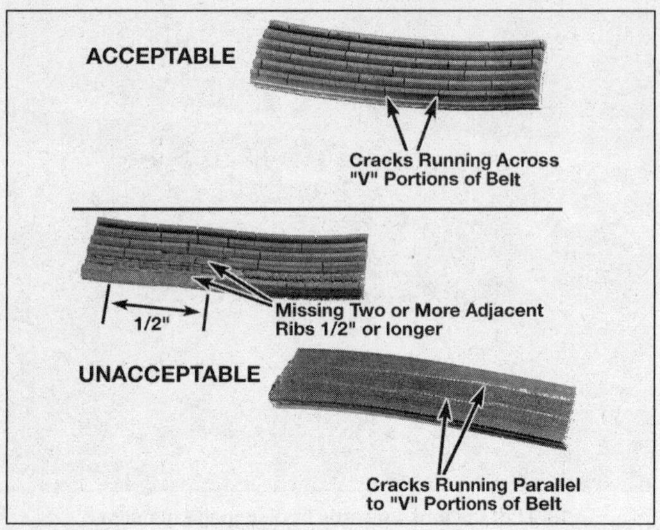

19.3 Here are some of the more common problems associated with drivebelts (check the belts very carefully to prevent an untimely breakdown)

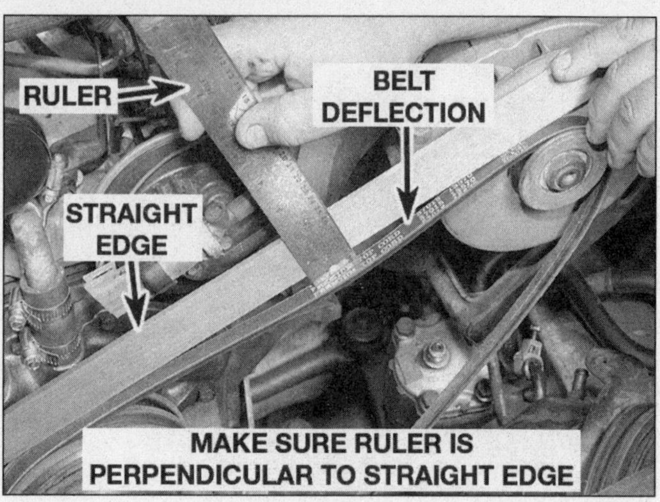

19.4 Measuring drivebelt deflection with a straightedge and ruler

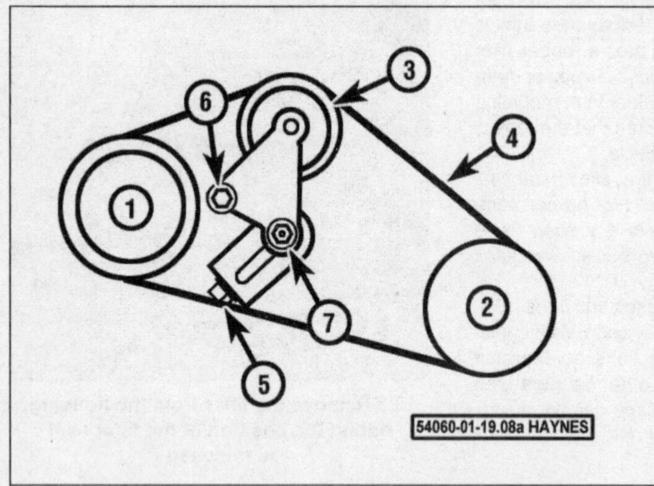

19.6 Power steering pump belt adjustment details

1 *Power steering pump*
2 *Crankshaft pulley*
3 *Tensioner pulley*
4 *Drive belt*
5 *Adjustment bolt*
6 *Pivot bolt*
7 *Adjustment bolt lock nut*

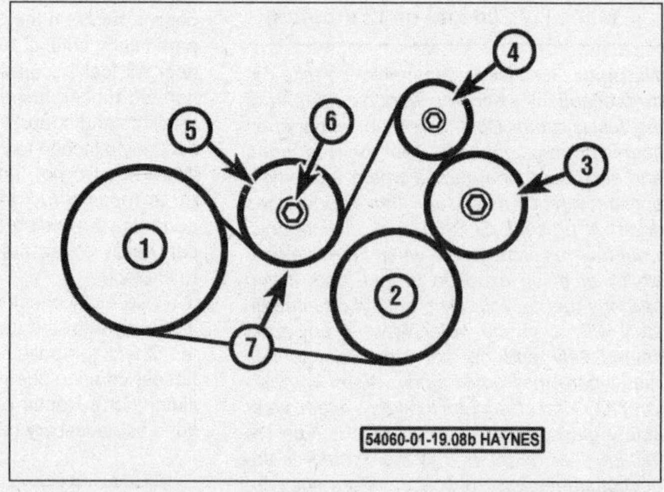

19.7 Air conditioning compressor/alternator belt adjustment details

1 *Crankshaft pulley*
2 *Air conditioning compressor*
3 *Idler pulley*
4 *Alternator*
5 *Tensioner pulley*
6 *Tensioner lock bolt*
7 *Tensioner adjusting bolt (accessed from underneath pulley)*

sary) to move along the belt, checking for cracks and separation of the belt plies. Also check for fraying and glazing, which gives the belt a shiny appearance (see illustration). Check the ribs on the underside of the belt. They should all be the same depth, with none of the surfaces uneven.

4 2005 and earlier models: The tension (deflection) of each drivebelt is checked by pushing on the belt at a distance halfway between the pulleys. Push firmly with your thumb and see how much the belt moves (deflects) (see illustration).The belt should deflect approximately 1/4-inch.

Adjustment (2005 and earlier models)

5 Both belts are adjusted in the same manner, although each has its own tensioner. To access the tensioners, loosen the right front wheel lug nuts, then raise the front of the vehicle and support it securely on jackstands. Remove the wheel and the inner fender splash shield or drivebelt splash shield, as applicable (see Chapter 11).

6 To adjust the power steering pump belt, loosen the tensioner hinge bolt and lock nut, then turn the adjuster bolt in or out to achieve the proper belt tension (see illustration). When proper tension is achieved, tighten the hinge bolt and lock nut securely.

7 To adjust the air conditioning compressor/alternator belt, loosen the tensioner pulley lock bolt, then turn the tensioner adjustment bolt in or out to achieve the proper belt tension (see illustration). When proper tension is achieved, tighten the pulley lock bolt securely.

Replacement

8 Apply the parking brake, loosen the right front wheel lug nuts, raise the front of the vehicle and support it securely on jackstands. Remove the wheel, then remove the inner fender splash shield or drivebelt splash shield, as applicable.

19.11 Place a wrench on the tensioner arm lug and rotate it counterclockwise to relieve the belt tension

19.15 Drivebelt tensioner mounting bolt(s) - 3.8L engine shown, 2011 and later 3.5L engine similar

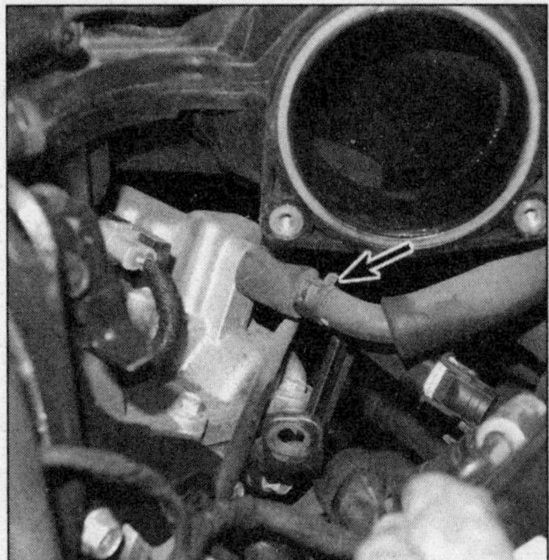

21.3a Squeeze the clamp and disconnect the PCV valve hose...

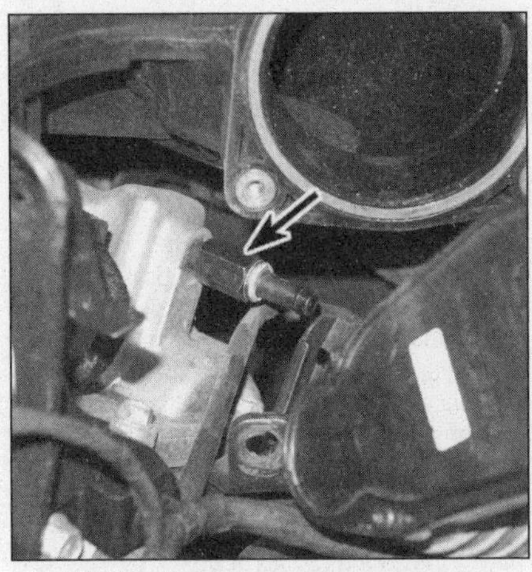

21.3b... then unscrew the valve (3.8L engine shown, 2011 and later 3.5L engine similar)

2005 and earlier models

9 Release the tension on the belt(s) so the belt(s) will slip off of the pulleys (see Steps 6 and 7).

10 Installation is the reverse of removal. When installing the belt, make sure the belt is centered on the pulleys and the belt tension is adjusted properly (see Steps 4 through 7).

2006 and later models

11 The automatic tensioner must be released to allow drivebelt replacement. Place a wrench on the tensioner arm lug and rotate it counterclockwise until the belt can be removed (see illustration). Remove the belt and slowly release the tensioner.

Warning: *Damage to the tensioner or possible injury can occur if the tensioner snaps back without the belt in place.*

12 Installation is the reverse of removal. When installing the belt, make sure the belt is centered on the pulleys.

13 Install the splash shield, wheel and lug nuts. Lower the vehicle and tighten the lug nuts to the torque listed in this Chapter's Specifications.

Automatic tensioner replacement (2006 and later models)

14 Remove the drivebelt as described previously in this Section.

15 Unscrew the mounting bolts of the tensioner and remove the tensioner (see illustration).

16 Install the new tensioner assembly by reversing the removal procedure. Tighten the mounting bolts to the torque listed in this Chapter's Specifications.

17 Install the drivebelt as described previously in this Section.

18 Install the drivebelt splash shield, wheel and lug nuts. Lower the vehicle and tighten the lug nuts to the torque listed in this Chapter's Specifications.

20 Brake fluid change (every 30,000 miles [48,000 km] or 30 months)

Warning: *Brake fluid can harm your eyes and damage painted surfaces, so use extreme caution when handling or pouring it. Do not use brake fluid that has been standing open or is more than one year old. Brake fluid absorbs moisture from the air. Excess moisture can cause a dangerous loss of braking effectiveness.*

1 At the specified intervals, the brake fluid should be drained and replaced. Since the brake fluid may drip or splash when pouring it, place plenty of rags around the master cylinder to protect any surrounding painted surfaces.

2 Before beginning work, purchase the specified brake fluid (see Recommended lubricants and fluids in this Chapter's Specifications).

3 Remove the cap from the master cylinder reservoir.

4 Using a hand suction pump or similar device, withdraw the fluid from the master cylinder reservoir.

5 Add new fluid to the master cylinder until it rises to the base of the filler neck.

6 Bleed the brake system at all four brakes until new and uncontaminated fluid is expelled from the bleeder screw (see Chapter 9). Be sure to maintain the fluid level in the master cylinder as you perform the bleeding process. If you allow the master cylinder to run dry, air will enter the system.

7 Refill the master cylinder with fluid and check the operation of the brakes. The pedal should feel solid when depressed, with no sponginess.

Warning:Do *not operate the vehicle if you are in doubt about the effectiveness of the brake system.*

21 Positive Crankcase Ventilation (PCV) valve check and replacement (every 60,000 miles or 60 months)

Warning: *Do not attempt to clean the PCV valve.*

Note: *If replacing the valve, compare the old and new valves to make sure they're identical.*

1 On 2005 and earlier models, the PCV valve and hose are located at the left end of the front valve cover. On 2006 and later models, it's located at the left end of the rear valve cover.

2 If you're working on a 2006 or later model, unbolt the throttle body and position it aside (see Chapter 4).

3 Detach the PCV hose and remove the valve (see illustrations).

4 Shake the valve. The valve should rattle freely - if it doesn't, replace it.

5 Replace the PCV valve with the correct one for your specific vehicle and tighten the it securely.

6 The remainder of installation is the reverse of removal.

22.5 The drain fitting is located at the bottom of the radiator

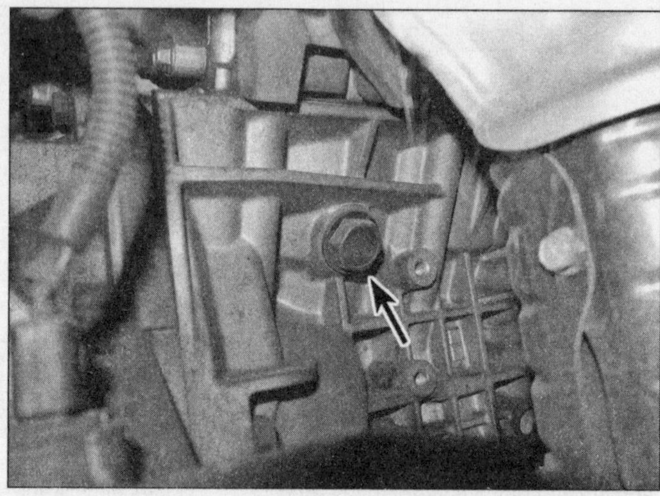

22.6 Remove the block drain plug(s). Some models only have one; this one is located on the rear cylinder bank, about five or six inches above the oil pan

22 Cooling system servicing (draining, flushing and refilling) (every 60 months)

Warning: *Do not allow antifreeze to come in contact with your skin or painted surfaces of the vehicle. Flush contaminated areas immediately with plenty of water. Do not store new coolant or leave old coolant lying around where it's accessible to children or pets - they're attracted by its sweet smell. Ingestion of even a small amount of coolant can be fatal! Wipe up garage floor and drip pan spills immediately. Keep antifreeze containers covered and repair cooling system leaks as soon as they're noticed. Check with local authorities about the disposal of used antifreeze. Many communities have collection centers which will see that antifreeze is disposed of properly.*

Warning: *The electric cooling fan(s) on these models can activate at any time the ignition switch is in the ON position. Make sure the ignition is OFF when working in the vicinity of the fan(s). As an added precaution, disconnect the cable from the negative terminal of the battery (see Chapter).*

1 Periodically, the cooling system should be drained, flushed and refilled to replenish the antifreeze mixture and prevent formation of rust and corrosion, which can impair the performance of the cooling system and cause engine damage.

2 At the same time the cooling system is serviced, all hoses and the radiator (pressure) cap should be inspected, tested and replaced if faulty (see Section 12).

Draining

Warning: *Wait until the engine is completely cool before beginning this procedure.*

3 With the engine cold, remove the radiator cap and set the heater control to maximum heat.

4 Move a large container, capable of holding at least 12 quarts, under the radiator drain fitting to catch the coolant mixture as it's drained.

5 Insert a blade screwdriver through the opening in the bottom of the radiator support and turn the drain fitting counter clockwise (see illustration). Allow the coolant to completely drain out.

6 After the coolant stops flowing out of the radiator, move the container under the engine block drain plugs and allow the coolant in the block to drain (see illustration).

7 While the coolant is draining, check the condition of the radiator hoses, heater hoses and clamps. Replace any damaged clamps or hoses (see Section 12).

Flushing

8 Close the radiator and engine block drain plugs. Fill the cooling system with clean water, following the Refilling procedure (see Step 15).

9 Start the engine and allow it to reach normal operating temperature, then rev up the engine a few times.

10 Turn the engine off and allow it to cool completely, then drain the system as described earlier.

11 Repeat Steps 8 through 10 until the water being drained is free of contaminants.

12 Severe cases of radiator contamination or clogging will require removing the radiator (see Chapter 3) and reverse flushing it. This involves inserting the hose in the bottom radiator outlet to allow the clean water to run against the normal flow, draining out through the top. A radiator repair shop should be consulted if further cleaning or repair is necessary.

13 When the coolant is regularly drained and the system refilled with the correct coolant mixture, there should be no need to employ chemical cleaners or descalers.

14 Disconnect the coolant reservoir hose, remove the reservoir from the vehicle and flush it with clean water (see Chapter 3). Inspect it for damage and replace if necessary.

Refilling

15 Install the coolant reservoir, reconnect the hose and close the radiator drain fitting.

16 Remove the radiator cap. Add the correct mixture of the proper type of antifreeze/coolant and water in the ratio specified on the antifreeze container or in this Chapter's Specifications through the filler neck until it reaches the radiator cap seat.

17 Add the same coolant mixture to the reservoir until the level is between the F and L marks. Install the radiator cap.

18 Run the engine until normal operating temperature is reached (the fans will cycle on, then off), then allow the engine to cool. With the engine cold, add coolant as necessary to bring it up to the correct level.

19 Keep a close watch on the coolant level and the various cooling system hoses during the first few miles of driving and check for any coolant leaks. Tighten the hose clamps and add more coolant mixture as necessary.

23 Spark plug check and replacement (see Maintenance schedule for intervals)

1 The spark plugs are located in the center of the valve covers on all models.

2 In most cases the tools necessary for spark plug replacement include a spark plug socket which fits onto a ratchet (this special socket is padded inside to protect the porcelain insulators on the new plugs and hold them in place), various extensions and a feeler gauge to check and adjust the spark plug gap (see illustration). Since these engines are equipped with aluminum cylinder heads, a torque wrench should be used when tightening the spark plugs.

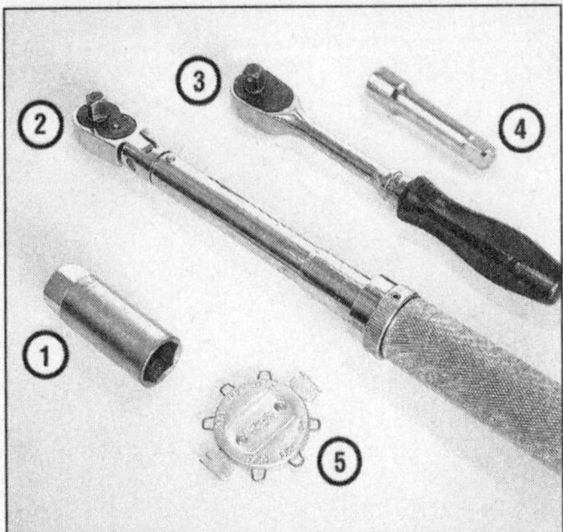

23.2 Tools required for changing spark plugs

1. ***Spark plug socket*** *- This will have special padding inside to protect the spark plug porcelain insulator*
2. ***Torque wrench*** *- Although not mandatory, use of this tool is the best way to ensure that the plugs are tightened properly*
3. ***Ratchet*** *- Standard hand tool to fit the plug socket*
4. ***Extension*** *- Depending on model and accessories, you may need special extensions and universal joints to reach one or more of the plugs*
5. ***Spark plug gap gauge*** *- This gauge for checking the gap comes in a variety of styles. Make sure the gap for your engine is included*

3 The best approach when replacing the spark plugs is to purchase the new spark plugs beforehand, adjust them to the proper gap and then replace each plug one at a time. When buying the new spark plugs, be sure to obtain the correct plug for your specific engine. This information can be found in this

23.5 Spark plug manufacturers recommend using a wire-type gauge when checking the gap - the wire should slide between the electrodes with a slight drag

Chapter's Specifications or in your owner's manual.

4 Allow the engine to cool completely before attempting to remove any of the plugs. During this cooling off time, each of the new spark plugs can be inspected for defects and the gaps can be checked.

5 The gap is checked by inserting the proper thickness gauge between the electrodes at the tip of the plug (see illustration). The gap between the electrodes should be as listed in this Chapter's Specifications or in your owner's manual. The wire should touch each of the electrodes. Also, at this time check for cracks in the spark plug body (if any are found, the plug must not be used).

Caution: *The manufacturer recommends against checking the gap on platinum-tipped spark plugs; the platinum coating could be scraped off.*

6 Cover the fender to prevent damage to the paint. Fender covers are available from auto parts stores but an old blanket will work

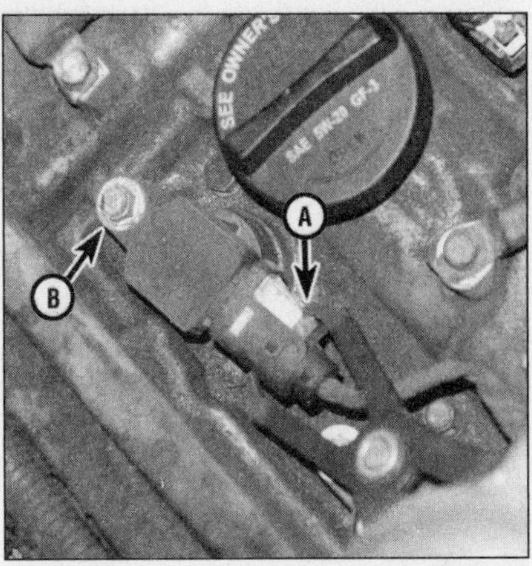

23.7 To remove an ignition coil(s), depress the tab (A), disconnect the electrical connector, remove the coil retaining bolt (B), then pull the coil straight up (2006 and later models)

just fine.

7 On 2006 and later models, remove the upper intake manifold (see Chapter 2A Section 5) to gain access to the rear ignition coils (see illustration).

8 On 2005 and earlier models, remove the spark plug wire from one spark plug, using a twisting motion. Pull only on the boot at the end of the wire - do not pull on the wire (see illustration), then remove the ignition coil from the corresponding cylinder as described in Step 7.

9 If compressed air is available, use it to blow any dirt or foreign material away from the spark plug area. The idea here is to eliminate the possibility of material falling into the cylinder through the spark plug hole as the spark plug is removed.

Warning: *Wear eye protection!*

10 Place the spark plug socket over the plug and remove it from the engine by turning it in a counterclockwise direction (see illustration).

11 Compare the spark plug with the chart

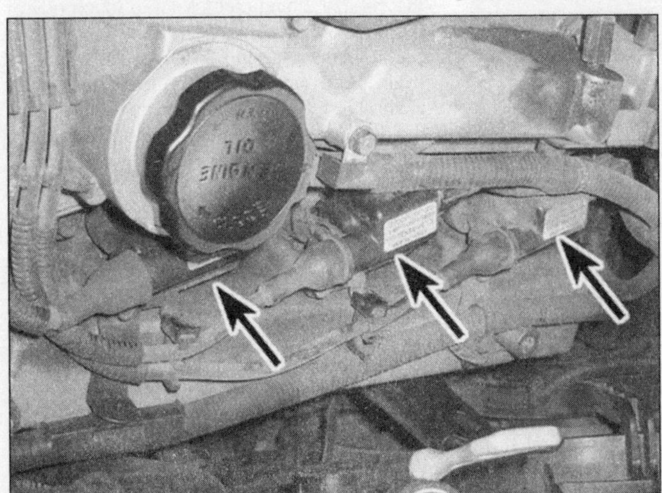

23.8 Use a spark plug boot pulling tool to remove each end of a spark plug wire - never pull on the wire itself (2005 and earlier models)

23.10 Use a ratchet, socket and long extension to remove the spark plugs (3.8L engine shown, all other engines similar)

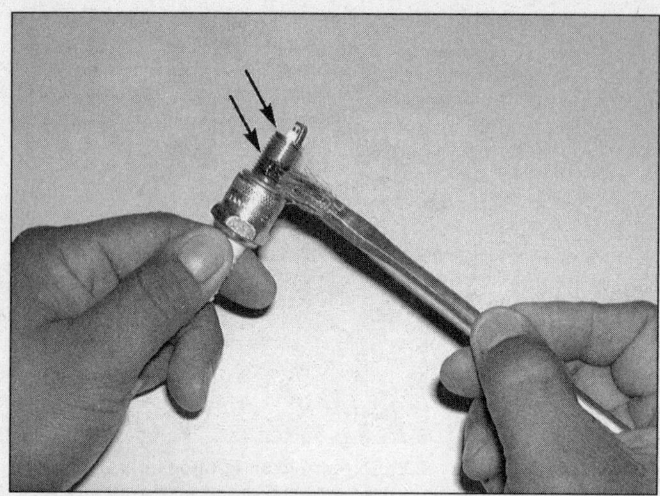

23.12 Apply a thin coat of anti-seize compound to the spark plug threads, but be careful not to get any of it near the electrodes

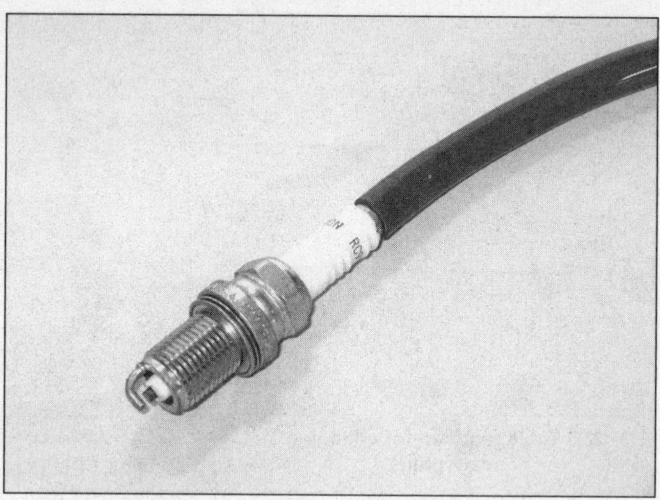

23.13 A length of snug-fitting rubber hose will save time and prevent damaged threads when installing the spark plugs

on the inside back cover of this manual to get an indication of the overall running condition of the engine.

12 It's a good idea to lightly coat the threads of the spark plugs with an anti-seize compound (see illustration) to insure that the spark plugs do not seize in the aluminum cylinder head.

13 It's often difficult to insert spark plugs into their holes without cross-threading them. To avoid this possibility, fit a piece of rubber hose over the end of the spark plug (see illustration). The flexible hose acts as a universal joint to help align the plug with the plug hole. Should the plug begin to cross-thread, the hose will slip on the spark plug, preventing thread damage. Install the spark plug and tighten it to the torque listed in this Chapter's Specifications.

14 On 2005 and earlier models, install the ignition coils then attach the plug wire to the new spark plug, again using a twisting motion on the boot until it is firmly seated on the end of the spark plug. On 2006 and later models, install the ignition coils.

15 Follow the above procedure for the remaining spark plugs.

24 Spark plug wire check and replacement (2005 and earlier models) (every 100,000 miles [160,000 km])

1 The spark plug wires should be replaced at the recommended intervals and/or checked when new spark plugs are installed.

2 Disconnect the spark plug wire from the corresponding ignition coil. Pull only on the boot at the end of the wire; don't pull on the wire itself. Use a twisting motion to free the boot/wire from the coil. Disconnect the same spark plug wire from the spark plug, using the same twisting method while pulling on the boot.

Note: *On 2005 and earlier models, only three ignition coils are used; the ignition coils are mounted over cylinders 2, 4 and 6 with spark plug wires that feed to the other cylinders. The ignition coil on cylinder 2 is connected to cylinder 5, cylinder 4 is connected to cylinder 1 and cylinder 6 is connected to cylinder 3.*

3 Check inside the boot for corrosion, which will look like a white, crusty powder (don't mistake the white dielectric grease used on some plug wire boots for corrosion protection).

4 Push the wire and boot back onto the end of the spark plug. It should be a tight fit on the plug end. If not, remove the wire and use a pair of pliers to carefully crimp the metal connector inside the wire boot until the fit is snug.

5 Push the wire and boot back into the end of the ignition coil terminal. It should be a tight fit in the terminal. If not, remove the wire and use a pair of pliers to carefully crimp the metal connector inside the wire boot until the fit is snug.

6 Using a cloth, clean each wire along its entire length. Remove all built-up dirt and grease. As this is done, inspect for burned areas, cracks and any other form of damage. Bend the wires in several places to ensure that the conductive material inside hasn't hardened. Repeat the procedure for the remaining wires.

7 If you are replacing the spark plug wires, purchase a complete set for your particular engine. The terminals and rubber boots should already be installed on the wires. Replace the wires one at a time to avoid mixing up the firing order and make sure the terminals are securely seated on the coil pack and the spark plugs.

8 Attach the plug wire to the new spark plug and to the ignition coil pack using a twisting motion on the boot until it is firmly seated.

25 Automatic transaxle fluid change (see Maintenance schedule for service intervals)

1 Before beginning work, purchase the specified transaxle fluid (see this Chapters Specifications).

2 The fluid should be drained immediately after the vehicle has been driven. Hot fluid is more effective than cold fluid at removing built up sediment.

Warning: *Fluid temperature can exceed 350-degrees F in a hot transaxle. Wear protective gloves.*

2010 and earlier models

3 After the vehicle has been driven to warm up the fluid, raise it and place it on jackstands for access to the transaxle drain plug.

4 Move the necessary equipment under the vehicle, being careful not to touch any of the hot exhaust components.

5 Place the drain pan under the transaxle drain plug and remove the drain plug (see illustration). Once the fluid is drained, reinstall the drain plug and tighten it to the torque listed in this Chapter's Specifications.

6 Lower the vehicle.

7 Add new fluid to the transaxle through the dipstick tube (see this Chapter's Specifications for recommended lubricants and fluids for the recommended fluid type and capacity). Use a funnel to prevent spills. It is best to add a little fluid at a time, continually checking the level with the dipstick (see Section 4).

Caution: *It's important not to overfill the transaxle.*

8 Start the engine and shift into all positions from P through L, then shift into N and apply the parking brake.

9 With the engine idling, check the fluid level. Add fluid up to the Cool (or lower) level mark on the dipstick.

10 If necessary, add more fluid (a little at a

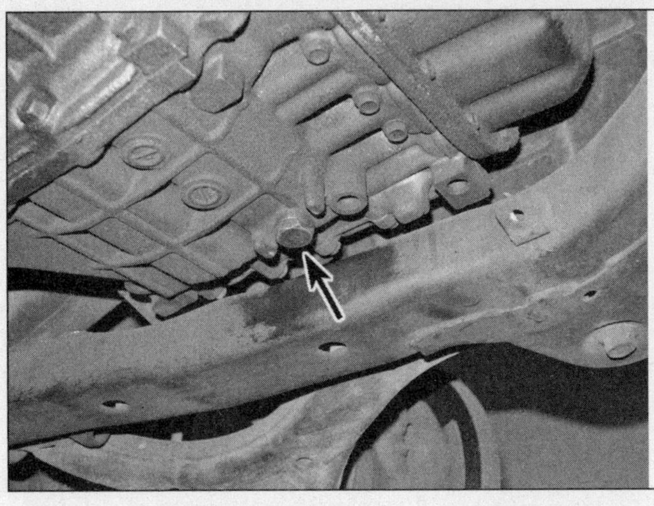

25.5 Remove the automatic transaxle drain plug (2006 model shown, later models similar)

time) until the level is between the Add and Full marks (be careful not to overfill it).

11 Drive the vehicle to warm up the transaxle to normal operating temperature, then recheck the fluid level.

2011 and later models

Warning:This *procedure is potentially dangerous and is best left to a professional shop with a safe lifting apparatus. The vehicle must be kept level while being safely raised high enough for access to the check plug on the transaxle.*

12 Raise the vehicle and support it securely on four jackstands (the vehicle must be level for this procedure).

13 Place a large drain pan under the transaxle. Remove the drain plug and allow the fluid to drain (see illustration 25.5).

14 Install the drain plug and tighten the plug to the torque listed in this Chapter's Specifications.

15 Remove the transaxle breather tube banjo-bolt from the top of the transaxle, then add approximately 5.2 quarts (5 liters) of transaxle fluid of the correct type (see this Chapter's Specifications) through the banjo-bolt hole.

Note: *A long-necked funnel will be necessary to add fluid through the banjo-bolt opening.*

16 Install the banjo bolt, using new sealing washers, then tighten it to the torque listed in this Chapter's Specifications.

17 Start the engine and allow it to idle until the fluid reaches approximately 122 to 140 degrees F (50 to 60 degrees C), then move the shift lever from Park to Drive, then Drive to Park. Repeat this step one more time at idle.

18 With the engine running, locate the fluid level check plug; it's located on the valve body cover on the driver's side of the transaxle.

19 Place a container under the check plug and remove it. The fluid should flow out in a thin steady stream, indicating correct fluid level. If the fluid level is correct, install the level check plug and tighten it to the torque listed in this Chapter's Specifications.

20 If no fluid drips from the check hole, remove the transaxle breather tube banjo-bolt from the top of the transaxle and add small amounts of fluid until the fluid has a thin, steady flow out of the check plug hole.

21 When the fluid level is correct, install the check plug and banjo bolt and tighten them to the torque values listed in this Chapter's Specifications.

Notes

Chapter 2 Part A V6 engines

Contents

	Section
Camshafts and valvetrain - removal, inspection, installation and valve adjustment	10
Crankshaft pulley/vibration damper - removal and installation	12
Cylinder heads - removal, inspection and installation	11
Driveplate - removal and installation	15
Exhaust manifold/catalytic converter assemblies - removal and installation	6
General information	1
Intake manifold - removal and installation	5
Oil pans - removal and installation	13
Oil pump - removal, inspection and installation	14
Oil seals - replacement	9
Powertrain mounts - check and replacement	17
Rear main oil seal - replacement	16
Repair operations possible with the engine in the vehicle	2
Timing belt and sprockets (2005 and earlier models) - removal, inspection and installation	8
Timing chain and sprockets (2006 and later models) - removal, inspection and installation	7
Top Dead Center (TDC) for number one piston - locating	3
Valve covers - removal and installation	4

General

Engine type	DOHC V6	
Displacement		
2005 and earlier 3.5L engine	213.3 cubic inches	3497 cc
3.8L engine	230.55 cubic inches	3778 cc
2011 and later 3.5L engine	211.75 cubic inches	3470 cc
Engine VIN code		
2004 and earlier 3.5L engine	1	
2005 3.5L engine	2	
2006 through 2010 3.8L engine	3	
2011 and later 3.5L engine	7	
3.8L engine	A	
Firing order	1-2-3-4-5-6	
Bore		
2005 and earlier 3.5L engine	3.66 inches	93 mm
3.8L engine	3.7795 inches	96 mm
2011 and later 3.5L engines	3.6220 inches	92 mm
Stroke		
2005 and earlier 3.5L engine	3.38 inches	85.8 mm
3.8L engine	3.4252 inches	87 mm
2011 and later 3.5L engine	3.4252 inches	87 mm
Compression ratio		
2005 and earlier 3.5L engine	10.0:1	
3.8L engines	10.4:1	
2011 and later 3.5L engine	10.6:1	
Compression pressure	See Chapter 2B	
Oil pressure	See Chapter 2B	

1 3 5

2 4 6

Front

54077-1-1b specs HAYNES

Cylinder numbering

Camshafts

Lobe height		
3.5L engine		
2005 and earlier		
Intake	1.3818 to 1.3897 inches	35.098 to 35.298 mm
Exhaust	1.3705 to 1.3783 inches	34.81 to 35.01 mm
2011 and later		
Intake	1.8582 inches	47.2 mm
Exhaust	1.8031 inches	45.8 mm
3.8L engine		
Intake	1.8425 inches	46.8 mm
Exhaust	1.8031 inches	45.8 mm
Journal diameter		
2005 and earlier 3.5L engine	1.0220 to 1.0224 inches	25.951 to 25.970 mm
All other V6 engine		
First journal	1.1009 to 1.1015 inches	27.964 to 27.978 mm
All other journals	0.9430 to 0.9437 inch	23.954 to 23.970 mm
Journal-to-bearing oil clearance (maximum)		
2005 and earlier 3.5L engine	0.0007 to 0.0024 inch	0.018 to 0.06 mm
All other engines		
First journal	0.0011 to 0.0022 inch	0.027 to 0.057 mm
All other journals	0.0012 to 0.0026 inch	0.030 to 0.067 mm
Endplay		
2005 and earlier 3.5L engine	0.0039 to 0.0059 inch	0.10 to 0.15 mm
All other engines	0.0008 to 0.0071 inch	0.02 to 0.18 mm

Valve clearances (engine cold)

All 2006 and later engines		
Intake valve	0.0067 to 0.0090 inch	0.17 to 0.23 mm
Exhaust valve	0.0106 to 0.0129 inch	0.27 to 0.33 mm

Timing belt tensioner

Timing belt tensioner pushrod protrusion (2005 and earlier 3.5L V6 engine)	0.15 to 0.18 inch	3.8 to 4.5 mm

Warpage limits

Cylinder head gasket surface	0.0019 inch	0.05 mm
Cylinder head intake gasket surface	0.0039 inch	0.10 mm
Cylinder head exhaust manifold gasket surface	0.0039 inch	0.10 mm
Lower intake manifold gasket surface	0.0039 inch	0.10 mm

Torque specifications

Note: *One foot-pound (ft-lb) of torque is equivalent to 12 inch-pounds (in-lbs) of torque. Torque values below approximately 15 foot-pounds are expressed in inch-pounds, because most foot-pound torque wrenches are not accurate at these smaller values.*

Torque specifications	Ft-lbs (unless otherwise indicated)	Nm
Camshaft bearing cap bolts		
2005 and earlier 3.5L engine		
Inner bolts	84 to 108 in-lbs	9.5 to 12
Outer bolts	14 to 15	19 to 20
All other engines	87 to 104 in-lbs	10 to 11.5
Camshaft sprocket bolt (2005 and earlier 3.5L engine)	58 to 72	79 to 98
Camshaft sprocket and Variable Camshaft Timing (CVVT) bolt	48 to 56	65 to 76
Crankshaft pulley bolt*		
2005 and earlier 3.5L engine	130 to 138	176 to 187
All other engines	210 to 224	285 to 304
Cylinder head bolts (in sequence - see illustration 11.22)*		
2005 and earlier 3.5L engine	76 to 83	105 to 115
All other engines		
Main bolts		
Step 1	28 to 30	38 to 40
Step 2	Tighten an additional 118 to 122-degrees	
Step 3	Tighten an additional 88 to 92-degrees	
M6 bolt (at the front of cylinder head)	14 to 17	19 to 23
Drivebelt tensioner (all models except 2005 and earlier 3.5L engine)		
M8 bolts	22 to 25	30 to 34
M12 bolts	60 to 63	81 to 85
Driveplate bolts	53 to 55	72 to 75
Exhaust manifold nuts		
2005 and earlier 3.5L engine	18 to 22	25 to 30
All other engines	29 to 33	35 to 45

Torque specifications (continued)	Ft-lbs (unless otherwise indicated)	Nm

Note: *One foot-pound (ft-lb) of torque is equivalent to 12 inch-pounds (in-lbs) of torque. Torque values below approximately 15 foot-pounds are expressed in inch-pounds, because most foot-pound torque wrenches are not accurate at these smaller values.*

Item	Ft-lbs	Nm
Intake manifold		
Lower manifold (in sequence - see illustration 5.20)		
2005 and earlier 3.5L engine	9 to 15	12 to 20
All other engines		
Step 1 (all bolts and nut)	36 to 48 in-lbs	4 to 5
Step 2		
Bolts	20 to 23	27 to 31
Nut	14 to 17	19 to 23
Step 3		
Bolts	20 to 23	27 to 31
Nut	14 to 17	19 to 23
Upper manifold		
2005 and earlier 3.5L engine	132 to 168 in-lbs	15 to 20
All 2006 and later engines	87 to 103 in-lbs	9.8 to 11.6
Oil control valve bolt	87 to 104 in-lbs	10 to 12
Lower oil pan bolts	87 to 104 in-lbs	10 to 12
Upper oil pan bolts		
3.5L engine		
2005 and earlier		
10 mm x 38 mm bolts	22 to 30	30 to 40
8 mm x 22 mm bolts	14 to 20	19 to 28
Oil pump case bolts	9 to 15	12 to 20
2011 and later	15 to 17	20 to 23
3.8L engine	14 to 17	19 to 23
Timing belt (2005 and earlier 3.5L engine)		
Tensioner pulley bolt	31 to 40	42 to 54
Idler pulley bolt	36 to 43	49 to 58
Tensioner arm (fixed bolt)	26 to 40	35 to 54
Automatic tensioner fixed bolt	14 to 20	19 to 27
Timing chain (all other engines)		
Timing chain cover bolts (in sequence - see illustration 7.42)		
Bolts B	14 to 16	19 to 22
Bolt C	87 to 104 in-lbs	10 to 12
Bolts D and E	43 to 51	58 to 69
Bolt F	18 to 20	25 to 27
Bolt G	16 to 17	22 to 23
Bolts H, I and J	87 to 104 in-lbs	10 to 12
Bolts K	96 in-lbs	11
Bolt L	16 to 19	22 to 26
Timing chain guides	87 to 104 in-lbs	10 to 12
Timing chain tensioner bolts	87 to 104 in-lbs	10 to 12
Valve cover bolts	87 to 104 in-lbs	10 to 12

* Use new bolt(s)

1 General information

1 2005 and earlier 3.5L engines use a timing belt, while all other engines use timing chains. All the V6 engines in this manual are DOHC (dual overhead cam) with aluminum heads, four valves per cylinder and a two-piece oil pan.

2 This Part of Chapter 2 is devoted to in-vehicle repair procedures for the V6 engine. Information concerning engine removal and installation and engine overhaul can be found in Chapter 2B.

3 The following repair procedures are based on the assumption that the engine is installed in the vehicle. If the engine has been removed from the vehicle and mounted on a stand, many of the steps outlined in this Part of Chapter 2 will not apply.

2 Repair operations possible with the engine in the vehicle

1 Many major repair operations can be accomplished without removing the engine from the vehicle.

2 Clean the engine compartment and the exterior of the engine with some type of degreaser before any work is done. It will make the job easier and help keep dirt out of the internal areas of the engine.

3 Depending on the components involved, it may be helpful to remove the hood to improve access to the engine as repairs are performed (see Chapter 11 if necessary). Cover the fenders to prevent damage to the paint. Special pads are available, but an old bedspread or blanket will also work.

4 If vacuum, exhaust, oil or coolant leaks develop, indicating a need for gasket or seal replacement, the repairs can generally be made with the engine in the vehicle. The intake and exhaust manifold gaskets, oil pan gasket, crankshaft oil seals and cylinder head gaskets are all accessible with the engine in place.

5 Exterior engine components, such as the intake and exhaust manifolds, the oil pan, the oil pump, the water pump, the starter motor, the alternator, and the fuel system components can be removed for repair with the engine in place.

6 Since the cylinder heads can be removed without pulling the engine, valve component servicing can also be accomplished with the engine in the vehicle. Replacement of the camshafts, timing belt/chain and sprockets is also possible with the engine in the vehicle.

3 Top Dead Center (TDC) for number one piston - locating

1 Top Dead Center (TDC) is the highest point in the cylinder that each piston reaches as it travels up the cylinder bore. Each piston reaches TDC on the compression stroke and again on the exhaust stroke, but TDC generally refers to piston position on the compression stroke.

2 Positioning the piston(s) at TDC is an essential part of certain procedures such as valve timing, camshaft, timing chain and timing belt and sprocket removal.

3 Before beginning this procedure, place the transaxle in Neutral and apply the parking brake or block the rear wheels. Disconnect the cable from the negative terminal of the battery (see Chapter 5).

4 Remove the number one spark plug (see Chapter 1) and install a compression pressure gauge in the spark plug hole. It should be a gauge with a screw-in fitting and a hose at least six inches long (see illustration).

5 Rotate the crankshaft with a socket and large ratchet or breaker bar while observing the compression gauge. When the compression stroke of the number one cylinder is reached, pressure will begin to show on the gauge; continue to rotate the crankshaft and align the notch on the crankshaft pulley with the 0 mark on the timing plate (2005 and earlier engines) or T mark (see illustration) on the timing chain cover (2006 and later engines). If you go past the marks, release the gauge pressure and rotate the crankshaft two more revolutions.

6 After the number one piston has been positioned at TDC on the compression stroke, TDC for the remaining cylinders can be located by turning the crankshaft 120-degrees (1/3-turn) at a time and following the firing order (see this Chapter's Specifications).

4 Valve covers - removal and installation

Removal

1 Disconnect the cable from the negative terminal of the battery (see Chapter 5).

2 Remove the engine cover.

3 Remove the upper intake manifold if you're working on the rear valve cover (see Section 5). On all other models the upper intake manifold must be removed for access to either valve cover.

4 Detach the engine wiring harnesses and pull them out of the way.

5 Disconnect all interfering wiring and hoses. Label them as you go to prevent confusion later.

6 Remove the ignition coils (see Chapter 5).

7 Remove the retaining bolts (see illustration), then detach the cover(s). If the cover is stuck to the head, bump the end with a wood block and a hammer to jar it loose. If that doesn't work, try to slip a flexible putty knife between the head and cover to break the seal.

Caution: *Don't pry at the cover-to-head joint or damage to the sealing surfaces may occur, leading to oil leaks after the cover is reinstalled.*

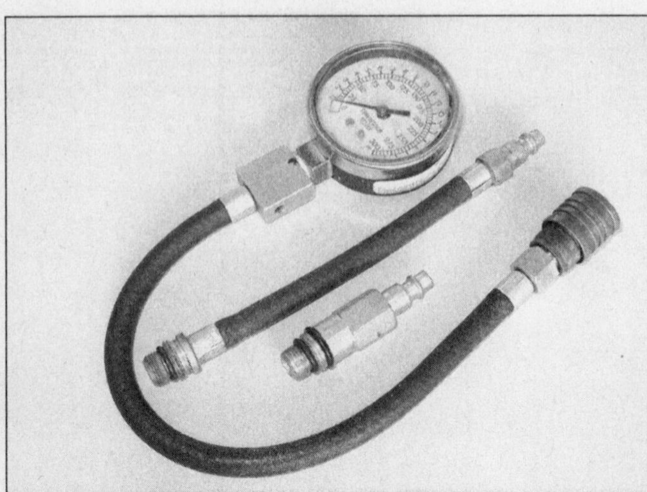

3.4 A compression gauge can be used in the number one plug hole to assist in finding TDC

3.5 Align the notch on the crankshaft pulley and the mark on the timing chain cover

4.7 Valve cover bolt locations - front cylinder bank shown

5.8a Remove the wiring harness support bracket bolt (shown), the upper support bracket mounting bolt. . .

5.8b. . . then, from under the vehicle, loosen the support bracket lower mounting bolt

5.8c At the left end of the manifold, remove the support bracket bolt at the bottom of the throttle body

Installation

8 The mating surfaces of the cylinder head and cover must be clean when the cover is installed. Use a gasket scraper to remove all traces of sealant and old gasket material, then clean the mating surfaces with brake system cleaner. If there's residue or oil on the mating surfaces when the cover is installed, oil leaks may develop.

9 Install new spark plug tube seals.

10 Apply RTV sealant to the gasket/seal joints at the front and rear camshaft bearing cap-to-cylinder head joints (2005 and earlier models), or timing chain cover-to-cylinder head joints (2006 and later models), then install the valve cover with a new gasket.

11 Tighten the bolts a little at a time, working from the center outwards, to the torque listed in this Chapter's Specifications.

12 Reinstall the remaining parts, run the engine and check for oil leaks.

5 Intake manifold - removal and installation

Warning: *Wait until the engine is completely cool before beginning this procedure.*

Removal

1 If you're working on a 2005 or earlier model or removing the lower manifold an any model, relieve the fuel system pressure (see Chapter 4), then disconnect the cable from the negative terminal of the battery (see Chapter 5).

2 Remove the engine cover.

3 On 2005 and earlier models, disconnect the accelerator and cruise control cables (see Chapter 6).

Upper intake manifold

4 Remove the air inlet tube and air filter housing (see Chapter 4).

5 Disconnect the PCV hose (see Chapter 6) and the brake booster hose (see Chapter 9).

6 Disconnect the ground strap, the electrical connectors and the vacuum lines from the upper intake manifold. Label each connector using tape and a marker to ensure correct reassembly. Pull the wiring harnesses aside.

7 On 2005 and earlier models, disconnect and plug the fuel supply line to the pressure regulator (see Chapter 4).

8 Disconnect and remove the upper intake manifold support brackets (see illustrations).

9 Disconnect the electrical connectors and hoses from the throttle body (see Chapter 6).

Caution: *Clamp-off the coolant hoses before detaching them, or plug them as soon as they are detached. Be prepared for coolant spillage.*

10 Disconnect the electrical connectors

5.11 Upper intake manifold mounting fastener locations

5.20 Lower intake manifold bolt tightening sequence

1 *On 2005 and earlier models, follow sequence 1 through 8*
2 *On 2006 and later models, Step 1: follow sequence A through H; Step 2 and Step 3: follow sequence 1 through 8*

from the various sensors and actuators and move the harnesses out of the way.

11 Remove the upper intake manifold mounting bolts/nuts (see illustration).

Lower intake manifold

12 Drain the cooling system (see Chapter 1).

13 On 2005 and earlier models, remove the thermostat housing and thermostat (see Chapter 3).

14 Disconnect the electrical connectors from the fuel injectors (see Chapter 4). Also detach the fuel line from the fuel rail (see Chapter 4). Pull the wiring harness aside.

15 On 2005 and earlier models, remove the fuel rail (see Chapter 4).

Note: *On 2006 and later models, the intake manifold can be removed with the injectors and fuel rails in place or removed, depending on the work to be done.*

16 Disconnect any remaining components from the lower manifold.

17 Remove the mounting bolts following the reverse of the tightening sequence (see illustration 5.20), then detach the lower intake manifold from the engine. If the manifold is stuck, don't pry between the gasket mating surfaces or damage may result.

Note: *Make note of each bolt as you remove them; they vary in lengths and must be installed in the same locations.*

18 Check the manifold's surface with a precision straightedge and compare your readings with those listed in this Chapter's Specifications. If it's excessively deformed, it must be replaced.

Installation

19 Use a scraper to remove all traces of old gasket material and sealant from the lower intake manifold and cylinder heads, then clean the mating surfaces with brake system cleaner.

20 Install new gaskets, then position the lower intake manifold on the engine. Make sure the gaskets haven't shifted, then install the bolts. Tighten the bolts in three or four equal steps, in the correct sequence (see illustration), to the torque listed in this Chapter's Specifications.

21 Install a new gasket between the lower and upper intake manifolds. Place the upper intake manifold on the lower intake manifold. Install the bolts and tighten them, a little at a time, to the torque listed in this Chapter's Specifications.

22 Refill the cooling system (see Chapter 1). Run the engine and check for fuel, vacuum and coolant leaks.

6 Exhaust manifold/catalytic converter assemblies - removal and installation

Warning: *The engine must be completely cool before beginning this procedure.*

Note: *All engines are equipped with exhaust manifold/catalytic converter assemblies; on 2005 and earlier models, the catalytic converters can be unbolted from the exhaust manifolds.*

1 Disconnect the cable from the negative terminal of the battery (see Chapter 5).

2 Spray penetrating oil on the exhaust manifold fasteners and allow it to soak in.

3 Raise the front of the vehicle and support it securely on jackstands, then remove the engine splash shield.

4 Disconnect the oxygen sensor electrical connector on the top of the manifold(s) (see Chapter 6), if you are replacing the manifold, remove the oxygen sensor.

5 Remove the exhaust manifold heat shield.

6 Remove the exhaust manifold brace, if equipped.

7 Remove the nuts retaining the exhaust pipe(s) to the exhaust manifold(s) or catalytic converter(s).

8 Unbolt the exhaust manifold(s) from the cylinder head(s), working from the ends toward the middle. Slip the manifold(s) off the mounting studs.

9 Carefully inspect the manifold(s) and fasteners for cracks and damage.

10 Use a scraper to remove all traces of old gasket material and carbon deposits from the manifold and cylinder head mating surfaces. If the gasket was leaking, check the manifold for warpage on the cylinder head mounting surface by placing a straightedge over the surface and trying to insert a feeler gauge. If the clearance exceeds the limit listed in this Chapter's Specifications, have the manifold resurfaced at an automotive machine shop.

11 Position a new gasket over the cylinder head studs.

12 Install the manifold(s) and thread the mounting nuts into place.

13 Working from the center out, tighten the nuts to the torque listed in this Chapter's Specifications in three or four equal steps.

14 The remainder of installation is the reverse of removal. Use new gaskets when connecting the exhaust pipes.

15 Run the engine and check for exhaust leaks.

7 Timing chain and sprockets (2006 and later models) - removal, inspection and installation

Warning: *Wait until the engine is completely cool before beginning this procedure.*

Caution: *The timing system is complex, and severe engine damage will occur if you make any mistakes. Do not attempt this procedure unless you are highly experienced with this type of repair. If you are at all unsure of your abilities, be sure to consult an expert. Double check all your work and be sure everything is correct before you attempt to start the engine.*

Removal

1 Disconnect the cable from the negative terminal of the battery (see Chapter 5), then remove the engine cover.

2 Remove the drivebelt (see Chapter 1).

3 Remove the alternator (see Chapter 5). Also unbolt the power steering pulley and secure it out of the way (don't disconnect the hoses).

4 Remove the tensioner and idler pulley (see Chapter 1).

5 Remove the air conditioning compressor (see Chapter 3), without opening the refrigerant lines, and secure the compressor out of the way.

6 Remove the intake manifold (see Section 5).

7 Raise the front of the vehicle and support it securely on jackstands. Apply the parking brake and block the rear wheels. Remove the right front wheel.

8 Drain the engine oil and coolant (see Chapter 1).

9 Remove the lower oil pan (see Section 13).

10 Remove the radiator and coolant reservoir (see Chapter 3).

11 Support the engine from below, using a jack and a block of wood under the oil pan.

12 Remove the upper engine mount bracket (see Section 13).

13 Remove the valve covers (see Section 4).

14 Set the number one cylinder to TDC on the compression stroke (see Section 3).

15 Remove the crankshaft pulley (see Section 12).

16 On 2006 through 2010 (3.8L) models, remove the water pump pulley (see Chapter 3). On 2011 and later models, remove the water pump pulley and water pump (see Chapter 3).

17 Remove the timing chain cover. Lay out the bolts carefully (in order) as you remove them, as there are many different sizes used and each must be reinstalled in its proper position.

18 Verify the number one cylinder is still at TDC on the compression stroke. Paint match marks on the sprockets so the entire assembly can be reinstalled in its original position. There are existing colored links on the chains for this purpose, but very often they become faint or totally erased during use (see illustration).

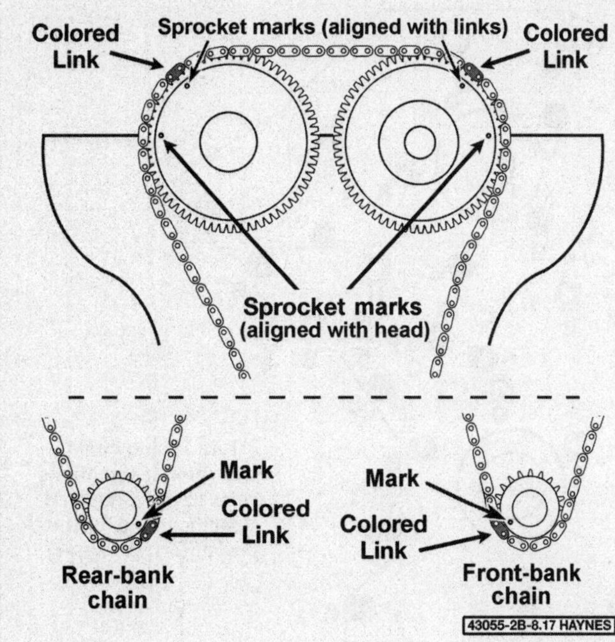

7.18 Camshaft timing chain alignment; the alignment is the same for both chains on both heads - however, the marks on the crankshaft sprocket are in different places

19 Compress the rear-bank chain tensioner and put a small drill bit or other steel pin through the hole to hold it in the retracted position.

20 Remove the rear-bank upper chain guide that is between the sprockets.

21 Remove the rear-bank tensioner and the tensioner arm, then lift off the rear-bank chain.

22 Remove the rear-bank chain guide.

23 Remove the oil pump chain cover, chain tensioner, oil pump sprocket and chain (see Section 14).

24 Remove the crankshaft gear for the oil pump and rear-bank timing chain.

25 Remove the components for the front-bank timing chain in the same order as for the rear-bank chain.

Note: *If the chains are not being replaced, make sure to mark chains front bank or rear bank so they can be installed on their original sides.*

Inspection

26 Inspect all parts for wear and damage. Check the timing chain for loose pins, cracks, worn rollers and worn side plates. Check the sprockets for hooked-shaped, chipped and missing teeth. Always replace the timing chain and sprockets as a set if the engine has high mileage or fails inspection of any component.

27 Check the chain guides for excessive wear. Note that some scoring and wear is normal.

28 Check the automatic tensioners for looseness. The piston should move smoothly when the pawl of the ratchet mechanism has been pushed back using a small Allen wrench or similar rod. All idler and tensioner sprockets must turn smoothly and freely. Again, if any component fails inspection, all other components are suspect.

Installation

29 Remove all dirt, oil and grease from the front of the engine.

30 Note that the crankshaft key will be at the 11 o'clock position, aligned with the mark on the block, when the number one piston is at TDC.

31 Make sure the camshafts are still aligned with their TDC marks at the top surface of the cylinder heads. Verify that all other marks are set correctly during this procedure. If you are installing new timing chains, align the colored links on the chains with the marks on the camshaft and crankshaft sprockets. If you're reusing the old timing chains, align the paint marks you made.

32 Install the timing chain guide.

33 Install the chains over the crankshaft sprocket first, followed by the guide and the camshaft sprockets. There should be no slack between these components.

Note: *Install the front-bank chain first, then the rear-bank chain.*

34 Install the tensioner arm, then the tensioner. Then install the upper cam-to-cam guide. This sequence should be followed for both timing chains.

35 Pull the pins out of both chain tensioners.

36 Install the oil pump chain guide and tensioner (see Section 14).

37 Rotate the engine two complete turns clockwise so that the marks are again aligned (use a socket and breaker bar on the crankshaft pulley center-bolt).

Caution: *If you feel any resistance, STOP! There is something wrong - most likely, the valves are contacting the pistons. You must find the problem before proceeding.*

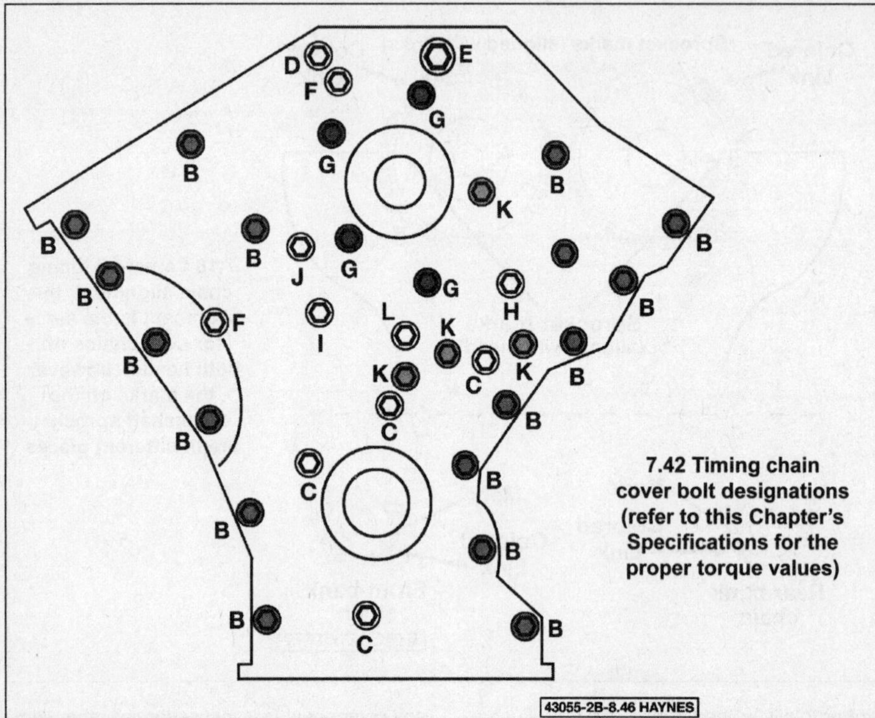

7.42 Timing chain cover bolt designations (refer to this Chapter's Specifications for the proper torque values)

8.10 Special camshaft sprocket holding tools can be obtained at most auto parts stores

38 Verify that the marks on all six sprockets are properly set. The colored links on the chains will not align with the marks on the sprockets (unless the crankshaft is rotated many turns) but the sprocket marks should be exact for the TDC setting (see illustration 7.18).

39 Clean the timing chain cover sealing surfaces and the mating surfaces of the block with brake system cleaner.

40 Apply a small dab of RTV silicone sealant to the four spots where the cylinder heads mate with the block under the timing cover.

41 Apply a continuous 3/16-inch bead of RTV silicone sealant along the sealing surface of the timing chain cover. Also replace the two small upper timing chain cover gaskets, if equipped.

42 Install and tighten the timing chain cover bolts (see illustration) to the torque listed in this Chapter's Specifications.

43 The remainder of installation is the reverse of removal.

8 Timing belt and sprockets (2005 and earlier models) - removal, inspection and installation

Caution: *The timing system is complex, and severe engine damage will occur if you make any mistakes. Do not attempt this procedure unless you are highly experienced with this type of repair. If you are at all unsure of your abilities, be sure to consult an expert. Double check all your work and be sure everything is correct before you attempt to start the engine.*

Removal

1 Disconnect the cable from the negative terminal of the battery (see Chapter 5).

2 Remove the engine cover.

3 Raise the front of the vehicle and support it securely on jackstands. Apply the parking brake and block the rear wheels.

4 Remove the drivebelt and drivebelt tensioner (see Chapter 1), then remove the crankshaft pulley (see Section 12).

5 Remove the power steering pump (see Chapter 10).

6 Remove the timing belt cover fasteners and covers.

7 Support the engine from below, using a jack and a block of wood under the oil pan.

8 Remove the right side engine mount and bracket (see Section 17).

9 Temporarily reinstall the crankshaft sprocket (without the bolt) and set the engine at TDC for number one cylinder (see Section 3). Verify that all timing marks are aligned before proceeding (see illustration 8.26).

10 Once all of the timing marks are aligned, secure the cam sprockets in place to prevent them from turning under valve spring pressure and causing any damage to the valves. We strongly recommend using special tools, available at most auto parts stores, meant for holding camshaft sprockets in place (see illustration).

11 If you intend to reuse the belt, mark it with an arrow indicating direction of travel and put match marks from the belt to the sprockets so it can be realigned easily.

12 Remove the tensioner and the timing belt.

13 The camshaft sprockets can be removed now, if necessary. Remove the valve covers and hold the hex area of the camshaft securely with a wrench while removing the bolts.

Inspection

14 Check the belt for the presence of oil or dirt, and inspect for visible defects (see illustration).

15 Check the belt tensioner for visible oil leakage. If there's only a faint trace of oil on the pushrod side, the tensioner seal is in satisfactory condition.

16 Push the tensioner forcefully against an immovable object (see illustration). If the pushrod moves, replace the tensioner.

17 Check that the idler pulleys turn smoothly.

Installation

18 Remove all dirt, oil and grease from the timing belt area at the front of the engine.

19 Install the camshaft sprocket(s) (if they were removed) on the camshaft(s). Align the pin hole in the sprocket with the pin in the end of the camshaft.

20 Install the camshaft sprocket bolt(s) and tighten it to the torque listed in this Chapter's Specifications.

21 Carefully align all of the camshaft sprocket marks with the marks on the engine.

22 Install all the sprockets and pulleys if they were removed. Verify that the engine is still at TDC.

23 Make sure that the crankshaft sprocket is installed with the spacer first, then the sensor blade between the spacer and the sprocket.

24 Align the marks on the front (left) camshafts with the marks on the engine. The right camshafts may have to be rotated counterclockwise about 50 degrees before final positioning.

25 Using a press or vise, compress the timing belt tensioner pushrod extremely slowly. Insert a metal pin, drill bit or Allen wrench through the holes in the pushrod and housing. Remove the tensioner from the press or vise and install it on the engine with the pin in place.

26 Align all of the timing marks and place the timing belt around the sprockets and pul-

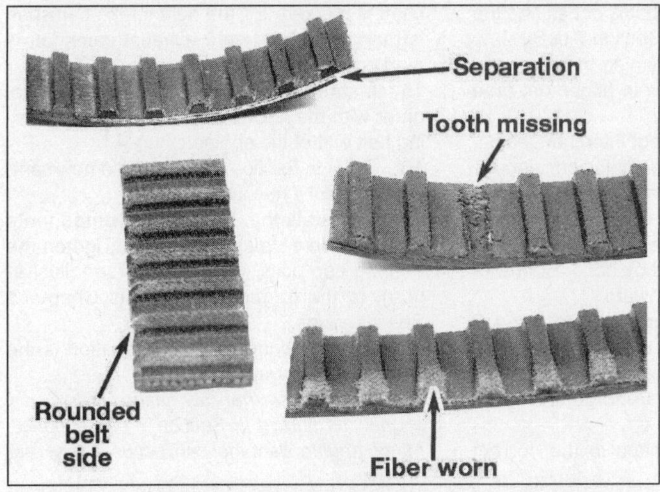

8.14 Check the timing belt for cracked or missing teeth; if the belt is cracked or worn, also check the pulleys for nicks or burrs - wear on one side of the belt indicates pulley misalignment problems

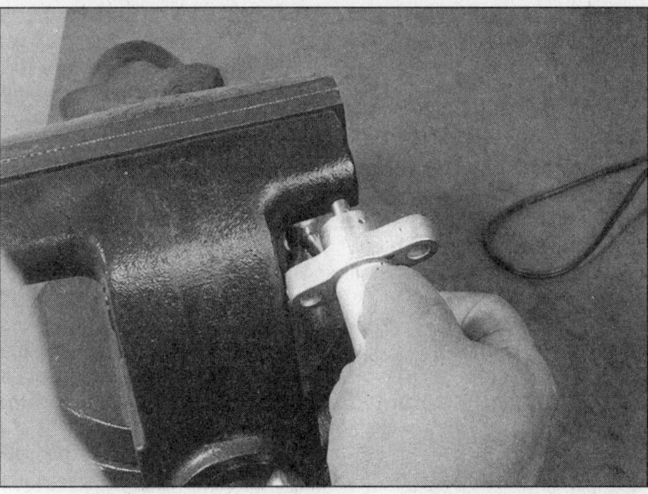

8.16 Check the tensioner for signs of leakage and test for leakdown by forcing it against an immovable object

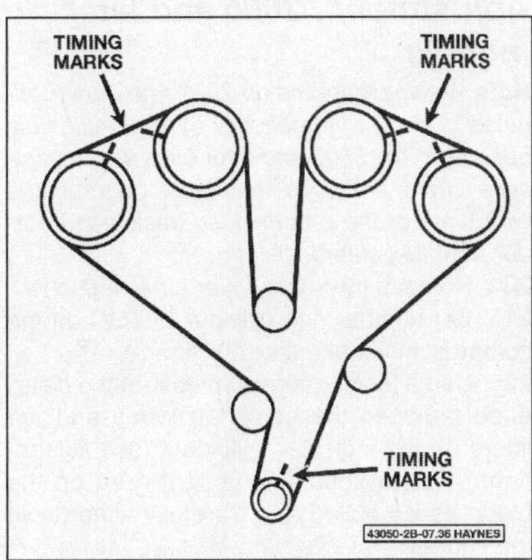

8.26 Timing belt alignment marks

8.27 Using the special tensioner pulley tool and an inch-pound torque wrench, rotate the pulley against the belt and apply 44 in-lbs of torque, then tighten the pulley center bolt to the torque listed in this Chapter's Specifications

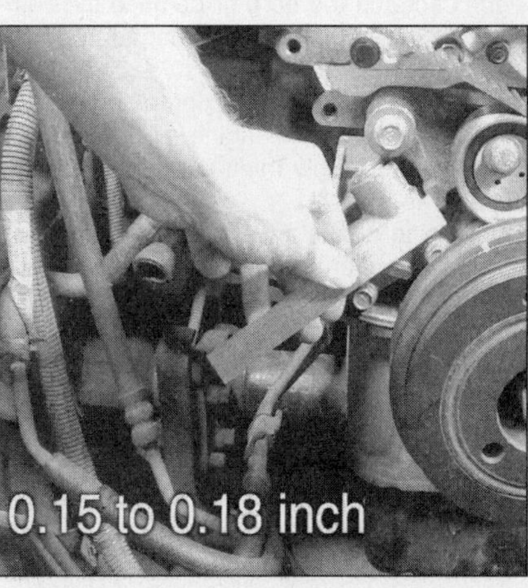

8.32 Measure the protrusion of the timing belt tensioner rod

leys in this order: Crankshaft, idler, camshafts, tensioner (see illustration).

27 With the tensioner pulley center bolt loose, use special tool no. 09244-28100 or equivalent to rotate the hub of the tensioner pulley counterclockwise, applying a torque of 44 in-lbs (50 kg-cm). While maintaining this torque on the pulley, tighten the pulley bolt to the torque listed in this Chapter's Specifications (see illustration).

28 Temporarily install the crankshaft pulley and turn it 90-degrees counterclockwise, then 90-degrees clockwise back into its original position.

29 Again verify that all timing marks are aligned, then pull the pin from the tensioner, allowing it to extend into position.

30 Turn the crankshaft slowly (clockwise) through two complete revolutions (720-degrees). Recheck the timing marks.

Caution: *Stop turning the crankshaft immediately if you feel resistance; the valves could be contacting the pistons.*

31 If the timing marks are not aligned exactly as shown in illustration 8.26, repeat the timing belt installation procedure. DO NOT start the engine until you're absolutely certain that the timing belt is installed correctly. Serious and costly engine damage could occur if the belt is installed incorrectly.

32 Let the engine sit for five minutes at TDC, then check the protrusion of the tensioner rod (see illustration). Compare your measurement to this Chapter's Specifications. If it isn't correct, replace the tensioner or determine if there's another problem.

33 The remainder of installation is the reverse of removal.

9 Oil seals - replacement

Crankshaft front oil seal

1 On 2005 and earlier models, remove the timing belt and crankshaft sprocket (see Section 8). Slip off the sensor ring and the spacer behind it. On 3.8L and 2011 and later 3.5L models, remove the crankshaft pulley (see Section 12).

2 Carefully pry the seal out with a screwdriver or seal removal tool. If you use a screwdriver, wrap tape around the tip - don't scratch the housing bore or damage the crankshaft (if the crankshaft is damaged, the new seal will end up leaking).

3 Clean the bore in the engine and coat the outer edge of the new seal with engine

oil or multi-purpose grease. Apply the same lubricant to the seal lip.

4 Using a seal driver or a socket with an outside diameter slightly smaller than the outside diameter of the seal, carefully drive the new seal into place with a hammer. Make sure it's installed squarely and driven in to the same depth as the original. Check the seal after installation to make sure the spring didn't pop out of place.

5 The remainder of installation is the reverse of removal.

6 Run the engine and check for oil leaks at the front seal.

Camshaft oil seals - 2005 and earlier models

7 Remove the timing belt and camshaft sprocket(s) (see Section 8).

8 Remove the bolts and detach the rear timing belt cover.

9 Note how far the seal is seated in the bore, then carefully pry it out with a screwdriver. Wrap the screwdriver tip with tape - don't scratch the bore or dámage the camshaft (if the camshaft is damaged, the new seal will end up leaking).

10 Clean the bore and coat the outer edge of the new seal with engine oil or multi-purpose grease. Apply multi-purpose grease to the seal lip.

11 Using a seal driver or a socket with an outside diameter slightly smaller than the outside diameter of the seal, carefully drive the new seal into place with a hammer. Make sure it's installed squarely and driven in to the same depth as the original.

12 Reinstall the rear timing belt cover and tighten the bolts.

13 Reinstall the camshaft sprocket(s) and timing belt (see Section 8).

Caution: *Verify that all timing marks are aligned as shown in illustration 8.25. Major engine damage can occur if they are not.*

14 Run the engine and check for oil leaks at the camshaft seal.

10 Camshafts and valvetrain - removal, inspection, installation and valve adjustment

Removal

Caution: *Don't try to disassemble the Continuous Variable Valve Timing (CVVT) assembly on the camshafts, if equipped. These assemblies must be removed and installed intact. To remove the sprocket and CVVT assembly, simply remove the center bolt from the end of the camshaft.*

1 Position the engine at TDC (see Section 3), then remove the valve covers (see Section 4).

2 On 2006 and later models, remove the Oil Control Valve (OCV) mounting bolts and remove the valves from the front camshaft bearing caps.

3 Remove the timing chains or belt and the camshaft sprockets (see Section 7 or 8).

4 Make sure the cam timing marks on the sprockets and engine are in alignment (see Section 7 or Section 8).

5 The camshafts are not interchangeable. Mark them clearly to avoid confusion later.

6 Loosen the camshaft bearing cap bolts in 1/4-turn increments in the reverse order of the tightening sequence (see illustration 10.17) until they can be removed by hand. Start with the outer caps and work inward.

7 The bearing caps are marked I and E for intake and exhaust and numbered. Mark the caps with your own numbers if necessary. Remove the bearing caps and gently lift out the camshaft.

8 Store the bearing caps in the correct order.

9 If necessary, the valve hydraulic adjusters and rocker arms can now be removed on 2006 and earlier 3.5L engines. On all other models, remove the bucket-style lifters. Store them separately so they can be reinstalled in their original locations.

Inspection

10 Refer to Section 10 for camshaft, lifter and related component inspection procedures, but use the Specifications in this Chapter.

Installation

11 Apply camshaft installation lubricant to the camshaft lobes and bearing journals.

12 Install the lifters (2006 and later models) or lash adjusters and rocker arms (2005 and earlier models) in their original positions.

13 On all 2006 and later models, install the timing chains around the sprockets of each pair of camshafts and set them in their journals. Make sure that the timing marks on the sprockets are aligned with the marks on the timing chains.

14 On 2005 and earlier models, place each camshaft in its original position and verify that the timing marks on the sprockets are lined up with the marks on the engine. The left intake camshaft is marked "I," the left exhaust camshaft is marked "E," the right intake camshaft is marked "J," the right exhaust camshaft is marked "H."

15 Install the bearing caps in numerical order with the arrows pointing toward the timing belt end of the engine.

16 Refer to Section 9 and install a new camshaft oil seal if necessary.

17 Reinstall the remaining components in the reverse order of removal. Tighten the bearing cap bolts, in sequence (see illustration), to the torque listed in this Chapter's Specifications.

18 The remainder of the installation is the reverse of removal.

Caution: *Verify that all timing marks are aligned as shown in Section 7 or Section 8. Major engine damage can occur if they are not.*

19 Run the engine, then check for leaks and proper operation. If the hydraulic valve adjusters have been somewhat drained, it may take several minutes for valvetrain noise to disappear.

Adjustment - 2006 and later models

Note: *Valve clearance on 2005 and earlier engines is done automatically by hydraulic lash adjusters. On 2006 and later engines, bucket-style lifters are used and must be replaced with ones of the proper head thickness in order to adjust clearance.*

20 Remove the valve cover (see Section 4).

21 Set number one cylinder to TDC on the compression stroke (see Section 3).

22 Use a feeler gauge to measure the clearance between the camshaft lobes and the lifters on the indicated cylinders (see illustrations). There should be a light drag on the blade as it's pulled out. Carefully write down the figures.

23 Rotate the engine exactly one turn clockwise and repeat the procedure on the remaining valves (see illustration).

24 If the clearances are outside of the limits (see this Chapter's Specifications), new lifters of the proper thickness will have to be installed in the location(s) with incorrect clearance(s).

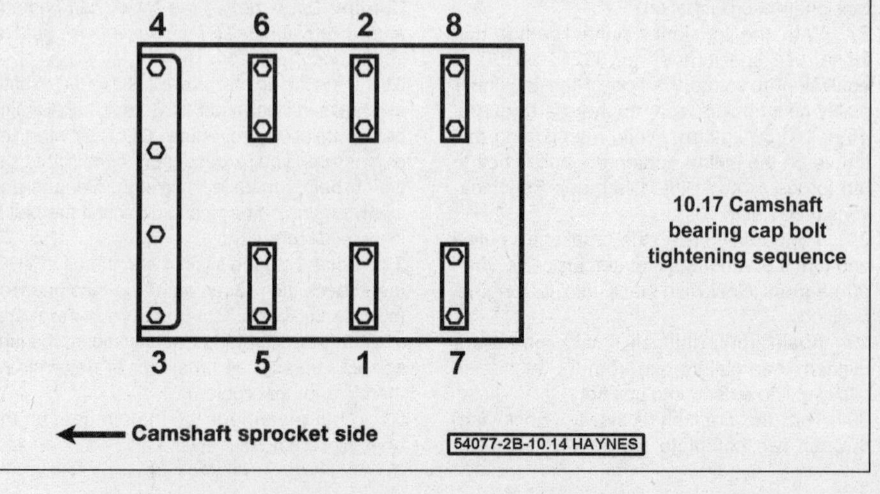

10.17 Camshaft bearing cap bolt tightening sequence

To do so, proceed to the next step.

25 Remove the camshaft(s) as described earlier in this Section.

26 Remove the lifter from the location with the incorrect clearance and measure it with a micrometer (see illustration).

27 To calculate the correct thickness of a lifter, use this formula:

N = T + (A - V)
N = Thickness of the new lifter
T = Thickness of the old lifter
A = Valve clearance measured
V = Valve clearance specified in this Chapter's Specifications

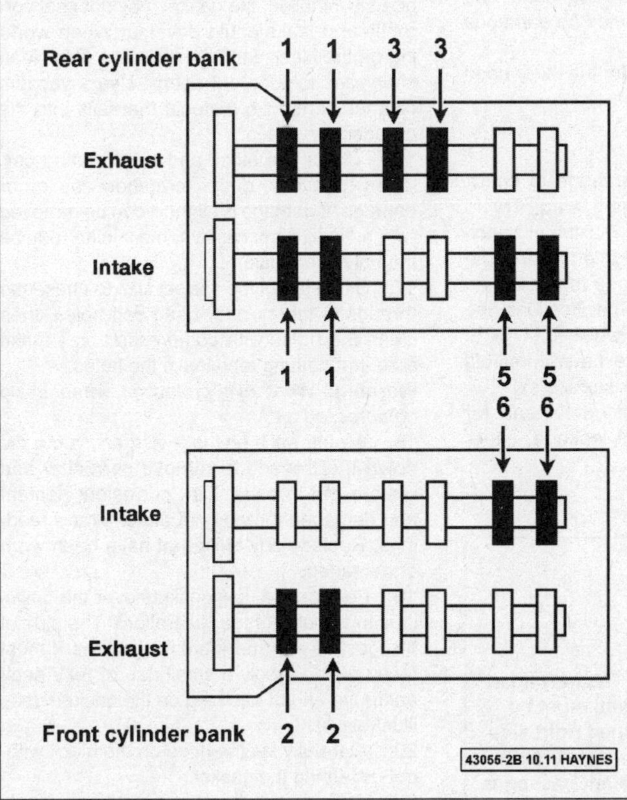

10.22a When the no. 1 piston is at TDC on the compression stroke, the valve clearance for the no.1 intake and exhaust valves, the number 3 exhaust valves, number 5 intake valve, number 2 exhaust valve and number 6 intake valve can be measured

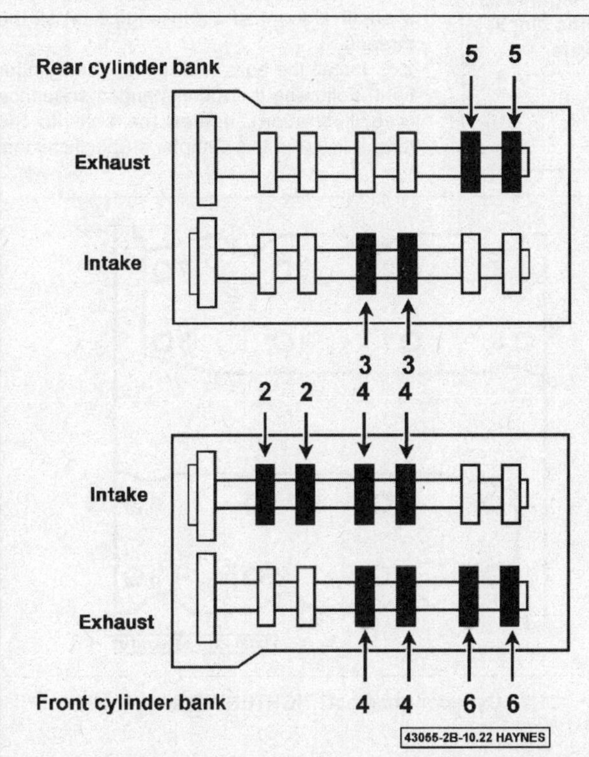

10.23 When the no. 4 piston is at TDC on the compression stroke, the valve clearance for the nos. 2, 3 and 4 intake valves and the nos. 4, 5 and 6 exhaust valves can be measured

28 Purchase replacement lifters of the correct thickness.

29 After installing the lifters and camshafts, check the clearances again and make sure they are within specification before proceeding.

30 Apply camshaft installation lubricant to the camshaft lobes and bearing journals.

31 Install the lash adjusters in their original positions.

32 Place each camshaft in its original position and verify that the timing marks on the sprockets are lined up with the marks on the engine.

33 Install the bearing caps in its original position, by numerical order with the arrows pointing toward the timing chain end of the engine.

34 Tighten the bearing cap bolts in sequence (see illustration 10.17), in 1/4-turn increments, to the torque listed in this Chapter's Specifications.

10.22b Measure the clearance for each valve with a feeler gauge of the specified thickness - if the clearance is correct, you should feel a slight drag on the gauge as you pull it out

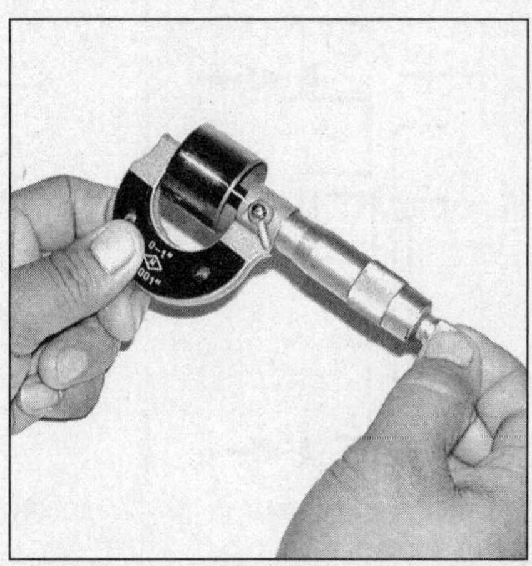

10.26 Measure the thickness of the lifter head with a micrometer

11 Cylinder heads - removal, inspection and installation

Warning: *Wait until the engine is completely cool before beginning this procedure.*

Removal

1 Relieve the fuel system pressure (see Chapter 4), then disconnect the cable from the negative terminal of the battery (see Chapter 5).

2 Drain the cooling system, including the engine block (see Chapter 1).

3 Remove the upper and lower intake manifolds (see Section 5).

4 Remove the exhaust manifold(s) (see Section 6).

5 Remove the timing belt (see Section 8) or timing chain (see Section 7) from the camshaft sprockets.

6 Remove the camshafts (see Section 10).

7 Disconnect any remaining sensors or hoses.

8 Loosen the cylinder head bolts in 1/4-turn increments until they can be removed by hand, along with their hardened washers. Follow the reverse order of the recommended tightening sequence (see illustration 11.22). **Note:** *On 2006 and later models, be sure to remove the M6 bolt at the front of the cylinder heads.*

9 Lift the cylinder head off the engine block. If the head is stuck, place a wood block against it and strike the wood with a hammer. **Caution:** *Don't pry between the head and block. The gasket surfaces may be damaged and leaks could result.*

10 Repeat the procedure for the other head if necessary.

Inspection

11 Use a precision straightedge to check the gasket surfaces of each head. Try to insert a feeler gauge of the maximum specified size between the straightedge and the head surface. If the clearance is more than that listed in this Chapter's Specifications, the head must be resurfaced or replaced.

12 Check the intake and exhaust manifold surfaces as well as the block surface(s).

13 Examine all areas of each head for signs of cracks and coolant leakage, especially around the valve seats.

Installation

14 The mating surfaces of the cylinder heads and block must be perfectly clean when the heads are installed.

15 Use a gasket scraper to remove all traces of carbon and old gasket material, then clean the mating surfaces with brake cleaner. If there's oil on the mating surfaces when the head is installed, the gasket may not seal correctly and leaks could develop. When working on the block, stuff the cylinders with clean shop rags to keep out debris. Use a vacuum cleaner to remove material that falls into the cylinders.

16 Check the block and head mating surfaces for nicks, deep scratches and other damage. If damage is slight, it can be removed with a file; if it's excessive, machining may be the only alternative.

17 Use a tap of the correct size to chase the threads in the cylinder head bolt holes, then clean the holes with compressed air - make sure that nothing remains in the holes. **Warning:** *Wear eye protection when using compressed air!*

18 Mount each bolt in a vise and run a die down the threads to remove corrosion and restore the threads. Dirt, corrosion, sealant and damaged threads will affect torque readings. Replace any bolts that have been worn or damaged.

19 Position the new gaskets over the dowel pins in the block (see illustration). The side of the gasket with the identification mark must face upward. Apply a small dab of RTV sealant to the end of each leg on the gaskets (see illustration).

20 Carefully set the head on the block without disturbing the gasket.

21 Before installing the head bolts, apply a small amount of clean engine oil to the threads.

22 Install the bolts and tighten them finger tight. Following the recommended sequence (see illustration), tighten the bolts to the torque listed in this Chapter's Specifications.

11.19a The new head gaskets must be positioned right side up (check all holes and coolant passages for correct alignment) and over the block dowels

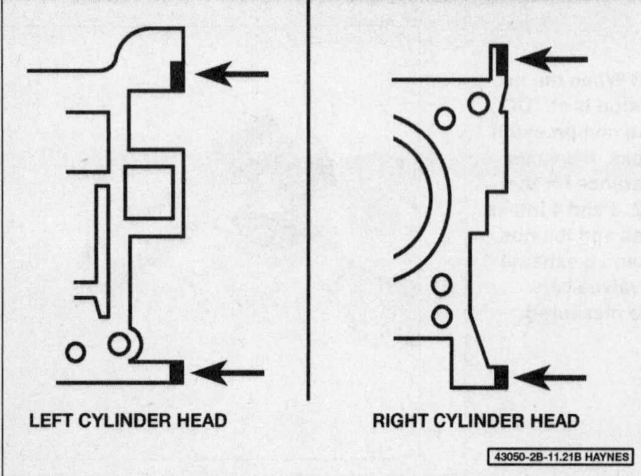

11.19b On 2006 and later models, apply sealant to the specified areas above and below the cylinder head gasket

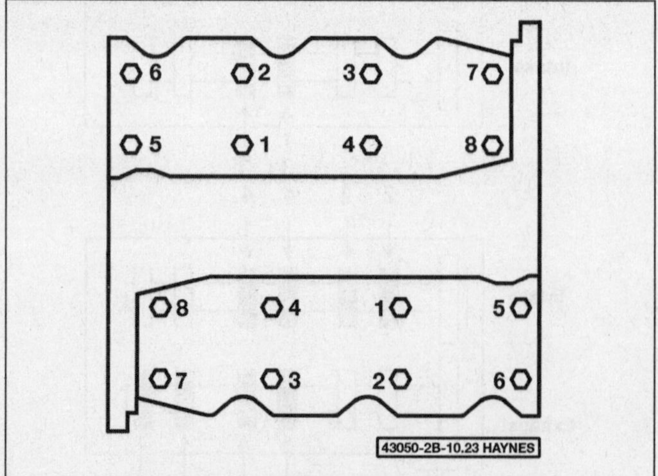

11.22 Cylinder head bolt TIGHTENING sequence

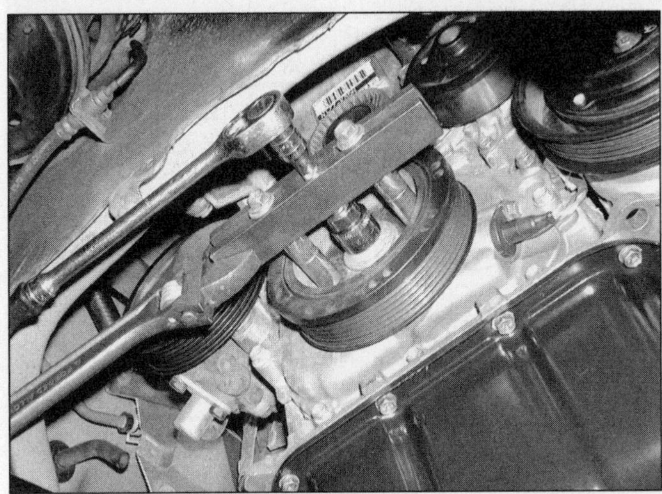
12.5 If it's necessary to use a puller, use one that bolts to the hub of the pulley. Do not use a jaw-type puller - it will damage the pulley/damper assembly

12.6 Align the keyway in the crankshaft pulley hub with the Woodruff key in the crankshaft

If you don't have a torque angle gauge attachment, apply a paint mark to the socket you will be using to act as a reference point.

23 Install and tighten the small bolt at the front of the cylinder heads to the torque listed in this Chapter's Specifications.

24 The remainder of installation is the reverse of removal.

25 Refill the cooling system, change the engine oil and filter (see Chapter 1), then run the engine and check for leaks.

12 Crankshaft pulley/vibration damper - removal and installation

1 Disconnect the cable from the negative terminal of the battery (see Chapter 5).

2 Remove the drivebelt (see Chapter 1).

3 With the parking brake applied and the shifter in Park, loosen the lug nuts from the right front wheel, then raise the front of the vehicle and support it securely on jackstands. Remove the engine splash shield (if equipped), the front wheel and the inner fender splash shield (see Chapter 11).

4 Remove the bolt from the front of the crankshaft. A breaker bar will be necessary, since the bolt is very tight. There are two ways to prevent the crankshaft from turning: Remove the starter and install a driveplate locking tool or wedge a large screwdriver in the ring gear teeth, or remove the torque converter access plate and install a driveplate locking tool or wedge a large screwdriver in the ring gear teeth.

Caution: *Discard the bolt and obtain a new one for installation.*

5 A puller should not be necessary, but if the pulley is stuck, only use a puller that bolts to the hub of the pulley (see illustration). Be sure to use the proper adapter to prevent damage to the end of the crankshaft.

6 To install the crankshaft pulley, slide the pulley onto the crankshaft, aligning it with the Woodruff key in the end of the crankshaft (see illustration).

7 Tighten the new crankshaft pulley bolt to the torque listed in this Chapter's Specifications.

8 The remainder of installation is the reverse of removal.

13 Oil pans - removal and installation

Removal

1 Disconnect the cable from the negative terminal of the battery (see Chapter 5).

2 Raise the vehicle and support it securely on jackstands.

3 Remove the engine splash shields, if equipped.

4 Drain the engine oil and remove the oil filter (see Chapter 1). The oil pan is a two-piece assembly, with an aluminum casting attached to the block and transaxle, and a lower stamped-steel pan section at the bottom.

5 Disconnect the exhaust pipe from both exhaust manifolds.

6 Disconnect the oxygen sensors (if necessary) and support the pipe temporarily. Unbolt the pipe at the rear, disconnect it from the hangers and remove it from the vehicle.

7 On 2006 and later models, remove the two lower bolts holding the upper aluminum oil pan section to the transaxle.

8 Remove any interfering components. These components vary by year and model; be sure you have enough clearance for oil pan removal.

Note: *It may be easier to attach an engine hoist and raise the engine (see Chapter 2B) to make enough room to remove the upper oil pan.*

9 Remove the bolts and detach the lower steel pan (see illustration). If it's stuck, pry it

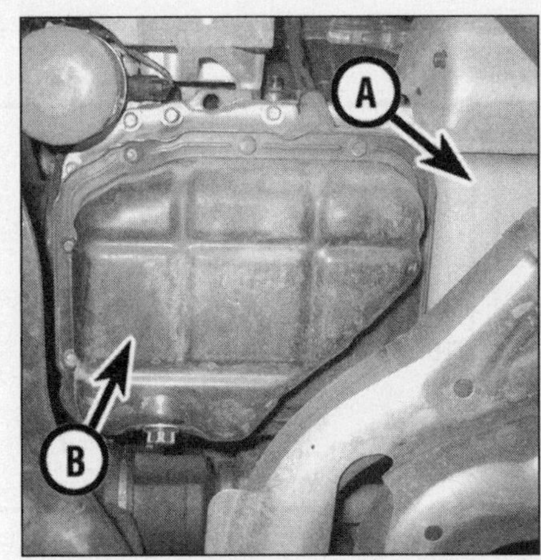

13.9 There are two oil pans: an upper cast aluminum pan (A) and a lower stamped steel pan (B)

loose very carefully with a small screwdriver or putty knife. Don't damage the mating surfaces of the pan or oil leaks could develop.

10 Remove the lower baffle (if equipped) and the oil pump strainer/pickup if necessary.

11 Remove the bolts securing the aluminum oil pan to the block.

Note: *Some bolts are within the area formerly covered by the steel pan.*

Installation

12 Use a scraper to remove all traces of old sealant from the block and oil pan. Clean the mating surfaces with lacquer thinner or acetone.

13 Make sure the threaded bolt holes in the block are clean.

14 Check the flange of the steel pan section for distortion, particularly around the bolt holes. If necessary, place the pan on a wood block and use a hammer to flatten and restore the gasket surface.

15 If the baffle has been removed, reinstall it now.

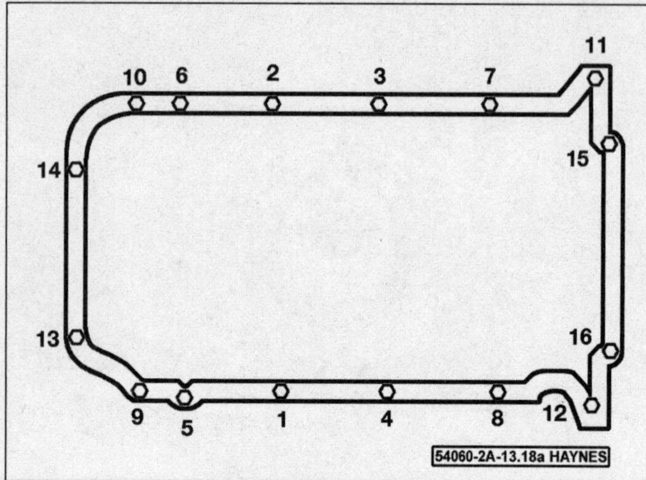

13.18a Upper oil pan bolt TIGHTENING sequence - 2005 and earlier models

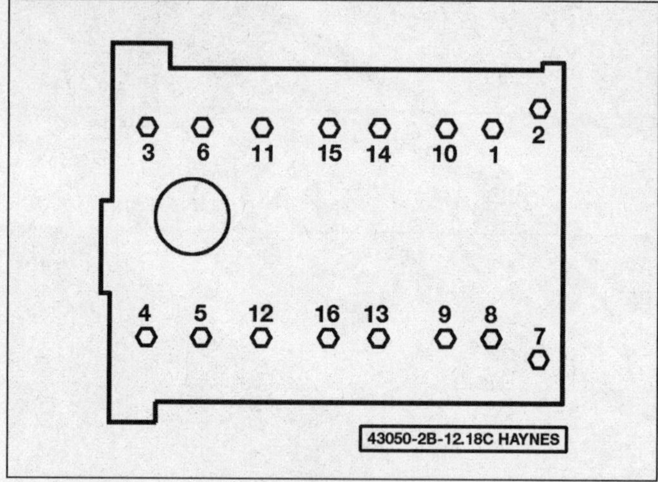

13.18b Upper oil pan bolt TIGHTENING sequence - 2006 and later models

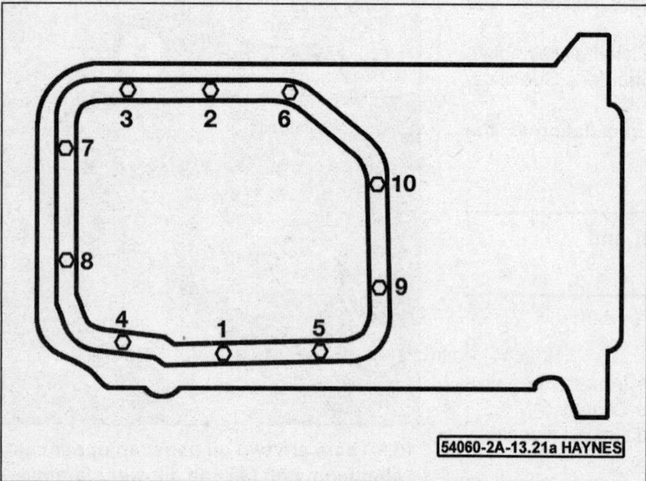

13.21a Lower oil pan bolt TIGHTENING sequence - 2005 and earlier models

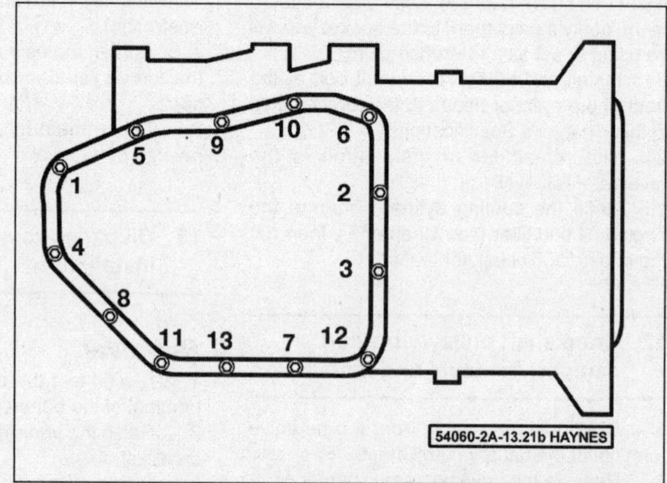

13.21b Lower oil pan bolt TIGHTENING sequence - 2006 and later models

16 Clean the mating surfaces of the engine block and aluminum pan section, being careful not to gouge the soft metal, which could lead to leaks.

17 Apply a 3/16-inch wide bead of RTV sealant to the aluminum pan section.

18 Install the aluminum pan section within five minutes, and uniformly tighten the bolts, in several steps, to the torque listed in this Chapter's Specifications. Follow the tightening sequence (see illustrations).

19 Inspect the oil pump pick-up/strainer assembly for cracks and a blocked strainer. If the pick-up was removed, clean it with solvent or thinner and install it now, using a new gasket (see Section 14). Tighten the fasteners to the torque listed in this Chapter's Specifications.

20 Apply a 3/16-inch wide bead of RTV sealant to the flange of the steel oil pan section.

Note: *The steel pan section must be installed within five minutes once the sealant has been applied.*

21 Carefully position the steel pan on the aluminum section and install the bolts, tightening them, in three or four steps, to the torque listed in this Chapter's Specifications. Follow the tightening sequence (see illustrations).

Note: *The manufacturer recommends applying a small amount of RTV sealant to the lower oil pan bolt threads before installing the bolts to help prevent leaks.*

22 The remainder of installation is the reverse of removal. Allow the sealant to set for at least two hours before adding new oil and a new oil filter.

23 Run the engine and check for oil pressure and leaks.

14 Oil pump - removal, inspection and installation

Removal

1 Disconnect the cable from the negative battery terminal (see Chapter 5).

2 Drain the engine oil and remove the oil filter (see Chapter 1).

2005 and earlier models

3 Remove the timing belt and sprocket (see Section 8).

4 Remove the oil filter bracket and gasket.

5 Remove the upper oil pan-to-oil pump bolts.

6 Remove the oil pump-to-engine block mounting bolts and remove the pump from

14.15a Measure the driven rotor-to-body clearance with a feeler gauge

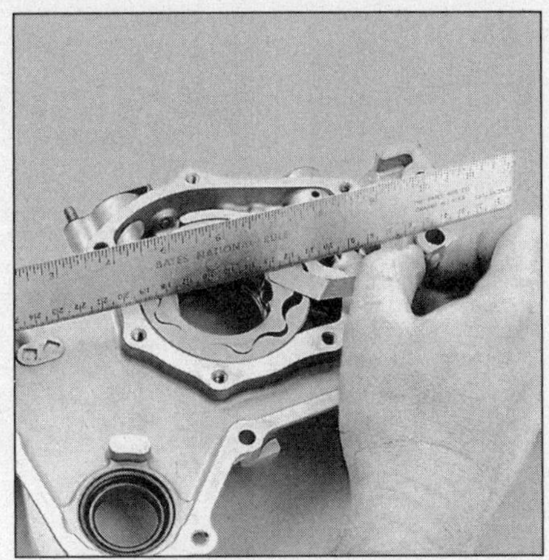

14.15b Measure the rotor side clearance with a precision straightedge and feeler gauge

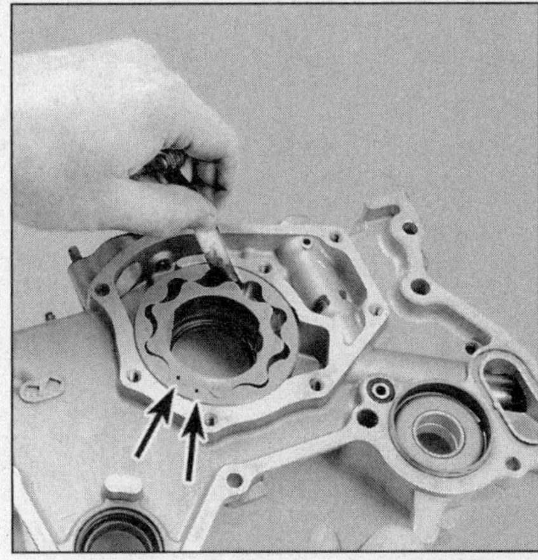

14.15c Measure the rotor tip clearance with a feeler gauge - note the rotor marks are facing out (when the pump body cover is installed, the marks will be against the cover)

the front of the engine.

7 Remove the pump cover fasteners, then remove the cover and pump rotors.

8 Use a gasket scraper to remove all traces of sealant and old gasket material from the pump body and engine block, then clean the mating surfaces with brake cleaner.

Note: *Keep the front of the oil pan covered to prevent debris from falling into the oil pans.*

2006 and later models

9 Remove the lower oil pan (see Section 13).

10 Remove the oil pump chain cover fasteners and remove the cover.

11 Remove the oil pump sprocket bolt, sprocket and chain and set them to the side.

12 Remove the oil pump mounting bolts and pump. On these models, the oil pump is normally serviced as a unit; don't try to replace individual parts.

Inspection

13 Clean all components with solvent, then inspect them for wear and damage.

2005 and earlier models

14 Check the oil pressure relief valve sliding surface and valve spring. If either the spring or the valve is damaged, they must be replaced as a set.

15 Check the clearance of the following components with a feeler gauge and compare the measurements to this Chapter's Specifications (see illustrations):

- *a) Driven rotor-to-oil pump body clearance*
- *b) Rotor side clearance*
- *c) Rotor tip clearance*

2006 and later models

16 If there is any problem suspected with the pump, replace it with a new one.

Installation

2005 and earlier models

17 Pry the old crankshaft seal out with a screwdriver.

18 Apply multi-purpose grease or engine oil to the outer edge of the new seal and carefully drive it into place with a seal driver and a hammer. Also apply multi-purpose grease to the seal lip.

19 Place the drive and driven rotors into the pump body.

20 Pack the pump cavity with white grease and install the cover using either a new gasket or RTV sealant. Tighten the screws in a criss-cross pattern to the torque listed in this Chapter's Specifications.

21 Lubricate the oil pressure relief valve with engine oil and install the valve components in the pump body.

22 Use brake cleaner and a clean rag to remove all traces of oil from the case gasket surfaces.

23 Install the oil pump case with a new gasket. Install the mounting bolts and tighten them in a criss-cross pattern to the torque listed in this Chapter's Specifications.

24 Using a new gasket, install the oil pick-up tube and tighten the fasteners to the torque listed in this Chapter's Specifications.

2006 and later models

25 Replace the oil pump O-ring with a new one.

26 Tighten the oil pump bolts to the torque listed in this Chapter's Specifications.

27 Replace the drive chain and sprocket and tighten the sprocket bolt to the torque listed in this Chapter's Specifications.

All models

28 Reinstall the remaining parts in the reverse order of removal.

29 Add oil, start the engine and check oil pressure and leaks.

30 Recheck the engine oil level.

15 Driveplate - removal and installation

Removal

1 Disconnect the cable from the negative terminal of the battery (see Chapter 5).

2 Remove the transaxle (see Chapter 7).

3 Using a center-punch or paint, apply alignment marks on the crankshaft flange and driveplate to ensure correct alignment on installation.

4 Remove the bolts retaining the driveplate to the crankshaft. Use a driveplate holding tool (available at auto parts stores) or wedge a screwdriver or prybar through one of the holes in the driveplate to keep it from turning while you loosen the bolts.

5 Remove the driveplate, taking note of spacers used and on which side of the driveplate they were installed.

Installation

6 Inspect the driveplate. Look for any fractures in the driveplate. Inspect the driveplate carefully for any other type of damage.

7 Position the driveplate on the crankshaft flange, aligning the marks made during removal. Align the bolt holes; note that some models may have a staggered bolt pattern to ensure correct installation.

8 Apply non-hardening thread locking compound to the threads of the bolts. Install the bolts and tighten them in a criss cross pattern to the torque listed in this Chapter's Specifications. Work up to the final torque in several steps.

9 Install the transaxle (see Chapter 7).

17.8a Right side mount (engine-to-body) bolt/nut locations

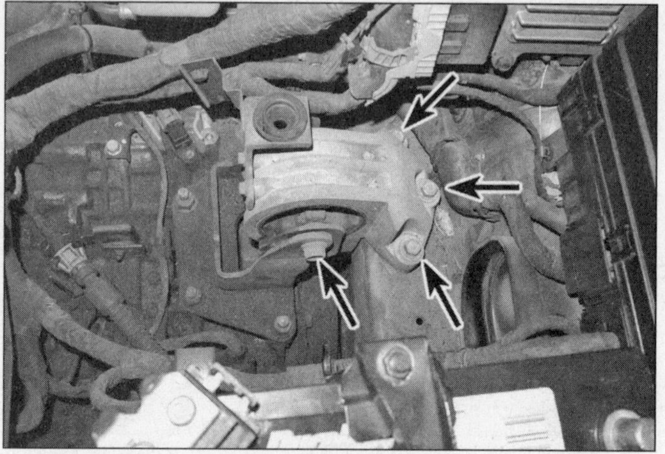

17.8b Left side mount (transaxle-to-body) bolt locations

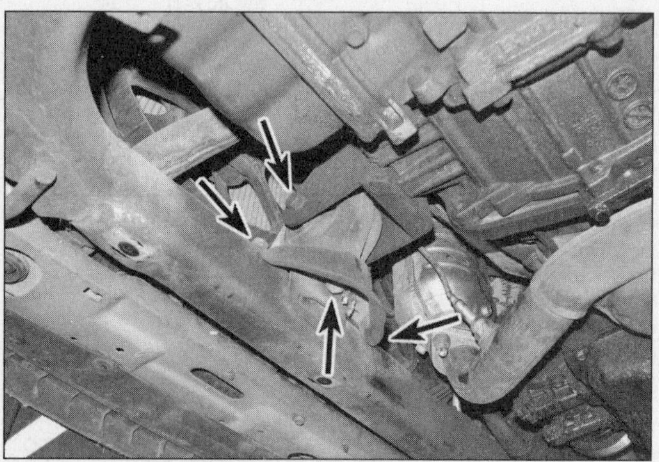

17.8c Front mount (front roll stopper mount-to-subframe) bolt/nut locations

17.8d Rear mount (rear roll stopper mount-to-subframe) bolt/nut locations

16 Rear main oil seal - replacement

1 Remove the driveplate (see Section 15).
2 Pry the oil seal from the seal housing at the rear of the engine with a seal removal tool or a screwdriver. Be careful not to nick or scratch the crankshaft or the seal bore. Thoroughly clean the seal bore in the housing with a shop towel. Remove all traces of oil and dirt.
3 Lubricate the outside diameter of the seal and install the seal over the end of the crankshaft. Make sure the lip of the seal points toward the engine. Preferably, a seal installation tool (available at most auto parts stores) should be used to press the new seal back into place.
4 Install the driveplate (see Section 15).
5 Install the transaxle (see Chapter 7).

17 Powertrain mounts - check and replacement

1 Powertrain mounts seldom require attention, but broken or deteriorated mounts should be replaced immediately or the added strain placed on driveline components may cause damage and wear.

Check

2 During the check, the engine (or transaxle) must be raised slightly to remove the weight from the mounts.
3 Raise the vehicle and support it securely on jackstands. Remove the engine splash shield (if so equipped) and position a jack under the engine oil pan. Place a large block of wood between the jack and the oil pan, then carefully raise the engine just enough to take the weight off the mounts. Do not position the wood block under the oil drain plug.

Warning: *DO NOT place any part of your body under the engine when only a jack supports it!*
4 Check the mounts to see if the rubber is cracked, hardened or separated from the bushing in the center of the mount.
5 Check for relative movement between the mount and the engine or frame (use a large screwdriver or prybar to attempt to move the mounts).
6 If movement is noted, lower the engine and tighten the mount fasteners.

Replacement

7 All engine mounts are replaced in the same manner. Use the jack to securely support the weight of the engine, then use it to remove all force from the mount in question.
8 Remove the bolts from both sides of the mount, then remove the mount (see illustrations).
9 Install the replacement mount and tighten all fasteners securely.

Notes

Notes

Chapter 2 Part B
General engine overhaul procedures

Contents

	Section		Section
Crankshaft - removal and installation	10	Engine removal - methods and precautions	6
Cylinder compression check	3	General information	1
Engine - removal and installation	7	Initial start-up and break-in after overhaul	12
Engine overhaul - disassembly sequence	8	Oil pressure check	2
Engine overhaul - reassembly sequence	11	Pistons and connecting rods - removal and installation	9
Engine rebuilding alternatives	5	Vacuum gauge diagnostic checks	4

Specifications

General

Cylinder compression	Lowest cylinder must be within 75% of the highest cylinder
Oil pressure	
2005 and earlier 3.5L (@ idle)	11 psi (80 kPa)
All other V6 engines (@ 1000 rpm)	18 psi (130 kPa)

Torque specifications

Note: *One foot-pound (ft-lb) of torque is equivalent to 12 inch-pounds (in-lbs) of torque. Torque values below approximately 15 foot-pounds are expressed in inch-pounds, because most foot-pound torque wrenches are not accurate at these smaller values.*

	Ft-lbs (unless otherwise indicated)	Nm
Connecting rod bolts/nuts		
2005 and earlier 3.5L engine (nuts)		
Step 1	26	34
Step 2	Tighten an additional 90- degrees	
All other V6 engines		
Step 1	13 to 16	18 to 22
Step 2	Tighten an additional 88 to 92-degrees	
Main bearing bolts		
2005 and earlier 3.5L engine	51 to 57	69 to 78
All other V6 engines		
Step 1, M11 (inner) bolts	36.2	49
Step 2, M11 (inner) bolts	Tighten an additional 90-degrees	
Step 3, M8 (outer) bolts	173 in-lbs	19.6
Step 4, M8 (outer) bolts	Tighten an additional 120-degrees	
Step 5, M8 (side) bolts	22 to 23	30 to 31
Baffle plate (3.8L and 2011 and later 3.5L engines)	87 to 104 in-lbs	10 to 11.5

1.10a An engine block being bored - an engine rebuilder will use special machinery to recondition the cylinder bores

1.10b If the cylinders are bored, the machine shop will normally hone the engine on a machine like this

1 General information - engine overhaul

1 Included in this portion of Chapter 2 are general information and diagnostic testing procedures for determining the overall mechanical condition of your engine.

2 The information ranges from advice concerning preparation for an overhaul and the purchase of replacement parts and/or components to detailed, step-by-step procedures covering removal and installation.

3 The following Sections have been written to help you determine whether your engine needs to be overhauled and how to remove and install it once you've determined it needs to be rebuilt. For information concerning in-vehicle engine repair, see Chapter 2A.

4 The Specifications included in this Part are general in nature and include only those necessary for testing the oil pressure, checking the engine compression, and bottom-end torque specifications. Refer to Chapter 2A for additional engine Specifications.

5 It's not always easy to determine when, or if, an engine should be completely overhauled, because a number of factors must be considered.

6 High mileage is not necessarily an indication that an overhaul is needed, while low mileage doesn't preclude the need for an overhaul. Frequency of servicing is probably the most important consideration. An engine that's had regular and frequent oil and filter changes, as well as other required maintenance, will most likely give many thousands of miles of reliable service. Conversely, a neglected engine may require an overhaul very early in its service life.

7 Excessive oil consumption is an indication that piston rings, valve seals and/or valve guides are in need of attention. Make sure that oil leaks aren't responsible before deciding that the rings and/or guides are bad. Perform a cylinder compression check to determine the extent of the work required (see Section 3). Also check the vacuum readings under various conditions (see Section 4).

8 Check the oil pressure with a gauge installed in place of the oil pressure sending unit and compare it to this Chapter's Specifications (see Section 2). If it's extremely low, the bearings and/or oil pump are probably worn out.

9 Loss of power, rough running, knocking or metallic engine noises, excessive valve train noise and high fuel consumption rates may also point to the need for an overhaul, especially if they're all present at the same time. If a complete tune-up doesn't remedy the situation, major mechanical work is the only solution.

10 An engine overhaul involves restoring the internal parts to the specifications of a new engine. During an overhaul, the piston rings are replaced and the cylinder walls are reconditioned (rebored and/or honed) (see illustrations 1.10a and 1.10b). If a rebore is done by an automotive machine shop, new oversize pistons will also be installed. The main bearings, connecting rod bearings and camshaft bearings are generally replaced with new ones and, if necessary, the crankshaft may be reground to restore the journals (see illustration 1.10c). Generally, the valves are serviced as well, since they're usually in less-than-perfect condition at this point. While the engine is being overhauled, other components, such as the distributor, starter and alternator, can be rebuilt as well. The end result should be a like-new engine that will give many trouble-free miles.

Note: *Critical cooling system components such as the hoses, drivebelts, thermostat and water pump should be replaced with new parts when an engine is overhauled. The radiator should be checked carefully to ensure that it isn't clogged or leaking (see Chapter 3). If you purchase a rebuilt engine or short block, some rebuilders will not warranty their engines unless the radiator has been professionally flushed. Also, we don't recommend overhauling the oil pump - always install a new one when an engine is rebuilt.*

11 Overhauling the internal components on today's engines is a difficult and time-consuming task which requires a significant amount of specialty tools and is best left to a professional engine rebuilder (see illustrations 1.11a, 1.11b and 1.11c). A competent engine rebuilder will handle the inspection of your old parts and offer advice concerning the reconditioning or replacement of the original engine.

1.10c A crankshaft having a main bearing journal ground

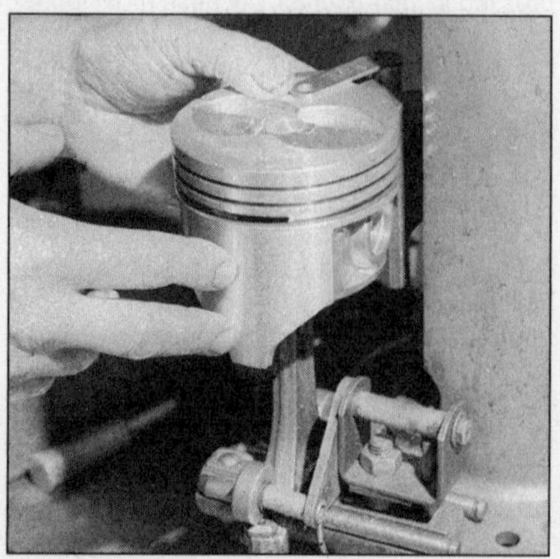
1.11a A machinist checks for a bent connecting rod, using specialized equipment

Never purchase parts or have machine work done on other components until the block has been thoroughly inspected by a professional machine shop. As a general rule, time is the primary cost of an overhaul, especially since the vehicle may be tied up for a minimum of two weeks or more. Be aware that some engine builders only have the capability to rebuild the engine you bring them while other rebuilders have a large inventory of rebuilt exchange engines in stock. Also be aware that many machine shops could take as much as two weeks time to completely rebuild your engine depending on shop workload. Sometimes it makes more sense to simply exchange your engine for another engine that's already rebuilt to save time.

1.11b A bore gauge being used to check the main bearing bore

1.11c Uneven piston wear like this indicates a bent connecting rod

2 Oil pressure check

1 Low engine oil pressure can be a sign of an engine in need of rebuilding. A low oil pressure indicator (often called an idiot light) is not a test of the oiling system. Such indicators only come on when the oil pressure is dangerously low. Even a factory oil pressure gauge in the instrument panel is only a relative indication, although much better for driver information than a warning light. A better test is with a mechanical (not electrical) oil pressure gauge.

2 Locate the oil pressure indicator sending unit. On 2005 and earlier 3.5L V6 models, it's located above the oil filter (see illustration). On 3.8L V6 engines, it's located at the rear of the left cylinder head. On 2011 and later 3.5L V6 engines, it's located under the intake manifold next to the coolant pipe.

3 Unscrew and remove the oil pressure sending unit, then screw in the hose for your oil pressure gauge (see illustration). If necessary, install an adapter fitting. Use Teflon tape or thread sealant on the threads of the adapter and/or the fitting on the end of your gauge's hose.

4 Check the oil pressure with the engine running (normal operating temperature) at idle, and compare it to this Chapter's Specifications. If it's extremely low, the bearings and/or oil pump are probably worn out.

3 Cylinder compression check

1 A compression check will tell you what mechanical condition the upper end of your engine (pistons, rings, valves, head gaskets) is in. Specifically, it can tell you if the compression is down due to leakage caused by worn piston rings, defective valves and seats or a blown head gasket.

Note: *The engine must be at normal operating temperature and the battery must be fully charged for this check.*

2 Begin by cleaning the area around the spark plugs before you remove them (compressed air should be used, if available). The idea is to prevent dirt from getting into the cylinders as the compression check is being done.

3 Disable the fuel pump circuit by relieving the fuel pressure (see Chapter 4).

4 Remove all of the spark plugs from the engine (see Chapter 1). Disconnect the primary (low voltage) electrical connector(s) from the coil pack(s).

5 Block the throttle wide open.

6 Install a compression gauge in the spark plug hole (see illustration).

7 Crank the engine over at least seven compression strokes and watch the gauge. The compression should build up quickly in a healthy engine. Low compression on the first stroke, followed by gradually increasing pressure on successive strokes, indicates worn piston rings. A low compression reading on the first stroke, which doesn't build up during successive strokes, indicates leaking valves or a blown head gasket (a cracked head could also be the cause). Deposits on the undersides of the valve heads can also cause low compression. Record the highest gauge reading obtained.

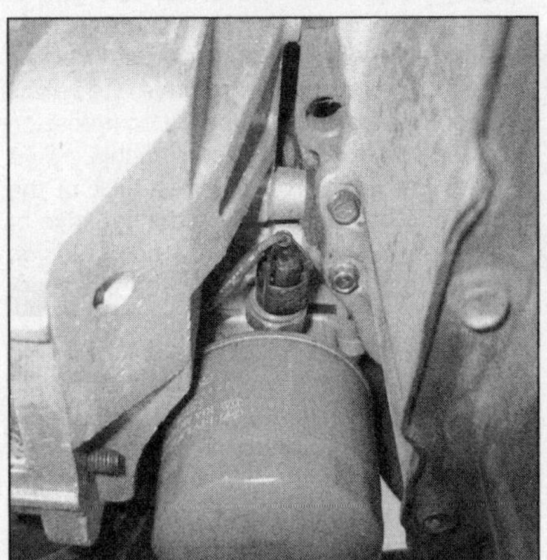

2.2 On 2005 and earlier 3.5L V6 models, the oil pressure sending unit is located above the oil filter

2.3 The oil pressure can be checked by removing the sending unit and installing a pressure gauge in its place

3.6 Use a compression gauge with a threaded fitting for the spark plug hole, not the type that requires hand pressure to maintain the seal - open the throttle valve as far as possible during the test

4.4 A simple vacuum gauge can be handy in diagnosing engine condition and performance

8 Repeat the procedure for the remaining cylinders and compare the results to this Chapter's Specifications.

9 Add some engine oil (about three squirts from a plunger-type oil can) to each cylinder, through the spark plug hole, and repeat the test.

10 If the compression increases after the oil is added, the piston rings are definitely worn. If the compression doesn't increase significantly, the leakage is occurring at the valves or head gasket. Leakage past the valves may be caused by burned valve seats and/or faces or warped, cracked or bent valves.

11 If two adjacent cylinders have equally very low compression, there's a strong possibility that the head gasket between them is blown. The appearance of coolant in the combustion chambers or the crankcase would verify this condition.

12 If one cylinder is slightly lower than the others, and the engine has a slightly rough idle, a worn lobe on the camshaft could be the cause.

13 If the compression is unusually high, the combustion chambers are probably coated with carbon deposits. If that's the case, the cylinder head(s) should be removed and decarbonized.

14 If compression is way down or varies greatly between cylinders, it would be a good idea to have a leak-down test performed by an automotive repair shop. This test will pinpoint exactly where the leakage is occurring and how severe it is.

4 Vacuum gauge diagnostic checks

1 A vacuum gauge provides inexpensive but valuable information about what is going on in the engine. You can check for worn rings or cylinder walls, leaking head or intake manifold gaskets, incorrect carburetor adjustments, restricted exhaust, stuck or burned valves, weak valve springs, improper ignition or valve timing and ignition problems.

2 Unfortunately, vacuum gauge readings are easy to misinterpret, so they should be used in conjunction with other tests to confirm the diagnosis.

3 Both the absolute readings and the rate of needle movement are important for accurate interpretation. Most gauges measure vacuum in inches of mercury (in-Hg). The following references to vacuum assume the diagnosis is being performed at sea level. As elevation increases (or atmospheric pressure decreases), the reading will decrease. For every 1,000-foot increase in elevation above approximately 2000 feet, the gauge readings will decrease about one inch of mercury.

4 Connect the vacuum gauge directly to the intake manifold vacuum, not to ported (throttle body) vacuum (see illustration). Be sure no hoses are left disconnected during the test or false readings will result.

5 Before you begin the test, allow the engine to warm up completely. Block the wheels and set the parking brake. With the transmission in Park, start the engine and allow it to run at normal idle speed.

Warning: *Keep your hands and the vacuum gauge clear of the fans and drivebelts.*

6 Read the vacuum gauge; an average, healthy engine should normally produce about 17 to 22 in-Hg with a fairly steady needle (see illustration). Refer to the following vacuum gauge readings and what they indicate about the engine's condition:

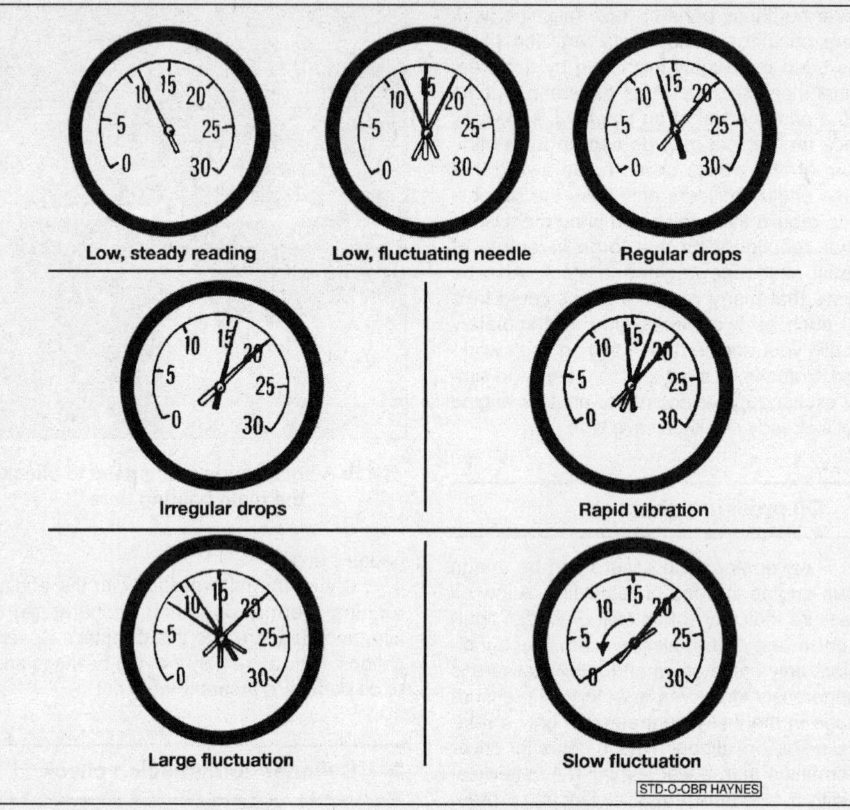

4.6 Typical vacuum gauge readings

7 A low steady reading usually indicates a leaking gasket between the intake manifold and cylinder head(s) or throttle body, a leaky vacuum hose, late ignition timing or incorrect camshaft timing. Check ignition timing with a timing light and eliminate all other possible causes, utilizing the tests provided in this Chapter before you remove the timing belt cover to check the timing marks.

8 If the reading is three to eight inches below normal and it fluctuates at that low reading, suspect an intake manifold gasket leak at an intake port or a faulty fuel injector.

9 If the needle has regular drops of about two-to-four inches at a steady rate, the valves are probably leaking. Perform a compression check or leak-down test to confirm this.

10 An irregular drop or down-flick of the needle can be caused by a sticking valve or an ignition misfire. Perform a compression check or leak-down test and read the spark plugs.

11 A rapid vibration of about four in-Hg vibration at idle combined with exhaust smoke indicates worn valve guides. Perform a leak-down test to confirm this. If the rapid vibration occurs with an increase in engine speed, check for a leaking intake manifold gasket or head gasket, weak valve springs, burned valves or ignition misfire.

12 A slight fluctuation, say one inch up and down, may mean ignition problems. Check all the usual tune-up items and, if necessary, run the engine on an ignition analyzer.

6.3a After tightly wrapping water-vulnerable components, use a spray cleaner on everything, with particular concentration on the greasiest areas, usually around the valve cover and lower edges of the block. If one section dries out, apply more cleaner

6.3b Depending on how dirty the engine is, let the cleaner soak in according to the directions and then hose off the grime and cleaner. Get the rinse water down into every area you can get at; then dry important components with a hair dryer or paper towels

13 If there is a large fluctuation, perform a compression or leak-down test to look for a weak or dead cylinder or a blown head gasket.

14 If the needle moves slowly through a wide range, check for a clogged PCV system, incorrect idle fuel mixture, throttle body or intake manifold gasket leaks.

15 Check for a slow return after revving the engine by quickly snapping the throttle open until the engine reaches about 2,500 rpm and let it shut. Normally the reading should drop to near zero, rise above normal idle reading (about 5 in-Hg over) and then return to the previous idle reading. If the vacuum returns slowly and doesn't peak when the throttle is snapped shut, the rings may be worn. If there is a long delay, look for a restricted exhaust system (often the muffler or catalytic converter). An easy way to check this is to temporarily disconnect the exhaust ahead of the suspected part and redo the test.

5 Engine rebuilding alternatives

1 The do-it-yourselfer is faced with a number of options when purchasing a rebuilt engine. The major considerations are cost, warranty, parts availability and the time required for the rebuilder to complete the project. The decision to replace the engine block, piston/connecting rod assemblies and crankshaft depends on the final inspection results of your engine. Only then can you make a cost effective decision whether to have your engine overhauled or simply purchase an exchange engine for your vehicle.

2 Some of the rebuilding alternatives include:

3 Individual parts - If the inspection procedures reveal that the engine block and most engine components are in reusable condition, purchasing individual parts and having a rebuilder rebuild your engine may be the most economical alternative. The block, crankshaft and piston/connecting rod assemblies should all be inspected carefully by a machine shop first.

4 Short block - A short block consists of an engine block with a crankshaft and piston/connecting rod assemblies already installed. All new bearings are incorporated and all clearances will be correct. The existing camshafts, valve train components, cylinder head and external parts can be bolted to the short block with little or no machine shop work necessary.

5 Long block - A long block consists of a short block plus an oil pump, oil pan, cylinder head, valve cover, camshaft and valve train components, timing sprockets and belt or gears and timing cover. All components are installed with new bearings, seals and gaskets incorporated throughout. The installation of manifolds and external parts is all that's necessary.

6 Low mileage used engines - Some companies now offer low mileage used engines that are a very cost effective way to get your vehicle up and running again. These engines often come from vehicles that have been totaled in accidents or come from other countries that have a higher vehicle turn over rate. A low mileage used engine also usually has a similar warranty like the newly remanufactured engines.

7 Give careful thought to which alternative is best for you and discuss the situation with local automotive machine shops, auto parts dealers and experienced rebuilders before ordering or purchasing replacement parts.

6 Engine removal - methods and precautions

1 If you've decided that an engine must be removed for overhaul or major repair work, several preliminary steps should be taken. Read all removal and installation procedures carefully prior to committing to this job. These engines are removed by lowering the engine to the floor, along with the transaxle, and then raising the vehicle sufficiently to slide the assembly out; this will require a vehicle hoist as well as an engine hoist.

2 Locating a suitable place to work is extremely important. Adequate work space, along with storage space for the vehicle, will be needed. If a shop or garage isn't available, at the very least a flat, level, clean work surface made of concrete or asphalt is required.

3 Cleaning the engine compartment and engine before beginning the removal procedure will help keep tools clean and organized (see illustrations 6.3a and 6.3b).

4 An engine hoist will also be necessary. Make sure the hoist is rated in excess of the combined weight of the engine and transaxle. Safety is of primary importance, considering the potential hazards involved in removing the engine from the vehicle.

5 If you're a novice at engine removal, get at least one helper. One person cannot easily do all the things you need to do to remove a big heavy engine and transaxle assembly from the engine compartment. Also helpful is to seek advice and assistance from someone who's experienced in engine removal.

6 Plan the operation ahead of time. Arrange for or obtain all of the tools and equipment you'll need prior to beginning the job

6.6 Get an engine stand sturdy enough to firmly support the engine while you're working on it. Stay away from three-wheeled models: they have a tendency to tip over more easily, so get a four-wheeled unit

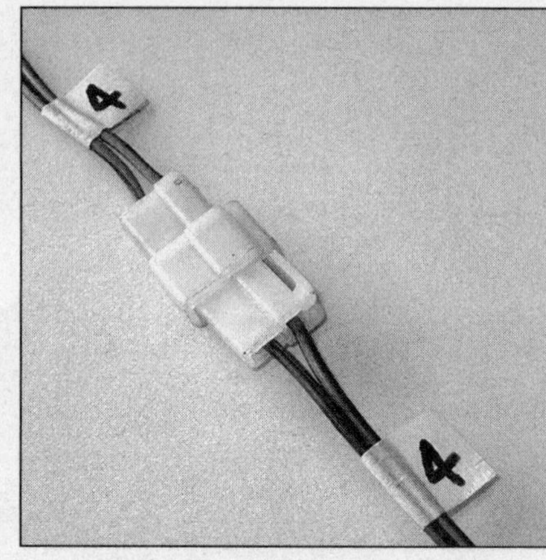

7.9 Label each wire before unplugging the connector

(see illustration 6.6). Some of the equipment necessary to perform engine removal and installation safely and with relative ease are (in addition to a vehicle hoist and an engine hoist) a heavy duty floor jack (preferably fitted with a transmission jack head adapter), complete sets of wrenches and sockets as described in the front of this manual, wooden blocks, plenty of rags and cleaning solvent for mopping up spilled oil, coolant and gasoline.

7 Plan for the vehicle to be out of use for quite a while. A machine shop can do the work that is beyond the scope of the home mechanic. Machine shops often have a busy schedule, so before removing the engine, consult the shop for an estimate of how long it will take to rebuild or repair the components that may need work.

7 Engine - removal and installation

Warning: *Gasoline is extremely flammable, so take extra precautions when you work on any part of the fuel system. Don't smoke or allow open flames or bare light bulbs near the work area, and don't work in a garage where a gas-type appliance (such as a water heater or clothes dryer) is present. Since gasoline is carcinogenic, wear fuel-resistant gloves when there's a possibility of being exposed to fuel, and, if you spill any fuel on your skin, rinse it off immediately with soap and water. Mop up any spills immediately and do not store fuel-soaked rags where they could ignite. The fuel system is under constant pressure, so, if any fuel lines are to be disconnected, the fuel pressure in the system must be relieved first (see Chapter for more information). When you perform any kind of work on the fuel system, wear safety glasses and have a Class B type fire extinguisher on hand.*

Warning: *The engine must be completely cool before beginning this procedure.*

Warning: *The air conditioning system is under high pressure. Do not loosen any hose fittings or remove any components until after the system has been discharged. Air conditioning refrigerant must be properly discharged into an EPA-approved recovery/recycling unit at a dealer service department or an automotive air conditioning repair facility. Always wear eye protection when disconnecting air conditioning system fittings.*

Note: *Engine removal on these models is a difficult job, especially for the do-it-yourself mechanic working at home. Because of the vehicle's design, the manufacturer states that the engine and transaxle have to be removed as a unit from the bottom of the vehicle, not the top. With a floor jack and jackstands, the vehicle can't be raised high enough and supported safely enough for the engine/transaxle assembly to slide out from underneath. The manufacturer recommends that removal of the engine transaxle assembly only be performed on a frame-contact type vehicle hoist.*

Note: *Read through the entire Section before beginning this procedure. The engine and transaxle are removed as a unit from below, then separated outside the vehicle.*

Removal

1 Have the air conditioning system discharged by an automotive air conditioning technician.

2 Park the vehicle on a frame-contact type vehicle hoist, then engage the arms of the hoist with the jacking points of the vehicle. Raise the hoist arms until they contact the vehicle, but not so much that the wheels come off the ground.

3 Remove the engine cover (see Chapter 1) then relieve the fuel system pressure (see Chapter 4).

4 Place protective covers on the fenders and cowl and remove the hood (see Chapter 11).

5 Remove the FAM mounting bolts and FAM from the fuse and relay box (see Chapter 12).

6 Remove the air filter housing (see Chapter 4).

7 Remove the battery and the battery tray cover (see Chapter 5).

8 Remove the lower splash shield from under the vehicle.

9 Clearly label and disconnect all vacuum lines, emissions hoses, wiring harness connectors, ground straps and fuel lines. Masking tape and/or a touch up paint applicator work well for marking items (see illustration). Take instant photos or sketch the locations of components and brackets.

10 Detach the ground cable from the cylinder head.

11 Loosen the front wheel lug nuts and the driveaxle/hub nuts (see Chapter 8), then raise the vehicle on the hoist.

Note: *Keep in mind that during this procedure you'll have to adjust the height of the vehicle to perform certain operations.*

12 Drain the cooling system and engine oil and remove the drivebelt (see Chapter 1).

13 Remove the alternator and its brackets (see Chapter 5).

14 Remove the power steering fluid reservoir and set it off to the side without disconnecting the fluid lines (see Chapter 10).

15 Lower the vehicle and detach the heater hoses at the firewall.

16 Detach the lower radiator hose from the engine and the upper radiator hose from the thermostat housing.

17 Remove the upper radiator support crossmember (see Chapter 11).

18 Remove the cooling fan(s), shroud(s) and radiator (see Chapter 3).

19 Disconnect the shift cable from the transaxle (see Chapter 7). Also disconnect any wiring harness connectors from the transaxle.

20 Disconnect the upper air conditioning line from the condenser for additional clearance.

21 Disconnect the air conditioning lines at the compressor and the junction inside the engine compartment. Remove the air conditioning compressor (see Chapter 3).

22 Remove the power steering pump and bracket (see Chapter 10).

23 Raise the vehicle on the hoist. Remove the front wheels.

24 Remove the driveaxles (see Chapter 8).

25 Unplug the downstream oxygen sensor electrical connector.

26 Detach the front exhaust pipe from the

exhaust manifolds (see Chapter 4).

Note: *The exhaust manifold and catalytic converters are combined and are referred to as "maniverters."*

27 Remove the power steering fluid cooler, if equipped.

28 Remove the front subframe bolts and subframe (see Chapter 10).

Note: *The subframe bolts and nuts have different torque specifications, make sure to note each bolt location so they can be reinstalled in their the original locations.*

29 Mark the position of the driveplate and remove the torque converter bolts (see Chapter 7).

30 Lower the vehicle.

31 Support the engine with a floor jack and block of wood. Remove the right (passenger's) side engine mount, including the portion that bolts to the engine. Using one of the mount-to-engine bolts, attach one end of an engine lifting sling or chain to the mount boss. Tighten the bolt securely. Attach the other end of the sling or chain to the other side of the engine, using one of the transaxle-to-engine bolts. Be sure the positioning of the chain or sling will support the engine and transaxle in a balanced attitude.

Note: *The sling or chain must be long enough to allow the engine hoist to lower the engine/transaxle assembly to the ground, without letting the hoist arm contact the vehicle.*

32 Roll the hoist into position and attach the sling or chain to it. Take up the slack until there is slight tension on the hoist, then remove the jack from under the engine. Remember that the transaxle end of the engine will be heavier, so position the chain on the hoist so it balances the engine and the transaxle level with the vehicle.

Note: *Depending on the design of the engine hoist, it may be helpful to position the hoist from the side of the vehicle, so that when the engine/transaxle assembly is lowered, it will fit between the legs of the hoist.*

33 Recheck to be sure nothing except the remaining mount is still connecting the engine or transaxle to the vehicle. Disconnect and label anything still remaining.

34 Remove the driver's side transaxle mount (see Chapter 2A).

35 Slowly lower the engine/transaxle to the ground.

36 Once the engine/transaxle assembly is on the floor, disconnect the engine lifting hoist and raise the vehicle until it clears the assembly.

37 Reconnect the chain or sling and raise the engine and transaxle. Support the engine with blocks of wood or another floor jack, while leaving the sling or chain attached to the right-side mounting boss. Support the transaxle with another floor jack, preferably one with a transmission jack head adapter. At this point the transaxle can be unbolted and removed from the engine. Be very careful to ensure that the components are supported securely so they won't topple off their supports during disconnection.

38 Reconnect the lifting chain to the engine, then raise the engine and attach it to an engine stand.

Installation

39 Installation is the reverse of removal, noting the following points:

a) *Check the engine/transaxle mounts. If they're worn or damaged, replace them.*
b) *Inspect the torque converter seal and bushing.*
c) *Attach the transaxle to the engine (see Chapter 7).*
d) *Add coolant, oil, power steering and transmission fluids as needed (see Chapter 1).*
e) *Run the engine and check for proper operation and leaks. Shut off the engine and recheck fluid levels.*

8 Engine overhaul - disassembly sequence

1 It's much easier to disassemble the engine if it's mounted on a portable engine stand. A stand can often be rented quite cheaply from an equipment rental yard. Before the engine is mounted on a stand, the driveplate should be removed from the engine.

2 If a stand isn't available, it's possible to remove the external engine components with it blocked up on the floor. Be extra careful not to tip or drop the engine when working without a stand.

3 If you're going to obtain a rebuilt engine, all external components must come off first, to be transferred to the replacement engine. These components include:

- *Flywheel/driveplate*
- *Ignition system components*
- *Emissions-related components*
- *Engine mounts and mount brackets*
- *Fuel injection components*
- *Intake/exhaust manifolds*
- *Upper and lower oil pans*
- *Oil filter*
- *Thermostat and housing assembly*
- *Water pump*

Note: *When removing the external components from the engine, pay close attention to details that may be helpful or important during installation. Note the installed position of gaskets, seals, spacers, pins, brackets, washers, bolts and other small items.*

4 If you're going to obtain a short block (assembled engine block, crankshaft, pistons and connecting rods), you should remove the timing belt/chain, cylinder head, oil pan, oil pump pick-up tube, oil pump and water pump from your engine so that you can turn in your old short block to the rebuilder as a core. See Section 5 for additional information regarding the different possibilities to be considered.

9 Pistons and connecting rods - removal and installation

Removal

Note: *Prior to removing the piston/connecting rod assemblies, remove the cylinder head, oil pan, and the upper (aluminum) oil pan (see Chapter 2A).*

1 Use your fingernail to feel if a ridge has formed at the upper limit of ring travel (about 1/4-inch down from the top of each cylinder). If carbon deposits or cylinder wear have produced ridges, they must be completely removed with a special tool (see illustration). Follow the manufacturer's instructions provided with the tool. Failure to remove the ridges before attempting to remove the piston/connecting rod assemblies may result in piston breakage.

2 After the cylinder ridges have been removed, turn the engine so the crankshaft is facing up.

3 Before the pistons and connecting rods are removed, check the connecting rod endplay with feeler gauges. Slide them between the first connecting rod and the crankshaft throw until the play is removed (see illustration). Repeat this procedure for each connecting rod. The endplay is equal to the thickness

9.1 Before you try to remove the pistons, use a ridge reamer to remove the raised material (ridge) from the top of the cylinders

9.3 Checking the connecting rod endplay (side clearance)

9.4 If the connecting rods and caps are not marked, use a center punch or numbered impression stamps to mark the caps to the rods by cylinder number

9.13 Install the piston ring into the cylinder, then push it down into position using a piston so the ring will be square in the cylinder

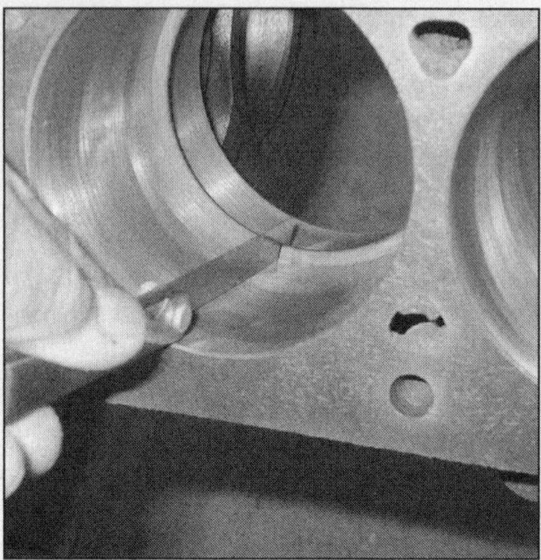

9.14 With the ring square in the cylinder, measure the ring end gap with a feeler gauge

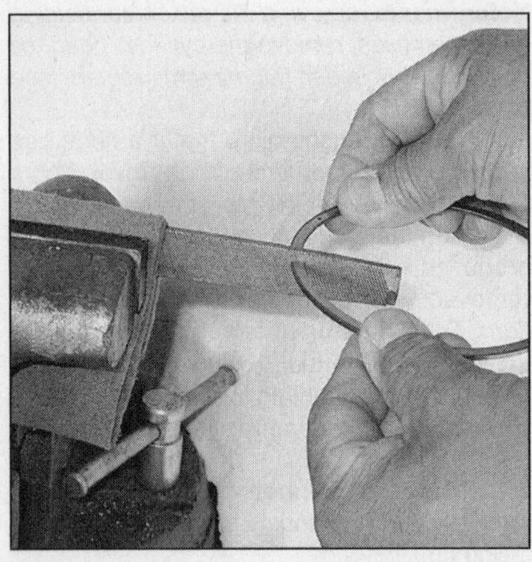

9.15 If the ring end gap is too small, clamp a file in a vise as shown and file the piston ring ends - file the ends squarely and finish by removing all raised material or burrs with a fine stone

of the feeler gauge(s). Check with an automotive machine shop for the endplay service limit. If the play exceeds the service limit, new connecting rods will be required. If new rods (or a new crankshaft) are installed, the endplay may fall under the minimum allowable clearance. If it does, the rods will have to be machined to restore it. If necessary, consult an automotive machine shop for advice.

4 Check the connecting rods and caps for identification marks (see illustration). If they aren't plainly marked, use a small centerpunch to make the appropriate number of indentations on each rod and cap (1, 2, 3, etc., depending on the cylinder they're associated with).

5 Loosen each of the connecting rod cap bolts 1/2-turn at a time until they can be removed by hand. Remove the number one connecting rod cap and bearing insert. Don't drop the bearing insert out of the cap.

6 Remove the bearing insert and push the connecting rod/piston assembly out through the top of the engine. Use a wooden or plastic hammer handle to push on the upper bearing surface in the connecting rod. Be careful to avoid scratching the crankshaft bearing journals with the rod bolts.

Note: *Slip a short section of rubber hose over the rod bolts before pushing the piston/rod assemblies out to make sure the crankshaft isn't damaged.*

7 If resistance is felt, double-check to make sure that the entire ridge was removed from the cylinder.

8 Repeat the procedure for the remaining cylinders.

9 After removal, reassemble the connecting rod caps and bearing inserts in their respective connecting rods and install the cap bolts finger tight. Leaving the old bearing inserts in place until reassembly will help prevent the connecting rod bearing surfaces from being accidentally nicked or gouged.

10 The pistons and connecting rods are now ready for inspection and overhaul at an automotive machine shop.

Piston ring installation

11 Before installing the new piston rings, the ring end gaps must be checked. It's assumed that the piston ring side clearance has been checked and verified correct.

Note: *Pistons and rods can only be installed after the crankshaft has been installed (see Section 10).*

12 Lay out the piston/connecting rod assemblies and the new ring sets so the ring sets will be matched with the same piston and cylinder during the end gap measurement and engine assembly.

13 Insert the top (number one) ring into the first cylinder and square it up with the cylinder walls by pushing it in with the top of the piston (see illustration). The ring should be near the bottom of the cylinder, at the lower limit of ring travel.

14 To measure the end gap, slip feeler gauges between the ends of the ring until a gauge equal to the gap width is found (see illustration). The feeler gauge should slide between the ring ends with a slight amount of drag. Check with an automotive machine shop for the correct end gap for your engine. If the gap is larger or smaller than specified, double-check to make sure you have the correct rings before proceeding.

15 If the gap is too small, it must be enlarged or the ring ends may come in contact with each other during engine operation, which can cause serious damage to the engine. The end gap can be increased by filing the ring ends very carefully with a fine file. Mount the file in a vise equipped with soft jaws, slip the ring over the file with the ends contacting the file face and slowly move the ring to remove material from the ends. When performing this operation, file only by pushing the ring from the outside end of the file towards the vise (see illustration).

16 Excess end gap isn't critical unless it's greater than approximately 0.030-inch. Again, double-check to make sure you have the correct ring type.

17 Repeat the procedure for each ring that will be installed in the first cylinder and for each ring in the remaining cylinders. Remember to keep rings, pistons and cylinders matched up.

18 Once the ring end gaps have been checked/corrected, the rings can be installed on the pistons.

19 The oil control ring (lowest one on the piston) is usually installed first. It's composed of three separate components. Slip the spacer/expander into the groove (see illustration). If an anti-rotation tang is used, make sure it's inserted into the drilled hole in the ring groove. Next, install the upper side rail in the same manner (see illustration). Don't use a piston ring installation tool on the oil ring side rails, as they may be damaged. Instead, place one end of the side rail into the groove between the spacer/expander and the ring

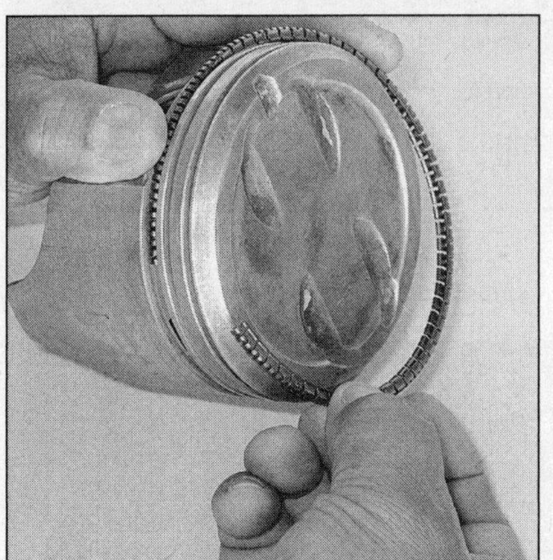

9.19a Installing the spacer/expander in the oil ring groove

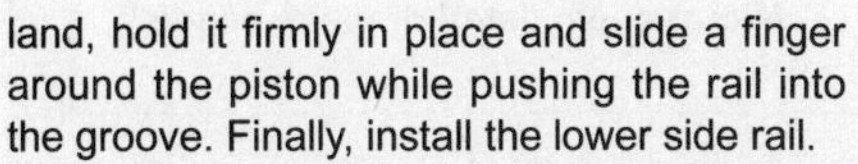

land, hold it firmly in place and slide a finger around the piston while pushing the rail into the groove. Finally, install the lower side rail.

20 After the three oil ring components have been installed, check to make sure that both the upper and lower side rails can be rotated smoothly inside the ring grooves.

21 The number two (middle) ring is installed next. It's usually stamped with a mark that must face up, toward the top of the piston. Do not mix up the top and middle rings, as they have different cross-sections.

Note: *Always follow the instructions printed on the ring package or box - different manufacturers may require different approaches.*

22 Use a piston ring installation tool and make sure the identification mark is facing the top of the piston, then slip the ring into the middle groove on the piston (see illustration). Don't expand the ring any more than necessary to slide it over the piston.

23 Install the number one (top) ring in the same manner. Make sure the mark is facing up. Be careful not to confuse the number one and number two rings.

24 Repeat the procedure for the remaining pistons and rings.

Installation

25 Before installing the piston/connecting rod assemblies, the cylinder walls must be perfectly clean, the top edge of each cylinder bore must be chamfered, and the crankshaft must be in place.

26 Remove the cap from the end of the number one connecting rod (refer to the marks made during removal - the bearing locating tangs must be together).

27 Remove the original bearing inserts and wipe the bearing surfaces of the connecting rod and cap with a clean, lint-free cloth. They must be kept spotlessly clean.

Connecting rod bearing oil clearance check

28 Clean the rear of the new upper bearing insert, then lay it in place in the connecting rod. Make sure the tab on the bearing fits into the recess in the rod. Don't hammer the bearing insert into place and be very careful not to nick or gouge the bearing face. Don't lubricate the bearing at this time.

29 Clean the back of the other bearing insert and install it in the rod cap. Again, make sure the tab on the bearing fits into the recess in the cap, and don't apply any lubricant. It's critically important that the mating surfaces of the bearing and connecting rod are perfectly clean and oil free when they're assembled.

30 Position the piston ring gaps around the piston as shown (see illustration).

31 Lubricate the piston and rings with clean engine oil and attach a piston ring compressor to the piston. Leave the skirt protruding about 1/4-inch to guide the piston into the cylinder. The rings must be compressed until they're flush with the piston.

Note: *Slip pieces of rubber hose about 6 inches long over each rod bolt. These will guide the connecting rod into position and keep the rod bolts from damaging the crankshaft.*

32 Rotate the crankshaft until the number one connecting rod journal is at Bottom Dead Center (BDC) and apply a liberal coat of engine oil to the cylinder walls.

33 With the mark on top of the piston facing the front (timing belt end) of the engine, gently insert the piston/connecting rod assembly into the number one cylinder bore and rest the bottom edge of the ring compressor on the engine block.

Note: *The connecting rod also has a mark on it that must face the correct direction.*

34 Tap the top edge of the ring compressor to make sure it's contacting the block around its entire circumference.

35 Gently tap on the top of the piston with the end of a wooden or plastic hammer handle (see illustration) while guiding the end of the connecting rod into place on the crankshaft journal. The piston rings may try to pop out of

9.19b DO NOT use a piston ring installation tool when installing the oil control side rails

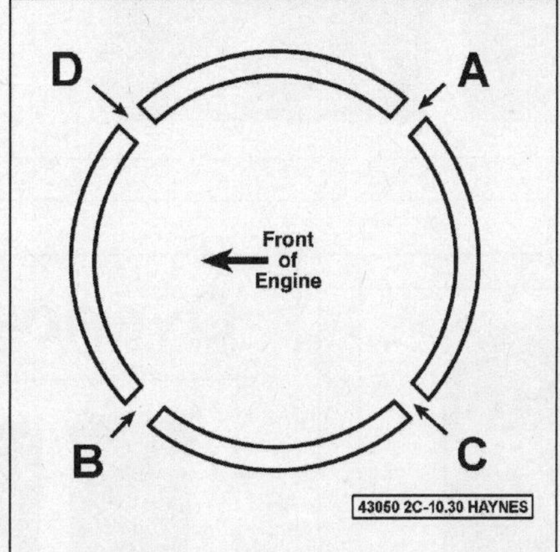

9.30 Position the piston ring end gaps as shown here before installing the piston/connecting rod assemblies into the engine

A Top compression ring gap and oil ring spacer gap
B Second compression ring
C Upper oil ring gap
D Lower oil ring gap

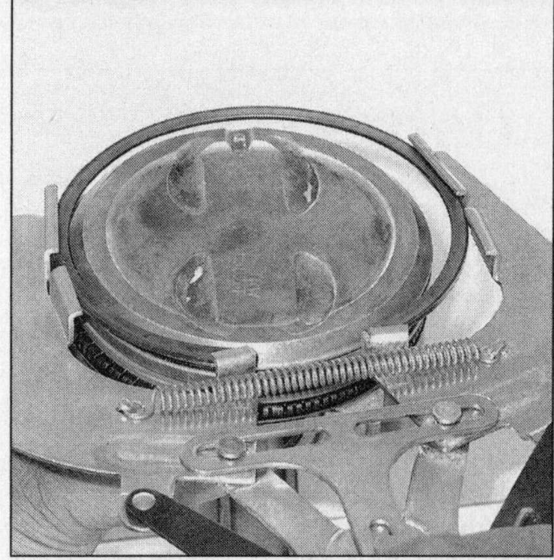

9.22 Use a piston ring installation tool to install the number 2 and the number 1 (top) rings - the directional mark on the piston ring(s) must face toward the top of the piston

9.35 Use a plastic or wooden hammer handle to push the piston into the cylinder

ENGINE BEARING ANALYSIS

Debris

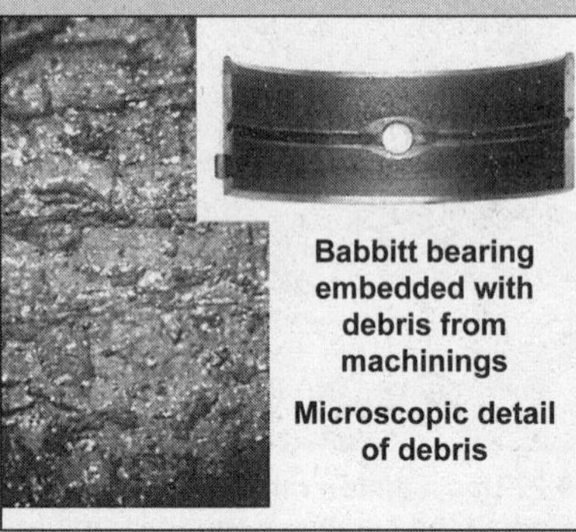

Babbitt bearing embedded with debris from machinings

Microscopic detail of debris

Microscopic detail of gouges

Overplated copper alloy bearing gouged by cast iron debris

Aluminum bearing embedded with glass beads

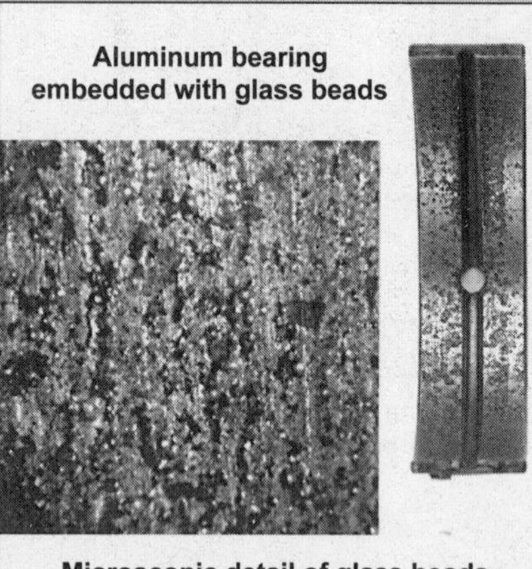

Microscopic detail of glass beads

Damaged lining caused by dirt left on the bearing back

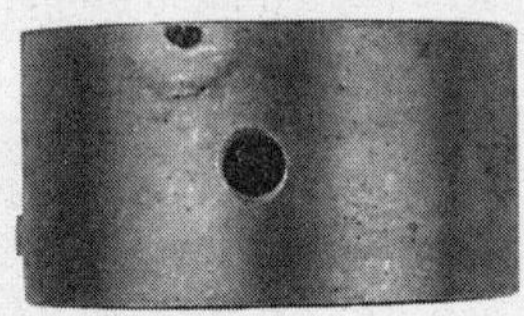

Misassembly

Result of a lower half assembled as an upper - blocking the oil flow

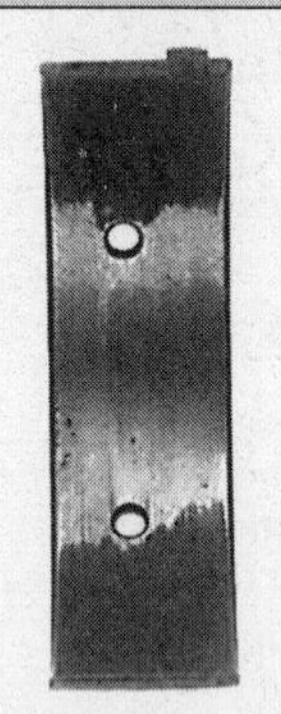

Excessive oil clearance is indicated by a short contact arc

Polished and oil-stained backs are a result of a poor fit in the housing bore

Result of a wrong, reversed, or shifted cap

Overloading

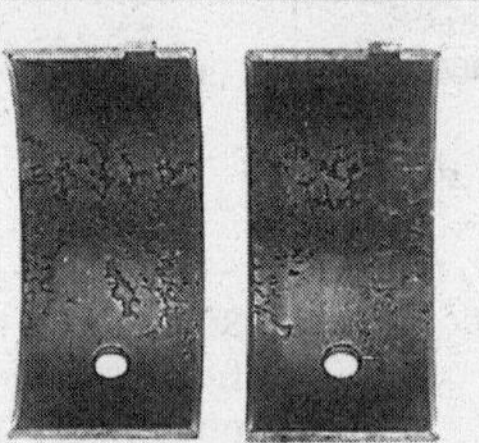

Damage from excessive idling which resulted in an oil film unable to support the load imposed

Damaged upper connecting rod bearings caused by engine lugging; the lower main bearings (not shown) were similarly affected

The damage shown in these upper and lower connecting rod bearings was caused by engine operation at a higher-than-rated speed under load

Misalignment

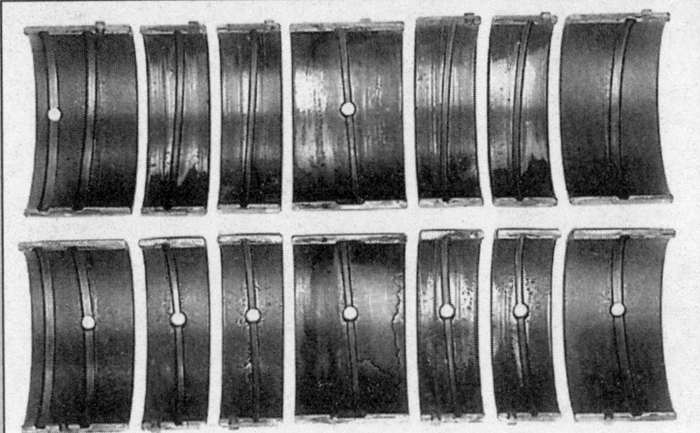

A warped crankshaft caused this pattern of severe wear in the center, diminishing toward the ends

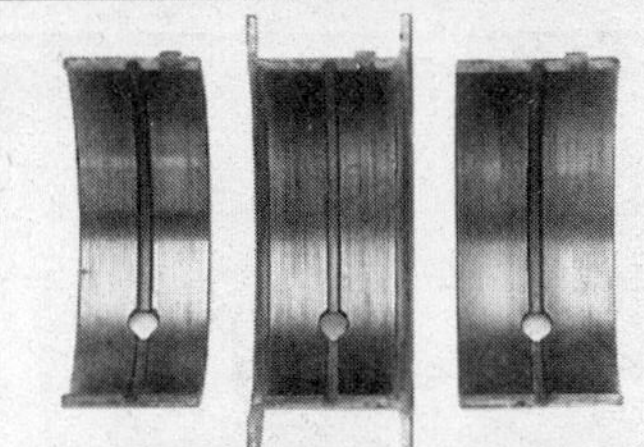

A poorly finished crankshaft caused the equally spaced scoring shown

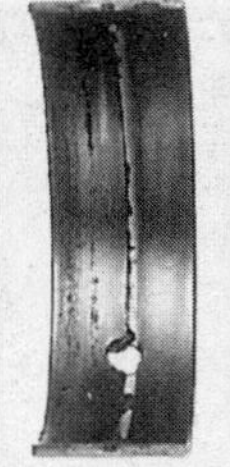

A tapered housing bore caused the damage along one edge of this pair

A bent connecting rod led to the damage in the "V" pattern

Lubrication

Result of dry start: The bearings on the left, farthest from the oil pump, show more damage

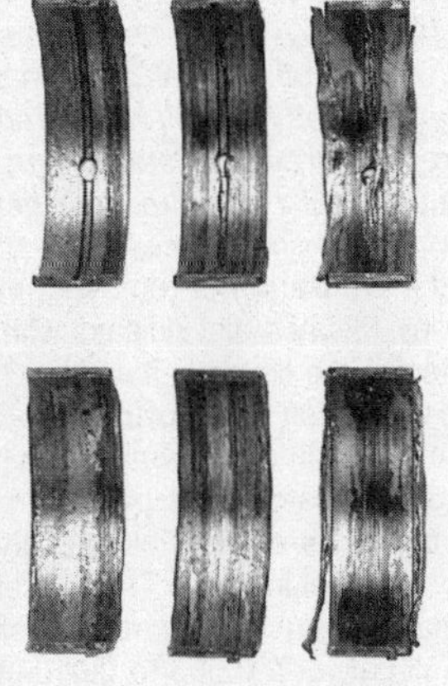

Result of a low oil supply or oil starvation

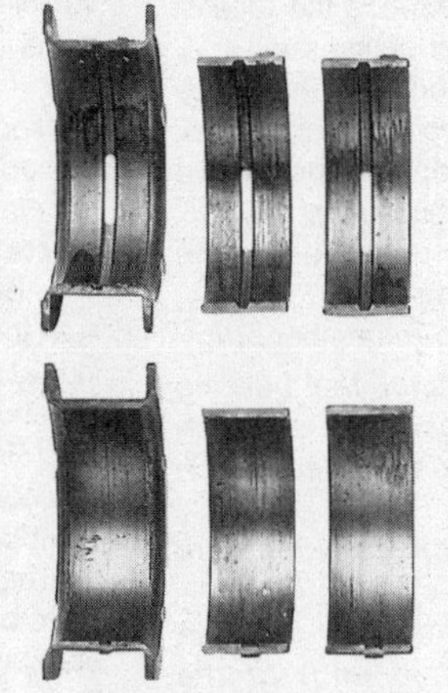

Severe wear as a result of inadequate oil clearance

Corrosion

Microscopic detail of corrosion

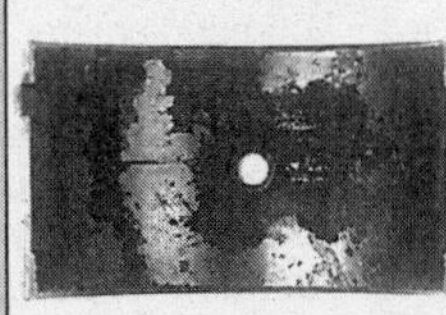

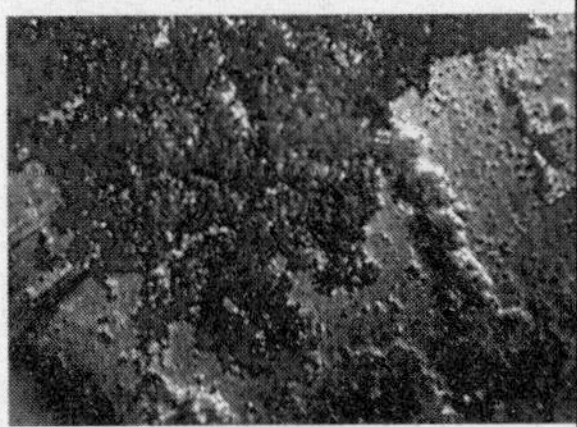

Corrosion is an acid attack on the bearing lining generally caused by inadequate maintenance, extremely hot or cold operation, or inferior oils or fuels

Microscopic detail of cavitation

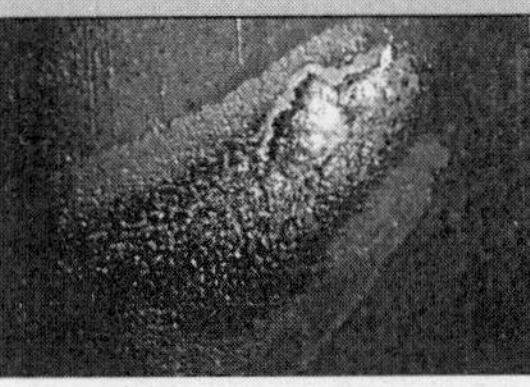

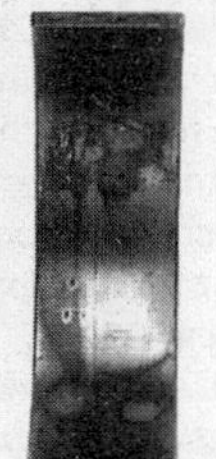

Example of cavitation - a surface erosion caused by pressure changes in the oil film

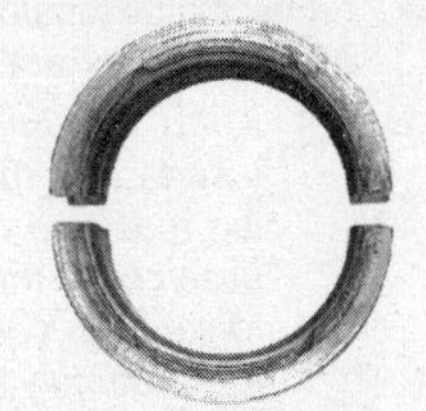

Damage from excessive thrust or insufficient axial clearance

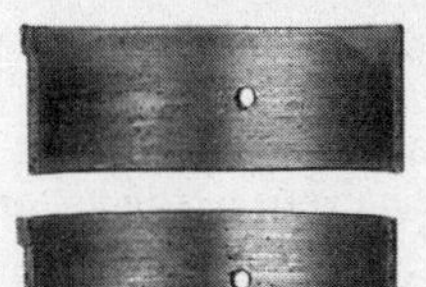

Bearing affected by oil dilution caused by excessive blow-by or a rich mixture

9.37 Place Plastigage on each connecting rod bearing journal parallel to the crankshaft centerline

9.41 Use the scale on the Plastigage package to determine the bearing oil clearance - be sure to measure the widest part of the Plastigage and use the correct scale; it comes with both standard and metric scales

10.1 Checking crankshaft endplay with a dial indicator

the ring compressor just before entering the cylinder bore, so keep some downward pressure on the ring compressor. Work slowly, and if any resistance is felt as the piston enters the cylinder, stop immediately. Find out what's hanging up and fix it before proceeding. Do not, for any reason, force the piston into the cylinder - you might break a ring and/or the piston.

36 Once the piston/connecting rod assembly is installed, the connecting rod bearing oil clearance must be checked before the rod cap is permanently installed.

37 Cut a piece of the appropriate size Plastigage slightly shorter than the width of the connecting rod bearing and lay it in place on the number one connecting rod journal, parallel with the journal axis (see illustration).

38 Clean the connecting rod cap bearing face and install the rod cap. Make sure the mating mark on the cap is on the same side as the mark on the connecting rod.

39 Install the rod bolts and tighten them in two steps to the torque listed in this Chapter's Specifications.

Note: *Use a thin-wall socket to avoid erroneous torque readings that can result if the socket is wedged between the rod cap and the bolt. If the socket tends to wedge itself between the fastener and the cap, lift up on it slightly until it no longer contacts the cap. DO NOT rotate the crankshaft at any time during this operation.*

40 Remove the fasteners and detach the rod cap, being very careful not to disturb the Plastigage.

41 Compare the width of the crushed Plastigage to the scale printed on the Plastigage envelope to obtain the oil clearance (see illustration). The connecting rod oil clearance is usually about 0.001 to 0.002 inch. Consult an automotive machine shop for the clearance specified for the rod bearings on your engine.

42 If the clearance is not as specified, the bearing inserts may be the wrong size (which means different ones will be required). Before deciding that different inserts are needed, make sure that no dirt or oil was between the bearing inserts and the connecting rod or cap when the clearance was measured. Also, recheck the journal diameter. If the Plastigage was wider at one end than the other, the journal may be tapered. If the clearance still exceeds the limit specified, the bearing will have to be replaced with an undersize bearing.

Caution: *When installing a new crankshaft always use a standard size bearing.*

Final installation

43 Carefully scrape all traces of the Plastigage material off the rod journal and/or bearing face. Be very careful not to scratch the bearing - use your fingernail or the edge of a plastic card.

44 Make sure the bearing faces are perfectly clean, then apply a uniform layer of clean moly-base grease or engine assembly lube to both of them. You'll have to push the piston into the cylinder to expose the face of the bearing insert in the connecting rod.

45 Slide the connecting rod back into place on the journal, install the rod cap and bolts, tightening them in two steps to the torque listed in this Chapter's Specifications.

46 Repeat the entire procedure for the remaining pistons/connecting rods.

47 The important points to remember are:

a) *Keep the back sides of the bearing inserts and the insides of the connecting rods and caps perfectly clean when assembling them.*
b) *Make sure you have the correct piston/rod assembly for each cylinder.*
c) *The mark on the piston must face the front (timing belt/chain end) of the engine.*
d) *Lubricate the cylinder walls liberally with clean oil.*
e) *Lubricate the bearing faces when installing the rod caps after the oil clearance has been checked.*

48 After all the piston/connecting rod assemblies have been correctly installed, rotate the crankshaft a number of times by hand to check for any obvious binding.

49 As a final step, check the connecting rod endplay again. If it was correct before disassembly and the original crankshaft and rods were reinstalled, it should still be correct. If new rods or a new crankshaft were installed, the endplay may be inadequate. If so, the rods will have to be removed and taken to an automotive machine shop for resizing.

10 Crankshaft - removal and installation

Removal

Note: *The crankshaft can be removed only after the engine has been removed from the vehicle. It's assumed that the flywheel/driveplate, crankshaft pulley, timing belt/chains, oil pan, oil pump body, oil filter and piston/connecting rod assemblies have already been removed. The rear main oil seal retainer must be unbolted and separated from the block before proceeding with crankshaft removal.*

1 Before the crankshaft is removed, measure the endplay. Mount a dial indicator with the indicator in line with the crankshaft and touching the end of the crankshaft (see illustration).

2 Pry the crankshaft all the way to the rear and zero the dial indicator. Next, pry the crankshaft to the front as far as possible and check the reading on the dial indicator. The distance traveled is the endplay. A typical crankshaft endplay will fall between 0.003 to 0.010-inch. If it's greater than that, check the crankshaft thrust surfaces for wear after it's removed. If no wear is evident, new main bearings should correct the endplay.

3 If a dial indicator isn't available, feeler gauges can be used. Gently pry the crankshaft all the way to the front of the engine. Slip

10.3 Checking crankshaft endplay with feeler gauges at the thrust bearing journal

10.17 Place the Plastigage onto the crankshaft bearing journal as shown

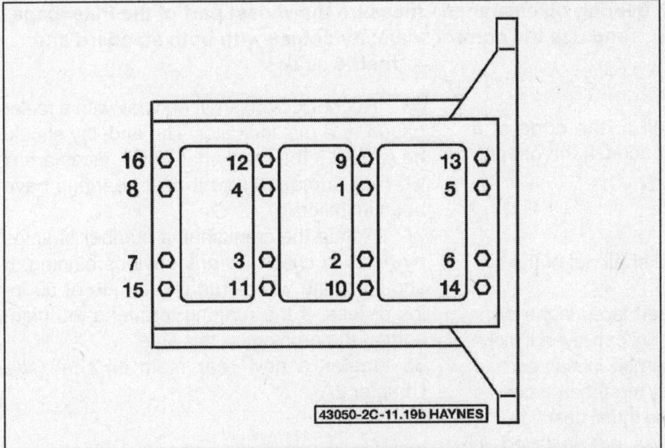

10.19a Main bearing cap bolt tightening sequence - 2005 and earlier 3.5L V6 models

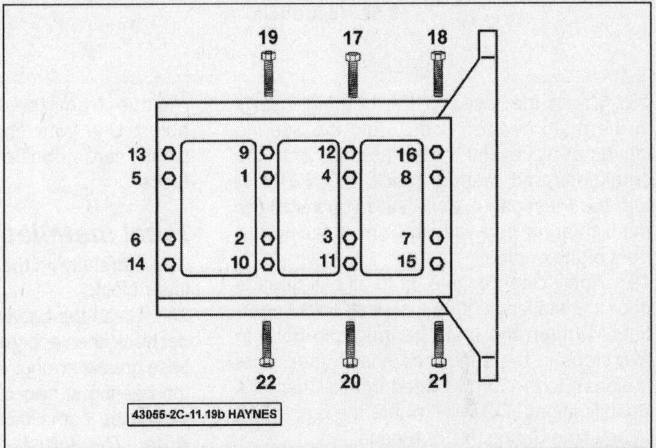

10.19b Main bearing cap bolt tightening sequence - 3.8L V6 models

feeler gauges between the crankshaft and the front face of the thrust bearing or washer to determine the clearance (see illustration).

4 Loosen the main bearing cap bolts (bearing cap assembly on 2005 and earlier 3.5L engines) (and side bolts if equipped), 1/4-turn at a time each, until they can be removed by hand in the reverse order of the tightening sequence (see illustration 10.19a, 10.19b or 10.19c).

5 Gently tap the main bearing caps with a soft-face hammer. Pull the main bearing cap straight up and off the cylinder block. Try not to drop the bearing inserts if they come out with the cap.

Note: *2005 and earlier 3.5L V6 engines use a mono-bearing cap that be removed as a unit.*

6 Carefully lift the crankshaft out of the engine. It may be a good idea to have an assistant available, since the crankshaft is quite heavy and awkward to handle. With the bearing inserts in place inside the engine block and main bearing caps, reinstall the main bearing caps onto the engine block and tighten the bolts finger tight. Make sure you install the main bearing cap(s) with the arrow facing the front end of the engine.

Installation and main bearing oil clearance check

7 Crankshaft installation is the first step in engine reassembly. It's assumed at this point that the engine block and crankshaft have been cleaned, inspected and repaired or reconditioned.

8 Position the engine block with the bottom facing up.

9 Remove the mounting bolts and lift off the main bearing cap(s).

10 If they're still in place, remove the original bearing inserts from the block and from the main bearing caps. Wipe the bearing surfaces of the block and main bearing caps with a clean, lint-free cloth. They must be kept spotlessly clean. This is critical for determining the correct bearing oil clearance.

11 Without mixing them up, clean the backs of the new upper main bearing inserts (with grooves and oil holes) and lay one in each main bearing saddle in the block. Each upper bearing has an oil groove and oil hole in it. Install the thrust washers with the grooved side facing out. Clean the back sides of the lower main bearing inserts (without grooves) and lay them in the corresponding caps. Make sure the tab on the bearing insert fits into the recess in the block or main bearing cap.

Caution: *The oil holes in the block must line up with the oil holes in the upper bearing inserts.*

Caution: *Do not hammer the bearing insert into place and don't nick or gouge the bearing faces. DO NOT apply any lubrication at this time.*

12 Clean the faces of the bearing inserts in the block and the crankshaft main bearing journals with a clean, lint-free cloth.

13 Check or clean the oil holes in the crankshaft, as any dirt here can go only one way - straight through the new bearings.

14 Once you're certain the crankshaft is clean, carefully lay it in position in the cylinder block.

15 Before the crankshaft can be permanently installed, the main bearing oil clearance must be checked.

16 Cut several strips of the appropriate size of Plastigage (they must be slightly shorter than the width of the main bearing journal).

17 Place one piece on each crankshaft main bearing journal, parallel with the journal axis (see illustration).

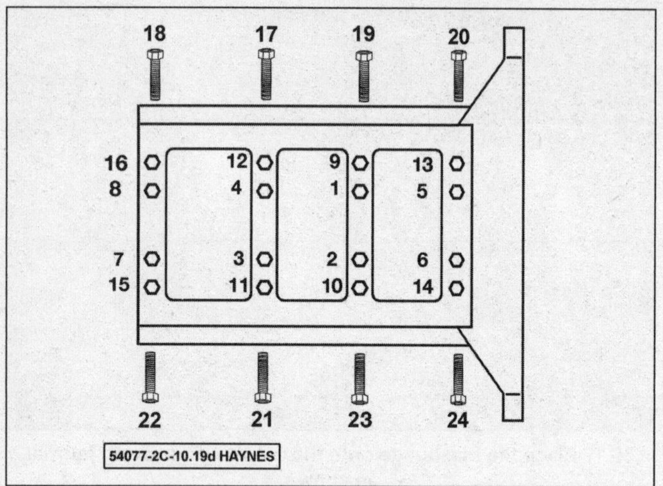

10.19c Main bearing cap bolt tightening sequence - 2011 and later 3.5L V6 models

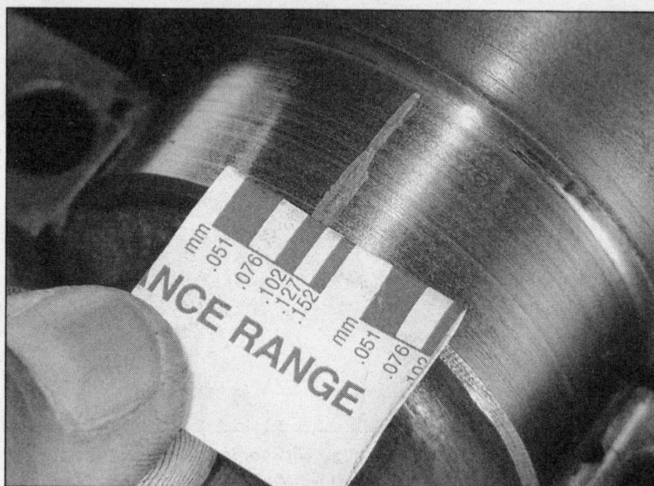

10.21 Use the scale on the Plastigage package to determine the bearing oil clearance - measure the widest part of the Plastigage and use the correct scale; itv comes with both standard and metric scales

18 Clean the faces of the bearing inserts in the main bearing caps. Hold the bearing inserts in place and install the caps onto the crankshaft and cylinder block. DO NOT disturb the Plastigage. Make sure you install the main bearing cap with the arrow facing the front of the engine.

19 Apply clean engine oil to all bolt threads prior to installation, then install all bolts finger-tight. Tighten the main bearing cap bolts in two steps in the sequence shown (see illustrations), to the torque listed in this Chapter's Specifications. DO NOT rotate the crankshaft at any time during this operation.

20 Remove the bolts in the reverse order of the tightening sequence and carefully lift the main bearing cap straight up and off the block. Do not disturb the Plastigage or rotate the crankshaft. If the main bearing cap is difficult to remove, tap it gently from side-to-side with a soft-face hammer to loosen it.

21 Compare the width of the crushed Plastigage on each journal to the scale printed on the Plastigage envelope to determine the main bearing oil clearance (see illustration). A typical main bearing oil clearance should fall between 0.0015 to 0.0023-inch. Check with an automotive machine shop for the clearance specified for your engine.

22 If the clearance is not as specified, the bearing inserts may be the wrong size (which means different ones will be required). Before deciding if different inserts are needed, make sure that no dirt or oil was between the bearing inserts and the cap or block when the clearance was measured. If the Plastigage was wider at one end than the other, the crankshaft journal may be tapered. If the clearance still exceeds the limit specified, the bearing insert(s) will have to be replaced with an undersize bearing insert(s).

Caution: *When installing a new crankshaft, always install a standard bearing insert set.*

23 Carefully scrape all traces of the Plastigage material off the main bearing journals and/or the bearing insert faces. Remove all residue from the oil holes. Use your fingernail or the edge of a plastic card - don't nick or scratch the bearing faces.

Final installation

24 Carefully lift the crankshaft out of the cylinder block.

25 Clean the bearing insert faces in the cylinder block, then apply a thin, uniform layer of moly-base grease or engine assembly lube to each of the bearing surfaces. Coat the thrust faces as well as the journal face of the thrust bearing.

Note: *The thrust bearings are installed in the no. 3 main cap/saddle position (counting from the front) on all engines covered by this manual.*

26 Make sure the crankshaft journals are clean, then lay the crankshaft back in place in the cylinder block.

27 Clean the bearing insert faces and apply the same lubricant to them.

28 Hold the bearing inserts in place and install the main bearing caps (cap assembly on 2005 and earlier 3.5L engines) on the crankshaft and cylinder block. Tap the bearing caps into place with a brass punch or a soft-face hammer.

29 Apply clean engine oil to the bolt threads, wipe off any excess oil and install the bolts finger-tight.

30 Tighten the main bearing cap bolts, to 10 or 12 foot-pounds, in the correct sequence (see illustration 10.19a, 10.19b or 10.19c).

31 Push the crankshaft forward using a screwdriver or prybar to seat the thrust bearing. Once the crankshaft is pushed fully forward to seat the thrust bearing, leave the screwdriver in position so that force stays on the crankshaft until after all main bearing cap bolts have been tightened.

32 Tighten the main bearing cap bolts in two steps, in sequence (see illustration 10.19a, 10.19b or 10.19c) and to the torque and angle listed in this Chapter's Specifications.

33 Recheck crankshaft endplay with a feeler gauge or a dial indicator. The endplay should be correct if the crankshaft thrust faces aren't worn or damaged and if new bearings have been installed.

34 Rotate the crankshaft a number of times by hand to check for any obvious binding. It should rotate with a running torque of 50 in-lbs or less. If the running torque is too high, correct the problem at this time.

35 Install a new rear main oil seal (see Chapter 2A).

11 Engine overhaul - reassembly sequence

1 Before beginning engine reassembly, make sure you have all the necessary new parts, gaskets and seals as well as the following items on hand:

Common hand tools
A 1/2-inch drive torque wrench
New engine oil
Gasket sealant
Thread locking compound

2 If you obtained a short block, it will be necessary to install the cylinder head, the oil pump and pick-up tube, the oil pan, the water pump, the timing belt/chain and timing cover, and the valve cover (see Chapter 2A). In order to save time and avoid problems, the external components must be installed in the following general order:

Thermostat and housing cover
Water pump
Intake and exhaust manifolds
Fuel injection components
Emission control components
Spark plugs
Ignition coils
Oil filter
Engine mounts and mount brackets
Driveplate (automatic transmission/transaxle)

12 Initial start-up and break-in after overhaul

Warning: *Have a fire extinguisher handy when starting the engine for the first time.*

1 Once the engine has been installed in the vehicle, double-check the engine oil and coolant levels.

2 With the spark plugs out of the engine and the ignition system and fuel pump disabled (see Section 3 to disable the ignition system and Chapter 4 to disable the fuel pump), crank the engine until oil pressure registers on the gauge or the light goes out.

3 Install the spark plugs and ignition coils and restore the fuel pump and ignition functions.

4 Start the engine. It may take a few moments for the fuel system to build up pressure, but the engine should start without a great deal of effort.

5 After the engine starts, it should be allowed to warm up to normal operating temperature. While the engine is warming up, make a thorough check for fuel, oil and coolant leaks.

6 Shut the engine off and recheck the engine oil and coolant levels.

7 Drive the vehicle to an area with minimum traffic, accelerate from 30 to 50 mph, then allow the vehicle to slow to 30 mph with the throttle closed. Repeat the procedure 10 or 12 times. This will load the piston rings and cause them to seat properly against the cylinder walls. Check again for oil and coolant leaks.

8 Drive the vehicle gently for the first 500 miles (no sustained high speeds) and keep a constant check on the oil level. It is not unusual for an engine to use oil during the break-in period.

9 At approximately 500 to 600 miles, change the oil and filter.

10 For the next few hundred miles, drive the vehicle normally. Do not pamper it or abuse it.

11 After 2,000 miles, change the oil and filter again and consider the engine broken in.

COMMON ENGINE OVERHAUL TERMS

B

Backlash - The amount of play between two parts. Usually refers to how much one gear can be moved back and forth without moving the gear with which it's meshed.

Bearing Caps - The caps held in place by nuts or bolts which, in turn, hold the bearing surface. This space is for lubricating oil to enter.

Bearing clearance - The amount of space left between shaft and bearing surface. This space is for lubricating oil to enter.

Bearing crush - The additional height which is purposely manufactured into each bearing half to ensure complete contact of the bearing back with the housing bore when the engine is assembled.

Bearing knock - The noise created by movement of a part in a loose or worn bearing.

Blueprinting - Dismantling an engine and reassembling it to EXACT specifications.

Bore - An engine cylinder, or any cylindrical hole; also used to describe the process of enlarging or accurately refinishing a hole with a cutting tool, as to bore an engine cylinder. The bore size is the diameter of the hole.

Boring - Renewing the cylinders by cutting them out to a specified size. A boring bar is used to make the cut.

Bottom end - A term which refers collectively to the engine block, crankshaft, main bearings and the big ends of the connecting rods.

Break-in - The period of operation between installation of new or rebuilt parts and time in which parts are worn to the correct fit. Driving at reduced and varying speed for a specified mileage to permit parts to wear to the correct fit.

Bushing - A one-piece sleeve placed in a bore to serve as a bearing surface for shaft, piston pin, etc. Usually replaceable.

C

Camshaft - The shaft in the engine, on which a series of lobes are located for operating the valve mechanisms. The camshaft is driven by gears or sprockets and a timing chain. Usually referred to simply as the cam.

Carbon - Hard, or soft, black deposits found in combustion chamber, on plugs, under rings, on and under valve heads.

Cast iron - An alloy of iron and more than two percent carbon, used for engine blocks and heads because it's relatively inexpensive and easy to mold into complex shapes.

Chamfer - To bevel across (or a bevel on) the sharp edge of an object.

Chase - To repair damaged threads with a tap or die.

Combustion chamber - The space between the piston and the cylinder head, with the piston at top dead center, in which air-fuel mixture is burned.

Compression ratio - The relationship between cylinder volume (clearance volume) when the piston is at top dead center and cylinder volume when the piston is at bottom dead center.

Connecting rod - The rod that connects the crank on the crankshaft with the piston. Sometimes called a con rod.

Connecting rod cap - The part of the connecting rod assembly that attaches the rod to the crankpin.

Core plug - Soft metal plug used to plug the casting holes for the coolant passages in the block.

Crankcase - The lower part of the engine in which the crankshaft rotates; includes the lower section of the cylinder block and the oil pan.

Crank kit - A reground or reconditioned crankshaft and new main and connecting rod bearings.

Crankpin - The part of a crankshaft to which a connecting rod is attached.

Crankshaft - The main rotating member, or shaft, running the length of the crankcase, with offset throws to which the connecting rods are attached; changes the reciprocating motion of the pistons into rotating motion.

Cylinder sleeve - A replaceable sleeve, or liner, pressed into the cylinder block to form the cylinder bore.

D

Deburring - Removing the burrs (rough edges or areas) from a bearing.

Deglazer - A tool, rotated by an electric motor, used to remove glaze from cylinder walls so a new set of rings will seat.

E

Endplay - The amount of lengthwise movement between two parts. As applied to a crankshaft, the distance that the crankshaft can move forward and back in the cylinder block.

F

Face - A machinist's term that refers to removing metal from the end of a shaft or the face of a larger part, such as a flywheel.

Fatigue - A breakdown of material through a large number of loading and unloading cycles. The first signs are cracks followed shortly by breaks.

Feeler gauge - A thin strip of hardened steel, ground to an exact thickness, used to check clearances between parts.

Free height - The unloaded length or height of a spring.

Freeplay - The looseness in a linkage, or an assembly of parts, between the initial application of force and actual movement. Usually perceived as slop or slight delay.

Freeze plug - See Core plug.

G

Gallery - A large passage in the block that forms a reservoir for engine oil pressure.

Glaze - The very smooth, glassy finish that develops on cylinder walls while an engine is in service.

H

Heli-Coil - A rethreading device used when threads are worn or damaged. The device is installed in a retapped hole to reduce the thread size to the original size.

I

Installed height - The spring's measured length or height, as installed on the cylinder head. Installed height is measured from the spring seat to the underside of the spring retainer.

J

Journal - The surface of a rotating shaft which turns in a bearing.

K

Keeper - The split lock that holds the valve spring retainer in position on the valve stem.

Key - A small piece of metal inserted into matching grooves machined into two parts fitted together - such as a gear pressed onto a shaft - which prevents slippage between the two parts.

Knock - The heavy metallic engine sound, produced in the combustion chamber as a result of abnormal combustion - usually detonation. Knock is usually caused by a loose or worn bearing. Also referred to as detonation, pinging and spark knock. Connecting rod or main bearing knocks are created by too much oil clearance or insufficient lubrication.

L

Lands - The portions of metal between the piston ring grooves.

Lapping the valves - Grinding a valve face and its seat together with lapping compound.

Lash - The amount of free motion in a gear train, between gears, or in a mechanical assembly, that occurs before movement can begin. Usually refers to the lash in a valve train.

Lifter - The part that rides against the cam to transfer motion to the rest of the valve train.

M

Machining - The process of using a machine to remove metal from a metal part.

Main bearings - The plain, or babbit, bearings that support the crankshaft.

Main bearing caps - The cast iron caps, bolted to the bottom of the block, that support the main bearings.

O

O.D. - Outside diameter.

Oil gallery - A pipe or drilled passageway in the engine used to carry engine oil from one area to another.

Oil ring - The lower ring, or rings, of a piston; designed to prevent excessive amounts of oil from working up the cylinder walls and into the combustion chamber. Also called an oil-control ring.

Oil seal - A seal which keeps oil from leaking out of a compartment. Usually refers to a dynamic seal around a rotating shaft or other moving part.

O-ring - A type of sealing ring made of a special rubber-like material; in use, the O-ring is compressed into a groove to provide the sealing action.

Overhaul - To completely disassemble a unit, clean and inspect all parts, reassemble it with the original or new parts and make all adjustments necessary for proper operation.

P

Pilot bearing - A small bearing installed in the center of the flywheel (or the rear end of the crankshaft) to support the front end of the input shaft of the transmission.

Pip mark - A little dot or indentation which indicates the top side of a compression ring.

Piston - The cylindrical part, attached to the connecting rod, that moves up and down in the cylinder as the crankshaft rotates. When the fuel charge is fired, the piston transfers the force of the explosion to the connecting rod, then to the crankshaft.

Piston pin (or wrist pin) - The cylindrical and usually hollow steel pin that passes through the piston. The piston pin fastens the piston to the upper end of the connecting rod.

Piston ring - The split ring fitted to the groove in a piston. The ring contacts the sides of the ring groove and also rubs against the cylinder wall, thus sealing space between piston and wall. There are two types of rings: Compression rings seal the compression pressure in the combustion chamber; oil rings scrape excessive oil off the cylinder wall.

Piston ring groove - The slots or grooves cut in piston heads to hold piston rings in position.

Piston skirt - The portion of the piston below the rings and the piston pin hole.

Plastigage - A thin strip of plastic thread, available in different sizes, used for measuring clearances. For example, a strip of plastigage is laid across a bearing journal and mashed as parts are assembled. Then parts are disassembled and the width of the strip is measured to determine clearance between journal and bearing. Commonly used to measure crankshaft main-bearing and connecting rod bearing clearances.

Press-fit - A tight fit between two parts that requires pressure to force the parts together. Also referred to as drive, or force, fit.

Prussian blue - A blue pigment; in solution, useful in determining the area of contact between two surfaces. Prussian blue is commonly used to determine the width and location of the contact area between the valve face and the valve seat.

R

Race (bearing) - The inner or outer ring that provides a contact surface for balls or rollers in bearing.

Ream - To size, enlarge or smooth a hole by using a round cutting tool with fluted edges.

Ring job - The process of reconditioning the cylinders and installing new rings.

Runout - Wobble. The amount a shaft rotates out-of-true.

S

Saddle - The upper main bearing seat.

Scored - Scratched or grooved, as a cylinder wall may be scored by abrasive particles moved up and down by the piston rings.

Scuffing - A type of wear in which there's a transfer of material between parts moving against each other; shows up as pits or grooves in the mating surfaces.

Seat - The surface upon which another part rests or seats. For example, the valve seat is the matched surface upon which the valve face rests. Also used to refer to wearing into a good fit; for example, piston rings seat after a few miles of driving.

Short block - An engine block complete with crankshaft and piston and, usually, camshaft assemblies.

Static balance - The balance of an object while it's stationary.

Step - The wear on the lower portion of a ring land caused by excessive side and back-clearance. The height of the step indicates the ring's extra side clearance and the length of the step projecting from the back wall of the groove represents the ring's back clearance.

Stroke - The distance the piston moves when traveling from top dead center to bottom dead center, or from bottom dead center to top dead center.

Stud - A metal rod with threads on both ends.

T

Tang - A lip on the end of a plain bearing used to align the bearing during assembly.

Tap - To cut threads in a hole. Also refers to the fluted tool used to cut threads.

Taper - A gradual reduction in the width of a shaft or hole; in an engine cylinder, taper usually takes the form of uneven wear, more pronounced at the top than at the bottom.

Throws - The offset portions of the crankshaft to which the connecting rods are affixed.

Thrust bearing - The main bearing that has thrust faces to prevent excessive endplay, or forward and backward movement of the crankshaft.

Thrust washer - A bronze or hardened steel washer placed between two moving parts. The washer prevents longitudinal movement and provides a bearing surface for thrust surfaces of parts.

Tolerance - The amount of variation permitted from an exact size of measurement. Actual amount from smallest acceptable dimension to largest acceptable dimension.

U

Umbrella - An oil deflector placed near the valve tip to throw oil from the valve stem area.

Undercut - A machined groove below the normal surface.

Undersize bearings - Smaller diameter bearings used with re-ground crankshaft journals.

V

Valve grinding - Refacing a valve in a valve-refacing machine.

Valve train - The valve-operating mechanism of an engine; includes all components from the camshaft to the valve.

Vibration damper - A cylindrical weight attached to the front of the crankshaft to minimize torsional vibration (the twist-untwist actions of the crankshaft caused by the cylinder firing impulses). Also called a harmonic balancer.

W

Water jacket - The spaces around the cylinders, between the inner and outer shells of the cylinder block or head, through which coolant circulates.

Web - A supporting structure across a cavity.

Woodruff key - A key with a radiused backside (viewed from the side).

Notes

Chapter 3
Cooling, heating and air conditioning systems

Contents

	Section
Air conditioning and heating system - check and maintenance	3
Air conditioning compressor - removal and installation	12
Air conditioning condenser - removal and installation	14
Air conditioning receiver-drier - removal and installation	13
Blower motor resistor/power module and blower motor assembly - replacement	9
Coolant reservoir - removal and installation	6
Engine cooling fan - replacement	5
Expansion valve - removal and installation	15
General information	1
Heater/air conditioner control assembly - removal and installation	11
Heater core - replacement	10
Radiator - removal and installation	7
Rear heating and air conditioning housing - removal and installation	16
Thermostat - replacement	4
Troubleshooting	2
Water pump - replacement	8

Specifications

General

Radiator cap pressure rating	14 to 18 psi	94 to 122 kPa
Thermostat rating		
Normal opening temperature	180 degrees F	82 degrees C
Wide open temperature	192 degrees F	95 degrees C
Cooling system capacity	See Chapter 1	
R134a Refrigerant capacity*		
2005 and earlier models	35.27 +/- 0.88 ounces	1000 +/- 25 grams
2006 and later models	31.7 +/- 0.88 ounces	900 +/- 25 grams

** Check the refrigerant capacity listed on the underhood HVAC label; if the charge capacity listed on the label differs from that shown here, assume the label is correct.*

Torque specifications

Note: *One foot-pound (ft-lb) of torque is equivalent to 12 inch-pounds (in-lbs) of torque. Torque values below approximately 15 ft-lbs are expressed in inch-pounds, since most foot-pound torque wrenches are not accurate at these smaller values.*

	Ft-lbs (unless otherwise indicated)	**Nm**
Thermostat housing bolts	144 to 180 in-lbs	17 to 19.5
Water inlet tube bolts		
2005 and earlier models	156 to 174 in-lbs	17 to 19.5
2006 and later models	14 to 17	19 to 24
Water pump mounting bolts		
2005 and earlier models (see illustration 8.10)		
Bolt A	132 to 192 in-lbs	15 to 21
Bolt B	24 to 36	32 to 49
Bolt C	15 to 19	20 to 26
2006 through 2010 models		
8 mm bolts	90 to 102 in-lbs	10 to 11.5
10 mm and 12 mm bolts	16 to 17	22 to 23
2011 and later models (see illustration 8.13)		
Bolt A	16 to 17	22 to 23
Bolt B, C, D and E	90 to 102 in-lbs	10 to 11.5
Bolt F*	16 to 19	22 to 26

**Use new bolt*

2.2 The cooling system pressure tester is connected in place of the pressure cap, then pumped up to pressurize the system

2.5a The combustion leak detector consists of a bulb, syringe and test fluid

2.5b Place the tester over the cooling system filler neck and use the bulb to draw a sample into the tester

1 General Information

Warning: *Do not allow antifreeze to come in contact with your skin or painted surfaces of the vehicle. Rinse off spills immediately with plenty of water. Antifreeze is highly toxic if ingested. Never leave antifreeze lying around in an open container or in puddles on the floor; children and pets are attracted by its sweet smell and may drink it. Check with local authorities about disposing of used antifreeze. Many communities have collection centers which will see that antifreeze is disposed of safely. Never dump used antifreeze on the ground or pour it into drains.*

Engine cooling system

1 All modern vehicles employ a pressurized engine cooling system with thermostatically controlled coolant circulation. The cooling system consists of a radiator, an expansion tank or coolant reservoir, a pressure cap (located on the expansion tank or radiator), a thermostat, a cooling fan, and a water pump.

2 The water pump circulates coolant through the engine. The coolant flows around each cylinder and around the intake and exhaust ports, near the spark plug areas and in close proximity to the exhaust valve guides.

3 A thermostat controls engine coolant temperature. During warm up, the closed thermostat prevents coolant from circulating through the radiator. As the engine nears normal operating temperature, the thermostat opens and allows hot coolant to travel through the radiator, where it's cooled before returning to the engine.

Heating system

4 The heating system consists of a blower fan and heater core located in a housing under the dash, the hoses connecting the heater core to the engine cooling system and the heater/air conditioning control head on the dashboard. Hot engine coolant is circulated through the heater core. When the heater mode is activated, a flap door in the housing opens to expose the heater core to the passenger compartment through air ducts. A fan switch on the control head activates the blower motor, which forces air through the core, heating the air.

Air conditioning system

5 The air conditioning system consists of a condenser mounted in front of the radiator, an evaporator mounted adjacent to the heater core, a compressor mounted on the engine, a receiver-drier or accumulator and the plumbing connecting all of the above components.

6 A blower fan forces the warmer air of the passenger compartment through the evaporator core (sort of a radiator-in-reverse), transferring the heat from the air to the refrigerant. The liquid refrigerant boils off into low pressure vapor, taking the heat with it when it leaves the evaporator.

2 Troubleshooting

Coolant leaks

1 A coolant leak can develop anywhere in the cooling system, but the most common causes are:

- *a) A loose or weak hose clamp*
- *b) A defective hose*
- *c) A faulty pressure cap*
- *d) A faulty pressure cap*
- *e) A damaged radiator*
- *f) A bad heater core*
- *g) A faulty water pump*
- *h) A faulty water pump*

2 Coolant leaks aren't always easy to find. Sometimes they can only be detected when the cooling system is under pressure. Here's where a cooling system pressure tester comes in handy. After the engine has cooled completely, the tester is attached in place of the pressure cap, then pumped up to the pressure value equal to that of the pressure cap rating (see illustration). Now, leaks that only exist when the engine is fully warmed up will become apparent. The tester can be left connected to locate a nagging slow leak.

Coolant level drops, but no external leaks

3 If you find it necessary to keep adding coolant, but there are no external leaks, the probable causes include:

- *a) A blown head gasket*
- *b) A leaking intake manifold gasket (only on engines that have coolant passages in the manifold)cracked cylinder head or cylinder block*

4 Any of the above problems will also usually result in contamination of the engine oil, which will cause it to take on a milkshake-like appearance. A bad head gasket or cracked head or block can also result in engine oil contaminating the cooling system.

5 Combustion leak detectors (also known as block testers) are available at most auto parts stores. These work by detecting exhaust gases in the cooling system, which indicates a compression leak from a cylinder into the coolant. The tester consists of a large bulb-type syringe and bottle of test fluid (see illustration). A measured amount of the fluid is added to the syringe. The syringe is placed over the cooling system filler neck and, with the engine running, the bulb is squeezed and a sample of the gases present in the cooling system are drawn up through the test fluid (see illustration). If any combustion gases are present in the sample taken, the test fluid will change color.

6 If the test indicates combustion gas is present in the cooling system, you can be sure that the engine has a blown head gasket or a crack in the cylinder head or block, and will require disassembly to repair.

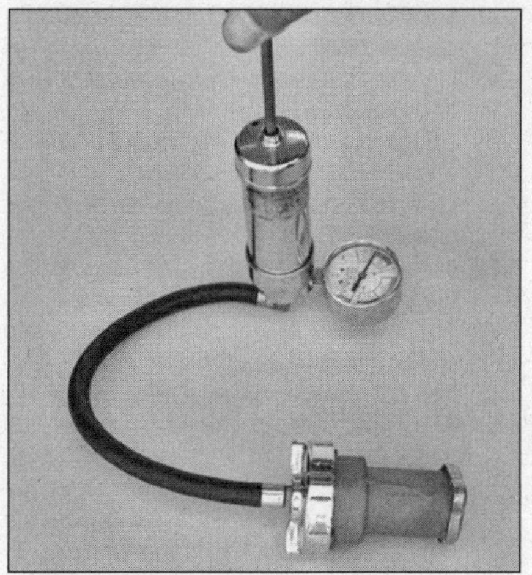

2.8 Checking the cooling system pressure cap with a cooling system pressure tester

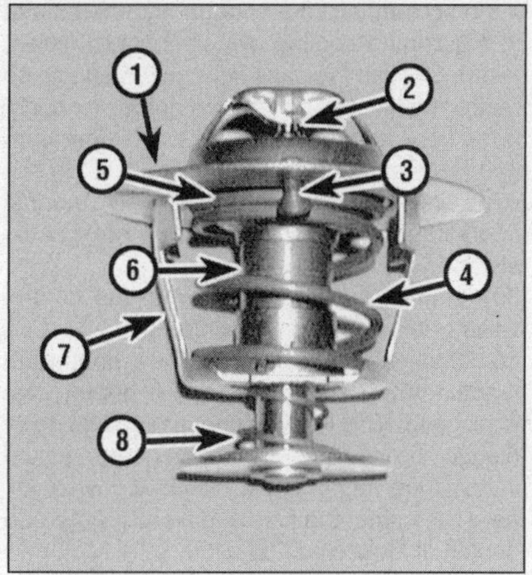

2.10 Typical thermostat

1 Flange
2 Piston
3 Jiggle valve
4 Main coil spring
5 Valve seat
6 Valve
7 Frame
8 Secondary coil spring

2.28 The water pump weep hole is generally located on the underside of the pump

Pressure cap

Warning: *Wait until the engine is completely cool before beginning this check.*

7 The cooling system is sealed by a spring-loaded cap, which raises the boiling point of the coolant. If the cap's seal or spring are worn out, the coolant can boil and escape past the cap. With the engine completely cool, remove the cap and check the seal; if it's cracked, hardened or deteriorated in any way, replace it with a new one.

8 Even if the seal is good, the spring might not be; this can be checked with a cooling system pressure tester (see illustration). If the cap can't hold a pressure within approximately 1-1/2 lbs of its rated pressure (which is marked on the cap), replace it with a new one.

9 The cap is also equipped with a vacuum relief spring. When the engine cools off, a vacuum is created in the cooling system. The vacuum relief spring allows air back into the system, which will equalize the pressure and prevent damage to the radiator (the radiator tanks could collapse if the vacuum is great enough). If, after turning the engine off and allowing it to cool down you notice any of the cooling system hoses collapsing, replace the pressure cap with a new one.

Thermostat

10 Before assuming the thermostat (see illustration) is responsible for a cooling system problem, check the coolant level (see Chapter 1), drivebelt tension (see Chapter 1) and temperature gauge (or light) operation.

11 If the engine takes a long time to warm up (as indicated by the temperature gauge or heater operation), the thermostat is probably stuck open. Replace the thermostat with a new one.

12 If the engine runs hot or overheats, a thorough test of the thermostat should be performed.

13 Definitive testing of the thermostat can only be made when it is removed from the vehicle. If the thermostat is stuck in the open position at room temperature, it is faulty and must be replaced.

Caution: *Do not drive the vehicle without a thermostat. The computer may stay in open loop and emissions and fuel economy will suffer.*

14 To test a thermostat, suspend the (closed) thermostat on a length of string or wire in a pot of cold water.

15 Heat the water on a stove while observing thermostat. The thermostat should fully open before the water boils.

16 If the thermostat doesn't open and close as specified, or sticks in any position, replace it.

Cooling fan

Electric cooling fan

17 If the engine is overheating and the cooling fan is not coming on when the engine temperature rises to an excessive level, unplug the fan motor electrical connector(s) and connect the motor directly to the battery with fused jumper wires. If the fan motor doesn't come on, replace the motor.

18 If the radiator fan motor is okay, but it isn't coming on when the engine gets hot, the fan relay might be defective. A relay is used to control a circuit by turning it on and off in response to a control decision by the Powertrain Control Module (PCM). These control circuits are fairly complex, and checking them should be left to a qualified automotive technician. Sometimes, the control system can be fixed by simply identifying and replacing a bad relay.

19 Locate the fan relays in the engine compartment fuse/relay box.

20 Test the relay (see Chapter 12).

21 If the relay is okay, check all wiring and connections to the fan motor. Refer to the wiring diagrams at the end of Chapter 12. If no obvious problems are found, the problem could be the Engine Coolant Temperature (ECT) sensor or the Powertrain Control Module (PCM). Have the cooling fan system and circuit diagnosed by a dealer service department or repair shop with the proper diagnostic equipment.

Belt-driven cooling fan

22 Disconnect the cable from the negative terminal of the battery and rock the fan back and forth by hand to check for excessive bearing play.

23 With the engine cold (and not running), turn the fan blades by hand. The fan should turn freely.

24 Visually inspect for substantial fluid leakage from the clutch assembly. If problems are noted, replace the clutch assembly.

25 With the engine completely warmed up, turn off the ignition switch and disconnect the negative battery cable from the battery. Turn the fan by hand. Some drag should be evident. If the fan turns easily, replace the fan clutch.

Water pump

26 A failure in the water pump can cause serious engine damage due to overheating.

Drivebelt-driven water pump

27 There are two ways to check the operation of the water pump while it's installed on the engine. If the pump is found to be defective, it should be replaced with a new or rebuilt unit.

28 Water pumps are equipped with weep (or vent) holes (see illustration). If a failure occurs in the pump seal, coolant will leak from the hole.

29 If the water pump shaft bearings fail, there may be a howling sound at the pump

while it's running. Shaft wear can be felt with the drivebelt removed if the water pump pulley is rocked up and down (with the engine off). Don't mistake drivebelt slippage, which causes a squealing sound, for water pump bearing failure.

Timing chain or timing belt-driven water pump

30 Water pumps driven by the timing chain or timing belt are located underneath the timing chain or timing belt cover.

31 Checking the water pump is limited because of where it is located. However, some basic checks can be made before deciding to remove the water pump. If the pump is found to be defective, it should be replaced with a new or rebuilt unit.

32 One sign that the water pump may be failing is that the heater (climate control) may not work well. Warm the engine to normal operating temperature, confirm that the coolant level is correct, then run the heater and check for hot air coming from the ducts.

33 Check for noises coming from the water pump area. If the water pump impeller shaft or bearings are failing, there may be a howling sound at the pump while the engine is running.

Note: *Be careful not to mistake drivebelt noise (squealing) for water pump bearing or shaft failure.*

34 It you suspect water pump failure due to noise, wear can be confirmed by feeling for play at the pump shaft. This can be done by rocking the drive sprocket on the pump shaft up and down. To do this you will need to remove the tension on the timing chain or belt as well as access the water pump.

All water pumps

35 In rare cases or on high-mileage vehicles, another sign of water pump failure may be the presence of coolant in the engine oil. This condition will adversely affect the engine in varying degrees.

Note: *Finding coolant in the engine oil could indicate other serious issues besides a failed water pump, such as a blown head gasket or a cracked cylinder head or block.*

36 Even a pump that exhibits no outward signs of a problem, such as noise or leakage, can still be due for replacement. Removal for close examination is the only sure way to tell. Sometimes the fins on the back of the impeller can corrode to the point that cooling efficiency is diminished significantly.

Heater system

37 Little can go wrong with a heater. If the fan motor will run at all speeds, the electrical part of the system is okay. The three basic heater problems fall into the following general categories:

- a) *Not enough heat*
- b) *Heat all the time*
- c) *No heat*

38 If there's not enough heat, the control valve or door is stuck in a partially open position, the coolant coming from the engine isn't hot enough, or the heater core is restricted. If the coolant isn't hot enough, the thermostat in the engine cooling system is stuck open, allowing coolant to pass through the engine so rapidly that it doesn't heat up quickly enough. If the vehicle is equipped with a temperature gauge instead of a warning light, watch to see if the engine temperature rises to the normal operating range after driving for a reasonable distance.

39 If there's heat all the time, the control valve or the door is stuck wide open.

40 If there's no heat, coolant is probably not reaching the heater core, or the heater core is plugged. The likely cause is a collapsed or plugged hose, core, or a frozen heater control valve. If the heater is the type that flows coolant all the time, the cause is a stuck door or a broken or kinked control cable.

Air conditioning system

41 If the cool air output is inadequate:

- a) *Inspect the condenser coils and fins to make sure they're clear*
- b) *Check the compressor clutch for slippage*
- c) *Check the blower motor for proper operation*
- d) *Inspect the blower discharge passage for obstructions*
- e) *Check the system air intake filter for clogging*

42 If the system provides intermittent cooling air:

- a) *Check the circuit breaker, blower switch and blower motor for a malfunction*
- b) *Make sure the compressor clutch isn't slipping*
- c) *Inspect the plenum door to make sure it's operating properly*
- d) *Inspect the evaporator to make sure it isn't clogged*
- e) *If the unit is icing up, it may be caused by excessive moisture in the system, incorrect super heat switch adjustment or low thermostat adjustment*

43 If the system provides no cooling air:

- a) *Inspect the compressor drivebelt. Make sure it's not loose or broken.*
- b) *Make sure the compressor clutch engages. If it doesn't, check for a blown fuse.*
- c) *Inspect the wire harness for broken or disconnected wires*
- d) *If the compressor clutch doesn't engage, bridge the terminals of the A/C pressure switch(es) with a jumper wire; if the clutch now engages, and the system is properly charged, the pressure switch is bad*
- e) *Make sure the blower motor is not disconnected or burned out*
- f) *Make sure the compressor isn't partially or completely seized*
- g) *Inspect the refrigerant lines for leaks*
- h) *Check the components for leaks*
- i) *Inspect the receiver-drier/accumulator or expansion valve/tube for clogged screens*

44 If the system is noisy:

- a) *Look for loose panels in the passenger compartment*
- b) *Inspect the compressor drivebelt. It may be loose or worn.*
- c) *Check the compressor mounting bolts. They should be tight.*
- d) *Listen carefully to the compressor. It may be worn out.*
- e) *Listen to the idler pulley and bearing and the clutch. Either may be defective.*
- f) *The winding in the compressor clutch coil or solenoid may be defective*
- g) *The compressor oil level may be low*
- h) *The blower motor fan bushing or the motor itself may be worn out*
- i) *If there is an excessive charge in the system, you'll hear a rumbling noise in the high pressure line, a thumping noise in the compressor, or see bubbles or cloudiness in the sight glass*
- j) *If there's a low charge in the system, you might hear hissing in the evaporator case at the expansion valve, or see bubbles or cloudiness in the sight glass*

3 Air conditioning and heating system - check and maintenance

Air conditioning system

Warning: *The air conditioning system is under high pressure. Do not loosen any hose fittings or remove any components until after the system has been discharged. Air conditioning refrigerant should be properly discharged into an EPA-approved recovery/recycling unit at a dealer service department or an automotive air conditioning repair facility. Always wear eye protection when disconnecting air conditioning system fittings.*

Caution: *All models covered by this manual use environmentally friendly R-134a. This refrigerant (and its appropriate refrigerant oils) are not compatible with R-12 refrigerant system components and must never be mixed or the components will be damaged.*

Caution: *When replacing entire components, additional refrigerant oil should be added equal to the amount that is removed with the component being replaced. Be sure to read the can before adding any oil to the system, to make sure it is compatible with the R-134a system.*

1 The following maintenance checks should be performed on a regular basis to ensure that the air conditioning continues to operate at peak efficiency.

- a) *Inspect the condition of the compressor drivebelt. If it is worn or deteriorated, replace it (see Chapter 1).*
- b) *Check the drivebelt tension (see Chapter 1).*
- c) *Inspect the system hoses. Look for cracks, bubbles, hardening and deterioration. Inspect the hoses and all fittings for oil bubbles or seepage. If there is any evidence of wear, damage or leakage, replace the hose(s).*

3.9 Insert a thermometer in the center vent, turn on the air conditioning system and wait for it to cool down;depending on the humidity, the output air should be 35 to 40 degrees cooler than the ambient air temperature

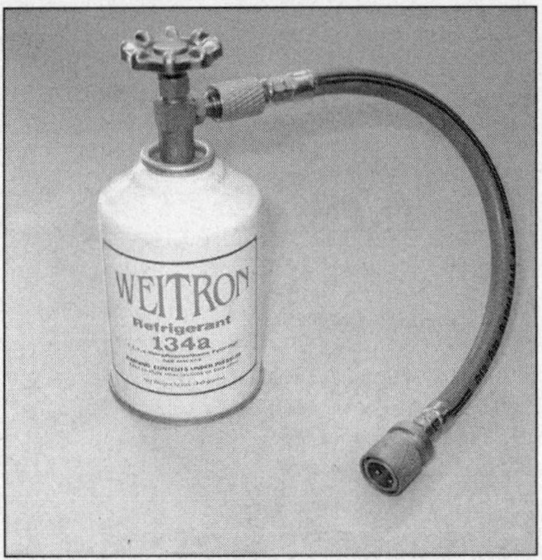

3.11 R-134a automotive air conditioning charging kit

3.13 Location of the low-side charging port

d) *Inspect the condenser fins for leaves, bugs and any other foreign material that may have embedded itself in the fins. Use a fin comb or compressed air to remove debris from the condenser.*

e) *Make sure the system has the correct refrigerant charge.*

f) *If you hear water sloshing around in the dash area or have water dripping on the carpet, check the evaporator housing drain tube and insert a piece of wire into the opening to check for blockage.*

2 It's a good idea to operate the system for about ten minutes at least once a month. This is particularly important during the winter months because long term non-use can cause hardening, and subsequent failure, of the seals. Note that using the Defrost function operates the compressor.

3 If the air conditioning system is not working properly, proceed to Step 6 and perform the general checks outlined below.

4 Because of the complexity of the air conditioning system and the special equipment necessary to service it, in-depth troubleshooting and repairs beyond checking the refrigerant charge and the compressor clutch operation are not included in this manual. However, simple checks and component replacement procedures are provided in this Chapter. For more complete information on the air conditioning system, refer to the Haynes Automotive Heating and Air Conditioning Manual.

5 The most common cause of poor cooling is simply a low system refrigerant charge. If a noticeable drop in system cooling ability occurs, one of the following quick checks will help you determine if the refrigerant level is low.

Checking the refrigerant charge

6 Warm the engine up to normal operating temperature.

7 Place the air conditioning temperature selector at the coldest setting and put the blower at the highest setting.

8 After the system reaches operating temperature, feel the larger pipe exiting the evaporator at the firewall. The outlet pipe should be cold (the tubing that leads back to the compressor). If the evaporator outlet pipe is warm, the system probably needs a charge.

9 Insert a thermometer in the center air distribution duct (see illustration) while operating the air conditioning system at its maximum setting - the temperature of the output air should be 35 to 40 degrees F below the ambient air temperature (down to approximately 40 degrees F). If the ambient (outside) air temperature is very high, say 110 degrees F, the duct air temperature may be as high as 60 degrees F, but generally the air conditioning is 35 to 40 degrees F cooler than the ambient air.

10 Further inspection or testing of the system requires special tools and techniques and is beyond the scope of the home mechanic.

Adding refrigerant

Caution: *Make sure any refrigerant, refrigerant oil or replacement component you purchase is designated as compatible with R-134a systems.*

11 Purchase an R-134a automotive charging kit at an auto parts store (see illustration). A charging kit includes a can of refrigerant, a tap valve and a short section of hose that can be attached between the tap valve and the system low side service valve.

Caution: *Never add more than one can of refrigerant to the system. If more refrigerant than that is required, the system should be evacuated and leak tested.*

12 Back off the valve handle on the charging kit and screw the kit onto the refrigerant can, making sure first that the O-ring or rubber seal inside the threaded portion of the kit is in place.

Warning: *Wear protective eyewear when dealing with pressurized refrigerant cans.*

13 Remove the dust cap from the low-side charging port and attach the hose's quick-connect fitting to the port (see illustration). Warning: DO NOT hook the charging kit hose to the system high side! The fittings on the charging kit are designed to fit only on the low side of the system.

14 Warm up the engine and turn On the air conditioning. Keep the charging kit hose away from the fan and other moving parts.

Note: *The charging process requires the compressor to be running. If the clutch cycles off, you can put the air conditioning switch on High and leave the car doors open to keep the clutch on and compressor working.The compressor can be kept on during the charging by removing the connector from the pressure switch and bridging it with a paper clip or jumper wire during the procedure.*

15 Turn the valve handle on the kit until the stem pierces the can, then back the handle out to release the refrigerant. You should be able to hear the rush of gas. Keep the can upright at all times, but shake it occasionally. Allow stabilization time between each addition.

Note: *The charging process will go faster if you wrap the can with a hot-water-soaked rag to keep the can from freezing up.*

16 If you have an accurate thermometer, you can place it in the center air conditioning duct inside the vehicle and keep track of the output air temperature. A charged system that is working properly should cool down to approximately 40 degrees F. If the ambient (outside) air temperature is very high, say 110 degrees F, the duct air temperature may be as high as 60 degrees F, but generally the air conditioning is 35 to 40 degrees F cooler than the ambient air.

17 When the can is empty, turn the valve handle to the closed position and release the

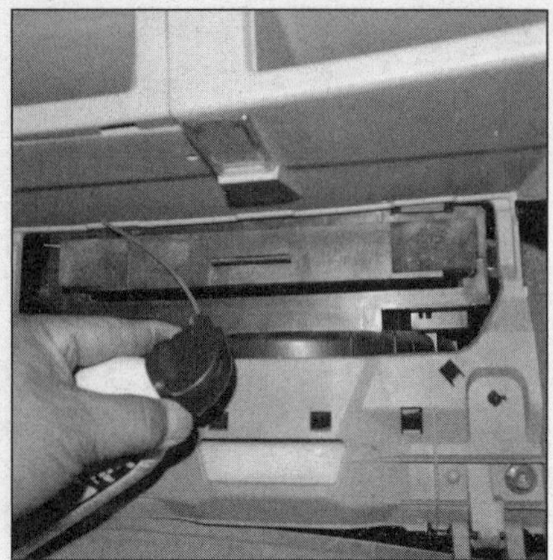

3.24 Insert the nozzle of the disinfectant can into the return-air intake behind the glove box

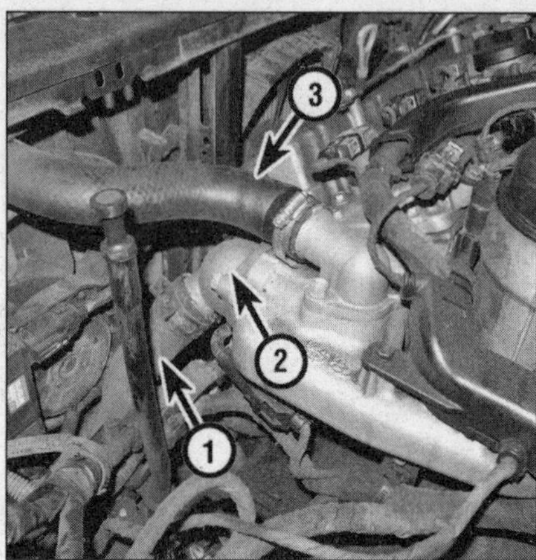

4.2 Both radiator hoses attach to the same area - the thermostat is in the housing at the end of the lower hose

1 *Lower radiator hose*
2 *Thermostat housing cover*
3 *Upper radiator hose*

4.3 Thermostat housing bolts

connection from the low-side port. Reinstall the dust cap.

18 Remove the charging kit from the can and store the kit for future use with the piercing valve in the UP position, to prevent inadvertently piercing the can on the next use.

Heating systems

19 If the carpet under the heater core is damp, or if antifreeze vapor or steam is coming through the vents, the heater core is leaking. Remove it (see Section 10) and install a new unit (most radiator shops will not repair a leaking heater core).

20 If the air coming out of the heater vents isn't hot, the problem could stem from any of the following causes:

a) *The thermostat is stuck open, preventing the engine coolant from warming up enough to carry heat to the heater core. Replace the thermostat (see Section 4).*
b) *There is a blockage in the system, preventing the flow of coolant through the heater core. Feel both heater hoses at the firewall. They should be hot. If one of them is cold, there is an obstruction in one of the hoses or in the heater core, or the heater control valve is shut. Detach the hoses and back flush the heater core with a water hose. If the heater core is clear but circulation is impeded, remove the two hoses and flush them out with a water hose.*
c) *If flushing fails to remove the blockage from the heater core, the core must be replaced (see Section 10).*

Eliminating air conditioning odors

21 Unpleasant odors that often develop in air conditioning systems are caused by the growth of a fungus, usually on the surface of the evaporator core. The warm, humid environment there is a perfect breeding ground for mildew to develop.

22 The evaporator core on most vehicles is difficult to access, and factory dealerships have a lengthy, expensive process for eliminating the fungus by opening up the evaporator case and using a powerful disinfectant and rinse on the core until the fungus is gone. You can service your own system at home, but it takes something much stronger than basic household germ-killers or deodorizers.

23 Aerosol disinfectants for automotive air conditioning systems are available in most auto parts stores, but remember when shopping for them that the most effective treatments are also the most expensive. The basic procedure for using these sprays is to start by running the system in the RECIRC mode for ten minutes with the blower on its highest speed. Use the highest heat mode to dry out the system and keep the compressor from engaging by disconnecting the wiring connector at the compressor.

24 The disinfectant can usually comes with a long spray hose. Insert the nozzle into an intake port inside the cabin filter housing, and spray according to the manufacturer's recommendations (see illustration). Try to cover the whole surface of the evaporator core, by aiming the spray up, down and sideways. Follow the manufacturer's recommendations for the length of spray and waiting time between applications.

25 Once the evaporator has been cleaned, the best way to prevent the mildew from coming back again is to make sure your evaporator housing drain tube is clear.

Automatic heating and air conditioning systems

26 Some vehicles are equipped with an optional automatic climate control system. This system has its own computer that receives inputs from various sensors in the heating and air conditioning system. This computer, like the PCM, has self-diagnostic capabilities to help pinpoint problems or faults within the system. Vehicles equipped with automatic heating and air conditioning systems are very complex and considered beyond the scope of the home mechanic. Vehicles equipped with automatic heating and air conditioning systems should be taken to a dealer service department or other qualified facility for repair.

4 Thermostat - replacement

Warning: *Do not attempt to remove the coolant reservoir (surge tank) cap, coolant or thermostat until the engine has cooled completely.*

Removal

1 Drain the cooling system (see Chapter 1).

2 Follow the radiator hose to the thermostat housing cover and disconnect the hose (see illustration).

3 Remove the thermostat housing cover mounting fasteners and remove the housing (see illustration). Be prepared for some coolant to spill as the gasket seal is broken.

4 Remove the thermostat, noting the direction in which it was installed in the housing, and thoroughly clean the sealing surfaces.

5 Install a new gasket onto the thermostat. Make sure it is evenly fitted all the way around (see illustration).

6 Install the thermostat and housing, positioning the jiggle pin at the highest point (see illustration).

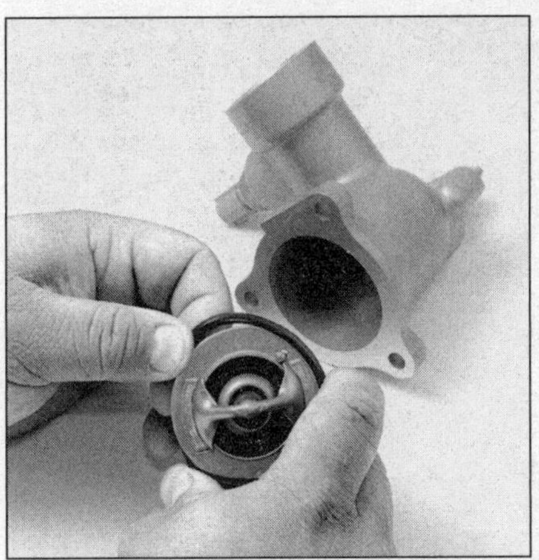

4.5 The thermostat seal fits around the edge of the thermostat

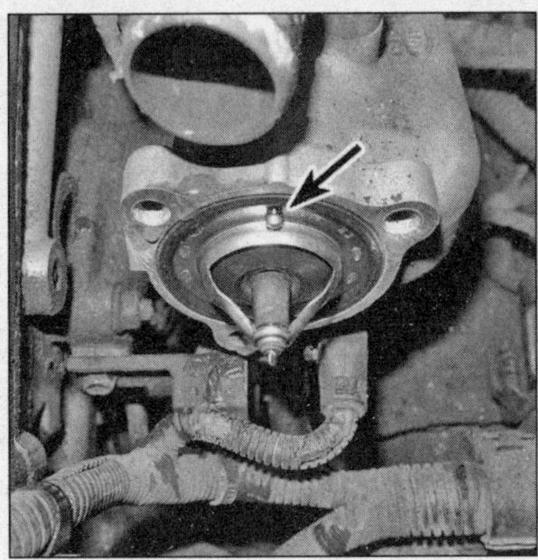

4.6 Note the position of the thermostat - the jiggle pin should be installed at the highest point

5.7 Remove the fan module fastener (A) then disconnect the electrical connectors (B)

7 Tighten the housing cover fasteners to the torque listed in this Chapter's Specifications and reinstall the remaining components in the reverse order of removal.

8 Refill the cooling system (see Chapter 1). Run the engine and check for leaks and proper operation.

5 Engine cooling fan - replacement

Warning: *To avoid possible injury or damage, DO NOT operate the engine with a damaged fan. Do not attempt to repair fan blades - replace a damaged fan with a new one.*

Warning: *The electric fans can start at any time; keep hands, clothes and tools away from the fan until the battery is disconnected to avoid possible injury or damage.*

1 If the engine is overheating and the cooling fan is not coming on when the engine temperature rises to an excessive level, see Section 2. Check the fan relays in the underhood fuse/relay box.

2 If the relays are okay, check all wiring and connections to the fan motor. Refer to the wiring diagrams at the end of Chapter 12. If no obvious problems are found, the problem could be the Engine Coolant Temperature (ECT) sensor or the Powertrain Control Module (PCM). Have the cooling fan system and circuit diagnosed by a dealer service department or repair shop with the proper diagnostic equipment.

Replacement

3 Disconnect the cable from the negative battery terminal (see Chapter 5), then disconnect the cooling fan electrical connector(s).

4 Remove the air inlet duct (see Chapter 4).

5 On 2005 and earlier models, remove the hood latch (see Chapter 11).

Note: *On some models, it may be necessary to disconnect the electrical connector and harness from the horns (see Chapter 12).*

6 Drain the cooling system (see Chapter 1).

7 Remove the fan control module fastener, then disconnect the electrical connectors and remove the module (see illustration).

8 Disconnect the upper radiator hose from the radiator.

9 Remove the cooling fan shroud mounting bolts.

10 Remove the cooling fan assembly by tilting it back and out of the engine compartment.

11 Installation is the reverse of removal. Place the fan assembly back into the retaining clips for the side and bottom.

6 Coolant reservoir - removal and installation

Warning: *Wait until the engine is completely cool before beginning this procedure.*

1 Place a drain pan and rags under the reservoir, then detach the reservoir hose. Plug the reservoir port to prevent leakage.

Note: *Be prepared for coolant spillage.*

2 Remove the fasteners and detach the reservoir from the inner fender panel (see illustration).

3 While the reservoir is off the vehicle, it should be cleaned with soapy water and a brush to remove any deposits inside. Inspect it for damage and replace it if necessary.

4 Installation is the reverse of removal. Fill the reservoir with the proper type and amount of coolant (see Chapter 1).

7 Radiator - removal and installation

Warning: *Wait until the engine is completely cool before beginning this procedure.*

6.2 Coolant reservoir fastener locations - 2006 model shown, other models similar

Removal

1 Disconnect the cable from the negative battery terminal (see Chapter 5).

2 Set the parking brake, raise the front of the vehicle and support it securely on jackstands.

3 Drain the cooling system (see Chapter 1).

4 Remove the air inlet duct (see Chapter 4).

5 Remove the radiator support cover trim panel (see Chapter 11 Section 8).

6 On 2005 and earlier models, remove the hood latch (see Chapter 11), then disconnect the electrical connector to the horn (see Chapter 12) and move the harness out of the way.

7 Remove the engine cooling fan assembly (see Section 5).

8 Detach the coolant reservoir hose from the radiator filler neck and retainer and move it aside.

9 Disconnect the upper and lower radiator hoses from the radiator.

7.10a Radiator mounting bracket fasteners (left side shown)

1 *Radiator mounting bracket bolts*
2 *Condenser bracket-to-radiator bolt*
3 *Condenser bracket-to-condenser bolts*

7.10b Radiator support bracket bolts (there's also another bolt at the bottom of the center vertical brace, accessed from under the vehicle)

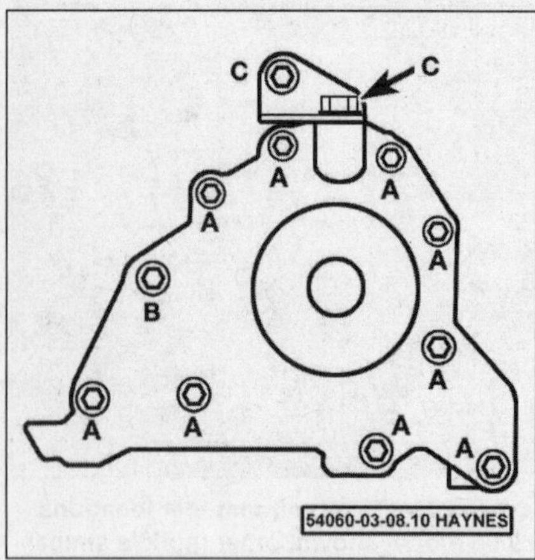

8.10 Water pump bolt designations for 2005 and earlier models (refer to this Chapter's Specifications for proper torque values)

10 Remove the radiator mounting bracket bolts, then unbolt the radiator support and reposition it to provide working room (see illustrations).

11 Remove the condenser mounting bracket bolts and carefully separate the air conditioning condenser from the radiator by disconnecting the condenser retaining tabs.

Note: *After separating the condenser, let it rest towards the front of the vehicle, being careful not to damage the cooling fins on it or the radiator.*

12 Lift the radiator from the vehicle.

13 Check the radiator for leaks and damage. If it needs repair, have a radiator shop or dealer service department perform the work, as special techniques are required.

14 Bugs and dirt can be removed from the radiator by spraying it from the back side with a garden hose. The radiator should be flushed out with a garden hose before reinstallation.

15 Check the radiator rubber mounts for deterioration and replace them if necessary.

Installation

16 Installation is the reverse of the removal procedure. Make sure the A/C condenser is properly attached to the radiator before seating the radiator into the lower rubber mounts.

Note: *Be sure that the flexible air seals on each side of the radiator are in the correct position while installing the radiator.*

17 After installation, fill the cooling system with the proper mixture of antifreeze and water (see Chapter 1).

18 Start the engine and check for leaks. Allow the engine to reach normal operating temperature, indicated by the upper radiator hose becoming hot. Recheck the coolant level and add more if required.

8 Water pump - replacement

Warning: *Do not start this procedure until the engine is completely cool. Do not allow antifreeze to come in contact with your skin or painted surfaces of the vehicle. Rinse off spills immediately with plenty of water. Antifreeze is highly toxic if ingested. Never leave antifreeze lying around in an open container or in puddles on the floor; children and pets are attracted by its sweet smell and may drink it. Check with local authorities on disposing of used antifreeze. Many communities have collection centers, which will see that antifreeze is disposed of safely. Never dump used antifreeze on the ground or into drains.*

Note: *Non-toxic coolant is available at local auto parts stores. Although the coolant is non-toxic when fresh, proper disposal of used coolant is still required.*

1 Disconnect the cable from the negative battery terminal (see Chapter 5).

2 Remove the drivebelt (see Chapter 1) and the alternator (see Chapter 5).

3 Drain the engine coolant (see Chapter 1).

2005 and earlier models

4 Remove the timing belt cover (see Chapter 2A).

5 Remove the fittings to the water pump and water outlet, remove the thermostat housing-to-engine bolts, and remove the complete housing as a unit.

Caution: *Every sprocket must maintain its position on the timing belt or severe engine damage can occur! If the marks are not legible later, it will be necessary to follow the timing belt installation procedure in Chapter 2A to ensure correct alignment.*

Note: *The belt can be secured to the pulleys with plastic zip-ties or a similar device to prevent them from coming off.*

6 Paint each sprocket with alignment marks onto the timing belt so that the belt can be installed in exactly the same position.

7 Remove the timing belt tensioner (see Chapter 2A).

Caution: *DO NOT rotate the crankshaft with the timing belt removed!*

8 Unscrew the water pump fasteners and remove the water pump. If necessary, tap the pump loose with a soft-face hammer.

9 Clean the water pump and block of any old gasket material or sealant, then clean with lacquer thinner.

10 Install a new gasket and install the water pump. Install the water pump bolts and nuts (see illustration) and tighten them to the torque listed in this Chapter's Specifications.

2006 and later models

11 Remove the water pump pulley mounting bolts and remove the pulley.

12 Remove the water pump mounting bolts,

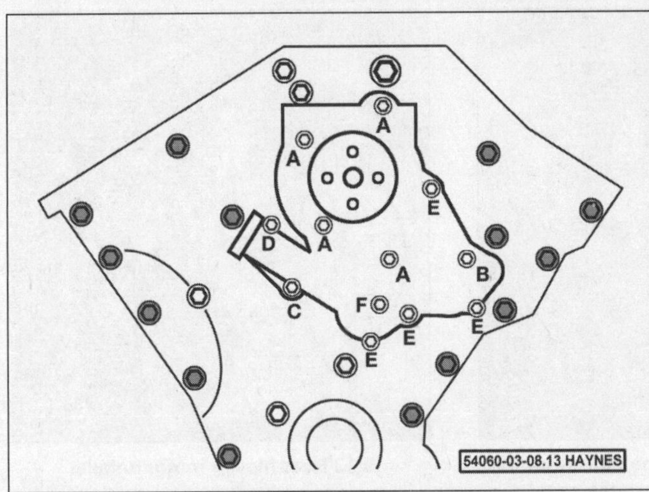

8.13 Water pump bolt designations for 2011 and later models (refer to this Chapter's Specifications for proper torque values)

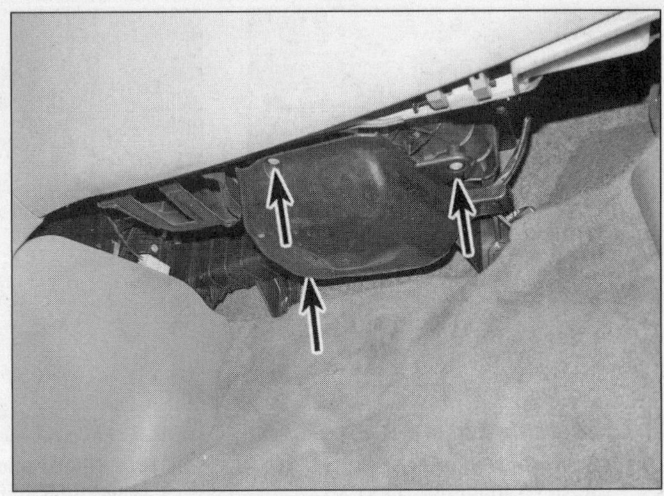

9.2 Remove the blower motor cover fasteners and cover

9.3 Blower motor power module details:

1 *Electrical connector* 2 *Mounting fasteners*

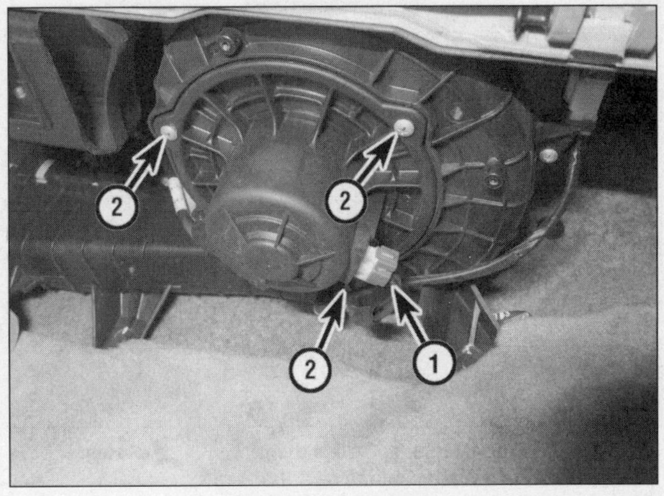

9.6 Blower motor details:

1 *Electrical connector* 2 *Mounting fasteners*

then remove the pump and gaskets; it may be necessary to use a soft-face hammer to loosen the pump.

13 Install a new gasket and install the water pump. Install the water pump bolts and nuts (see illustration) and tighten them to the torque listed in this Chapter's Specifications.

All models

14 The remainder of installation is the reverse of removal.

15 Refill the cooling system (see Chapter 1), then run the engine and check for leaks and proper operation.

9 Blower motor resistor/power module and blower motor assembly - replacement

Warning: *The models covered by this manual are equipped with Supplemental Restraint systems (SRS), more commonly known as airbags. Always disable the airbag system before working in the vicinity of any airbag system component to avoid the possibility of accidental deployment of the airbag, which could cause personal injury (see Chapter 12).*

1 Disconnect the cable from the negative battery terminal (see Chapter 5).

Front

2 Remove the blower motor cover fasteners (see illustration) and cover, if equipped, or pull down the insulation under the glove box.

Blower motor power module/ MOSFET

3 Disconnect the electrical connectors for the blower motor power module (see illustration).

Note: *Models equipped with automatic temperature control utilize a power module instead of a blower motor resistor. They are similar in the way they are mounted and connected.*

4 Remove the mounting fasteners and withdraw the unit from the heater/air conditioning housing.

5 Installation is the reverse of removal.

Blower motor assembly

Note: *The blower motor and blower wheel are balanced to each other at the factory and replaced only as an assembly.*

6 Disconnect the electrical connector for the blower motor (see illustration).

7 Remove the blower motor mounting fasteners, then remove the blower motor.

8 Installation is the reverse of removal.

Rear

Warning: *The air conditioning system is under high pressure. DO NOT loosen any fittings or remove any components until after the system has been discharged. Air conditioning refrigerant must be properly discharged into an EPA-approved container at a dealer service department or an automotive air conditioning repair facility. Always wear eye protection when dis-*

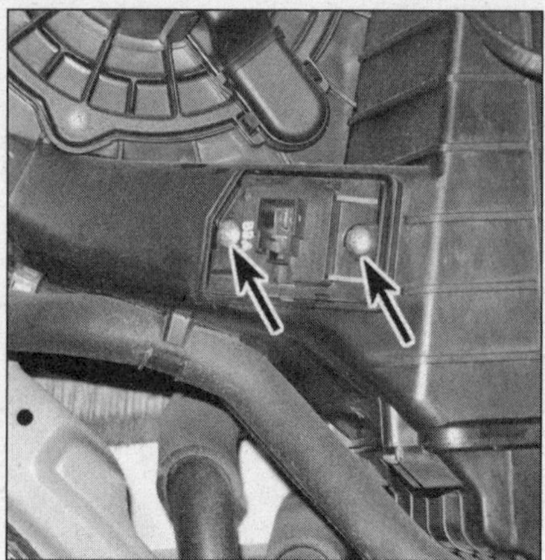

9.11a Remove the blower motor resistor/MOSFET mounting screws. . .

9.11b. . . then remove the blower motor resistor/MOSFET from the case

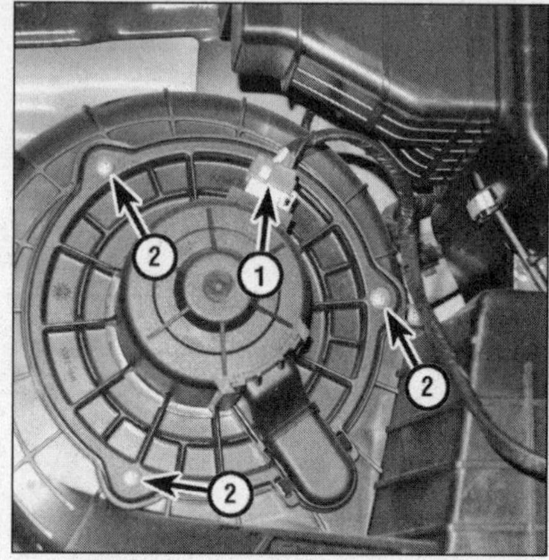

9.13 Rear blower motor details:

1 *Electrical connector*
2 *Mounting fasteners*

10.5 Squeeze the clamps and slide them back on the hoses, then disconnect the heater hoses from the heater core tubes at the firewall

10.7 Heater core tube cover fastener locations

connecting air conditioning system fittings.

Warning: *Wait until the engine is completely cool before beginning this procedure.*

9 Remove the rear heating and air conditioning housing (see Section 16).

Blower motor resistor/MOSFET

Note: *All 2006 and later models equipped with Power MOSFET instead of a blower motor resistor. They are similar in the way they are mounted and connected.*

10 Remove the rear quarter panel trim (see Chapter 11), disconnect the electrical connector for the blower motor resistor/MOSFET.

11 Remove the mounting fasteners and withdraw the unit from the heater/air conditioning housing (see illustrations).

12 Installation is the reverse of removal.

Blower motor assembly

Note: *The blower motor and blower wheel are balanced to each other at the factory and replaced as an assembly only.*

13 Disconnect the electrical connector for the blower motor (see illustration).

14 Remove the blower motor mounting screws on the rear of the housing.

15 Remove the blower motor from the housing.

16 Installation is the reverse of removal.

10 Heater core - replacement

Warning: *Wait until the engine is completely cool before beginning this procedure.*

1 Have the air conditioning system discharged and recovered by an air conditioning technician.

2 Disconnect the cable from the negative battery terminal (see Chapter 5). Drain the cooling system (see Chapter 1).

Front

3 Remove the instrument panel (see Chapter 11). Also remove the upper intake manifold (see Chapter 2A) for access to the heater hoses at the firewall.

4 Detach the expansion valve from the evaporator core at the firewall (see Section 15).

5 Detach the heater hoses from the heater core pipes at the firewall (see illustration).

6 Remove the fasteners and pull the heater and air conditioning housing away from the firewall.

7 Remove the heater core tube cover fasteners (see illustration).

8 Remove the fasteners securing the heater core cover, then remove the cover.

9 Pull the heater core out of the heater/air conditioning housing.

10 Installation is the reverse of removal. Use new seals for the heater core fittings and refill the cooling system (see Chapter 1).

11 Have the system evacuated, recharged and leak tested by the shop that discharged it.

Rear

Warning: *The air conditioning system is under high pressure. DO NOT loosen any fittings or remove any components until after the system has been discharged. Air conditioning refrigerant must be properly discharged into an EPA-approved container at a dealer service department or an automotive air conditioning repair facility. Always wear eye protection when disconnecting air conditioning system fittings.*

Warning: *Wait until the engine is completely cool before beginning this procedure.*

12 Remove the rear heater/air conditioning housing and set it on a bench (see Section 16).

13 Remove the fastener securing the heater core tube bracket to the housing.

14 Carefully release the two plastic retainers while pulling the heater core out of the heater/air conditioning housing.

15 Remove the heater core from the housing.

16 Installation is the reverse of removal. Pre-fill the heater core and quickly attach the hoses. Check the cooling system level after reassembly is complete (see Chapter 1).

Note: *If the heater core was replaced and not*

pre-filled, thermal cycle the vehicle TWICE. This procedure ensures that the heater core is filled completely.

17 To thermal cycle the vehicle, it must be operated until the thermostat opens, then turned off and allowed to cool. The coolant level in the reservoir must be maintained during this process. To verify that the rear unit is filled completely, follow this procedure:

- *a) Begin with the vehicle at room temperature*
- *b) Start the vehicle and bring the engine to operating temperature*
- *c) Set the temperature to the full HEAT position in the front A/C control, then turn off the front system*
- *d) Start the engine and turn the rear A/C system blower on HIGH with the temperature setting in the full HEAT position*
- *e) The discharge air temperature, measured at the dual register located on the C-pillar base, should be between 135-degrees and 145-degrees F*

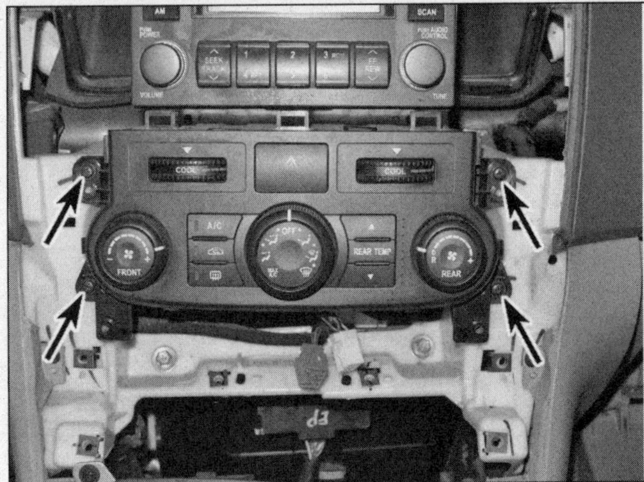

11.3 Remove control assembly fasteners and separate the assembly from the instrument panel

11 Heater/air conditioner control assembly - removal and installation

Warning: *The models covered by this manual are equipped with Supplemental Restraint systems (SRS), more commonly known as airbags. Always disable the airbag system before working in the vicinity of any airbag system component to avoid the possibility of accidental deployment of the airbag, which could cause personal injury (see Chapter 12).*

Front

1 Disconnect the cable from the negative battery terminal (see Chapter 5).

2 Remove the center trim panel, center console panel and both center vent assemblies (see Chapter 11).

3 Remove the control assembly mounting screws (see illustration) and pull the assembly forward.

4 Disconnect the electrical connectors from the back of the heater/air conditioning control assembly (see illustration).

5 Installation is the reverse of removal.

Rear

6 Disconnect the cable from the negative battery terminal (see Chapter 5).

7 Gently pry the rear heater/air conditioning control bezel assembly from the headliner (see illustration).

8 Disconnect the electrical connector from the back of the control assembly (see illustration).

9 Remove the mounting fasteners and remove the control assembly from the bezel.

10 Installation is the reverse of removal. If the heater/air conditioning control assembly is being replaced, calibration/diagnostic tests will be necessary. This will require a specialized scan tool; take the vehicle to a dealer service department or other qualified repair shop to have this service performed.

12 Air conditioning compressor - removal and installation

Warning: *The air conditioning system is under high pressure. Do not loosen any hose fittings or remove any components until the system has been discharged. Air conditioning refrigerant must be properly discharged into an EPA-approved recovery/recycling unit by a dealer service department or an automotive air conditioning repair facility. Always wear eye protection when disconnecting air conditioning system fittings.*

Caution: *The receiver/drier should be serviced whenever the compressor is replaced.*

1 Have the air conditioning system discharged and the refrigerant recovered by an automotive air conditioning technician.

2 Disconnect the cable from the negative battery terminal (see Chapter 5).

3 Raise the vehicle and support it securely on jackstands.

4 Remove the drivebelt from the compressor (see Chapter 1).

11.4 The heater/air conditioning electrical connectors

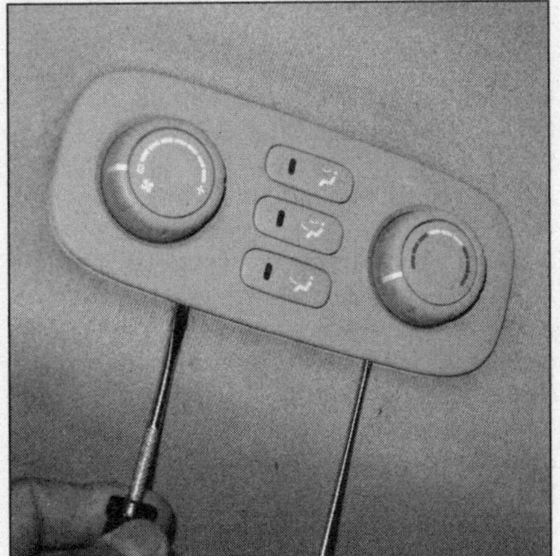

11.7 Using two screwdrivers, depress the tabs then gently pry out the rear heater/air conditioning control bezel assembly

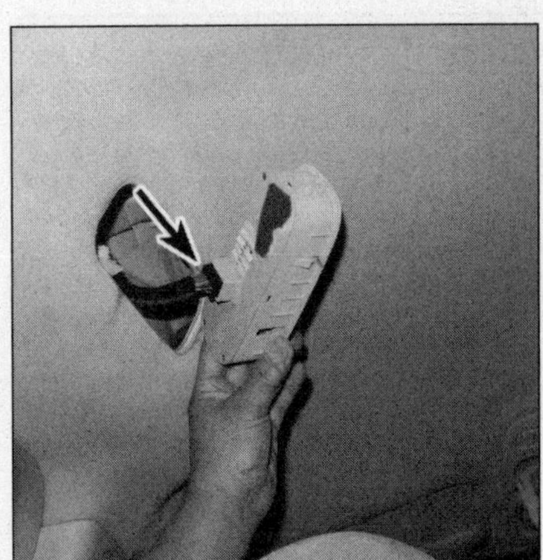

11.8 The rear control assembly electrical connector

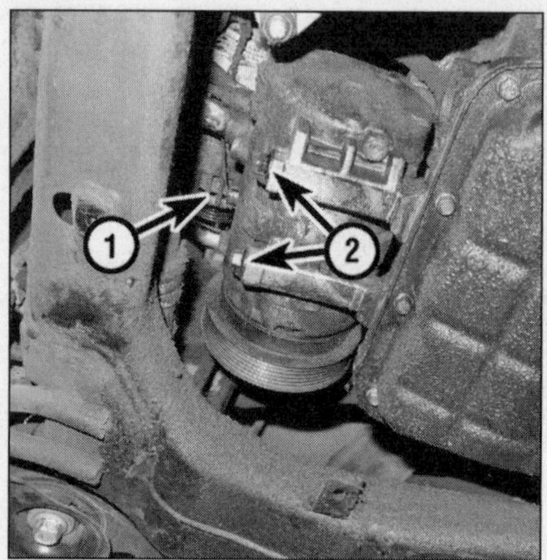

12.5 Air compressor details

1 *Electrical connector*
2 *Lower mounting bolts - upper mounting bolts not visible*

13.10 Remove the Allen plug and pull the dessicant cartridge from the tube on the condenser

14.4 Remove the mounting nuts and disconnect the refrigerant lines

5 Disconnect the electrical connector (see illustration).

6 Disconnect the refrigerant lines at the compressor. Seal the ends to prevent contamination.

7 Unbolt the compressor and lower it from the vehicle.

8 If a new or rebuilt compressor is being installed, follow the directions, which come with it regarding the proper level of oil prior to installation.

9 Installation is the reverse of removal. Replace any O-rings with new ones specifically made for the purpose and lubricate them with refrigerant oil. Tighten the compressor mounting bolts securely.

10 Have the system evacuated, recharged and leak tested by the shop that discharged it.

13 Air conditioning receiver-drier - removal and installation

Warning: *The air conditioning system is under high pressure. DO NOT loosen any fittings or remove any components until after the system has been discharged. Air conditioning refrigerant must be properly discharged into an EPA-approved container at a dealer service department or an automotive air conditioning repair facility. Always wear eye protection when disconnecting air conditioning system fittings.*

Caution: *When replacing entire components, additional refrigerant oil must be added equal to the amount that is removed with the component being replaced. Read the label on the oil container to verify that it is compatible with the R-134a system before adding any of it to the system.*

1 Have the system discharged and the refrigerant recovered by an air conditioning technician.

2005 and earlier models

Note: *The receiver-drier is located in front of the radiator on the right side.*

2 Remove both line fittings from the receiver-drier.

Note: *Plug all openings immediately to prevent contamination.*

3 Remove the mounting fastener retaining the receiver-drier bracket to the shock tower. Note the position of the ground strap (if equipped).

4 Remove the receiver-drier.

5 Installation is the reverse of removal. Install new O-rings onto the line fittings and lightly coat them with the correct refrigerant oil.

Note: *Only use O-rings that are designed specifically for A/C system applications.*

6 If you are replacing the receiver-drier with a new unit, add 0.8-ounce (25 ml) of refrigerant oil to the replacement.

7 Have the system evacuated, recharged and leak tested by the shop that discharged it.

2006 and later models

8 Disconnect the cable from the negative battery terminal (see Chapter 5).

9 Detach the condenser from the radiator and reposition it so the receiver-drier can clear the crossmember (see Section 14). If necessary, remove the condenser entirely.

10 Using an Allen wrench, detach the end plug (see illustration) and remove the desiccant from the condenser with a pair of needle-nose pliers.

11 Use new O-rings and a new bottom cap when installing the new desiccant, and tighten the end plug securely. Lubricate the O-rings with R-134a compatible refrigerant oil.

12 Installation is the reverse of removal.

13 Have the system evacuated, recharged and leak tested by the shop that discharged it.

14 Air conditioning condenser - removal and installation

Warning: *The air conditioning system is under high pressure. DO NOT loosen any fittings or remove any components until after the system has been discharged. Air conditioning refrigerant must be properly discharged into an EPA-approved container at a dealer service department or an automotive air conditioning repair facility. Always wear eye protection when disconnecting air conditioning system fittings.*

Caution: *When replacing entire components, additional refrigerant oil must be added equal to the amount that is removed with the component being replaced. Read the label on the oil container to verify that it is compatible with the R-134a system before adding any of it to the system.*

Note: *If the condenser is being replaced because of damage (cracked or punctured), the receiver-drier should also be replaced (see Section 13).*

1 Have the system discharged and the refrigerant recovered by an air conditioning technician.

2 Disconnect the cable from the negative battery terminal (see Chapter 5).

3 Remove the radiator (see Section 7).

4 Disconnect the refrigerant lines from the block at the right front corner of the engine compartment (see illustration). Plug all open fittings to prevent entry of dirt and moisture.

5 Carefully pull straight up to release the condenser from the lower clips, then remove the condenser from the vehicle.

6 Installation is the reverse of removal. Make certain to fully seat the condenser into the mounting clips and retainers. Install new O-rings onto the line fittings and lightly coat them with refrigerant oil.

Note: *Only use O-rings that are designed specifically for A/C system applications.*

7 If you are replacing the condenser with a

15.3 Location of the refrigerant line fitting fastener (A) at the expansion valve and the expansion valve mounting bolts (B)

15.8 Refrigerant line fitting fastener (A) at the rear expansion valve and expansion valve mounting bolts (B)

16.5 Heater hoses at the rear heater core connector pipes - make a note of the inlet and outlet hose locations

new unit, add 1.7-ounce (50 ml) of refrigerant oil to the replacement.

8 Have the system evacuated, recharged and leak tested by the shop that discharged it.

15 Expansion valve - removal and installation

Warning: *The air conditioning system is under high pressure. DO NOT loosen any fittings or remove any components until after the system has been discharged. Air conditioning refrigerant must be properly discharged into an EPA-approved container at a dealer service department or an automotive air conditioning repair facility. Always wear eye protection when disconnecting air conditioning system fittings.*

1 Have the air conditioning system refrigerant discharged and recovered by an air conditioning technician.

2 Disconnect the cable from the negative battery terminal (see Chapter 5). Remove the upper intake manifold (see Chapter 2A) for access to the expansion valve.

Front

3 Locate the expansion valve at the firewall just above the heater hoses. Remove the fastener securing both line fittings to the valve and remove the lines while discarding the seals. Plug all openings quickly to minimize contamination (see illustration).

4 Remove the mounting fasteners for the valve, then remove the valve while discarding any other seals. Again, plug all openings.

5 Installation is the reverse of removal. Install new O-rings onto the line fittings and lightly coat them with the correct refrigerant oil.

Note: *Only use O-rings that are designed specifically for A/C system applications.*

6 Have the system evacuated, recharged and leak tested by the shop that discharged it.

Rear

7 Raise the vehicle and support it securely on jackstands.

8 Remove the rear quarter panel trim (see Chapter 11), then remove the fastener securing both line fittings to the valve and remove the lines while discarding the seals (see illustration). Plug all openings quickly to minimize contamination.

9 Remove the mounting fasteners for the valve, then remove the valve while discarding any other seals. Again, plug all openings.

10 Installation is the reverse of removal. Install new O-rings onto the line fittings and lightly coat them with the correct refrigerant oil.

Note: *Only use O-rings that are designed specifically for A/C system applications.*

11 Have the system evacuated, recharged and leak tested by the shop that discharged it.

16 Rear heating and air conditioning housing - removal and installation

Warning: *The air conditioning system is under high pressure. DO NOT loosen any fittings or remove any components until after the system has been discharged. Air conditioning refrigerant must be properly discharged into an EPA-approved container at a dealer service department or an automotive air conditioning repair facility. Always wear eye protection when disconnecting air conditioning system fittings.*

Warning: *Wait until the engine is completely cool before beginning this procedure.*

1 Have the air conditioning system refrigerant discharged and recovered by an air conditioning technician.

2 Disconnect the cable from the negative battery terminal (see Chapter 5).

3 Remove the refrigerant lines and expansion valve from the heater/air conditioning housing under the vehicle (see Section 15) and plug or cap all open ends.

16.7 Upper air duct fastener

Note: *Discard the old refrigerant line seals; new seals will be required when the lines are reconnected.*

4 Remove the right rear trim panels (see Chapter 11).

5 Pinch off the heater hoses at the rear heater core with locking pliers, or equivalent, then detach them from the core (see illustration).

Caution: *Line the jaws of the pliers with a rag to prevent damage to the hose.*

6 Plug or cap the hose and core ends to minimize coolant loss.

Caution: *Make sure you mark or note the inlet and outlet hose locations. If the hoses are installed incorrectly the heating system will not function properly.*

Note: *Be prepared for some coolant to spill when disconnecting the hoses from the heater core.*

7 Remove the upper air duct fastener from the rear housing (see illustration).

16.8 Rear speaker bracket fastener locations

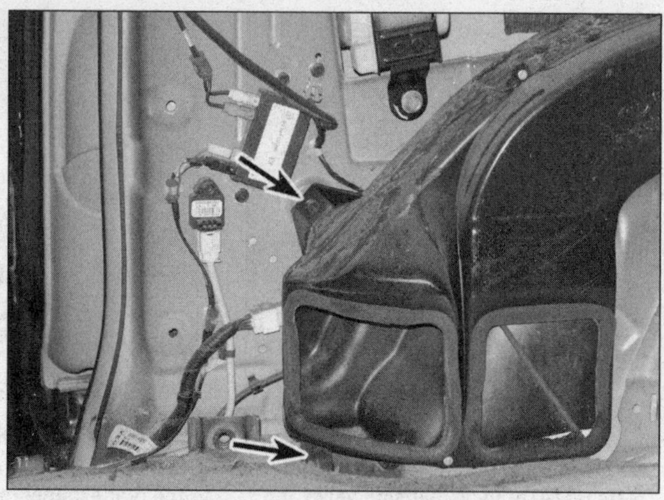

16.9 Remove the air duct fasteners - 2006 models shown other models similar

8 Remove the rear speaker (see Chapter 11) then remove the speaker bracket fasteners and bracket (see illustration).

9 Remove the air ducts from the heater/air conditioning housing (see illustration).

10 Remove the fasteners securing the heater core tubes to the floor and right quarter panel.

11 Disconnect the wiring harness from the heater/air conditioning harness connector.

16.12 Housing mounting nut locations - 2006 models shown other models similar

12 Remove the mounting fasteners that secure the housing to the body studs (see illustration).

13 Carefully lift the heater/air conditioning housing high enough to clear the floor and remove it from the vehicle. Be sure that no wires or brackets are still connected to the housing as it is being removed.

14 Installation is the reverse of removal. Install new seals (coated with clean refrigerant oil) at the refrigerant lines. Top off the cooling system and have the air conditioning system evacuated, recharged and leak tested.

Note: *If the heater core was emptied and not pre-filled, thermal cycle the vehicle TWICE. This procedure ensures that the heater core is filled completely.*

15 To thermal cycle the vehicle, refer to the procedure at the end of Section 10.

Notes

Notes

Chapter 4
Fuel and exhaust systems

Contents

	Section		Section
Air filter housing - removal and installation	10	Fuel pump module - component replacement	8
Exhaust system servicing - general information	6	Fuel rail and injectors - removal and installation	12
Fuel lines and fitting - general information and disconnection	5	Fuel tank - removal and installation	9
Fuel pressure - check	4	Fuel tank pressure sensor - replacement	14
Fuel pressure regulator - replacement	13	General information	1
Fuel pressure relief procedure	3	Throttle body - removal and installation	11
Fuel pump/fuel level sending unit - removal and installation	7	Troubleshooting	2

Specifications

General

Fuel system pressure (at idle)		
2002 through 2005 models		
Vacuum hose connected to regulator	39 psi	270 kPa
Vacuum hose disconnected from regulator	46 to 49 psi	320 to 340 kPa
2006 through 2010 models	54.3 to 55.8 psi	375 to 385 kPa
2011 and later models	55 psi	379 kPa

Torque specifications

Note: *One foot-pound (ft-lb) of torque is equivalent to 12 inch-pounds (in-lbs) of torque. Torque values below approximately 15 foot-pounds are expressed in inch-pounds, because most foot-pound torque wrenches are not accurate at these smaller values.*

	Ft-lbs (unless otherwise indicated)	Nm
Fuel tank strap bolts	28.9 to 39.8	39.2 to 53.9
Fuel rail mounting fasteners	78 to 104 in-lbs	8.8 to 11.8
Throttle body mounting fasteners	15 to 18	20 to 24

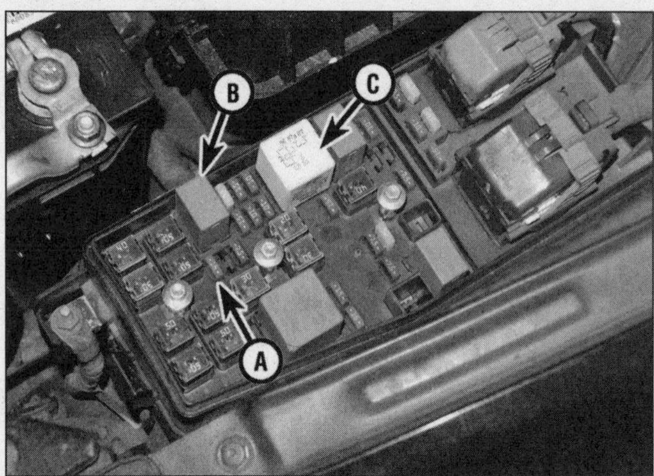

2.2 The fuel pump fuse (A) and fuel pump relay (B) are located in the engine compartment fuse box; (C) is the main relay (the locations of the fuses and relays may vary with model and year - refer to the guide on the underside of the fuse box cover and the guide in your owner's manual)

2.9 An automotive stethoscope is used to listen to the fuel injectors in operation

1 General Information

Fuel system warnings

Warning: *Gasoline is extremely flammable and repairing fuel system components can be dangerous. Consider your automotive repair knowledge and experience before attempting repairs which may be better suited for a professional mechanic.*

- *Don't smoke or allow open flames or bare light bulbs near the work area*
- *Don't work in a garage with a gas-type appliance (water heater, clothes dryer)*
- *Use fuel-resistant gloves. If any fuel spills on your skin, wash it off immediately with soap and water*
- *Clean up spills immediately*
- *Do not store fuel-soaked rags where they could ignite*
- *Prior to disconnecting any fuel line, you must relieve the fuel pressure (see Section 3)*
- *Wear safety glasses*
- *Have a proper fire extinguisher on hand*

Fuel system

1 The fuel system consists of the fuel tank, electric fuel pump/fuel level sending unit (located in the fuel tank), fuel rail and fuel injectors. The fuel injection system is a multi-port system which uses timed impulses to inject the fuel directly into the intake port of each cylinder. The Powertrain Control Module (PCM) controls the injectors. The PCM monitors various engine parameters and delivers the exact amount of fuel required for efficient operation.

2 Fuel is circulated from the fuel pump to the fuel rail, through fuel lines running along the underside of the vehicle. Various sections of the fuel line are either rigid metal or nylon, or flexible fuel hose. The various sections of the fuel hose are connected either by quick-connect fittings or threaded metal fittings.

Exhaust system

3 The exhaust system consists of the exhaust manifold(s), catalytic converter(s), muffler(s), tailpipe and all connecting pipes, flanges and clamps. The catalytic converters are an emission control device added to the exhaust system to reduce pollutants.

2 Troubleshooting

Fuel pump

1 The fuel pump is located inside the fuel tank. Sit inside the vehicle with the windows closed, turn the ignition key to ON (not START) and listen for the sound of the fuel pump as it's briefly activated. You will only hear the sound for a second or two, but that sound tells you that the pump is working. Alternatively, have an assistant listen at the fuel filler cap.

2 Check the fuel pump fuse and relay (see illustration). If the fuse and relay are okay, check the wiring back to the fuel pump. If the fuse, main relay, fuel pump relay and wiring are okay, the fuel pump is probably defective. If the pump runs continuously with the ignition key in the ON position, the Powertrain Control Module (PCM) is probably defective. Have the PCM checked by a professional mechanic.

Fuel injection system

Note: *The following procedure is based on the assumption that the fuel pump is working and the fuel pressure is adequate (see Section).*

3 Check all electrical connectors that are related to the system. Check the ground wire connections for tightness.

4 Verify that the battery is fully charged (see Chapter 5).

5 Inspect the air filter element (see Chapter 1).

6 Check all fuses related to the fuel system (see Chapter 12).

7 Check the air induction system between the throttle body and the intake manifold for air leaks. Also inspect the condition of all vacuum hoses connected to the intake manifold and to the throttle body.

8 Remove the air intake duct from the throttle body and look for dirt, carbon, varnish, or other residue in the throttle body, particularly around the throttle plate. If it's dirty, clean it with carb cleaner, a toothbrush and a clean shop towel.

9 With the engine running, place an automotive stethoscope against each injector, one at a time, and listen for a clicking sound that indicates operation (see illustration).

Warning: *Stay clear of the drivebelt and any rotating or hot components.*

Note: *On some models this check will not be possible, since the upper intake manifold is in the way.*

10 If you can hear the injectors operating, but the engine is misfiring, the electrical circuits are functioning correctly, but the injectors might be dirty or clogged. Try a commercial injector cleaning product (available at auto parts stores). If cleaning the injectors doesn't help, replace the injectors.

11 If an injector is not operating (it makes no sound), disconnect the injector electrical connector and measure the resistance across the injector terminals with an ohmmeter. Compare this measurement to the other injectors. If the resistance of the non-operational injector is quite different from the other injectors, replace it.

12 If the injector is not operating, but the resistance reading is within the range of resistance of the other injectors, the PCM or the circuit between the PCM and the injector might be faulty.

3.2a Pull up the carpet . . .

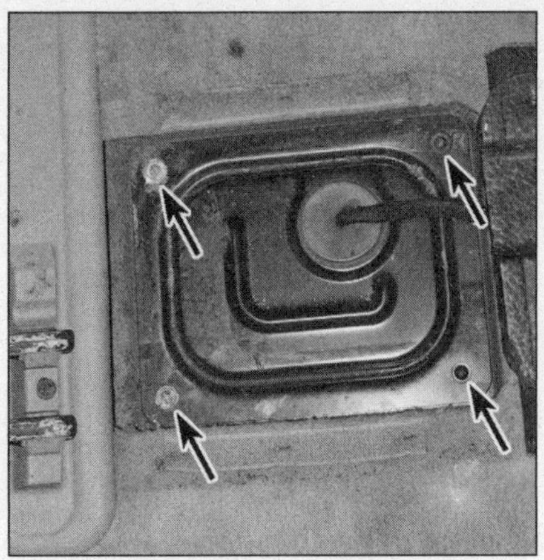

3.2b . . . then remove the screws and lift up the fuel pump access cover

3.3 Fuel pump electrical connector

3 Fuel pressure relief procedure

Warning: *Gasoline is extremely flammable, so take extra precautions when you work on any part of the fuel system. See Fuel system warnings in Section 1.*

1 Remove the fuel filler cap to release any built-up pressure in the fuel tank.

2 Remove the left-side second-row seat, then pull back the carpet and remove the fuel pump access cover (see illustrations).

Note: *On 2005 and earlier models it isn't necessary to remove the seat.*

3 Disconnect the fuel pump electrical connector (see illustration).

4 Attempt to start the engine; it should immediately stall. Crank the engine several more times to ensure the fuel system has been completely relieved. Disconnect the cable from the negative terminal of the battery before working on the fuel system.

Note: *It's a good idea to cover any fuel connection to be disassembled with rags to absorb the residual fuel that may leak out. Properly dispose of the rags.*

4 Fuel pressure - check

Warning: *Gasoline is extremely flammable, so take extra precautions when you work on any part of the fuel system. See Fuel system warnings in Section 1.*

Note: *The following procedure assumes that the fuel pump is receiving voltage and runs.*

1 Relieve the fuel system pressure (see Section 3).

2 Disconnect the fuel supply line at the fuel rail, then use an adapter to connect the fuel pressure gauge between the fuel line and the fuel rail (see illustration).

Return-type fuel systems (2005 and earlier models)

3 Turn off all accessories and turn the ignition switch key to ON. The fuel pump should run for about two seconds to pressurize the system. Note the reading on the gauge. After the pump stops running, the pressure should hold steady. After five minutes it should not drop below the minimum listed in this Chapter's Specifications.

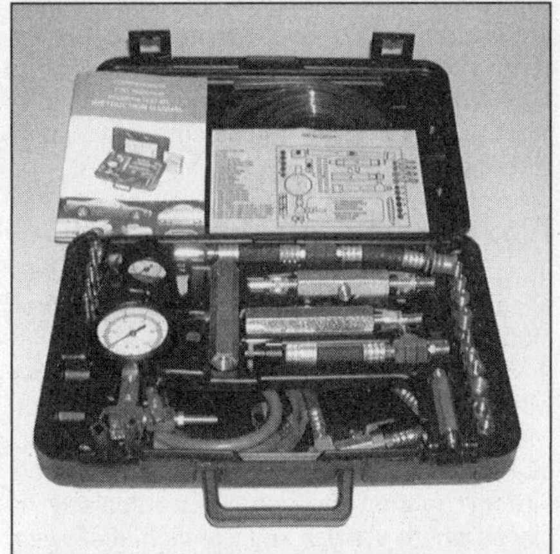

4.2a This fuel pressure testing kit contains all the necessary fittings and adapters, along with the fuel pressure gauge, to test most automotive fuel systems

4.2b Remove the nuts and disconnect the fuel line from the fuel rail, install an adapter (with gauge fitting) between the fuel line and fuel rail, then connect the gauge to the adapter fitting

4 Start the engine, allow it to warm up to its normal operating temperature, then measure the fuel pressure and compare your readings to the system pressure listed in this Chapter's Specifications.

a) *If the pressure is high, disconnect the vacuum hose from the fuel pressure regulator and connect a vacuum gauge to the hose. Make sure there is 12 in-Hg or more vacuum present at the hose. If there isn't, check the hose for a restriction or leak.*

b) *If there is adequate vacuum to the regulator but the pressure is high, check for a restricted fuel return hose or line. If the return hose and line are clear, replace the pressure regulator.*

c) *If the pressure is low, pinch the fuel return hose. If the pressure goes up, replace the fuel pressure regulator. If the pressure does not increase, replace the fuel filter (see Section 8) and recheck the pressure. If it's still low, check the fuel supply hose and line for a restriction. If there is no restriction, replace the fuel pump (see Section 8).*

d) *Another possibility of low fuel pressure is a leaking fuel injector, but that would most likely set a trouble code and turn on the CHECK ENGINE light (because the fuel mixture would be too rich).*

5 To check the operation of the fuel pressure regulator, disconnect the vacuum hose from the regulator with the engine idling and watch the fuel pressure gauge - the fuel pressure should increase 3 to 10 psi as soon as the hose is disconnected. If it doesn't, check for vacuum at the hose. If vacuum is present, replace the fuel pressure regulator.

6 Turn the key off and observe the pressure for five minutes. If the pressure drops

substantially, then there is either a leaking injector or a faulty check valve in the fuel pump.

7 Relieve the system fuel pressure (see Section 3), then disconnect the cable from the negative battery terminal (see Chapter 5). Remove the fuel pressure gauge and test hoses, then reconnect the fuel supply hose to the fuel rail. Reconnect the cable to the negative battery terminal, then start the engine and check for leaks.

Returnless fuel systems (2007 and later models)

8 Start the engine and let it warm up until it's idling at its normal operating temperature, then measure the fuel pressure and compare your reading to the fuel pressure listed in this Chapter's Specifications.

Note: *At the time of writing, the fuel pressure regulator was not available separately. Check with your local auto parts store or dealer parts department to see if the pressure regulator can be purchased separately.*

a) *If the indicated fuel pressure is low, inspect the fuel supply hose and line for an obstruction. If the hose and line are clear, replace the fuel filter, then recheck the fuel pressure. If the indicated fuel pressure is still low, replace the fuel pump/fuel pressure regulator, then recheck the fuel pressure.*

b) *If the indicated fuel pressure is high, replace the fuel pump/fuel pressure regulator, then recheck the fuel pressure. If the fuel pressure is still high, have the fuel system diagnosed by a dealer service department or other qualified repair shop.*

9 After the test is complete, relieve the system fuel pressure (see Section 3), then disconnect the cable from the negative battery terminal (see Chapter 5).

10 Remove the fuel pressure gauge.

11 Reconnect the cable to the negative battery terminal.

12 Start the engine and check for fuel leaks.

5 Fuel lines and fittings - general information and disconnection

Warning: *Gasoline is extremely flammable, so take extra precautions when you work on any part of the fuel system. See Fuel system warnings in Section 1.*

1 Relieve the fuel pressure before servicing fuel lines or fittings (see Section 3), then disconnect the cable from the negative battery terminal (see) before proceeding.

2 The fuel supply line connects the fuel pump in the fuel tank to the fuel rail on the engine. The Evaporative Emission (EVAP) system lines connect the fuel tank to the EVAP canister and connect the canister to the intake manifold.

3 Whenever you're working under the vehicle, be sure to inspect all fuel and EVAP lines for leaks, kinks, dents and other damage. Always replace a damaged fuel or EVAP line immediately.

4 If you find signs of dirt in the lines during disassembly, disconnect all lines and blow them out with compressed air. Inspect the fuel strainer on the fuel pump pick-up unit for damage and deterioration.

Steel tubing

5 It is critical that the fuel lines be replaced with lines of equivalent type and specification.

6 Some steel fuel lines have threaded fittings. When loosening these fittings, hold the stationary fitting with a wrench while turning the tube nut.

Plastic tubing

Warning: *When removing or installing plastic fuel line tubing, be careful not to bend or twist it too much, which can damage it. Also, plastic fuel tubing is NOT heat resistant, so keep it away from excessive heat.*

7 When replacing fuel system plastic tubing, use only original equipment replacement plastic tubing.

Flexible hoses

8 When replacing fuel system flexible hoses, use only original equipment replacements.

9 Don't route fuel hoses (or metal lines) within four inches of the exhaust system or within ten inches of the catalytic converter. Make sure that no rubber hoses are installed directly against the vehicle, particularly in places where there is any vibration. If allowed to touch some vibrating part of the vehicle, a hose can easily become chafed and it might start leaking. A good rule of thumb is to maintain a minimum of 1/4-inch clearance around a hose (or metal line) to prevent contact with the vehicle underbody.

Disconnecting Fuel Line Fittings

10 These are some of the fitting types you may encounter when working on the fuel system (see illustrations).

6 Exhaust system servicing - general information

Warning: *Allow exhaust system components to cool before inspection or repair. Also, when working under the vehicle, make sure it is securely supported on jackstands.*

1 The exhaust system consists of the exhaust manifolds, catalytic converter, muffler, tailpipe and all connecting pipes, flanges and clamps. The exhaust system is isolated from the vehicle body and from chassis components by a series of rubber hangers (see illustration). Periodically inspect these hangers for cracks or other signs of deterioration, replacing them as necessary.

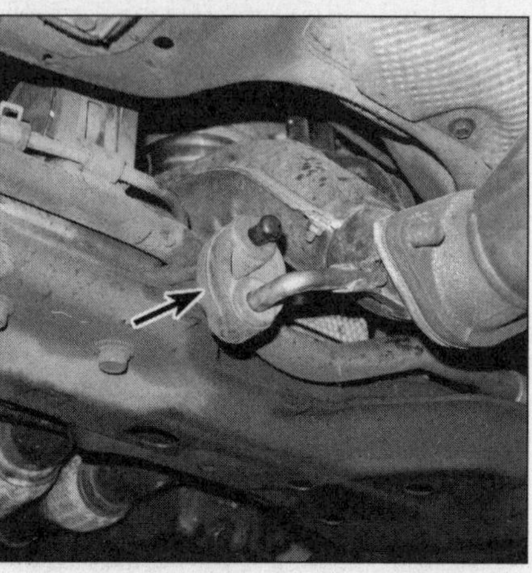

6.1 A typical exhaust system hanger. Inspect regularly and replace at the first sign of damage or deterioration

2 Conduct regular inspections of the exhaust system to keep it safe and quiet. Look for any damaged or bent parts, open seams, holes, loose connections, excessive corrosion or other defects which could allow exhaust fumes to enter the vehicle. Do not repair deteriorated exhaust system components; replace them with new parts.

3 If the exhaust system components are extremely corroded, or rusted together, a cutting torch is the most convenient tool for removal. Consult a properly-equipped repair shop. If a cutting torch is not available, you can use a hacksaw, or if you have compressed air, there are special pneumatic cutting chisels that can also be used. Wear safety goggles to protect your eyes from metal chips and wear work gloves to protect your hands.

4 Here are some simple guidelines to follow when repairing the exhaust system:

a) *Work from the back to the front when removing exhaust system components.*

b) *Apply penetrating oil to the exhaust system component fasteners to make them easier to remove.*

c) *Use new gaskets, hangers and clamps.*

d) *Apply anti-seize compound to the threads of all exhaust system fasteners during reassembly.*

e) *Be sure to allow sufficient clearance between newly installed parts and all points on the underbody to avoid overheating the floor pan and possibly damaging the interior carpet and insulation. Pay particularly close attention to the catalytic converter and heat shield.*

7 Fuel pump/fuel level sending unit - removal and installation

Warning: *Gasoline is extremely flammable, so take extra precautions when you work on any part of the fuel system. See Fuel system warnings in Section 1.*

1 Relieve the fuel system pressure (see

Disconnecting Fuel Line Fittings

Two-tab type fitting; depress both tabs with your fingers, then pull the fuel line and the fitting apart

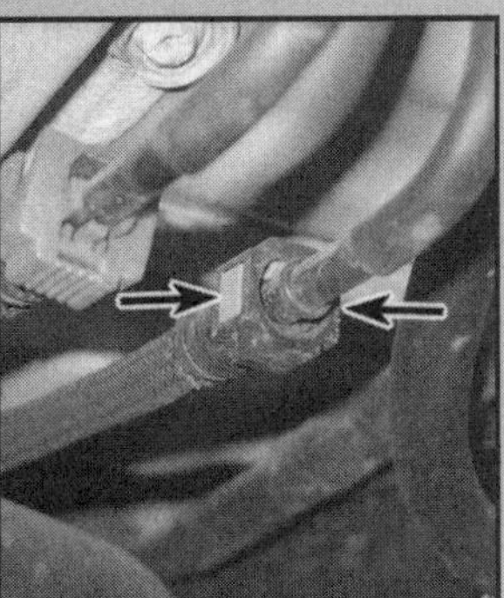

On this type of fitting, depress the two buttons on opposite sides of the fitting, then pull it off the fuel line

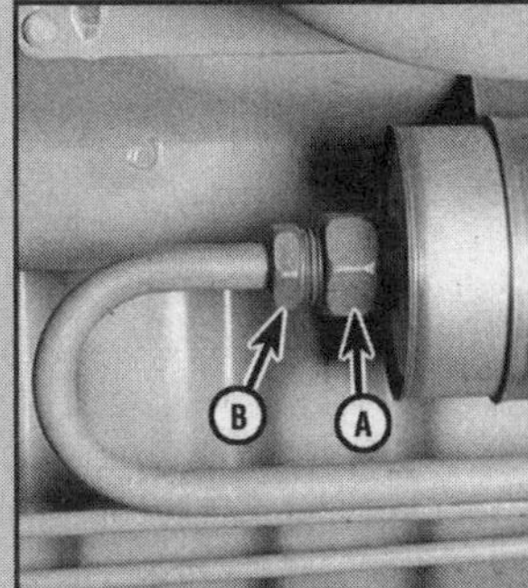

Threaded fuel line fitting; hold the stationary portion of the line or component (A) while loosening the tube nut (B) with a flare-nut wrench

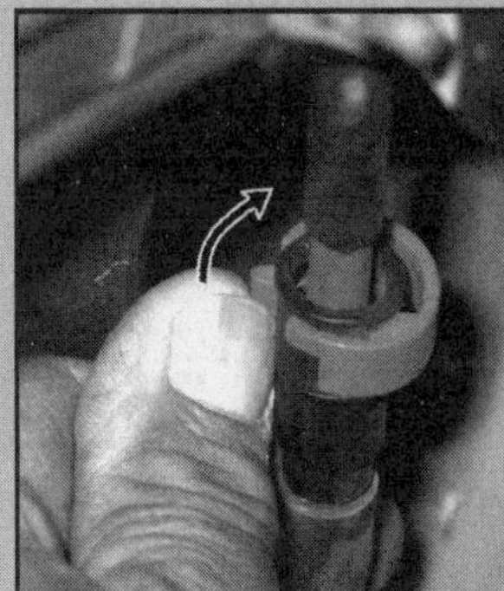

Plastic collar-type fitting; rotate the outer part of the fitting

Metal collar quick-connect fitting; pull the end of the retainer off the fuel line and disengage the other end from the female side of the fitting . . .

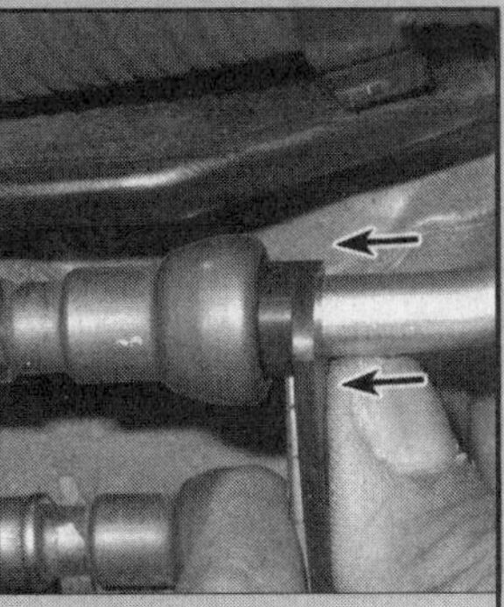

. . . insert a fuel line separator tool into the female side of the fitting, push it into the fitting and pull the fuel line off the pipe

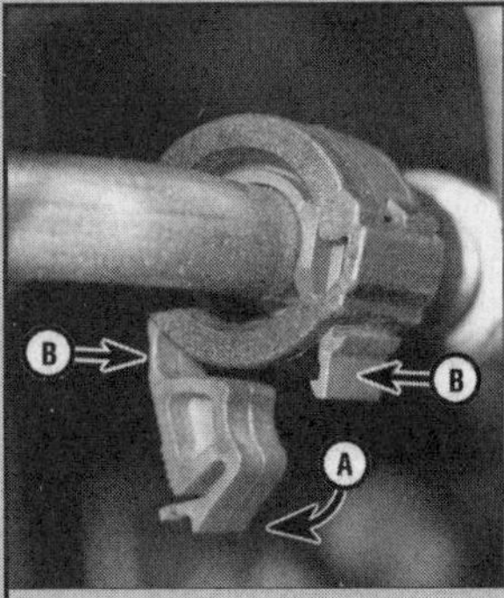

Some fittings are secured by lock tabs. Release the lock tab (A) and rotate it to the fully-opened position, squeeze the two smaller lock tabs (B) . . .

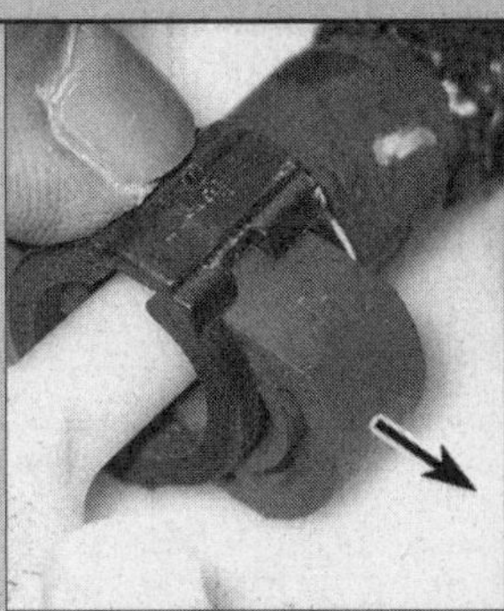

. . . then push the retainer out and pull the fuel line off the pipe

Spring-lock coupling; remove the safety cover, install a coupling release tool and close the tool around the coupling . . .

. . . push the tool into the fitting, then pull the two lines apart

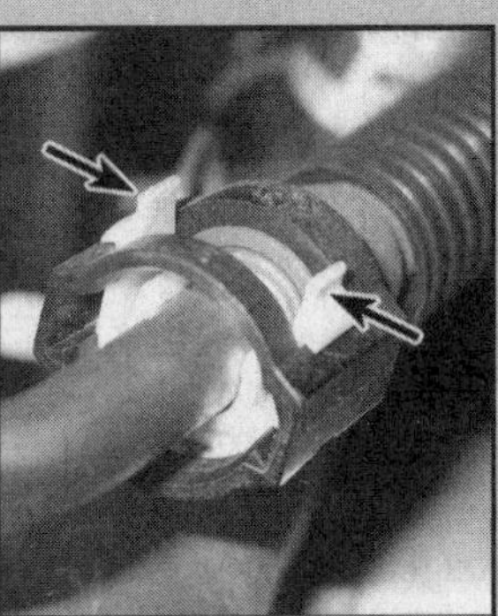

Hairpin clip type fitting: push the legs of the retainer clip together, then push the clip down all the way until it stops and pull the fuel line off the pipe

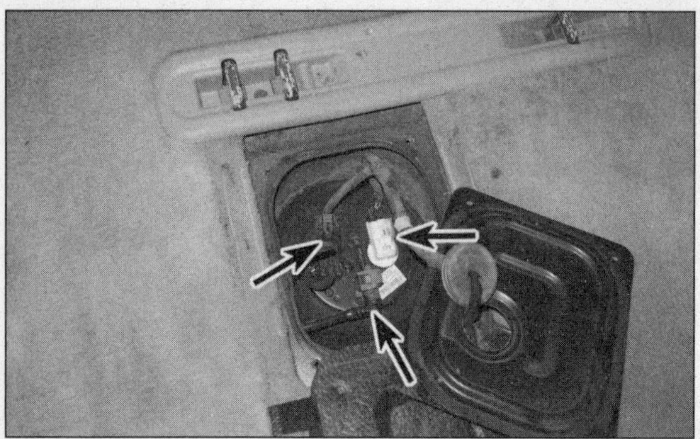
7.5 Disconnect the electrical connectors from the fuel pump module, then the fuel line(s)

7.8 The lock ring can be loosened with a punch

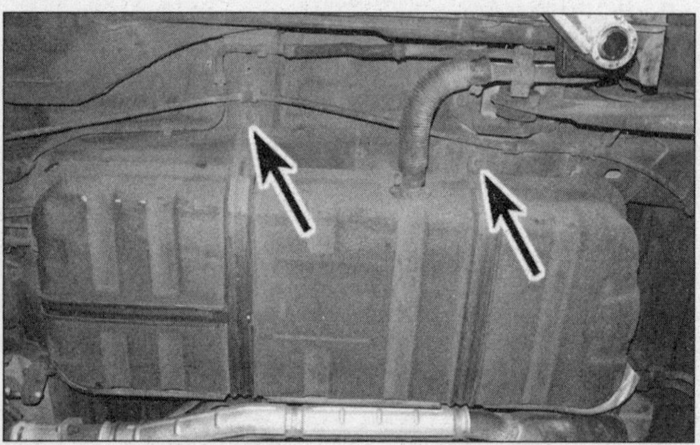
9.6a The fuel tank strap mounting bolts. . .

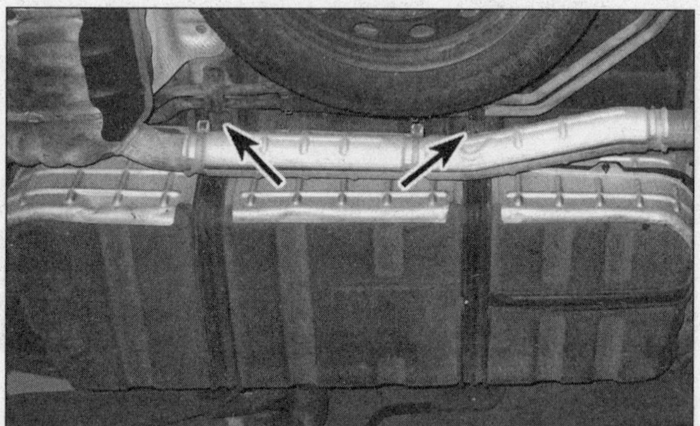
9.6b. . . must be removed from each end of the straps

Section 3) and remove the fuel filler cap.

2 Disconnect the cable from the negative battery terminal (see Chapter 5).

3 Remove the left-side second row rear seat (see Chapter 11), then pull the carpet back (see illustration 3.2a).

Note: *On 2005 and earlier models it isn't necessary to remove the seat.*

4 Remove the fuel pump/sending unit floor service hole cover (see illustration 3.2b).

5 Disconnect the fuel pump electrical connectors and the fuel lines from the top of the fuel pump unit (see illustration).

6 Remove the sound insulator, if equipped, then mark the fuel pump orientation for reference when installing.

7 On 2005 and earlier models, remove the fuel pump mounting screws.

8 On 2006 and later models, use special service tool 09310-2B200 (or equivalent) to rotate the lock ring counterclockwise and remove it. If you don't have access to such a tool, a punch can be used to drive the lock ring in a counterclockwise direction (see illustration).

9 Carefully lift the fuel pump/fuel level sending unit assembly from the fuel tank.

10 Installation is the reverse of removal.

8 Fuel pump module - component replacement

Warning: *Gasoline is extremely flammable, so take extra precautions when you work on any part of the fuel system. See Fuel system warnings in Section 1.*

1 At the time of writing, individual components of the fuel pump module (fuel pump motor, fuel pressure regulator [2006 and later models], fuel filter, fuel level sending unit) were not available separately. Check with your local auto parts store or dealer parts department to see if individual parts have become available.

9 Fuel tank - removal and installation

Warning: *Gasoline is extremely flammable, so take extra precautions when you work on any part of the fuel system. See Fuel system warnings in Section 1.*

1 Relieve the fuel system pressure (see Section 3).

2 Disconnect the cable from the negative battery terminal (see Chapter 5).

3 Remove the fuel pump/sending unit floor service hole cover and disconnect the hoses and electrical connectors from the fuel pump/fuel level sending unit (see Section 7).

4 Remove the fuel filler hose and vent hose, disconnect the fuel feed quick connector near the EVAP canister and any hoses that would interfere with tank removal.

5 Raise the vehicle and support it securely on jackstands.

6 Support the fuel tank and remove the strap mounting bolts (see illustrations).

7 Carefully lower the tank.

8 Installation is the reverse of removal. Tighten the fuel tank strap bolts to the torque listed in this Chapter's Specifications.

10 Air filter housing - removal and installation

Air intake duct and resonators

1 Disconnect the electrical connector at the MAF/IAT sensor (2010 and earlier models) or BARO/IAT sensor (2011 and later models).

2 Loosen the hose clamps at both ends of the air intake duct and remove the duct.

3 Installation is the reverse of removal.

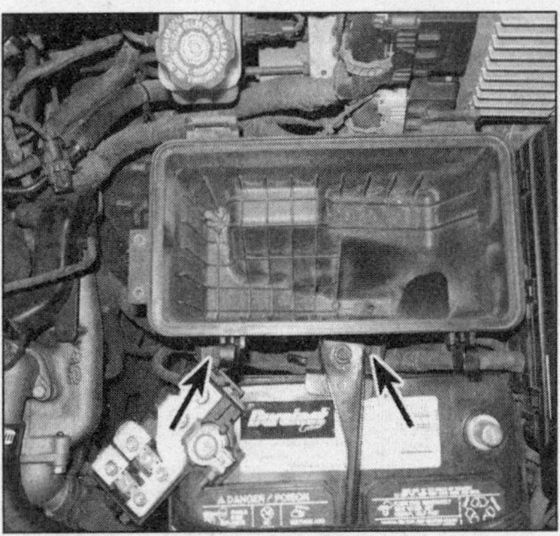

10.5 Air filter housing mounting bolts - 2006 and later models shown

11.3 Disconnect the electrical connectors on the throttle body

1 *ISC motor*
2 *Throttle position sensor*

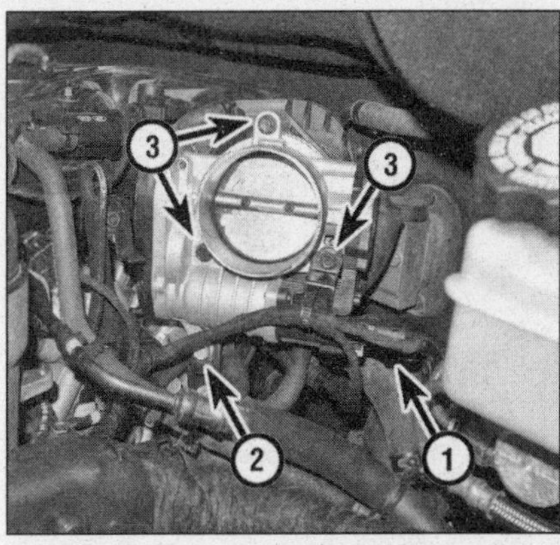

11.7 Remove the throttle body-to-support bracket bolt, then the throttle body mounting bolts

1 *Throttle control motor electrical connector*
2 *Throttle body-to-support bracket bolt*
3 *Throttle body mounting bolts*

Air filter housing

4 Remove the air filter housing cover and the filter element (see Chapter 1).
5 Remove the air filter housing mounting fasteners (see illustration).
6 Remove the air filter housing.
7 Installation is the reverse of removal.

11 Throttle body - removal and installation

Warning: *Wait until the engine is completely cool before beginning this procedure.*
1 Disconnect the cable from the negative battery terminal (see Chapter 5).
2 Remove the air intake duct (see Section 10).
3 On 2005 and earlier models, disconnect the electrical connectors from the Throttle Position Sensor (TPS) and Idle Speed Control (ISC) motor (see illustration).
4 On 2006 and later models, disconnect the wiring from the throttle control motor (see illustration 11.7).
5 If applicable, disconnect the vacuum hoses from the throttle body.
6 If applicable, clamp off the coolant hoses to the throttle body to minimize coolant loss.
7 Remove the throttle body mounting fasteners and remove the throttle body (see illustration). On 2006 and later models remove the throttle body support bracket bolt at the base of the throttle body.
Note: *On 2006 and later models remove the throttle body-to-support bracket bolt at the base of the throttle body.*
8 Disconnect the coolant hoses from the throttle body (see illustration).
9 Remove and discard the old throttle body gasket. Clean the gasket mating surfaces.

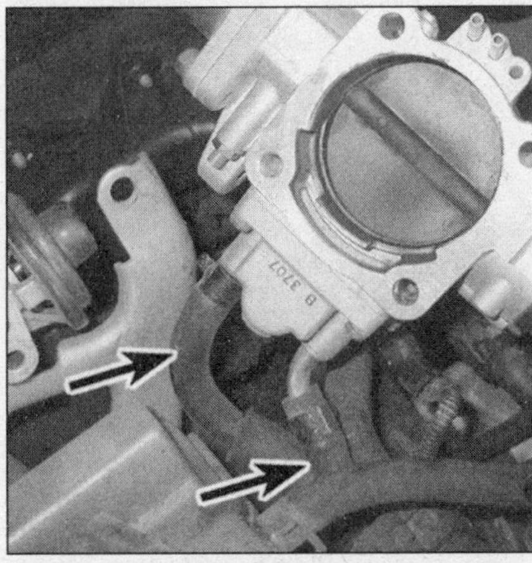

11.8 Pinch off the two coolant hoses prior to detaching them from the throttle body to avoid spillage

10 Installation is the reverse of removal. Use a new gasket and tighten the throttle body mounting bolts to the torque listed in this Chapter's Specifications. Check the coolant level, adding as necessary (see Chapter 1).

12 Fuel rail and injectors - removal and installation

Warning: *Gasoline is extremely flammable, so take extra precautions when you work on any part of the fuel system. See Fuel system warnings in Section 1.*
Note: *We recommend replacing all injector O-rings even when only one injector O-ring or seal is leaking. On most fuel rails, you have to remove the entire assembly anyway, so replace all of the O-rings/seals at one time to avoid having to remove the fuel rail later to replace another O-ring and/or seal.*

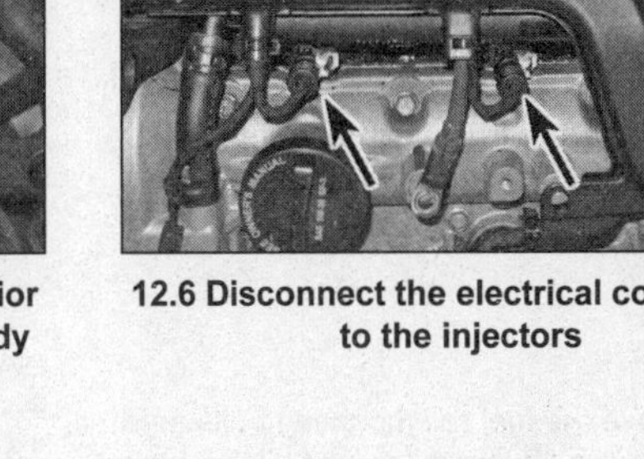

12.6 Disconnect the electrical connectors to the injectors

1 Relieve the fuel pressure (see Section 3).
2 Disconnect the cable from the negative battery terminal (see Chapter 5). Remove the engine cover, if equipped.
3 Remove the air intake duct and air filter housing (see Section 10).
4 Remove the upper intake manifold (see Chapter 2A).
5 Detach the fuel line from the fuel rail. On 2005 and earlier models, also detach the fuel return line from the fuel pressure regulator(see Section 13).
6 Disconnect the electrical connectors from the fuel injectors (see illustration) and set the injector harness aside.

12.7 Fuel rails mounting bolt locations

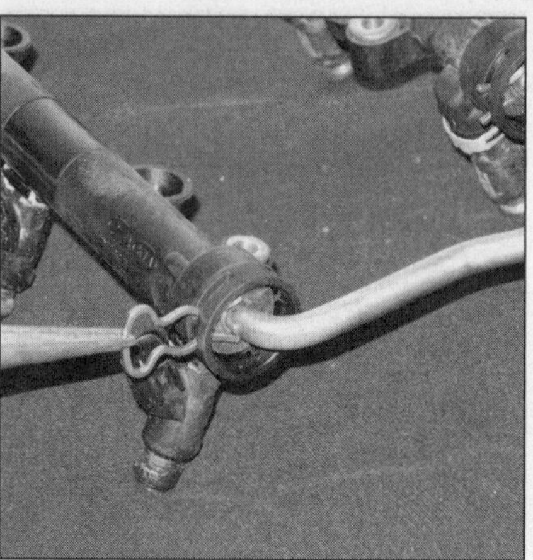
12.8a Pull the retaining clip out from the fuel rail. . .

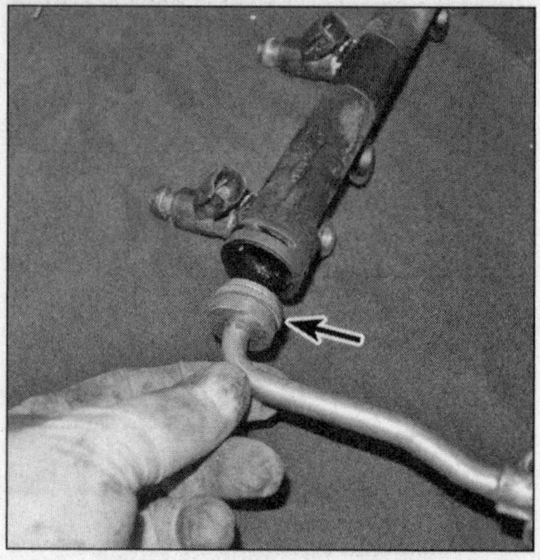
12.8b. . . then separate the supply tube from the fuel rail and replace the O-ring

12.9 Carefully pry the retaining clip up and off, then twist and pull the injector(s) out of the fuel rail

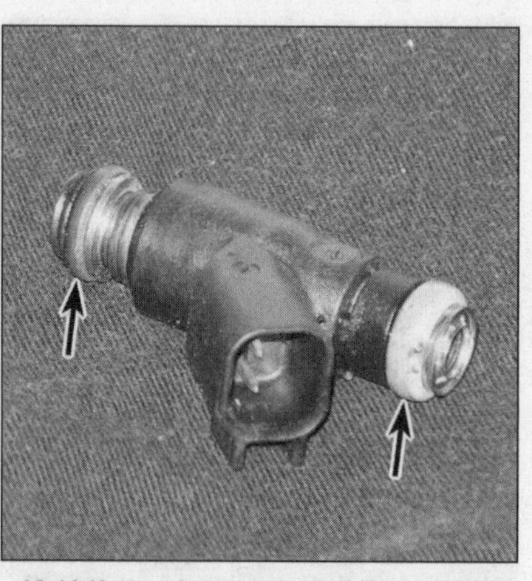
12.10 If you plan to reinstall the original injectors, remove and discard the old O-rings and grommets and replace them with new ones

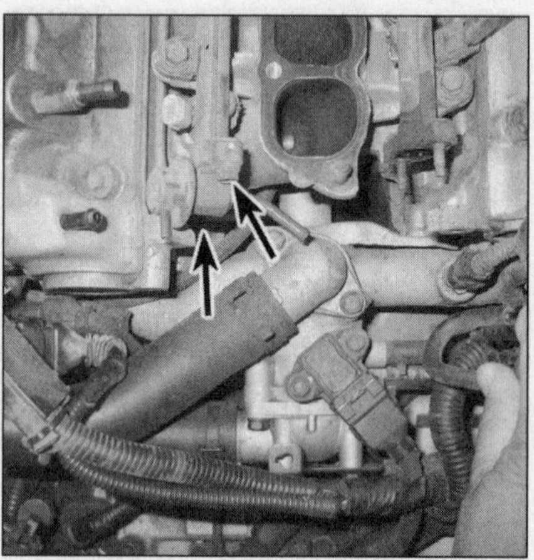
13.5 Pressure regulator mounting bolt locations

7 Remove the fuel rail mounting bolts (see illustration) and lift the rail assembly up from the intake manifold.

8 If necessary, disconnect the fuel tube from the fuel rails by pulling the retaining clip out, then pull the fuel supply tube from the fuel rail (see illustrations). Always replace the O-rings with new ones.

9 Remove the retaining clips, then remove the fuel injectors from the fuel rail (see illustration).

10 If you intend to re-use the same injectors, replace the washer seals (if equipped), grommets and O-rings (see illustration).

11 Installation is the reverse of removal. Use new injector O-rings and tighten the fuel rail mounting bolts to the torque listed in this Chapter's Specifications.

13 Fuel pressure regulator (2005 and earlier models) - replacement

Note: *On 2006 and later models, the fuel pressure regulator is part of the fuel pump module.*

1 Relieve the fuel system pressure (see Section 3), then disconnect the cable from the negative terminal of the battery (see Chapter 5).

2 Remove the upper intake manifold (see Chapter 2A).

3 Disconnect the vacuum hose from the fuel pressure regulator.

4 Disconnect the fuel return line from the regulator.

5 Remove the two bolts (see illustration) and detach the fuel pressure regulator from the fuel rail.

6 If you're installing the same regulator, check the condition of the O-ring, replacing it if necessary.

7 Installation is the reverse of removal.

14 Fuel tank pressure sensor - replacement

1 See Chapter 6 for the fuel tank pressure sensor replacement procedure.

Notes

Notes

Chapter 5
Engine electrical systems

Contents

	Section
Alternator - removal and installation	7
Battery - disconnection	3
Battery and battery tray - removal and installation	4
Battery cables - replacement	5
General information and precautions	1
Ignition coils - replacement	6
Starter motor - removal and installation	8
Troubleshooting	2

Specifications

Charging system

Battery voltage	12.6 to 12.9 volts
Charging voltage	14.0 to 15.0 volts

Ignition system

Ignition coil resistance (approximate)	
2005 and earlier models	
Primary	0.702 to 0.858 ohms (1)
Secondary	10.4 to 15.6 k-ohms
2006 and later models	
Primary	0.558 to 0.682 ohms
Secondary	5.9 to 8.0 K-ohms

(1) Connect a 3V source negative circuit (-) to coil terminal 1 and positive circuit (+) to coil terminal 2. Measure resistance between terminals 2 and 3.

Torque specifications	Ft-lbs (unless otherwise indicated)	Nm
Alternator bolts	19.5 to 24.6	26.5 to 33.3
Starter bolts	31.1 to 39.8	52.2 to 53.9

Note: *One foot-pound (ft-lb) of torque is equivalent to 12 inch-pounds (in-lbs) of torque. Torque values below approximately 15 ft-lbs are expressed in inch-pounds, since most foot-pound torque wrenches are not accurate at these smaller values.*

1 General information and precautions

General information

Ignition system

1 The electronic ignition system consists of the Crankshaft Position (CKP) sensor, the Camshaft Position (CMP) sensor, the Knock Sensor (KS), the Powertrain Control Module (PCM), the ignition switch, the battery, the individual ignition coils or a coil pack, and the spark plugs. For more information on the CKP, CMP and KS sensors, as well as the PCM, refer to Chapter 6.

Charging system

2 The charging system includes the alternator (with an integral voltage regulator), the Powertrain Control Module (PCM), the Body Control Module (BCM), a charge indicator light on the dash, the battery, a fuse or fusible link and the wiring connecting all of these components. The charging system supplies electrical power for the ignition system, the lights, the radio, etc. The alternator is driven by a drivebelt.

Starting system

3 The starting system consists of the battery, the ignition switch, the starter relay, the Powertrain Control Module (PCM), the Body Control Module (BCM), the Transmission Range (TR) switch, the starter motor and solenoid assembly, and the wiring connecting all of the components.

Precautions

4 Always observe the following precautions when working on the electrical system:

a) *Be extremely careful when servicing engine electrical components. They are easily damaged if checked, connected or handled improperly.*
b) *Never leave the ignition switched on for long periods of time when the engine is not running.*
c) *Never disconnect the battery cables while the engine is running.*
d) *Maintain correct polarity when connecting battery cables from another vehicle during jump starting - see "Booster battery (jump) starting" (Chapter 0 Section 8).*
e) *Always disconnect the cable from the negative battery terminal before working on the electrical system, but read the battery disconnection procedure first (see Chapter 5).*

5 It's also a good idea to review the safety-related information regarding the engine electrical systems located in "Safety first!" (Chapter 0 Section 10) before beginning any operation included in this Chapter.

2 Troubleshooting

Ignition system

1 If a malfunction occurs in the ignition system, do not immediately assume that any particular part is causing the problem. First, check the following items:

a) *Make sure that the cable clamps at the battery terminals are clean and tight.*
b) *Test the condition of the battery (see Steps 21 through 24). If it doesn't pass all the tests, replace it.*
c) *Check the ignition coil or coil pack connections.*
d) *Check any relevant fuses in the engine compartment fuse and relay box (see Chapter 12). If they're burned, determine the cause and repair the circuit.*

Check

Warning: *Because of the high voltage generated by the ignition system, use extreme care when performing a procedure involving ignition components.*

Note: *The ignition system components on these vehicles are difficult to diagnose. In the event of ignition system failure that you can't diagnose, have the vehicle tested at a dealer service department or other qualified auto repair facility.*

Note: *You'll need a spark tester for the following test. Spark testers are available at most auto supply stores.*

2 If the engine turns over but won't start, verify that there is sufficient ignition voltage to fire the spark plugs as follows.

3 On models with a coil-over-plug type ignition system, remove a coil and install the tester between the boot at the lower end of the coil and the spark plug (see illustration). On models with spark plug wires, disconnect a spark plug wire from a spark plug and install the tester between the spark plug wire boot and the spark plug.

Caution: *Do NOT crank the engine or allow it to run for more than five seconds; running the engine for more than five seconds may set a Diagnostic Trouble Code (DTC) for a cylinder misfire.*

4 Crank the engine and note whether or not the tester flashes.

Models with a coil-on-plug type ignition system

5 If the tester flashes during cranking, the coil is delivering sufficient voltage to the spark plug to fire it. Repeat this test for each cylinder to verify that the other coils are OK.

6 If the tester doesn't flash, remove a coil from another cylinder and swap it for the one being tested. If the tester now flashes, you know that the original coil is bad. If the tester still doesn't flash, the PCM or wiring harness is probably defective. Have the PCM checked out by a dealer service department or other qualified repair shop (testing the PCM is beyond the scope of the do-it-yourselfer because it requires expensive special tools).

7 If the tester flashes during cranking but a misfire code (related to the cylinder being tested) has been stored, the spark plug could be fouled or defective.

Models with spark plug wires

8 If the tester flashes during cranking, sufficient voltage is reaching the spark plug to fire it.

9 Repeat this test on the remaining cylinders.

10 Proceed on this basis until you have verified there is a good spark from each spark plug wire. If there is, then you have verified that the coils in the coil pack are functioning correctly and that the spark plug wires are OK.

11 If there is not spark from the spark plug wire, then either the coil is bad, the plug wire is bad or a connection at one end of the plug wire is loose. Assuming that you're using new plug wires or known good wires, then the coil is probably defective. Also inspect the coil pack electrical connector. Make sure that it's clean, tight and in good condition.

12 If all the coils are firing correctly, but the engine misfires, then one or more of the plugs might be fouled. Remove and check the spark plugs or install new ones (see Chapter 1).

13 No further testing of the ignition system is possible without special tools. If the prob-

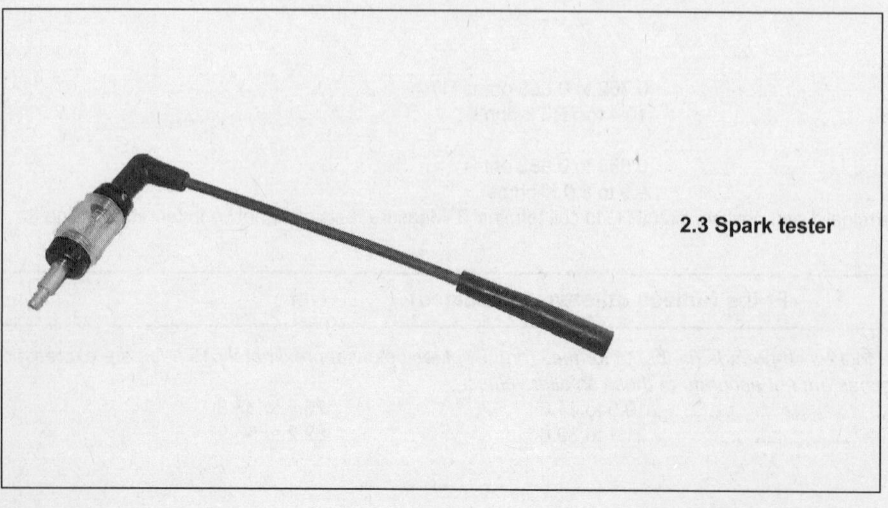

2.3 Spark tester

lem persists, have the ignition system tested by a dealer service department or other qualified repair shop.

Charging system

14 If a malfunction occurs in the charging system, do not automatically assume the alternator is causing the problem. First check the following items:

a) *Check the drivebelt tension and condition (see Chapter 1). Replace it if it's worn or deteriorated.*
b) *Make sure the alternator mounting bolts are tight.*
c) *Inspect the alternator wiring harness and the connectors at the alternator and voltage regulator. They must be in good condition, tight and have no corrosion.*
d) *Check the fusible link (if equipped) or main fuse in the underhood fuse/relay box. If it is burned, determine the cause, repair the circuit and replace the link or fuse (the vehicle will not start and/or the accessories will not work if the fusible link or main fuse is blown).*
e) *Start the engine and check the alternator for abnormal noises (a shrieking or squealing sound indicates a bad bearing).*
f) *Check the battery. Make sure it's fully charged and in good condition (one bad cell in a battery can cause overcharging by the alternator).*
g) *Disconnect the battery cables (negative first, then positive). Inspect the battery posts and the cable clamps for corrosion. Clean them thoroughly if necessary (see Chapter 1). Reconnect the cables (positive first, negative last).*

Alternator - check

15 Use a voltmeter to check the battery voltage with the engine off. It should be at least 12.6 volts (see illustration 2.21).

16 Start the engine and check the battery voltage again. It should now be approximately 13.5 to 15 volts.

17 If the voltage reading is more or less than the specified charging voltage, the voltage regulator is probably defective, which will require replacement of the alternator (the voltage regulator is not replaceable separately). Remove the alternator and have it bench tested (most auto parts stores will do this for you).

18 The charging system (battery) light on the instrument cluster lights up when the ignition key is turned to ON, but it should go out when the engine starts.

19 If the charging system light stays on after the engine has been started, there is a problem with the charging system. Before replacing the alternator, check the battery condition, alternator belt tension and electrical cable connections.

20 If replacing the alternator doesn't restore voltage to the specified range, have the charging system tested by a dealer service department or other qualified repair shop.

Battery - check

Note: *The battery's surface charge must be removed before accurate voltage measurements can be made. Turn on the high beams for ten seconds, then turn them off and let the vehicle stand for two minutes.*

21 Check the battery state of charge. Visually inspect the indicator eye on the top of the battery (if equipped with one); if the indicator eye is black in color, charge the battery (see Chapter 1). Next perform an open circuit voltage test using a digital voltmeter. With the engine and all accessories Off, touch the negative probe of the voltmeter to the negative terminal of the battery and the positive probe to the positive terminal of the battery (see illustration). The battery voltage should be 12.6 volts or slightly above. If the battery is less than the specified voltage, charge the battery before proceeding to the next test. Do not proceed with the battery load test unless the battery charge is correct.

22 Disconnect the negative battery cable, then the positive cable from the battery.

23 Perform a battery load test. An accurate check of the battery condition can only be performed with a load tester (see illustration). This test evaluates the ability of the battery to operate the starter and other accessories during periods of high current draw. Connect the load tester to the battery terminals. Load test the battery according to the tool manufacturer's instructions. This tool increases the load demand (current draw) on the battery.

24 Maintain the load on the battery for 15 seconds and observe that the battery voltage does not drop below 9.6 volts. If the battery condition is weak or defective, the tool will indicate this condition immediately.

Note: *Cold temperatures will cause the minimum voltage reading to drop slightly. Follow the chart given in the manufacturer's instructions to compensate for cold climates. Minimum load voltage for freezing temperatures (32 degrees F) should be approximately 9.1 volts.*

Starting system

The starter rotates, but the engine doesn't

25 Remove the starter (see Section 8). Check the overrunning clutch and bench test the starter to make sure the drive mechanism extends fully for proper engagement with the flywheel ring gear. If it doesn't, replace the starter.

26 Check the flywheel ring gear for missing teeth and other damage. With the ignition turned off, rotate the flywheel so you can check the entire ring gear.

The starter is noisy

27 If the solenoid is making a chattering noise, first check the battery (see Steps 21 through 24). If the battery is okay, check the cables and connections.

28 If you hear a grinding, crashing metallic

2.21 To test the open circuit voltage of the battery, touch the black probe of the voltmeter to the negative terminal and the red probe to the positive terminal of the battery; a fully charged battery should be at least 12.6 volts

2.23 Connect a battery load tester to the battery and check the battery condition under load following the tool manufacturer's instructions

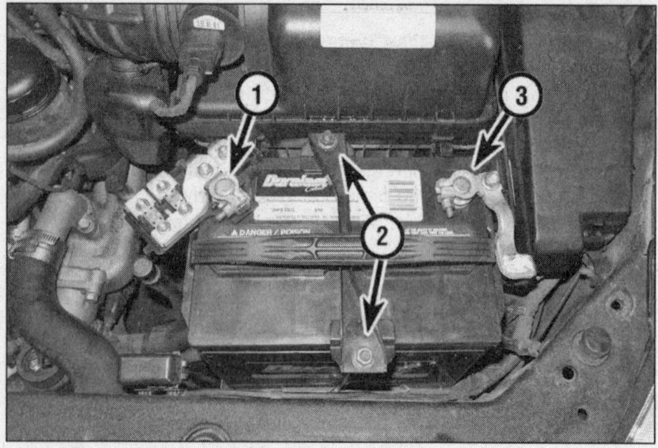

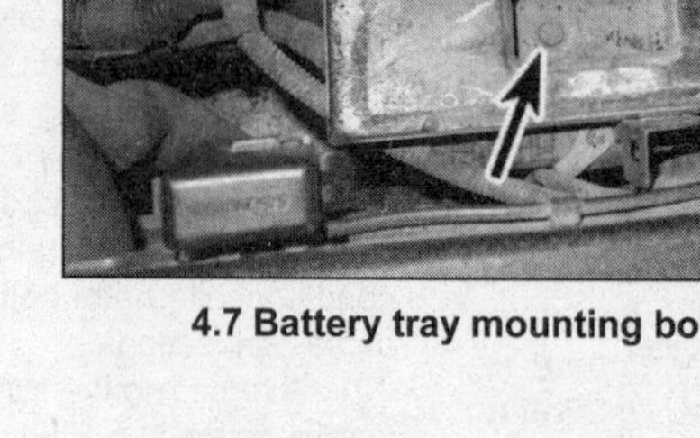

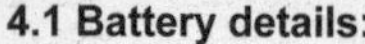

4.1 Battery details:

1 *Positive cable clamp*
2 *Hold-down bracket nuts*
3 *Negative cable clamp*

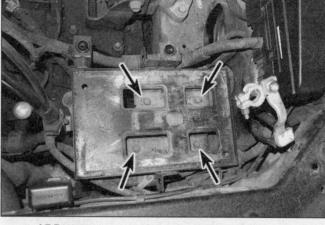

4.7 Battery tray mounting bolts (2006 model shown)

sound when you turn the key to Start, check for loose starter mounting bolts. If they're tight, remove the starter and inspect the teeth on the starter pinion gear and flywheel ring gear. Look for missing or damaged teeth.

29 If the starter sounds fine when you first turn the key to Start, but then stops rotating the engine and emits a zinging sound, the problem is probably a defective starter drive that's not staying engaged with the ring gear. Replace the starter.

The starter rotates slowly

30 Check the battery (see Steps 21 through 24).

31 If the battery is okay, verify all connections (at the battery, the starter solenoid and motor) are clean, corrosion-free and tight. Make sure the cables aren't frayed or damaged.

32 Check that the starter mounting bolts are tight so it grounds properly. Also check the pinion gear and flywheel ring gear for evidence of a mechanical bind (galling, deformed gear teeth or other damage).

The starter does not rotate at all

33 Check the battery (see Steps 21 through 24).

34 If the battery is okay, verify all connections (at the battery, the starter solenoid and motor) are clean, corrosion-free and tight. Make sure the cables aren't frayed or damaged.

35 Check all of the fuses in the underhood fuse/relay box.

36 Check that the starter mounting bolts are tight so it grounds properly.

37 Check for voltage at the starter solenoid "S" terminal when the ignition key is turned to the start position. If voltage is present, replace the starter/solenoid assembly. If no voltage is present, the problem could be the starter relay, the Transmission Range (TR) switch (see Chapter 7), or with an electrical connector somewhere in the circuit (see the wiring diagrams in Chapter 13). Also, on many modern vehicles, the Powertrain Control Module (PCM) and the Body Control Module (BCM) control the voltage signal to the starter solenoid; on such vehicles, a special scan tool is required for diagnosis.

3 Battery - disconnection

Caution: *Always disconnect the cable from the negative battery terminal FIRST and hook it up LAST or the battery may be shorted by the tool being used to loosen the cable clamps.*

1 Some systems on the vehicle require battery power to be available at all times, either to maintain continuous operation (alarm system, power door locks, etc.), or to maintain control unit memory (radio station presets, Powertrain Control Module and other control units). When the battery is disconnected, the power that maintains these systems is cut. So, before you disconnect the battery, please note that on a vehicle with power door locks, it's a wise precaution to remove the key from the ignition and to keep it with you, so that it does not get locked inside if the power door locks should engage accidentally when the battery is reconnected!

Warning: *Some memory savers deliver a considerable amount of current in order to keep vehicle systems operational after the main battery is disconnected. If you're using a memory saver, make sure that the circuit concerned is actually open before servicing it.*

Warning: *If you're going to work near any of the airbag system components, the battery MUST be disconnected and a memory saver must NOT be used. If a memory saver is used, power will be supplied to the airbag, which means that it could accidentally deploy and cause serious personal injury.*

2 Devices known as memory-savers can be used to avoid some of these problems. Precise details vary according to the device used. The typical memory saver is plugged into the cigarette lighter and is connected to a spare battery. Then the vehicle battery can be disconnected from the electrical system. The memory saver will provide sufficient current to maintain audio unit security codes, PCM memory, etc. and will provide power to always hot circuits such as the clock and radio memory circuits.

3 To disconnect the battery for service procedures requiring power to be cut from the vehicle, loosen the cable end bolt and disconnect the cable from the negative battery terminal (see illustration 4.1). Isolate the cable end to prevent it from coming into accidental contact with the battery terminal.

4 Battery and battery tray - removal and installation

Battery

1 Disconnect the cable from the negative battery terminal first, then from the positive battery terminal (see illustration).

2 Remove the battery hold-down clamp.

3 Lift out the battery. Be careful - it's heavy.

Note: *Battery straps and handlers are available at most auto parts stores for reasonable prices. They make it easier to remove and carry the battery.*

4 If you are replacing the battery, make sure you get one that's identical, with the same dimensions, amperage rating, cold cranking rating, etc. Remove the heat shield from the old battery and install it on the new battery.

5 Installation is the reverse of removal. Always connect the positive cable first and the negative cable last.

Battery tray

6 Remove the battery, then, if necessary for access, remove the air filter assembly (see Chapter 4).

7 Remove the battery tray bolts and the battery tray (see illustration).

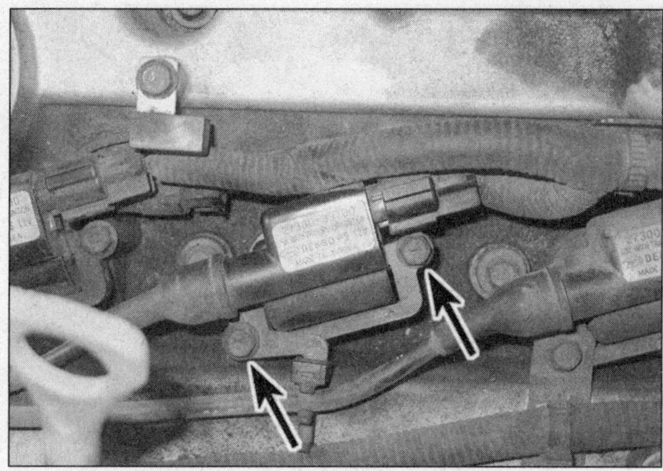

6.5a On 2005 and earlier models, each ignition coil is secured by two bolts

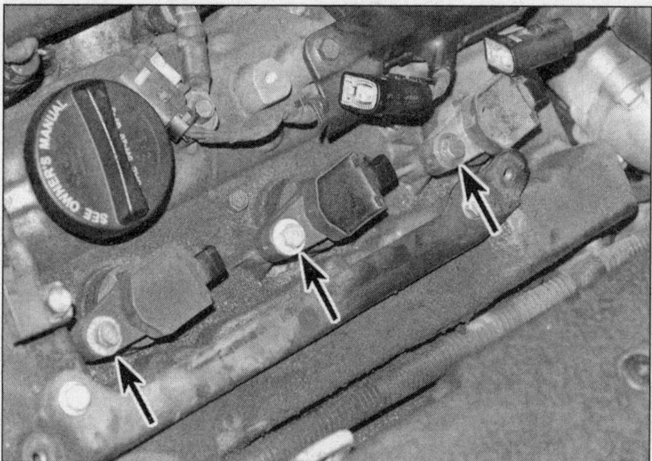

6.5b On 2006 and later models, each ignition coil is secured by one bolt

8 Installation is the reverse of removal. Always connect the positive cable first and the negative cable last.

5 Battery cables - replacement

1 When removing the cables, always disconnect the cable from the negative battery terminal first and hook it up last, or you might accidentally short out the battery with the tool you're using to loosen the cable clamps. Even if you're only replacing the cable for the positive terminal, be sure to disconnect the negative cable from the battery first.
2 Disconnect the old cables from the battery, then trace each of them to their opposite ends and disconnect them. Note the routing of each cable before disconnecting it to ensure correct installation.
3 If you are replacing any of the old cables, take them with you when buying new cables. It is vitally important that you replace the cables with identical parts.
4 Clean the threads of the solenoid or ground connection with a wire brush to remove rust and corrosion. Apply a light coat of battery terminal corrosion inhibitor or petroleum jelly to the threads to prevent future corrosion.
5 Attach the cable to the solenoid or ground connection and tighten the mounting nut/bolt securely.
6 Before connecting a new cable to the battery, make sure that it reaches the battery post without having to be stretched.
7 Connect the cable to the positive battery terminal first, then connect the ground cable to the negative battery terminal.

6 Ignition coils - replacement

1 Disconnect the cable from the negative battery terminal (see Section 3).
2 Remove the engine cover, if equipped.

6.6 After removing the bolt(s), pull the coil straight up and out. Make sure the boot is in good condition (2006 and later models shown)

3 On 2006 and later models, remove the upper intake manifold to allow access to the rear bank ignition coils (see Chapter 2A Section 5).
4 On 2005 and earlier models, disconnect the spark plug wire. Pull on the boot only - not on the wire.
5 Disconnect the electrical connector from the ignition coil, then remove the mounting fastener(s) (see illustrations).
Note: *On 2005 and earlier 3.5L V6 engines, only three ignition coils are used; the ignition coils are mounted over cylinders 2, 4 and 6 with spark plug wires that feed to the other cylinders. The ignition coil on cylinder 2 is connected to cylinder 5, cylinder 4 is connected to cylinder 1 and cylinder 6 is connected to cylinder 3.*
6 Pull the coil straight up and out of the valve cover (see illustration).
7 Installation is the reverse of removal. Apply dielectric grease to the spark plug boot or coil boot prior to installation.

7.3 Alternator electrical connectors - 2006 and later models shown, other models similar

7 Alternator - removal and installation

Removal

Note: *On 2005 and earlier models, the alternator is located on the back side of the engine and accessed through the passenger fenderwell. On 2006 and later models, the alternator is located on the front side of the engine.*
Note: *Access is very limited on these models. It will be necessary to remove various components to gain access (such as the engine cooling fan on some models - see Chapter 3). These components vary from model to model. Raise and support the vehicle as necessary to gain access to the alternator.*
1 Disconnect the cable from the negative battery terminal (see Section 3).
2 Remove the engine cover (if necessary) and the drivebelt (see Chapter 1).
3 Disconnect the electrical connectors from the alternator (see illustration).

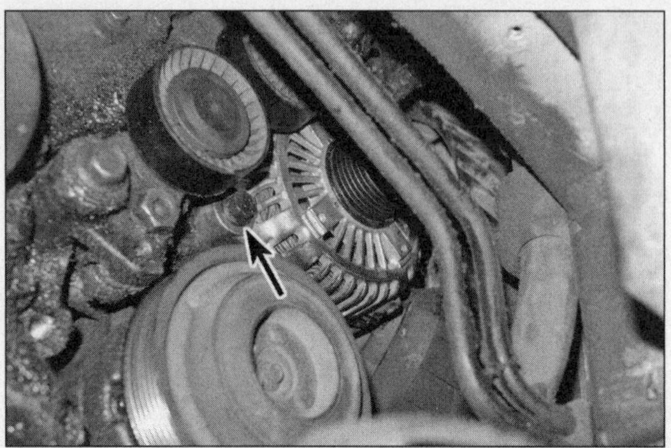

7.4a Remove the lower mounting bolt. . .

7.4b. . . then the upper mounting bolt - 2006 and later models shown, earlier models similar

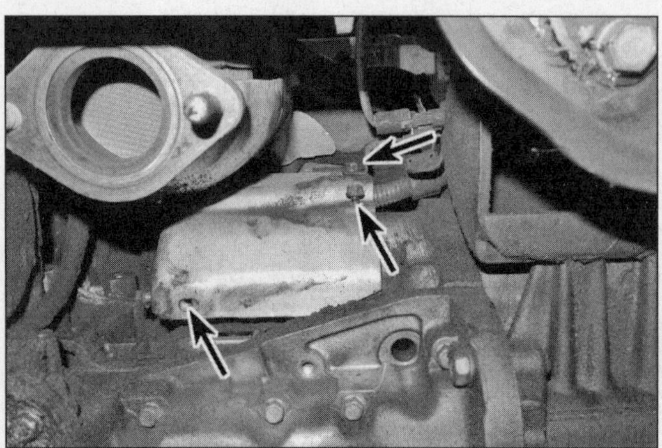

8.3 Starter shield mounting bolt locations

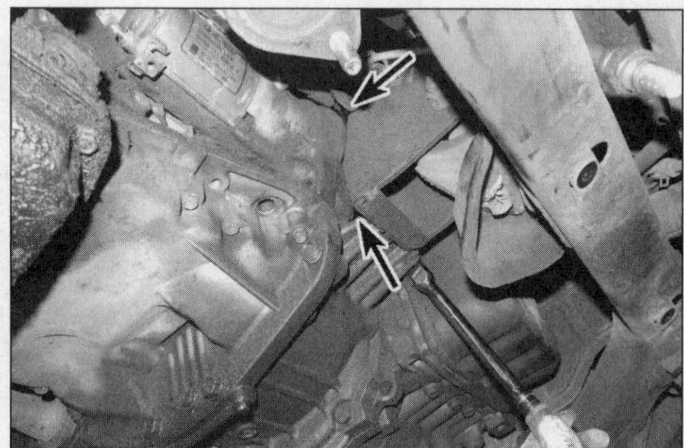

8.5 The starter is retained by two bolts (approximate locations)

4 Remove the mounting bolts (see illustrations) and remove the alternator.

Installation

5 If you're replacing the alternator, take the old alternator with you when purchasing a replacement unit. Make sure that the new/rebuilt unit is identical to the old alternator. Look at the terminals - they should be the same in number, size and locations as the terminals on the old alternator. Finally, look at the identification markings - they will be stamped in the housing or printed on a tag or plaque affixed to the housing. Make sure that these numbers are the same on both alternators.

6 If the replacement alternator doesn't have a pulley installed, you might have to switch the pulley from the old unit to the replacement unit. When buying a new or rebuilt alternator, ask about the shop's policy regarding pulley swapping. Some shops will perform this service for free.

7 Installation is the reverse of removal. After the alternator is installed, check the charging voltage to verify that the alternator is operating correctly (see Section 2).

8 Starter motor - removal and installation

1 Disconnect the cable from the negative battery terminal (see Section 3). Raise and the front of the vehicle and support it securely on jackstands. Remove the engine undercover.

2 Unbolt the exhaust pipes from the exhaust manifolds and remove the pipes for access to the starter.

3 Remove the starter shield, if equipped (see illustration).

4 Detach the electrical connectors from the starter/solenoid assembly.

5 Remove the starter motor mounting bolts from the transaxle side and remove the starter (see illustration).

6 Installation is the reverse of removal.

Notes

Notes

Chapter 6
Emissions and engine control systems

Contents

	Section
Accelerator Pedal Position (APP) sensor - replacement	4
Camshaft Position (CMP) sensor - replacement	5
Catalytic converters - replacement	21
Crankshaft Position (CKP) sensor - replacement	6
CVVT Oil Control Valve (OCV) - replacement	15
CVVT Oil Temperature Sensor (OTS) - replacement	14
Engine Coolant Temperature (ECT) sensor - replacement	7
Evaporative emissions control (EVAP) system - component replacement	22
Fuel tank pressure sensor - replacement	13
General information	1
Knock sensor - replacement	8
Manifold Absolute Pressure (MAP) sensor - replacement	9
Mass Air Flow/Intake Air Temperature (MAF/IAT), Barometric Pressure/Intake Air Temperature (BARO/IAT) sensors - replacement	10
Obtaining and clearing Diagnostic Trouble Codes (DTCs)	3
On Board Diagnosis (OBD) system	2
Oxygen sensors - general information and replacement	11
Positive Crankcase Ventilation (PCV) valve - replacement	23
Powertrain Control Module (PCM) - replacement	20
Throttle Position (TP) sensor - replacement and adjustment	12
Transmission Range (TR) sensor - removal, installation and adjustment	18
Transmission speed sensors - replacement	19
Variable Charge Motion Actuator - replacement	17
Variable Intake Solenoid (VIS) control valve - replacement	16

Specifications

Torque specifications

Note: One foot-pound (ft-lb) of torque is equivalent to 12 inch-pounds (in-lbs) of torque. Torque values below approximately 15 foot-pounds are expressed in inch-pounds, because most foot-pound torque wrenches are not accurate at these smaller values.

	Ft-lbs (unless otherwise indicated)	Nm
Knock sensor	17	23
Oxygen sensor		
2005 and earlier models	29 to 34	40 to 50
2006 through 2010 models	36.2 to 43.4	49 to 59
2011 and later models	26 to 33.3	35.3 to 45.1
Engine coolant temperature sensor		
2005 and earlier models	90 to 102 in-lbs	10 to 12
2006 through 2010 models	14.5 to 28.9	19.6 to 39.2
Camshaft position sensor bolt		
2005 and earlier models	Not available	
2006 and later models	61.2 to 86.4 in-lbs	6.9 to 9.8
Crankshaft position sensor bolt(s)		
2005 and earlier models	Not available	
2006 and later models	69.6 to 104.4 in-lbs	7.8 to 11.8
CVVT oil control valve mounting bolts	86.4 to 104.4 in-lbs	9.8 to 11.8
CVVT oil temperature sensor (2006 and later models)	26 to 32	35 to 44
Variable Intake Solenoid control valve bolts		
2006 through 2012 models	78 to 104.4 in-lbs	8.8 to 11.8
2014 model	48 to 74.4 in-lbs	5.4 to 8.3
Variable Charge Motion Actuator bolts	70.8 to 97.2 in-lbs	8 to 11

1 General information

1 To prevent pollution of the atmosphere from incompletely burned and evaporating gases, and to maintain good driveability and fuel economy, a number of emission control systems are incorporated. They include the:

Catalytic converter

2 A catalytic converter is an emission control device in the exhaust system that reduces certain pollutants in the exhaust gas stream. There are two types of converters: oxidation converters and reduction converters.

3 Oxidation converters contain a monolithic substrate (a ceramic honeycomb) coated with the semi-precious metals platinum and palladium. An oxidation catalyst reduces unburned hydrocarbons (HC) and carbon monoxide (CO) by adding oxygen to the exhaust stream as it passes through the substrate, which, in the presence of high temperature and the catalyst materials, converts the HC and CO to water vapor (H2O) and carbon dioxide (CO2).

4 Reduction converters contain a monolithic substrate coated with platinum and rhodium. A reduction catalyst reduces oxides of nitrogen (NOx) by removing oxygen, which in the presence of high temperature and the catalyst material produces nitrogen (N) and carbon dioxide (CO2).

5 Catalytic converters that combine both types of catalysts in one assembly are known as three-way catalysts (TWCs). A TWC can reduce all three pollutants.

Evaporative Emissions Control (EVAP) system

6 The Evaporative Emissions Control (EVAP) system prevents fuel system vapors (which contain unburned hydrocarbons) from escaping into the atmosphere. On warm days, vapors trapped inside the fuel tank expand until the pressure reaches a certain threshold. Then the fuel vapors are routed from the fuel tank through the fuel vapor vent valve and the fuel vapor control valve to the EVAP canister, where they're stored temporarily until the next time the vehicle is operated. When the conditions are right (engine warmed up, vehicle up to speed, moderate or heavy load on the engine, etc.) the PCM opens the canister purge valve, which allows fuel vapors to be drawn from the canister into the intake manifold. Once in the intake manifold, the fuel vapors mix with incoming air before being drawn through the intake ports into the combustion chambers where they're burned up with the rest of the air/fuel mixture. The EVAP system is complex and virtually impossible to troubleshoot without the right tools and training.

Powertrain Control Module (PCM)

7 The Powertrain Control Module (PCM) is the brain of the engine management system. It also controls a wide variety of other vehicle systems. In order to program the new PCM, the dealer needs the vehicle as well as the new PCM. If you're planning to replace the PCM with a new one, there is no point in trying to do so at home because you won't be able to program it yourself.

Positive Crankcase Ventilation (PCV) system

8 The Positive Crankcase Ventilation (PCV) system reduces hydrocarbon emissions by scavenging crankcase vapors, which are rich in unburned hydrocarbons. A PCV valve or orifice regulates the flow of gases into the intake manifold in proportion to the amount of intake vacuum available.

9 The PCV system generally consists of the fresh air inlet hose, the PCV valve or orifice and the crankcase ventilation hose (or PCV hose). The fresh air inlet hose connects the air intake duct to a pipe on the valve cover. The crankcase ventilation hose (or PCV hose) connects the PCV valve or orifice in the valve cover to the intake manifold.

Information Sensors

10 Typical information sensors (see illustrations).

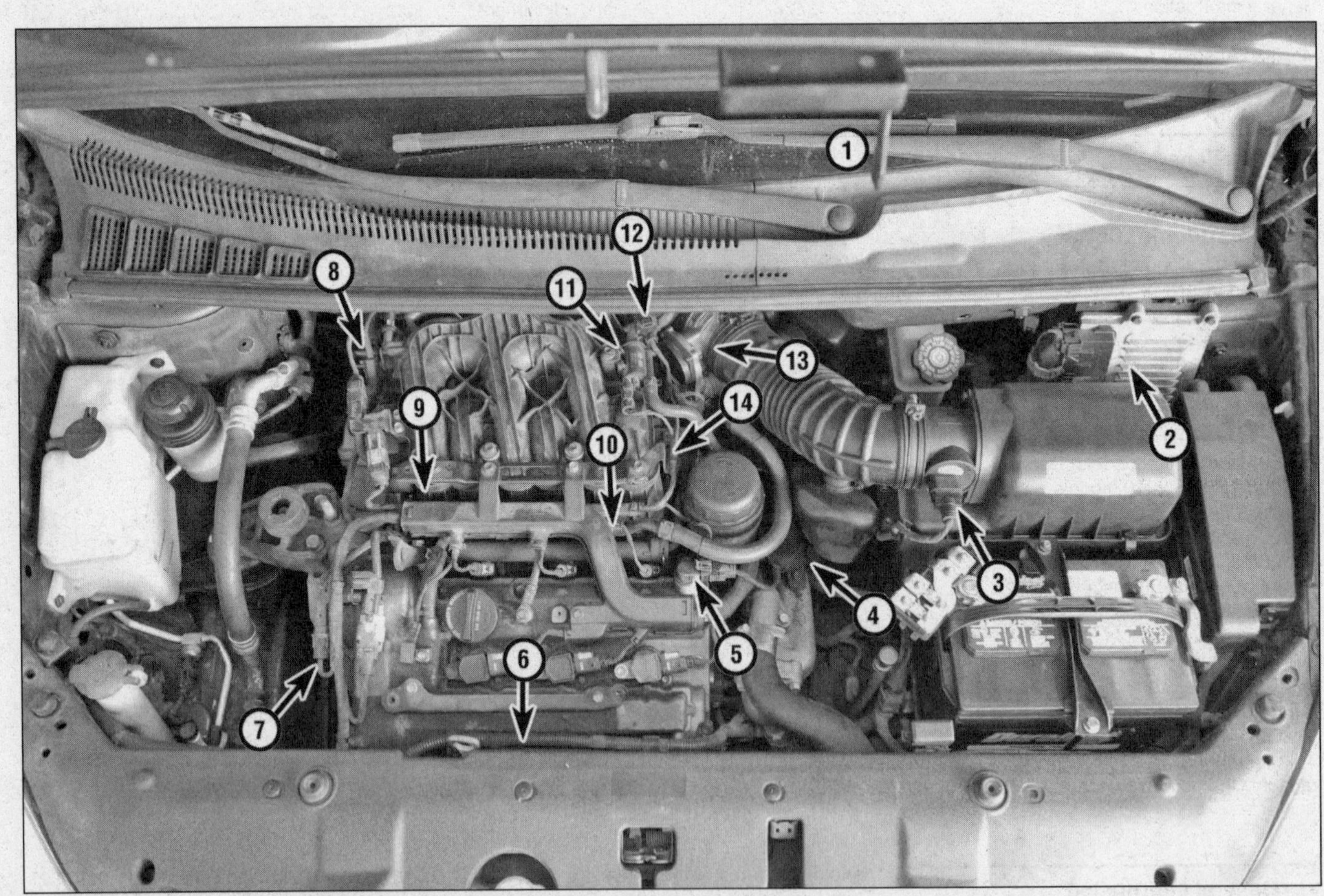

1.9 Emissions control and engine control components (2006 3.8L engine shown)

1 *Accelerator Pedal Position (APP) sensor*
2 *Powertrain Control Module (PCM)*
3 *Mass Air Flow (MAF) sensor & Intake Air Temperature (IAT) Sensor*
4 *Engine Coolant Temperature (ECT) sensor*
5 *Camshaft Position (CMP) sensor (Bank 1)*
6 *Heated oxygen sensor*
7 *CVVT Oil Control Valve (OCV)*
8 *Variable Intake Solenoid (VIS) valve*
9 *Knock sensor - under intake manifold*
10 *Knock sensor - under intake manifold*
11 *Purge control solenoid valve (PCSV)*
12 *Manifold Absolute Pressure (MAP) sensor*
13 *Electronic Throttle Control (ETC) module - Throttle Position Sensor (TPS)/ETC motor*
14 *Camshaft Position (CMP) sensor (Bank 2)*

Information Sensors

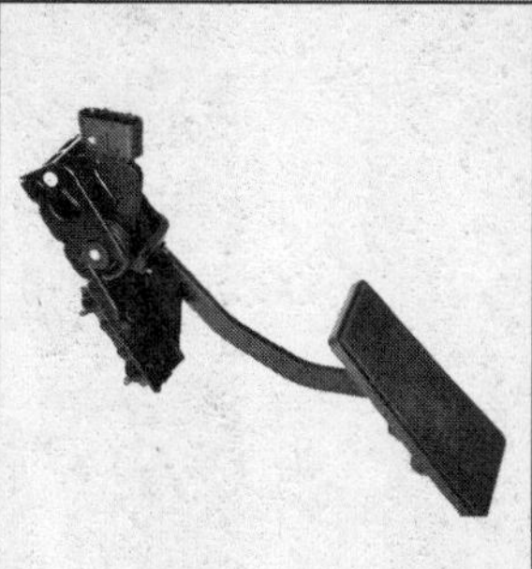

Accelerator Pedal Position (APP) sensor - as you press the accelerator pedal, the APP sensor alters its voltage signal to the PCM in proportion to the angle of the pedal, and the PCM commands a motor inside the throttle body to open or close the throttle plate accordingly

Camshaft Position (CMP) sensor - produces a signal that the PCM uses to identify the number 1 cylinder and to time the firing sequence of the fuel injectors

Crankshaft Position (CKP) sensor - produces a signal that the PCM uses to calculate engine speed and crankshaft position, which enables it to synchronize ignition timing with fuel injector timing, and to detect misfires

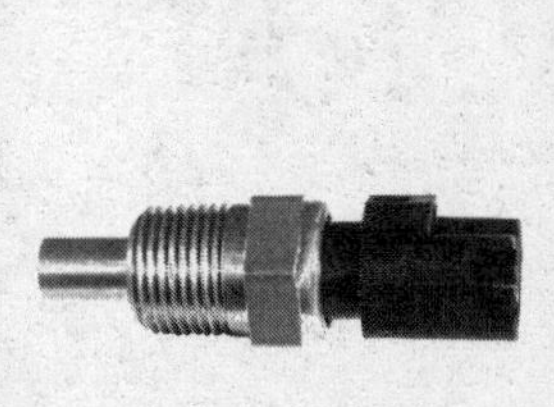

Engine Coolant Temperature (ECT) sensor - a thermistor (temperature-sensitive variable resistor) that sends a voltage signal to the PCM, which uses this data to determine the temperature of the engine coolant

Fuel tank pressure sensor - measures the fuel tank pressure and controls fuel tank pressure by signaling the EVAP system to purge the fuel tank vapors when the pressure becomes excessive

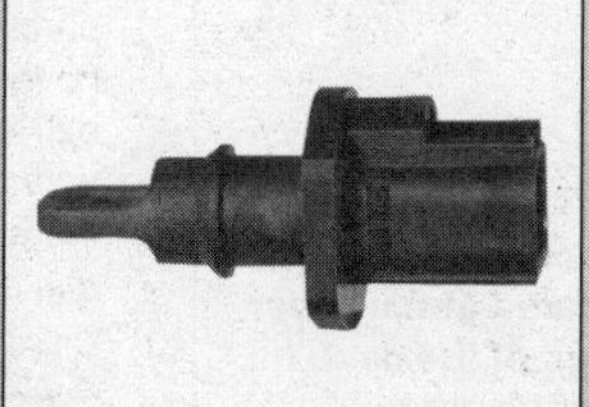

Intake Air Temperature (IAT) sensor - monitors the temperature of the air entering the engine and sends a signal to the PCM to determine injector pulse-width (the duration of each injector's on-time) and to adjust spark timing (to prevent spark knock)

Knock sensor - a piezoelectric crystal that oscillates in proportion to engine vibration which produces a voltage output that is monitored by the PCM. This retards the ignition timing when the oscillation exceeds a certain threshold

Manifold Absolute Pressure (MAP) sensor - monitors the pressure or vacuum inside the intake manifold. The PCM uses this data to determine engine load so that it can alter the ignition advance and fuel enrichment

Mass Air Flow (MAF) sensor - measures the amount of intake air drawn into the engine. It uses a hot-wire sensing element to measure the amount of air entering the engine

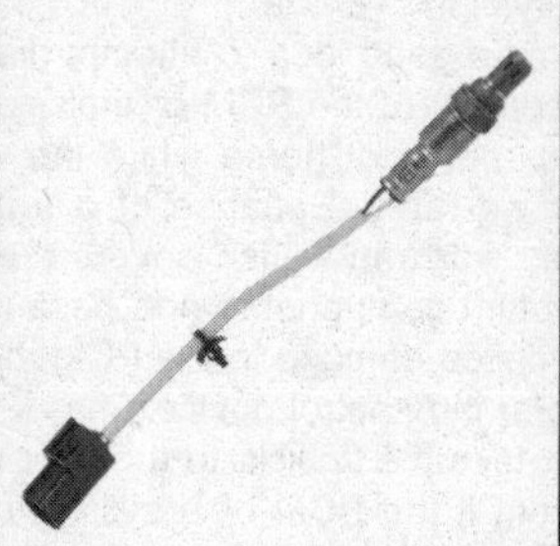

Oxygen sensors - generates a small variable voltage signal in proportion to the difference between the oxygen content in the exhaust stream and the oxygen content in the ambient air. The PCM uses this information to maintain the proper air/fuel ratio. A second oxygen sensor monitors the efficiency of the catalytic converter

Throttle Position (TP) sensor - a potentiometer that generates a voltage signal that varies in relation to the opening angle of the throttle plate inside the throttle body. Works with the PCM and other sensors to calculate injector pulse width (the duration of each injector's on-time)

Photos courtesy of Wells Manufacturing, except APP and MAF sensors.

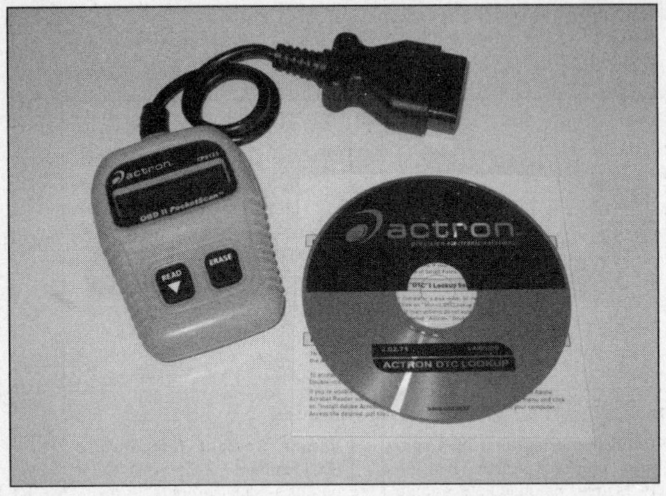

2.4a Simple code readers are an economical way to extract

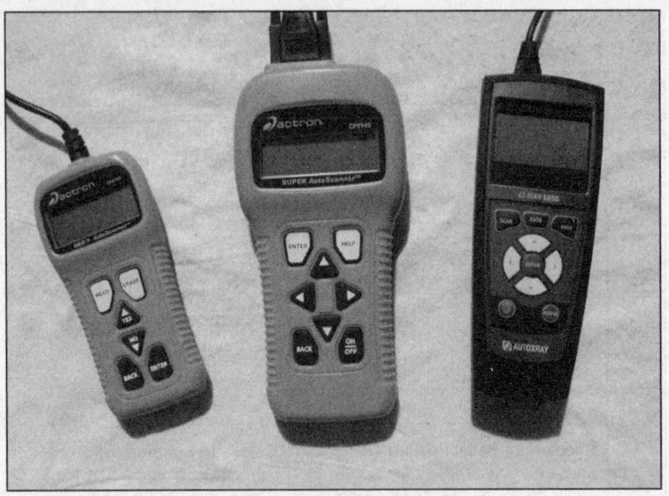

2.4b Hand-held scan tools like these can extract computer codes and also perform diagnostics

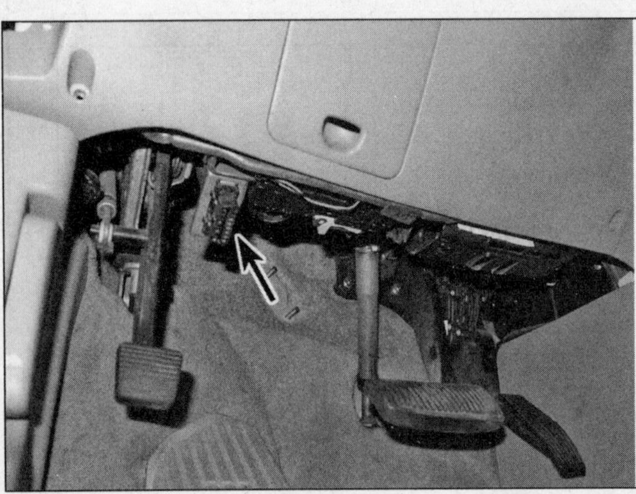

3.3 The Data Link Connector (DLC) is located at the lower edge of the dash on the left side

2 On Board Diagnosis (OBD) system

General description

1 All models are equipped with the second generation OBD-II system. This system consists of an on-board computer known as the Powertrain Control Module (PCM), and information sensors, which monitor various functions of the engine and send data to the PCM. This system incorporates a series of diagnostic monitors that detect and identify fuel injection and emissions control system faults and store the information in the computer memory. This system also tests sensors and output actuators, diagnoses drive cycles, freezes data and clears codes.

2 The PCM is the brain of the electronically controlled fuel and emissions system. It receives data from a number of sensors and other electronic components (switches, relays, etc.). Based on the information it receives, the PCM generates output signals to control various relays, solenoids (fuel injectors) and other actuators. The PCM is specifically calibrated to optimize the emissions, fuel economy and driveability of the vehicle.

3 It isn't a good idea to attempt diagnosis or replacement of the PCM or emission control components at home while the vehicle is under warranty. Because of a federally-mandated warranty which covers the emissions system components and because any owner-induced damage to the PCM, the sensors and/or the control devices may void this warranty, take the vehicle to a dealer service department if the PCM or a system component malfunctions.

Scan tool information

4 Because extracting the Diagnostic Trouble Codes (DTCs) from an engine management system is now the first step in troubleshooting many computer-controlled systems and components, a code reader, at the very least, will be required (see illustration). More powerful scan tools can also perform many of the diagnostics once associated with expensive factory scan tools (see illustration). If you're planning to obtain a generic scan tool for your vehicle, make sure that it's compatible with OBD-II systems. If you don't plan to purchase a code reader or scan tool and don't have access to one, you can have the codes extracted by a dealer service department or an independent repair shop.

Note: *Some auto parts stores even provide this service.*

3 Obtaining and clearing Diagnostic Trouble Codes (DTCs)

1 All models covered by this manual are equipped with on-board diagnostics. When the PCM recognizes a malfunction in a monitored emission or engine control system, component or circuit, it turns on the Malfunction Indicator Light (MIL) on the dash. The PCM will continue to display the MIL until the problem is fixed and the Diagnostic Trouble Code (DTC) is cleared from the PCM's memory. You'll need a scan tool to access any DTCs stored in the PCM.

2 Before outputting any DTCs stored in the PCM, thoroughly inspect ALL electrical connectors and hoses. Make sure that all electrical connections are tight, clean and free of corrosion. And make sure that all hoses are correctly connected, fit tightly and are in good condition (no cracks or tears).

Accessing the DTCs

3 The Diagnostic Trouble Codes (DTCs) can only be accessed with a code reader or scan tool. Professional scan tools are expensive, but relatively inexpensive generic code readers or scan tools (see illustrations 2.4a and 2.4b) are available at most auto parts stores. Simply plug the connector of the scan tool into the diagnostic connector (see illustration). Then follow the instructions included with the scan tool to extract the DTCs.

4 Once you have output all of the stored DTCs, look them up on the accompanying DTC chart.

5 After troubleshooting the source of each DTC, make any necessary repairs or replace the defective component(s).

Clearing the DTCs

6 Clear the DTCs with the code reader or scan tool in accordance with the instructions provided by the tool's manufacturer.

Diagnostic Trouble Codes

7 The accompanying tables are a list of the Diagnostic Trouble Codes (DTCs) that can be accessed by a do-it-yourselfer working at home (there are many, many more DTCs available to professional mechanics with proprietary scan tools and software, but those codes cannot be accessed by a generic scan tool). If, after you have checked and repaired the connectors, wire harness and vacuum hoses (if applicable) for an emission-related system, component or circuit, the problem persists, have the vehicle checked by a dealer service department or other qualified repair shop.

OBD-II trouble codes

Note: *Not all trouble codes apply to all models.*

Code	Code identification
P0010	Intake camshaft position actuator, open circuit (Bank 1)
P0011	Intake camshaft position timing over-advanced (Bank 1)
P0012	Intake camshaft position timing, over-retarded (Bank 1)
P013A	Oxygen sensor slow response, rich to lean (Bank 1, Sensor 2)
P013C	Oxygen sensor slow response, rich to lean (Bank 2, Sensor 2)
P013E	Oxygen sensor delayed response, rich to lean (Bank 1, Sensor 2)
P0014	Camshaft ‘B’ position sensor, over advanced
P014A	Oxygen sensor delayed response, rich to lean (Bank 2, Sensor 2)
P0016	Crankshaft position-to-camshaft position correlation (Bank 1, sensor A)
P0017	Crankshaft position – to intake camshaft position correlation (Bank 1, Sensor B)
P0018	Crankshaft position-to-camshaft position correlation (Bank 2, sensor A)
P0019	Crankshaft position – to intake camshaft position correlation (Bank 2, sensor B)
P0020	Intake camshaft position actuator, open circuit (Bank 2)
P0021	Camshaft position - timing over-advanced (Bank 2, sensor A)
P0021	Intake camshaft position timing over-advanced (Bank 2)
P0024	Camshaft position - timing over-advanced (Bank 2, sensor B)
P0022	Intake camshaft position timing over-retarded (Bank 2)
P025A	Fuel pump module control circuit open
P025B	Fuel pump module control circuit range or performance problem
P0030	Oxygen sensor heater control circuit (Bank 1, Sensor 1)
P0031	Oxygen sensor heater circuit low (Bank 1, Sensor 1)
P0032	Oxygen sensor heater circuit high (Bank 1, Sensor 1)
P0036	Oxygen sensor heater control circuit (Bank 1, Sensor 2)
P0037	Oxygen sensor heater circuit low (Bank 1, Sensor 2)

OBD-II trouble codes (continued)

Note: *Not all trouble codes apply to all models.*

Code	Code identification
P0038	Oxygen sensor heater circuit high (Bank 1, Sensor 2)
P0040	Oxygen sensor signals swapped (Bank 1, Sensor 1/Bank 2, Sensor 1)
P0041	Oxygen sensor signals swapped (Bank 1, Sensor 2/Bank 2, Sensor 2)
P0050	Oxygen sensor heater control circuit (Bank 2, Sensor 1)
P0050	Oxygen sensor heater circuit problem (Bank 1, Sensor 1)
P050A	Cold start idle air control performance
P050B	Cold start ignition timing performance
P050E	Cold start engine exhaust temperature out of range
P0051	Oxygen sensor heater circuit low (Bank 1, Sensor 1)
P0052	Oxygen sensor heater circuit high (Bank 1, Sensor 1)
P052A	Cold start camshaft position timing over-advanced (Bank 1)
P052B	Cold start camshaft position timing over-retarded (Bank 1)
P052C	Cold start camshaft position timing over-advanced (Bank 2)
P052D	Cold start camshaft position timing over-retarded (Bank 2)
P0053	Oxygen sensor heater resistance (Bank 1, Sensor 1)
P053A	Positive Crankcase Ventilation (PCV) heater control circuit open
P0054	Oxygen sensor heater resistance (Bank 1, Sensor 2)
P0055	Oxygen sensor heater resistance (Bank 1, Sensor 3)
P0056	Oxygen sensor heater control circuit problem (Bank 2, Sensor 2)
P0057	Oxygen sensor heater control circuit low (Bank 2, Sensor 2)
P0058	Oxygen sensor heater control circuit high (Bank 2, Sensor 2)
P0059	Oxygen sensor heater resistance (Bank 2, Sensor 1)
P0060	Oxygen sensor heater resistance (Bank 2, Sensor 2)
P060A	Internal control module monitoring processor performance
P060B	Internal control module analog/digital processing performance
P060C	Internal control module main processor performance
P060D	Internal control module accelerator pedal position performance
P061B	Internal control module torque calculation performance
P061C	Internal control module engine rpm performance

Code	Code identification
P061D	Internal control module engine air mass performance
P061F	Internal control module throttle actuator controller performance
P062C	Internal control module vehicle speed performance
P064D	Internal control module oxygen sensor processor performance (Bank 1)
P064E	Internal control module oxygen sensor processor performance (Bank 2)
P065B	Alternator control circuit range or performance problem
P0068	Manifold Absolute Pressure (MAP) sensor/Mass Air Flow (MAF) sensor-to-throttle position correlation
P0076	Intake control solenoid valve circuit low (four-cylinder)
P0077	Intake control solenoid valve circuit high (four-cylinder)
P0079	Exhaust control solenoid valve circuit low (four-cylinder)
P0080	Exhaust control solenoid valve circuit high (four-cylinder)
P0082	Intake valve control solenoid circuit-low (Bank 2)
P0083	Intake valve control solenoid circuit-high (Bank 2)
P0085	Exhaust valve control solenoid circuit-low (Bank 2)
P0086	Exhaust valve control solenoid circuit-high (Bank 2)
P0097	Intake Air Temperature (IAT) sensor 2 circuit, low voltage
P0098	Intake Air Temperature (IAT) sensor 2 circuit, high voltage
P0102	Mass or volume air flow A circuit, low voltage
P0104	Mass Air Flow (MAF) sensor A circuit, intermittent or erratic signal
P0106	Manifold Absolute Pressure (MAP)/(BARO) Barometric Pressure sensor circuit performance problem
P0106	Manifold Absolute Pressure (MAP) sensor circuit, range or performance problem
P0107	Manifold Absolute Pressure (MAP)/(BARO) Barometric Pressure circuit low
P0107	Manifold Absolute Pressure (MAP) sensor circuit, low voltage
P0108	Manifold Absolute Pressure (MAP)/(BARO) Barometric Pressure circuit high
P0108	Manifold Absolute Pressure (MAP) sensor circuit, high voltage
P0109	Manifold Absolute Pressure (MAP) sensor circuit, intermittent signal
P0111	Intake Air Temperature (IAT) sensor circuit, range or performance problem
P0112	Intake Air Temperature (IAT) sensor circuit, low voltage
P0113	Intake Air Temperature (IAT) sensor circuit, high voltage
P0114	Intake Air Temperature (IAT) sensor circuit, intermittent or erratic signal
P0116	Engine Coolant Temperature (ECT) sensor circuit, range or performance problem

OBD-II trouble codes (continued)

Note: *Not all trouble codes apply to all models.*

Code	Code identification
P0117	Engine Coolant Temperature (ECT) sensor circuit, low voltage
P0118	Engine Coolant Temperature (ECT) sensor circuit, high voltage
P0119	Engine Coolant Temperature (ECT) sensor circuit, intermittent or erratic signal
P0121	Throttle Position (TP) sensor A circuit, range or performance problem
P0122	Throttle Position (TP) sensor A circuit, low voltage
P0123	Throttle Position (TP) sensor A circuit, high voltage
P0125	Insufficient coolant temperature for closed loop fuel control
P0128	Coolant temperature below coolant thermostat's regulating temperature
P0130	Oxygen sensor circuit malfunction (Bank 1, Sensor 1)
P0131	Oxygen sensor circuit, low voltage (Bank 1, Sensor 1)
P0132	Oxygen sensor circuit, high voltage (Bank 1, Sensor 1)
P0133	Oxygen sensor circuit, slow response (Bank 1, Sensor 1)
P0134	Oxygen sensor circuit, no activity detected (Bank 1, Sensor 1)
P0135	Oxygen sensor heater circuit malfunction (Bank 1, Sensor 1)
P0137	Oxygen sensor circuit, low voltage (Bank 1, Sensor 2)
P0138	Oxygen sensor circuit, high voltage (Bank 1, Sensor 2)
P0139	Oxygen sensor circuit, slow response (Bank 1, Sensor 2)
P0140	Oxygen sensor circuit, no activity detected (Bank 1, Sensor 2)
P0144	Oxygen sensor circuit, high voltage (Bank 1, Sensor 3)
P0147	Oxygen sensor heater circuit malfunction (Bank 1, Sensor 3)
P0148	Fuel delivery error
P0150	Oxygen sensor circuit malfunction (Bank 2, Sensor 1)
P0151	Oxygen sensor circuit, low voltage (Bank 2, Sensor 1)
P0152	Oxygen sensor circuit, high voltage (Bank 2, Sensor 1)
P0153	Oxygen sensor circuit, slow response (Bank 2, Sensor 1)
P0154	Oxygen sensor circuit, no activity detected (Bank 2, Sensor 1)
P0155	Oxygen sensor heater circuit malfunction (Bank 2, Sensor 1)
P0157	Oxygen sensor circuit, low voltage (Bank 2, Sensor 2)
P0158	Oxygen sensor circuit, high voltage (Bank 2, Sensor 2)

Code	Code identification
P0159	Oxygen sensor circuit, slow response (Bank 2, Sensor 2)
P0160	Oxygen sensor circuit, no activity detected (Bank 2, Sensor 2)
P0161	Oxygen sensor heater circuit malfunction (Bank 2, Sensor 2)
P0171	System too lean (Bank 1)
P0172	System too rich (Bank 1)
P0174	System too lean (Bank 2)
P0175	System too rich (Bank 2)
P0180	Fuel temperature sensor circuit malfunction
P0181	Fuel temperature sensor circuit, range or performance problem
P0182	Fuel temperature sensor circuit, low voltage
P0183	Fuel temperature sensor circuit, high voltage
P0191	Fuel rail pressure sensor circuit, range or performance problem
P0192	Fuel rail pressure sensor circuit, low voltage
P0193	Fuel rail pressure sensor circuit, high voltage
P0196	Engine Oil Temperature (EOT) sensor circuit, range or performance problem
P0197	Engine Oil Temperature (EOT) sensor circuit, low voltage
P0198	Engine Oil Temperature (EOT) sensor circuit, high voltage
P0201	Injector open circuit, cylinder 1
P0202	Injector open circuit, cylinder 2
P0203	Injector open circuit, cylinder 3
P0204	Injector open circuit, cylinder 4
P0205	Injector open circuit, cylinder 5
P0206	Injector open circuit, cylinder 6
P0217	Engine coolant over-temperature condition
P0218	Transaxle fluid temperature over-temperature condition
P0219	Engine over-speed condition
P0221	Throttle Position (TP) sensor circuit, range or performance problem
P0222	Throttle Position (TP) sensor circuit, low voltage
P0223	Throttle Position (TP) sensor circuit, high voltage
P0230	Fuel pump primary circuit malfunction
P0231	Fuel pump secondary circuit, low voltage

OBD-II trouble codes (continued)

Note: *Not all trouble codes apply to all models.*

Code	Code identification
P0232	Fuel pump secondary circuit, high voltage
P0261	Cylinder 1 injector circuit, low voltage
P0262	Cylinder 1 injector circuit, high voltage
P0263	Cylinder 1 injector contribution/balance problem
P0264	Cylinder 2 injector circuit, low voltage
P0265	Cylinder 2 injector circuit, high voltage
P0266	Cylinder 2 injector contribution/balance problem
P0267	Cylinder 3 injector circuit, low voltage
P0268	Cylinder 3 injector circuit, high voltage
P0269	Cylinder 3 injector contribution/balance problem
P0270	Cylinder 4 injector circuit, low voltage
P0271	Cylinder 4 injector circuit, high voltage
P0272	Cylinder 4 injector contribution/balance problem
P0273	Cylinder 5 injector circuit, low voltage
P0274	Cylinder 5 injector circuit, high voltage
P0275	Cylinder 5 injector contribution/balance problem
P0276	Cylinder 6 injector circuit, low voltage
P0277	Cylinder 6 injector circuit, high voltage
P0278	Cylinder 6 injector contribution/balance problem
P0298	Engine oil over-temperature condition
P0300	Random misfire detected
P0301	Cylinder 1 misfire
P0302	Cylinder 2 misfire
P0303	Cylinder 3 misfire
P0304	Cylinder 4 misfire
P0305	Cylinder 5 misfire
P0306	Cylinder 6 misfire
P0315	Crankshaft position system variation not learned
P0316	Misfire detected on start-up (first 1000 revolutions)

Code	Code identification
P0320	Ignition/distributor engine speed input circuit
P0325	Knock sensor 1 circuit malfunction (Bank 1 or single sensor)
P0326	Knock sensor 1 circuit, range or performance problem (Bank 1 or single sensor)
P0330	Knock sensor 2 circuit malfunction (Bank 2)
P0331	Knock sensor 2 circuit, range or performance problem (Bank 2)
P0335	Crankshaft position sensor A circuit problem
P0336	Crankshaft position sensor A circuit, range performance problem
P0340	Camshaft Position (CMP) sensor circuit malfunction (Bank 1 or single sensor)
P0341	Camshaft Position (CMP) sensor circuit, range or performance problem (Bank 1 or single sensor)
P0344	Camshaft Position (CMP) sensor circuit, intermittent signal (Bank 1 or single sensor)
P0345	Camshaft Position (CMP) sensor circuit malfunction (Bank 2)
P0346	Camshaft Position (CMP) sensor circuit, range or performance problem (Bank 2)
P0349	Camshaft Position (CMP) sensor circuit, intermittent signal (Bank 2)
P0350	Ignition coil primary/secondary circuit malfunction
P0351	Ignition coil A primary/secondary circuit malfunction
P0352	Ignition coil B primary/secondary circuit malfunction
P0353	Ignition coil C primary/secondary circuit malfunction
P0354	Ignition coil D primary/secondary circuit malfunction
P0355	Ignition coil E primary/secondary circuit malfunction
P0356	Ignition coil F primary/secondary circuit malfunction
P0366	Camshaft position sensor B circuit, range performance problem (Bank 1)
P0391	Camshaft position sensor B circuit, range performance problem (Bank 2)
P0400	Exhaust Gas Recirculation (EGR) system flow
P0401	Exhaust Gas Recirculation (EGR) system, insufficient flow detected
P0402	Exhaust Gas Recirculation (EGR) system, excessive flow detected
P0403	Exhaust Gas Recirculation (EGR) system control circuit malfunction
P0405	Exhaust Gas Recirculation (EGR) system, differential pressure feedback sensor circuit, low voltage
P0406	Exhaust Gas Recirculation (EGR) system, differential pressure feedback sensor circuit, high voltage
P0410	Secondary Air Injection (AIR) system
P0412	Secondary Air Injection (AIR) system, switching valve circuit malfunction
P0420	Catalyst system efficiency below threshold (Bank 1)

OBD-II trouble codes (continued)

Note: *Not all trouble codes apply to all models.*

Code	Code identification
P0430	Catalyst system efficiency below threshold (Bank 2)
P0441	Evaporative Emission (EVAP) system, incorrect purge flow
P0442	Evaporative Emission (EVAP) system, small leak detected
P0443	Evaporative Emission (EVAP) system, purge control valve circuit malfunction
P0445	Evaporative Emission (EVAP) system, purge control valve circuit shorted
P0446	Evaporative Emission (EVAP) system, vent control circuit malfunction
P0447	Evaporative Emission (EVAP) system, vent control circuit open
P0448	Evaporative Emission (EVAP) system, vent control circuit shorted
P0451	Evaporative Emission (EVAP) system, pressure sensor range or performance problem
P0452	Evaporative Emission (EVAP) system, pressure sensor, low voltage
P0453	Evaporative Emission (EVAP) system, pressure sensor, high voltage
P0454	Evaporative Emission (EVAP) system, pressure sensor, intermittent signal
P0455	Evaporative Emission (EVAP) system, gross leak detected/no flow
P0456	Evaporative Emission (EVAP) system, very small leak detected
P0457	Evaporative Emission (EVAP) system, leak detected (fuel cap loose or off)
P0460	Fuel level sensor circuit malfunction
P0461	Fuel level sensor circuit, range or performance problem
P0462	Fuel level sensor circuit, low voltage
P0463	Fuel level sensor circuit, high voltage
P0464	Fuel level sensor circuit, intermittent
P0480	Fan 1 control circuit malfunction
P0481	Fan 2 control circuit malfunction
P0483	Fan performance
P0491	Secondary Air Injection (AIR) system, insufficient flow (Bank 1)
P0500	Vehicle Speed Sensor (VSS)
P0503	Vehicle Speed Sensor (VSS), intermittent, erratic or high signal
P0505	Idle Air Control (IAC) system
P0506	Idle Air Control (IAC) system, rpm lower than expected
P0507	Idle Air Control (IAC) system, rpm higher than expected

Code	Code identification
P0511	Idle Air Control (IAC) system circuit malfunction
P0512	Starter request circuit malfunction
P0528	Fan speed sensor circuit, no signal
P0532	Air conditioning refrigerant pressure sensor circuit, low voltage
P0533	Air conditioning refrigerant pressure sensor circuit, high voltage
P0534	Air conditioning refrigerant charge loss
P0537	Air conditioning evaporator temperature sensor circuit, low voltage
P0538	A/C evaporator temperature sensor circuit, high voltage
P0552	Power Steering Pressure (PSP) sensor circuit, low voltage
P0553	Power Steering Pressure (PSP) sensor circuit, high voltage
P0562	System voltage low
P0563	System voltage high
P0564	Cruise control multi-function input A circuit, problem
P0571	Brake switch circuit malfunction
P0572	Brake switch circuit, low voltage
P0573	Brake switch circuit, high voltage
P0579	Cruise control multifunction input circuit, ranger or performance problem
P0581	Cruise control multifunction input circuit, high voltage
P0600	Serial communication link
P0601	Powertrain Control Module (PCM), memory checksum error
P0602	Powertrain Control Module (PCM) programming error
P0603	Powertrain Control Module (PCM), Keep Alive Memory (KAM) error
P0604	Powertrain Control Module (PCM), Random Access Memory (RAM) error
P0605	Powertrain Control Module (PCM), Read Only Memory (ROM) error
P0606	Powertrain Control Module (PCM) processor
P0607	Powertrain Control Module (PCM) performance
P0610	Powertrain Control Module (PCM) options error
P0620	Alternator control circuit malfunction
P0622	Alternator field terminal, circuit malfunction
P0625	Alternator field terminal, low circuit voltage
P0626	Alternator field terminal, high circuit voltage

OBD-II trouble codes (continued)

Note: *Not all trouble codes apply to all models.*

Code	Code identification
P0627	Fuel pump, open control circuit
P062F	Internal control module EEPROM error
P0630	VIN not programmed or incompatible with ECM/PCM
P0638	Throttle actuator control, range performance (Bank 1)
P0641	Sensor reference voltage (VREF) circuit open
P0642	Sensor reference voltage (VREF) circuit below VREF minimum voltage
P0643	Sensor reference voltage (VREF) circuit, high voltage
P0645	Air conditioning clutch relay control circuit malfunction
P0646	Air conditioning clutch relay control circuit low
P0647	Air conditioning clutch relay control circuit high
P0657	Actuator supply voltage, open circuit
P065B	Alternator control circuit range or performance problem
P0660	Intake Manifold Tuning Valve (IMTV) control circuit, open circuit (Bank 1)
P0663	Intake Manifold Tuning Valve (IMTV) control circuit, open circuit (Bank 2)
P0685	Powertrain Control Module (PCM) power relay control circuit open
P0689	Powertrain Control Module (PCM) power relay sense circuit, low voltage
P0690	Powertrain Control Module (PCM) power relay sense circuit, high voltage
P0703	Brake switch input circuit malfunction
P0704	Clutch switch input circuit malfunction
P0705	Transmission Range (TR) sensor circuit (PRNDL) input problem
P0706	Transmission Range (TR) sensor circuit, range or performance problem
P0707	Transmission Range (TR) sensor circuit, low voltage
P0708	Transmission range sensor circuit, high voltage
P0711	Transmission fluid temperature sensor circuit, range or performance problem
P0712	Transmission fluid temperature sensor circuit, low input
P0713	Transmission fluid temperature sensor circuit, high input
P0715	Input/turbine speed sensor circuit malfunction
P0716	Input/turbine speed sensor circuit, range or performance problem
P0717	Input/turbine speed sensor circuit, no signal

Code	Code identification
P0720	Output Shaft Speed (OSS) sensor circuit malfunction
P0721	Output Shaft Speed (OSS) sensor circuit, range or performance problem
P0722	No signal from Output Shaft Speed (OSS) sensor
P0723	Output Shaft Speed (OSS) sensor circuit, intermittent signal
P06B8	Internal control module Non-volatile random access memory (NVRAM) error
P0729	Gear 6 incorrect ratio
P0730	Incorrect gear ratio
P0731	Incorrect gear ratio, first gear
P0732	Incorrect gear ratio, second gear
P0733	Incorrect gear ratio, third gear
P0734	Incorrect gear ratio, fourth gear
P0735	Incorrect gear ratio, fifth gear
P0736	Incorrect gear ratio, reverse gear
P0741	Torque converter clutch, circuit performance problem or stuck in Off position
P0742	Torque converter clutch circuit, stuck in On position
P0744	Torque converter clutch circuit, intermittent
P0745	Pressure control solenoid malfunction
P0751	Shift solenoid A, performance problem or stuck in Off position
P0752	Shift solenoid A, stuck in On position
P0753	Shift solenoid A, electrical problem
P0756	Shift solenoid B, performance problem or stuck in Off position
P0757	Shift solenoid B, stuck in On position
P0758	Shift solenoid B, electrical problem
P0761	Shift solenoid C, performance problem or stuck in Off position
P0762	Shift solenoid C, stuck in On position
P0763	Shift solenoid C, electrical problem
P0766	Shift solenoid D, performance problem or stuck in Off position
P0767	Shift solenoid D, stuck in On position
P0768	Shift solenoid D, electrical problem
P0771	Shift solenoid E, performance problem or stuck in Off position
P0772	Shift solenoid E, stuck in On position

OBD-II trouble codes (continued)

Note: *Not all trouble codes apply to all models.*

Code	Code identification
P0773	Shift solenoid E, electrical problem
P0777	Pressure control solenoid "B" stuck On
P0778	Pressure control solenoid "B" electrical
P0780	Shift malfunction
P0791	Intermediate shaft speed sensor circuit malfunction
P0812	Reverse input circuit malfunction
P0815	Upshift switch circuit malfunction
P0817	Starter disable circuit malfunction
P0830	Clutch pedal switch circuit malfunction
P0840	Transmission fluid pressure sensor circuit malfunction
P0841	Transmission fluid pressure sensor/switch "A" circuit range/performance problem
P0882	Transmission control module (TCM) power input signal low
P0894	Transmission component slipping
P0961	Pressure control (PC) solenoid A - control circuit range/performance problem
P0962	Pressure control (PC) solenoid A - control circuit low
P0963	Pressure control (PC) solenoid A - control circuit high
P0973	Shift solenoid (SS) A - control circuit low
P0974	Shift solenoid (SS) A - control circuit high
P0976	Shift solenoid (SS) B - control circuit low
P0977	Shift solenoid (SS) B - control circuit high
P0978	Shift solenoid (SS) C - control circuit range/performance problem
P0979	Shift solenoid (SS) C - control circuit low
P0980	Shift solenoid (SS) C - control circuit high
P0981	Shift solenoid (SS) D - control circuit range/performance problem
P0982	Shift solenoid (SS) D - control circuit low
P0983	Shift solenoid (SS) D - control circuit high
P0984	Shift solenoid (SS) E - control circuit range/performance problem
P0985	Shift solenoid (SS) E - control circuit low

Code	Code identification
P0986	Shift solenoid (SS) E - control circuit high
P0997	Shift solenoid (SS) F - control circuit range/performance problem
P0998	Shift solenoid (SS) F - control circuit low
P0999	Shift solenoid (SS) F - control circuit high

4 Accelerator Pedal Position (APP) sensor - replacement

Note: *This procedure applies to 2006 and later models only.*

1 Disconnect the cable from the negative battery terminal (see Chapter 5).

2 Working underneath the dash, disconnect the APP sensor electrical connector at the top of the accelerator pedal.

3 Remove the sensor mounting nuts and remove the sensor (see illustration).

4 Installation is the reverse of removal.

5 Camshaft Position (CMP) sensor - replacement

1 Disconnect the cable from the negative battery terminal (see 5 Section 3).

2005 and earlier models

Note: *The sensor is located under the timing belt cover, mounted next to the exhaust camshaft sprocket on the front cylinder bank.*

2 Remove the timing belt cover (see Chapter 2A).

3 Disconnect the sensor electrical connector.

4 Remove the two mounting bolts and remove the sensor (see illustration).

5 Installation is the reverse of removal, making sure to tighten the bolts securely.

2006 and later models

Note: *3.8L engines are equipped with two CMP sensors (one for each intake camshaft). The sensors are located on the top left ends of the valve covers.*

Note: *2011 and later 3.5L engines are equipped with four CMP sensors (one for each intake and one for each exhaust camshaft). The sensors are located on the left ends of the valve covers, on the top (intake) and side (exhaust).*

6 If you're removing a sensor from the rear cylinder bank (bank 1), remove the upper intake manifold if it's in the way (see Chapter 2A).

7 Disconnect the electrical connector from the CMP sensor (see illustration).

8 Remove the CMP sensor mounting bolt and remove the sensor.

9 If you're going to install the same sensor, check the condition of the O-ring. Replace the O-ring if it's damaged.

10 Installation is the reverse of removal. Tighten the CMP sensor bolt to the torque listed in this Chapter's Specifications.

4.3 The APP sensor is located at the top of the accelerator pedal. Disconnect the electrical connector (A) then remove the mounting nuts (B)

5.4 CMP sensor location - 2005 and earlier models

5.7 CMP sensor locations - intake manifold removed for clarity (3.8L engine shown)

1 *CMP sensor (Bank 1)*
2 *CMP sensor (Bank 2)*

6.4 CKP sensor mounting bolts

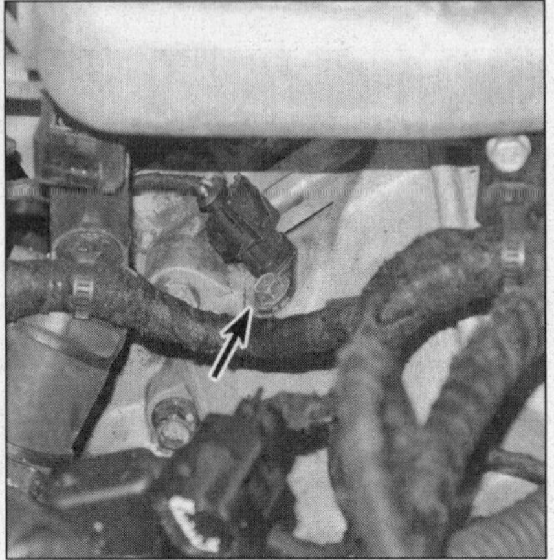
6.8 CKP sensor location

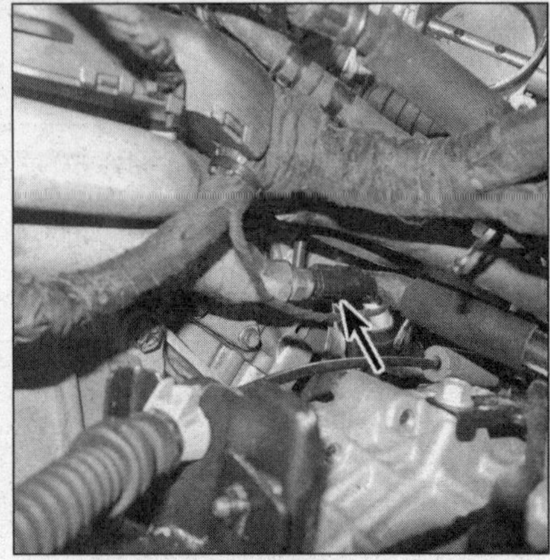
7.7 Disconnect the connector from the sensor

6 Crankshaft Position (CKP) sensor - replacement

1 Disconnect the negative battery cable (see Chapter 5).

2005 and earlier models

Note: *The crankshaft position (CKP) sensor is located on the front of the engine, behind the timing belt cover, next to the crankshaft sprocket.*

2 Remove the timing belt covers (see Chapter 2A).

3 Disconnect the sensor wiring harness.

4 Remove the sensor's mounting bolts and lift off the sensor (see illustration).

5 Installation is the reverse of removal making sure to tighten the bolts securely.

6 Installation is the reverse of removal.

2006 and later models

Note: *The CKP sensor is located on the top front side of the transaxle bellhousing, near the left end of the front-bank cylinder head.*

7 Remove the battery (see Chapter 5).

8 Disconnect the electrical connector from the sensor (see illustration).

9 Remove the CKP sensor mounting bolt and remove the CKP sensor.

10 Installation is the reverse of removal. Inspect the O-ring for damage and replace if necessary.

11 Tighten the CKP sensor bolt to the torque listed in this Chapter's Specifications.

7 Engine Coolant Temperature (ECT) sensor - replacement

Warning: *Wait until the engine is completely cool before beginning this procedure.*

Caution: *Handle the ECT sensor with care. Damage to the ECT sensor will affect the operation of the fuel injection system.*

1 Disconnect the cable from the negative battery terminal (see Chapter 5). Partially drain the cooling system (see Chapter 1).

2005 and earlier models

Note: *The ECT sensor is located on the coolant housing, above the thermostat housing cover.*

2 Remove the air filter housing (see Chapter 4).

3 Disconnect the ECT sensor electrical connector.

4 Remove the ECT sensor mounting bolts and lift the sensor off of the coolant housing.

5 Installation is the reverse of removal. Tighten the ECT sensor mounting bolts to the torque listed in this Chapter's Specifications. Refill the cooling system (see Chapter 3).

2006 through 2010 models

Note: *The ECT sensor is located on the coolant housing, below the throttle body, pointing towards the firewall.*

6 Remove the air inlet duct from between the throttle body and the top of the air filter housing (see Chapter 4).

7 Disconnect the ECT electrical connector (see illustration).

8 Unscrew the ECT sensor from the housing.

9 Apply a small amount of liquid sealant to the threads of the sensor before installing it.

Caution: *Don't seal the threads of the new sensor with Teflon tape, as this will interfere with the grounding of the sensor.*

10 Installation is the reverse of removal. Tighten the ECT sensor to the torque listed in this Chapter's Specifications. Refill the cooling system (see Chapter 1).

2011 and later models

Note: *The ECT sensor is located on the coolant housing, under the throttle body.*

11 Remove the air filter housing (see Chapter 4).

12 Disconnect the ECT sensor electrical connector.

13 Remove the spring clip, then pull the sensor out of the coolant housing.

14 Installation is the reverse of removal, making sure the spring clip is completely seated and the sensor is locked in place.

15 Refill the cooling system (see Chapter 1).

8 Knock sensor - replacement

Warning: *Wait until the engine is completely cool before beginning this procedure.*

Note: *There is one knock sensor on 2005 and earlier models and two knock sensors on 2006 and later models. They are located in the valley between the cylinder heads.*

1 Disconnect the cable from the negative battery terminal (see Chapter 5).

2 Remove the intake manifold (see Chapter 2A).

3 Disconnect the knock sensor(s) electrical connector(s).

4 On 2005 and earlier models, unscrew the knock sensor. On 2006 and later models, unscrew the knock sensor mounting bolt and remove the sensor.

5 Installation is the reverse of removal. Tighten the knock sensor or sensor mounting bolt to the torque listed in this Chapter's Specifications.

9 Manifold Absolute Pressure (MAP) sensor (2006 and later models only) - replacement

Note: *The MAP sensor is located in the upper intake manifold, near the throttle body.*

1 Disconnect the cable from the negative battery terminal (see Chapter 5).

2 Disconnect the electrical connector from the MAP sensor (see illustration).

3 Remove the mounting bolt(s) and pull the sensor straight up and out of the upper intake manifold.

4 Installation is the reverse of removal.

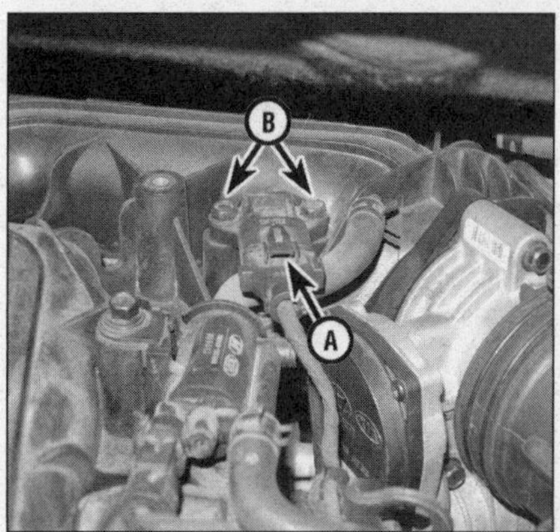

9.2 Disconnect the electrical connector (A) then remove the mounting bolts (B)

10.2a MAF/IAT sensor (2005 and earlier models)

10.2b MAF/IAT sensor location (2006 through 2010 models)

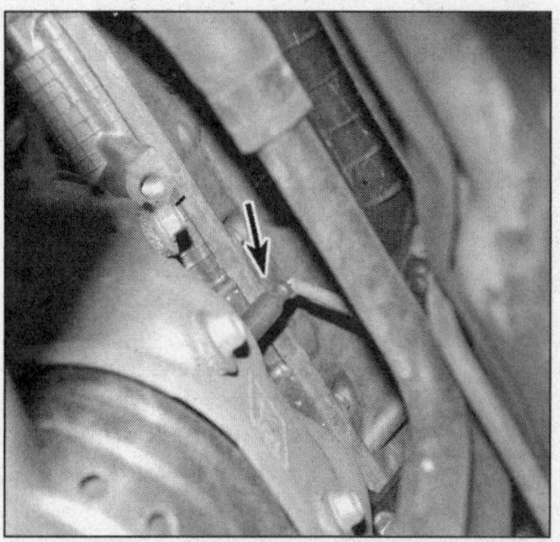
11.4a Upstream oxygen sensor location - Bank 1 (rear cylinder bank)

11.4b Upstream oxygen sensor location - Bank 2 (front cylinder bank)

11.4c After disconnecting the wiring, carefully unscrew the sensor with an oxygen sensor socket (shown) or with a large wrench - oxygen sensor sockets are handy where there's no room to turn a wrench

10 Mass Air Flow/Intake Air Temperature (MAF/IAT), Barometric Pressure/Intake Air Temperature (BARO/IAT) sensors - replacement

Note: *2005 and earlier models use an Intake Air Flow/Intake Air Temperature (IAF/IAT) sensor, which is now called a MAF/IAT sensor. It is located in the air inlet duct.*

Note: *2006 through 2010 models use a Mass Air Flow/Intake Air Temperature (MAF/IAT) sensor. It is located in the air filter housing outlet.*

Note: *On 2011 and later models, a Barometric Pressure/Intake Air Temperature (BARO/IAT) sensor is used, located in the air filter housing outlet.*

1 Disconnect the cable from the negative battery terminal (see 5 Section 3).

2 Disconnect the electrical connector from the sensor (see illustrations).

3 2005 and earlier models: Remove the screws and pull the sensor from the duct.

4 2006 through 2010 models: Loosen the clamp and disconnect the duct from the sensor housing, then remove the two bolts and detach the sensor from the air filter housing cover.

5 2011 and later models: Remove the bolt and detach the sensor from the air filter housing outlet.

6 Installation is the reverse of removal.

11 Oxygen sensors - general information and replacement

General information

1 Use special care when servicing an oxygen sensor:

a) *Oxygen sensors have a permanently attached pigtail and electrical connector that can't be removed from the sensor. Damage to or removal of the pigtail or the electrical connector will ruin the sensor.*

b) *Keep grease, dirt and other contaminants away from the electrical connector and the oxygen sensor.*

c) *Do not use cleaning solvents of any kind on an oxygen sensor.*

d) *Do not drop or roughly handle an oxygen sensor.*

Replacement

Note: *Because it is installed in the exhaust manifold/catalytic converter, both of which contract when cool, an oxygen sensor might be very difficult to loosen when the engine is cold. Rather than risk damage to the sensor, start and run the engine for a minute or two, then shut it off. Be careful not to burn yourself during the following procedure.*

Note: *The sensors are located at the inlet and outlet of each primary catalytic converter. These converters are bolted to the bases of the exhaust manifolds. There are a total of four oxygen sensors on all models.*

Upstream O2 sensor replacement

2 If you're replacing the Bank 1 (rear cylinder bank) sensor, raise the front of the vehicle and support it securely on jackstands.

3 Follow the lead from the sensor to the electrical connector, then disconnect the electrical connector.

4 Unscrew the sensor (see illustrations).

Note: *Special oxygen sensor sockets are available at most auto parts stores.*

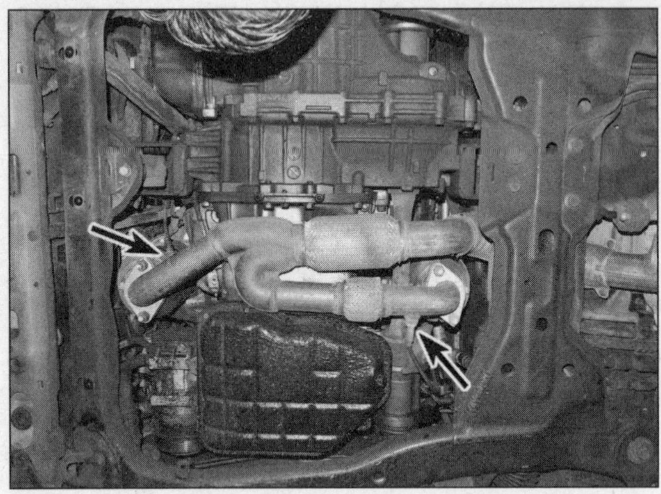
11.8 Locations of the downstream oxygen sensors

12.2 The Throttle Position sensor has slotted mounting holes to allow for adjustment

Downstream O2 sensor replacement

5 Raise the vehicle and support it securely on jackstands.

6 Remove any exhaust shields that block access to the O2 sensors.

7 Follow the lead from the sensor to the electrical connector, then disconnect the electrical connector.

8 Unscrew the sensor (see accompanying illustration and illustration 11.4c).

Upstream and downstream sensors

9 Installation is the reverse of removal. Coat the threads of the oxygen sensor with anti-seize compound and tighten it to the torque listed in this Chapter's Specifications.

Note: *New sensors may already be coated with anti-seize compound.*

12 Throttle Position (TP) sensor (2005 and earlier 3.5L V6 models) - replacement and adjustment

Note: *The TP sensor is located on the throttle body.*

Replacement

1 Disconnect the cable from the negative battery terminal (see Chapter 5).

2 Disconnect the TP sensor electrical connector (see illustration).

3 Mark the position of the sensor if you plan to reinstall the same one.

4 Remove the TP sensor mounting screws and remove the sensor from the throttle body.

5 Install the sensor and rotate it until the mounting holes in the TP sensor are aligned with the mounting holes in the throttle body.

6 Installation is otherwise the reverse of removal.

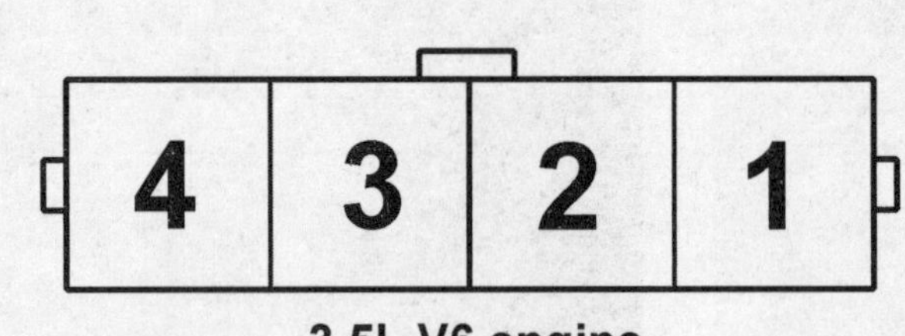

12.11 TP sensor connector terminal designations (harness-side shown)

Adjustment

Using a scan tool

7 Connect a scan tool to the 16-pin Data Link Connector (DLC), then bring up the Throttle Position sensor values parameter on the screen.

8 Turn the ignition key to the On position.

9 With the throttle fully closed, note the value on the scan tool - it should be as follows: 300 to 900 millivolts (mV)

10 If the sensor voltage doesn't fall within the specified range, loosen the TP sensor mounting screws and turn the sensor one way or the other until it does, then tighten the screws securely.

Using a voltmeter

11 Connect the negative lead of a high-impedance digital voltmeter to terminals 1 and 3 of the sensor (see illustration). It will be necessary to backprobe the sensor's connector using a straight-pin to take the voltage reading, or pierce the wire with a pin and connect the lead to it (although the latter method isn't recommended if at all possible to avoid).

Note: *Use only a high-impedance digital voltmeter for this procedure.*

12 Follow Steps 8 through 10 to check and, if necessary, adjust the TP sensor.

13 Fuel tank pressure sensor - replacement

Warning: *Gasoline and its vapors are extremely flammable. Read the* Fuel System Warning *in Chapter 4 Section 1.*

Note: *The fuel pressure sensor is located in the fuel line under the vehicle, near the right-front corner of the fuel tank.*

1 Disconnect the cable from the negative terminal of the battery (see Chapter 5).

2 Remove the fuel filler cap to release any pressure built up in the fuel tank.

3 Remove the left-side second row rear seat (see Chapter 11), then pull the carpet flap back.

4 Remove the fuel pump/sending unit floor service hole cover (see Chapter 4).

5 Disconnect the electrical connector from the fuel tank pressure sensor.

6 Remove the sensor mounting nuts (see illustration) and pull the sensor from the top of the fuel pump module.

7 Install a new O-ring or gasket, then install the fuel pressure sensor and tighten the nuts securely. Reconnect the electrical connector.

8 Reconnect the battery cable.

13.6 Remove the fuel tank pressure sensor mounting nuts

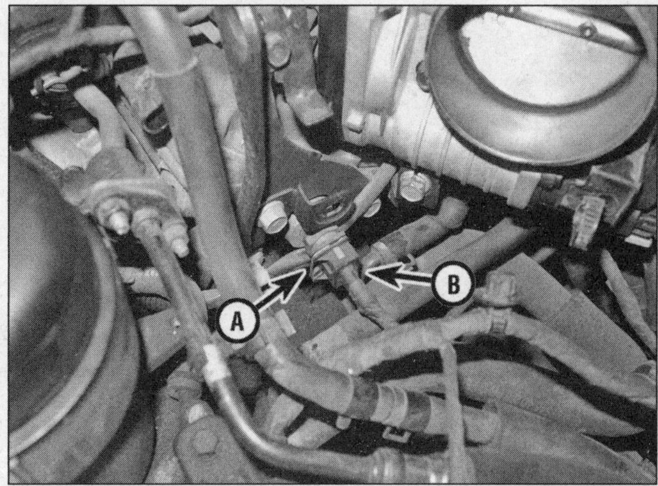

14.3 Remove the electrical connector retaining clip (A), then disconnect the connector (B) from the sensor

14 CVVT Oil Temperature Sensor (OTS) (2006 and later models) - replacement

Warning: *Wait until the engine has cooled completely before beginning this procedure.*

Note: *The Continuous Variable Valve Timing (CVVT) oil temperature sensor is located on the left end of the rear-bank cylinder head.*

1 Disconnect the cable from the negative battery terminal (see Chapter 5).

2 Remove the air filter housing and detach the intake duct from the throttle body (see Chapter 4).

3 Locate the sensor and disconnect the electrical connector (see illustration).

4 Place rags under the sensor catch any oil that leaks out.

5 Carefully clean around the sensor to avoid dropping bits of debris into the open hole.

6 Unscrew the sensor from the cylinder head.

7 Installation is the reverse of removal, making sure to tighten the oil temperature sensor to the torque this Chapter's Specifications.

15 CVVT Oil Control Valve (OCV) (2006 and later models) - replacement

Warning: *Wait until the engine has cooled completely before beginning this procedure.*

Note: *CVVT is used on 2006 and later models. 2006 through 2010 models (3.8L engines) use two CVVT valves; one for each intake camshaft. 2011 and later models (3.5L engines) use four CVVT valves; one for each camshaft.*

1 Disconnect the cable from the negative battery terminal (see Chapter 5).

2006 through 2010 models

Note: *The CVVT oil control valves are located in the valley between the two cylinder heads, on the timing chain end of the engine.*

2 Remove the intake manifold (see Chapter 2A).

3 Disconnect the oil control valve electrical connector (see illustration).

4 Remove the oil control valve mounting bolt.

5 Pull the oil control valve out of the cylinder head. Discard and replace the O-rings if re-using the valve.

6 Installation is the reverse of removal, making sure to tighten the mounting bolt to the torque listed in this Chapter's Specifications.

Caution: *Ensure that the electrical connectors are installed correctly or the engine may be damaged. The Bank 1 (rear cylinder head) connector is grey and the Bank 2 (front cylinder head) connector is black.*

7 Installation is the reverse of removal.

2011 and later models

Intake oil control valves

8 Remove the intake manifold (see Chapter 2A).

9 Disconnect the electrical connectors from the valve(s) (see illustration 15.3).

10 Remove the valve mounting bolt(s).

11 Pull the valve out of the cylinder head. Discard and replace the O-rings if re-using the CVVT valve(s).

12 Installation is the reverse of removal, making sure to tighten the CVVT mounting bolt to the torque listed in this Chapter's Specifications

15.3 Oil control valve locations

1 *Oil control valve connector - Bank 1 (grey connector)*

2 *Oil control valve connector - Bank 2 (black connector)*

Caution: *Ensure that the CVVT electrical connectors are installed correctly or the engine may be damaged. The Bank 1 (rear cylinder head) connector is grey and the Bank 2 (front cylinder head) connector is black.*

Exhaust oil control valves

13 Disconnect the electrical connectors from the valve(s).

14 Remove the valve covers (see Chapter 2A).

15 Remove the three valve mounting bolts.

16 Remove the valve from the cylinder head. Discard and replace the O-rings if re-using the CVVT valve(s).

17 Installation is the reverse of removal. Coat the O-rings with clean engine oil and tighten the mounting bolts to the torque listed in this Chapter's Specifications.

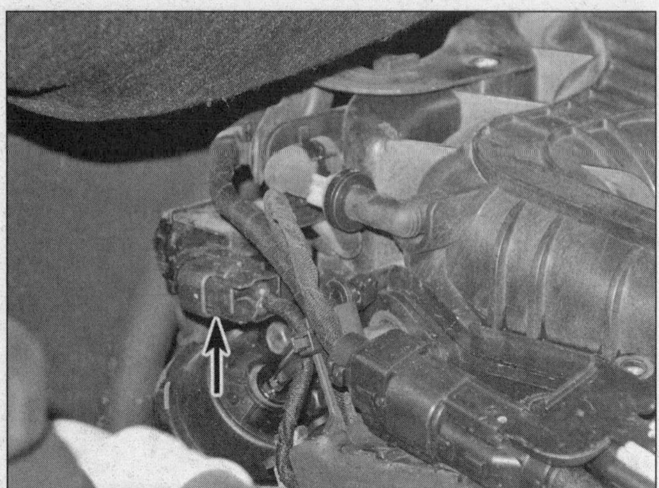

16.2 The VIS control valve solenoid and actuator is located at the right end of the upper intake manifold (3.8L engine)

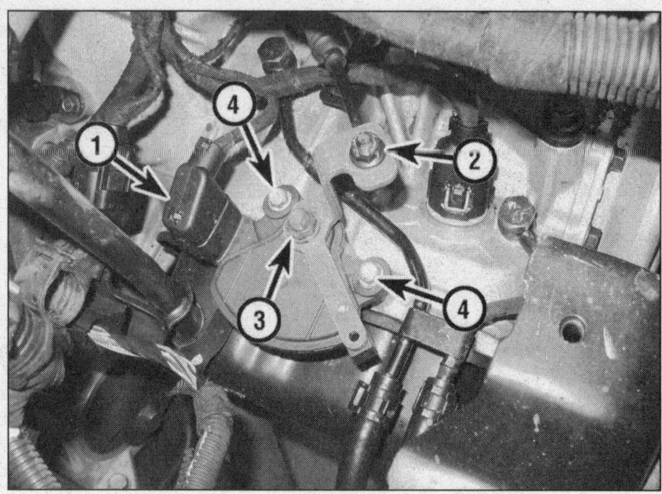

18.3 Transmission Range sensor details

1 *Electrical connector*
2 *Shift cable nut*
3 *Control shaft lever nut*
4 *TR sensor mounting bolts*

18.10 Insert a 4 mm drill bit through the hole in the manual lever and into the hole in the switch body to align it

16 Variable Intake Solenoid (VIS) control valve (2006 and later models) - replacement

Note: *The VIS valve is mounted in the upper intake manifold. 2006 through 2012 models use one VIS valve. 2014 models use two VIS valves, one on the upper intake manifold and the other on the lower intake manifold.*

1 Disconnect the cable from the negative battery terminal (see Chapter 5).

2 Locate and disconnect the electrical connector from the VIS control valve solenoid (see illustration).

3 Disconnect the vacuum hose from the VIS control valve.

4 Remove the VIS control valve mounting bolts.

5 Remove the VIS control valve from the intake manifold.

6 Installation is the reverse of removal. Tighten the mounting bolts to the torque listed in this Chapters Specifications.

17 Variable Charge Motion Actuator (2014 models) - replacement

Note: *The Variable Charge Motion Actuator (VCMA) is installed on the inlet side of the intake manifold. The valve creates turbulence in the air flow entering into the combustion chamber of each cylinder during cold start conditions, which helps to reduce emissions.*

1 Disconnect the cable from the negative battery terminal (see Chapter 5, Section 3).

2 Disconnect the electrical connector to the VCMA.

3 Remove the two VCMA mounting bolts from the intake manifold.

4 Separate the VCMA linkage rod from the attachment point on the VCMA lever using a trim clip removal tool.

5 Remove the VCMA actuator.

6 Installation is the reverse of removal, noting the following points:

a) *Make sure the VCM valve is completely closed before installing the actuator.*
b) *Tighten the VCMA mounting bolts to the torque listed in this Chapter's Specifications.*

18 Transmission Range (TR) sensor - removal, installation and adjustment

Removal

Note: *The TR sensor is located on the top of the transaxle.*

1 Disconnect the cable from the negative battery terminal (see Chapter 5). On 2005 and earlier models, remove the air filter housing (see Chapter 4).

2 Remove the battery and battery tray (see Chapter 5).

3 Disconnect the electrical connector from the TR sensor (see illustration).

4 Remove the nut that secures the shift control cable to the control shaft lever, and disconnect the cable from the lever.

5 Remove the nut and washer that secures the control shaft lever to the manual valve shaft and remove the control shaft lever from the manual valve shaft.

6 Remove the TR sensor mounting bolts and remove the sensor.

Installation

7 Slide the sensor onto the manual valve shaft, then loosely install the mounting bolts.

8 Install the lever on the manual valve shaft. Install the nut and tighten it securely. Turn the lever through the gears - it will click as it changes to the next gear - until it stops at Park, then turn it two clicks. It's now in the Neutral position.

9 Connect the cable to the manual valve shaft and install the nut, but don't tighten it yet.

10 Align the holes on the manual lever and the sensor; use an appropriately sized drill bit to insert into the holes to ensure alignment (see illustration), turning the sensor as necessary. When alignment is achieved, tighten the sensor mounting screws securely, being careful to avoid moving the sensor.

11 The remainder of installation is the reverse of removal.

12 Tighten the cable nut and check that the transmission and indicator operate properly. Make sure the engine only starts in Park and Neutral, and make sure the back-up lights come on when the shifter is placed in Reverse.

19.3 Input speed sensor location

19.6 Output speed sensor location

19.9 The vehicle speed sensor is located on the rear lower part of the transaxle case

19 Transmission speed sensors - replacement

2010 and earlier models

Input speed sensor

1 Remove the battery and battery tray (see Chapter 5) and the air filter housing (see Chapter 4).

2 Detach the shift cable from the manual shift lever on the transaxle, then unbolt the shift cable bracket and move it out of the way.

3 Remove the input speed sensor hold-down bolt and pull the sensor from the transaxle case (see illustration).

4 Installation is the reverse of removal. Lubricate the O-ring with clean automatic transmission fluid and tighten the hold-down bolt securely.

Output speed sensor

5 Remove the air filter housing (see Chapter 4).

6 Remove the output speed sensor hold-down bolt and pull the sensor from the transaxle case (see illustration).

7 Installation is the reverse of removal. Lubricate the O-ring with clean automatic transmission fluid and tighten the hold-down bolt securely.

Vehicle speed sensor

Note: *The vehicle speed sensor is located on the rear lower portion of the transaxle case, above the inner end of the right driveaxle. It is accessed from above, however.*

8 Remove the air filter housing and the throttle body (see Chapter 4).

9 Remove the vehicle speed sensor hold-down bolt and pull the sensor from the transaxle case (see illustration).

10 Installation is the reverse of removal. Lubricate the O-ring with clean automatic transmission fluid and tighten the hold-down bolt securely.

2011 and later models

11 The speed sensors on these models are internally mounted, requiring valve body removal; we don't recommend replacing them at home.

20.7a Pull the safety lock up and out. . .

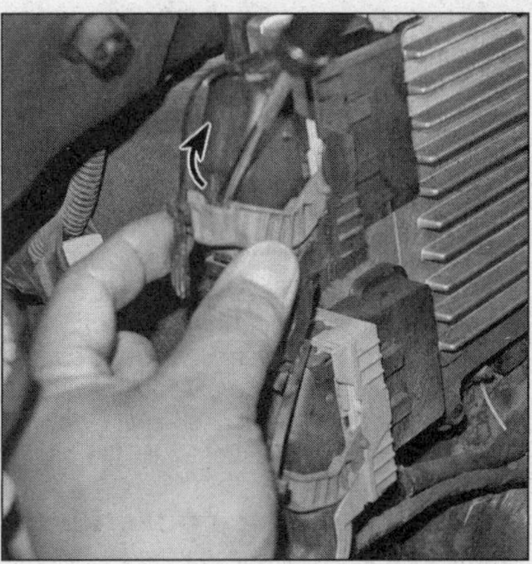
20.7b. . . then flip open the locking levers and unplug the electrical connectors from the PCM

20 Powertrain Control Module (PCM) - replacement

Warning: *The models covered by this manual are equipped with Supplemental Restraint systems (SRS), more commonly known as airbags. Always disable the airbag system before working in the vicinity of any airbag system component to avoid the possibility of accidental deployment of the airbag, which could cause personal injury (see Chapter 12).*

Caution: *To avoid electrostatic discharge damage to the PCM, handle the PCM only by its case. Do not touch the electrical terminals during removal and installation. If available, ground yourself to the vehicle with an anti-static ground strap, available at computer supply stores, and use a special anti-static pad to store the PCM on once it is removed.*

Note: *On 2005 and earlier models, the PCM is located in the passenger's side footwell, under the carpet and a metal cover. On 2006 and later models, the PCM is next to the air filter housing.*

1 Disconnect the cable from the negative battery terminal (see Chapter 5).

2005 and earlier models

2 Pull back the carpet from the passenger's side footwell, starting at the top.

3 Remove the nuts securing the sheet metal cover to the floor, then remove the cover.

4 Remove the PCM mounting fasteners, detach the PCM from the floor, then unplug the electrical connectors.

5 Installation is the reverse of the removal procedure.

2006 and later models

6 Remove the air filter housing (see Chapter 4).

7 Disconnect the electrical connectors from the PCM (see illustrations).

8 Remove the PCM mounting bracket upper and lower fasteners and carefully remove the PCM (see the Caution above).

9 Installation is the reverse of removal.

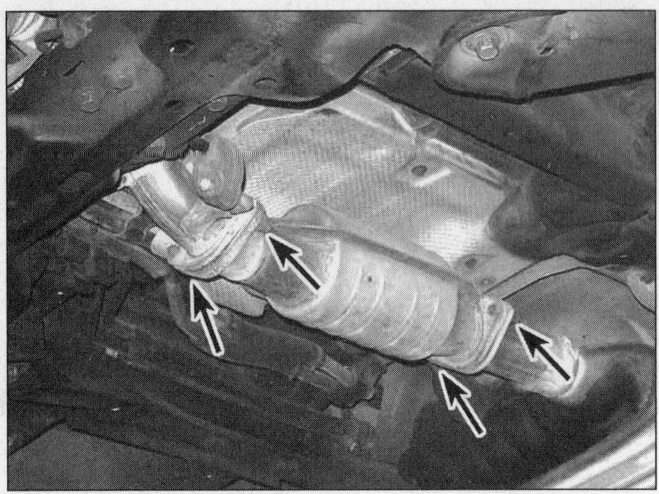

21.9 Secondary catalytic converter fasteners

22.3 Location of the purge control solenoid valve (3.8L engine shown, other models similar)

21 Catalytic converters - replacement

Warning: *Do NOT service a catalytic converter until it has completely cooled down.*

Note: *Before attempting to loosen any exhaust system fastener, apply penetrating oil to the fastener and allow it to soak in for awhile. Replace damaged fasteners with new ones.*

Primary catalytic converters

2005 and earlier models

Note: *On these models, the primary catalytic converters are bolted to the undersides of the exhaust manifolds.*

1 Raise the vehicle and support it securely on jackstands.

2 Unbolt the exhaust pipe from the bottom of the catalytic converter.

3 Disconnect the rubber exhaust pipe supports under the vehicle and carefully lower the front of the pipe as much as possible for access to the catalytic converters.

4 Disconnect the oxygen sensor electrical connector.

5 Unbolt the converter from the exhaust manifold and remove it from beneath the vehicle.

6 Installation is the reverse of the removal procedure. Be sure to use new gaskets. Apply anti-seize compound to the threads of the fasteners and tighten them securely.

2006 and later models

Note: *On these models, the primary catalytic converters are integral parts of the exhaust manifolds.*

7 Refer to Chapter 2A for the exhaust manifold removal and installation procedure.

Secondary catalytic converter

8 Raise the vehicle and support it securely on jackstands.

9 Remove the fasteners from the flanges at each end of the catalytic converter (see illustration).

10 Push the converter to the rear and detach it from the front portion of the exhaust system, then lower the front of the converter and detach it from the rear portion of the exhaust system.

11 Installation is the reverse of the removal procedure. Be sure to use new gaskets. Apply anti-seize compound to the threads of the fasteners and tighten them securely.

22 Evaporative emissions control (EVAP) system - component replacement

Warning: *Gasoline and gasoline vapor are extremely flammable, so take extra precautions when you work on any part of the fuel or EVAP systems. Don't smoke or allow open flames or bare light bulbs near the work area, and don't work in a garage where a gas-type appliance (such as a water heater or a clothes dryer) is present. Since gasoline is carcinogenic, wear fuel resistant gloves when there's a possibility of being exposed to fuel, and, if you spill any fuel on your skin, rinse it off immediately with soap and water. Mop up any spills immediately and do not store fuel-soaked rags where they could ignite. When you perform any kind of work on the fuel system, wear safety glasses and have a Class B type fire extinguisher on hand.*

1 Disconnect the cable from the negative terminal of the battery (see Chapter 5).

Purge control solenoid valve

2 Remove the engine cover, if applicable (see Chapter 2A).

3 Disconnect the electrical connector from the purge control solenoid valve (see illustration).

4 Disconnect the vacuum hoses from the purge valve.

5 Remove the purge valve mounting fasteners and remove the purge valve.

6 Installation is the reverse of removal.

Other components (under vehicle)

7 Raise the rear of the vehicle and support it securely on jackstands.

8 Remove the protective cover from the EVAP canister assembly, if so equipped.

Two-way valve

Note: *The two-way valve is located in the line between the fuel tank and the canister.*

9 Disconnect the EVAP hoses from the two-way valve.

10 Installation is the reverse of removal. The valve must be installed facing the correct direction, indicated by the arrow on the valve.

EVAP canister

Note: *The EVAP canister is mounted under the vehicle, near the fuel tank.*

11 Remove the EVAP canister shield fasteners (see illustration) and shield.

12 Disconnect the hoses from the canister (see illustration).

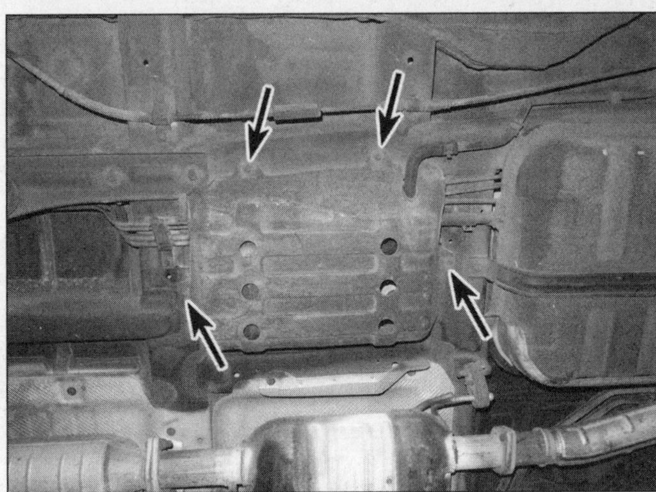
22.11 EVAP canister shield fastener locations

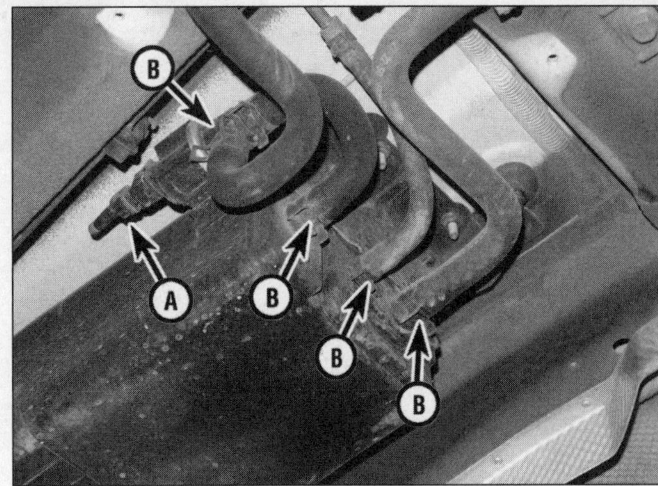

22.12 Disconnect the canister closed valve electrical connector (A), then disconnect the hoses (B)

22.14 Evaporator canister mounting fastener locations

23.2 Disconnect the PCV valve hose

13 Disconnect the electrical connector from the canister closed valve.

14 Remove the EVAP canister mounting bracket fasteners (see illustration) and remove the EVAP canister and mounting bracket as a single assembly.

15 Installation is the reverse of removal.

Vapor pressure sensor

Note: *This sensor is mounted to the rear end of the fuel tank in the line connecting the fuel tank and the canister.*

16 Disconnect the wiring harness from the sensor.

17 Disconnect the fuel hoses.

18 Remove the sensor along with its mounting bracket. The bracket can be removed from the sensor after it is out of the vehicle.

19 Installation is the reverse of removal.

Canister closed valve

Note: *This valve is connected to the canister.*

20 Disconnect the electrical connector from the valve.

21 Remove the valve from the canister.

22 Installation is the reverse of removal.

23 Positive Crankcase Ventilation (PCV) valve - replacement

1 Remove the throttle body (see Chapter 4) to access the PCV valve on the rear valve cover.

2 Remove the hose clamp and disconnect the hose from the valve (see illustration).

3 Unscrew the PCV valve from the valve cover.

4 Installation is the reverse of removal.

Notes

Chapter 7
Automatic transaxle

Contents

	Section
Automatic transaxle - removal and installation	8
Automatic transaxle overhaul - general information	9
Brake Transmission Shift Interlock (BTSI) system - description, check and replacement	6
Diagnosis - general	2
Driveaxle oil seals - replacement	3
General information	1
Shift cable - removal and installation	5
Shift lever - replacement	4
Transaxle oil cooler - removal and installation	7

Specifications

General

Lubricant type and capacity	See Chapter 1

Torque specifications

Note: *One foot-pound (ft-lb) of torque is equivalent to 12 inch-pounds (in-lbs) of torque. Torque values below approximately 15 ft-lbs are expressed in inch-pounds, since most foot-pound torque wrenches are not accurate at these smaller values.*

Torque specifications	**Ft-lbs** (unless otherwise indicated)	**Nm**
Shift cable adjustment nut/bolt		
2010 and earlier 5-speed models	90 to 120 in-lbs	10 to 14
2011 and later 6-speed models	13 to 18	18 to 24
Torque converter-to-driveplate bolts	34 to 38	46 to 52
Transaxle-to-engine bolts		
2010 and earlier 5-speed models	47 to 61	65 to 85
2011 and later 6-speed models		
Upper bolts		
Center and right side (3)	47 to 61	64 to 83
Left side (1)	24 to 36	33 to 49
Middle, right side (1)	58 to 72	79 to 98
Lower bolts (4)	29 to 34	40 to 46
Transaxle brace	70	
2011 and later transaxle fluid check plug	26 to 32	35 to 44
2011 and later transaxle drain plug	26 to 32	35 to 44
2011 and later transaxle breather banjo-bolt	26 to 32	35 to 44

1 General Information

1 These models are equipped with either a F5A51-3, A5MF1 (5-speed) or the A6LF2 (6-speed) automatic transaxle. The automatic transaxle and the differential are housed in a compact, lightweight, two-piece aluminum alloy housing.

2 These models are equipped with a Transmission Control Module (TCM) which is the brain of the transaxle. The TCM monitors engine and transaxle operating parameters through numerous sensors, then generates output signals to various relays and solenoids to regulate hydraulic pressures, optimize drivability, provide efficient torque management and maintain maximum fuel economy. All models incorporate the TCM into the PCM. The TCM is part of the On-Board Diagnostic system OBD-II. For more information, see Chapter 6.

3 Because of the complexity of the automatic transaxles and the specialized equipment necessary to perform most service operations, this Chapter contains only those procedures related to general diagnosis, adjustment and removal and installation procedures.

4 If the transaxle requires major repair work, it should be left to a dealer service department or an automotive or transmission repair shop. Once properly diagnosed you can, however, remove and install the transaxle yourself and save the expense, even if the repair work is done by a transmission shop.

2 Diagnosis - general

1 Automatic transaxle malfunctions may be caused by five general conditions:

- a) *Poor engine performance*
- b) *Improper adjustments*
- c) *Hydraulic malfunctions*
- d) *Mechanical malfunctions*
- e) *Malfunctions in the computer or its signal network*

2 Diagnosis of these problems should always begin with a check of the easily repaired items: fluid level and condition (see Chapter 1), shift cable adjustment and shift lever installation. Next, perform a road test to determine if the problem has been corrected or if more diagnosis is necessary. If the problem persists after the preliminary tests and corrections are completed, additional diagnosis should be performed by a dealer service department or other qualified transmission repair shop. Refer to the "Troubleshooting" Section at the front of this manual for information on symptoms of transaxle problems.

Preliminary checks

3 Drive the vehicle to warm the transaxle to normal operating temperature.

4 Check the fluid level as described in Chapter 1 :

- a) *If the fluid level is unusually low, add enough fluid to bring the level within the designated area of the dipstick, then check for external leaks (see following).*
- b) *If the fluid level is abnormally high, drain off the excess, then check the drained fluid for contamination by coolant. The presence of engine coolant in the automatic transaxle fluid indicates that a failure has occurred in the internal radiator oil cooler walls that separate the coolant from the transaxle fluid (see Chapter 3).*
- c) *If the fluid is foaming, drain it and refill the transaxle, then check for coolant in the fluid, or a high fluid level.*

5 Check the engine idle speed.

Note: *If the engine is malfunctioning, do not proceed with the preliminary checks until it has been repaired and runs normally.*

6 Check and adjust the shift cable, if necessary (see Section 5).

7 If hard shifting is experienced, inspect the shift cable under the center console and at the manual lever on the transaxle (see Section 5).

Fluid leak diagnosis

8 Most fluid leaks are easy to locate visually. Repair usually consists of replacing a seal or gasket. If a leak is difficult to find, the following procedure may help.

9 Identify the fluid. Make sure it's transaxle fluid and not engine oil or brake fluid (automatic transaxle fluid is a deep red color).

10 Try to pinpoint the source of the leak. Drive the vehicle several miles, then park it over a large sheet of cardboard. After a minute or two, you should be able to locate the leak by determining the source of the fluid dripping onto the cardboard.

11 Make a careful visual inspection of the suspected component and the area immediately around it. Pay particular attention to gasket mating surfaces. A mirror is often helpful for finding leaks in areas that are hard to see.

12 If the leak still cannot be found, clean the suspected area thoroughly with a degreaser or solvent, then dry it thoroughly.

13 Drive the vehicle for several miles at normal operating temperature and varying speeds. After driving the vehicle, visually inspect the suspected component again.

14 Once the leak has been located, the cause must be determined before it can be properly repaired. If a gasket is replaced but the sealing flange is bent, the new gasket will not stop the leak. The bent flange must be straightened.

15 Before attempting to repair a leak, check to make sure that the following conditions are corrected or they may cause another leak.

Note: *Some of the following conditions cannot be fixed without highly specialized tools and expertise. Such problems must be referred to a qualified transmission shop or a dealer service department.*

Gasket leaks

16 Check the pan periodically. Make sure the bolts are tight, no bolts are missing, the gasket is in good condition and the pan is flat (dents in the pan may indicate damage to the valve body inside).

17 If the pan gasket is leaking, the fluid level or the fluid pressure may be too high, the vent may be plugged, the pan bolts may be too tight, the pan sealing flange may be warped, the sealing surface of the transaxle housing may be damaged, the gasket may be damaged or the transaxle casting may be cracked or porous. If sealant instead of gasket material has been used to form a seal between the pan and the transaxle housing, it may be the wrong type of sealant.

Seal leaks

18 If a transaxle seal is leaking, the fluid level may be too high, the vent may be plugged, the seal bore may be damaged, the seal itself may be damaged or improperly installed, the surface of the shaft protruding through the seal may be damaged or a loose bearing may be causing excessive shaft movement.

19 Make sure the dipstick tube seal is in good condition and the tube is properly seated. Periodically check the area around the sensors for leakage. If transaxle fluid is evident, check the seals for damage.

Case leaks

20 If the case itself appears to be leaking, the casting is porous and will have to be repaired or replaced.

21 Make sure the oil cooler hose fittings are tight and in good condition.

Fluid comes out vent pipe or fill tube

22 If this condition occurs, the possible causes are: the transaxle is overfilled, there is coolant in the fluid, the dipstick is incorrect, the vent is plugged or the drain-back holes are plugged.

3 Driveaxle oil seals - replacement

1 The driveaxle oil seals are located on the sides of the transaxle, where the inner ends of the driveaxles are splined into the differential side gears. If you suspect that a driveaxle oil seal is leaking, raise the vehicle and support it securely on jackstands. If the seal is leaking, you'll see lubricant on the side of the transaxle, below the seal.

2 Remove the driveaxle or mid-shaft (see Chapter 8).

3 Using a screwdriver or prybar, carefully pry the oil seal out of the transaxle bore (see illustration).

4 If the oil seal cannot be removed with a screwdriver or prybar, a special oil seal removal tool (available at auto parts stores) will be required.

3.3 Using a large screwdriver or prybar, carefully pry the oil seal out of the transaxle (if you can't remove the oil seal with a screwdriver or prybar, you may need to obtain a special seal removal tool, available at most auto parts stores)

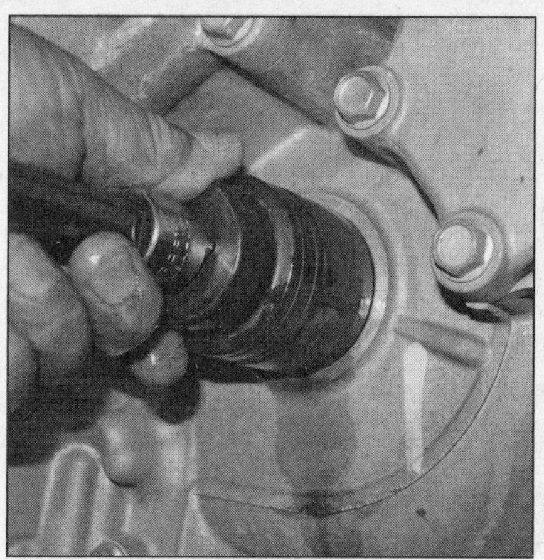

3.5 Using a seal installer, large section of pipe or a large deep socket as a drift, drive the new seal squarely into the bore and make sure that it's completely seated; lubricate the lip of the new seal with multi-purpose grease

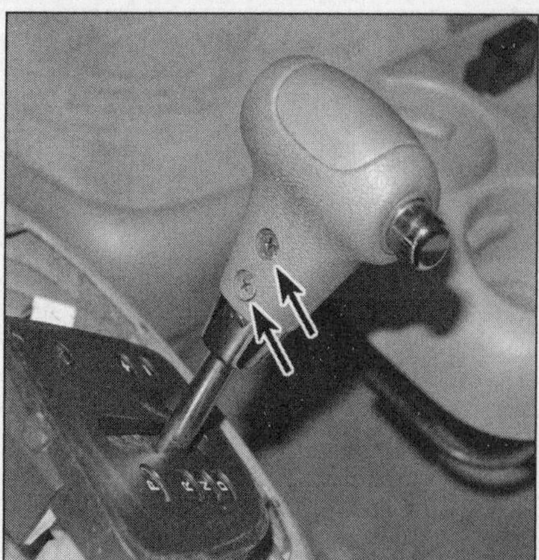

4.1 There are two small screws on the sides of the shift handle; when replacing the handle, align the push button with the plunger to allow the handle to slip into the correct position, allowing the screws to line up with their holes

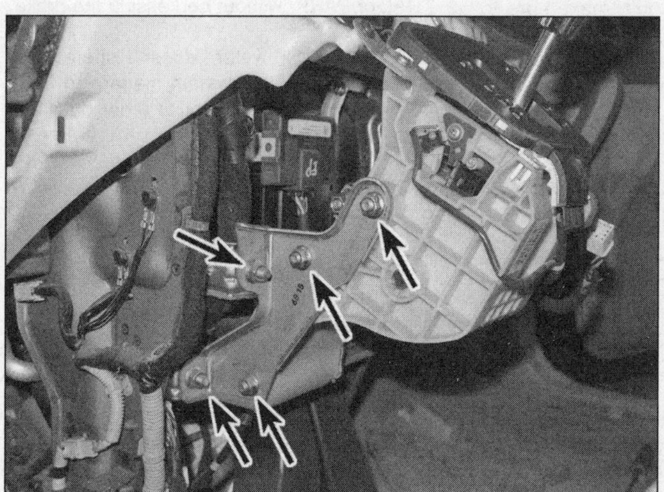

4.5a Remove the left side bracket mounting nuts. . .

4.5b. . . and the right side bracket nuts and bracket

5 Using a seal installer, install the new oil seal. Drive it into the bore squarely until it bottoms (see illustration).

6 Install the driveaxle (see Chapter 8).

7 Check the fluid level (see Chapter 1) and adjust as necessary.

4 Shift lever - replacement

1 To replace the shift lever handle, loosen the two small screws on the sides of the handle, then remove it (see illustration). If you remove the button and spring from the handle, be sure to note the direction the button is installed.

2 Remove the center console (see Chapter 11).

3 Disconnect the shift cable and the key lock cable, if equipped (see Section 5).

4 Disconnect the inhibitor switch electrical connector.

5 Remove the shift lever bracket mounting nuts (see illustrations) and brackets.

6 Remove the shift lever housing-to-instrument panel screws and remove the assembly.

7 Installation is the reverse of removal.

5 Shift cable - removal and installation

Warning: *The models covered by this manual are equipped with Supplemental Restraint systems (SRS), more commonly known as airbags. Always disarm the airbag system before working in the vicinity of any airbag system component to avoid the possibility of accidental deployment of the airbag, which could cause personal injury (see Chapter 12). Do not use a memory saving device to preserve the PCM's memory when working on or near airbag system components.*

Warning: *Do not attempt this procedure until the vehicle has cooled completely. The exhaust system components must be cold to avoid physical harm.*

Removal

1 Raise the hood and place a blanket over the left (driver's) fender to protect it.

2 Remove the air filter housing (see Chapter 4).

3 Remove the battery and battery tray (see Chapter 5).

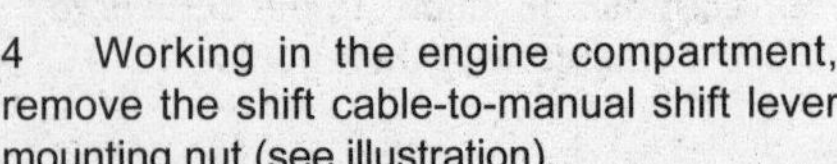
5.4 Remove the shift cable-to-shift lever mounting bolt

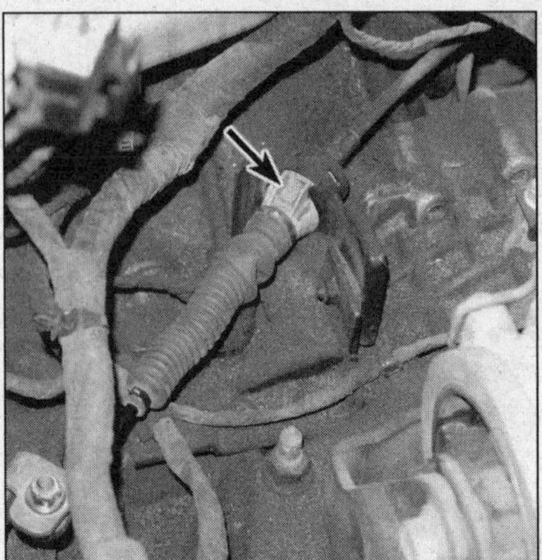

5.5 Depress the tab then pull the shift cable up off the bracket on the transaxle

4 Working in the engine compartment, remove the shift cable-to-manual shift lever mounting nut (see illustration).

5 Disconnect the shift cable from the bracket (see illustration).

6 Working inside the vehicle, remove the front console (see Chapter 11).

7 Remove the shift cable-to-shift lever nut and disconnect the cable (see illustration), then remove the cable from the housing.

8 Remove the grommet fasteners from the panel opening between the engine compartment and the passenger compartment.

Note: *It may be necessary to remove the shift lever mounting nuts and bracket on the driver's side of the shift lever to allow enough room to remove the shift cable.*

9 Pull out and remove the cable from the passenger compartment.

Installation

10 Working under the steering column, install the shift cable through the panel opening into the engine compartment.

11 Place the shift cable onto the shift lever stud and install the mounting nut, tightening the nut securely.

12 Push the shift cable into the shift lever housing until it snaps into place.

13 Working in the engine compartment, place the shift cable to the manual shift lever and install the mounting bolt, make sure to tighten the bolt securely.

14 Place the cable housing into the mounting bracket and install the retaining clip.

15 The remainder of installation is the reverse of removal.

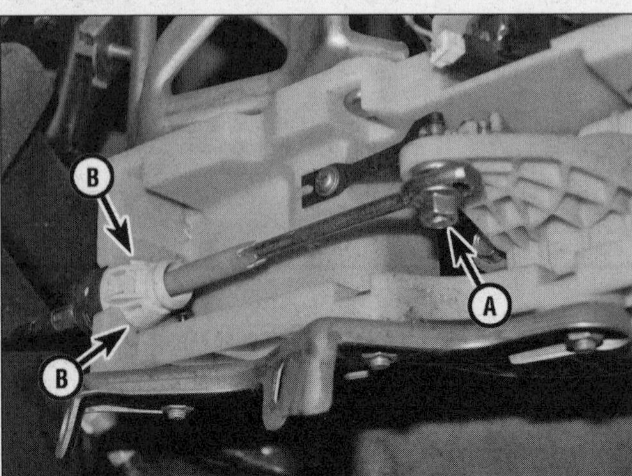

5.7 Remove the shift cable mounting nut (A) then depress the locking tabs (B) and slide cable off the housing

6 Brake Transmission Shift Interlock (BTSI) system - description, check and replacement

Description

1 The Brake Transmission Shift Interlock (BTSI) system prevents the shift lever from being moved out of PARK unless the brake pedal is depressed. The BTSI system also prevents the ignition key from being turned to the LOCK or ACCESSORY position unless the shift lever is fully locked into the PARK position.

Check

2 Verify that the ignition key can be removed only when the shift lever is in the PARK position.

3 When the shift lever is in the PARK position, you should be able to rotate the ignition key from OFF to LOCK. But when the shift lever is in any gear position other than PARK (including NEUTRAL), you should not be able to rotate the ignition key to the LOCK position.

4 You should be able to move the shift lever out of the PARK position when the ignition key is turned to the OFF position.

5 You should not be able to move the shift lever out of the PARK position when the ignition key is turned to the RUN or START position until you depress the brake pedal.

6 With the shifter in any gear selection other than Park, you should not be able to turn the key back to the ACC or LOCK position.

7 Once in gear, with the ignition key in the RUN position, you should be able to move the shift lever between gears, or put it into NEUTRAL or PARK, without depressing the brake pedal.

8 If the BTSI system doesn't operate as described, have the system diagnosed by a dealer service department or other qualified auto repair facility.

Replacement

9 Disconnect the negative battery cable (see Chapter 5).

2005 and earlier models

10 Remove the knee bolster and center console (see Chapter 11).

11 Depress the lock tab at the shifter housing then pull the interlock cable end from the shifter housing.

12 Remove the clevis pin retaining clip with pliers and pull out the pin to disconnect the cable from the steering column.

13 Installation is the reverse of removal.

2006 and later models

Note: *On 2006 and later models the Brake Transmission Shift Interlock (BTSI) system is controlled by a solenoid assembly mounted to the shift lever assembly.*

14 Remove the center console (see Chapter 11).

15 Remove the shift knob retaining screws and lift the knob off of the shift lever.

16 Disconnect the electrical connector to the shift indicator panel then release the indicator panel clips and remove the panel.

17 Remove the indicator switch assembly fasteners and switch assembly from the top of the shift lever.

18 Disconnect the electrical connector to the interlock solenoid (see illustration) then remove the solenoid mounting fasteners. Lift the lever and solenoid off the side of the shift lever housing.

19 Installation is the reverse of removal.

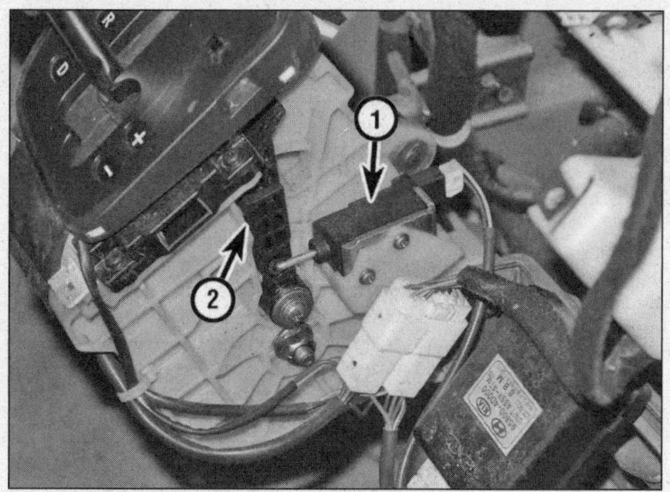

6.18 Brake Transmission Shift Interlock (BTSI) system details

1 *Interlock solenoid* 2 *Interlock solenoid lever*

7.6 Transaxle cooler details

1 *Transaxle cooler lines and clamps* 2 *Transaxle cooler mounting bolts*

7 Transaxle oil cooler - removal and installation

Note: *The transaxle oil cooler and air conditioning condenser are serviced as an assembly. See Chapter 3 for the condenser removal procedure.*

1 Disconnect the cable from the negative battery terminal (see Chapter 5).

2 Raise the front of the vehicle and place it securely on jackstands.

3 To remove the lines from the oil cooler end, remove the front bumper cover (see Chapter 11).

4 Put a drain pan underneath the oil cooler line fittings to catch any spilled transaxle fluid.

5 Using a pair of pliers, loosen the cooler line clamps and slide the clamps down the lines. Using a twisting motion disconnect the lines from the cooler. Plug the lines and fittings to prevent fluid spills.

6 Once both ends of the lines are disconnected remove the transaxle cooler mounting bolts (see illustration) and the cooler from the vehicle.

7 Installation is the reverse of removal, making sure the fluid line clamps are secure.

8 Check the transaxle fluid level and add some if necessary (see Chapter 1).

8 Automatic transaxle - removal and installation

Removal

1 Remove the battery and the battery tray (see Chapter 5).

2 Loosen the front wheel lug nuts and the driveaxle/hub nuts (see Chapter 8), then raise the vehicle and support it securely on jackstands. Remove the wheels.

Note: *Depending on the type of wheels installed on the vehicle and the thickness of the socket you are using, you may have to loosen the driveaxle/hub nuts after the wheels have been removed (see Chapter 8).*

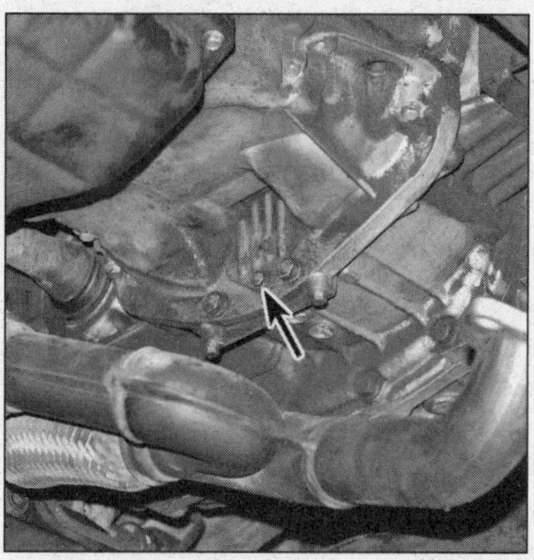

8.16 Location of the torque converter cover bolts

8.17 Mark the relationship of the torque converter to the driveplate

3 Remove the lower splash shield (see Chapter 1).

4 Remove the air filter housing and air intake duct assembly (see Chapter 4).

5 Remove the coolant reservoir (see Chapter 3).

6 Detach the transaxle oil cooler lines and plug them to prevent fluid from spilling (see Section 7).

7 Remove the heater hose bracket bolts and move the hoses back. Clearly label, and unplug, all electrical connectors from the transaxle.

8 Disconnect the shift cable from the manual lever and bracket (see Section 5).

9 Disconnect and remove the crankshaft sensor (see Chapter 6).

10 Drain the transaxle fluid (see Chapter 1 or 7).

11 Remove both driveaxles (see Chapter 8).

12 Support the engine from above with a hoist or engine support fixture, or place a jack and a block of wood under the transaxle.

13 Remove the engine mount subframe (see Chapter 10).

14 Remove the transaxle brace mounting bolts and braces.

15 Remove the starter motor (see Chapter 5).

16 Remove the torque converter cover (see illustration).

17 Mark the relationship of the torque converter to the driveplate so they can be installed in the same position (see illustration).

18 Wedge a screwdriver between the teeth on the driveplate and the engine block at the transaxle to prevent the engine from turning while loosening the torque converter bolts.

19 Remove the torque converter-to-driveplate bolts. After all the bolts are removed, push the torque converter into the bellhousing so it doesn't stay with the engine when the transaxle is removed.

20 Support the transaxle with a transmis-

sion jack, if available, or use a floor jack. Secure the transaxle to the jack using straps or chains so it doesn't fall off during removal.

21 Remove the transaxle upper mount-to-bracket bolts (see Chapter 2A). Remove the upper transaxle-to-engine bolts.

22 Remove the front transaxle/engine bracket and the rear engine mount and bracket (see Chapter 2A).

23 Remove the lower transaxle-to-engine bolts.

24 Make a final check that all wires and hoses have been disconnected from the transaxle, then move the transaxle jack toward the side of the vehicle until the transaxle is clear of the engine locating dowels. Make sure you keep the transaxle level as you do this.

Installation

25 Installation of the transaxle is a reversal of the removal procedure, but note the following points:

- a) *As the torque converter is reinstalled, ensure that the drive tangs at the center of the torque converter hub engage with the recesses in the automatic transaxle fluid pump inner gear. This can be confirmed by turning the torque converter while pushing it towards the transaxle. If it isn't fully engaged, it will "clunk" into place.*
- b) *When installing the transaxle, make sure the match marks you made on the torque converter and driveplate line up.*
- c) *Install all of the driveplate-to-torque converter bolts before tightening any of them.*
- d) *Tighten the driveplate-to-torque converter bolts to the torque listed in this Chapter's Specifications.*
- e) *Tighten the driveaxle/hub nuts to the torque value listed in the Chapter 8 Specifications.*
- f) *Tighten the wheel lug nuts to the torque listed in the Chapter 1 Specifications.*
- g) *Fill the transaxle with the correct type and amount of fluid as described in Chapter 1.*
- h) *On completion, adjust the shift cable (see Section 5).*

9 Automatic transaxle overhaul - general information

1 In the event of a problem occurring, it will be necessary to establish whether the fault is electrical, mechanical or hydraulic in nature, before repair work can be contemplated. Diagnosis requires detailed knowledge of the transaxle's operation and construction, as well as access to specialized test equipment, and so is deemed to be beyond the scope of this manual. It is therefore essential that problems with the automatic transaxle are referred to a dealer service department or other qualified repair facility for assessment.

2 Note that a faulty transaxle should not be removed before the vehicle has been diagnosed by a knowledgeable technician equipped with the proper tools, as trouble-shooting must be performed with the transaxle installed in the vehicle.

Chapter 8
Driveaxles

Contents

	Section		Section
Driveaxle boot replacement	3	Driveaxle - removal and installation	2
Driveaxles - general information and inspection	1		

Torque specifications	Ft-lbs (unless otherwise indicated)	Nm
Driveaxle/hub nut	177 to 199	240 to 270
Intermediate shaft bearing support bracket-to-cylinder block bolts		
2005 and earlier models	31 to 46	42 to 62
2006 and later models	36 to 47	50 to 65
Wheel lug nuts	See Chapter 1	

1 Driveaxles - general information and inspection

1 Power is transmitted from the transaxle to the wheels through a pair of driveaxles. The driveaxles are two equal length halfshafts, consisting of "short" halfshafts on both sides and an intermediate shaft on the right side. The inner end of the left driveaxle, and the right intermediate shaft, are splined to the differential side gears. The inner end of the right driveaxle is splined to the intermediate shaft. The driveaxles can be pulled out to replace the oil seals (see Chapter 7). The outer ends of the driveaxles are splined to the front hubs and locked in place by a large nut.

2 Each driveaxle assembly consists of an inner and outer constant velocity (CV) joint connected together by a driveaxle shaft. The inner ends of the driveaxles are equipped with a tri-pot type joint. The design is capable of both angular and axial motion. In other words, the inner CV joints are free to slide in-and-out as the driveaxle moves up-and-down with the wheel.

3 The outer CV joints use a ball-and-cage design, or "Rzeppa" joint, capable of angular but not axial movement.

4 The boots should be inspected periodically for damage and leaking lubricant. Torn CV joint boots must be replaced immediately or the joints can be damaged. Boot replacement involves removal of the driveaxle (see Section 2).

5 The most common symptom of worn or damaged CV joints, besides lubricant leaks, is a clicking noise in turns, a clunk when accelerating after coasting and vibration at highway speeds. To check for wear in the CV joints and driveaxle shafts, grasp each axle (one at a time) and rotate it in both directions while holding the CV joint housings, feeling for play indicating worn splines or sloppy CV joints. Also check the axleshafts for cracks, dents and distortion.

2.4 Use a punch or chisel and unstake the driveaxle/hub nut

2.5 To prevent the hub from turning while you're loosening the driveaxle/hub nut, wedge a punch or screwdriver into the slots of the brake disc and let it rest against the brake caliper

2.10 If it's stuck, push the driveaxle out of the hub splines using a puller

2.13 Using a large pry bar, pry the inner CV joint out sharply to disengage the snap-ring from the differential gears inside the transaxle

2 Driveaxle - removal and installation

Removal

1 Set the parking brake. Remove the wheel cover or hubcap, if equipped.

2 Loosen, but do not remove, the wheel lug nuts.

3 Raise the vehicle and support it securely on jackstands, then remove the lug nuts and the wheel.

4 Unstake the driveaxle/hub nut with a small punch or chisel (see illustration).

5 Loosen the driveaxle/hub nut with a large socket and breaker bar (see illustration), then remove the driveaxle/hub nut from the axle and discard it.

6 Remove the brake caliper and disc (see Chapter 9).

7 If equipped with antilock brakes, remove the speed sensor cable routing bracket from the steering knuckle (see Chapter 9).

8 Disconnect the tie-rod end from the steering knuckle (see Chapter 10).

9 Separate the control arm balljoint from the steering knuckle (see Chapter 10).

10 Pull out on the steering knuckle while sliding the driveaxle out of the hub. If necessary, strike the end of the stub shaft with a soft-faced hammer to break loose the splines from the hub and bearing assembly. If it still sticks, use a puller to push it out (see illustration).

11 Place a drain pan under the inner CV joint.

12 If you're removing the right-side driveaxle, remove the heat shield fastener and shield, then remove the intermediate shaft support bearing bracket bolts.

13 If you're removing the left driveaxle, support the outer end of the driveaxle and insert a prybar between the inner CV joint and the transaxle case (see illustration). Pry out sharply to disengage the inner CV joint from the transaxle. If you're removing the right driveaxle/intermediate shaft, slide the intermediate shaft out of the transaxle.

Installation

14 Installation is the reverse of removal, noting the following additional points:

a) *Thoroughly clean the splines and bearing shield on the outer CV joint. This is very important, as the bearing shield protects the wheel bearings from water and contamination. Also clean the wheel bearing area of the steering knuckle.*

b) *Thoroughly clean the splines and oil seal sealing surface on the inner CV joint. Apply an even bead of multi-purpose grease around the oil seal sealing surface of the inner CV joint.*

c) *When installing the driveaxle, push it sharply in to seat the snap-ring on the inner CV joint stub shaft into its groove in the differential gears inside the transaxle. Pull out on the inner CV joint housing to ensure it's seated.*

d) *On the right-side driveaxle, insert the splined intermediate shaft into the splined differential gears inside the transaxle, then install the support bearing mounting bolts and tighten them to the torque listed in this Chapter's Specifications. Install the bearing heat shield and tighten the mounting bolts securely.*

e) *Tighten the steering knuckle-to-strut bolts to the torque listed in Chapter 10.*

f) *The steering knuckle-to-balljoint stud pinch bolt and nut should not be reused. A new pinch bolt and nut should always be used; tighten it to the torque listed in the Chapter 10 Specifications.*

g) *Tighten the driveaxle/hub nut to the torque listed in this Chapter's Specifications. Stake the driveaxle/hub nut using a hammer and punch.*

h) *Check the transaxle lubricant, adding some if necessary (see Chapter 1).*

i) *Tighten the lug nuts to the torque listed in the Chapter 1 Specifications.*

3 Driveaxle boot replacement

Note: *If the CV joints or boots must be replaced, explore all options before beginning the job. Complete, rebuilt driveaxles are available on an exchange basis, eliminating much time and work. Whichever route you choose to*

3.5 Remove the snap-ring with a pair of snap-ring pliers or small screwdriver

3.6 Mark the relationship of the tri-pot bearing assembly to the axleshaft

3.7 Drive the tri-pot joint off the axleshaft with a brass punch and hammer; be careful not to damage the bearing surfaces or the splines on the shaft

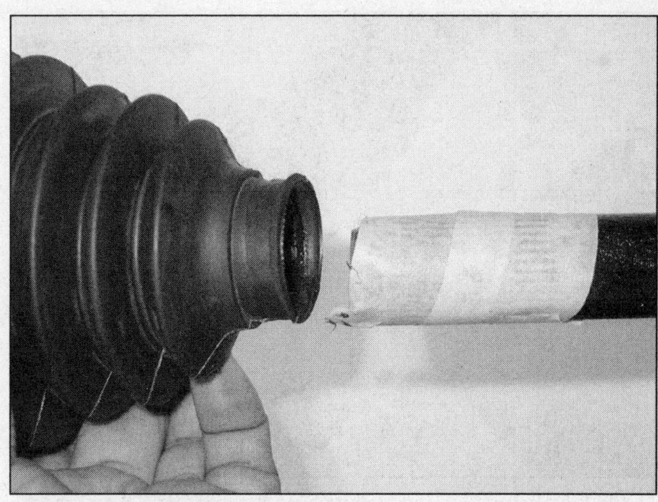
3.10a Wrap the axleshaft splines with tape to prevent damaging the boot as it's slid onto the shaft

take, check on the cost and availability of parts before disassembling the vehicle.

1 Remove the driveaxle (see Section 2).

2 Mount the driveaxle in a vise with wood-lined jaws, to prevent damage to the axleshaft. Check the CV joints for excessive play in the radial direction, which indicates worn parts. Check for smooth operation throughout the full range of motion for each CV joint. If a boot is torn, the recommended procedure is to disassemble the joint, clean the components and inspect for damage due to loss of lubrication and possible contamination by foreign matter. If the CV joint is in good condition, lubricate it with CV joint grease and install a new boot.

Disassembly

3 Cut the boot clamps with side-cutters, then remove and discard them.

4 Using a screwdriver, pry up on the edge of the boot, pull it off the CV joint housing and slide it down the axleshaft, exposing the tri-pot spider assembly. Pull the CV joint housing straight off.

Note: *When removing the housing, hold the rollers in place on the spider trunnion to prevent the rollers and the needle bearings from falling free.*

5 Remove the spider assembly snap-ring with a pair of snap-ring pliers (see illustration).

6 Mark the tri-pot to the axleshaft to ensure that they are reassembled properly (see illustration).

7 Use a hammer and a brass drift to drive the spider assembly from the axleshaft (see illustration).

Note: *It may be necessary to use a two-puller to remove the spider assembly from the axleshaft available from most auto parts stores.*

8 Slide the boot off the shaft.

Inspection

9 Thoroughly clean all components with solvent until the old CV joint grease is completely removed. Inspect the bearing surfaces of the inner tri-pots and housings for cracks, pitting, scoring and other signs of wear. If any part of the inner CV joint is worn, you must replace the entire driveaxle assembly (inner tri-pot joint, axleshaft and outer CV joint). The only components that can be purchased separately are the boots themselves and the boot clamps.

Reassembly

10 Wrap the splines on the inner end of the axleshaft with tape to protect the boots from the sharp edges of the splines, then slide the clamps and boot onto the axleshaft (see illustration). Remove the tape and place the tri-pot spider on the axleshaft with the chamfer

3.10b Install the tri-pot spider on the axleshaft (make sure your match mark is facing out and aligned with the mark on the axleshaft)

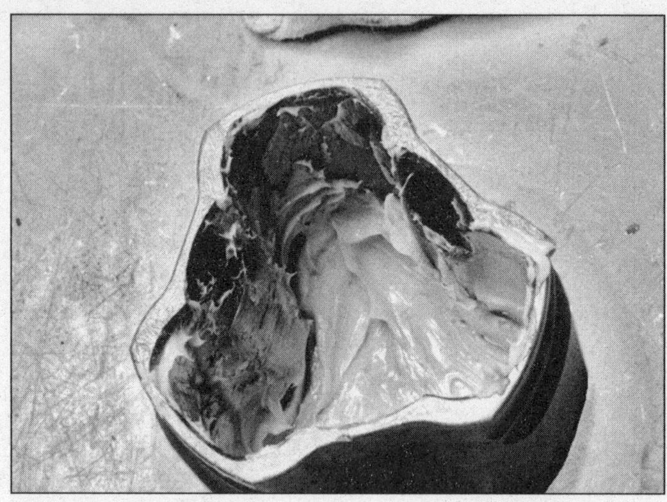

3.10c Place grease at the bottom of the CV joint housing

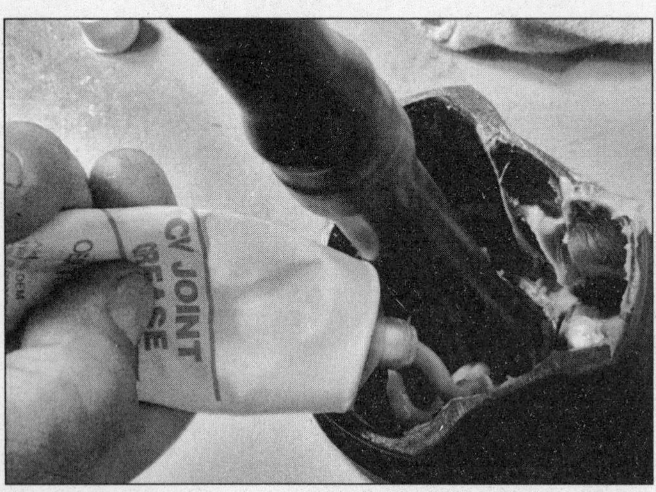

3.10d Install the boot and clamps onto the axleshaft, then insert the tri-pot into the housing, followed by the rest of the grease

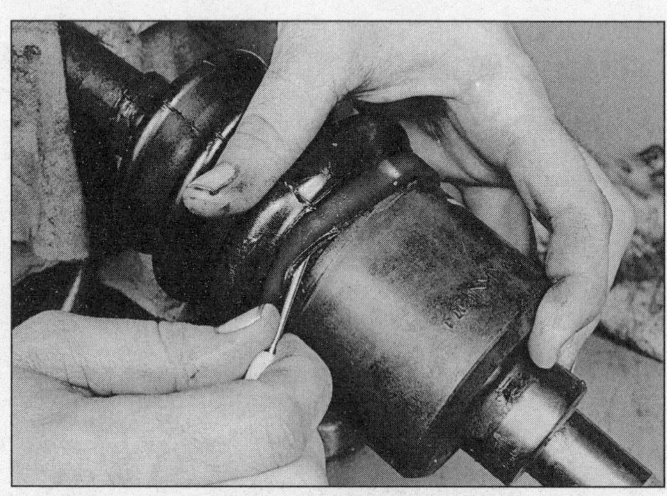

3.12 Equalize the pressure inside the boot by inserting a screwdriver between the boot and the CV joint housing

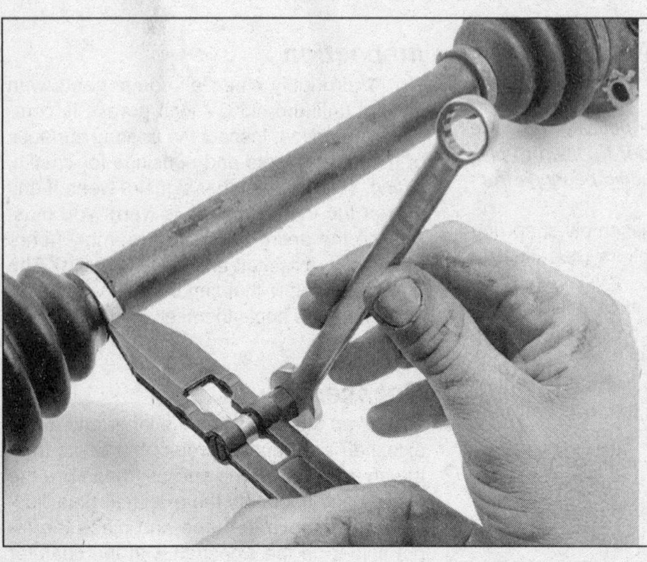

3.14a You'll need a special tightening tool to install "band" type boot clamps: Install the band with its end pointing in the direction of axle rotation and tighten it securely...

toward the shaft (see illustration). Tap the spider onto the shaft (aligning the marks made in Step 6) with a brass drift until it's seated, then install the snap-ring. Apply grease to the tri-pot assembly and inside the housing (see illustration). Insert the tri-pot into the housing and pack the remainder of the grease around the tri-pot (see illustration).

11 Slide the boot into place, making sure both ends seat into the grooves.

12 Position the CV joint mid-way through its travel, then equalize the pressure in the boot (see illustration).

13 Make sure each end of the boot is seated properly, and the boot is not distorted.

14 Install the boot clamps. There are three types of clamps you're likely to encounter: the band type, which requires a special tightening tool, the crimp type (which also requires a special tool), or the fold-over type (see illustrations).

15 Install the driveaxle (see Section 2).

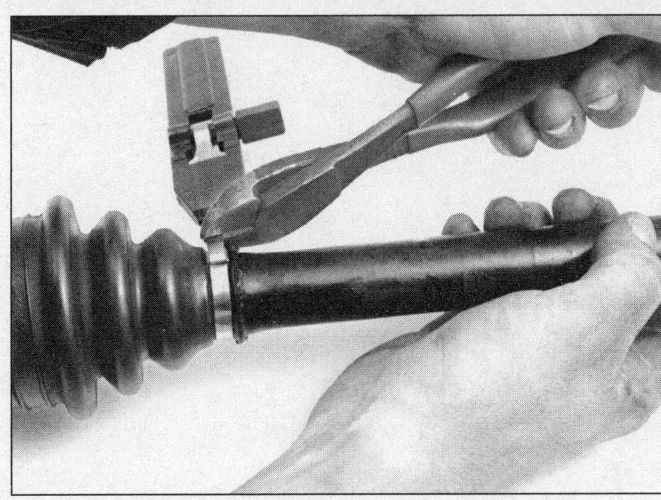

3.14b... then bend the end of the clamp back and cut off the excess

3.14c If you're installing crimp-type boot clamps, you'll need a pair of special crimping pliers (available at most auto parts stores)

3.14d To install fold-over type boot clamps, bend the tang down...

3.14e... then tap the tabs over to hold it in place

Notes

Chapter 9
Brakes

Contents

	Section		Section
Anti-lock Brake System (ABS) - general information	3	Drum brake shoes - replacement	7
Brake disc - inspection, removal and installation	6	General information	1
Brake hoses and lines - inspection and replacement	10	Master cylinder - removal and installation	9
Brake light switch - removal, installation and adjustment	15	Parking brake - adjustment	14
Brake pedal - adjustment	16	Parking brake shoes - inspection and replacement	13
Brake system - bleeding	11	Power brake booster - check, replacement and adjustment	12
Disc brake caliper - removal and installation	5	Troubleshooting	2
Disc brake pads - replacement	4	Wheel cylinder - removal and installation	8

Specifications

General

Brake fluid type	See Chapter 1	
Brake pedal height		
2005 and earlier models	Not available	
2006 and later models	7.57 inches	192.3 mm
Brake pedal free play	13/64 to 5/16 inch	5 to 8 mm
Brake light switch plunger protrusion		
2005 and earlier models	1/64 to 3/32 inch	0.4 to 2.5 mm
2006 and later models	3/64 to 1/16 inch	1.0 to 1.5 mm
Parking brake pedal travel (with 45 lbs (20.4 kg) applied	3-15/32 to 3-27/32 inches	88 to 98 mm

Disc brakes

Brake pad minimum thickness	See Chapter 1	
Disc lateral runout limit	0.005 inch	0.13 mm
Disc minimum thickness	Cast into disc	
Thickness variation (parallelism)	0.0005 inch	0.015 mm

Power brake booster

Booster pushrod-to-master cylinder piston clearance (2005 and earlier models)		
With no vacuum applied to booster	0.016 to 0.024 inch	0.4 to 0.6 mm
With 19.7 in-Hg (500 mm-Hg) applied to booster	0.0039 to 0.016 inch	0.01 to 0.04 mm)
Booster-to-clevis hole center dimension	4.411 to 4.449 inches	111.5 to 112.5 mm

Torque specifications

Note: *One foot-pound (ft-lb) of torque is equivalent to 12 inch-pounds (in-lbs) of torque. Torque values below approximately 15 ft-lbs are expressed in inch-pounds, since most foot-pound torque wrenches are not accurate at these smaller values.*

Torque specifications	Ft-lbs (unless otherwise indicated)	Nm
Brake booster mounting nuts		
2005 and earlier models	14 to 19	19 to 26
2006 and later models	114 to 138 in-lbs	13 to 15
Brake hose banjo bolt-to-caliper	19 to 21	25 to 30
Caliper mounting bolts	16 to 23	22 to 32
Caliper mounting bracket bolts		
Front		
2005 and earlier models	73 to 94	98 to 127
2006 and later models	62 to 72	98 to 127
Rear	37 to 43	50 to 60
Master cylinder-to-brake booster mounting nuts		
2005 and earlier models	108 to 192 in-lbs	13 to 21
2006 and later models	53 to 106 in-lbs	8 to 12
Wheel speed sensor bolt	62 to 88 in-lbs	7 to 10
Wheel lug nuts	See Chapter 1	

1 General Information

1 The vehicles covered by this manual are equipped with hydraulically operated front and rear brake systems. The front brakes are disc type and the rear brakes are disc or drum type. Both the front and rear brakes are self adjusting. The disc brakes automatically compensate for pad wear, while the drum brakes incorporate an adjustment mechanism that is activated as the parking brake is applied.

Hydraulic system

2 The hydraulic system consists of two separate circuits. The master cylinder has separate reservoir chambers for the two circuits, and, in the event of a leak or failure in one hydraulic circuit, the other circuit will remain operative. A dynamic proportioning valve, integral with the ABS hydraulic unit, provides brake balance to each individual wheel.

Power brake booster and vacuum pump

3 The power brake booster, utilizing engine manifold vacuum, and atmospheric pressure to provide assistance to the hydraulically operated brakes, is mounted on the firewall in the engine compartment. An auxiliary vacuum pump, mounted below the power brake booster in the left side of the engine compartment, provides additional vacuum to the booster under certain operating conditions.

Parking brake

4 The parking brake operates the rear brakes only, through cable actuation. It's activated by a lever mounted in the center console.

Service

5 After completing any operation involving disassembly of any part of the brake system, always test drive the vehicle to check for proper braking performance before resuming normal driving. When testing the brakes, perform the tests on a clean, dry, flat surface. Conditions other than these can lead to inaccurate test results.

6 Test the brakes at various speeds with both light and heavy pedal pressure. The vehicle should stop evenly without pulling to one side or the other. Avoid locking the brakes, because this slides the tires and diminishes braking efficiency and control of the vehicle.

7 Tires, vehicle load and wheel alignment are factors which also affect braking performance.

Precautions

8 There are some general cautions and warnings involving the brake system on this vehicle:

a) *Use only brake fluid conforming to DOT 3 specifications.*

b) *The brake pads and linings contain fibers that are hazardous to your health if inhaled. Whenever you work on brake system components, clean all parts with brake system cleaner. Do not allow the fine dust to become airborne. Also, wear an approved filtering mask.*

c) *Safety should be paramount whenever any servicing of the brake components is performed. Do not use parts or fasteners that are not in perfect condition, and be sure that all clearances and torque specifications are adhered to. If you are at all unsure about a certain procedure, seek professional advice. Upon completion of any brake system work, test the brakes carefully in a controlled area before putting the vehicle into normal service. If a problem is suspected in the brake system, don't drive the vehicle until it's fixed.*

d) *Used brake fluid is considered a hazardous waste and it must be disposed of in accordance with federal, state and local laws. DO NOT pour it down the sink, into septic tanks or storm drains, or on the ground. Clean up any spilled brake fluid immediately and then wash the area with large amounts of water. This is especially true for any finished or painted surfaces.*

2 Troubleshooting

PROBABLE CAUSE	CORRECTIVE ACTION
No brakes - pedal travels to floor	
1 Low fluid level 2 Air in system	1 and 2 Low fluid level and air in the system are symptoms of another problem a leak somewhere in the hydraulic system. Locate and repair the leak
3 Defective seals in master cylinder	3 Replace master cylinder
4 Fluid overheated and vaporized due to heavy braking	4 Bleed hydraulic system (temporary fix). Replace brake fluid (proper fix)
Brake pedal slowly travels to floor under braking or at a stop	
1 Defective seals in master cylinder	1 Replace master cylinder
2 Leak in a hose, line, caliper or wheel cylinder	2 Locate and repair leak
3 Air in hydraulic system	3 Bleed the system, inspect system for a leak
Brake pedal feels spongy when depressed	
1 Air in hydraulic system	1 Bleed the system, inspect system for a leak
2 Master cylinder or power booster loose	2 Tighten fasteners
3 Brake fluid overheated (beginning to boil)	3 Bleed the system (temporary fix). Replace the brake fluid (proper fix)
4 Deteriorated brake hoses (ballooning under pressure)	4 Inspect hoses, replace as necessary (it's a good idea to replace all of them if one hose shows signs of deterioration)

PROBABLE CAUSE	CORRECTIVE ACTION

Brake pedal feels hard when depressed and/or excessive effort required to stop vehicle

1 Power booster faulty	1 Replace booster
2 Engine not producing sufficient vacuum, or hose to booster clogged, collapsed or cracked	2 Check vacuum to booster with a vacuum gauge. Replace hose if cracked or clogged, repair engine if vacuum is extremely low
3 Brake linings contaminated by grease or brake fluid	3 Locate and repair source of contamination, replace brake pads or shoes
4 Brake linings glazed	4 Replace brake pads or shoes, check discs and drums for glazing, service as necessary
5 Caliper piston(s) or wheel cylinder(s) binding or frozen	5 Replace calipers or wheel cylinders
6 Brakes wet	6 Apply pedal to boil-off water (this should only be a momentary problem)
7 Kinked, clogged or internally split brake hose or line	7 Inspect lines and hoses, replace as necessary

Excessive brake pedal travel (but will pump up)

1 Drum brakes out of adjustment	1 Adjust brakes
2 Air in hydraulic system	2 Bleed system, inspect system for a leak

Excessive brake pedal travel (but will not pump up)

1 Master cylinder pushrod misadjusted	1 Adjust pushrod
2 Master cylinder seals defective	2 Replace master cylinder
3 Brake linings worn out	3 Inspect brakes, replace pads and/or shoes
4 Hydraulic system leak	4 Locate and repair leak

Brake pedal doesn't return

1 Brake pedal binding	1 Inspect pivot bushing and pushrod, repair or lubricate
2 Defective master cylinder	2 Replace master cylinder

Brake pedal pulsates during brake application

1 Brake drums out-of-round	1 Have drums machined by an automotive machine shop
2 Excessive brake disc runout or disc surfaces out-of-parallel	2 Have discs machined by an automotive machine shop
3 Loose or worn wheel bearings	3 Adjust or replace wheel bearings
4 Loose lug nuts	4 Tighten lug nuts

Brakes slow to release

1 Malfunctioning power booster	1 Replace booster
2 Pedal linkage binding	2 Inspect pedal pivot bushing and pushrod, repair/lubricate
3 Malfunctioning proportioning valve	3 Replace proportioning valve
4 Sticking caliper or wheel cylinder	4 Repair or replace calipers or wheel cylinders
5 Kinked or internally split brake hose	5 Locate and replace faulty brake hose

Brakes grab (one or more wheels)

1 Grease or brake fluid on brake lining	1 Locate and repair cause of contamination, replace lining
2 Brake lining glazed	2 Replace lining, deglaze disc or drum

Troubleshooting (continued)

PROBABLE CAUSE	CORRECTIVE ACTION
Vehicle pulls to one side during braking	
1 Grease or brake fluid on brake lining	1 Locate and repair cause of contamination, replace lining
2 Brake lining glazed	2 Deglaze or replace lining, deglaze disc or drum
3 Restricted brake line or hose	3 Repair line or replace hose
4 Tire pressures incorrect	4 Adjust tire pressures
5 Caliper or wheel cylinder sticking	5 Repair or replace calipers or wheel cylinders
6 Wheels out of alignment	6 Have wheels aligned
7 Weak suspension spring	7 Replace springs
8 Weak or broken shock absorber	8 Replace shock absorbers
Brakes drag (indicated by sluggish engine performance or wheels being very hot after driving)	
1 Brake pedal pushrod incorrectly adjusted	1 Adjust pushrod
2 Master cylinder pushrod (between booster and master cylinder)	2 Adjust pushrod incorrectly adjusted
3 Obstructed compensating port in master cylinder	3 Replace master cylinder
4 Master cylinder piston seized in bore	4 Replace master cylinder
5 Contaminated fluid causing swollen seals throughout system	5 Flush system, replace all hydraulic components
6 Clogged brake lines or internally split brake hose(s)	6 Flush hydraulic system, replace defective hose(s)
7 Sticking caliper(s) or wheel cylinder(s)	7 Replace calipers or wheel cylinders
8 Parking brake not releasing	8 Inspect parking brake linkage and parking brake mechanism, repair as required
9 Improper shoe-to-drum clearance	9 Adjust brake shoes
10 Faulty proportioning valve	10 Replace proportioning valve
Brakes fade (due to excessive heat)	
1 Brake linings excessively worn or glazed	1 Deglaze or replace brake pads and/or shoes
2 Excessive use of brakes	2 Downshift into a lower gear, maintain a constant slower speed (going down hills)
3 Vehicle overloaded	3 Reduce load
4 Brake drums or discs worn too thin	4 Measure drum diameter and disc thickness, replace drums or discs as required
5 Contaminated brake fluid	5 Flush system, replace fluid
6 Brakes drag	6 Repair cause of dragging brakes
7 Driver resting left foot on brake pedal	7 Don't ride the brakes
Brakes noisy (high-pitched squeal)	
1 Glazed lining	1 Deglaze or replace lining
2 Contaminated lining (brake fluid, grease, etc.)	2 Repair source of contamination, replace linings
3 Weak or broken brake shoe hold-down or return spring	3 Replace springs
4 Rivets securing lining to shoe or backing plate loose	4 Replace shoes or pads
5 Excessive dust buildup on brake linings	5 Wash brakes off with brake system cleaner
6 Brake drums worn too thin	6 Measure diameter of drums, replace if necessary
7 Wear indicator on disc brake pads contacting disc	7 Replace brake pads
8 Anti-squeal shims missing or installed improperly	8 Install shims correctly

PROBABLE CAUSE	CORRECTIVE ACTION

Brakes noisy (scraping sound)

1 Brake pads or shoes worn out; rivets, backing plate or brake	1 Replace linings, have discs and/or drums machined (or replace) shoe metal contacting disc or drum

Brakes chatter

1 Worn brake lining	1 Inspect brakes, replace shoes or pads as necessary
2 Glazed or scored discs or drums	2 Deglaze discs or drums with sandpaper (if glazing is severe, machining will be required)
3 Drums or discs heat checked	3 Check discs and/or drums for hard spots, heat checking, etc. Have discs/drums machined or replace them
4 Disc runout or drum out-of-round excessive	4 Measure disc runout and/or drum out-of-round, have discs or drums machined or replace them
5 Loose or worn wheel bearings	5 Adjust or replace wheel bearings
6 Loose or bent brake backing plate (drum brakes)	6 Tighten or replace backing plate
7 Grooves worn in discs or drums	7 Have discs or drums machined, if within limits (if not, replace them)
8 Brake linings contaminated (brake fluid, grease, etc.)	8 Locate and repair source of contamination, replace pads or shoes
9 Excessive dust buildup on linings	9 Wash brakes with brake system cleaner
10 Surface finish on discs or drums too rough after machining	10 Have discs or drums properly machined (especially on vehicles with sliding calipers)
11 Brake pads or shoes glazed	11 Deglaze or replace brake pads or shoes

Brake pads or shoes click

1 Shoe support pads on brake backing plate grooved or	1 Replace brake backing plate excessively worn
2 Brake pads loose in caliper	2 Loose pad retainers or anti-rattle clips
3 Also see items listed under Brakes chatter	

Brakes make groaning noise at end of stop

1 Brake pads and/or shoes worn out	1 Replace pads and/or shoes
2 Brake linings contaminated (brake fluid, grease, etc.)	2 Locate and repair cause of contamination, replace brake pads or shoes
3 Brake linings glazed	3 Deglaze or replace brake pads or shoes
4 Excessive dust buildup on linings	4 Wash brakes with brake system cleaner
5 Scored or heat-checked discs or drums	5 Inspect discs/drums, have machined if within limits (if not, replace discs or drums)
6 Broken or missing brake shoe attaching hardware	6 Inspect drum brakes, replace missing hardware

Rear brakes lock up under light brake application

1 Tire pressures too high	1 Adjust tire pressures
2 Tires excessively worn	2 Replace tires
3 Defective proportioning valve	3 Replace proportioning valve

Brake warning light on instrument panel comes on (or stays on)

1 Low fluid level in master cylinder reservoir (reservoirs with fluid level sensor)	1 Add fluid, inspect system for leak, check the thickness of the brake pads and shoes
2 Failure in one half of the hydraulic system	2 Inspect hydraulic system for a leak
3 Piston in pressure differential warning valve not centered	3 Center piston by bleeding one circuit or the other (close bleeder valve as soon as the light goes out)

Troubleshooting (continued)

PROBABLE CAUSE	CORRECTIVE ACTION
Brake warning light on instrument panel comes on (or stays on) (continued)	
4 Defective pressure differential valve or warning switch	4 Replace valve or switch
5 Air in the hydraulic system	5 Bleed the system, check for leaks
6 Brake pads worn out (vehicles with electric wear sensors - small	6 Replace brake pads (and sensors) probes that fit into the brake pads and ground out on the disc when the pads get thin)
Brakes do not self adjust	
Disc brakes	
1 Defective caliper piston seals	1 Replace calipers. Also, possible contaminated fluid causing soft or swollen seals (flush system and fill with new fluid if in doubt)
2 Corroded caliper piston(s)	2 Same as above
Drum brakes	
1 Adjuster screw frozen	1 Remove adjuster, disassemble, clean and lubricate with high-temperature grease
2 Adjuster lever does not contact star wheel or is binding	2 Inspect drum brakes, assemble correctly or clean or replace parts as required
3 Adjusters mixed up (installed on wrong wheels after brake job)	3 Reassemble correctly
4 Adjuster cable broken or installed incorrectly (cable-type adjusters)	4 Install new cable or assemble correctly
Rapid brake lining wear	
1 Driver resting left foot on brake pedal	1 Don't ride the brakes
2 Surface finish on discs or drums too rough	2 Have discs or drums properly machined
3 Also see Brakes drag	

3.2 The integrated electronic and hydraulic control unit is located below the brake master cylinder

3 Anti-lock Brake System (ABS) - general information

General information

1 The Anti-lock Brake System is designed to maintain vehicle steerability, directional stability and optimum deceleration under severe braking conditions on most road surfaces. It does so by monitoring the rotational speed of each wheel and controlling the brake line pressure to each wheel during braking. This prevents the wheels from locking up.

2 The ABS system has three main components: the wheel speed sensors, an electronic control unit and a hydraulic unit. Four wheel speed sensors - one at each wheel - send a variable voltage signal to the control unit, which monitors these signals, compares them to its program and determines whether a wheel is about to lock up. When a wheel is about to lock up, the control unit signals the hydraulic unit to reduce hydraulic pressure (or not increase it further) at that wheel's brake caliper. Pressure modulation is handled by electrically-operated solenoid valves within the hydraulic control unit (see illustration).

3 If a problem develops within the system, an ABS warning light will glow on the dashboard. Sometimes, a visual inspection of the ABS system can help you locate the problem. Carefully inspect the ABS wiring harness. Pay particularly close attention to the harness and connections near each wheel. Look for signs of chafing and other damage caused by incorrectly routed wires. If a wheel sensor harness is damaged, it must be replaced along with the sensor (if they are assembled together).

Warning: *Do NOT try to repair an ABS wiring harness. The ABS system is sensitive to even the smallest changes in resistance. Repairing the harness could alter resistance values and cause the system to malfunction. If the ABS wiring harness is damaged in any way, it must be replaced.*

Caution: *Make sure the ignition is turned off before unplugging or reattaching any electrical connections.*

3.9a The front wheel speed sensor is mounted to the steering knuckle

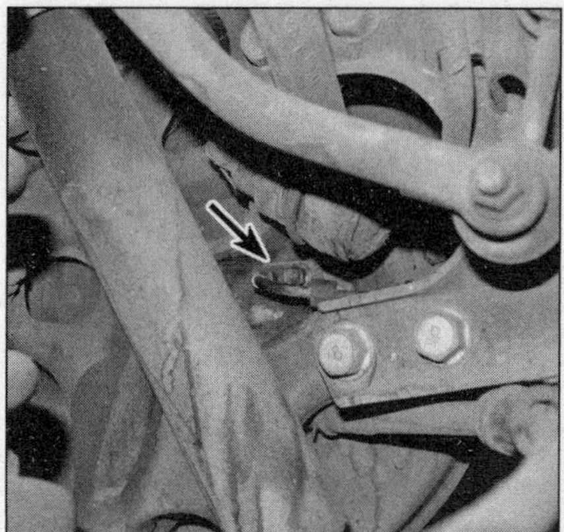

3.9b The rear wheel speed sensor is mounted to the rear knuckle (hub carrier)

4.5 Before removing the caliper, slowly depress the piston in the caliper bore by using a large C-clamp between the outer brake pad and the back of the caliper

Diagnosis and repair

4 If the ABS warning light comes on and stays on while the vehicle is in operation, the ABS system requires attention. Although special electronic ABS diagnostic testing tools are necessary to properly diagnose the system, you can perform a few preliminary checks before taking the vehicle to a dealer service department.

- *a) Check the brake fluid level in the reservoir.*
- *b) Verify that the computer electrical connectors are securely connected.*
- *c) Check the electrical connectors at the hydraulic control unit.*
- *d) Check the fuses.*
- *e) Follow the wiring harness to each wheel and verify that all connections are secure and that the wiring is undamaged.*

5 If the above preliminary checks do not solve the problem, the vehicle should be diagnosed by a dealer service department or other qualified repair shop. Due to the complex nature of the ABS system, all actual repair work must be done by a qualified automotive technician.

Wheel speed sensor - removal and installation

6 Loosen the wheel lug nuts, raise the vehicle and support it securely on jackstands. Remove the wheel.

7 Make sure the ignition key is turned to the Off position.

8 Trace the wiring back from the sensor, detaching all brackets and clips while noting its correct routing, then disconnect the electrical connector.

9 Remove the mounting fastener and carefully detach the sensor from the knuckle (front) or rear knuckle/hub carrier (rear) (see illustrations).

10 Installation is the reverse of removal procedure. Tighten the bolt to the torque listed in this Chapter's Specifications.

11 Install the wheel and lug nuts, lower the vehicle and tighten the lug nuts to the torque listed in the Chapter 1 Specifications.

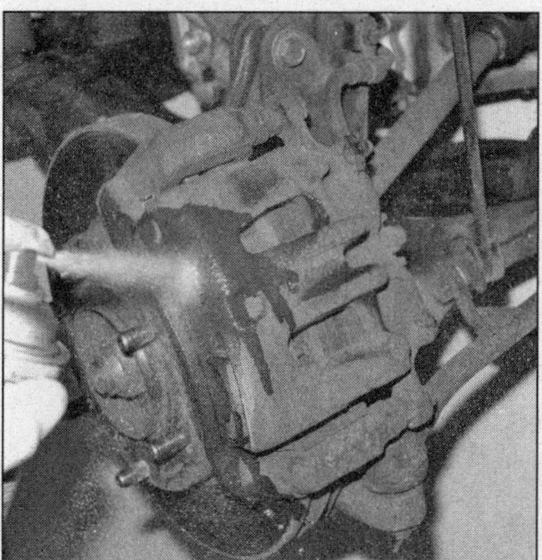

4.6a Always wash the brakes with brake cleaner before disassembling anything

4.6b Remove the lower caliper bolt. Hold the slide pin with an open-end wrench wile loosening the bolt

4 Disc brake pads - replacement

Warning: *Disc brake pads must be replaced on both front or rear wheels at the same time - never replace the pads on only one wheel. Also, the dust created by the brake system is harmful to your health. Never blow it out with compressed air and don't inhale any of it. An approved filtering mask should be worn when working on the brakes. Do not, under any circumstances, use petroleum-based solvents to clean brake parts. Use brake system cleaner only!*

Note: *The following procedure applies to both the front and rear disc brakes.*

1 Remove the cap from the brake fluid reservoir.

2 Loosen the wheel lug nuts, raise the front or rear of the vehicle and support it securely on jackstands. Block the wheels at the opposite end.

3 Remove the wheels. Work on one brake assembly at a time, using the assembled brake for reference if necessary.

4 Inspect the brake disc carefully as outlined in Section 6. If machining is necessary, follow the information in that Section to remove the disc, at which time the pads can be removed as well.

5 Push the piston back into its bore to provide room for the new brake pads. A C-clamp can be used to accomplish this (see illustration). As the piston is depressed to the bottom of the caliper bore, the fluid in the master cylinder will rise. Make sure that it doesn't overflow. If necessary, siphon off some of the fluid.

6 Follow the accompanying photos, beginning with illustration 4.6a. Be sure to stay in order and read the caption accompanying each illustration.

7 When reinstalling the caliper, tighten the mounting bolts to the torque listed in this Chapter's Specifications. After the job has been completed, firmly depress the brake pedal a few times to bring the pads into contact with the disc. Check the level of the brake fluid, adding some if necessary. Check the operation of the brakes carefully before placing the vehicle into normal service.

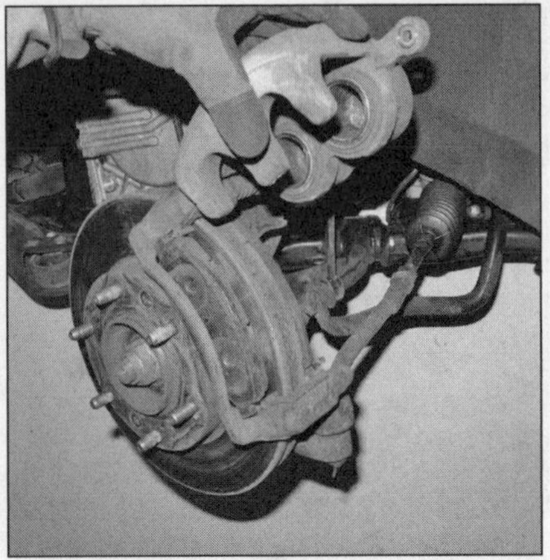

4.6c Pivot the caliper up (be careful not to damage the boot for the upper slide pin)

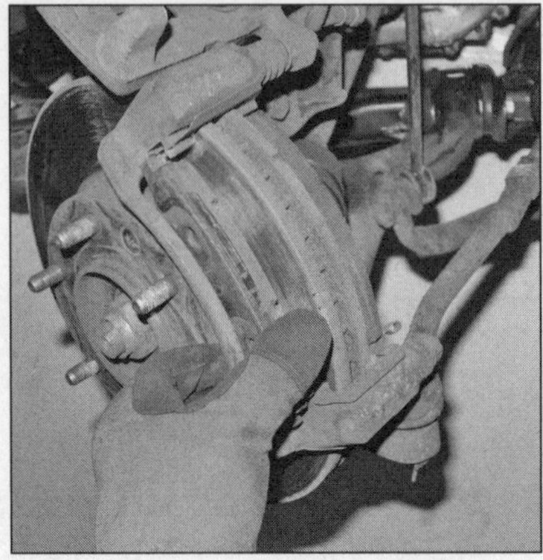

4.6d Remove the outer pad. . .

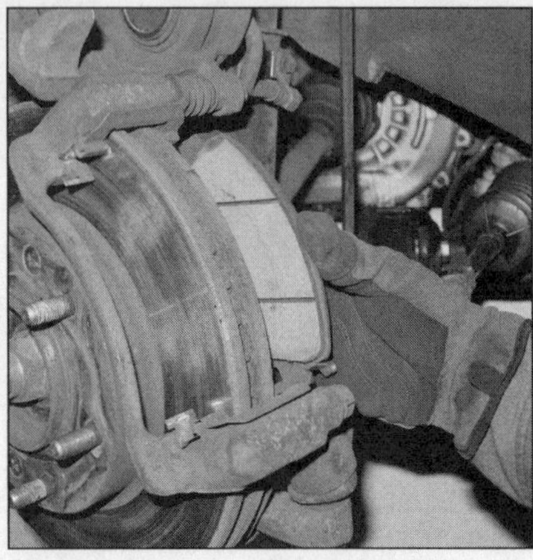

4.6e. . . and the inner pad

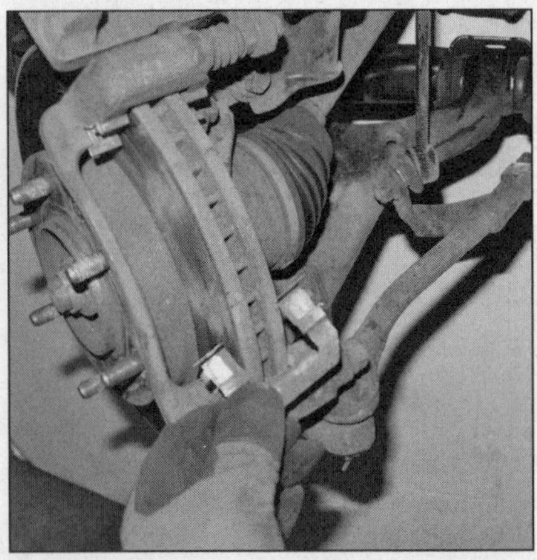

4.6f Remove the upper and lower pad support plates; make sure they are a tight fit and aren't worn. If necessary, replace them

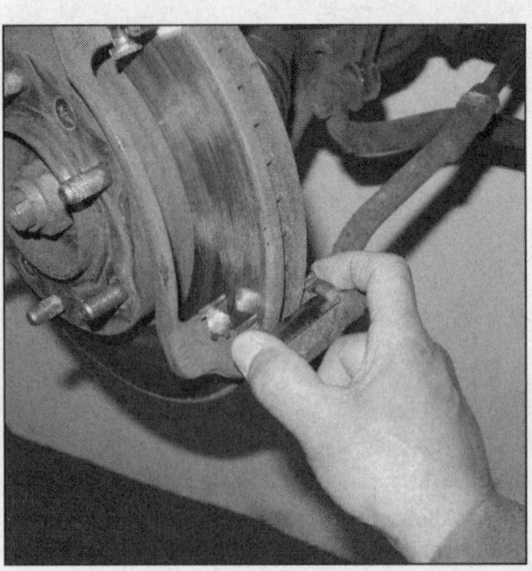

4.6g Install the upper and lower pad support plates

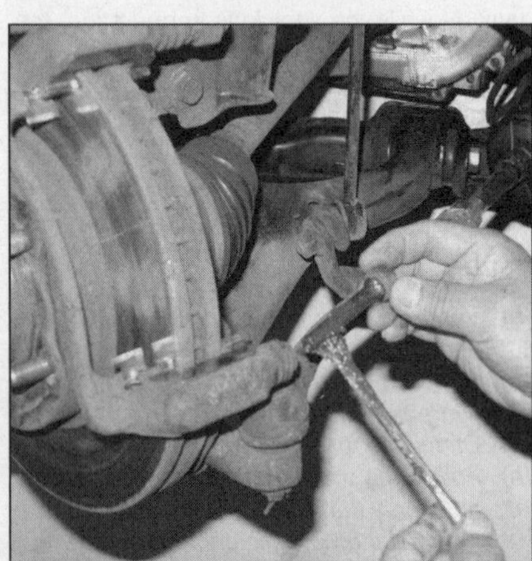

4.6h Pull out the upper and lower sliding pins and clean them. Apply a coat of high-temperature grease to the pins and reinstall them. Be careful not to damage the pin boots, replace any boots that are worn or damaged

4.6i Install the inner pad, making sure that the ends are seated correctly on the pad support plates

4.6j Install the outer pad, making sure that the ends are seated correctly on the pad support plates

4.6k Swing the caliper down and tighten the caliper lower mounting bolt to the torque listed in this Chapter's Specifications

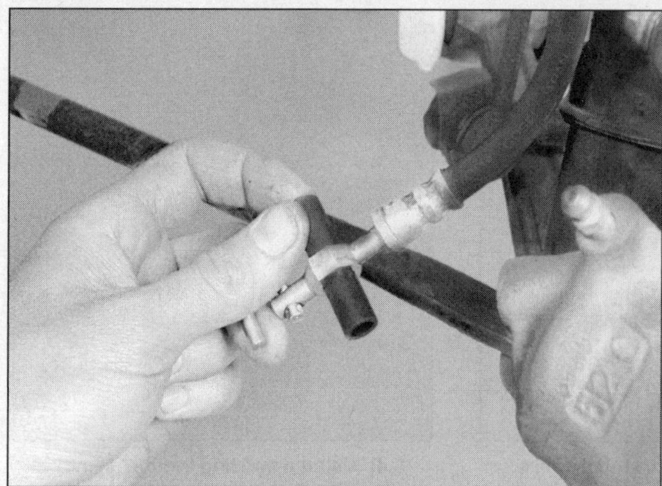

5.2a Using a piece of rubber hose of the appropriate size, plug the brake line banjo fitting to prevent brake fluid from leaking out and to prevent dirt and moisture from contaminating the fluid in the hose

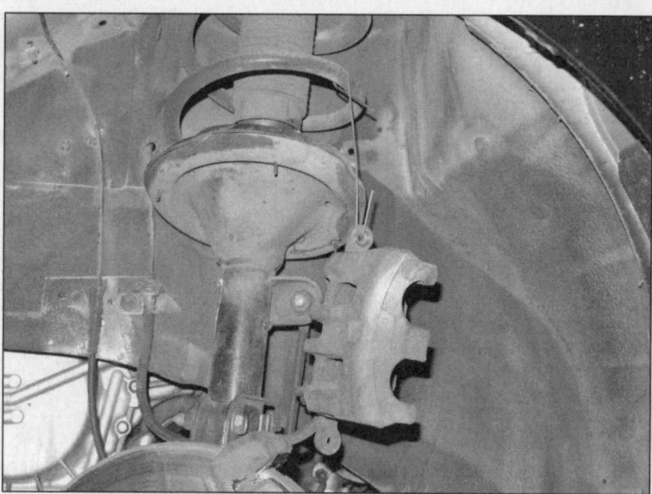

5.2b If you're just removing the caliper for access to other components, hang it from the spring with a piece of wire; do not allow the caliper to hang by the flexible brake hose

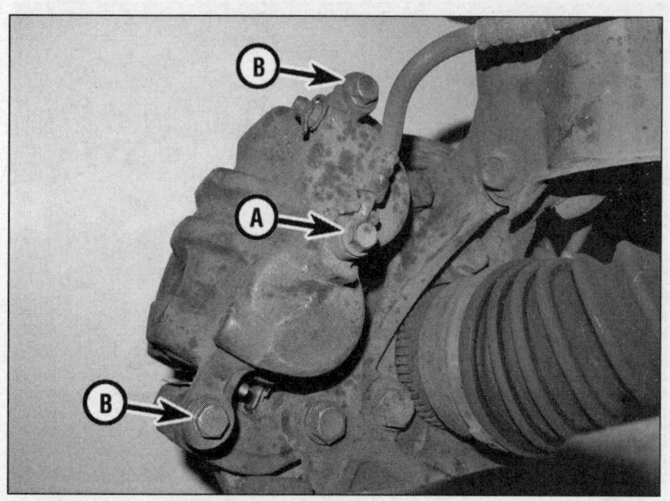

5.3a Front brake caliper mounting details

A Brake hose banjo fitting bolt   B Caliper mounting bolts

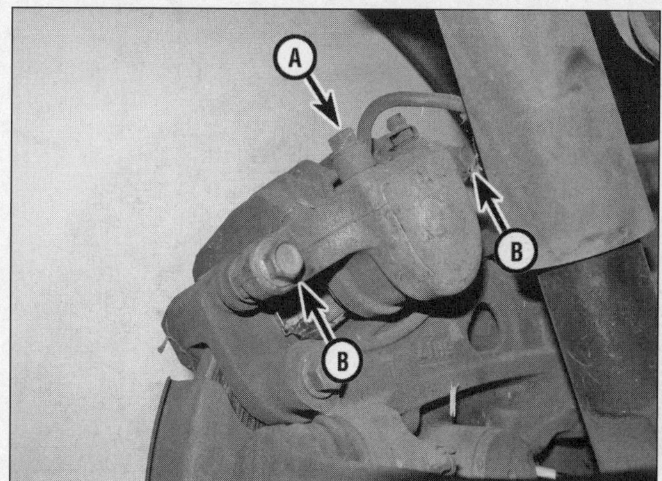

5.3b Rear brake caliper mounting details

A Brake hose banjo fitting bolt   B Caliper mounting bolts

5 Disc brake caliper - removal and installation

Warning: *Dust created by the brake system is harmful to your health. Never blow it out with compressed air and don't inhale any of it. An approved filtering mask should be worn when working on the brakes. Do not, under any circumstances, use petroleum-based solvents to clean brake parts. Use brake system cleaner only!*

Note: *Always replace the calipers in pairs on the same axle (front or rear) - never replace just one of them.*

Removal

1 Loosen the wheel lug nuts, raise the vehicle and support it securely on jackstands. Remove the wheels.

2 Remove the brake hose banjo bolt and disconnect the hose from the caliper. Plug the hose to keep contaminants out of the brake system and to prevent losing any more brake fluid than is necessary (see illustration).

Note: *If you're just removing the caliper for access to other components, don't detach the hose, but be sure to support the caliper with a piece of wire - don't let it hang by the hose (see illustration).*

3 Remove the caliper mounting bolts (see illustrations).

4 Remove the caliper. If necessary, remove the caliper mounting bracket from the steering knuckle or rear knuckle.

Installation

5 Installation is the reverse of removal. Tighten the caliper mounting bolts (and mounting bracket bolts, if removed) to the torque listed in this Chapter's Specifications. Install new sealing washers on both sides of the brake hose banjo fitting, then tighten the banjo bolt to the torque listed in this Chapter's Specifications.

6 Bleed the brake system (see Section 11).

7 Install the wheels and lug nuts. Lower the vehicle and tighten the lug nuts to the torque listed in the Chapter 1 Specifications.

Warning: *Depress the brake pedal several times before moving the vehicle to bring the brake pads into contact with the discs. Failure to do so will result in an initial loss of braking.*

8 Check the operation of the brakes carefully before driving the vehicle.

6.3 The brake pads on this vehicle were obviously neglected - they wore down completely and cut deep grooves into the disc (wear this severe means the disc must be replaced)

6.4 Use a dial indicator to measure disc runout - if the reading exceeds the maximum allowable runout limit, the disc will have to be machined or replaced

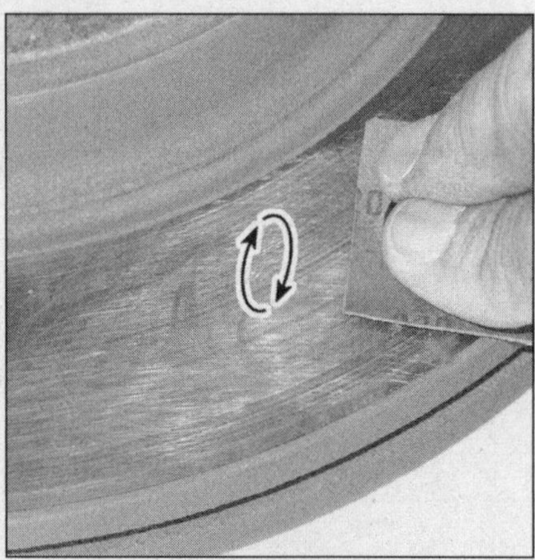

6.4b Using a swirling motion, remove the glaze from the disc surface with sandpaper or emery cloth

6.5a The minimum wear dimension is cast into the back side of the disc (typical)

6.5b Use a micrometer to measure disc thickness

6 Brake disc - inspection, removal and installation

Warning: *Dust created by the brake system is harmful to your health. Never blow it out with compressed air and don't inhale any of it. An approved filtering mask should be worn when working on the brakes. Do not, under any circumstances, use petroleum-based solvents to clean brake parts. Use brake system cleaner only.*

Note: *This procedure applies to both front and rear brake discs.*

Inspection

1 Loosen the wheel lug nuts, raise the vehicle and support it securely on jackstands. Remove the wheel(s) and if the rear brake disc is being worked on, release the parking brake.

2 Remove the brake caliper and pads (see Sections 4 and 5). Don't disconnect the brake hose from the caliper, or you'll have to bleed the brakes when everything is reassembled. After removing the caliper, suspend it out of the way with a piece of wire.

3 Inspect the disc surface for score marks and other damage. Light scratches and shallow grooves are normal after use and may not always be detrimental to brake operation, but deep scoring requires disc removal and refinishing by an automotive machine shop. Check both sides of the disc (see illustration). If pulsating has been noticed during application of the brakes, suspect excessive disc runout.

4 To check disc runout, place a dial indicator at a point about 1/2-inch from the outer edge of the disc (see illustration). Set the indicator to zero and turn the disc. The indicator reading should not exceed the specified allowable runout limit. If it does, the disc should be refinished by an automotive machine shop.

Note: *The discs should be resurfaced regardless of the dial indicator reading, as this will impart a smooth finish and ensure a perfectly flat surface, eliminating any brake pedal pulsation or other undesirable symptoms related to questionable discs. At the very least, if you elect not to have the discs resurfaced, remove the glaze from the surface with emery cloth using a swirling motion (see illustration).*

5 It's absolutely critical that the disc not be machined to a thickness under the specified minimum allowable thickness. The minimum thickness is cast into the inside of the disc (see illustration). The disc thickness can be checked with a micrometer (see illustration).

Note: *The rear disc has the minimum thickness specification cast into it as well, although the location may vary.*

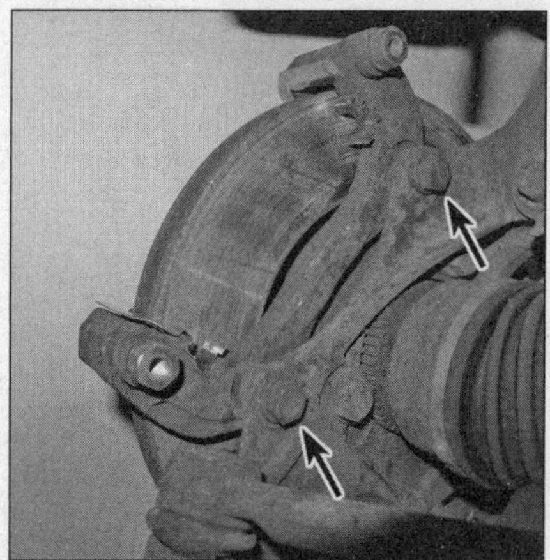
6.6a Caliper mounting bracket bolts - front brake

6.6b Caliper mounting bracket bolts - rear brake

6.6c Rear discs have two retaining screws

Removal

6 Remove the caliper mounting bracket bolts (see illustrations). On rear discs, remove the Phillips head screws that hold the disc in place.

7 Remove the lug nuts that were put on to hold the disc in place, then remove the disc from the hub.

Note: *Remove and discard any retaining clips on the wheel studs that hold the disc to the hub. These clips are not necessary for reinstallation of the brake disc.*

Installation

8 Place the disc in position over the wheel studs. Install the mounting bracket, tightening the bolts to the torque listed in this Chapter's Specifications.

9 Install the brake pads and caliper (see Section 4). Tighten the caliper mounting bolts to the torque listed in this Chapter's Specifications.

10 Install the wheel, lower the vehicle and tighten the lug nuts to the torque listed in the Chapter 1 Specifications1,0.

11 Pump the brake pedal a few times to bring the brake pads into contact with the disc. Bleeding won't be necessary unless the brake hose was disconnected from the caliper. Check the operation of the brakes carefully before driving the vehicle.

7 Drum brake shoes - replacement

Warning: *Drum brake shoes must be replaced on both wheels at the same time - never replace the shoes on only one wheel. Also, the dust created by the brake system is harmful to your health. Never blow it out with compressed air and don't inhale any of it. An approved filtering mask should be worn when working on the brakes. Do not, under any circumstances, use petroleum-based solvents to clean brake parts. Use brake system cleaner only!*

Caution: *Whenever the brake shoes are replaced, the return and hold-down springs should also be replaced. Due to the continuous heating/cooling cycle the springs are subjected to, they can lose tension over a period of time and may allow the shoes to drag on the drum and wear at a much faster rate than normal.*

1 Loosen the wheel lug nuts, then raise the rear of the vehicle and support it securely on jackstands. Block the front wheels to keep the vehicle from rolling off the stands.

2 Remove the rear wheels. Release the parking brake. Loosen the parking brake cable adjuster (see illustration 14.5) to create slack in the parking brake cables.

3 Pull off the brake drums. The brake drums may be difficult to remove if the shoes have worn the drums excessively. If you can't pull off the drums, remove the access hole plug for the adjuster from the backing plate and, using a brake adjuster tool and a narrow screwdriver (or two screwdrivers), push the adjuster lever off the star wheel and turn the star wheel to retract the shoes.

4 Wash the brake assembly thoroughly with brake system cleaner before beginning work. Do NOT use compressed air to blow off the brake assembly.

5 Clean the brake drums and check them for score marks, deep grooves, hard spots (which will appear as small discolored areas) and cracks. If the drums are worn, scored or out-of-round, they can be resurfaced by an automotive machine shop.

Note: *Professionals recommend resurfacing the drums whenever a brake job is done. Resurfacing will eliminate the possibility of out-of-round drums. If the drums are worn so much they can't be resurfaced without exceeding the maximum allowable diameter (stamped or cast on the drum), new ones will be required. At the very least, if you elect not to have the drums resurfaced, remove the glazing from the surface with sandpaper or emery cloth using a swirling motion.*

6 Work on only one drum brake assembly at a time. Do not begin disassembling the other brake until you have reassembled the first one. That way, you can use the other one as a reference, if necessary.

7 Using a hold-down spring tool, push down and give each hold-down cup a 90-degree twist, disconnect the hold-down cups and remove the hold-down springs.

8 Disconnect the lower shoe return spring from the brake shoes.

9 Remove the leading and trailing shoes and the adjuster mechanism from the backing plate.

10 Disconnect the parking brake cable from the parking brake lever.

11 Place the brake shoe and adjuster assembly on a workbench and remove the rest of the parts.

12 Inspect and, if necessary, replace the wheel cylinder (see Section 8).

13 Clean off the backing plate and apply brake grease or high-temperature grease to the raised pads, the slots in the wheel cylinder pistons and the ends of the lower shoe retaining plate.

14 Apply brake grease to the threaded portion of the adjuster and to the tips of the adjuster, where it engages the brake shoes. Engage the slots in the brake shoes with the ends of the adjuster. Attach the upper return spring to both shoes to hold them in place.

15 Position the shoes and adjuster on the brake backing plate and engage the upper ends of the shoes, one at a time, with the slots on the ends of the wheel cylinder pistons.

16 Attach the lower return spring to the leading and trailing shoes.

17 Install the hold-down pins, springs and cups.

18 Repeat this procedure for the other rear brake assembly.

19 Install the brake drums. To adjust the brake shoes, turn the adjuster until the drum stops turning, then back off the adjuster slightly. The wheel should now turn freely and you shouldn't be able to hear the shoes

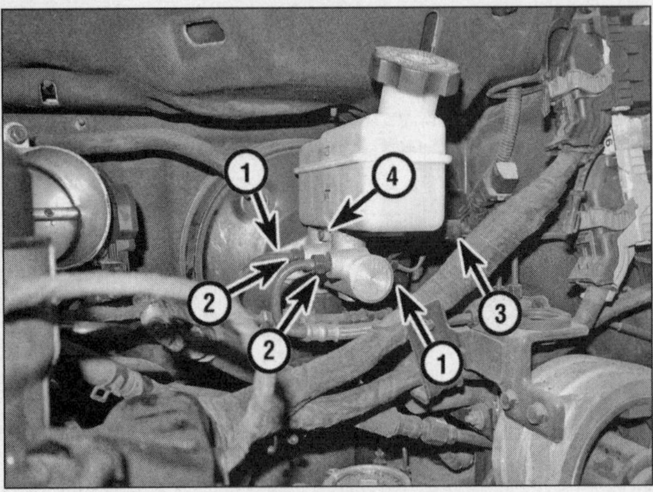

9.6 Master cylinder details:

1 *Mounting nuts (not visible)*
2 *Brake line fitting*
3 *Brake fluid level sensor connector*
4 *Reservoir retaining screw*

9.10 The best way to bleed air from the master cylinder before installing it on the vehicle is with a pair of bleeder tubes that direct brake fluid into the reservoir during bleeding

dragging on the drum; if it doesn't turn freely and you can hear the shoes drag, back off the adjuster a little more.

20 Adjust the parking brake cable (see Section 14).

21 Install the wheels and lug nuts, lower the vehicle and tighten the lug nuts to the torque listed in the Chapter 1 Specifications. Test the brakes for proper operation before driving the vehicle in traffic.

8 Wheel cylinder - removal and installation

Warning: *The dust created by the brake system is harmful to your health. Never blow it out with compressed air and don't inhale any of it. An approved filtering mask should be worn when working on the brakes. Do not, under any circumstances, use petroleum-based solvents to clean brake parts. Use brake system cleaner only!*

Note: *If replacement is indicated (usually because of fluid leakage or sticky operation), it is recommended that the wheel cylinders be replaced, not overhauled. Always replace the wheel cylinders in pairs - never replace just one of them.*

Removal

1 Remove the brake drum and brake shoes (see Section 7).

2 Remove the brake line fitting from the rear of the wheel cylinder with a flare-nut wrench. Don't pull the metal line out of the wheel cylinder - it could bend, making installation difficult.

3 Remove the wheel cylinder-to-brake backing plate fasteners.

4 Remove the wheel cylinder.

5 Plug the end of the brake line to prevent the loss of brake fluid and the entry of dirt.

Installation

6 Place the wheel cylinder in position and, while it's still loose, connect the brake line to it, being careful not to cross-thread the fitting. Don't tighten the fitting yet.

7 Install the fasteners and tighten them securely, then tighten the brake line fitting securely.

8 Bleed the brakes (see Section 11). Don't drive the vehicle in traffic until the operation of the brakes has been thoroughly tested.

9 Master cylinder - removal and installation

Caution: *Brake fluid will quickly damage paint. Cover all body parts and be careful not to spill fluid during any of the following procedures. Wipe up any spilled fluid immediately and then flush the area thoroughly with water.*

Removal

1 The master cylinder is located in the engine compartment, mounted to the power brake booster.

2 If you're working on a 2005 or earlier model, remove the battery (see Chapter 5). If you're working on a 2006 or later model, remove the air filter housing (see Chapter 4).

3 With the engine off, pump the brake pedal several times to relieve the vacuum reserve inside the power brake booster.

Note: *This step will prevent contaminants from being sucked into the power brake booster when the cylinder is removed.*

4 Using a syringe or equivalent, remove the brake fluid from the master cylinder reservoir and dispose of it properly.

5 Disconnect the brake fluid level switch connector and move the harness out of the way.

6 Place rags under the fluid fittings and prepare caps or plastic bags to cover the ends of the lines once they are disconnected. Loosen the fittings at the ends of the brake lines where they enter the master cylinder (see illustration). Pull the brake lines slightly away from the master cylinder and quickly plug the ends to prevent contamination.

Note: *To prevent rounding off the corners on these fitting nuts, the use of a flare-nut wrench, which wraps around the nut, is preferred.*

7 Thoroughly clean the area where the master cylinder mounts to the power booster. Remove the nuts attaching the master cylinder to the power booster (see illustration 9.6). Pull the master cylinder off the studs and out of the engine compartment. Again, be careful not to spill any fluid as this is done.

8 If necessary, remove the reservoir mounting screw and the old reservoir and transfer it to the new master cylinder.

Note: *Install new seals between the master cylinder and reservoir.*

Installation

9 Bench bleed the new master cylinder before installing it. Mount the master cylinder in a vise, with the jaws of the vise clamping on the mounting flange.

10 Attach a pair of master cylinder bleeder tubes to the outlet ports of the master cylinder (see illustration).

11 Fill the reservoir with brake fluid of the recommended type (see Chapter 1).

12 Slowly push the pistons into the master cylinder (a large Phillips screwdriver can be used for this) - air will be expelled from the pressure chambers and into the reservoir. Because the tubes are submerged in fluid, air can't be drawn back into the master cylinder when you release the pistons.

13 Repeat the procedure until no more air bubbles are present.

14 Remove the bleed tubes, one at a time, and install plugs in the open ports to prevent

fluid leakage and air from entering. Install the reservoir cap.

15 Install a new vacuum seal onto the master cylinder where it mates with the power booster.

Warning: *Do not skip this step or a vacuum leak could occur and render the power booster ineffective; this results in greatly increased pedal effort and longer stopping distances.*

16 Install the master cylinder over the studs on the power brake booster and tighten the attaching nuts only finger tight at this time.

17 Carefully thread the brake line fittings into the master cylinder. Since the master cylinder is still a bit loose, it can be moved slightly in order for the fittings to thread in easily. Do not strip the threads as the fittings are tightened.

18 Fully tighten the mounting nuts, and then the brake line fittings. Tighten the nuts to the torque listed in this Chapter's Specifications.

19 Fill the master cylinder reservoir with fluid, then bleed the master cylinder and the brake system (see Section 11). To bleed the cylinder on the vehicle, have an assistant depress the brake pedal and hold the pedal to the floor. Loosen the fitting to allow air and fluid to escape. Repeat this procedure on both fittings until the fluid is clear of air bubbles.

Caution: *Have plenty of rags on hand to catch the fluid - brake fluid will ruin painted surfaces. After the bleeding procedure is completed, rinse the area under the master cylinder thoroughly with clean water.*

20 Test the operation of the brake system carefully before placing the vehicle into normal service.

Warning: *Do not operate the vehicle if you are in doubt about the effectiveness of the brake system. It is possible for air to become trapped in the anti-lock brake system hydraulic control unit; if the pedal continues to feel spongy after repeated bleedings or the BRAKE or ANTI-LOCK light stays on, have the vehicle towed to a dealer service department or other qualified shop to be bled with the aid of a scan tool.*

10 Brake hoses and lines - inspection and replacement

Inspection

1 About every six months, with the vehicle raised and placed securely on jackstands, the flexible hoses which connect the steel brake lines with the front and rear brake assemblies should be inspected for cracks, chafing of the outer cover, leaks, blisters and other damage. These are important and vulnerable parts of the brake system and inspection should be complete. A light and mirror will be needed for a thorough check. If a hose exhibits any of the above defects, replace it with a new one.

Replacement

2 Loosen the wheel lug nuts, raise the vehicle and support it securely on jackstands. Remove the wheel.

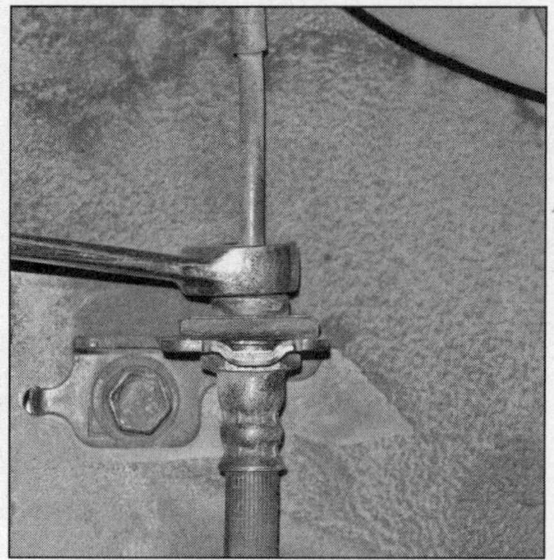

10.3 Unscrew the brake line threaded fitting with a flare-nut wrench to protect the fitting corners from being rounded off

10.4 Remove the brake hose-to-bracket U-clip with a pair of pliers

Flexible brake hoses

3 At the frame bracket, unscrew the brake line fitting from the hose (see illustration). Use a flare-nut wrench to prevent rounding off the corners.

4 Use a pair of pliers to remove the U-clip from the female fitting at the bracket (see illustration), then pass the hose through the bracket.

5 Detach any hose brackets from the suspension components, if applicable.

6 At the caliper end of the hose, remove the banjo-fitting bolt, then separate the hose from the caliper. Note that there are two copper sealing washers on each side of the fitting; they should be replaced with new ones during installation.

7 To install the hose, connect the fitting to the caliper with the banjo bolt and new sealing washers. Make sure the fitting is engaged with the casting protrusions on the caliper, then tighten the bolt to the torque listed in this Chapter's Specifications. Route the hose into the frame bracket, making sure it isn't twisted, and reconnect the hose brackets. Thread the tube nut into the fitting, then install the U-clip. Tighten the tube nut securely.

8 Bleed the caliper (see Section 11).

9 Install the wheel and lug nuts, lower the vehicle and tighten the lug nuts to the torque listed in the Chapter 1 Specifications.

Metal brake lines

10 When replacing brake lines, be sure to use the correct parts. Don't use copper tubing for any brake system components. Purchase genuine steel brake lines from a dealer or auto parts store.

11 Prefabricated brake line, with the tube ends already flared and fittings installed, is available at auto parts stores and dealer parts departments.

12 When installing the new line, make sure it's securely supported in the brackets and has plenty of clearance between moving or hot components.

13 After installation, check the master cylinder fluid level and add fluid as necessary. Bleed the brake system (see Section 11) and test the brakes carefully before driving the vehicle in traffic.

11 Brake system - bleeding

Warning: *The following procedure is a manual bleeding procedure. This is the only bleeding procedure which can be performed at home without special tools. However, if air has found its way into the hydraulic control unit, the entire system must be bled manually, then with a scan tool, then manually a second time. If the brake pedal feels spongy even after bleeding the brakes, or the ABS or brake light on the instrument panel does not go off, or if you have any doubts whatsoever about the effectiveness of the brake system, have the vehicle towed to a dealer service department or other repair shop equipped with the necessary tools for bleeding the system.*

Warning: *Wear eye protection when bleeding the brake system. If the fluid comes in contact with your eyes, immediately rinse them with water and seek medical attention.*

Note: *Bleeding the hydraulic system is necessary to remove any air that manages to find its way into the system when it's been opened during removal and installation of a hydraulic component.*

1 It will be necessary to bleed the complete system if air has entered the system due to low fluid level, or if the brake lines have been disconnected at the master cylinder.

2 If a brake line was disconnected only at a wheel, then only that caliper or wheel cylinder must be bled.

3 If a brake line is disconnected at a fitting located between the master cylinder and any of the brakes, that part of the system served by the disconnected line must be bled. The following procedure describes bleeding the entire system, however.

4 Remove any residual vacuum from the brake power booster by applying the brake

11.8 When bleeding the brakes, a hose is connected to the bleed screw at the caliper or wheel cylinder and then submerged in clean brake fluid - air will be seen as bubbles exiting the tube (all air must be expelled before moving to the next wheel)

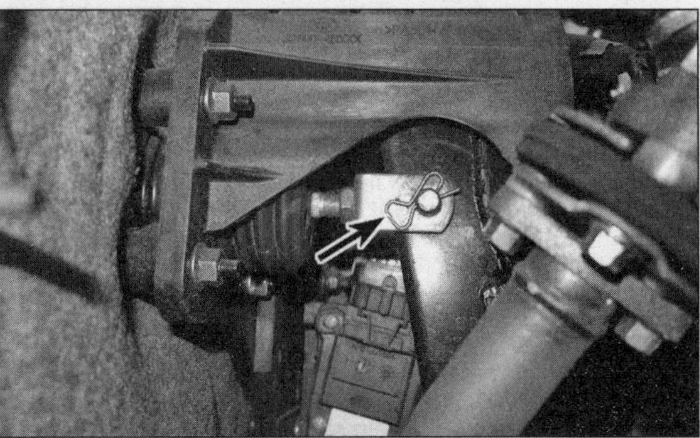

12.12 Remove the retaining clip from the clevis pin

several times with the engine off.

5 Remove the cap from the master cylinder reservoir and fill the reservoir with brake fluid. Reinstall the cap.

Note: *Check the fluid level often during the bleeding operation and add fluid as necessary to prevent the fluid level from falling low enough to allow air bubbles into the master cylinder.*

6 Have an assistant on hand, as well as a supply of new brake fluid, a clear container partially filled with clean brake fluid, a length of clear tubing to fit over the bleeder valve and a wrench to open and close the bleeder valve.

7 Begin the bleeding process by bleeding the first wheel in the bleeding sequence, loosen the bleeder valve slightly, then tighten it to a point where it is snug but can still be loosened quickly and easily. The bleeding sequence is as follows:

2005 and earlier models

Right front
Left front
Right rear
Left rear

2006 and later models

Conventional (non-ABS) brakes

Right rear
Left front
Left rear
Right front

ABS brakes

Left front
Right rear
Left rear
Right front

8 Place one end of the hose over the bleeder valve and submerge the other end in brake fluid in the container (see illustration).

9 Have the assistant push the brake pedal slowly to the floor, then hold the pedal firmly depressed.

10 While the pedal is held depressed, open the bleeder valve just enough to allow a flow of fluid to leave the valve. Watch for air bubbles to exit the submerged end of the tube. When the fluid flow slows after a couple of seconds, close the valve and have your assistant release the pedal.

11 Repeat Steps 9 and 10 until no more air is seen leaving the tube, then tighten the bleeder valve and proceed to bleed the other calipers/wheel cylinders, in the proper sequence, using the same procedure. Check the fluid in the master cylinder reservoir frequently.

Note: *Be careful not to over-tighten the bleeder valve.*

12 Never use old brake fluid. It contains moisture which can boil, rendering the brakes inoperative.

13 Refill the master cylinder with fluid at the end of the operation.

14 Check the operation of the brakes. The pedal should feel solid when depressed, with no sponginess. If necessary, repeat the entire process.

Warning: *If, after bleeding the system, you do not have a firm brake pedal, if the ABS or brake light on the instrument panel does not go off, or if you have any doubts whatsoever about the effectiveness of the brake system, have it towed to a dealer service department or other repair shop to have the system bled.*

12 Power brake booster - check, replacement and adjustment

Operating check

1 Depress the pedal and start the engine. If the pedal goes down slightly, operation is normal.

2 Depress the brake pedal several times with the engine running and make sure that there is no change in the pedal reserve distance.

Airtightness check

3 Start the engine and turn it off after one or two minutes. Depress the brake pedal several times slowly. If the pedal goes down farther the first time but gradually rises after the second or third depression, the booster is airtight.

4 Depress the brake pedal while the engine is running, then stop the engine with the pedal depressed. If there is no change in the pedal reserve travel after holding the pedal for 30 seconds, the booster is airtight.

Replacement

5 The power brake booster unit requires no special maintenance apart from periodic inspection of the vacuum hoses and the case. The booster should never be disassembled. If a problem develops, it must be replaced with a new one.

6 Remove any vacuum from the booster by pumping the pedal several times with the engine off, until the pedal feels hard to push.

7 If you're working on a 2005 or earlier model, remove the battery (see Chapter 5). If you're working on a 2006 or later model, remove the air filter housing (see Chapter 4).

8 Clean the area where the master cylinder attaches to the power brake booster.

9 Detach the master cylinder from the brake booster and carefully move it aside while keeping it supported (see Section 9).

Note: *It is not necessary to disconnect the brake lines from the master cylinder when detaching it from the brake booster. Be careful not to kink or damage the brake lines when placing it aside.*

10 Disconnect the vacuum hose from the check valve that's located on the outside of the brake booster.

Warning: *Do not remove the check valve from the booster.*

11 Working under the dash, disconnect and remove the brake light switch (see Section).

12 Remove the clevis pin retaining clip with pliers and pull out the pin to disconnect the brake pedal pushrod from the top of the brake pedal (see illustration).

12.13 Power brake booster mounting nut locations

12.18 Measure the distance that the pushrod protrudes from the brake booster at the master cylinder mounting surface

13 Remove the nuts attaching the booster to the firewall (see illustration).

14 Working inside the engine compartment, carefully withdraw the brake booster unit from the firewall and out of the engine compartment.

15 Before installing the new booster, measure the booster pushrod-to-master cylinder piston clearance (2005 and earlier models) (see Steps 18 through 22) or booster input rod length (see Step 23) and adjust as necessary.

16 To install the booster, place it into position on the firewall, then tighten the retaining nuts to the torque listed in this Chapter's Specifications. Connect the brake pedal to the brake booster pushrod with the clevis pin and secure the pin in place with the retaining clip.

17 Installation is the reverse of removal. Use a new gasket between the booster and the firewall.

Adjustment

2005 and earlier models

Note: *If a new power brake booster unit is being installed, check the pushrod-to-master cylinder piston clearance as follows:*

18 Using a hand-held vacuum pump, apply a vacuum of 19.7 in-Hg (500 mm-Hg) to the booster. Measure the distance that the pushrod protrudes from the master cylinder mounting surface on the front of the power brake booster, including the gasket (if used). Write down this measurement (see illustration). This is "dimension A".

19 Measure the distance from the mounting flange to the end of the master cylinder (see illustration). Write down this measurement. This is "dimension B".

20 Measure the distance from the end of the master cylinder to the bottom of the pocket in the piston (see illustration). Write down this measurement. This is "dimension C".

21 Subtract measurement B from measurement C, then subtract measurement A from the difference between B and C. This is the pushrod clearance.

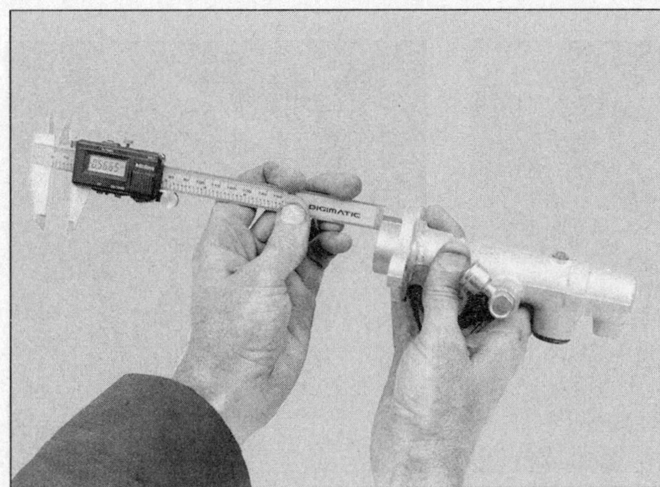

12.19 Measure the distance from the mounting flange to the end of the master cylinder

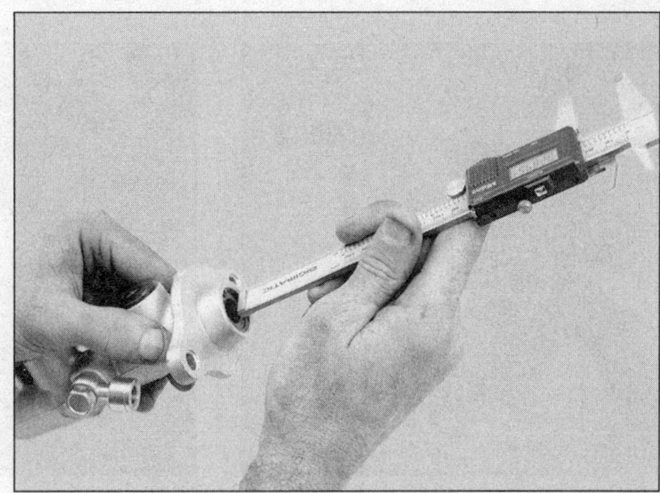

12.20 Measure the distance from the piston pocket to the end of the master cylinder

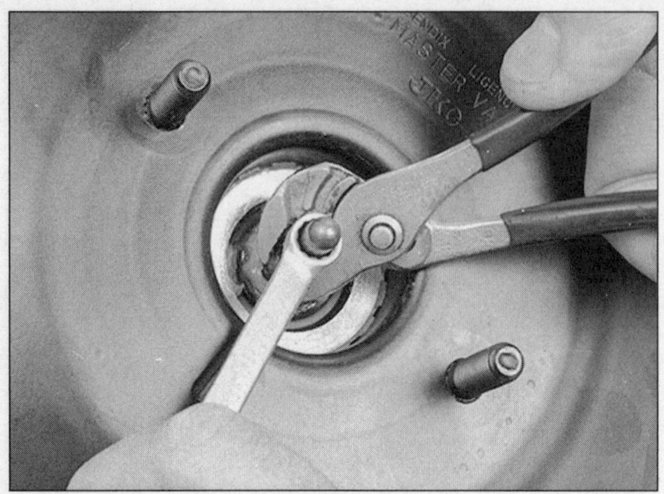

12.22 To adjust the length of the booster pushrod, hold the serrated portion of the rod with a pair of pliers and turn the adjusting screw in or out, as necessary, to achieve the desired setting

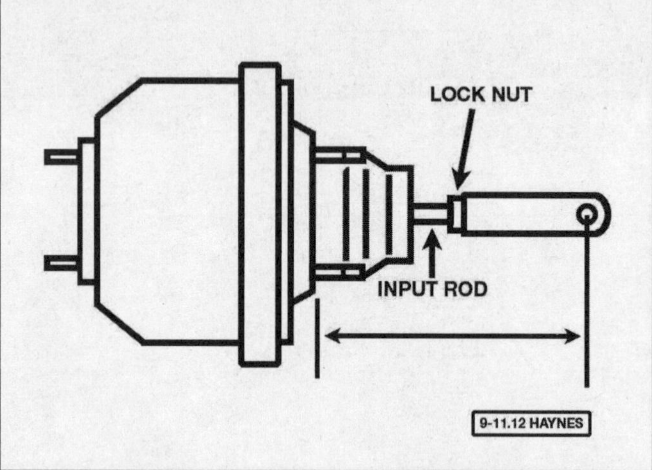

12.23 Measure the distance between the power brake booster and the hole in the clevis and compare your measurement to the dimension listed in this Chapter's Specifications; if necessary, adjust the clevis before installing the power brake booster

22 Compare your calculated pushrod clearance to the pushrod clearance listed in this Chapter's Specifications. If necessary, adjust the pushrod length to achieve the correct clearance (see illustration).

2006 and later models

23 Measure the distance between the power brake booster and the hole in the input rod clevis (see illustration) and compare it to the dimension listed in this Chapter's Specifications. If necessary, loosen the adjusting nut and turn the clevis in or out to the specified length, then install the booster, connect the clevis to the brake pedal, and tighten the nut securely.

13 Parking brake shoes (rear disc brake models) - inspection and replacement

Warning: *Dust created by the brake system is hazardous to your health. Never blow it out with compressed air and don't inhale any of it. An approved filtering mask should be worn when working on the brakes. Do not, under any circumstances, use petroleum-based solvents to clean brake parts. Use brake system cleaner only!*

Warning: *Parking brake shoes must be replaced on both wheels at the same time - never replace the shoes on only one wheel.*

1 Remove the rear brake discs (see Section 6).

2 Inspect the thickness of the lining material on the shoes. If the lining has worn down to 1/32-inch or less, the shoes must be replaced.

3 Wash off the brake parts with brake system cleaner (see illustration) then remove the hub assembly (see Chapter 10).

4 Follow the accompanying illustrations for the brake shoe replacement procedure (see illustrations 13.4a through 13.4r). Be sure to stay in order and read the caption accompanying each illustration.

5 Install the hub assembly (see Chapter 10) and brake disc. Temporarily thread

13.3 Always wash the brakes with brake cleaner before disassembling anything

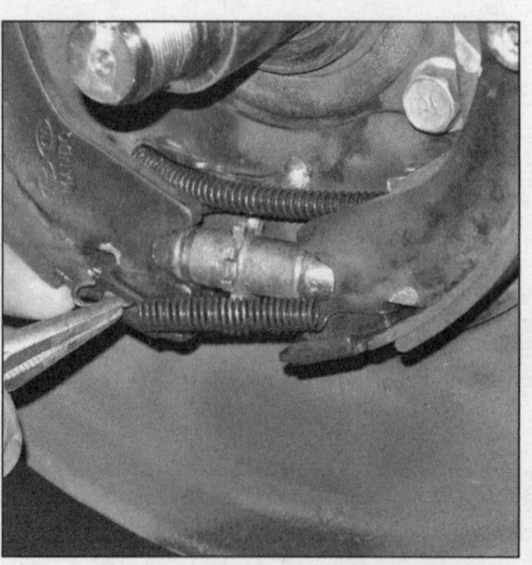

13.4a Remove the lower return spring

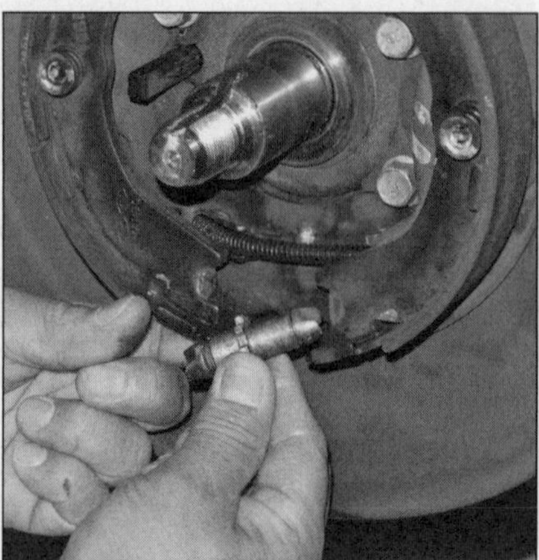

13.4b Spread the shoes and remove the adjuster, noting which way it is oriented

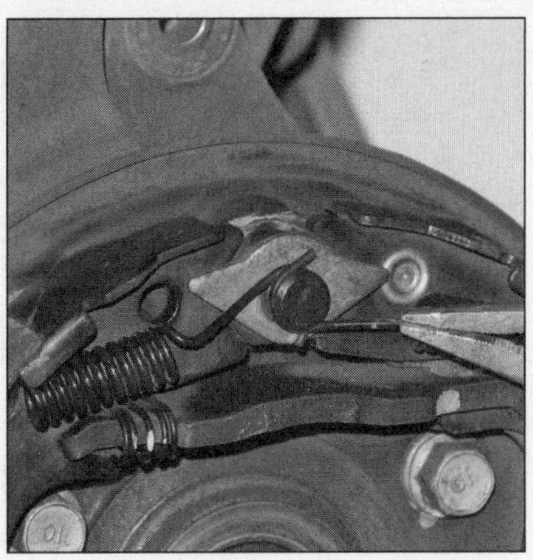

13.4c Remove the upper rear return spring. . .

13.4d. . . the the upper front return spring

13.4e Spread the shoes and remove the strut

13.4f Remove the front shoe hold-down retainer and spring

13.4g Remove the shoe from the backing plate

13.4h Remove the rear shoe hold-down retainer, spring and rear shoe

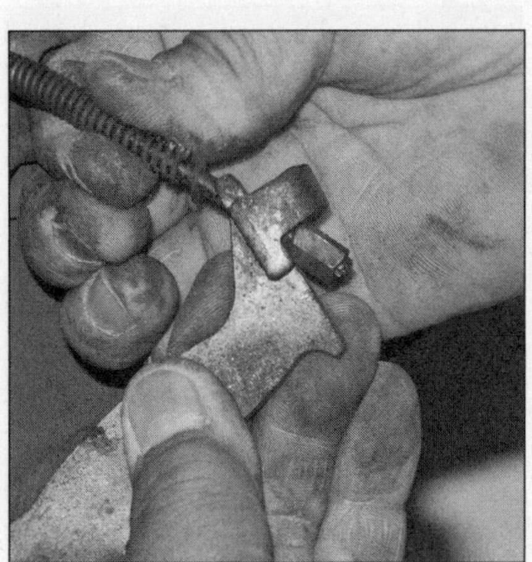

13.4i Disconnect the parking brake cable from the lever attached to the rear shoe

13.4j Clean the backing plate with brake system cleaner, then lubricate shoe contact areas with a light film of high-temperature brake grease

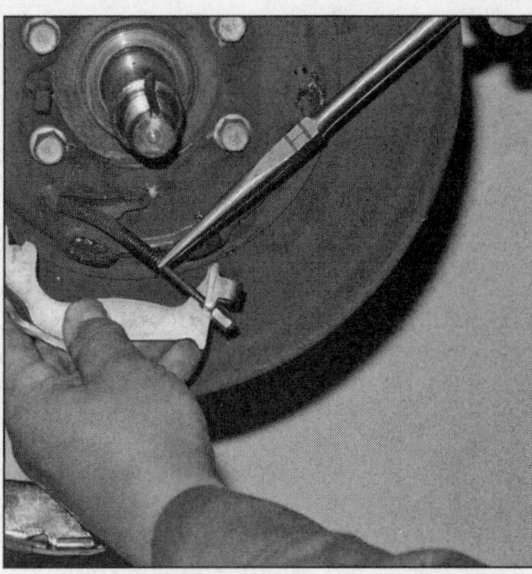

13.4k Use a pair of needle-nose pliers to pull back the spring and connect the parking brake cable to the lever

13.4l Install the rear shoe and hold-down spring and retainer. . .

13.4m. . . then install the front shoe and hold-down spring and retainer

13.4n Install the strut with damper spring between the shoes

13.4o Install the front and rear return springs

13.4p Clean the adjuster assembly and lubricate the moving components with the same grease

three of the wheel lug nuts onto the studs to hold the disc in place.

6 Remove the hole plugs from the brake discs. Adjust the parking brake shoe clearance by turning the adjuster star wheel with a brake adjusting tool or screwdriver until the shoes contact the discs and the discs can't be turned (see illustration). Back off the adjusters five notches, then install the hole plugs.

7 Install the brake mounting bracket, pads and caliper (see Section 5). Tighten the bolts to the torque listed in this Chapter's Specifications.

8 Install the wheel and tighten the lug nuts to the torque listed in the Chapter 1 Specifications.

9 Set the parking brake with about 45 pounds of force and measure the distance that the pedal travels. It should be within the range listed in this Chapter's Specifications - if not, adjust the parking brake (see Section 14).

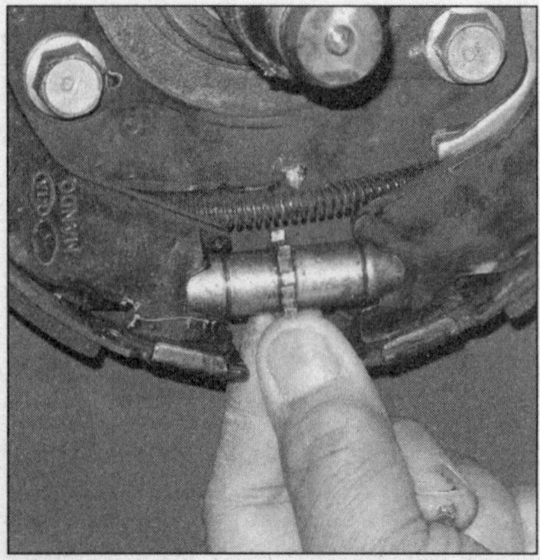

13.4q Install the adjuster, making sure it's facing the proper direction. . .

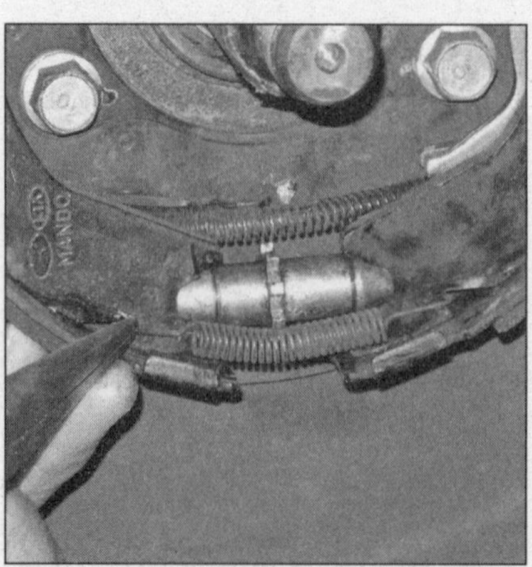

13.4r. . . then install the upper return spring

13.6 To adjust the parking brake shoes, remove the rubber plug, then use a screwdriver to rotate the star-wheel until the shoes lock, then back them off until the disc doesn't drag when turned

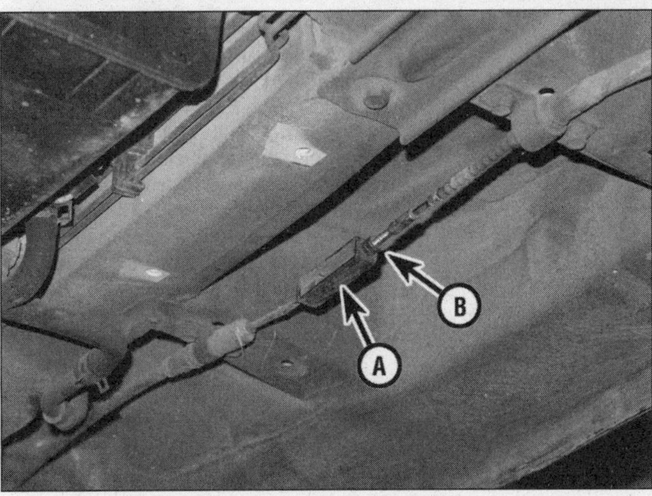

14.5 Parking brake cable adjuster (A) and locknut (B)

15.1 The brake light switch is located on a bracket near the top of the brake pedal. Loosen the locknut and unscrew the switch from its bracket

14 Parking brake - adjustment

1 The parking brake is a mechanically operated system utilizing a series of cables to apply brake shoes located in the rear wheels. The parking brake system will need to be periodically adjusted to compensate for brake shoe wear. Additionally, adjustment may be needed in the event of cable stretch, which can occur as the vehicle ages.

Operating check

2 Adjust the parking brake shoe clearance (see Section 13) prior to adjusting the parking brake pedal travel.

3 Depress the parking brake pedal using about 45 pounds (20.4 kg) of force, observe the stroke of the parking brake pedal and compare that to the travel listed in this Chapter's Specifications. If the travel is less than that specified, there's a chance the parking brake might not be releasing completely. If it travels more than specified, the parking brake may not hold adequately on an incline, allowing the vehicle to roll.

4 If adjustment is needed, raise the rear of the vehicle and support it securely on jackstands. Block the front wheels, then release the parking brake.

5 Locate the parking brake cable adjuster under the vehicle in the area beneath the driver's door (see illustration).

6 With the parking brake released, loosen the locknut while holding the adjuster. Tighten or loosen the adjuster to achieve the proper parking brake pedal travel. Operate the pedal several times to set the brakes between adjustments, then re-check the travel.

7 Confirm that the parking brake is fully engaged within the specified range of travel, then tighten the locknut.

8 With the pedal released, turn the rear wheels by hand to make sure that the parking brake isn't dragging.

9 Lower the vehicle.

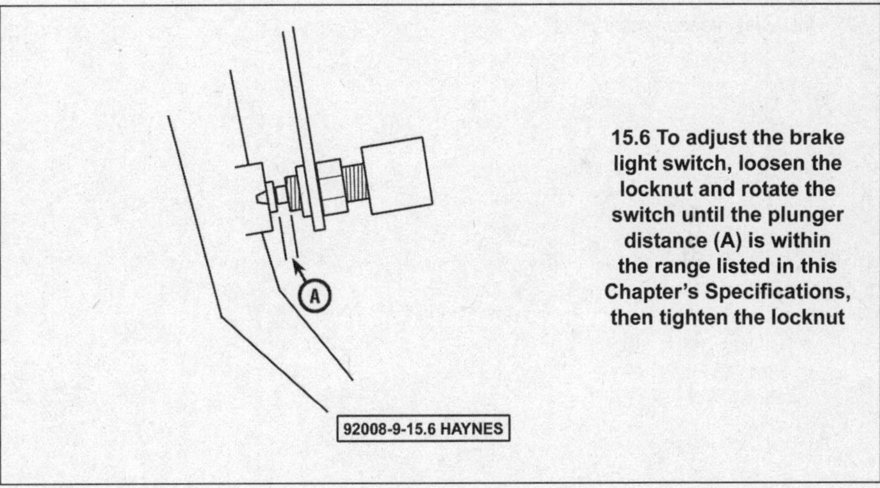

15.6 To adjust the brake light switch, loosen the locknut and rotate the switch until the plunger distance (A) is within the range listed in this Chapter's Specifications, then tighten the locknut

15 Brake light switch - removal, installation and adjustment

Removal and installation

1 The brake light switch is located on a bracket at the top of the brake pedal (see illustration).

2 Disconnect the electrical connector from the switch.

3 Loosen the locknut and unscrew the switch from the pedal bracket.

4 Installation is the reverse of removal.

Adjustment

5 Check and, if necessary, adjust brake pedal height (see Section 16).

6 Loosen the switch locknut, adjust the switch so that the plunger protrusion is as listed in this Chapter's Specifications (see illustration).

7 Plug the electrical connector into the switch. Make sure the brake lights come on when the brake pedal is depressed and go off when the pedal is released. If not, repeat the adjustment procedure until the brake lights function properly.

8 Check and, if necessary, adjust brake pedal freeplay (see Section 16).

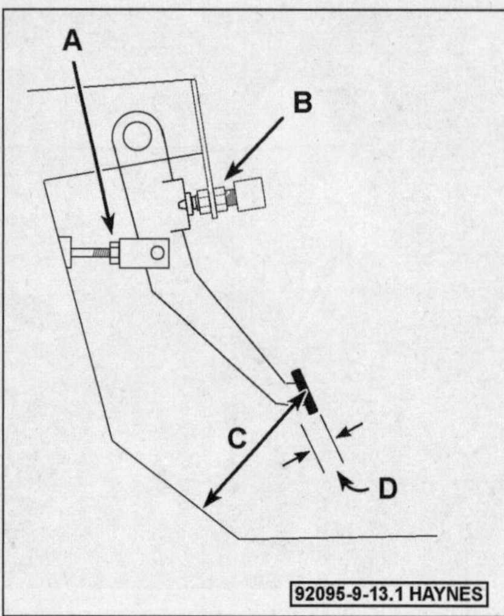

16.3 Brake pedal height and freeplay measuring and adjustment points

A Clevis locknut
B Brake light switch adjusting nut/locknut
C Pedal height measurement (to steel floor)
D Freeplay measurement point

16 Brake pedal - adjustment

Brake pedal height

1 Disconnect the electrical connector from the brake light switch (see Section 15).

2 Loosen the locknut on the brake light switch and rotate the switch until it does not contact the brake pedal arm.

3 With the brake pedal fully released, measure the distance from the top of the pad to the floor (see illustration).

4 Compare the height measurement to this Chapter's Specifications. Continue to the next Step for the pedal height adjustment.

5 Loosen the clevis locknut on the pushrod, then turn the pushrod with a pair of pliers to attain the proper pedal height.

6 With the pedal height adjusted, tighten the locknut securely.

Brake pedal freeplay

7 Press the brake pedal several times with the engine OFF; this will deplete the vacuum in the brake booster.

8 Press down lightly on the brake pedal by hand and measure the distance that it moves freely before resistance is felt (see illustration 16.3). The freeplay should be within the values listed in this Chapter's Specifications.

9 If there is less freeplay than specified, check to be sure the outer case of the brake light switch is not contacting the brake pedal arm.

10 If there is too much freeplay, check the clevis, clevis pin and the hole in the brake pedal arm for excessive wear and replace faulty parts as needed.

Chapter 10
Suspension and steering systems

Contents

	Section
Balljoints - replacement	6
Coil springs (rear) - removal and installation	9
Control arm and tension arm - removal, inspection and installation	5
General information	1
Hub and bearing assembly (front) - removal and installation	7
Hub and bearing assembly (rear) - removal and installation	13
Power steering pump - removal and installation	19
Power steering system - bleeding	20
Shock absorbers (rear) - removal and installation	11
Stabilizer bar, bushings and links (front) - removal and installation	2
Stabilizer bar, bushings and links (rear) - removal and installation	10
Steering column - removal and installation	18
Steering gear - removal and installation	17
Steering knuckle - removal and installation	8
Steering wheel - removal and installation	15
Strut assembly (front) - removal, inspection and installation	3
Strut/coil spring assembly - replacement	4
Subframe - removal and installation	14
Suspension arms and rear axle beam (rear) removal and installation	12
Tie-rod ends - removal and installation	16
Wheel alignment - general information	22
Wheels and tires - general information	21

Specifications

Torque specifications

Note: *One foot-pound (ft-lb) of torque is equivalent to 12 inch-pounds (in-lbs) of torque. Torque values below approximately 15 ft-lbs are expressed in inch-pounds, since most foot-pound torque wrenches are not accurate at these smaller values.*

Front suspension	Ft-lbs (unless otherwise indicated)	Nm
Balljoint-to-control arm mounting bolt/nuts (2006 and later models only)	66 to 86	90 to 120
Balljoint-to-steering knuckle pinch bolt/nut		
2005 and earlier models	69 to 85	93 to 115
2006 and later models	66 to 86	90 to 120
Control arm		
2005 and earlier models		
Control arm-to-subframe pivot bolt/nut	88 to 101	120 to 137
Control arm-to-tension arm bolts/nuts (2005 and earlier models)	88 to 101	120 to 137
Tension arm-to-subframe nut	115 to 130	157 to 180
2006 and later models (pivot bolts-to-subframe)	116 to 130	160 to 180
Driveaxle/hub nut	See Chapter 8	
Hub and bearing assembly-to-steering knuckle bolts (2006 and later models only)	116 to 130	160 to 180
Stabilizer bar link nuts		
2005 and earlier models	69 to 85	93 to 115
2006 and later models	73 to 86	100 to 120
Stabilizer bar bushing bracket bolts		
2005 and earlier models	16 to 20	21 to 26
2006 and later models	28 to 43	39 to 60
Strut upper mounting nuts	33 to 43	45 to 60

Torque specifications	Ft-lbs (unless otherwise indicated)	Nm
Note: One foot-pound (ft-lb) of torque is equivalent to 12 inch-pounds (in-lbs) of torque. Torque values below approximately 15 ft-lbs are expressed in inch-pounds, since most foot-pound torque wrenches are not accurate at these smaller values.		
Strut damper shaft nut		
2005 and earlier models	88 to 101	120 to 137
2006 and later models	44 to 50	60 to 70
Strut-to-steering knuckle nuts		
2005 and earlier models	88 to 101	119 to 137
2006 and later models	73 to 86	100 to 120
Subframe		
2005 and earlier models	88 to 101	120 to 137
2006 and later models		
Subframe-to-body bolts	116 to 130	160 to 180
Guide bracket bolts	33 to 43	45 to 60
Rear suspension		
Hub and bearing nut		
2005 and earlier models	20 to 25	27 to 33
2006 and later models	145 to 188	200 to 260
Stabilizer bar		
2005 and earlier models		
Link nut/bolt	17 to 20	24 to 28
Bracket bolts	32 to 40	43 to 54
2006 and later models		
Link nuts	37 to 47	50 to 65
Bracket-to-subframe bolts	29 to 43	39 to 60
Shock absorber		
2005 and earlier models		
Upper bracket mounting bolts	55 to 69	74 to 93
Upper mounting nuts	45 to 47	55 to 64
Lower mounting bolt/nut	55 to 69	74 to 93
2006 and later models		
Upper bracket mounting bolts	58 to 79	80 to 110
Upper bracket mounting nut	66 to 86	90 to 120
Shock absorber-to-upper bracket bolt/nut	116 to 130	160 to 180
Lower mounting nut	116 to 130	160 to 180
Trailing arm (2006 and later models)		
Trailing arm bracket-to-body bolts	58 to 79	80 to 110
Trailing arm-to-bracket through-bolt	116 to 130	160 to 180
Trailing arm-to-knuckle bolts	58 to 79	80 to 110
Upper arm		
2005 and earlier models	55 to 69	74 to 93
2006 and later models		
Upper arm-to-rear subframe nut	116 to 130	160 to 180
Upper arm-to-knuckle nut	66 to 79	90 to 110
Lower arm		
2005 and earlier models	87 to 101	118 to 137
2006 and later models		
Lower arm-to-knuckle bolt/nut	87 to 116	120 to 160
Lower arm-to-subframe bracket	145 to 195	200 to 270
Lateral control arm (2006 and later models)		
Arm-to-subframe nut	66 to 86	90 to 120
Arm-to-knuckle nut	116 to 130	160 to 180
Panhard rod (2005 and earlier models)		
Rod-to-axle housing bolt/nuts	99 to 116	134 to 157
Rod-to-body bracket bolt/nuts	135 to 155	183 to 210
Subframe-to-body bolts		
2005 and earlier models	116 to 130	160 to 180
2006 and later models	Not available	
Steering system		
Airbag module screws		
2005 and earlier models	Not available	
2006 and later models	72 to 96	8 to 11
Power steering pump mounting bolt/nuts		
2005 and earlier models	Not available	
2006 and later models	25 to 36	35 to 50

Torque specifications

	Ft-lbs (unless otherwise indicated)	Nm
Note: One foot-pound (ft-lb) of torque is equivalent to 12 inch-pounds (in-lbs) of torque. Torque values below approximately 15 ft-lbs are expressed in inch-pounds, since most foot-pound torque wrenches are not accurate at these smaller values.		
Power steering pump pressure line banjo-bolt		
2005 and earlier models	Not available	
2006 and later models	47 to 54	65 to 75
Steering column coupler pinch bolts		
2005 and earlier models	16 to 20	21 to 26
2006 and later models		
Upper pinch bolt	133 to 177 in-lbs	15 to 20
Lower pinch bolt	115 to 159 in-lbs	13 to 18
Steering column mounting nuts	12 to 17	16 to 23
Steering gear mounting bolts	65 to 80	90 to 110
Steering wheel retaining nut	29 to 36	40 to 50
Tie-rod end-to-steering knuckle nut	36 to 40	50 to 55
Wheel lug nuts	See Chapter 1	

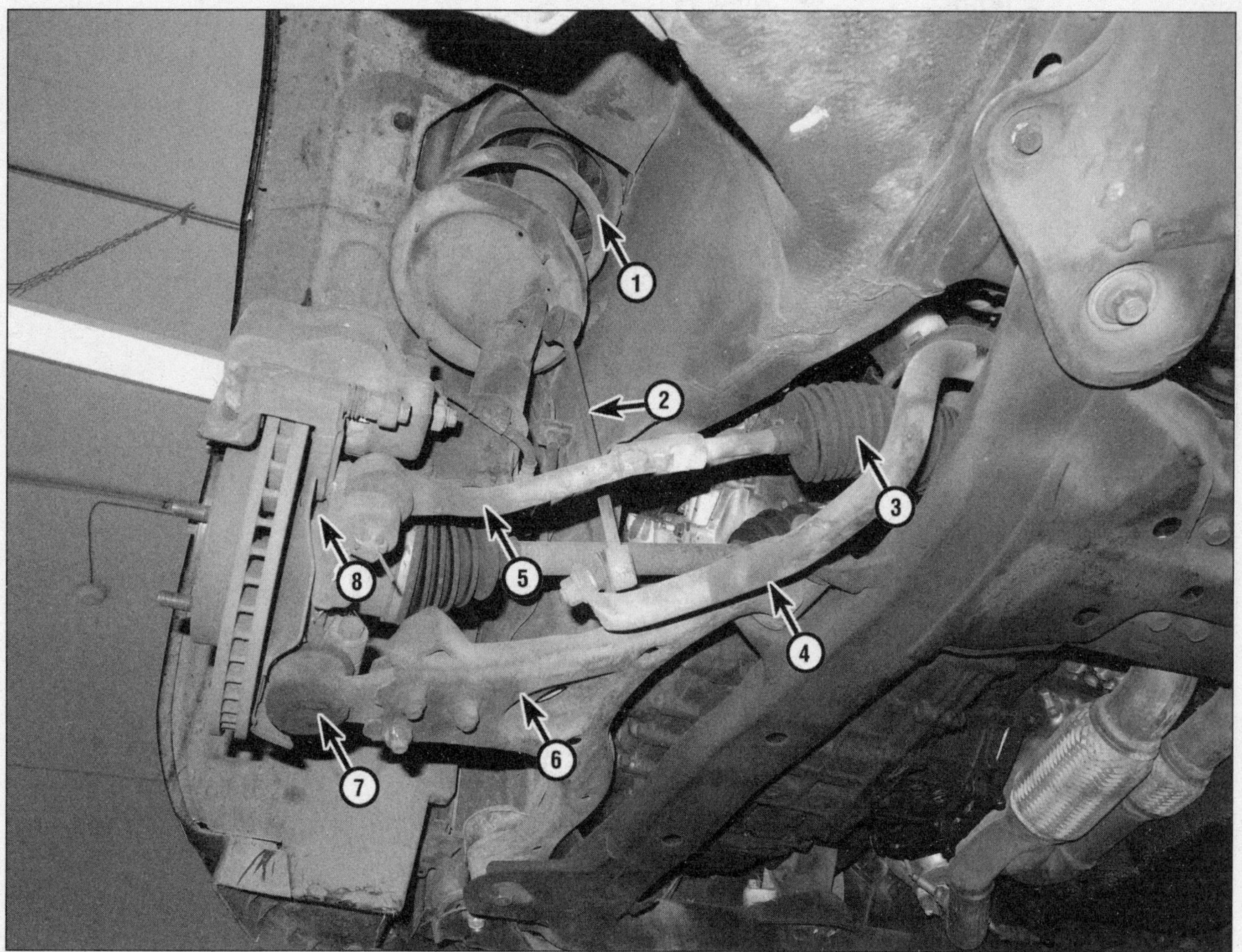

1.1 Front suspension and steering components

1 *Strut/coil spring assembly*
2 *Stabilizer bar link*
3 *Steering gear boot*
4 *Stabilizer bar*
5 *Tie-rod end*
6 *Control arm*
7 *Balljoint*
8 *Steering knuckle*

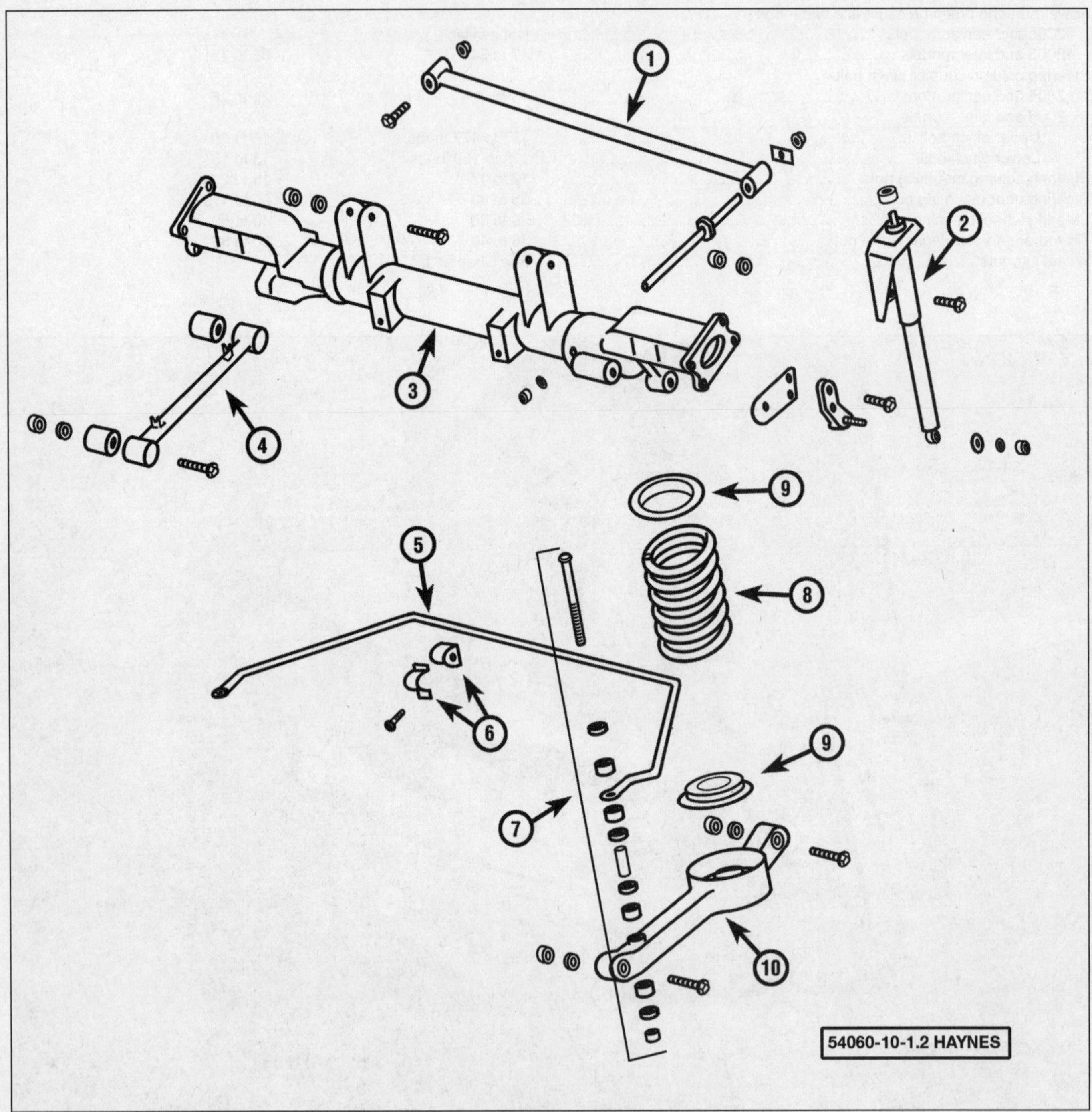

1.2 Rear suspension components - 2005 and earlier models

1 Panhard rod
2 Shock absorber and upper mounting bracket
3 Axle beam
4 Upper control arm
5 Stabilizer bar
6 Stabilizer bar bushing and bracket
7 Stabilizer bar link bolt, bushings and washers
8 Coil spring
9 Coil spring insulator
10 Lower control arm

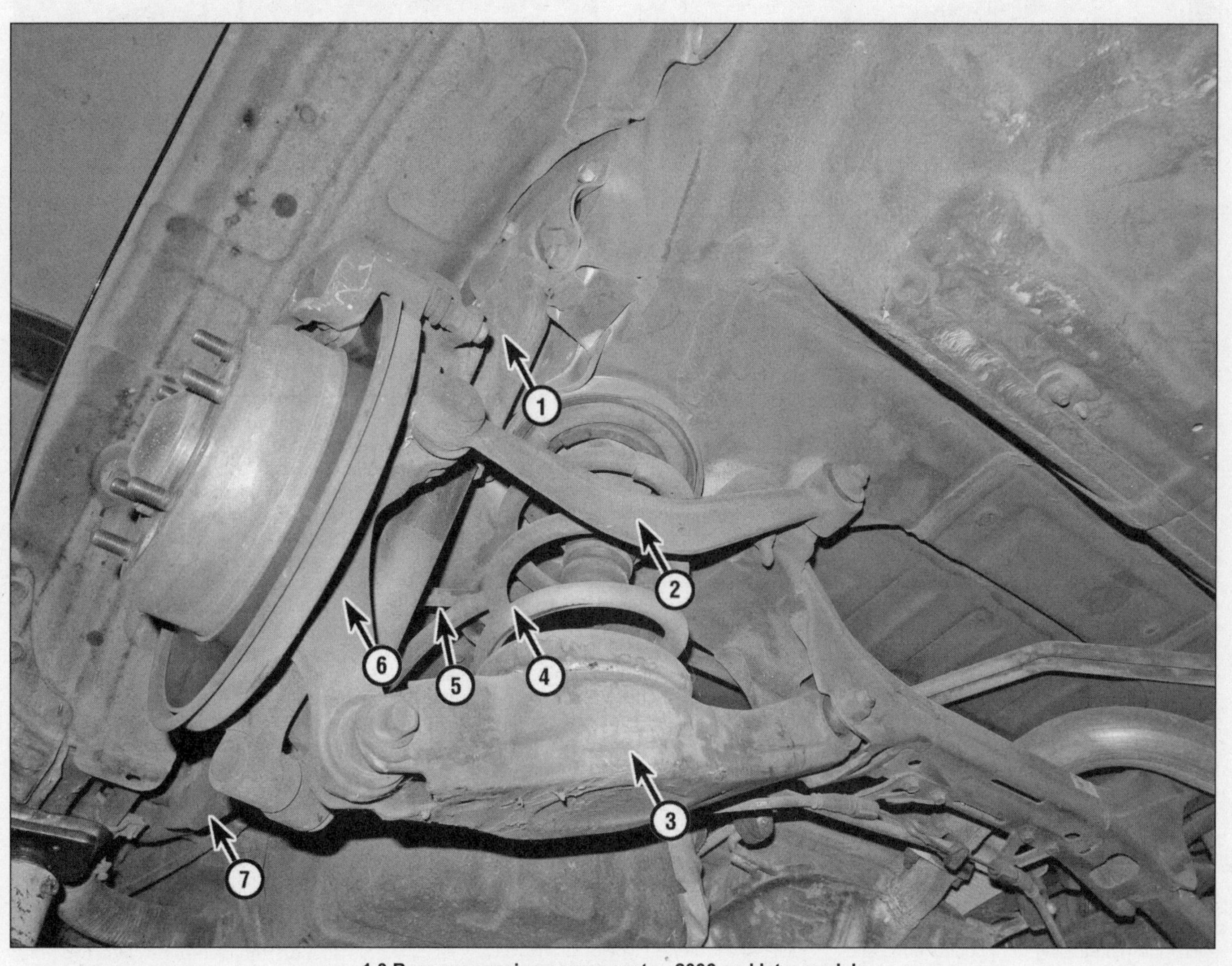

1.3 Rear suspension components - 2006 and later models

1 Shock absorber
2 Upper arm
3 Lower arm
4 Coil spring
5 Lateral control arm
6 Knuckle
7 Trailing arm

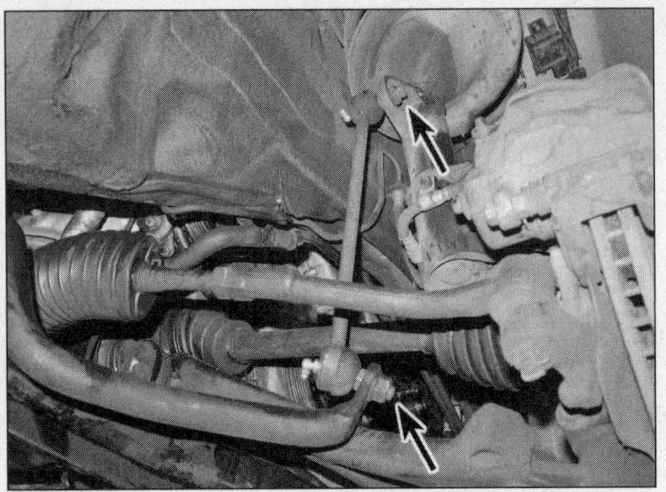

2.2 Stabilizer bar link nuts (2006 and later models shown; on 2005 and earlier models, the link connects to the control arm)

2.7 Stabilizer bar bracket bolts

1 General Information

1 The front suspension (see illustration) on these vehicles is a MacPherson strut design. The upper end of each strut is attached to the vehicle's body strut support. The lower end of the strut is connected to the upper end of the steering knuckle. The steering knuckle is attached by a balljoint mounted to the outer end of the suspension control arm. The control arm is held longitudinally by the front suspension subframe/cradle. A stabilizer bar, mounted to the subframe/cradle and connected to the strut, reduces body roll while cornering.

2 On 2005 and earlier models, the rear suspension is composed of a beam-type axle with upper and lower control arms, coil springs and shock absorbers. Side-to-side axle movement is controlled by a Panhard rod (track bar) attached to the axle beam and the chassis.

3 On 2006 and later models, the rear suspension (see illustration) uses a trailing arm, an upper and lower control arm, a lateral control arm, a coil spring and a shock absorber on each side. The trailing arm, control arms and lateral control arm connect to a rear knuckle/hub assembly and the rear subframe. A stabilizer bar reduces body roll on turns.

4 The power-assisted rack-and-pinion steering gear is attached to the front suspension subframe/cradle. The steering gear actuates the tie-rods, which are attached to the steering knuckles. The steering column is designed to collapse in the event of an accident.

5 Frequently, when working on the suspension or steering system components, you may come across fasteners that seem impossible to loosen. These fasteners on the underside of the vehicle are continually subjected to water, road grime, mud, etc., and can become rusted or frozen, making them extremely difficult to remove. In order to unscrew these stubborn fasteners without damaging them (or other components), use lots of penetrating oil and allow it to soak in for a while. Using a wire brush to clean exposed threads will also ease removal of the nut or bolt and prevent damage to the threads. Sometimes a sharp blow with a hammer and punch will break the bond between a nut and bolt threads, but care must be taken to prevent the punch from slipping off the fastener and ruining the threads. Heating the stuck fastener and surrounding area with a torch sometimes helps too, but isn't recommended because of the obvious dangers associated with fire. Long breaker bars and extension, or cheater, pipes will increase leverage, but never use an extension pipe on a ratchet - the ratcheting mechanism could be damaged. Sometimes tightening the nut or bolt first will help to break it loose. Fasteners that require drastic measures to remove should always be replaced with new ones.

6 Since most of the procedures dealt with in this Chapter involve jacking up the vehicle and working underneath it, a good pair of jackstands will be needed. A hydraulic floor jack is the preferred type of jack to lift the vehicle, and it can also be used to support certain components during various operations.

Warning: *Never, under any circumstances, rely on a jack to support the vehicle while working on it.*

7 Whenever any of the suspension or steering fasteners are loosened or removed they must be inspected and, if necessary, replaced with new ones of the same part number or of original equipment quality and design. Torque specifications must be followed for proper reassembly and component retention. Never attempt to heat or straighten any suspension or steering components. Instead, replace any bent or damaged part with a new one.

2 Stabilizer bar, bushings and links (front) - removal and installation

1 Park the vehicle with the wheels pointing straight ahead. Loosen the front wheel lug nuts, then raise the front of the vehicle and support it securely on jackstands. Remove the wheels and the under-vehicle splash shield.

2 Disconnect the stabilizer bar links from the bar (see illustration).

3 If you're working on a 2005 or earlier model, remove the front section of the exhaust pipe (see Chapter 4).

4 Lock the steering wheel in the straight-ahead position. Mark the relationship of the steering shaft to the steering gear, then remove the nut and detach the steering shaft U-joint from the steering gear input shaft (see Section).

5 Remove the through-bolts from the front and rear powertrain mounts (roll stopper mounts) (see Chapter 2A).

6 If you're working on a 2006 or later model, detach the tie-rod ends and control arm balljoints from the steering knuckles (see Section 16 and Section 5).

7 Support the subframe with two floor jacks (one positioned on each side). Loosen the subframe mounting bolts a few turns (see Section 14), then lower the floor jacks far enough to access the stabilizer bar bracket bolts (see illustration).

Note: *On some models, it may be necessary to completely remove the subframe mounting bolts in order to lower the subframe far enough to provide clearance to remove the stabilizer bar.*

8 Maneuver the stabilizer bar out from between the subframe and the body.

9 Slide off the bushings and inspect them. If they're cracked, worn or deteriorated,

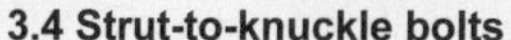

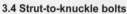

3.4 Strut-to-knuckle bolts

3.6 Strut upper mounting nuts

replace them. Also inspect the stabilizer bar links for loose ballstuds.

10 Clean the bushing area of the stabilizer bar with a stiff wire brush to remove any rust or dirt.

11 Install the bushings onto the stabilizer bar. Guide the bar into place and install the bushing brackets, tightening the bolts to the torque listed in this Chapter's Specifications.

12 Raise the subframe against the body and tighten the bolts to the torque listed in this Chapter's Specifications.

13 Reconnect the steering shaft U-joint to the steering gear and tighten the bolt to the torque listed in this Chapter's Specifications.

14 Install the links, tightening the link nuts to the torque listed in this Chapter's Specifications.

15 The remainder of installation is the reverse of removal, tightening the fasteners to the torque values listed in this Chapter's Specifications.

16 Tighten the lug nuts to the torque listed in the Chapter 1 Specifications.

17 It's a good idea to have the front wheel alignment checked and, if necessary, adjusted.

3 Strut assembly (front) - removal, inspection and installation

Removal

Warning: *Always replace the struts and/or coil springs in pairs - never replace just one strut or one coil spring; this could cause dangerous handling peculiarities.*

Note: *If both strut assemblies are going to be removed, mark the assemblies Right and Left so they will be reinstalled on the correct side.*

1 Loosen the wheel lug nuts, then raise the vehicle and support it securely on jackstands. Remove the wheels and detach the ABS speed sensor wiring harness (if equipped) from the strut (see Chapter 9).

2 On 2006 and later models, disconnect the stabilizer bar link from the strut assembly (see Section 2).

3 Remove the brake hose bracket mounting bolt and secure the hose away from the strut.

4 Remove the cotter pins (if equipped), then remove the nuts and bolts (see illustration). Separate the strut from the steering knuckle, being careful not to overextend the inner CV joint. Also, don't let the steering knuckle fall outward and strain the brake hose.

Caution: *The bolts are serrated and must not be turned. Hold the bolts with a wrench, then remove the strut-to-knuckle nuts. Knock the bolts out with a hammer and punch, noting which way the bolt heads face.*

Note: *Some models do use cotter pins on the strut-to-steering knuckle bolts.*

5 Remove the cowl cover (see Chapter 11).

6 If you're working on a 2005 or earlier model, mark one of the upper mounting studs to the body to preserve wheel alignment. On all models, have an assistant support the strut and spring assembly, then remove the three strut-to-body nuts (see illustration). Remove the assembly from the fenderwell.

Inspection

7 Check the strut body for leaking fluid, dents, cracks and other obvious damage which would warrant repair or replacement.

8 Check the coil spring for chips or cracks in the spring coating (this will cause premature spring failure due to corrosion). Inspect the spring seat for cuts, hardness and general deterioration.

9 If any undesirable conditions exist, proceed to the strut disassembly procedure (see Section).

Installation

10 Guide the strut assembly up into the fenderwell and insert the upper mounting studs through the holes in the body (on 2005 and earlier models be sure to align the marked stud with the marked hole on the body). Once the studs protrude, install the nuts so the strut won't fall back through. This is most easily accomplished with the help of an assistant, as the strut is quite heavy and awkward.

11 Tighten the upper mounting nuts to the torque listed in this Chapter's Specifications.

12 Slide the steering knuckle into the strut flange and insert the two bolts. Install the nuts and tighten them to the torque listed in this Chapter's Specifications. Install new cotter pins, where applicable.

Note: *Make sure that the bolts are installed in their original directions.*

13 If the vehicle is equipped with ABS, install the speed sensor wiring harness bracket.

14 Connect the stabilizer bar link to the strut. Tighten the nut to the torque listed in this Chapter's Specifications.

15 Install the wheel and lug nuts, then lower the vehicle and tighten the lug nuts to the torque listed in the Chapter 1 Specifications

16 Have the front end alignment checked, and if necessary, adjusted.

4 Strut/coil spring assembly - replacement

Warning: *Always replace strut/coil spring assemblies in pairs - never replace just one of them.*

1 If the struts or coil springs exhibit the telltale signs of wear (leaking fluid, loss of damping capability, chipped, sagging or cracked coil springs), explore all options before beginning any work. The strut/shock absorber assemblies are not serviceable and must be

4.3 Install the spring compressor in accordance with the tool manufacturer's instructions and compress the spring until all pressure is relieved from the upper spring seat

4.4 Remove the damper shaft nut

4.5 Lift the suspension support off the damper shaft

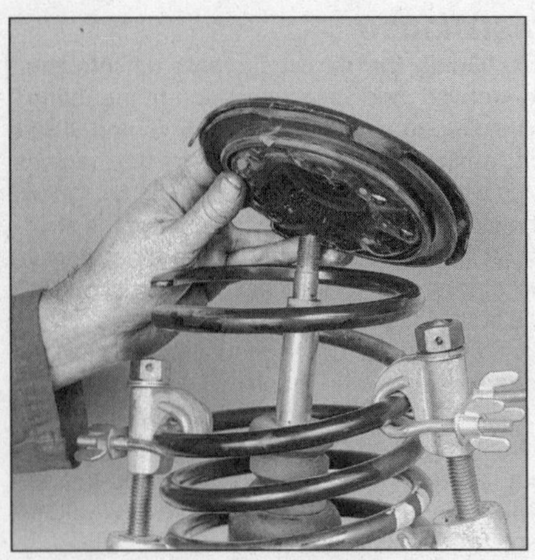
4.6 Remove the spring seat from the damper shaft

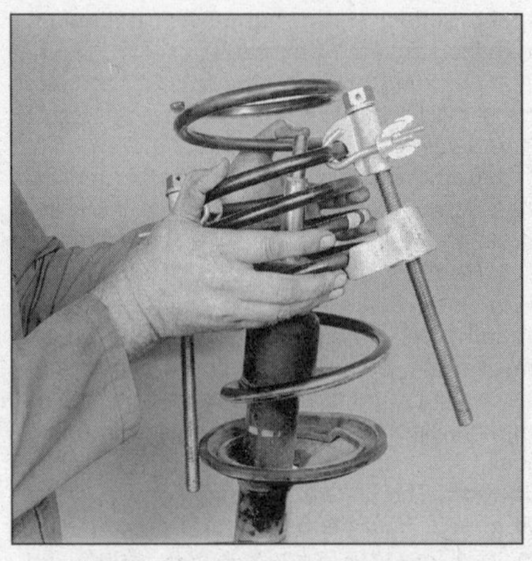
4.7 Remove the compressed spring assembly - keep the ends of the spring pointed away from your body

4.11 When installing the spring, make sure the end fits into the recessed portion of the lower seat

replaced if a problem develops. However, strut assemblies complete with springs may be available on an exchange basis, which eliminates much time and work. Whichever route you choose to take, check on the cost and availability of parts before disassembling your vehicle.

Warning: *Disassembling a strut is potentially dangerous and utmost attention must be directed to the job, or serious injury may result. Use only a high-quality spring compressor and carefully follow the manufacturer's instructions furnished with the tool. After removing the coil spring from the strut assembly, set it aside in a safe, isolated area.*

Disassembly

2 Remove the strut and spring assembly (see Section 3). Mount the strut assembly in a vise. Line the vise jaws with wood or rags to prevent damage to the unit and don't tighten the vise excessively.

3 Following the tool manufacturer's instructions, install the spring compressor (which can be obtained at most auto parts stores or equipment yards on a daily rental basis) on the spring and compress it sufficiently to relieve all pressure from the upper spring seat (see illustration). This can be verified by wiggling the spring.

4 Unscrew the damper shaft nut (see illustration).

5 Remove the nut and suspension support (see illustration). Inspect the bearing in the suspension support for smooth operation. If it doesn't turn smoothly, replace the suspension support. Check the rubber portion of the suspension support for cracking and general deterioration. If there is any separation of the rubber, replace it.

6 Remove the upper spring seat from the damper shaft (see illustration). Check the spring seat for cracking and hardness; replace it if necessary. Remove the upper insulator.

7 Carefully lift the compressed spring from the assembly (see illustration) and set it in a safe place.

Warning: *Never place your head near the end of the spring!*

8 Slide the rubber bumper off the damper shaft.

9 Check the lower insulator for wear, cracking and hardness and replace it if necessary.

Reassembly

10 If the lower insulator is being replaced, set it into position with the dropped portion seated in the lowest part of the seat. Extend the damper rod to its full length and install the rubber bumper.

11 Carefully place the coil spring onto the lower insulator, with the end of the spring resting in the lowest part of the insulator (see illustration).

12 Install the upper insulator on the spring. Install the spring seat, making sure that the flats in the hole in the seat match up with the

4.12 The flats on the damper shaft must match up with the flats in the spring seat

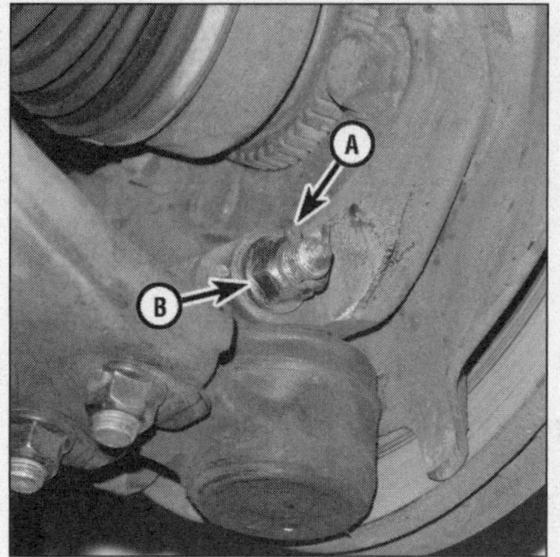

5.3a Remove the cotter pin (A, if equipped) and the balljoint-to-steering knuckle pinch bolt/nut (B)

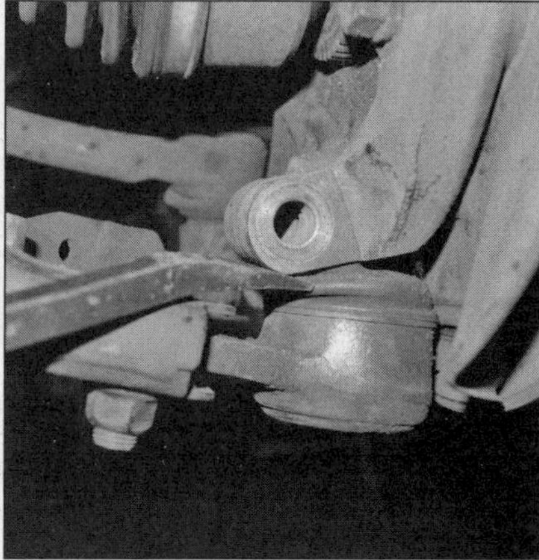
5.3b Carefully pry the control arm downwards to release the balljoint from the steering knuckle

flats on the damper shaft (see illustration).

13 Align the holes in the upper spring seat with those in the lower.

14 Install the damper nut and tighten it to the torque listed in this Chapter's Specifications. Don't allow the holes in the spring seats to become misaligned. Remove the spring compressor tool.

15 Install the strut/spring assembly.

5 Control arm and tension arm - removal, inspection, and installation

Note: *Only 2005 and earlier models are equipped with tension arms.*

Control arm

Removal

1 Loosen the wheel lug nuts, raise the front of the vehicle and support it securely on jackstands. Remove the wheel.

2 On 2005 and earlier models, detach the stabilizer bar link from the control arm.

3 Remove the cotter pin (if equipped) and the balljoint-to-steering knuckle pinch bolt, then separate the balljoint from the steering knuckle (see illustrations).

Caution: *Be careful not to damage the balljoint boot.*

4 On 2005 and earlier models remove the tension arm-to-control arm mounting nuts/bolts and the control arm-to-subframe nut/pivot bolt. Remove the control arm.

5 On 2006 and later models, remove the front bolt attaching the control arm to the subframe (see illustration). Remove the rear nut/pivot bolt and detach the control arm from the subframe.

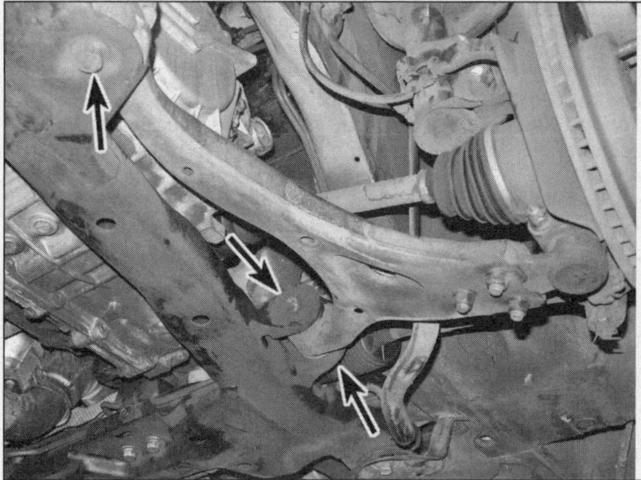
5.5 Control arm-to-subframe bolts (2006 and later models)

Inspection

6 Make sure the control arm is straight. If it is bent, replace it. Do not attempt to straighten a bent control arm.

7 Inspect all bushings for cracks, distortion, and tears. If a bushing is torn or worn, take the assembly to an automotive machine shop and have it replaced (a hydraulic press and proper adapters are required).

Installation

8 Position the control arm in the subframe. Install the bolts and nuts but do not tighten them yet.

9 On 2005 and earlier models, install the tension arm-to-control arm bolts and nuts but do not tighten them yet.

10 Reinstall the balljoint to the steering knuckle and tighten the balljoint-to-steering knuckle pinch bolt/nut to the torque listed in this Chapter's Specifications.

11 Place a floor jack under the control arm (as close to the balljoint as possible). Raise the control arm to simulate normal ride height.

12 Tighten the control arm bolt(s) and tension arm nuts/bolts (2005 and earlier models) to the torque listed in this Chapter's Specifications.

13 Install the wheel and lug nuts, lower the vehicle and tighten the lug nuts to the torque listed in the Chapter 1 Specifications.

14 Have the front wheel alignment checked and, if necessary, adjusted.

Tension arm (2005 and earlier models only)

15 Loosen the wheel lug nuts, raise the front of the vehicle and support it securely on jackstands. Remove the wheel.

16 Remove the tension arm-to-control arm mounting nuts/bolts.

17 Mark the relationship of the tension arm nuts to the tension arm.

18 Unscrew the forward tension arm nut, then detach the tension arm and bushings from the subframe.

19 Installation is the reverse of removal. Align the marks on the tension arm nuts with the mark made onthe arm, then tighten the forward nut to the torque listed in this Chapter's Specifications.

20 Install the wheel and lug nuts, lower the vehicle and tighten the lug nuts to the torque listed in the Chapter 1 Specifications.

21 Have the front wheel alignment checked and, if necessary, adjusted.

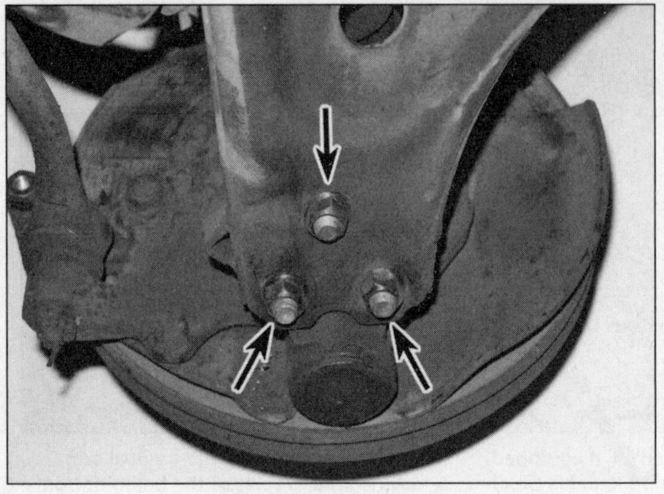

6.2 Balljoint mounting nuts/bolts

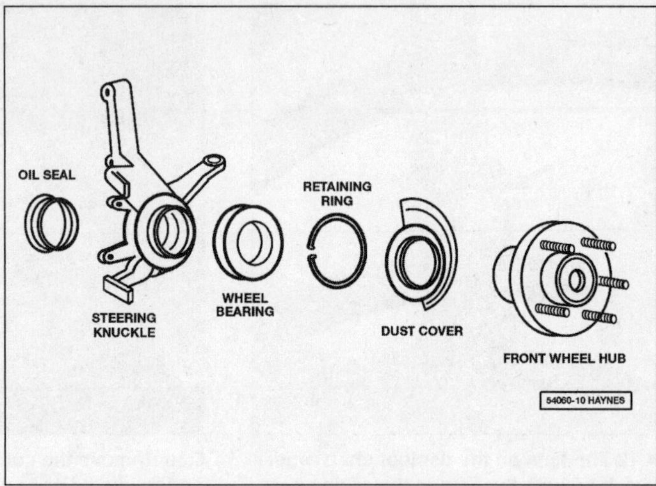

7.3 Exploded view of the front hub and bearing assembly (2005 and earlier models)

6 Balljoints - replacement

Note: *This procedure applies to 2006 and later models only. If a balljoint on 2005 and earlier models requires replacement, the entire control arm must be replaced.*

1 Separate the control arm balljoint from the steering knuckle (see Section 5).

2 Remove the balljoint mounting bolts (see illustration) and pull the balljoint out of the control arm.

3 Insert the balljoint into the end of the control arm, then install the mounting bolts/nuts and tighten them to the torque listed in this Chapter's Specifications.

4 Reconnect the balljoint to the steering knuckle (see Section 5).

7 Hub and bearing assembly (front) - removal and installation

1 Loosen the wheel lug nuts, raise the front of the vehicle and support it securely on jackstands. Remove the wheel.

2005 and earlier models

Note: *This procedure requires a hydraulic press and special adapters.*

2 Remove the steering knuckle (see Section 8).

3 Pry out the oil seal (see illustration).

4 Using two press plates, block-up the steering knuckle, face-down, on a hydraulic press.

5 Using a properly sized bearing driver adapter, press the hub/axle flange out of the wheel bearing.

6 Remove the retaining ring.

7 The bearing inner race will probably be stuck to the hub spindle. If so, grind off part of the race (being careful not to grind all the way through it) until it is approximately 1/64-inch (0.4 mm) thick. Then, using a hammer and chisel, cut through the race and remove it from the hub spindle.

8 Using a properly sized bearing driver adapter, press the wheel bearing out of the steering knuckle.

9 Clean the steering knuckle bore of all corrosion and grime. Also remove all corrosion, grime and burrs from the hub/axle flange spindle.

10 Block-up the steering knuckle, face-up, on the press.

11 Using the proper bearing driver, press the new wheel bearing into the steering knuckle until it seats.

12 Install the retaining ring.

13 Press the hub/axle flange into the bearing until it seats.

14 Using a hammer and a seal driver, install the new oil seal.

15 Install the steering knuckle (see Section 8).

2006 and later models

Removal

Note: *If the hub/bearing assembly cannot be removed easily and appears frozen in the steering knuckle, it will have to be pressed out of the steering knuckle. If this is the case, remove the steering knuckle (see Section 8) and take it to an automotive machine shop or other repair facility for service.*

16 Unstake the driveaxle/hub nut using a hammer and chisel, then loosen the nut (see Chapter 8).

17 Loosen the wheel lug nuts, then raise the vehicle and support it securely on jackstands. Remove the wheel.

18 Remove the brake caliper, the caliper mounting bracket, and the brake disc from the steering knuckle (see Chapter 9).

Note: *Be sure to support the brake caliper as described in Chapter 9.*

19 Remove the driveaxle/hub nut.

20 Remove the hub/bearing assembly mounting bolts from the rear of the steering knuckle (see illustration).

21 Remove the hub/bearing assembly from the steering knuckle. If the driveaxle splines stick in the hub, push the driveaxle out of the hub with a puller.

Note: *If the driveaxle splines stick in the hub, push the driveaxle out of the hub with a two-jaw puller. Be careful not to overextend the driveaxle inner CV joint.*

Installation

22 Make sure that the mounting surface inside the steering knuckle and on the driveaxle splines is smooth and free of burrs and nicks prior to installing the hub/bearing assembly.

23 Lubricate the driveaxle splines with multi-purpose grease. Install the hub/bearing assembly onto the driveaxle and into the steering knuckle until it is seated on the steering knuckle.

24 Install the hub/bearing assembly-to-steering knuckle bolts. Tighten the bolts equally, a little at a time, until the hub/bearing assembly is seated securely against the steering knuckle. Tighten the bolts to the torque listed in this Chapter's Specifications.

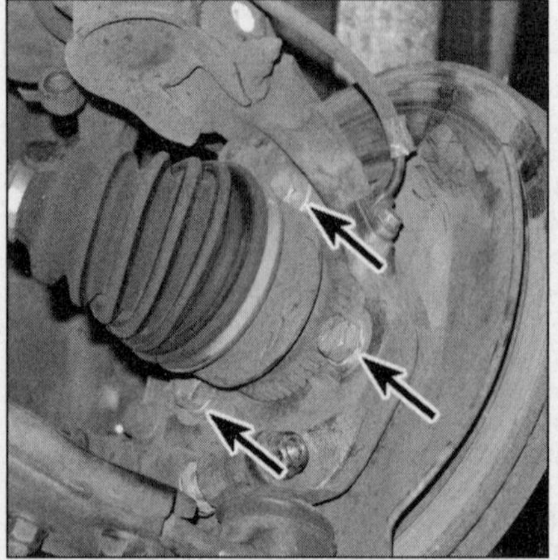

7.20 Remove the hub/bearing three mounting bolts

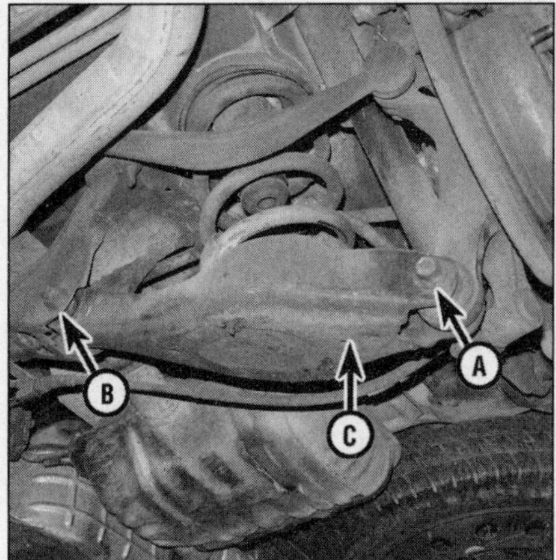

9.15 Lower control arm-to-rear knuckle nut/bolt (A) and control arm-to-subframe nut/pivot bolt (B). Support the lower control arm with a floor jack placed underneath the spring seat (C)

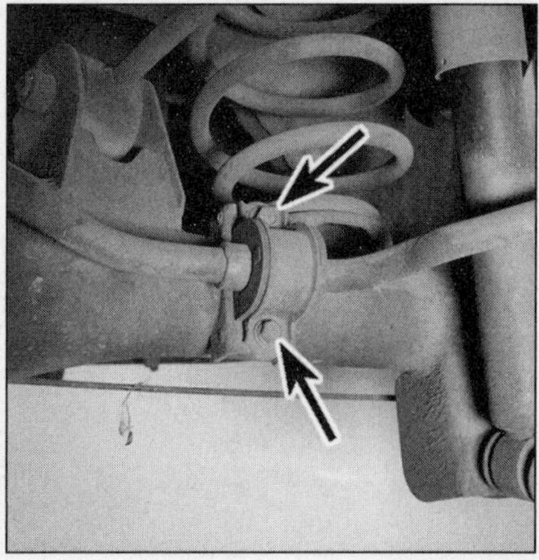

10.4 Remove the stabilizer bar bushing brackets

25 Install the driveaxle/hub nut. Do not tighten the nut yet.

26 Install the brake disc, the caliper mounting bracket and the caliper; tighten the fasteners to the torque values listed in the Chapter 9 Specifications.

27 Install the wheel and lug nuts, remove the jackstands, and lower the vehicle.

28 Tighten the driveaxle/hub nut to the torque listed in the Chapter 8 Specifications.

29 Tighten the lug nuts to the torque listed in the Chapter 1 Specifications.

8 Steering knuckle - removal and installation

Note: *The steering knuckle is not a repairable component. It must be replaced if it is damaged in any way.*

Removal

1 Loosen the wheel lug nuts and the driveaxle/hub nut (see Chapter 8), then raise the vehicle and support it securely on jackstands.

2 Remove the wheel.

3 Remove the driveaxle/hub nut.

4 Remove the brake disc and, if equipped, the ABS front wheel speed sensor (see Chapter 9).

5 Detach the tie-rod end from the steering knuckle (see Section 16).

6 Separate the control arm balljoint from the steering knuckle (see Section 5).

7 Remove the two strut-to-steering knuckle bolts, noting their installed direction (see Section 3).

Caution: *The strut-to-steering knuckle bolts are serrated and must not be turned during removal - turn the nuts only.*

8 Remove the knuckle from the strut, while pulling the driveaxle stub shaft out of the hub splines.

Caution: *Do not overextend the inner CV joint, and do not allow the driveaxle to hang by the inner CV joint.*

Note: *If the driveaxle splines stick in the hub, push the driveaxle out with a puller.*

Installation

9 Installation is the reverse of the removal procedure. Tighten all suspension fasteners to the torque listed in this Chapter's Specifications. Tighten the brake fasteners to the torque listed in the Chapter 9 Specifications.

10 Install the wheel, lower the vehicle and tighten the lug nuts and driveaxle/hub nut to the torque listed in the Chapter 1 and 8 Specifications.

11 Have the front end alignment checked and, if necessary, adjusted.

9 Coil springs (rear) - removal and installation

1 Raise the vehicle and support it securely on jackstands. Block the front tires to keep the vehicle from moving.

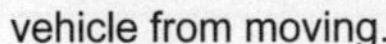

2005 and earlier models

Removal

2 Place a floor jack under the axle beam and raise it slightly.

3 Remove the Panhard rod-to-chassis bolt (see Section 12).

4 Remove the shock absorber lower mounting bolt (see Section 11).

5 Remove the rear brake hose bracket fastener and allow the hose to hang freely.

6 Slowly lower the floor jack until each spring can be removed from its seat.

7 Remove the lower spring seat insulator.

Installation

8 Place the lower spring seat insulator onto the spring seat.

9 Insert the spring between the upper seat in the body and the lower seat on the axle beam.

10 Using the jack, raise the axle beam and compress the spring until the shock absorber lower mounting bolts can be installed. Do not tighten them yet.

11 Connect the Panhard rod to the chassis and install the bolt. Do not tighten it yet.

12 The remainder of installation is the reverse of removal.

13 Lower the vehicle to the floor. With the full weight of the vehicle on the wheels, tighten the shock absorber lower mounting bolts and the Panhard rod bolt to the torque values listed in this Chapter's Specifications.

2006 and later models

14 Support the lower control arm with a floor jack placed under the area of the coil spring.

15 Loosen the lower control arm-to-subframe nut/pivot bolt, then unbolt the lower control arm from the rear knuckle (see illustration).

16 Use the floor jack to slowly and carefully lower the arm until the spring can be removed from the seat in the arm.

17 Inspect the coil spring for chips and distortion. Check the insulators for deterioration. Replace parts as necessary.

18 Installation is the reverse of removal. Raise the lower control arm with the floor jack to simulate normal ride height, then tighten the lower control arm fasteners to the torque listed in this Chapter's Specifications. Tighten the lug nuts to the torque listed in the Chapter 1 Specifcations.

Note: *The control arm bolt/nut should be tightened with the vehicle at normal ride height. This can be done after the vehicle has been assembled, lowered to the ground and bounced a few times (as if inspecting the shock absorbers). Alternatively, the normal ride height can be simulated by raising the lower control arm with a floor jack.*

10 Stabilizer bar, bushings and links (rear) - removal and installation

1 Loosen the rear wheel lug nuts. Raise the rear of the vehicle and support it securely on jackstands. Remove the wheels.

2005 and earlier models

2 Support the rear axle beam with a floor jack and raise the axle slightly.

3 Remove the nuts from the stabilizer bar link bolts, then pull the link bolts out, noting the order of the spacers, washers and rubber insulators.

4 Unbolt the stabilizer bar bushing brackets (see illustration).

5 The stabilizer bar can now be removed from the vehicle. Remove the bushings from the stabilizer bar, noting their positions.

6 Check the bushings for wear, hardness, distortion, cracking and other signs of deterioration, replacing them if necessary. Check the stabilizer bar links for loose ballstuds.

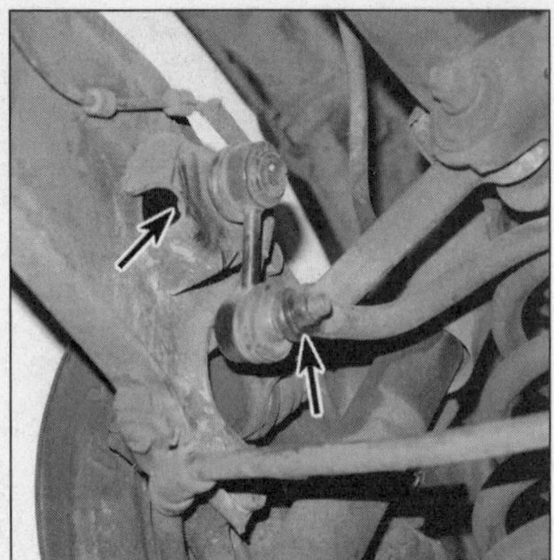
10.9 Stabilizer bar link nuts

10.10 Stabilizer bar bushing bracket bolts

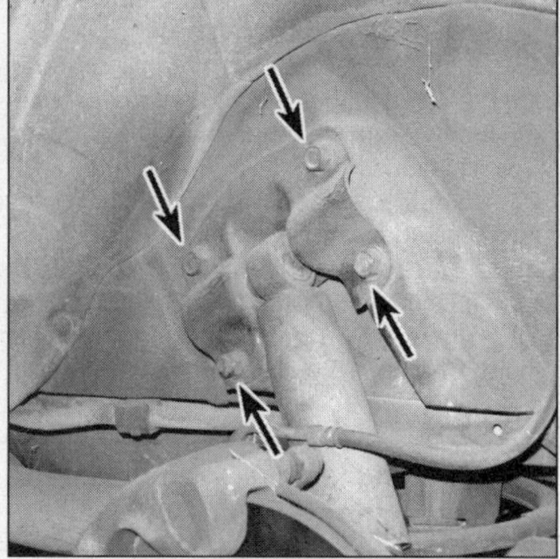
11.11 Shock absorber upper mounting bracket fasteners

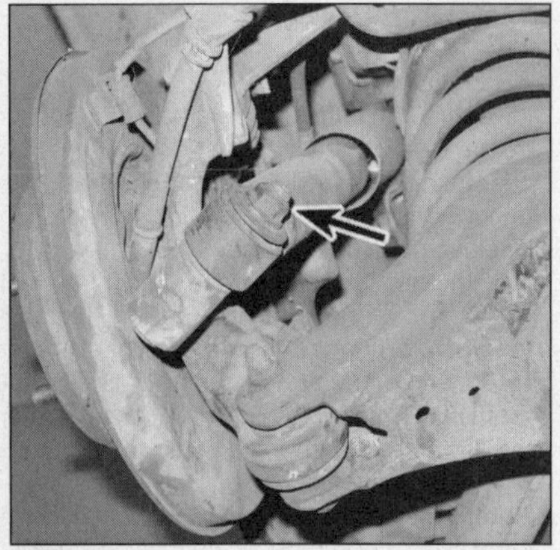
11.12 Shock absorber lower mounting nut

7 Using a wire brush, clean the areas of the bar where the bushings ride.

8 Installation is the reverse of removal. Tighten the bushing bracket bolts to the torque listed in this Chapter's Specifications. Tighten the link nuts until 3/8 to 5/8-inch (9.4 to 15.4 mm) of thread is exposed, then tighten the outer nut against the inner nut to the torque listed in this Chapter's Specifications.

2006 and later models

9 Remove the nuts and detach the stabilizer bar links from the trailing arm (see illustration).

10 Remove the bolts from the stabilizer bar bushing brackets and detach the bar from the subframe (see illustration).

11 Check the bushings for wear, hardness, distortion, cracking and other signs of deterioration, replacing them if necessary. Check the stabilizer bar links for loose ballstuds.

12 Using a wire brush, clean the areas of the bar where the bushings ride.

13 Installation is the reverse of removal. Tighten the bushing bracket bolts and the link nuts to the torque values listed in this Chapter's Specifications. Tighten the wheel lug nuts to the torque listed in the Chapter 1 Specifications.

11 Shock absorbers (rear) - removal and installation

1 Raise the vehicle and support it securely on jackstands placed under the unibody structure (not the axle or control arms). Block the front wheels to keep the vehicle from moving.

2005 and earlier models

Removal

2 Support the axle beam with a floor jack near the shock absorber to be removed.

3 Remove the shock absorber upper mounting nuts.

4 Remove the shock absorber lower mounting nut/bolt and remove the shock absorber.

Installation

5 Position the lower end of the shock absorber in the axle bracket and allow the top of the shock absorber to extend into the top bracket.

6 Install the shock absorber mounting bolts and nuts finger tight. Raise the axle beam to simulate normal ride height.

7 Tighten the shock absorber lower bolt and nut to the torque listed in this Chapter's Specifications.

8 Tighten the upper nuts until there is approximately 13/32 to 29/64-inch (10.5 to 11.5 mm) of threads exposed above the top nut then tighten the top nut against the lower nut to the torque listed in this Chapter's Specifications.

9 Install the wheel and lug nuts, then lower the vehicle. Tighten the lug nuts to the torque listed in the Chapter 1 Specifications.

2006 and later models

Removal

10 Support the lower control arm with a floor jack placed under the area of the coil spring.

11 Remove the shock absorber upper mounting bracket nut and bolts (see illustration).

12 Remove the shock absorber lower mounting nut (see illustration).

13 Slide the lower end of the shock absorber off of the stud and remove the shock absorber and bracket assembly.

14 Remove the upper mounting bolt/nut and separate the shock absorber from the bracket.

Installation

15 Install the upper end of the shock absorber into the bracket then install the nut and bolt and tighten to the torque listed in this Chapter's Specifications.

16 Install the lower end of the shock absorber onto the stud, then install the washer and nut and tighten it finger-tight.

17 Install the bracket nut and bolts, tightening them to the torque listed in this Chapter's Specifications.

18 Raise the lower control arm to simulate normal ride height, then tighten the lower mounting nut to the torque listed in this Chapter's Specifications.

19 Install the wheel and lug nuts, then lower the vehicle. Tighten the lug nuts to the torque listed in the Chapter 1 Specifications.

12 Suspension arms and rear axle beam (rear) - removal and installation

1 Only 2005 and earlier models have a rear axle beam.

2005 and earlier models

2 Loosen the rear wheel lug nuts, then raise the rear of the vehicle and support it securely on jackstands placed under the unibody frame rails. Remove the rear wheel.

Lower arm

3 Support the rear axle beam with a floor jack nearest the arm to be removed.

4 Remove the coil spring (see Section 9).

5 Disconnect the rear stabilizer bar link bolt from the front of the trailing arm.

6 Remove the nuts and pivot bolts from each end of the arm, then remove the arm (see illustration 1.2).

7 Check the bushings for wear and deterioration. If necessary, take the arm to an automotive machine shop or other repair facility to have the old bushings pressed out and new ones pressed in.

8 Installation is the reverse of removal. Tighten the fasteners to the torque listed in this Chapter's Specifications. Tighten the lug nuts to the torque listed in the Chapter 1 Specifications.

Note: *When installing any rear suspension arm, loosely tighten all the bolts, move the suspension to its normal ride-height angle and position (a floor jack can be used to do this), then fully tighten the bolts.*

Upper arm/Panhard rod

9 Support the rear axle beam with a floor jack.

10 Remove the nuts and pivot bolts from each end of the control arm or Panhard rod, then remove the bar/rod (see illustration 1.1).

11 Check the bushings for wear and deterioration. If necessary, take the control arm or Panhard rod to an automotive machine shop or other repair facility to have the old bushings pressed out and new ones pressed in.

12 Installation is the reverse of removal. Tighten the fasteners to the torque listed in this Chapter's Specifications. Tighten the lug nuts to the torque listed in the Chapter 1 Specifications.

Note: *When installing any rear suspension arm, loosely tighten all of the bolts, move the suspension to its normal ride-height angle and position (a floor jack can be used to do this), then fully tighten the bolts.*

Axle beam

13 Remove the rear drum brake assemblies (see Chapter 9) and detach the brake hydraulic fluid line fitting. Plug the fittings to prevent fluid leakage.

14 Remove the coil springs (see Section 9).

15 Remove the upper and lower arms and Panhard rod as described earlier in this Section.

16 Make sure no wires or hoses are attached to the axle beam, then lower the beam with the floor jack.

17 Installation is the reverse of the removal procedure. Bleed the brake system (see Chapter 9).

18 Tighten the lug nuts to the torque listed in the Chapter 1 Specifications.

2006 and later models

19 Loosen the rear wheel lug nuts, then raise the rear of the vehicle and support it securely on jackstands under the unibody frame rails. Remove the rear wheel.

Upper control arm

20 Remove the rear brake caliper (see Chapter 9).

21 Remove the cotter pin and unscrew the castle nut a few turns, then break loose the balljoint stud with a balljoint separator or a suitable puller (see illustration) from the steering knuckle.

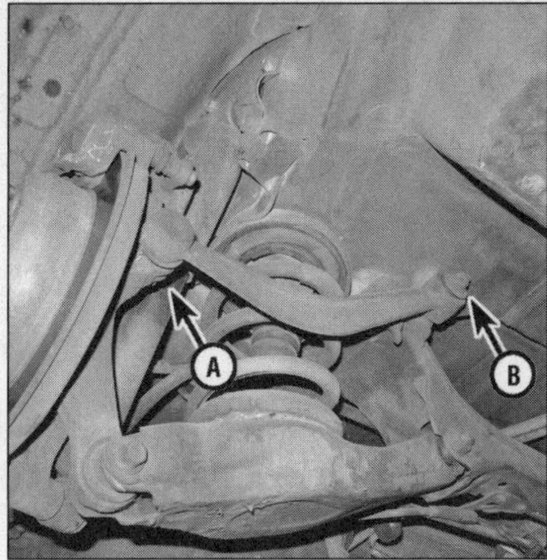

12.21 Upper control arm balljoint-to-rear knuckle nut (A) and arm-to-subframe nut (B)

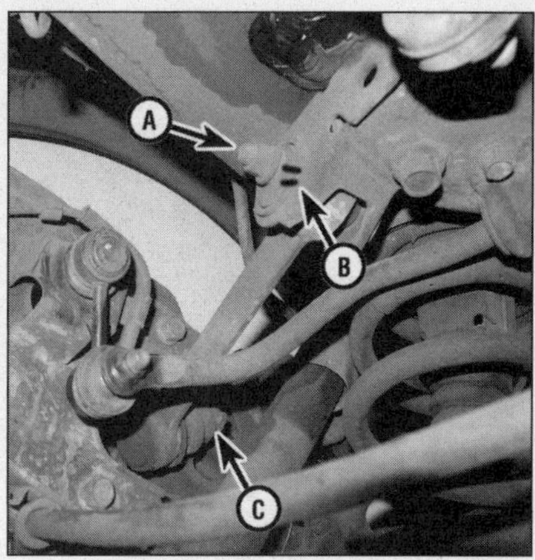

12.32 Lateral control rod details

A *Inner pivot bolt/nut*
B *Alignment marks*
C *Lateral control arm-to-knuckle nut*

22 Remove the inner pivot nut and detach the upper control arm from the subframe. Check the bushings for wear and deterioration. Check the balljoint for excessive play. If necessary, take the arm to an automotive machine shop or other repair facility to have the old bushing pressed out and new ones pressed in. If the balljoint has excessive play the upper control must be replaced.

23 Installation is the reverse of removal. Tighten all suspension fasteners to the torque listed in this Chapter's Specifications and use a new cotter pin on the balljoint castle nut. If necessary, tighten the castle nut a little more to align the hole in the ballstud with the slots in the nut - don't loosen the nut to achieve this alignment. Tighten the brake caliper bolts to the torque listed in the Chapter 9 Specifications. Tighten the lug nuts to the torque listed in the Chapter 1 Specifications.

Note: *When installing any rear suspension arm equipped with a bushing, loosely tighten all of the bolts, move the suspension to its normal ride-height angle and position (a floor jack can be used to do this), then fully tighten the bolts.*

Lower control arm

24 Remove the coil spring (see Section 9).

25 Remove the nut and inner pivot bolt, then detach the arm from the subframe (see illustration 9.15).

26 Check the bushing for wear and deterioration. If necessary, take the arm to an automotive machine shop or other repair facility to have the old bushing pressed out and a new one pressed in.

27 Installation is the reverse of removal. Tighten all suspension fasteners to the torque values listed in this Chapter's Specifications. Tighten the lug nuts to the torque listed in the Chapter 1 Specifications.

Note: *When installing any rear suspension arm, loosely tighten all of the bolts, move the suspension to its normal ride-height angle and position (a floor jack can be used to do this), then fully tighten the bolts.*

28 Have the rear wheel alignment checked and, if necessary, adjusted.

Lateral control arm

29 Remove the rear brake caliper (see Chapter 9).

30 Support the lower control arm with a floor jack. Mark the position of the cam washer on the arm's inner pivot bolt to the subframe.

31 Remove the cotter pin and loosen the castle nut on the outer end of the arm several turns, then break loose the balljoint stud with a balljoint separator or a suitable puller (see illustration 12.21). Remove the nut and detach the arm from the knuckle.

32 Remove the nut and inner pivot bolt from the rod and detach the rod from the subframe (see illustration).

33 Remove the nut and inner pivot bolt from the rod and detach the rod from the subframe.

34 Check the bushing for wear and deterioration. If necessary, take the arm to an automotive machine shop or other repair facility to have the old bushing pressed out and a new one pressed in.

35 Installation is the reverse of removal. Be sure to align the previously made match marks, then tighten all suspension fasteners to the torque values listed in this Chapter's Specifications, and use a new cotter pin on on the balljoint castle nut. If necessary, tighten the castle nut a little more to align the hole in the ballstud with the slots in the nut - don't loosen the nut to achieve this alignment. Tighten the brake caliper bolts to the torque listed in the Chapter 9 Specifications. Tighten the lug nuts to the torque listed in the Chapter 1 Specifications.

Note: *When installing any rear suspension arm, loosely tighten all of the bolts, move the suspension to its normal ride-height angle and position (a floor jack can be used to do this), then fully tighten the bolts.*

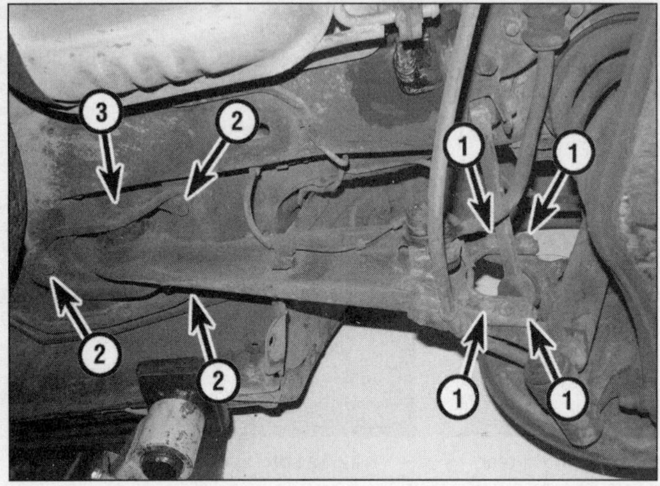

12.39 Trailing arm details

1 *Trailing arm-to-knuckle bolts*
2 *Trailing arm bracket-to-body bolts*
3 *Trailing arm pivot bolt/nut*

13.23 Carefully separate the dust cap from the hub

Trailing arm

36 Support the rear suspension with a floor jack placed under the outer end of the lower control arm.

37 Remove the wheel speed sensor harness bracket bolt and parking brake cable bracket from the trailing arm.

38 Detach the stabilizer bar link from the trailing arm (see Section 10).

39 Remove the bolts securing the trailing arm to the rear knuckle (see illustration).

40 Remove the trailing arm bracket-to-body bolts and remove the trailing arm.

41 Remove the trailing arm-to-bracket pivot bolt/nut and separate the trailing arm from the bracket.

42 Check the bushing for wear and deterioration. If necessary, take the arm to an automotive machine shop or other repair facility to have the old bushing pressed out and a new one pressed in.

43 Installation is the reverse of removal. Tighten all suspension fasteners to the torque values listed in this Chapter's Specifications. Tighten the lug nuts to the torque listed in the Chapter 1 Specifications.

Note: *Don't tighten the trailing arm-to-bracket pivot bolt/nut until the lower control arm has been raised with the jack to simulate normal ride height.*

13 Hub and bearing assembly (rear) - removal and installation

1 Loosen the rear wheel lug nuts, raise the rear of the vehicle, support it securely on jackstands and remove the wheels.

2005 and earlier models

2 Remove the rear brake drum (see Chapter 9).

3 Pry the dust cap out of the hub using a screwdriver or hammer and chisel.

4 Use needle-nose pliers or a screwdriver to straighten the ends of the cotter pin then pull the cotter pin out of the cover set. Discard the cotter pin and use a new one during reassembly.

5 Remove the cover set, hub lock nut and washer from the end of the stub shaft.

6 Pull the hub out slightly and then push it back into its original position. This should force the outer bearing off the stub shaft enough so that it can be removed.

7 Pull the hub assembly off of the stub shaft.

8 On the rear side of the hub, use a screwdriver to pry out the seal. Before removing the seal, note the direction in which the seal is installed.

9 Remove the inner wheel bearing, noting the direction the bearing faces.

10 Use high-temperature wheel bearing grease to pack the bearings, if necessary. Work the grease completely into the bearings, forcing it between the rollers, cone and cage from the back side.

11 Apply a thin coat of grease to the stub shaft, at the outer bearing seat, inner bearing seat, shoulder and seal seat.

12 Put a small quantity of grease inboard of each bearing race inside the hub, using your finger to prevent the grease from flowing out of the bearing.

13 Place the grease-packed inner bearing into the rear of the hub applying a small amount of grease on the outboard side of the bearing.

14 Place the new seal over the inner bearing end of the hub and tap the seal evenly into place with a hammer and block of wood until the seal is flush with the hub.

15 Carefully place the hub assembly onto the stub shaft and push the grease-packed outer bearing into position on the stub shaft and into the hub.

16 Install the washer and lock nut. Tighten the lock nut to the lower torque value listed in this Chapter's Specifications.

17 Place the cover set over the hub lock nut and install the cotter pin through the slots in the cover set and hole in the stub shaft. If the slots in the cover set do not line up, tighten the lock nut slightly until they do. Don't exceed the higher torque value listed in this Chapter's Specifications.

18 Bend the ends of the cotter pin until they are flat against the cover set and lock nut. Cut off any extra length which could interfere with the dust cap.

19 Install the dust cap, tapping it into place with a hammer. Try not to dent the cap with the hammer.

20 Install the brake drum.

21 Install the wheel and lug nuts. Lower the vehicle and tighten the lug nuts to the torque listed in the Chapter 1 Specifications.

2006 and later models

22 Remove the brake disc, rear wheel speed sensor (if equipped) (see Chapter 9), and parking brake cable bracket fasteners.

23 Pry the dust cap out of the hub using a screwdriver or hammer and chisel (see illustration).

24 Unstake the hub nut with a small punch or chisel (see illustration).

25 Loosen the hub nut with a socket and breaker bar, then remove the hub nut from the stub axle and discard it.

26 Remove the tang-washer (see illustration) and hub assembly from the stub shaft (see illustration).

27 Due to the special tools and expertise required to press the hub bearings in and out of the hub, this job should be left to a professional shop. Take the hub assembly to a qualified repair shop or machine shop to have the bearings replaced.

28 Installation is the reverse of removal.

13.24 Use a small punch to un-stake the nut

13.26a Remove the tang-washer, then. . .

13.26b . . then side the hub assembly off of the stub shaft

Tighten the new hub nut to the torque listed in this Chapter's Specifications.

29 Stake the collar of the new hub nut onto the slot in the stub axle using a hammer and punch.

30 Install the dust cap, tapping it into place with a hammer. Try not to dent the cap with the hammer.

31 Installation is the reverse of removal.

32 Install the wheel and lug nuts. Lower the vehicle and tighten the lug nuts to the torque listed in the Chapter 1 Specifications.

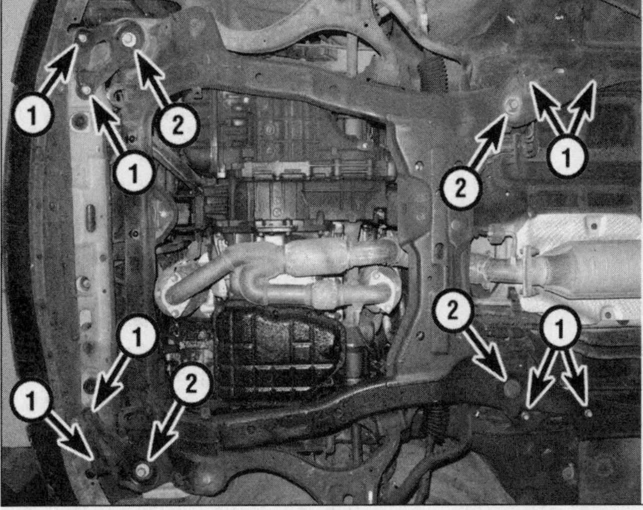

14.13 Subframe mounting fasteners (2006 and later models shown)

1 *Support bracket bolts*
2 *Subframe bolts*

14 Subframe - removal and installation

Front

Removal

1 Disconnect the cable from the negative battery terminal (see Chapter 5).

2 Loosen the front wheel lug nuts, raise the front of the vehicle and support it securely on jackstands. Remove both front wheels.

Note: *The jackstands must be behind the front suspension subframe, not supporting the vehicle by the subframe.*

3 If you're working on a 2005 or earlier model, remove the front portion of the exhaust system.

4 Disconnect the stabilizer bar links from the bar (see Section 2).

5 Disconnect the tie-rod ends from the steering knuckles (see Section 16).

6 Disconnect the control arms from the steering knuckles (see Section 5).

7 Mark the relationship of the intermediate shaft to the steering shaft U-joint and remove the pinch bolt (see Section 18).

8 Inspect the subframe for any hose, line or harness brackets that may be attached, and detach them. Plug all disconnected hoses and lines.

Warning: *Do not disconnect any refrigerant line fittings.*

9 Before the subframe is removed, be sure to disconnect the power steering line-to-subframe retainers.

10 Support the engine from above using an engine hoist or support fixture (see Chapter 2A).

Warning: *DO NOT place any part of your body under the engine when it's supported only by a hoist or other lifting device.*

11 Detach the front and rear roll stoppers (front and rear engine mounts) from the subframe (see Chapter 2A).

12 Using two floor jacks, support the subframe. Position one jack on each side of the subframe, midway between the front and rear mounting points.

13 With the jacks sufficiently supporting the subframe, remove the subframe mounting fasteners (see illustration).

14 With the help of an assistant to steady the subframe, carefully lower the jacks until the subframe is sufficiently resting on the ground.

Note: *Once the subframe is lowered a few inches, disconnect the power steering fluid lines from the steering gear.*

Installation

15 Installation is the reverse of removal. Tighten all suspension and subframe fasteners to the torque listed in this Chapter's Specifications. Tighten the engine roll stopper (mount) fasteners to torque listed in the Chapter 2A Specifications.

Rear

16 Loosen the rear wheel lug nuts, raise the rear of the vehicle and support it securely on jackstands. Remove the wheels.

17 Remove the rear portion of the exhaust system.

18 If you're working on a 2006 or later model, remove the brake calipers (see Chapter 9). Hang the calipers with lengths of wire or rope; don't disconnect the hoses.

19 Remove the rear axle beam and detach the control arms and Panhard rod from the subframe (2005 and earlier models) or rear suspension arms (2006 and later models) (see Section 12).

20 Support the crossmember with a floor jack (or a pair of floor jacks). A jack with a transmission adapter works well.

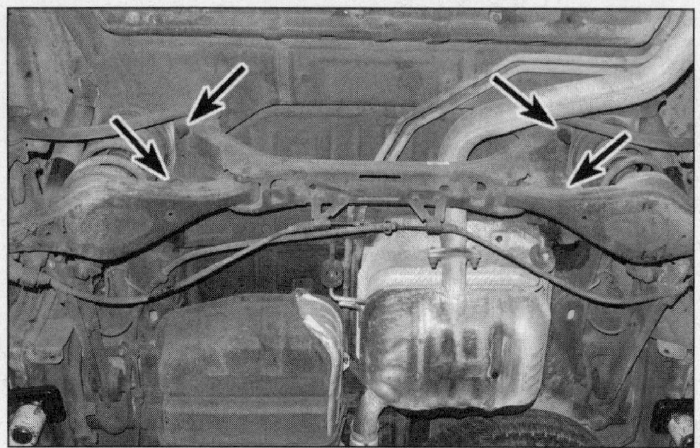

14.21 Subframe mounting fasteners (2006 and later models shown)

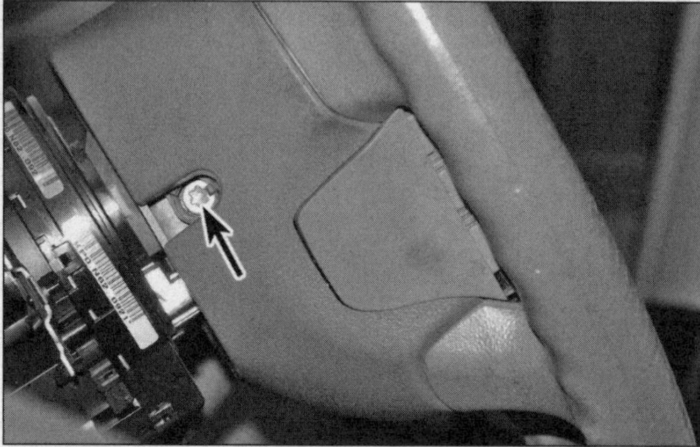

15.6 Locate the airbag module bolts, then remove them using the proper Torx bit

15.7 The airbag connectors have safety latches that must be released prior to disconnect the connectors (pry them up)

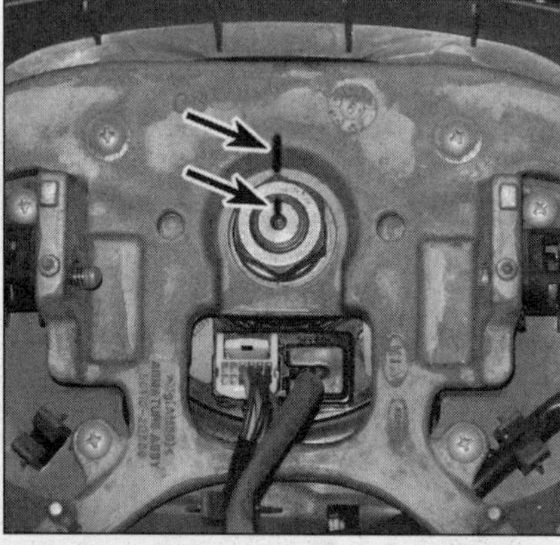

15.9 The steering shaft and steering wheel must have matching marks made so they can be reassembled in the same position

15.10 Use a puller with bolts threaded into the steering wheel to pull the wheel from the steering shaft

21 Remove the crossmember mounting fasteners and lower it to the floor (see illustration).

22 Installation is the reverse of removal. Tighten tighten the subframe and suspension component fasteners to the torque listed in this Chapter's Specifications. Tighten the brake system fasteners to the torque listed in the Chapter 9 Specifications. If you're working on a 2005 or earlier model, bleed the brake system (see Chapter 9). Tighten the wheel lug nuts to the torque listed in the Chapter 1 Specifications.

15 Steering wheel - removal and installation

Warning: *These models have airbags. Always disarm the airbag system before working in the vicinity of the impact sensors, steering column, or instrument panel to avoid accidental deployment of the airbag, which could cause personal injury (see Chapter 12).*

Warning: *Do not use a memory saving device to preserve the PCM's memory when working on or near airbag system components.*

Removal

1 Park the vehicle with the wheels pointing straight ahead and the steering wheel centered. Disconnect the cable from the negative terminal of the battery (see Chapter 5).

Warning: *Wait at least two minutes before proceeding with the following steps.*

2005 and earlier models

2 Remove the steering column lower cover (see Chapter 11) then lower the steering wheel. There are airbag retainer access holes on the back side of the steering wheel hub.

Note: *The steering wheel must be rotated to the top or 12 o'clock position for each of the access holes to disengage the retaining wires.*

3 With an access hole in the 12 o'clock position, insert special tool 10187 (or the tip of a blade screwdriver) into the access hole. Pry the retaining wire loop up until it disengages from the hook of the steering wheel, while carefully pulling the airbag outwards.

4 Repeat Step 3 for all the retainer wires. Once all three retaining wires are free, rotate the steering wheel to the center position.

Note: *The lower retainer wire loop has a V-shape and must always be installed at the bottom hook of the steering wheel.*

2006 and later models

5 Remove the steering column covers (see Chapter 11).

6 Remove the fasteners holding the airbag module to the steering wheel (see illustration).

All models

7 Remove the airbag module from the steering wheel and disconnect the electrical connectors (see illustration).

8 Set the module aside in a safe, isolated area, with the airbag side of the module facing UP.

Warning: *When carrying the airbag module, keep the driver's (trim) side facing away from you.*

9 Remove the steering wheel retaining nut and mark the position of the steering wheel to the shaft (see illustration), if marks don't already exist or don't line up.

10 Remove the steering wheel using a puller (see illustration).

Caution: *Do not hammer on the steering shaft or the steering wheel in an attempt to free the steering wheel from the shaft. Also, do not use a slide hammer puller to remove the steering wheel from the shaft.*

16.2 Hold the tie-rod end while breaking loose the jam nut

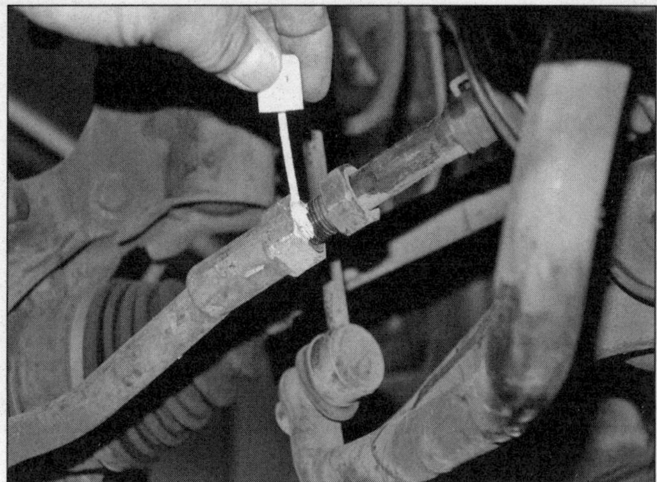

16.3 Back-off the jam nut and mark the exposed threads

Caution: *While the steering wheel is removed, DO NOT turn the steering shaft. If you do so, the airbag clockspring could be damaged when the vehicle is put back in service. Apply a piece of tape across the clockspring housing and the hub of the clockspring to prevent it from becoming uncentered.*

Installation

11 Make sure the clockspring is still centered. If it isn't, make sure that the front wheels are facing straight ahead, then turn the hub in either direction until it stops (don't apply too much force). Now, rotate the hub in the other direction, counting the number of turns it takes to reach the opposite stop. Divide that number by two, then turn the hub back that many turns, approximately, until the wiring is at the 6 o'clock position.

12 Install the wheel on the steering shaft, making sure to align the marks.

Note: *Make sure the clockspring wires are routed correctly through the steering wheel.*

13 Install the steering wheel retaining nut and tighten it to the torque listed in this Chapter's Specifcations 0.

14 Reconnect the electrical connectors and place the airbag module on the steering wheel.

15 On 2005 and earlier models, hook the lower retainer wire (6 o'clock position) first, then hook the remaining two retaining wires.

16 On 2006 and later models, install the airbag module fasteners and tighten them to the torque listed in this Chapter's Specifications.

17 Connect the cable to the negative battery terminal (see Chapter 5).

18 Turn the ignition key On and verify that the airbag system is operating properly by watching the airbag warning light in the instrument cluster (see Chapter 12).

Warning: *If the airbag system is not operating properly (as indicated by the airbag warning light), DO NOT drive the vehicle. Have the airbag system repaired at a dealership service department or other qualified repair shop.*

16 Tie-rod ends - removal and installation

Removal

1 Loosen the wheel lug nuts, raise the front of the vehicle and support it securely on jackstands. Apply the parking brake and block the rear wheels to keep the vehicle from rolling off the jackstands. Remove the wheel.

2 Loosen the tie-rod end jam nut (see illustration).

3 Mark the relationship of the tie-rod end to the threaded portion of the tie-rod. This will ensure the toe-in setting is restored when reassembled (see illustration).

4 Remove the cotter pin then loosen the castellated nut from the tie-rod end ballstud a few turns. Disconnect the tie-rod end ballstud from the steering knuckle arm with a puller (see illustration).

5 Remove the nut from the ballstud, separate the tie-rod end from the steering knuckle, then unscrew the tie-rod end from the tie-rod.

Installation

6 Thread the tie-rod end onto the tie-rod to the marked position and connect the tie-rod end to the steering arm. Install the nut on the ballstud and tighten it to the torque listed in this Chapter's Specifications.

7 Install a new cotter pin through the castellated nut and bend the ends of the cotter pin up.

Note: *It may be necessary to slightly tighten the castellated nut a little to line-up the slots in the nut with the hole in the ballstud.*

8 Tighten the jam nut securely and install the wheel. Lower the vehicle and tighten the lug nuts to the torque listed in the Chapter 1 Specifications.

9 Have the front end alignment checked and, if necessary, adjusted.

16.4 Use a two-jaw puller to push the tie-rod end out of the steering knuckle

17 Steering gear - removal and installation

Removal

Warning: *Make sure the steering shaft is not turned while the steering gear is detached or you could damage the airbag system clockspring. To prevent the shaft from turning, place the ignition key in the LOCK position or thread the seat belt through the steering wheel and clip it into place.*

1 Park the vehicle with the front wheels pointing straight ahead. Loosen the front wheel lug nuts, then raise the front of the vehicle and support it securely on jackstands. Apply the parking brake and remove the wheels. Remove the under-vehicle splash shield.

2 Place a drain pan under the steering gear. Detach the power steering pressure and return lines and cap the ends to prevent excessive fluid loss and contamination.

Caution: *Use a flare-nut wrench for detaching*

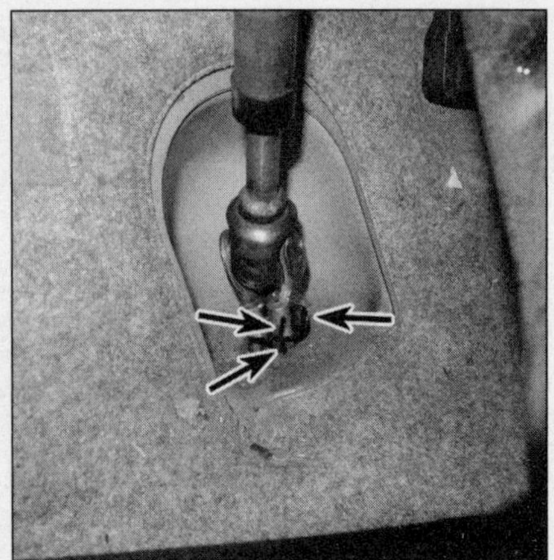

17.3 Steering column intermediate shaft pinch bolt and matchmarks

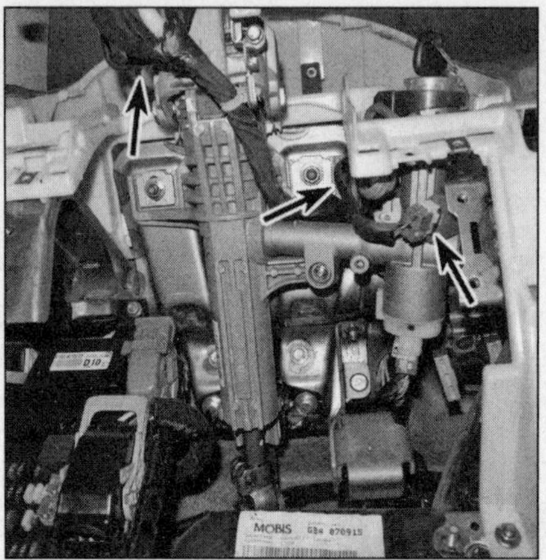

18.4 Disconnect all electrical connectors from the steering column components (not all are shown here)

18.7 Steering column mounting fasteners

the lines from the steering gear or the fittings could be damaged.

3 Mark the relationship of the intermediate shaft to the steering shaft U-joint and remove the pinch bolt (see illustration).

4 Separate the tie-rod ends from the steering knuckle arms (see Section 16).

2005 and earlier models

5 Remove the steering gear mounting fasteners.

6 Separate the intermediate shaft U-joint from the steering gear input shaft, then maneuver the steering gear down and out from the right side of the vehicle.

7 Check the steering gear bushings for excessive wear or deterioration, replacing them if necessary.

2006 and later models

8 Remove the subframe (see Section 14).

Note: *Before the subframe is removed make sure to disconnect the power steering line-to-subframe retainers. Once the subframe is lowered a few inches there is greater access to disconnect the power steering lines at the steering gear.*

9 Remove the bolts and detach the steering gear from the subframe.

Installation

10 Installation is the reverse of removal, noting the following points:

a) *Align the marks on the intermediate shaft U-joint and the steering gear input shaft. If you're installing a new steering gear, center the pinion in the center of its travel by counting the number of turns lock to lock and setting the pinion midway.*

b) *Tighten all fasteners to the torque listed in this Chapter's Specifications.*

c) *Connect the power steering pressure and return hoses to the steering gear and fill the power steering pump reservoir with the recommended fluid (see Chapter 1).*

d) *Lower the vehicle and bleed the steering system (see Section 20).*

e) *Have the alignment checked by a dealer service department or an alignment shop.*

18 Steering column - removal and installation

Warning: *These models have airbags. Always disarm the airbag system before working in the vicinity of the impact sensors, steering column, or instrument panel to avoid accidental deployment of the airbag, which could cause personal injury (see Chapter 12).*

Warning: *Do not use a memory saving device to preserve the PCM's memory when working on or near airbag system components.*

Removal

1 Park the vehicle with the wheels pointing straight ahead. Disconnect the cable from the negative terminal of the battery (see Chapter 5).

2 Remove the steering wheel (see Section 15).

Warning: *Do not move the steering shaft after the steering wheel has been removed or damage to the clockspring could occur when the vehicle is put back into service. To ensure this doesn't happen, make sure the steering column is locked.*

3 Remove the steering column covers and the lower knee bolster (see Chapter 11).

4 Disconnect all electrical connectors coming from the large harness on the side of the steering column and any ground wires that may be attached to the steering column from the other side (see illustration).

5 On 2005 and earlier models, disconnect the brake transmission shift interlock (BTSI) cable from the steering column, if equipped (see Chapter 7).

6 Mark the relationship of the intermediate shaft to the steering column coupler. Remove the pinch bolt and separate the intermediate shaft from the coupler by compressing the shaft (see illustration 17.4).

7 Remove the steering column mounting fasteners; carefully lower the column, making sure nothing is still connected, and remove it (see illustration).

Installation

8 Guide the steering column into position, then install the steering column mounting fasteners and tighten them to the torque listed in this Chapter's Specifications.

9 Connect the steering column coupler to the intermediate shaft and install the pinch bolt and nut, tightening it to the torque listed in this Chapter's Specifications.

10 The remainder of installation is the reverse of removal. Reconnect the negative battery cable (see Chapter 5).

19 Power steering pump - removal and installation

Removal

1 Disconnect the cable from the negative terminal of the battery (see Chapter 5).

2 Remove the fluid from the reservoir using a suction pump or equivalent.

Caution: *Be careful not to tear any mesh filter that may be present just under the surface of the fluid.*

3 Raise the vehicle and support it securely on jackstands.

4 Remove the drivebelt (see Chapter 1).

5 Disconnect the power steering return line hose clamp and pull the hose from the pump then cap the hose fitting at the pump (see illustration). Remove the pressure line banjo-bolt and line from the pump. Make sure to replace the banjo-bolt sealing washers and plug the lines to avoid total excessive fluid loss.

6 Remove the power steering pump mounting bolts and remove the pump.

19.5 Power steering pressure line banjo bolt (A) and return line bolts (B) (as seen from below)

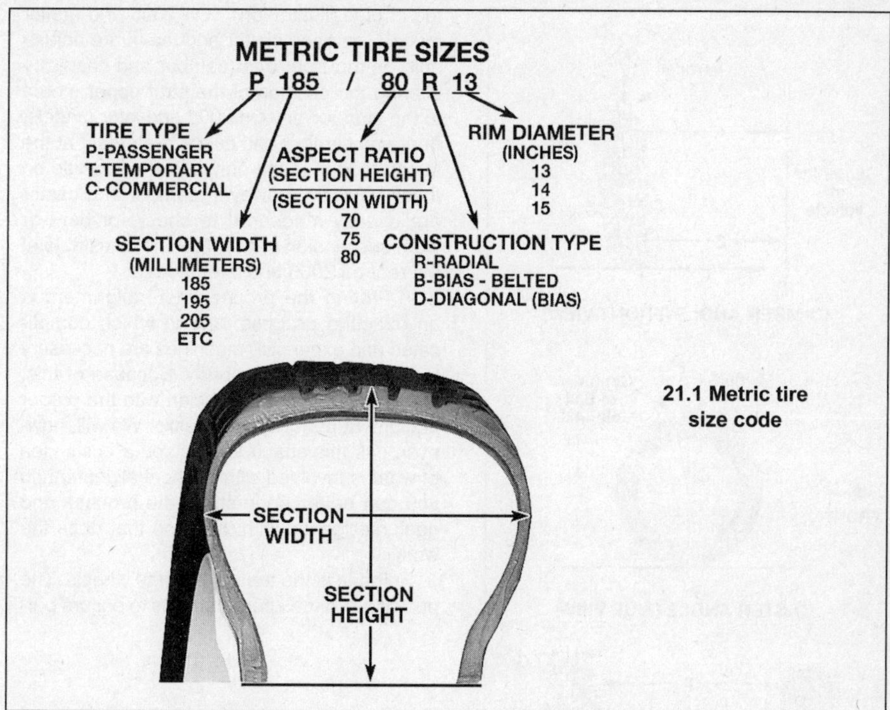

21.1 Metric tire size code

Installation

7 Installation is the reverse of removal.

8 Tighten all power steering mounting fasteners to the torque listed in this Chapter's Specifications.

9 Tighten the pressure line-to-pump banjo bolt to the torque listed in this Chapter's Specifications.

10 Make sure the hoses are properly routed and the return line hose clamp is securely tightened.

11 Fill the power steering fluid reservoir with the recommended fluid (see Chapter 1).

12 Install and adjust the drive belt (see Chapter 1).

13 Connect the negative battery cable to the battery (see Chapter 5).

14 Bleed the power steering system (see Section 20). Stop the engine, check the fluid level, and inspect the system for leaks.

20 Power steering system - bleeding

1 Following any operation in which the power steering fluid lines have been disconnected, the power steering system must be bled to remove all air and obtain proper steering performance.

2 With the front wheels in the straight ahead position, check the power steering fluid level (see Chapter 1).

3 Start the engine and allow it to run at fast idle. Recheck the fluid level and add fluid if necessary.

4 Bleed the system by turning the wheels from side to side, without hitting the stops. This will work the air out of the system. Maintain the proper fluid level as this is done.

5 When the air is worked out of the system, return the wheels to the straight ahead position and leave the vehicle running for several more minutes before shutting it off.

6 Road test the vehicle to be sure the steering system is functioning normally and noise free.

7 Recheck the fluid level to be sure it is correct. Add fluid if necessary.

21 Wheels and tires - general information

1 All vehicles covered by this manual are equipped with metric-sized fiberglass or steel belted radial tires (see illustration). Use of other size or type of tires may affect the ride and handling of the vehicle. Don't mix different types of tires, such as radials and bias belted, on the same vehicle as handling may be seriously affected. It's recommended that tires be replaced in pairs on the same axle, but if only one tire is being replaced, be sure it's the same size, structure and tread design as the other.

2 Because tire pressure has a substantial effect on handling and wear, the pressure on all tires should be checked at least once a month or before any extended trips (see Chapter 1).

3 Wheels must be replaced if they are bent, dented, leak air, have elongated bolt holes, are heavily rusted, out of vertical symmetry or if the lug nuts won't stay tight. Wheel repairs that use welding or peening are not recommended.

4 Tire and wheel balance is important in the overall handling, braking and performance of the vehicle. Unbalanced wheels can adversely affect handling and ride characteristics as well as tire life. Whenever a tire is installed on a wheel, the tire and wheel should be balanced by a shop with the proper equipment.

22 Wheel alignment - general information

1 A wheel alignment refers to the adjustments made to the wheels so they are in proper angular relationship to the suspension and the ground. Wheels that are out of proper alignment not only affect vehicle control, but also increase tire wear. The angles normally measured are camber, caster and

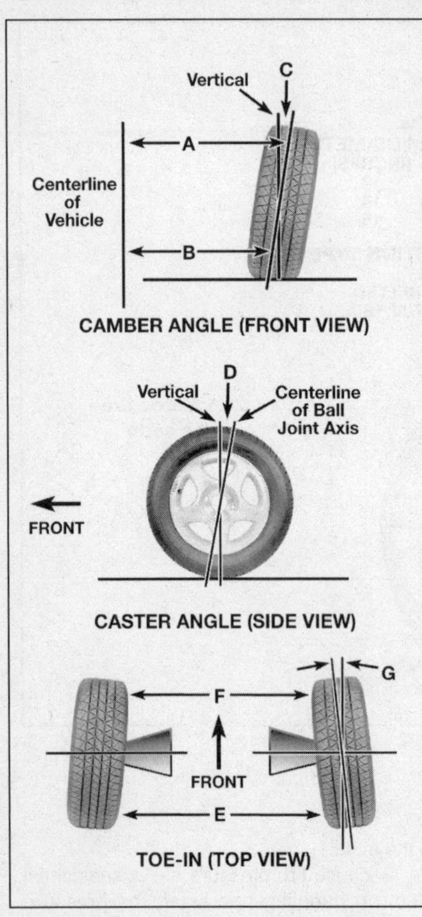

22.1 Camber, caster and toe-in angles

A minus B = C (degrees camber)
D = degrees caster
E minus F = toe-in (measured in inches)
G = toe-in (expressed in degrees)

toe-in (see illustration). On 2005 and earlier models, camber, caster and toe-in are adjustable on the front end (camber and caster by altering the position of the strut upper mount to the strut tower). On 2006 and later models, front-end camber and caster are preset at the factory; toe-in is the only adjustable angle on these vehicles (however, camber and caster are usually measured to check for bent or worn suspension parts). Toe-inis adjustable at the rear on 2006 and later models.

2 Getting the proper wheel alignment is an exacting process, one in which complicated and expensive machines are necessary to perform the job properly. Because of this, you should have a technician with the proper equipment perform these tasks. We will, however, use this space to give you a basic idea of what is involved with a wheel alignment so you can better understand the process and deal intelligently with the shop that does the work.

3 Toe-in is the turning in of the wheels. The purpose of a toe specification is to ensure parallel rolling of the wheels. In a vehicle with zero toe-in, the distance between the front edges of the wheels will be the same as the distance between the rear edges of the wheels. The actual amount of toe-in is normally only a fraction of an inch. Incorrect toe-in will cause the tires to wear improperly by making them scrub against the road surface.

4 Camber is the tilting of the wheels from vertical when viewed from one end of the vehicle. When the wheels tilt out at the top, the camber is said to be positive (+). When the wheels tilt in at the top the camber is negative (-). The amount of tilt is measured in degrees from vertical and this measurement is called the camber angle. This angle affects the amount of tire tread which contacts the road and compensates for changes in the suspension geometry when the vehicle is cornering or traveling over an undulating surface.

5 Caster is the tilting of the front steering axis from the vertical. A tilt toward the rear is positive caster and a tilt toward the front is negative caster.

Notes

Notes

Chapter 11 Body

Contents

	Section
Body repair - major damage	4
Body repair - minor damage	3
Bumper covers - removal and installation	10
Center floor console - removal and installation	27
Cowl cover - removal and installation	12
Dashboard trim panels - removal and installation	23
Door - removal and installation	14
Door module, latch, lock and handle - removal and installation	16
Door trim panels - removal and installation	13
Door window glass - removal and installation	17
Fastener and trim removal	6
Front fender - removal and installation	11
General information	1
Hood - removal, installation and adjustment	7
Hood and liftgate struts - replacement	15
Hood latch and cable - removal and installation	8
Instrument panel - removal and installation	24
Mirrors - removal and installation	20
Overhead console - removal and installation	21
Power liftgate motor assembly - removal and installation	28
Quarter window glass - removal and installation	18
Radiator grille - removal and installation	9
Rear trim panels - removal and installation	25
Repair minor paint scratches	2
Seats - removal and installation	26
Steering column covers - removal and installation	22
Upholstery, carpets and vinyl trim - maintenance	5
Window glass regulators - removal and installation	19

Specifications

Torque specifications	Ft-lbs (unless otherwise indicated)	Nm
Seat belt mounting bolts	29 ft-lbs	39

1 General information

Warning: *The models covered by this manual are equipped with Supplemental Restraint Systems (SRS), more commonly known as airbags. Always disable the airbag system before working in the vicinity of any airbag system components to avoid the possibility of accidental deployment of the airbags, which could cause personal injury (see Chapter 12).*

Certain body components are particularly vulnerable to accident damage and can be unbolted and repaired or replaced. Among these parts are the hood, doors, tailgate, liftgate, bumpers and front fenders.

Only general body maintenance practices and body panel repair procedures within the scope of the do-it-yourselfer are included in this Chapter.

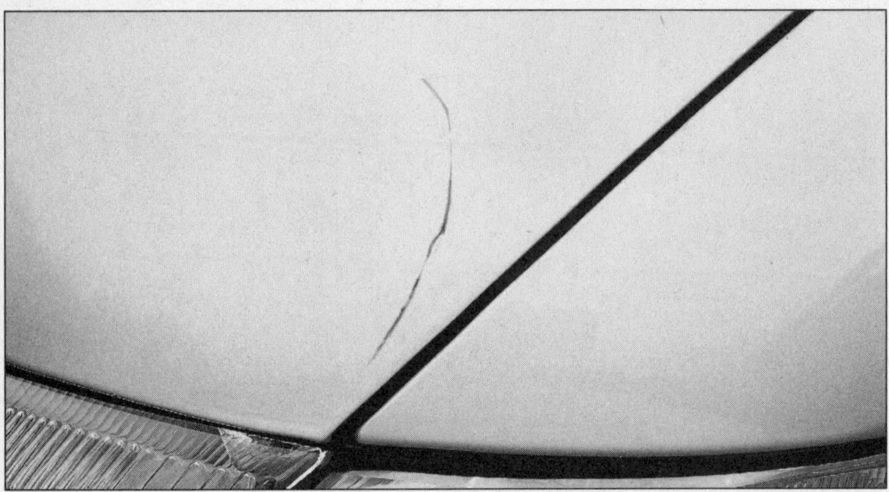

Make sure the damaged area is perfectly clean and rust free. If the touch-up kit has a wire brush, use it to clean the scratch or chip. Or use fine steel wool wrapped around the end of a pencil. Clean the scratched or chipped surface only, not the good paint surrounding it. Rinse the area with water and allow it to dry thoroughly

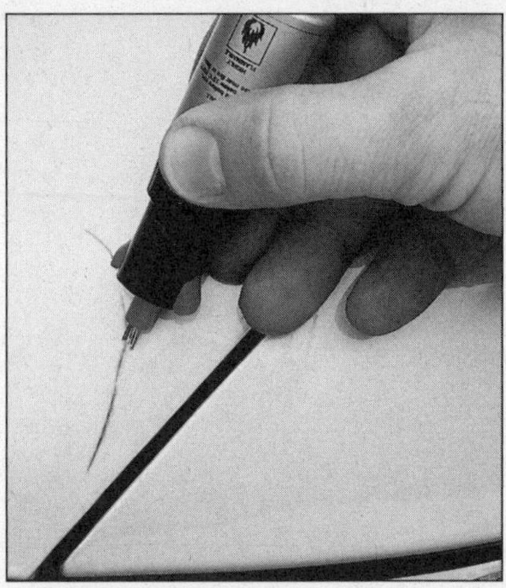

Thoroughly mix the paint, then apply a small amount with the touch-up kit brush or a very fine artist's brush. Brush in one direction as you fill the scratch area. Do not build up the paint higher than the surrounding paint

2 Repair minor paint scratches

No matter how hard you try to keep your vehicle looking like new, it will inevitably be scratched, chipped or dented at some point. If the metal is actually dented, seek the advice of a professional. But you can fix minor scratches and chips yourself. Buy a touch-up paint kit from a dealer parts department or an auto parts store. To ensure that you get the right color, you'll need to have the specific make, model and year of your vehicle and, ideally, the paint code, which is located on a special metal plate under the hood or in the door jamb.

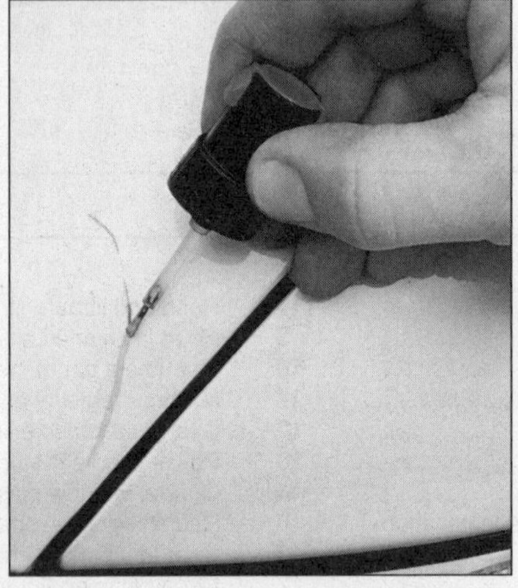

If the vehicle has a two-coat finish, apply the clear coat after the color coat has dried

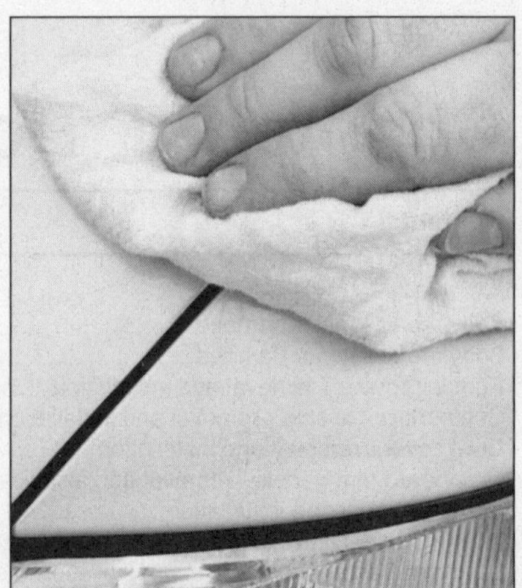

Wait a few days for the paint to dry thoroughly, then rub out the repainted area with a polishing compound to blend the new paint with the surrounding area. When you're happy with your work, wash and polish the area

3 Body repair - minor damage

Plastic body panels

The following repair procedures are for minor scratches and gouges. Repair of more serious damage should be left to a dealer service department or qualified auto body shop. Below is a list of the equipment and materials necessary to perform the following repair procedures on plastic body panels.

Wax, grease and silicone removing solvent
Cloth-backed body tape
Sanding discs
Drill motor with three-inch disc holder
Hand sanding block
Rubber squeegees
Sandpaper
Non-porous mixing palette
Wood paddle or putty knife
Curved-tooth body file
Flexible parts repair material

Flexible panels (bumper trim)

1 Remove the damaged panel, if necessary or desirable. In most cases, repairs can be carried out with the panel installed.

2 Clean the area(s) to be repaired with a wax, grease and silicone removing solvent applied with a water-dampened cloth.

3 If the damage is structural, that is, if it extends through the panel, clean the backside of the panel area to be repaired as well. Wipe dry.

4 Sand the rear surface about 1-1/2 inches beyond the break.

5 Cut two pieces of fiberglass cloth large enough to overlap the break by about 1-1/2 inches. Cut only to the required length.

6 Mix the adhesive from the repair kit according to the instructions included with the kit, and apply a layer of the mixture approximately 1/8-inch thick on the backside of the panel. Overlap the break by at least 1-1/2 inches.

7 Apply one piece of fiberglass cloth to the adhesive and cover the cloth with additional adhesive. Apply a second piece of fiberglass cloth to the adhesive and immediately cover the cloth with additional adhesive in sufficient quantity to fill the weave.

8 Allow the repair to cure for 20 to 30 minutes at 60-degrees to 80-degrees F.

9 If necessary, trim the excess repair material at the edge.

10 Remove all of the paint film over and around the area(s) to be repaired. The repair material should not overlap the painted surface.

11 With a drill motor and a sanding disc (or a rotary file), cut a "V" along the break line approximately 1/2-inch wide. Remove all dust and loose particles from the repair area.

12 Mix and apply the repair material. Apply a light coat first over the damaged area; then continue applying material until it reaches a level

slightly higher than the surrounding finish.

13 Cure the mixture for 20 to 30 minutes at 60-degrees to 80-degrees F.

14 Roughly establish the contour of the area being repaired with a body file. If low areas or pits remain, mix and apply additional adhesive.

15 Block sand the damaged area with sandpaper to establish the actual contour of the surrounding surface.

16 If desired, the repaired area can be temporarily protected with several light coats of primer. Because of the special paints and techniques required for flexible body panels, it is recommended that the vehicle be taken to a paint shop for completion of the body repair.

Steel body panels

See photo sequence

Repair of dents

17 When repairing dents, the first job is to pull the dent out until the affected area is as close as possible to its original shape. There is no point in trying to restore the original shape completely as the metal in the damaged area will have stretched on impact and cannot be restored to its original contours. It is better to bring the level of the dent up to a point that is about 1/8-inch below the level of the surrounding metal. In cases where the dent is very shallow, it is not worth trying to pull it out at all.

18 If the backside of the dent is accessible, it can be hammered out gently from behind using a soft-face hammer. While doing this, hold a block of wood firmly against the opposite side of the metal to absorb the hammer blows and prevent the metal from being stretched.

19 If the dent is in a section of the body which has double layers, or some other factor makes it inaccessible from behind, a different technique is required. Drill several small holes through the metal inside the damaged area, particularly in the deeper sections. Screw long, self-tapping screws into the holes just enough for them to get a good grip in the metal. Now pulling on the protruding heads of the screws with locking pliers can pull out the dent.

20 The next stage of repair is the removal of paint from the damaged area and from an inch or so of the surrounding metal. This is easily done with a wire brush or sanding disk in a drill motor, although it can be done just as effectively by hand with sandpaper. To complete the preparation for filling, score the surface of the bare metal with a screwdriver or the tang of a file or drill small holes in the affected area. This will provide a good grip for the filler material. To complete the repair, see the Section on filling and painting.

Repair of rust holes or gashes

21 Remove all paint from the affected area and from an inch or so of the surrounding metal using a sanding disk or wire brush mounted in a drill motor. If these are not available, a few sheets of sandpaper will do the job just as effectively.

22 With the paint removed, you will be able to determine the severity of the corrosion and decide whether to replace the whole panel, if possible, or repair the affected area. New body panels are not as expensive as most people think and it is often quicker to install a new panel than to repair large areas of rust.

23 Remove all trim pieces from the affected area except those which will act as a guide to the original shape of the damaged body, such as headlight shells, etc. Using metal snips or a hacksaw blade, remove all loose metal and any other metal that is badly affected by rust. Hammer the edges of the hole in to create a slight depression for the filler material.

24 Wire-brush the affected area to remove the powdery rust from the surface of the metal. If the back of the rusted area is accessible, treat it with rust inhibiting paint.

25 Before filling is done, block the hole in some way. This can be done with sheet metal riveted or screwed into place, or by stuffing the hole with wire mesh.

26 Once the hole is blocked off, the affected area can be filled and painted. See the following subsection on filling and painting.

Filling and painting

27 Many types of body fillers are available, but generally speaking, body repair kits which contain filler paste and a tube of resin hardener are best for this type of repair work. A wide, flexible plastic or nylon applicator will be necessary for imparting a smooth and contoured finish to the surface of the filler material. Mix up a small amount of filler on a clean piece of wood or cardboard (use the hardener sparingly). Follow the manufacturer's instructions on the package, otherwise the filler will set incorrectly.

28 Using the applicator, apply the filler paste to the prepared area. Draw the applicator across the surface of the filler to achieve the desired contour and to level the filler surface. As soon as a contour that approximates the original one is achieved, stop working the paste. If you continue, the paste will begin to stick to the applicator. Continue to add thin layers of paste at 20-minute intervals until the level of the filler is just above the surrounding metal.

29 Once the filler has hardened, the excess can be removed with a body file. From then on, progressively finer grades of sandpaper should be used, starting with a 180-grit paper and finishing with 600-grit wet-or-dry paper. Always wrap the sandpaper around a flat rubber or wooden block, otherwise the surface of the filler will not be completely flat. During the sanding of the filler surface, the wet-or-dry paper should be periodically rinsed in water. This will ensure that a very smooth finish is produced in the final stage.

30 At this point, the repair area should be surrounded by a ring of bare metal, which in turn should be encircled by the finely feathered edge of good paint. Rinse the repair area with clean water until all of the dust produced by the sanding operation is gone.

31 Spray the entire area with a light coat of primer. This will reveal any imperfections in the surface of the filler. Repair the imperfections with fresh filler paste or glaze filler and once more smooth the surface with sandpaper. Repeat this spray-and-repair procedure until you are satisfied that the surface of the filler and the feathered edge of the paint are perfect. Rinse the area with clean water and allow it to dry completely.

32 The repair area is now ready for painting. Spray painting must be carried out in a warm, dry, windless and dust free atmosphere. These conditions can be created if you have access to a large indoor work area, but if you are forced to work in the open, you will have to pick the day very carefully. If you are working indoors, dousing the floor in the work area with water will help settle the dust that would otherwise be in the air. If the repair area is confined to one body panel, mask off the surrounding panels. This will help minimize the effects of a slight mismatch in paint color. Trim pieces such as chrome strips, door handles, etc., will also need to be masked off or removed. Use masking tape and several thickness of newspaper for the masking operations.

33 Before spraying, shake the paint can thoroughly, then spray a test area until the spray painting technique is mastered. Cover the repair area with a thick coat of primer. The thickness should be built up using several thin layers of primer rather than one thick one. Using 600-grit wet-or-dry sandpaper, rub down the surface of the primer until it is very smooth. While doing this, the work area should be thoroughly rinsed with water and the wet-or-dry sandpaper periodically rinsed as well. Allow the primer to dry before spraying additional coats.

34 Spray on the top coat, again building up the thickness by using several thin layers of paint. Begin spraying in the center of the repair area and then, using a circular motion, work out until the whole repair area and about two inches of the surrounding original paint is covered. Remove all masking material 10 to 15 minutes after spraying on the final coat of paint. Allow the new paint at least two weeks to harden, then use a very fine rubbing compound to blend the edges of the new paint into the existing paint. Finally, apply a coat of wax

4 Body repair - major damage

1 Major damage must be repaired by an auto body shop specifically equipped to perform body and frame repairs. These shops have the specialized equipment required to do the job properly.

2 If the damage is extensive, the frame must be checked for proper alignment or the vehicle's handling characteristics may be adversely affected and other components may wear at an accelerated rate.

3 Due to the fact that all of the major body components (hood, fenders, etc.) are separate and replaceable units, any seriously damaged components should be replaced rather than repaired. Sometimes the components can be found in a wrecking yard that specializes in used vehicle components, often at considerable savings over the cost of new parts.

These photos illustrate a method of repairing simple dents. They are intended to supplement *Body repair - minor damage* in this Chapter and should not be used as the sole instructions for body repair on these vehicles.

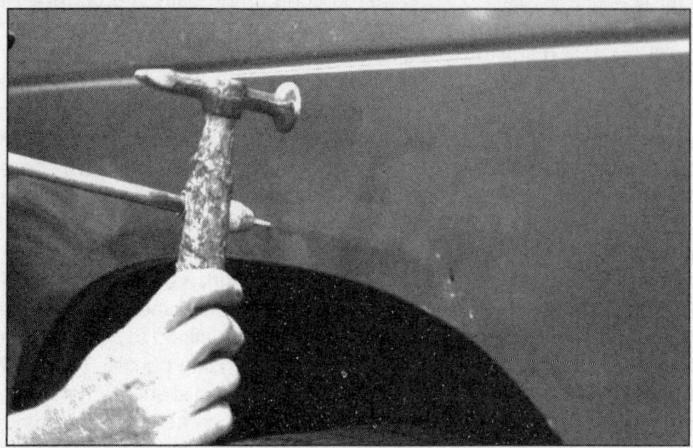

1 If you can't access the backside of the body panel to hammer out the dent, pull it out with a slide-hammer-type dent puller. Tap with a hammer near the edge of the dent to help 'pop' the metal back to its original shape, about 1/8-inch below the surface of the surrounding metal

2 Using coarse-grit sandpaper, remove the paint down to the bare metal. Clean the repair area with wax/silicone remover.

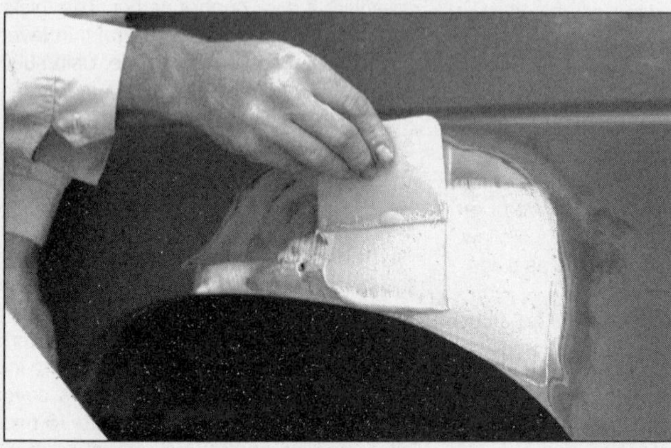

3 Following label instructions, mix up a batch of plastic filler and hardener, then quickly press it into the metal with a plastic applicator. Work the filler until it matches the original contour and is slightly above the surrounding metal

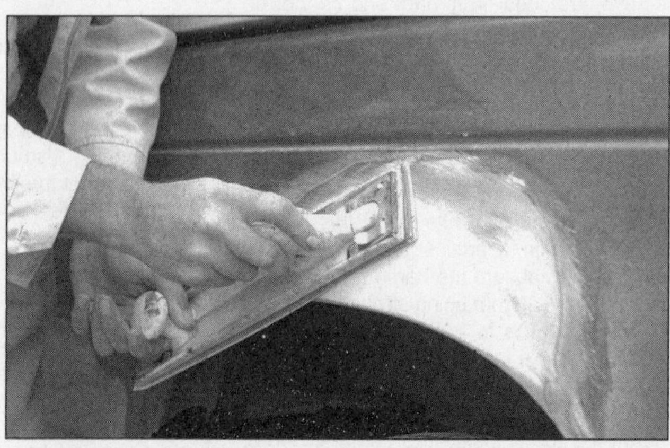

4 Let the filler harden until you can just dent it with your fingernail. File, then sand the filler down until it's smooth and even. Work down to finer grits of sandpaper - always using a board or block - ending up with 360 or 400 grit

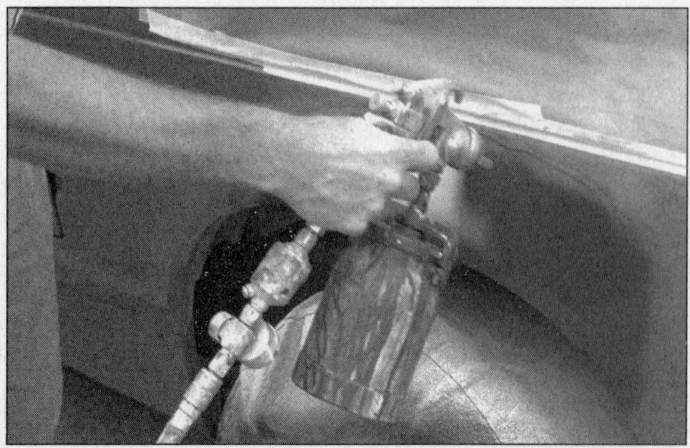

5 When the area is smooth to the touch, clean the area and mask around it. Apply several layers of primer to the area. A professional-type spray gun is being used here, but aerosol spray primer works fine

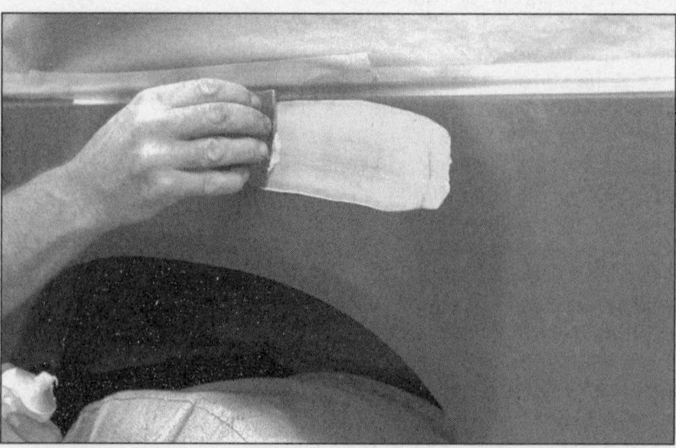

6 Fill imperfections or scratches with glazing compound. Sand with 360 or 400-grit and re-spray. Finish sand the primer with 600 grit, clean thoroughly, then apply the finish coat. Don't attempt to rub out or wax the repair area until the paint has dried completely (at least two weeks)

5 Upholstery, carpets and vinyl trim - maintenance

Upholstery and carpets

1 Every three months remove the floormats and clean the interior of the vehicle (more frequently if necessary). Use a stiff whiskbroom to brush the carpeting and loosen dirt and dust, then vacuum the upholstery and carpets thoroughly, especially along seams and crevices.

2 Dirt and stains can be removed from carpeting with basic household or automotive carpet shampoos available in spray cans. Follow the directions and vacuum again, then use a stiff brush to bring back the "nap" of the carpet.

3 Most interiors have cloth or vinyl upholstery, either of which can be cleaned and maintained with a number of material-specific cleaners or shampoos available in auto supply stores. Follow the directions on the product for usage, and always spot-test any upholstery cleaner on an inconspicuous area (bottom edge of a backseat cushion) to ensure that it doesn't cause a color shift in the material.

4 After cleaning, vinyl upholstery should be treated with a protectant. **Note:** *Make sure the protectant container indicates the product can be used on seats - some products may make a seat too slippery.* **Caution:** *Do not use protectant on vinyl-covered steering wheels.*

5 Leather upholstery requires special care. It should be cleaned regularly with saddlesoap or leather cleaner. Never use alcohol, gasoline, nail polish remover or thinner to clean leather upholstery.

6 After cleaning, regularly treat leather upholstery with a leather conditioner, rubbed in with a soft cotton cloth. Never use car wax on leather upholstery.

7 In areas where the interior of the vehicle is subject to bright sunlight, cover leather seating areas of the seats with a sheet if the vehicle is to be left out for any length of time.

Vinyl trim

8 Don't clean vinyl trim with detergents, caustic soap or petroleum-based cleaners. Plain soap and water works just fine, with a soft brush to clean dirt that may be ingrained. Wash the vinyl as frequently as the rest of the vehicle.

9 After cleaning, application of a high-quality rubber and vinyl protectant will help prevent oxidation and cracks. The protectant can also be applied to weather-stripping, vacuum lines and rubber hoses, which often fail as a result of chemical degradation, and to the tires.

6 Fastener and trim removal

Refer to illustration 6.4

1 There is a variety of plastic fasteners used to hold trim panels, splash shields and other parts in place in addition to typical screws, nuts and bolts. Once you are familiar with them, they can usually be removed without too much difficulty.

2 The proper tools and approach can prevent added time and expense to a project by minimizing the number of broken fasteners and/or parts.

3 The following illustration shows various types of fasteners that are typically used on most vehicles and how to remove and install them **(see illustration)**. Replacement fasten-

Fasteners

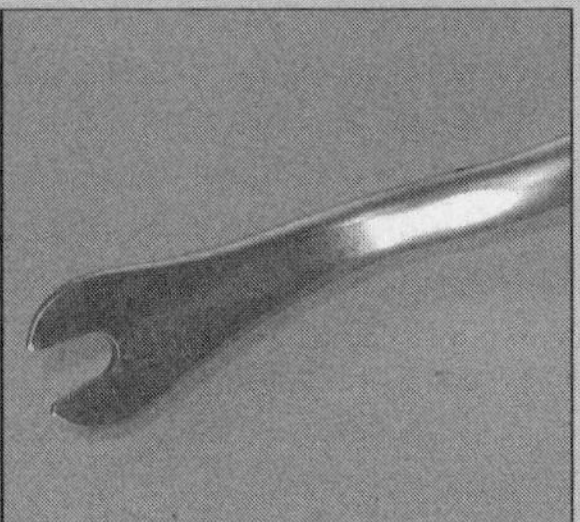

This tool is designed to remove special fasteners. A small pry tool used for removing nails will also work well in place of this tool

A Phillips head screwdriver can be used to release the center portion, but light pressure must be used because the plastic is easily damaged. Once the center is up, the fastener can easily be pried from its hole

Here is a view with the center portion fully released. Install the fastener as shown, then press the center in to set it

This fastener is used for exterior panels and shields. The center portion must be pried up to release the fastener. Install the fastener with the center up, then press the center in to set it

This type of fastener is used commonly for interior panels. Use a small blunt tool to press the small pin at the center in to release it . . .

. . . the pin will stay with the fastener in the released position

Reset the fastener for installation by moving the pin out. Install the fastener, then press the pin flush with the fastener to set it

This fastener is used for exterior and interior panels. It has no moving parts. Simply pry the fastener from its hole like the claw of a hammer removes a nail. Without a tool that can get under the top of the fastener, it can be very difficult to remove

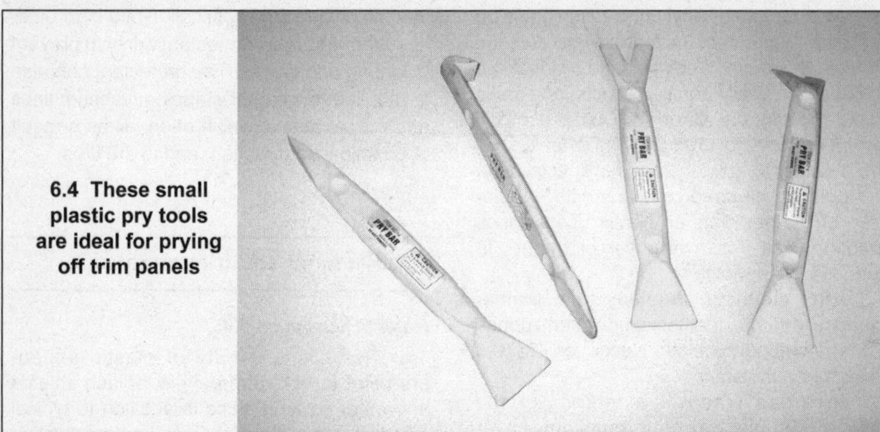

6.4 These small plastic pry tools are ideal for prying off trim panels

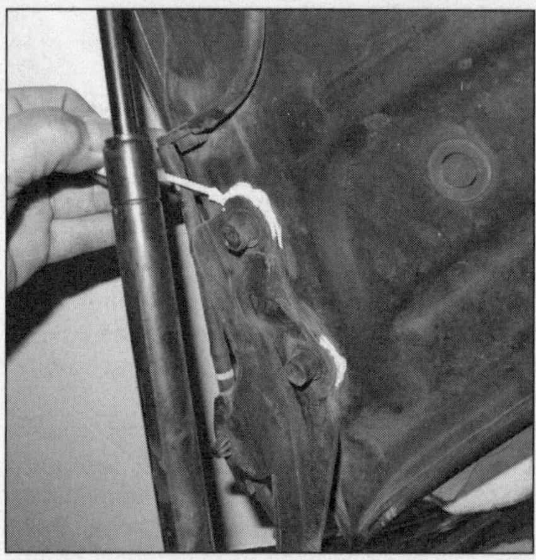

7.2 Mark the hinge plate and bolt head locations and loosen the bolts for latch adjustment or removal

ers are commonly found at most auto parts stores, if necessary.

4 Trim panels are typically made of plastic and their flexibility can help during removal. The key to their removal is to use a tool to pry the panel near its retainers to release it without damaging surrounding areas or breaking-off any retainers. The retainers will usually snap out of their designated slot or hole after force is applied to them. Stiff plastic tools designed for prying on trim panels are available at most auto parts stores (see illustration). Tools that are tapered and wrapped in protective tape, such as a screwdriver or small pry tool, are also very effective when used with care.

7 Hood - removal, installation and adjustment

Note: *The hood is heavy and somewhat awkward to remove and install - at least two people should perform this procedure.*

Removal and installation

1 Use blankets or pads to cover the cowl area of the body and the fenders. This will protect the body and paint as the hood is lifted off.

2 Scribe alignment marks around the bolt heads and hinge attachment locations to insure proper alignment during installation - a permanent-type felt-tip marker also will work for this (see illustration).

3 Remove the top bolts holding the hood to the hinge and loosen the bottom bolts until they can be removed by hand.

4 Have an assistant on the opposite side of the vehicle support the weight of the hood. On 2006 and later models, disconnect the support struts from the ball studs and lay the supports down. Take turns removing the hinge-to-hood bolts and lift off the hood (see illustration).

5 Installation is the reverse of removal.

Adjustment

6 Front-and-back and side-to-side adjustment of the hood is done by moving the hood in relation to the hinge plate after loosening the bolts.

7 Scribe or trace a line around the entire hinge plate so you can judge the amount of movement.

8 Loosen the bolts or nuts and move the hood into correct alignment. Move it only a little at a time. Tighten the hinge bolts or nuts and carefully lower the hood to check the alignment.

9 Adjust the hood bumpers on the radiator support or fenders so the hood is flush with the fenders when closed (see illustration).

10 Mark the hood latch as a guide for adjustment (or removal and replacement). The hood latch assembly can also be adjusted up-and-down and side-to-side after loosening the bolts (see Section 8).

11 The hood latch assembly, as well as the hinges, should be periodically lubricated with white lithium-base grease to prevent sticking and wear.

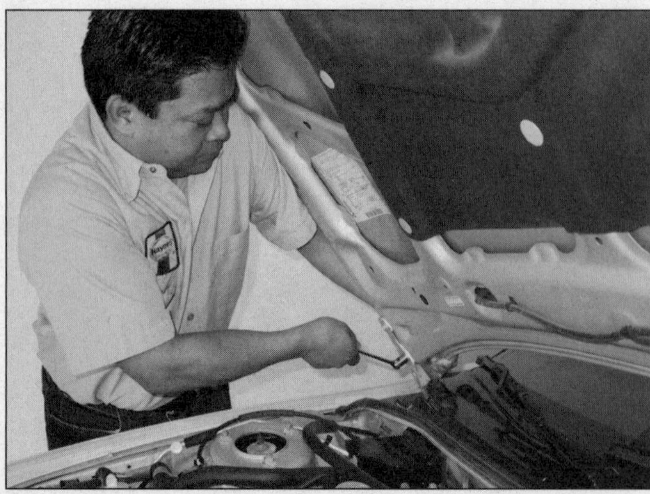

7.4 Support the hood with your shoulder while removing the hood bolts

7.9 Adjust the hood height by screwing the hood bumpers in or out

8.1 Radiator support trim panel plastic fastener locations

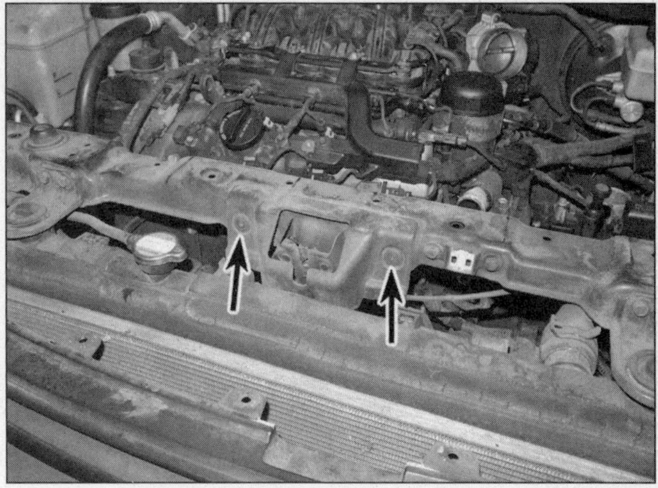

8.2 Hood latch trim panel fastener locations

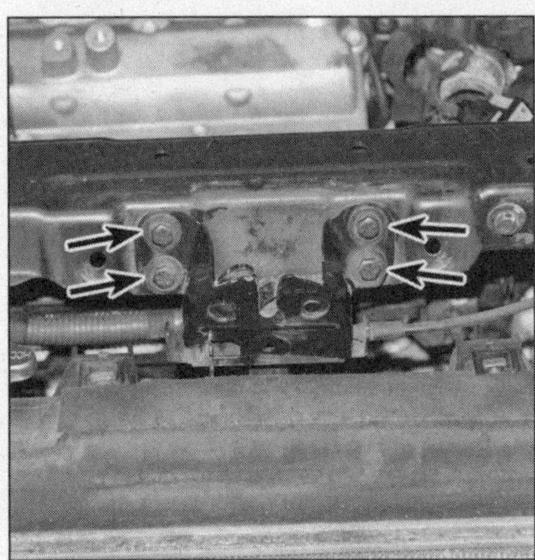

8.3 Hood latch mounting bolt locations

8.6 Detach the cable end (A) and cable body (B) from the latch lever

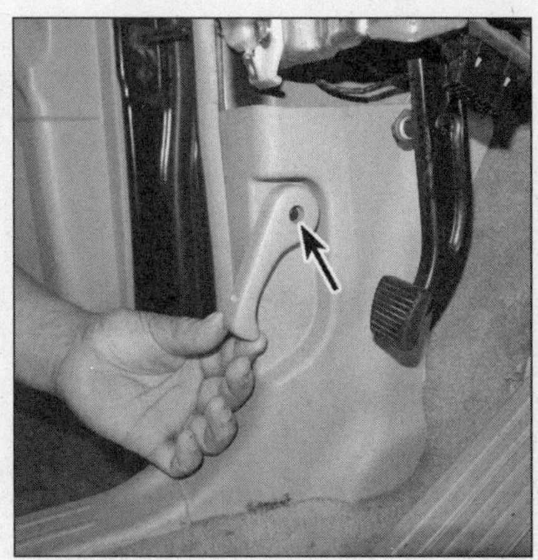

8.9a Remove the center screw and release handle. . .

8 Hood latch and cable - removal and installation

Latch

1 Remove the radiator support trim panel fasteners and panel (see illustration), if equipped.

2 On 2006 and later models, remove the hood latch trim cover plastic fasteners (see illustration) and cover.

3 Remove the bolts holding the hood latch to the radiator support and detach the latch assembly (see illustration).

4 Detach the hood release cable (see Step 6), then remove the latch from the radiator support.

5 Installation is the reverse of removal.

Cable

6 Release the cable end, then slide the cable case end sideways in the keyhole slot of the hood latch while pinching the barb on the cable case closed (see illustration).

7 Remove the cable from the latch.

8 On 2005 and earlier models, working in the passenger compartment, remove the screws and detach the hood release cable and handle assembly from the instrument panel.

9 On 2006 and later models, working in the passenger compartment, remove the center screw on the release handle and slide the handle off. Remove the kick panel (see Section 23), then detach the hood release cable and handle assembly. Detach the cable end from the hood release handle(see illustrations).

10 Under the dash remove the rubber cable insulator from the hole in the dash panel.

11 Connect a string or piece of wire to the engine compartment end of the cable, then detach the cable and pull it through the firewall into the passenger compartment.

12 Connect the string or wire to the new cable and pull it through the firewall into the engine compartment.

13 The remainder of installation is the reverse of removal.

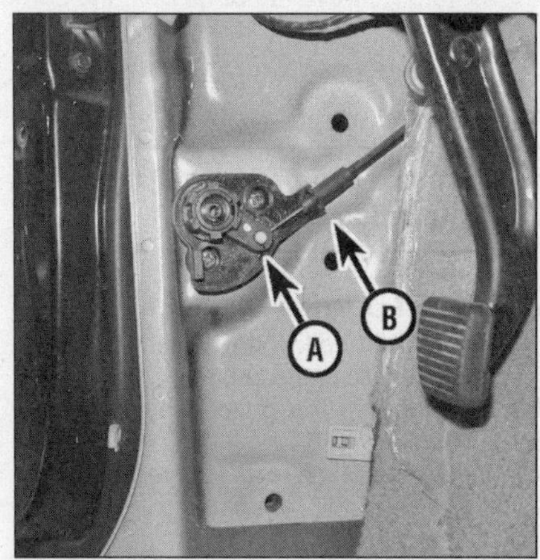

8.9b Detach the cable end (A) and cable body (B) from the hood release lever

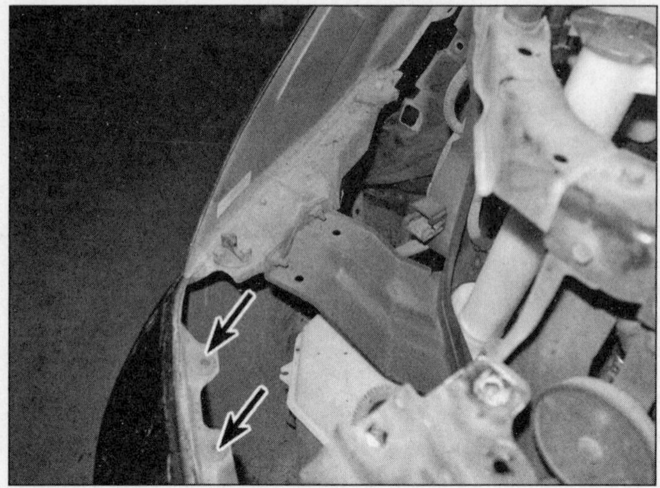

10.5a On 2006 and later models, remove the fasteners along the top of the bumper cover

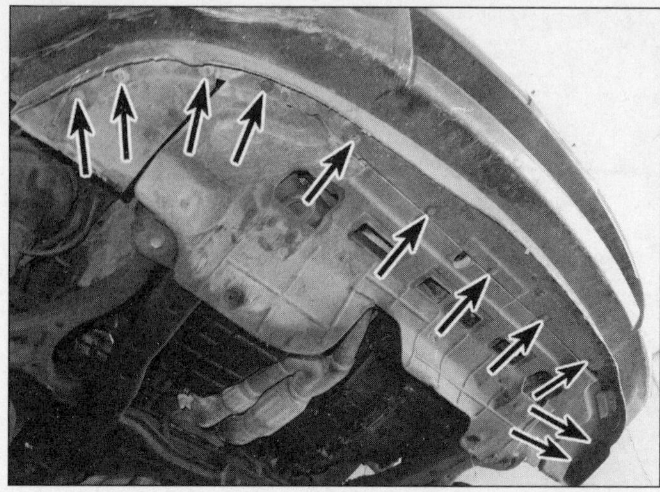

10.5b Remove the fasteners along the bottom of the bumper cover

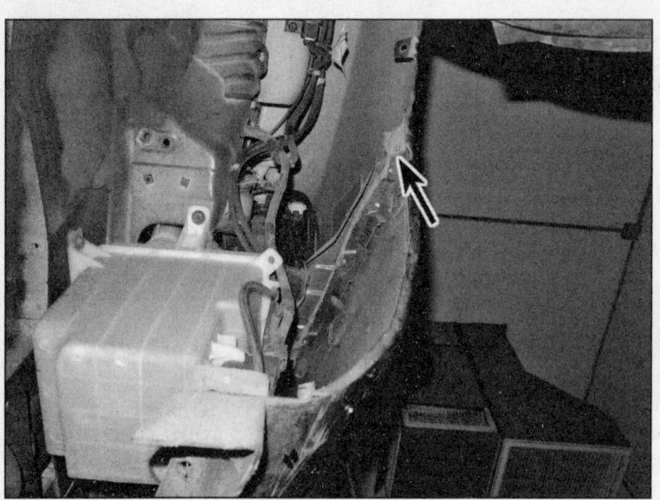

10.6 Remove the bolts from the corners of the cover

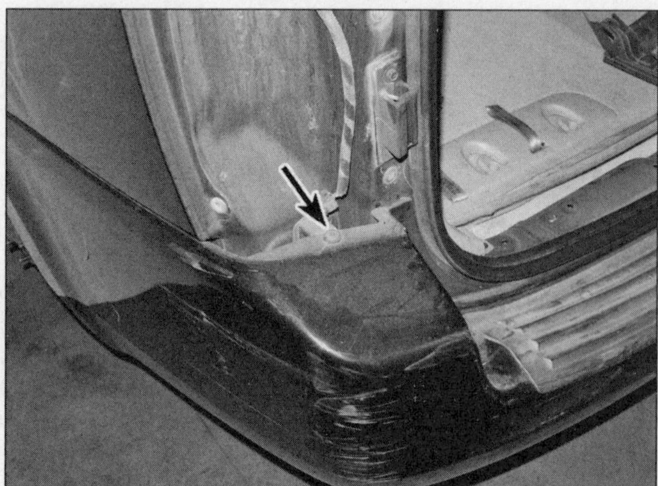

10.14 Remove the rear bumper cover upper mounting fastener from each side

9 Radiator grille - removal and installation

2005 and earlier models

1 Open the hood, then detach the clips securing the grille to the hood.

2 Carefully lift the grille away from the hood.

3 Installation is the reverse of removal.

2006 and later models

4 Remove the bumper cover (see Section 10).

5 Remove the grille retaining fasteners from the backside of the bumper cover and detach the grille from the bumper cover.

6 Installation is the reverse of removal.

10 Bumper covers - removal and installation

Front bumper cover

1 Release the hood latch and open the hood.

2 Remove the headlight housings (see Chapter 12).

3 Raise the vehicle and support it securely on jackstands.

4 Remove the inner fenderwell splash shield (see Section 11).

5 Remove the fasteners securing the top and bottom of the bumper cover (see illustrations).

6 Remove the fasteners securing the corners of the bumper cover to the fenders (see illustration).

7 On 2005 and earlier models, remove the fasteners securing the top center section of the bumper cover and remove the cover from the bumper reinforcement.

8 Disconnect the fog light/parking and turn signal light electrical connector, if necessary.

9 Remove the bumper cover from the vehicle.

10 Installation is the reverse of removal.

Rear bumper cover

11 Open the liftgate.

12 Remove the taillight assemblies (see Chapter 12).

13 Raise the vehicle and support it securely on jackstands.

14 Remove the upper mounting fasteners (see illustration).

15 Remove the fasteners securing the bot-

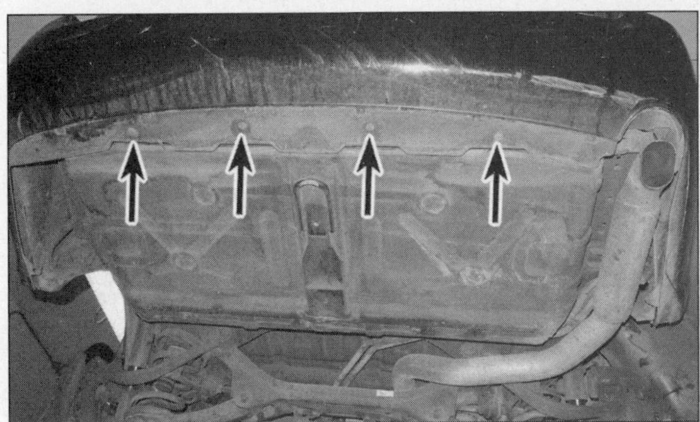

10.15a Remove the rear bumper cover lower mounting fasteners. . .

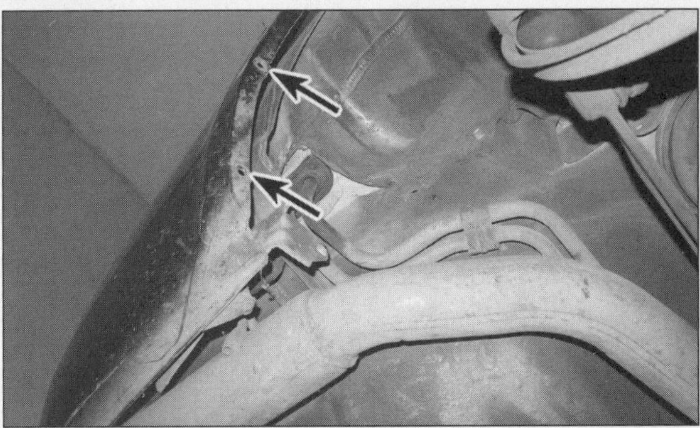

10.15b. . . and the fasteners in the wheel well

11.2 Remove the fender inner splash shield mounting fasteners

11.6 Fender front mounting bolt locations

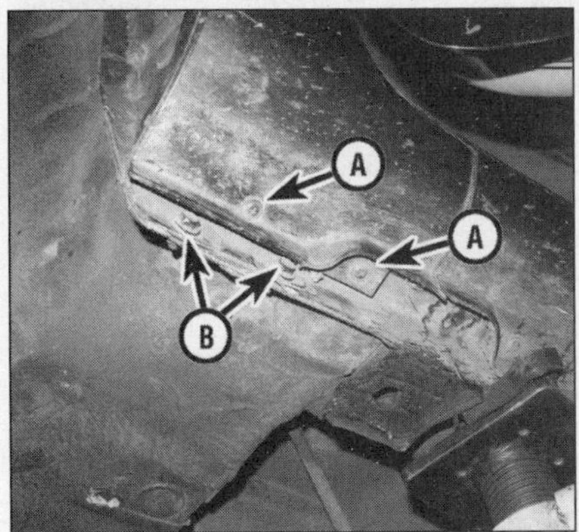

11.7a Remove the fender-to-rocker panel cover fasteners (A) and panel, then remove the fasteners (B) securing the fender to the body

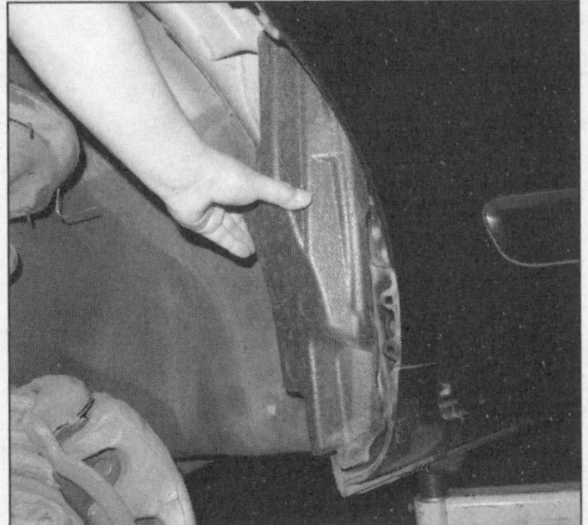

11.7b Working inside the inner fenderwell, remove the insulator. . .

11.7c. . . then the fender-to-door panel bolt

tom of the bumper cover (see illustrations).

16 Disconnect the parking assist electrical connector, if equipped.

17 Release the hooks on the sides of the bumper cover from the tabs in the rear cover brackets.

18 Remove the rear bumper cover from the vehicle.

19 Installation is the reverse of removal.

11 Front fender - removal and installation

1 Loosen the wheel lug nuts. Raise the vehicle and support it securely on jackstands, then remove the front wheel.

2 Remove the fasteners retaining the fender inner splash shield (see illustration).

3 Remove the headlight housing (see Chapter 12).

4 Remove the front bumper cover (see Section 10).

5 Remove the mud guard fasteners and guards from the lower section of the fender.

6 Remove the fender front mounting bolts (see illustration).

7 Remove the fender-to-rocker panel bolt and the fender-to-door pillar bolt (see illustrations).

11.8 Remove the fender upper mounting bolts and lift off the fender

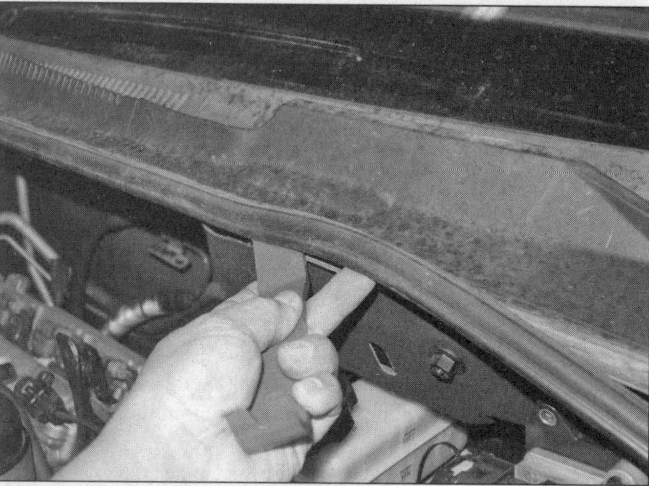
12.2 Use a trim tool to separate the weather strip from the cowl

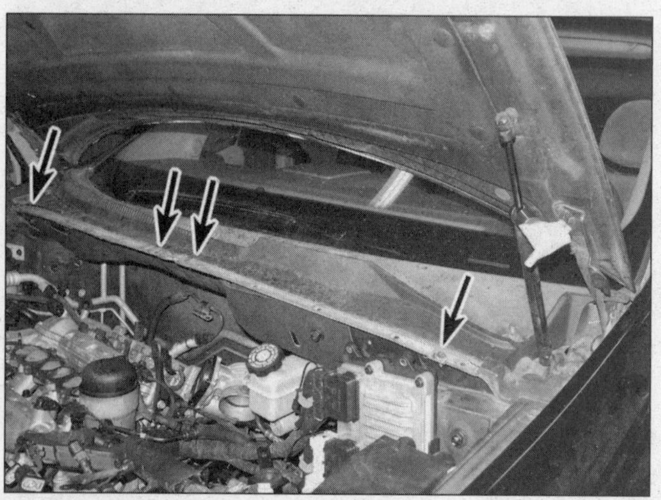
12.3 Cowl cover mounting fastener locations

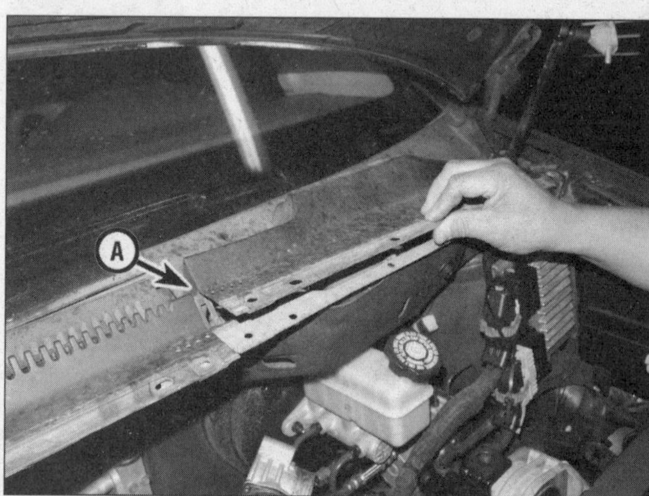

12.4a Disengage the clip (A) on the left-side cowl cover from the right side and lift cover off the vehicle. . .

8 Remove the remaining fender mounting bolts (see illustration).

9 Detach the fender. It's a good idea to have an assistant support the fender while it's being moved away from the vehicle to prevent damage to the surrounding body panels. If you're removing the right-side fender, disconnect the antenna cable (see Chapter 12).

10 Installation is the reverse of removal.

12 Cowl cover - removal and installation

1 Remove the windshield wiper arms (see Chapter 12).

2 Remove the weatherstrip (see illustration).

3 Disengage the plastic fasteners that hold the two cowl covers to the body (see illustration).

4 Remove the left side of the cowl cover first, then the right side cowl cover (see illustrations).

5 Installation is the reverse of removal.

12.4b. . . then remove the right side

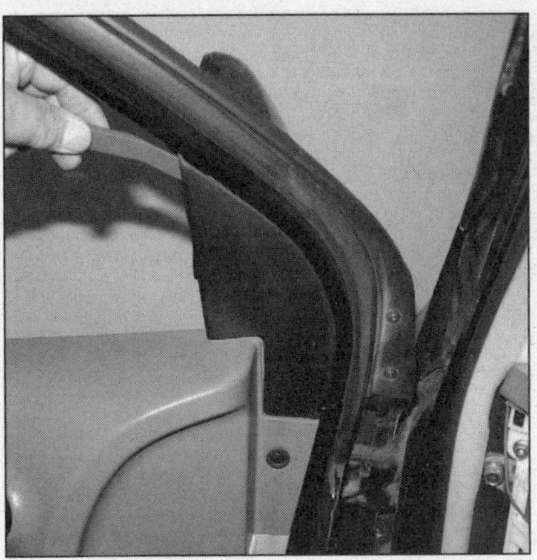

13.1 Pry the sail panel out from the door

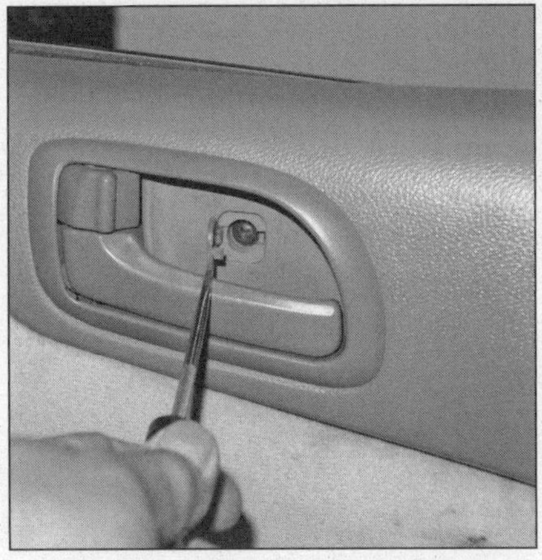

13.2a Pry out the screw cover, then remove the fastener securing the inside door handle

13.2b Remove the inside handle trim cover

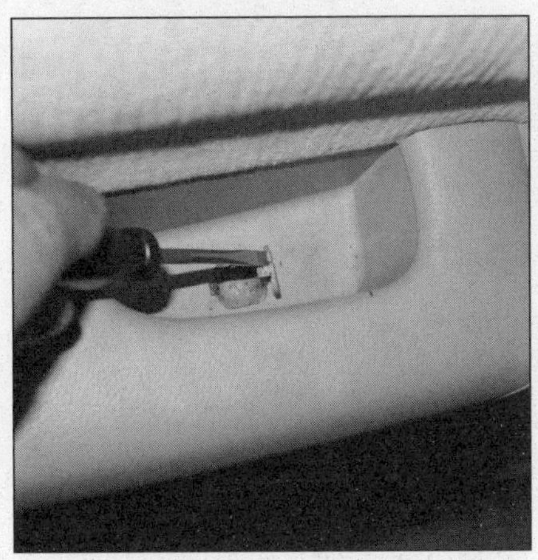

13.2c Pry off the screw cover. . .

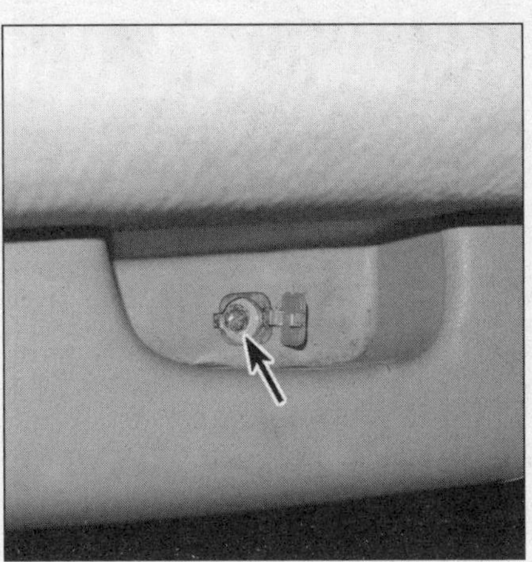

13.2d. . . then remove the fastener securing the inside door pull/armrest

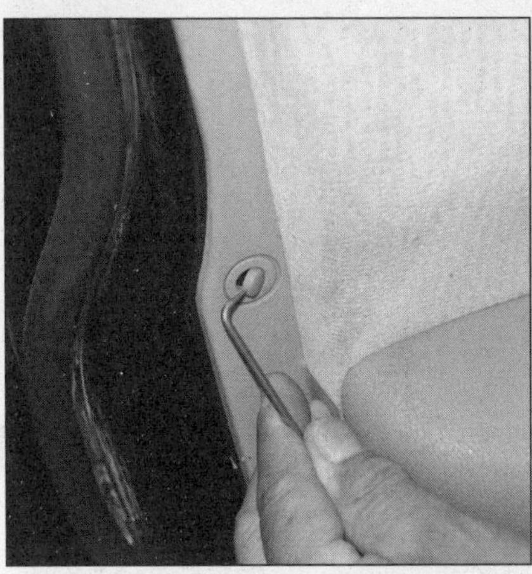

13.2e Pry the trim covers off the door panel mounting screws. . .

13 Door trim panels - removal and installation

Removal

Front door trim panel

1 Use a small flat-bladed pry tool to remove the door sail panel (see illustration).

2 Remove all door trim panel retaining screws and door pull/armrest assemblies (see illustrations).

3 Carefully pry the door trim panel loose from the door (see illustration). Start from the bottom of the trim panel and work around the perimeter until all the fasteners have been released from the door.

4 Disconnect the inner door handle lock cable from the handle and lift the panel off the door.

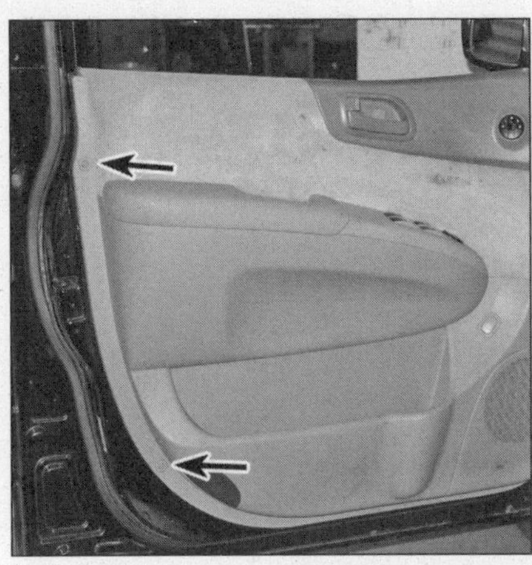

13.2f. . . then remove the panel mounting screws

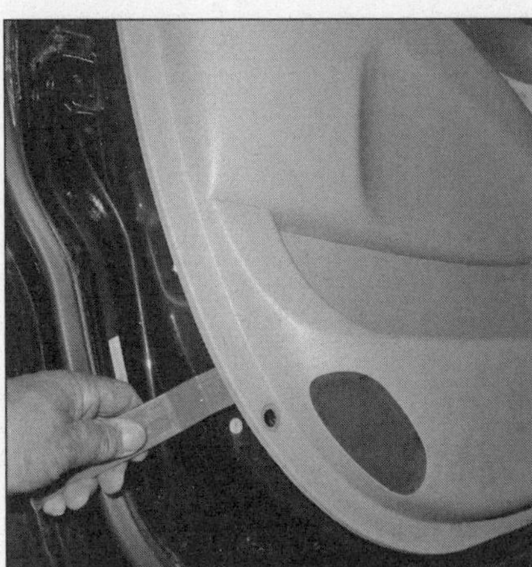

13.3 Carefully pry the clips free so the door trim panel can be removed

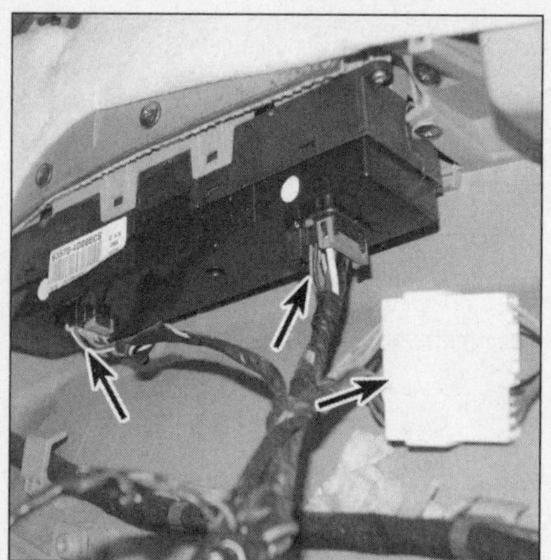

13.5 Disconnect the door harness connectors from the switch and the door panel harness

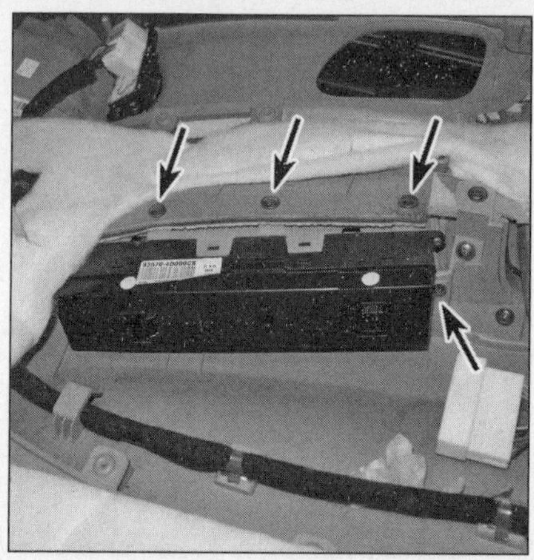

13.6a Remove the power window/door lock switch mounting screws and switch from the door panel

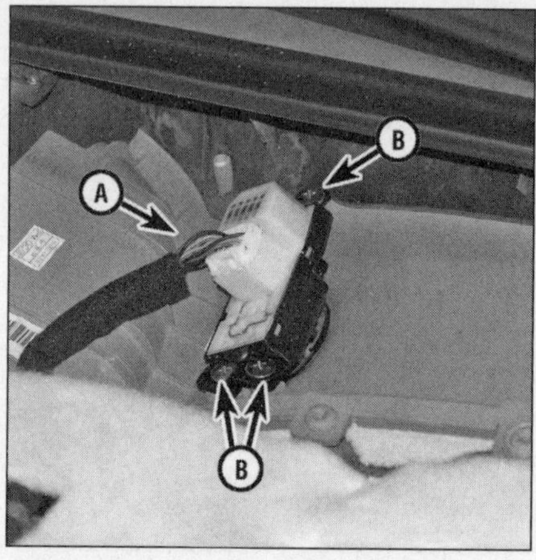

13.6b Disconnect the door panel harness (A) from the power mirror switch then remove the mounting screws (B) and switch

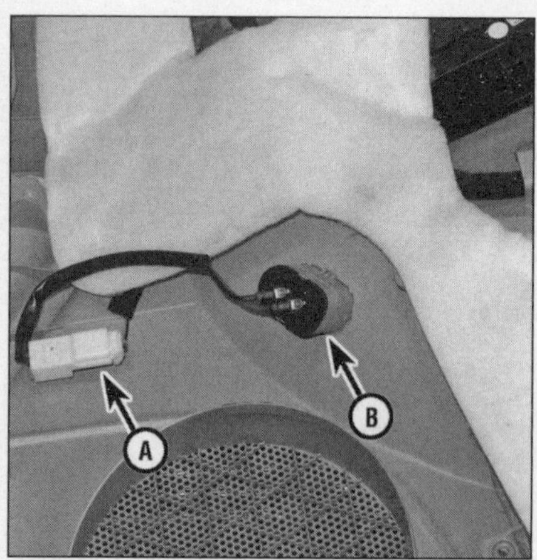

13.6c Disconnect the door panel harness (A) from the fuel door switch harness and press the switch (B) out of the panel

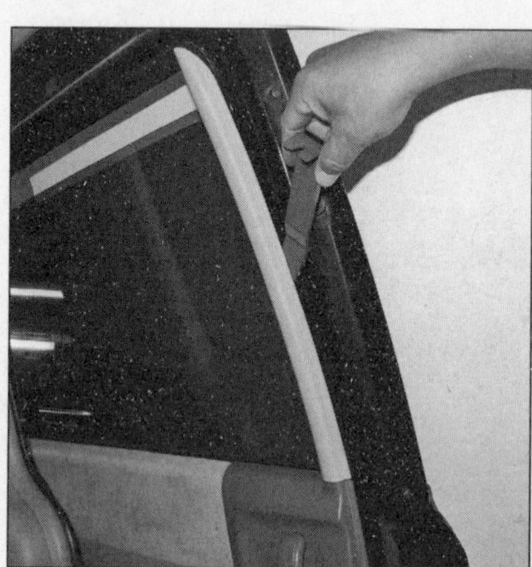

13.7 Carefully pry off the front side trim panel

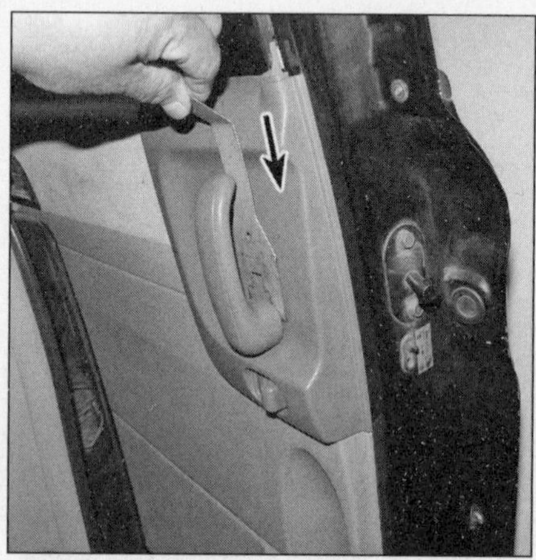

13.8a Insert a window regulator handle removal tool in between the trim and handle to pop the handle retaining clip loosen. . .

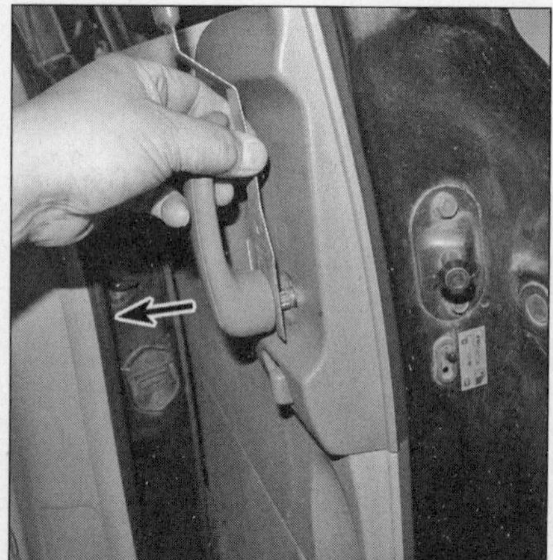

13.8b. . . then slide the handle off

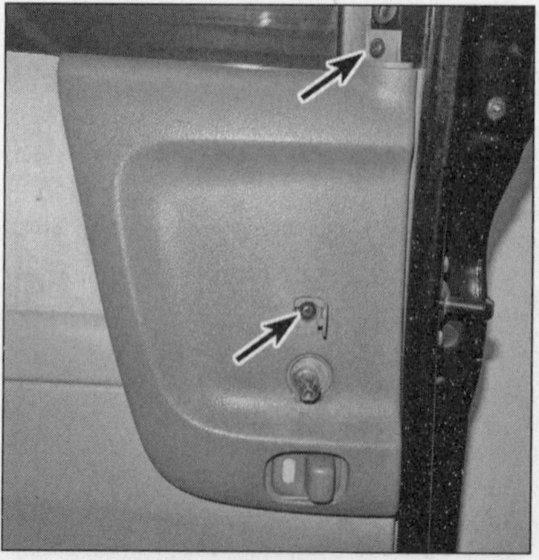

13.9a Pry off the screw cover then remove the screws securing the handle assembly trim

5 Working from the back side of the panel, unplug the harness from the power window/door lock switch and door panel harness (see illustration).

6 Remove the switches from the door panel (see illustrations).

Sliding door trim panel

7 Pry the front side trim panel out to disengage the mounting clips (see illustration) and remove the panel.

8 Remove the inside door handle (see illustrations).

Note: *If you don't have a window regulator handle removal tool, work a clean shop rag down between the handle and the door trim panel from above and pull down on the rag to pop the handle clip loose then remove the handle.*

9 Remove the screws holding the handle assembly trim panel to the door (see illustrations).

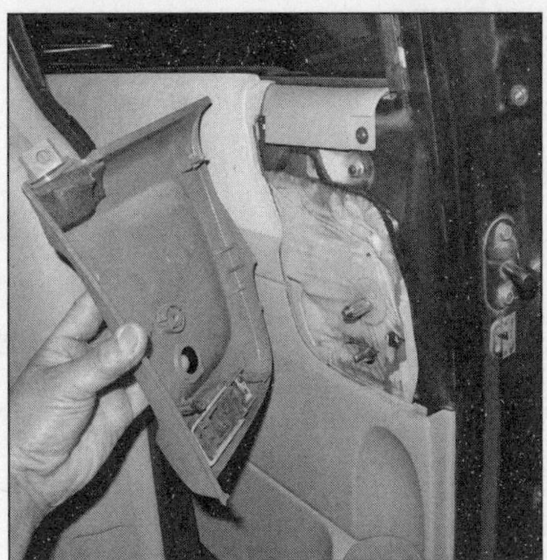

13.9b Remove the trim from the door

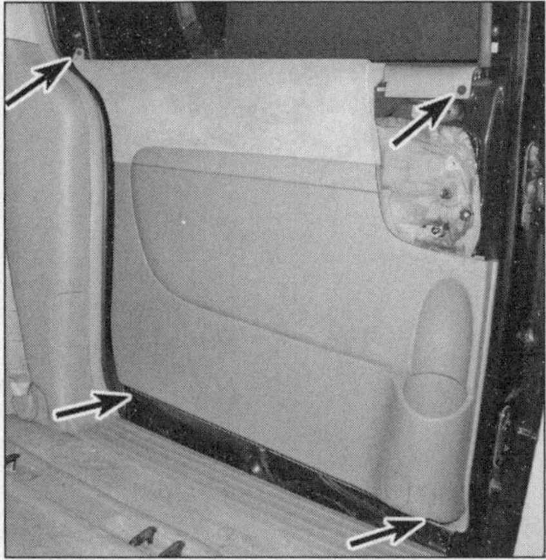

13.10 Sliding door trim panel screw locations

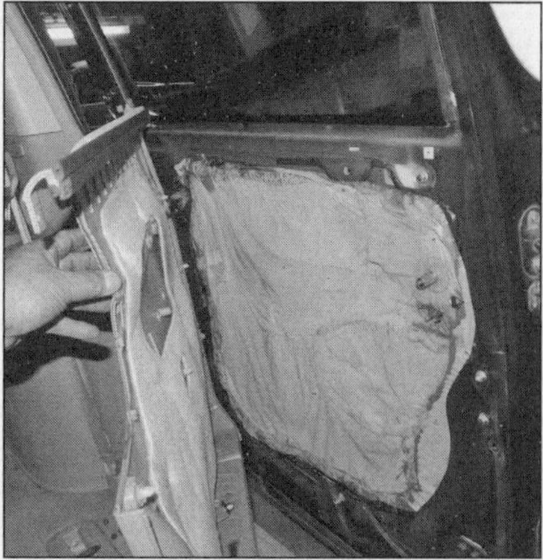

13.11 Remove the sliding door trim panel from the door

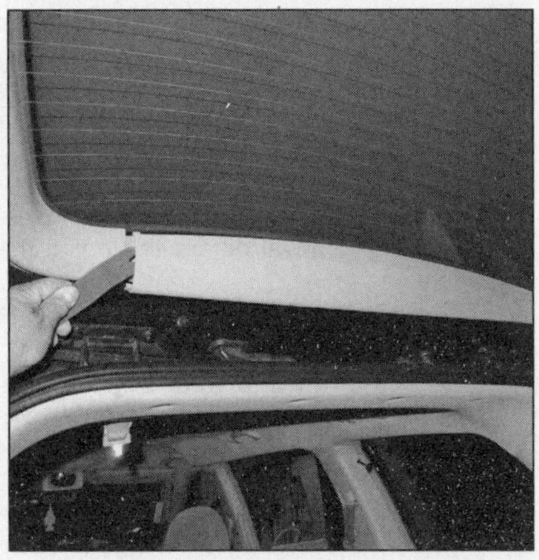

13.13a Using a trim removal tool, remove the upper frame molding

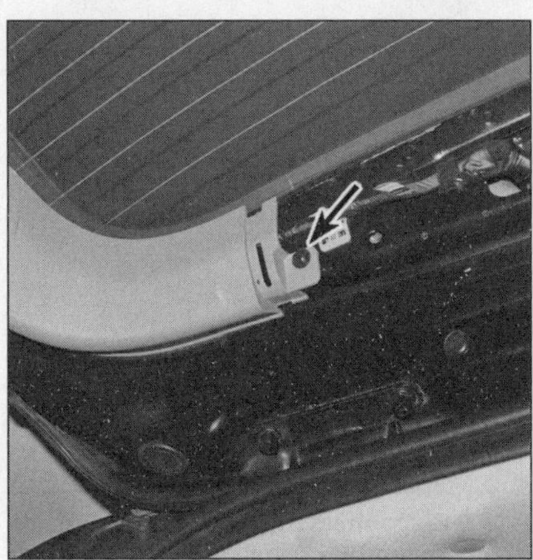

13.13b Remove the side trim mounting screw. . .

13.13c. . . then use a trim tool to remove the side trim - left side shown, right side identical

10 Remove the door trim panel mounting screws and panel (see illustration).

11 Remove the door trim panel using a door panel removal tool. Start from the bottom of the trim panel and work around the perimeter until all the fasteners have been released from the door and remove the panel (see illustration).

Liftgate trim panel

12 Using a small screwdriver, detach the cover from the power liftgate motor link rod (if equipped), then pry or pull sharply to detach the liftgate motor link rod from the door.

13 Remove the liftgate window trim panels (see illustration).

14 Remove the rear cargo light lens (see Chapter 12, Section 17) then pry the liftgate switch out from the bottom of the panel and disconnect the electrical connector, if equipped.

15 Remove the liftgate pull handle fasteners and handle (see illustration).

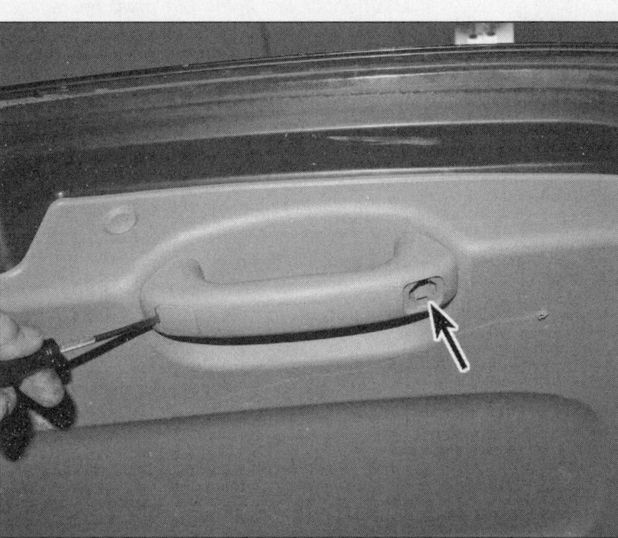

13.15 Pry out the screw covers, then remove the fastener securing the pull handle

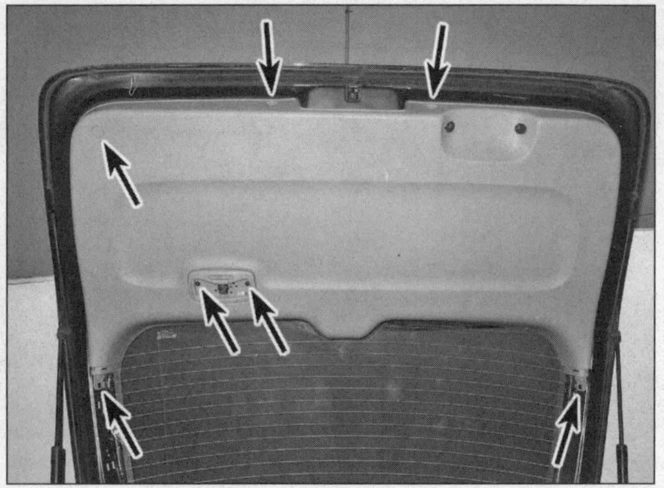
13.16 Remove the fasteners securing the door panel

14.4a Remove the fasteners holding the door stop strut to the body (A) and the lower hinge to the door (B). . .

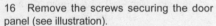

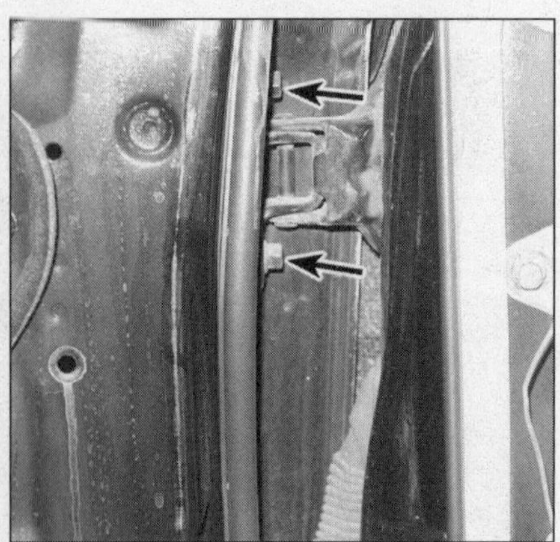
14.4b. . . then remove the upper hinge to door bolts

14.9 Disconnect the electrical connector for the motor mechanism at the bottom front roller

16 Remove the screws securing the door panel (see illustration).

17 Remove the door trim panel using a door panel removal tool. Start from the bottom of the trim panel and work around the perimeter until all the fasteners have been released from the door.

Note: *There are approximately 14 retaining clips used to hold the liftgate trim panel, depending on the year. Make sure all are released before trying to remove the panel.*

18 Disconnect the electrical connector from the courtesy lamps and remove the trim panel.

Installation

19 Prior to installation of the door trim panels and/or the tailgate trim panel, be sure to reinstall any clips in the panel which may have come out when you removed the panel.

20 Position the wire harness connectors for the power door lock switch and the power window switch (if equipped) on the back of the panel, then place the panel in position in the door. Press the door panel into place until the clips are seated.

21 The remainder of installation is the reverse of removal.

14 Door - removal and installation

Front door

Caution: *If the hinge pin must be removed from the hinge, do not reuse the original pin. If you plan to remove the pin be sure you have a new one before starting the job. The retaining clips used on the door hinge pins should also be replaced with new ones.*

1 Remove the door panel (see Section 13), then disconnect all the electrical connections and harness retaining clips from the door.

Note: *Its a good idea to label all the connections to aid in the reassembly process.*

2 From the door side, detach the rubber conduit between the body and the door. Pull wiring harness through the conduit hole and remove it from the door.

3 Scribe around both the hinges with a marking pen, then place a jack under the door or have an assistant on hand to support it when the hinge fasteners are removed.

Note: *If a jack is used, place a towel between it and the door to protect the door's painted surfaces.*

4 Remove the fasteners holding door stop strut and the lower hinge to the door end frame (see illustration). Keeping the door steady, remove the fasteners holding the upper hinge to the door end frame and carefully lift off the door (see illustration).

5 Installation is the reverse of removal, making sure to align the hinge with the marks made during removal before tightening the fasteners.

6 Following installation of the door, check the alignment and adjust it if necessary as follows:

- a) *Up-and-down and in-and-out adjustments are made by loosening the hinge-to-door fasteners and moving the door as necessary.*
- b) *Forward-and-backward adjustments are made by loosening the hinge-to-body fasteners and moving the door as necessary*
- c) *The door lock striker can also be adjusted both up-and-down and sideways to provide positive engagement with the lock mechanism. This is done by loosening the mounting screws and moving the striker as necessary.*

Sliding door

Caution: *Apply several layers of masking tape to the body around the rear end of the upper roller channel and the forward edge of the quarter glass to avoid damaging the paint.*

Note: *This procedure applies to both the manual and electrically operated sliding door removal and installation and applies to both right and left side sliding doors. It does not apply to the electrically operated mechanism for the door.*

7 Open the door. Apply masking tape to the outside surface of the quarter panel below the center roller channel, rearward of the door opening.

8 Apply masking tape to the door jamb area, rearward of the upper roller channel.

9 Disconnect the electrical connector at the front bottom roller (see illustration).

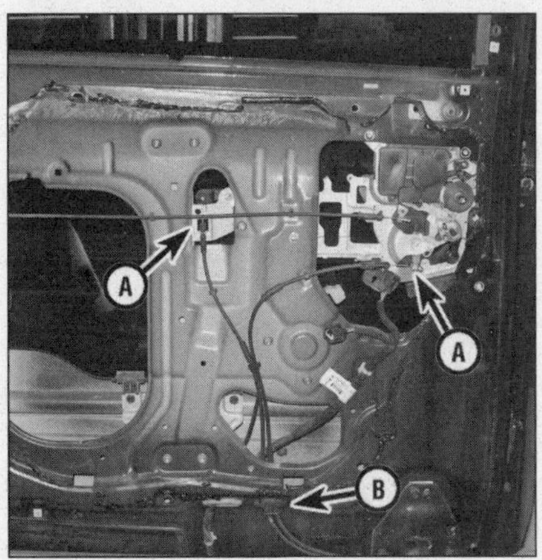

14.11 Disconnect the cables (A) then feed the cable and rubber conduit (B) out of the door

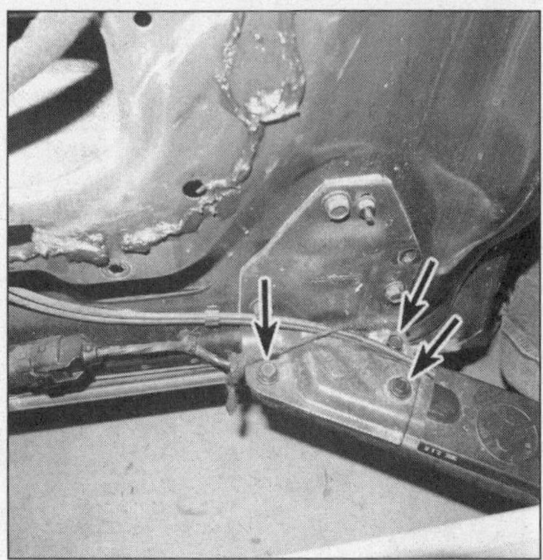

14.13a Remove the lower roller bracket bolts. . .

14.13b. . . then remove the rear roller brackets bolts. . .

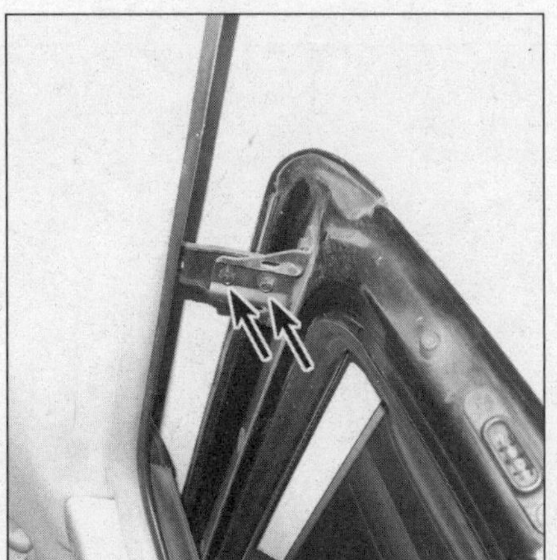

14.13c. . . and the upper roller bracket bolts

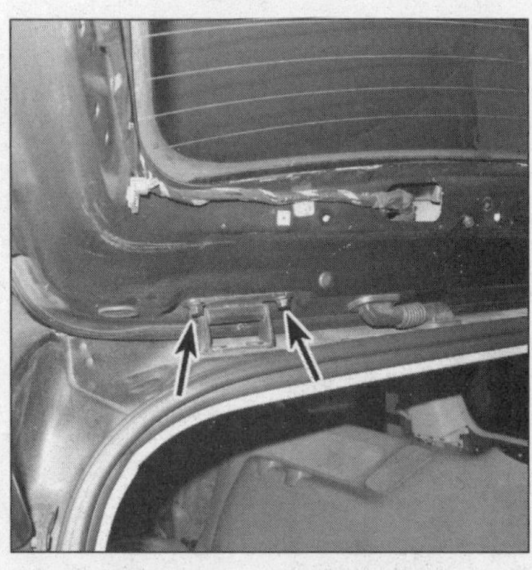

14.21 Liftgate hinge-to-liftgate bolts - left side shown; opposite side identical

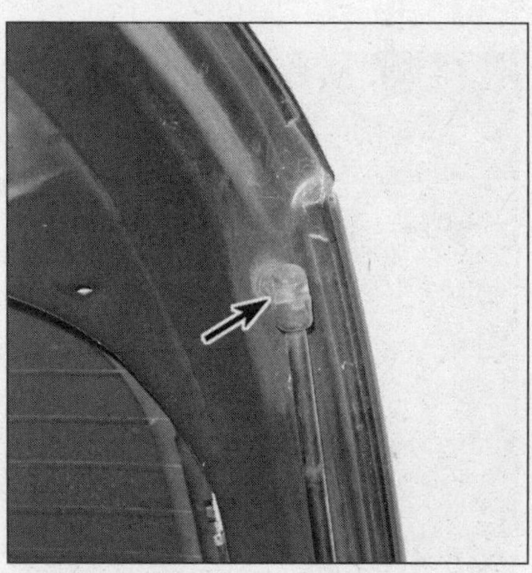

15.2a Pry the clip out of the upper end of support strut and pull the end off of the ball stud

10 Remove the door panel (see Section 13). and the water shield.

11 Disconnect the cables to the door controller (see illustration) and feed the cable out of the door.

12 Support the sliding door on a suitable lifting device that has a padded upper surface. The door must be moveable while on the lifting device.

13 Have an assistant on the out side of the door to support the weight of the door. Remove the sliding door roller bracket bolts (see illustration) and separate the brackets.

14 Remove the sliding door from the vehicle.

15 Installation is the reverse of removal.

Liftgate

16 Have an assistant support the liftgate in its fully open position.

17 Disconnect all cables and wire harness connectors that would interfere with removal of the liftgate.

18 Remove the liftgate upper frame molding and disconnect the rear window washer hose from the spray nozzle.

19 On power liftgate models, disconnect the lift mechanism actuator rod from the liftgate.

20 While an assistant supports the liftgate, detach the support struts (see Section 15).

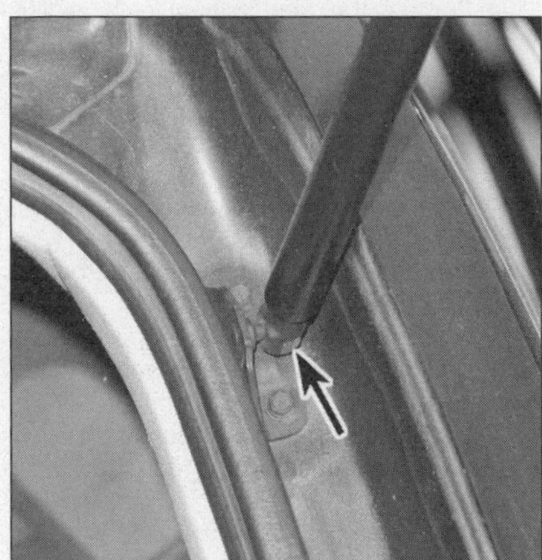

15.2b Pry the clip out of the lower end and remove the support strut - liftgate shown hood similar

21 Mark or scribe around the hinges, then remove the hinge bolts and detach the liftgate from the vehicle (see illustration).

22 Installation is the reverse of removal.

23 Close the liftgate and make sure it is in proper alignment with the surrounding body panels. Adjustments are made by changing the position of the hinge bolts in the slots. Loosen the hinge bolts and reposition the hinges either side-to-side or front and back the desired amount and retighten the bolts.

24 The engagement of the liftgate can be adjusted by loosening the lock striker bolts, repositioning the striker and retightening the bolts.

15 Hood and liftgate struts - replacement

1 Have an assistant support the hood or liftgate in its fully open position.

2 Disconnect the support struts (see illustrations).

3 Installation is the reverse of removal.

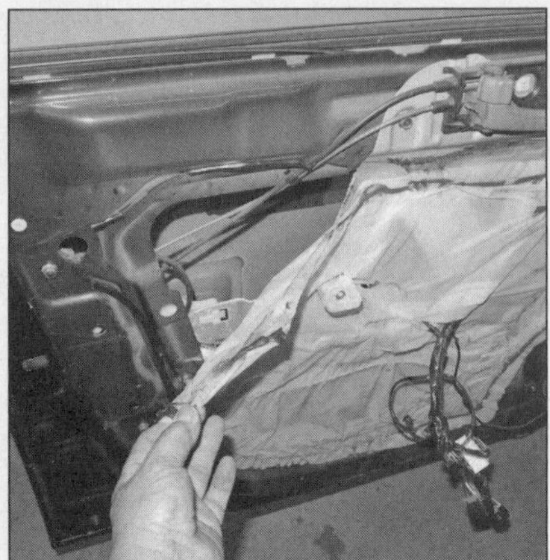

16.3 Carefully peel back the water shield from the door

16.5 Door latch mounting screws

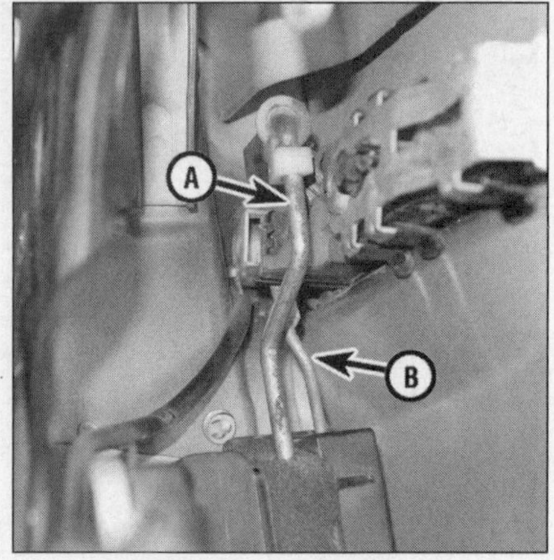

16.9 Pry the end of the lock rod (A) and outside door handle rod (B) retaining clips outwards then rotate the clips up and pull the rods out of the handle

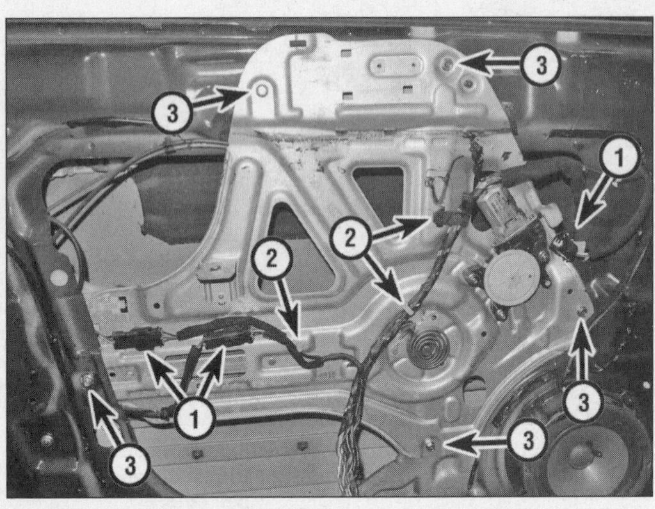

16.11 Remove the front door module fastener

1 Electrical connectors
2 Harness retainers and clips
3 Door module fasteners

16.15 Remove the door latch-to-front door module fastener

16 Door module, latch, lock and handle - removal and installation

Warning: *Models covered by this manual are equipped with a Supplemental Restraint System (SRS), more commonly known as airbags. Always disable the airbag system before working in the vicinity of any airbag system component to avoid the possibility of accidental deployment of the airbag, which could cause personal injury (see Chapter 12).*

Front door module

1 Lower the window a quarter of the way down and tape the window in place, then remove the door trim panel (see Section 13).

Note: *If the glass can't be moved, remove the power window motor (see Section 19) and lower the glass by hand, then tape it inplace to prevent it from falling.*

2 Disconnect the cable from the negative battery terminal (see Chapter 5).

3 Remove the door water shield (see illustration).

4 Remove the inside door handle (see Steps 19 and 20).

5 Remove the door latch mounting bolts (see illustration).

6 Remove the door speaker (see Chapter 12).

7 Disconnect the window glass from the window regulator (see Section 17).

8 Working inside the door remove the lock cylinder shield fasteners and shield, if equipped.

9 From inside the door disconnect the lock rod and outside door handle rod (see illustration).

10 Disconnect the electrical connectors, disengage the harness retainers and remove the harness from the module.

11 Remove the door module fasteners (see illustration) then pull the module away from the door to release the retaining tabs.

12 Pull the front end of the module away and maneuver the rear of the module with the latch assembly from the door.

13 Installation is the reverse of removal.

Front door latch

14 Remove the front door module as previously described.

15 Remove the door latch-to-door module fasteners then lift the latch off of the stud and separate the latch from the module (see illustration).

16 Installation is the reverse of removal.

Inside door handle

17 Remove the door trim panel (see Section 13).

18 Remove the water shield (see illustration 16.3).

19 Remove the inside door handle fastener (see illustration) and separate the handle from

16.19 Remove the handle fastener then slide the handle back to disconnect it from the module

16.20 Pull the cables out from the retainers in the handle

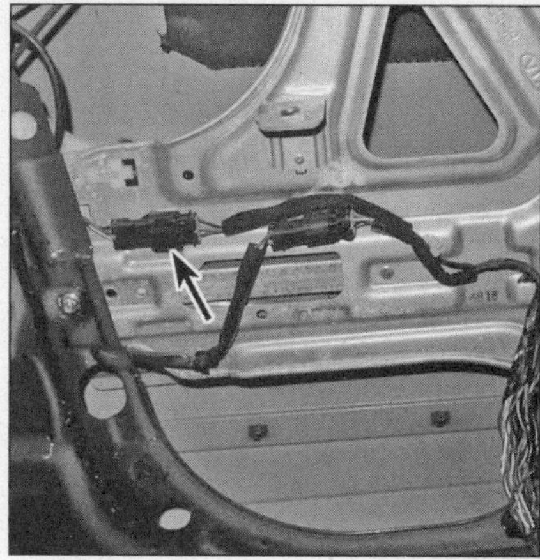
16.24 Disengage the connector retainer the disconnect the electrical connector to the harness

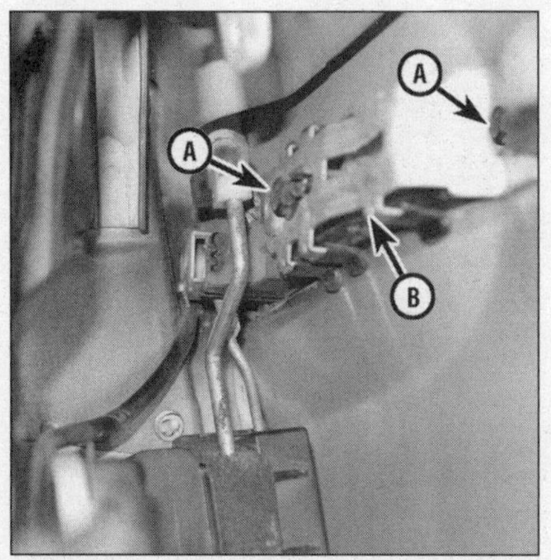

16.27 Loosen the outside handle mounting bolts (A), then remove the outside handle support bracket (B)

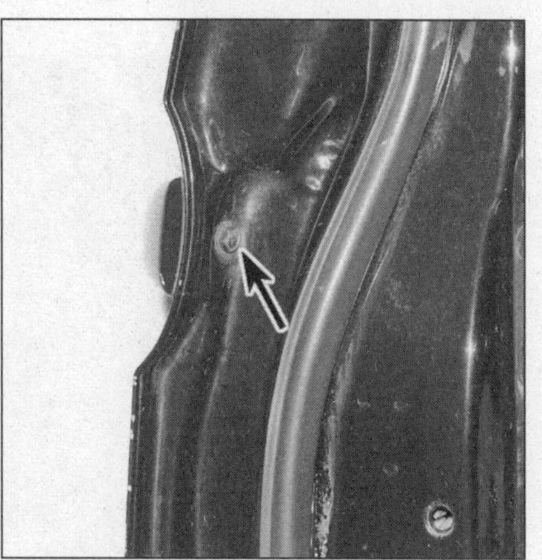
16.28 Remove the outside door handle outer bolt

16.29a Remove the handle assembly from the door. . .

the door module.

20 Rotate the handle and pull the cables from the handle (see illustration) then disconnect the cables from the handle.

21 Installation is the reverse of removal.

Front door outside handle

22 Close the window completely and remove the front door trim panel (see Section 13).

23 Remove the water shield (see illustration 16.3).

24 Disconnect the electrical connector to the lock (see illustration).

25 Working inside the door remove the lock cylinder shield fasteners and shield, if equipped.

26 From inside the door disconnect the lock rod and outside door handle rod (see illustration 16.9).

27 Loosen the outside handle mounting bolts and remove the outside handle support bracket (see illustration).

28 Remove the bolt holding the outside door handle to the door outer panel (see illustration).

29 From inside the door, remove the bolts holding the outside door handle (see illustration 16.27) to the door outer panel and remove the handle from the vehicle (see illustrations).

30 Installation is the reverse of removal.

Front door lock cylinder

31 Remove the front door outside handle (see Steps 22 through 29) and pull the lock from the door handle.

32 Install the lock cylinder into the door handle. The remainder of installation is the reverse of removal.

Sliding door actuator/module

Note: *A door initialization procedure must be performed any time a component or power is removed from the power sliding door.*

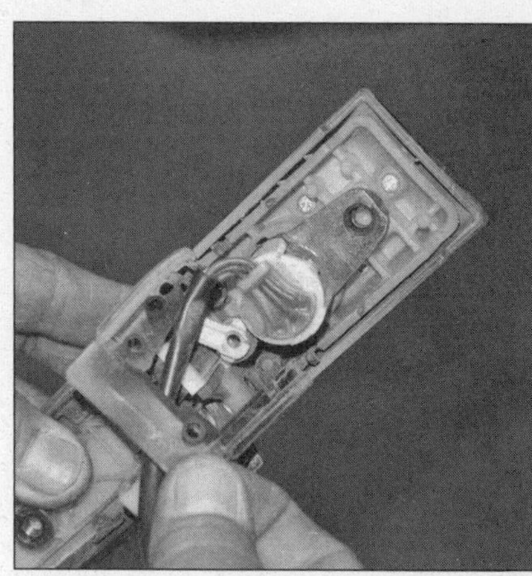
16.29b. . . then remove the gasket from the handle

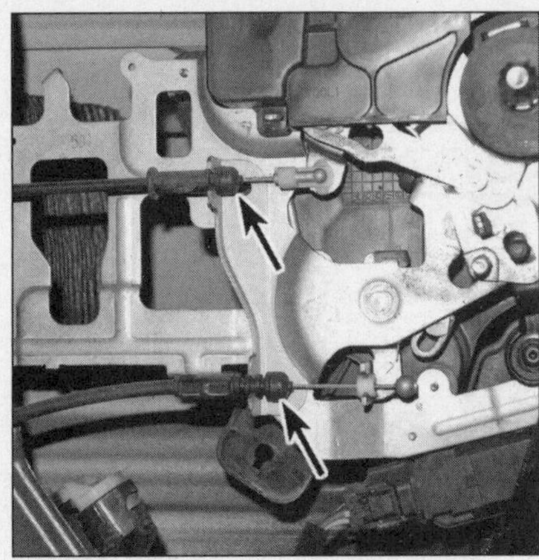
16.35 Pull the cables out from the retainers in the actuator/module

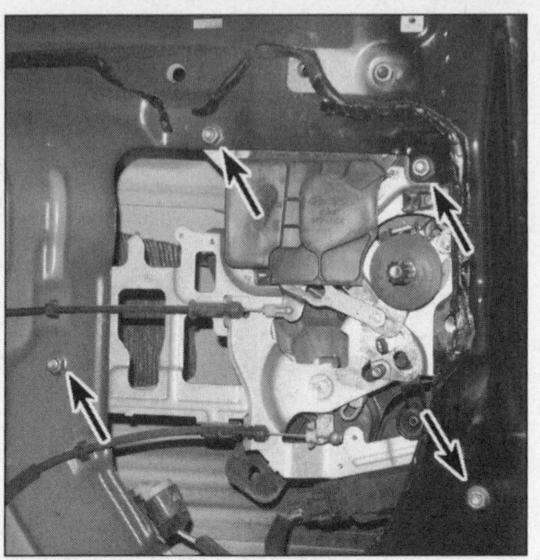
16.36 Sliding door actuator/module fastener locations

16.37 Disconnect the lock cable from the outside door handle

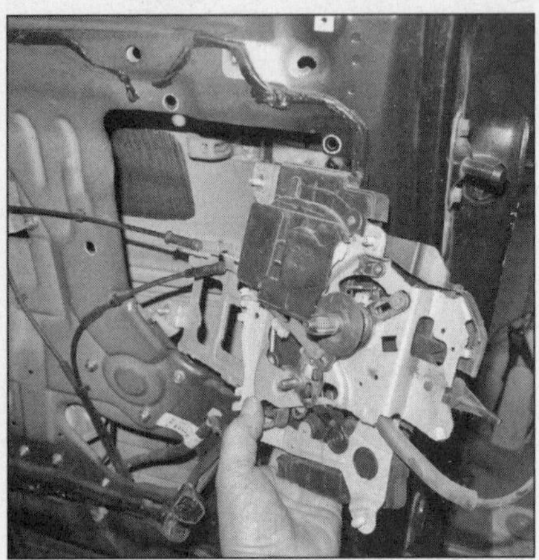
16.38 Maneuver the module assembly through the opening in the door

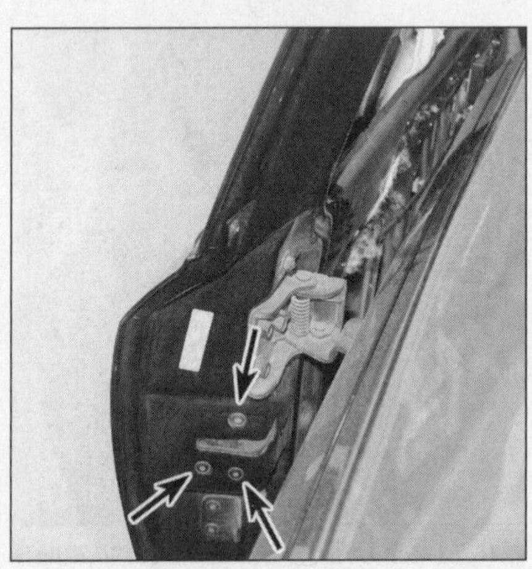
16.41 Latch mounting screw locations

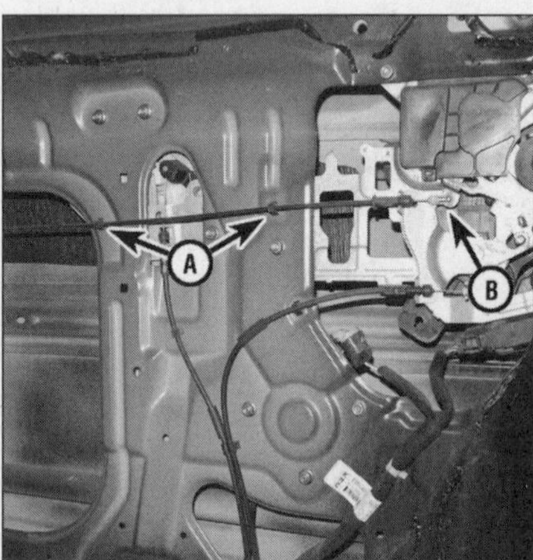

16.42 Unclip the cable retainers (A) then release the cable end (B) from the actuator/module

16.47 Remove the access plug from the door then remove the handle mounting bolt

33 Disconnect the cable from the negative battery terminal (see Chapter 5).
34 Remove the sliding door trim panel and weather shield (see Section 13).
35 Disconnect the cables to the actuator (see illustration).
36 Remove the door actuator/module fasteners (see illustration) and lower the module.
37 Disconnect the lock cable from the outside door handle (see illustration).
38 Maneuver the module with the latch assembly from the door by rotating the panel at an angle with the front end slightly down and the back end slightly raised (see illustration).
39 Installation is the reverse of removal.

Sliding door latch

40 Remove the sliding door trim panel and weather shield (see Section 13).
41 Open the sliding door half way, remove the latch mounting screws (see illustration) and lower the latch from the end of the door.
42 Disconnect the external cable from the door and actuator/module (see installation).
43 Reach inside the door and remove the latch with cable from the vehicle.
44 Installation is the reverse of removal.

Sliding door outside handle

45 Remove the sliding door trim panel (see Section 13)
46 Remove the actuator/module and release the cable from the outside door handle (see Steps 33 through 38).
47 Remove the access plug for the outside handle retaining bolt and remove the bolt (see illustration).

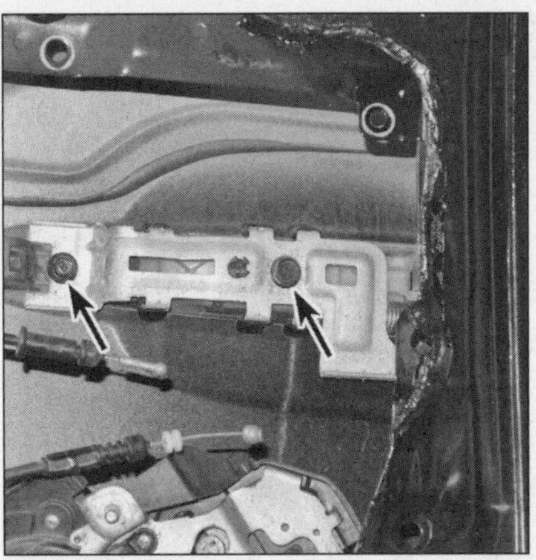
16.48 Remove the mounting bolts through the close-out opening

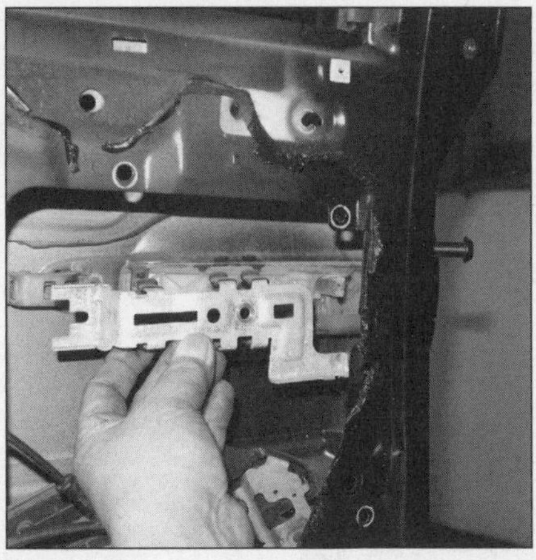
16.49 Remove the support bracket

16.50 Remove the handle assembly from the door

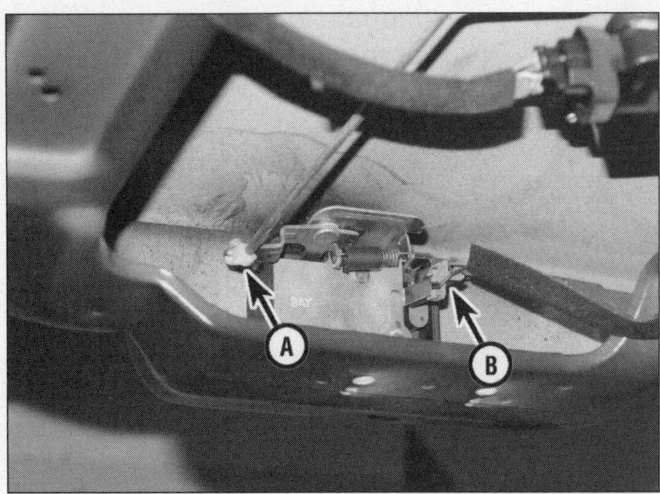

16.60 Pry the end of the handle rod (A) retaining clip outwards then rotate the clips up and pull the rod out of the latch then disconnect the electrical connector (B)

16.61 Liftgate latch mounting screws

48 Remove the bolts holding the outside door handle to the door outer panel (see illustration).

49 Remove the outside handle support bracket from the handle (see illustration).

50 Pull the handle outwards (see illustration) and remove the handle.

51 Installation is the reverse of removal.

Sliding door initialization procedure

Note: *In the event the power sliding door system needs to be reset, remove the memory fuse from the interior fuse box. Wait one minute then reinstall the fuse and start the door initialization procedure.*

52 The door initialization procedure or learn cycle must be performed any time a component or power is removed from the power sliding door. The learn cycle programs the power sliding door control module (PSDM) travel limits and effort to operate the sliding door in a safe and fully functional manner.

53 Manually close the sliding door making sure the door is latched.

54 Power the sliding door, to the fully open position using either the open/close switch, B-pillar switch or the handle.

55 Power the door closed, from the fully open position all the way to the fully closed position.

56 Power the door open to the fully open position.

Liftgate latch

57 Disconnect the cable from the negative battery terminal (see Chapter 5).

58 Remove the liftgate trim panels (see Section 13).

59 If the liftgate is stuck closed, pry the access panel out from the liftgate trim panel, then rotate the release lever up.

60 Disconnect the handle rod and the electrical connector to the latch (see illustration).

61 Remove the screws holding the latch to the liftgate and remove it from the vehicle (see illustration).

62 Remove the latch assembly from the liftgate and disconnect the cable and electrical connector.

63 Installation is the reverse of removal.

Liftgate outside handle

64 Remove the liftgate trim panels (see Section 13).

65 Disconnect the electrical connectors for the liftgate outside handle, if equipped.

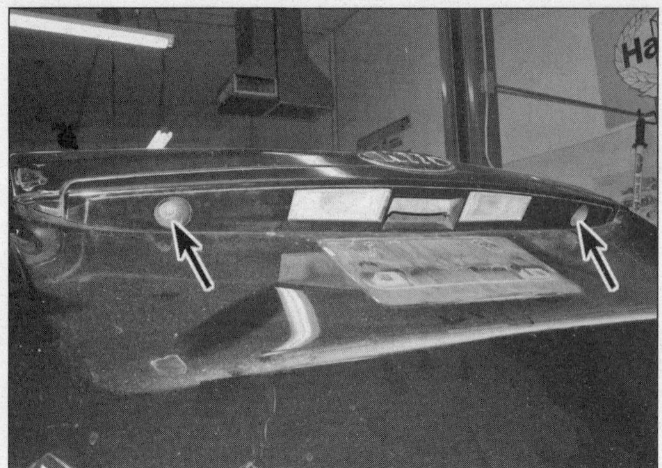

16.66 Remove the two mounting bolts from the outside

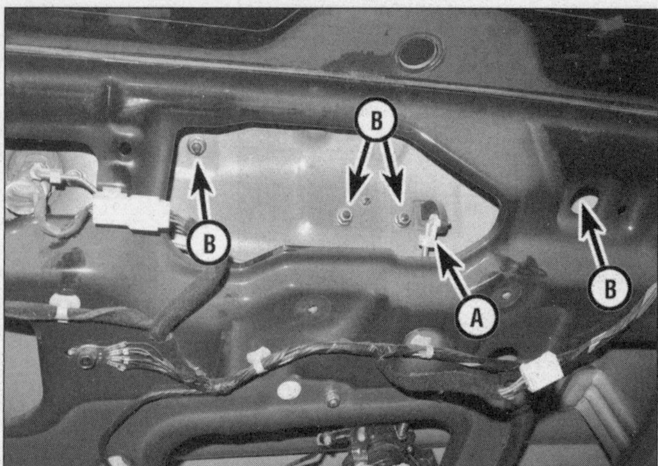

16.67 Pry the end of the handle rod (A) retaining clip outwards then rotate the clips up and pull the rod out of the handle then remove the handle mounting nuts (B)

66 Remove the liftgate exterior trim panel two outside mounting screws (see illustration).

67 Remove the two outside and two inside handle mounting screws (see illustration).

68 Remove the liftgate exterior trim panel out, disconnect the electrical connectors to the lights.

69 Remove the handle from the vehicle.

70 Installation is the reverse of removal.

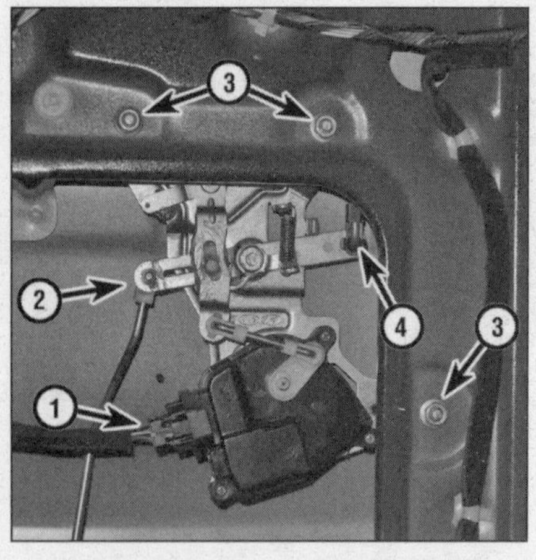

16.73 Lock/actuator assembly details

1 *Lock/actuator electric connector*
2 *Key lock rod*
3 *Mounting nuts*
4 *Actuator rod*

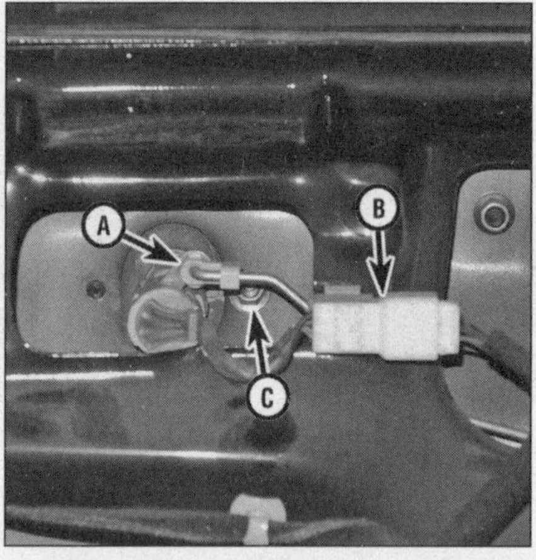

16.77 Pry the end of the lock rod (A) retaining clip outwards then rotate the clip up and pull the rod out of the lock then disconnect the electrical connector (B) and remove the handle mounting nut (C)

17.5 Window glass-to-regulator bolt locations

Liftgate lock/actuator assembly

71 Remove the liftgate trim panels (see Section 13).

72 Disengage the outside handle rod, actuator rod, key cylinder lock rod and disconnect the electrical connector.

73 Remove the actuator mounting nuts (see illustration) and remove the actuator assembly from the liftgate.

74 Installation is the reverse of removal.

Key lock

75 Remove the liftgate trim panels (see Section 13).

76 Remove the liftgate exterior trim panel (see Steps 66 through 68).

77 Disengage the lock rod and disconnect the electrical connector (see illustration) and remove the mounting nut.

78 From the outside of the liftgate remove the two mounting screws and remove the key lock from the liftgate.

79 Installation is the reverse of removal.

17 Door window glass - removal and installation

Front door

1 Remove the door trim panel (see Section 13).

2 Remove the door water shield (see illustration 16.3).

3 Lower the window glass about a quarter of the way down.

Note: *If the glass can't be moved, remove the power window motor (see Section 19) and lower the glass by hand, then tape it inplace to prevent it from falling.*

4 Remove the door speaker (see Chapter 12).

5 Working through both openings remove the window glass-to-regulator bolts (see illustration).

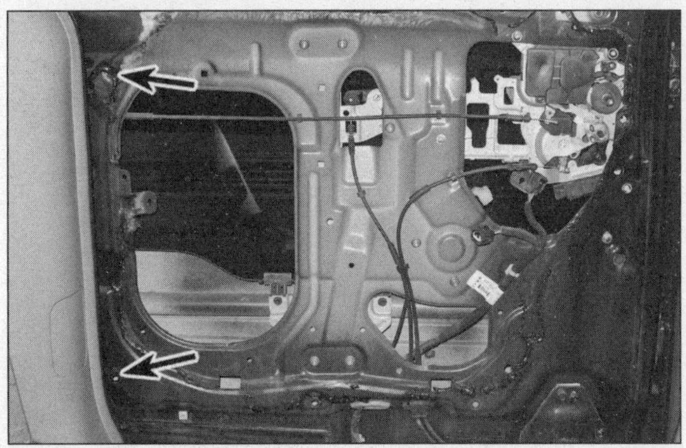
17.10 Remove the the rear channel fasteners

17.12 Remove the window glass-to-regulator bracket nuts

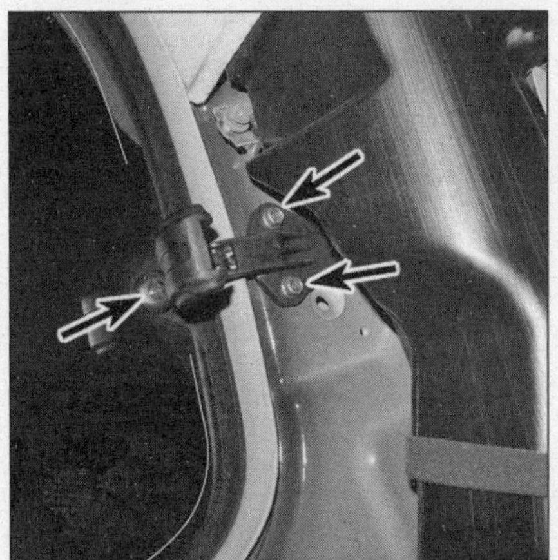
18.3 Vent arm fastener locations

18.4 Pull the seal back and remove the mounting bolt - upper bolt shown lower bolt identical

19.9 Power window motor mounting nut locations

6 Carefully tilt the front end of the glass downwards and separate the glass from the channel, then lift the glass upward and out of the exterior opening at the top of the door.
7 Installation is the reverse of removal.

Sliding door

8 Remove the sliding door trim panel (see Section 13).
9 Remove the door water shield (see illustration 16.3).

Moveable glass

10 Remove the window rear channel fasteners (see illustration) and slide the channel to the side.
11 Lower the window glass about a quarter of the way down and secure the window.
Note: *If the glass can't be moved, remove the power window motor (see Section 19) and lower the glass by hand, then tape it inplace to prevent it from falling.*
12 Working through both openings, remove the window glass-to-window regulator bracket mounting bolts (see illustration).
13 Carefully tip the top of the glass outwards, then lift the glass upward and out of the opening at the top of the door.
14 Installation is the reverse of removal.

Fixed glass

15 Remove the window glass mounting fasteners and lower the glass into the door.
16 Remove the mounting bracket mounting fasteners and separate the bracket form the glass.
17 Carefully lift the glass out of the opening at the top of the door.
18 Installation is the reverse of removal.

18 Quarter window glass - removal and installation

1 Remove the interior trim from around the window to be removed (see Section 25), then open the window to the vent position.
2 On power window models, disconnect the vent arm from the quarter window retainer (see Section 19).
3 On manual window models, remove the vent fasteners (see illustration).
4 Remove the nuts that hold the glass to the pillar (see illustration) and remove the glass from the vehicle.
5 Installation is the reverse of removal.

19 Window glass regulators - removal and installation

Front door

1 Remove the door trim panel (see Section 13).
2 Remove the weather shield (see illustration 16.3).
3 Remove the door glass (see Section 17).

2005 and earlier models

4 Disconnect the electrical connector to the power window motor.
5 Remove the mounting bolts and maneuver the regulator of of the door through the access hole.
6 Once the regulator assembly is out, remove the power window motor fasteners and separate the motor from the regulator.
7 Installation is the reverse of removal.

2006 and later models

8 Remove the door module (see Section 16).
9 Remove the power window motor mounting nuts (see illustration).

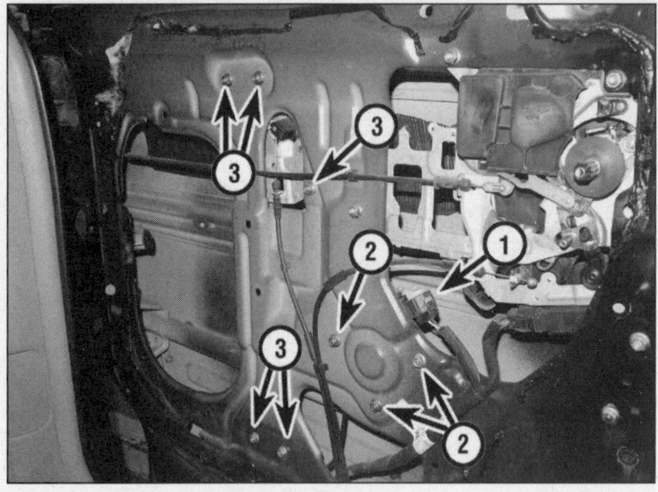

19.20 Unplug the electrical connector and remove regulator assembly fasteners

1 *Power window motor electrical connector*
2 *Power window motor fasteners*
3 *Regulator fasteners*

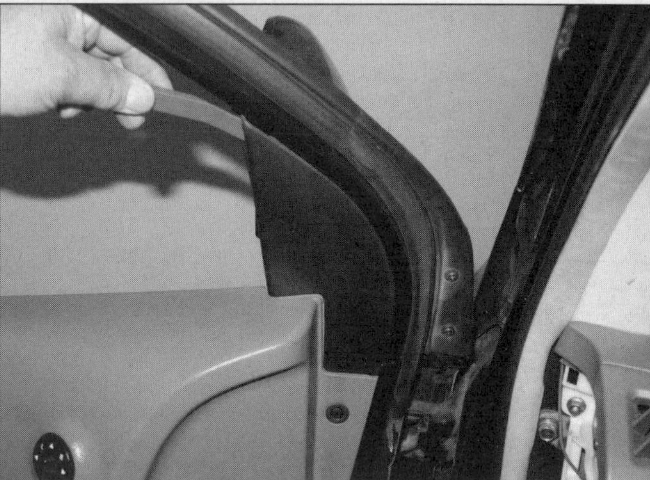

20.1 Pry out the sail panel from the corner of the door

Note: *The power window motor can be removed with out removing the door module assembly.*

10 Remove the power window motor from the module.

11 The window glass regulator is mot serviceable separately from the door module. The assembly must be replaced as a unit.

12 Installation is the reverse of removal.

Quarter window

13 Remove the rear trim panel (see Section 25).

14 Disconnect the electrical connector from the vent motor.

15 Remove the circular actuator link tab, then remove the arm from the window ball socket.

16 Remove the vent motor mounting fasteners and remove the vent motor.

17 Installation is the reverse of removal.

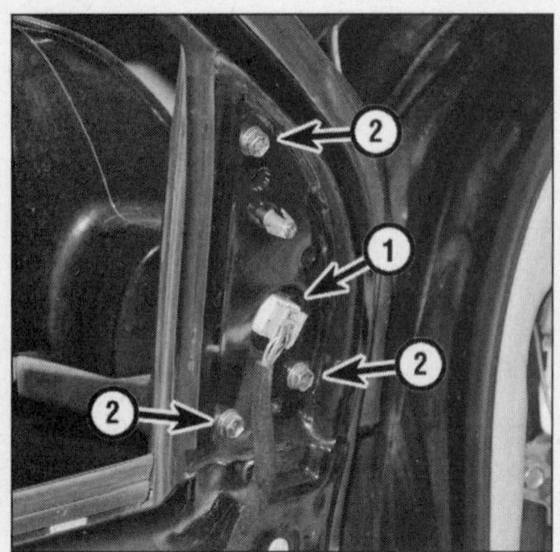

20.2 Power mirror details

1 *Power mirror electrical connector*
2 *Mirror mounting bolt – identical for manual mirrors*

Sliding door window - 2006 and later models only

18 Remove the door trim panel (see Section 13).

19 Remove the door glass from the regulator (see Section 17).

20 Unplug the electrical connector to the power window motor, if equipped then remove the motor fasteners, regulator fasteners and maneuver the assembly out through the access hole at the rear of the door (see illustration).

21 Installation is the reverse of removal.

20 Mirrors - removal and installation

Outside mirrors

1 Carefully pry the interior sail panel from the corner of the door (see illustration).

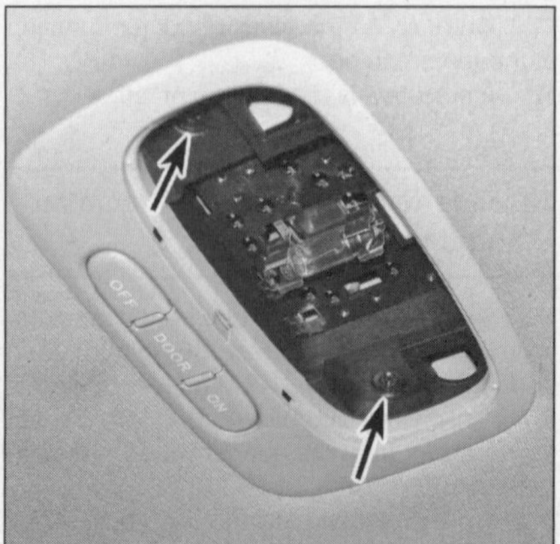

21.5 Rear overhead console mounting screw locations

2 If equipped with power mirrors, remove the door trim panel (see Section 13), disconnect the electrical connectors and disengage the harness retainer for the mirror (see illustration).

3 Remove the mirror mounting bolt and detach the mirror (see illustration 20.2).

4 Installation is the reverse of removal.

Inside mirror

5 If equipped, disconnect the electrical connector to the back of the mirror. Use a Phillips head screwdriver to remove the set screw, then slide the mirror up off the button on the windshield.

Note: *If the mount plate itself has come off the windshield, adhesive kits are available at auto parts stores to re-secure it. Follow the instructions included with the kit.*

6 Installation is the reverse of removal.

21 Overhead console - removal and installation

Front

1 Insert a plastic trim tool at the front of the overhead console and carefully pry the console from the headliner to disengage the snap clips at the front and rear of the console.

2 Lower the overhead console sufficiently to gain access to the electrical connectors. Disconnect the electrical connectors and remove the overhead console.

3 Installation is the reverse of removal.

Rear

4 Insert a plastic trim tool at the front of the overhead console and carefully pry the console trim panel out from the console.

5 Remove the console mounting screws (see illustration) and lower the overhead con-

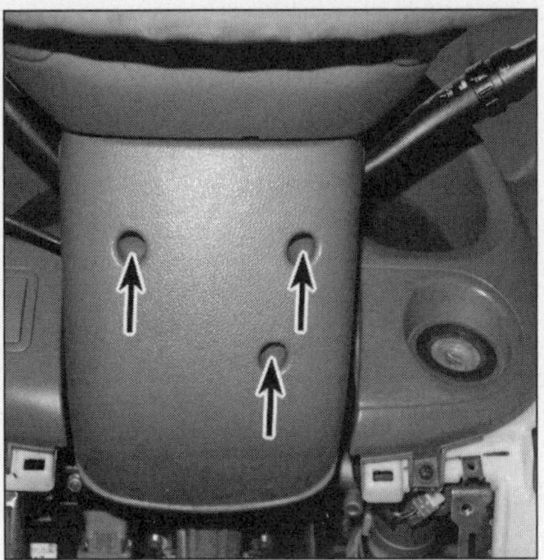
22.3 Remove the screws from the lower steering column cover

22.4 Using a small trim tool, disengage the retaining clips from the cover halves

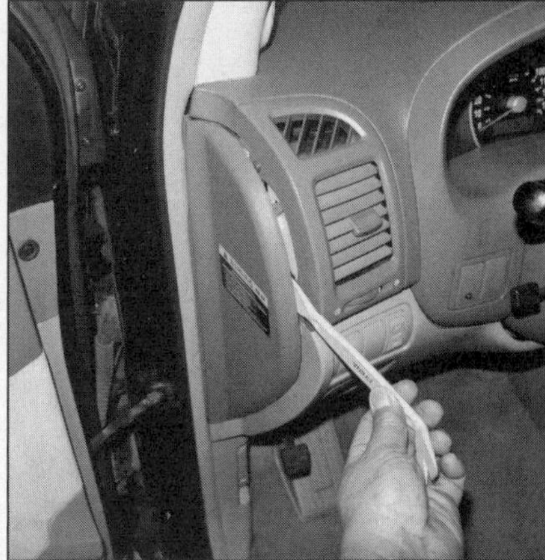
23.2 Pry the instrument panel end cap out to disconnect the mounting clips - left side shown, right side identical

23.6 Instrument cluster bezel mounting screw locations

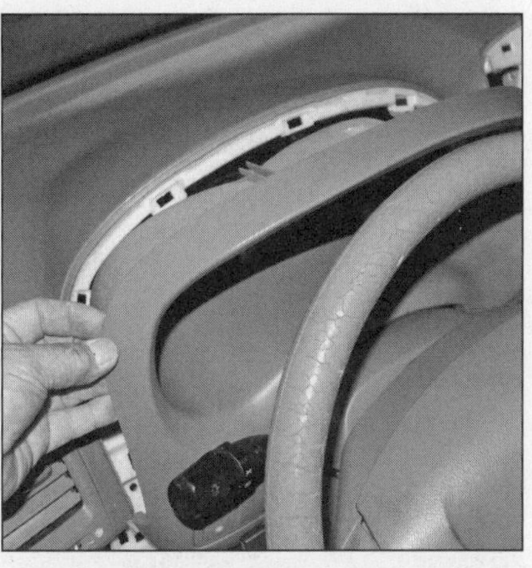
23.7 Pry the instrument cluster bezel out to disconnect the mounting clips

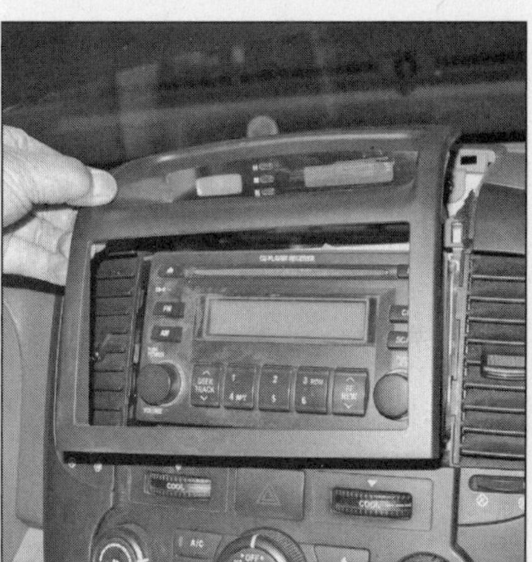
23.10 Pry the center upper trim panel out from around the radio

sole sufficiently to gain access to the electrical connectors.

6 Disconnect the electrical connectors and remove the overhead console.

7 Installation is the reverse of removal.

22 Steering column covers - removal and installation

Warning: *Models covered by this manual are equipped with a Supplemental Restraint System (SRS), more commonly known as airbags. Always disable the airbag system before working in the vicinity of any airbag system component to avoid the possibility of accidental deployment of the airbag, which could cause personal injury (see Chapter 12).*

1 Disconnect the cable from the negative battery terminal (see Chapter 5).

2 Remove the knee bolster panel (see Section 23).

3 Remove the screws from the lower steering column cover (see illustration).

4 Using a trim tool, disengage the retaining clips around the perimeter of the cover halves (see illustration).

5 Separate the cover halves and detach them from the steering column.

6 Installation is the reverse of removal.

23 Dashboard trim panels - removal and installation

Warning: *Models covered by this manual are equipped with a Supplemental Restraint System (SRS), more commonly known as airbags. Always disable the airbag system before working in the vicinity of any airbag system component to avoid the possibility of accidental deployment of the airbag, which could cause personal injury (see Chapter 12).*

1 Disconnect the cable from the negative battery terminal (Chapter 5).

Instrument panel end caps

2 Using a trim tool pry the end cap out (see illustration), then detach it from the dashboard.

3 If you're working on the right side end cap, grasp the cover securely and pull sharply to remove it.

4 Installation is the reverse of removal.

Instrument cluster trim bezel

5 Remove the knee bolster (see Steps 32 through 36).

6 Remove the bezel mounting screws at the bottom edge of the bezel (see illustration).

7 Using a trim tool pry around the perimeter of the bezel (see illustration), until all the clips are detached then remove it from the dashboard.

8 If you're working on the right side end cap, grasp the cover securely and pull sharply to remove it.

9 Installation is the reverse of removal.

Instrument panel center trim panels

Upper trim panel

10 Using a trim stick, carefully pry around the edges of the center, upper trim panel to release the mounting clips (see illustration).

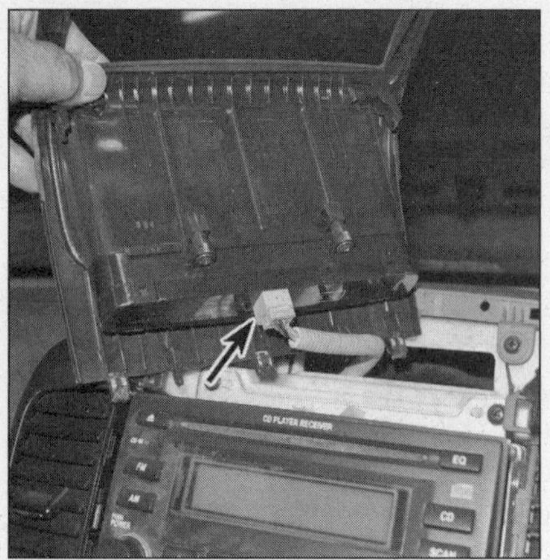
23.11 Disconnect the electrical connector and remove the panel

23.13 Pry the center lower trim panel out and manuever it around the shift handle

23.14 Disconnect the electrical connector and remove the panel

23.17 Remove the center vents fasteners from bottom edge of the panels

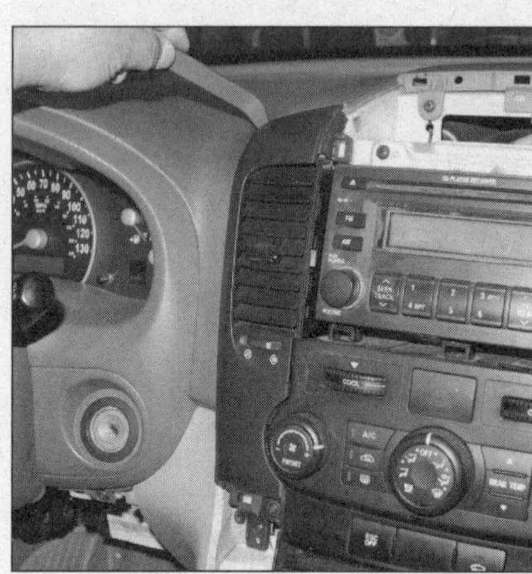
23.18a Pry the left center vent. . .

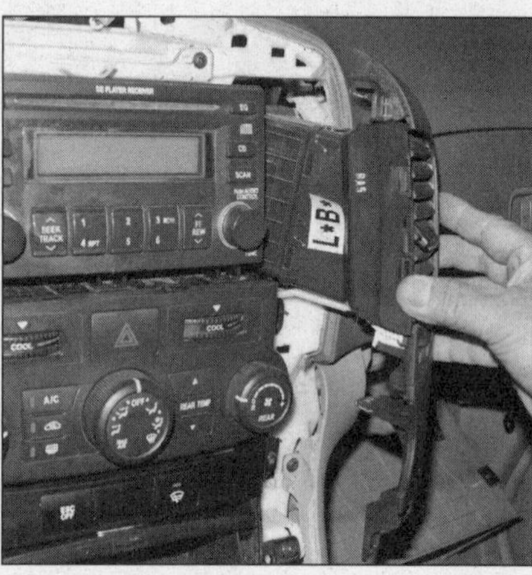
23.18b. . . and the right center vent out of the instrument panel

23.22 Center storage compartment mounting screw locations

11 Remove the panel enough to disconnect the electrical connector to the clock (see illustration) then remove the panel.

12 Installation is the reverse of removal.

Lower trim panel

13 Using a trim stick, carefully pry around the edges of the center, lower trim panel to release the mounting clips (see illustration).

14 Remove the panel enough to disconnect the electrical harness for the power outlets (see illustration) then remove the panel.

15 Installation is the reverse of removal.

Instrument panel center vents

16 Remove the center trim panels (see Steps 10 and 11, 13 and 14).

17 Remove the mounting screws at the bottom edge of the center vent panels (see illustration).

18 Using a trim tool, pry the center vents out from the dash (see illustrations).

19 Installation is the reverse of removal.

Instrument panel center storage compartment

20 Remove the center trim panels (see Steps 10 and 11, 13 and 14).

21 Remove the instrument panel switches (see Chapter 12 Section 10).

22 Remove the center storage compartment mounting screws (see illustration).

23 Pull the storage compartment out from the dash.

24 Installation is the reverse of removal.

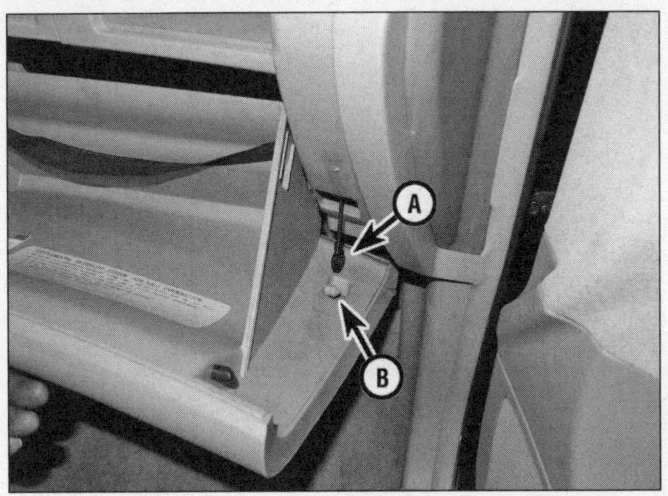

23.25 Pull the damper rod end (A) off of the door tab (B)

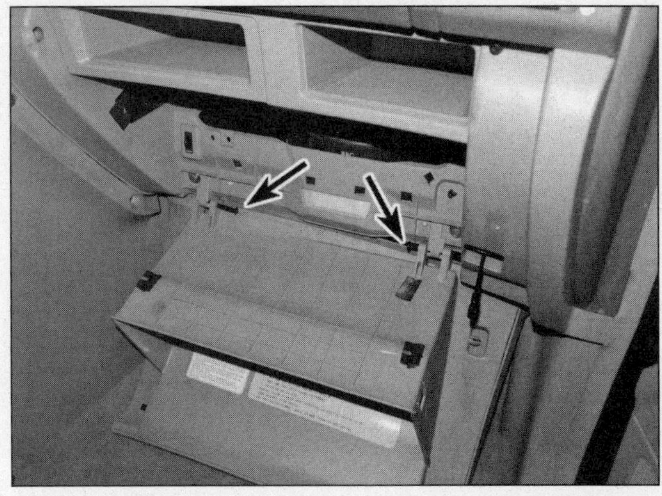
23.26 Slide the pins inwards to remove them, then remove the door

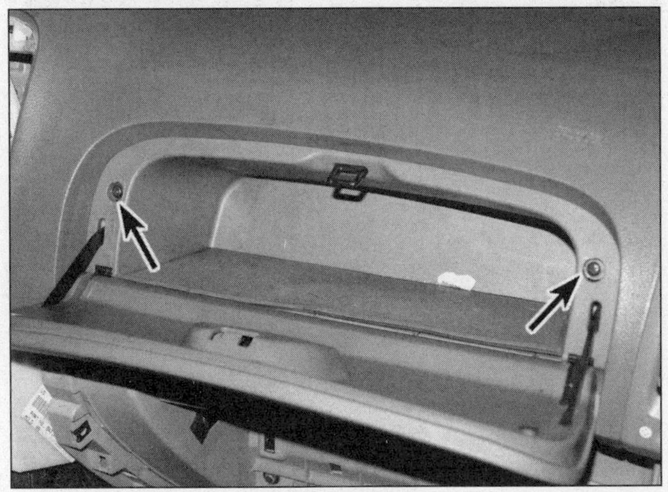
23.28 With the screw covers removed the upper mounting screws can be accessed

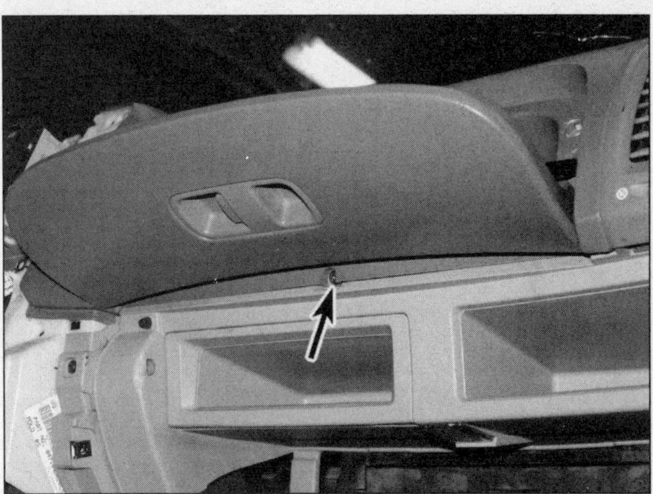
23.29 Upper glove box lower fastener

Lower glove box

25 Open the glove box, and pull the damper rod off of the door tab, then lower the door (see illustration).

26 Pivot the glove box in a downward position and slide the pins out (see illustration) and remove the lower glove box door

27 Installation is the reverse of removal.

Upper glove box

28 Open the upper glove box, use a small screwdriver to pry out the upper mounting screw covers then remove the screws (see illustration).

29 Remove the glove box lower mounting screw (see illustration).

30 Pull the glove box out from the instrument panel (see illustration).

31 Installation is the reverse of removal.

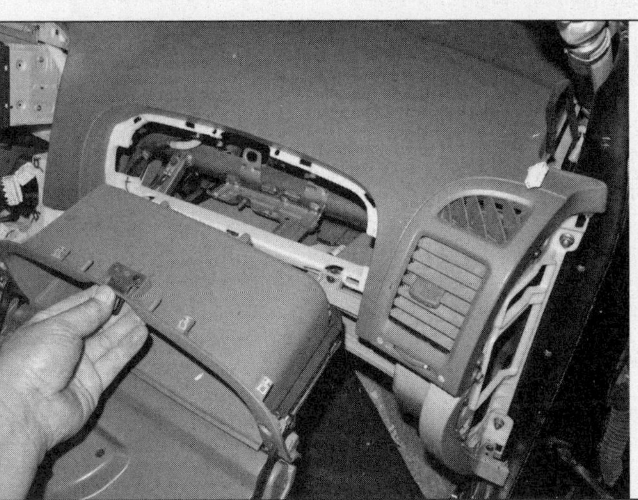
23.30 Pull the glove box straight out

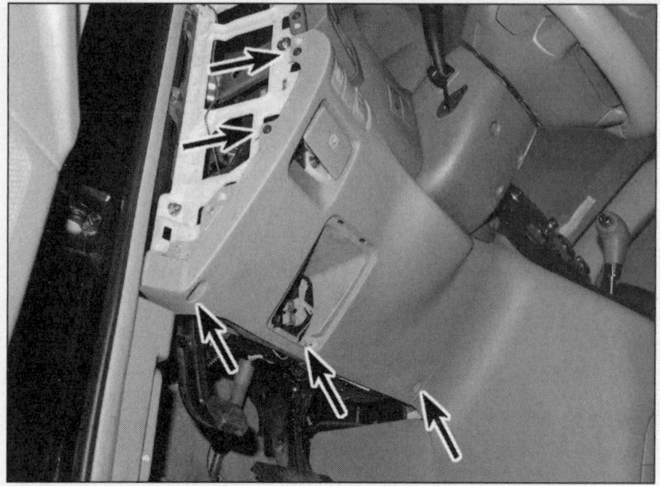
23.33 Knee bolster fastener locations

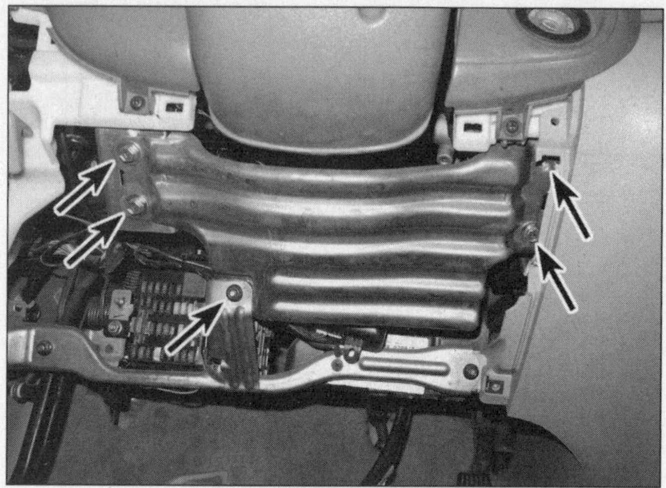
23.37 Knee bolster support fastener locations

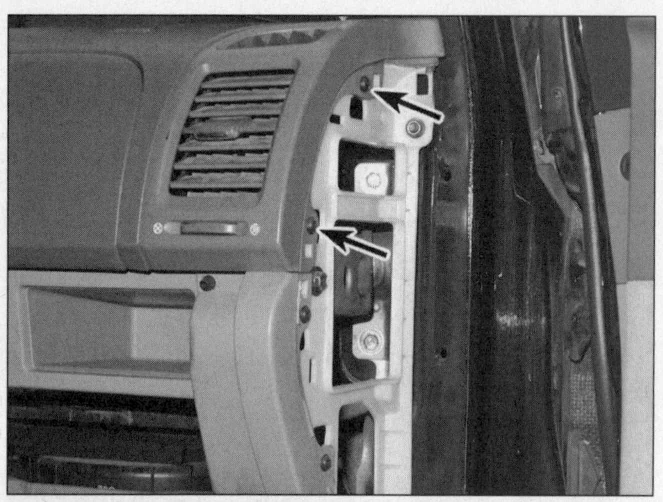
23.45 Remove the center vents fasteners from bottom edge of the panels

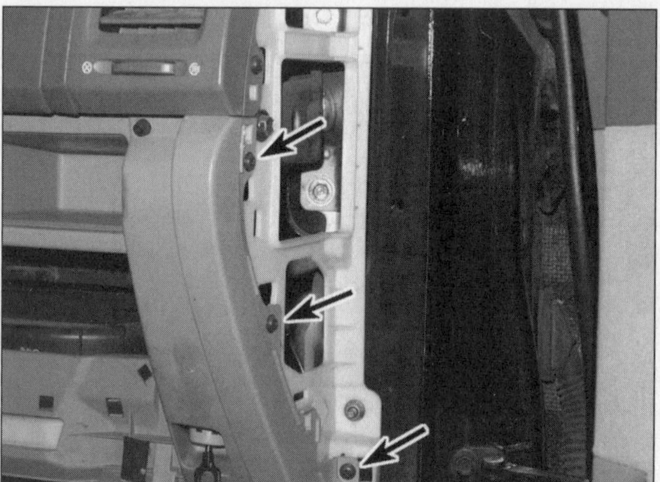
23.51a Remove the passenger's side lower trim panel fasteners from the side. . .

Knee bolster

32 Remove the instrument panel end cap (see Steps 2 and 3), then remove the fuse panel cover from the panel.
33 Remove the knee bolster upper fasteners (see illustration).
34 Grasp the cover with both hands and pull straight out to disengage the panel from the instrument panel.
35 Maneuver the panel around the parking brake release handle.
36 Disconnect the electrical connectors to the switches and remove the panel.
37 Remove the knee bolster support fasteners and support (see illustration).
38 Installation is the reverse of removal.

Instrument panel side vents

Driver's side vent

39 Remove the end cap (see Steps 2 and 3).
40 Remove the knee bolster (see Steps 32 through 36).
41 Remove the side vent mounting screws and pry the vent from the instrument panel.
42 Installation is the reverse of removal.

Passenger's side vent

43 Remove the end cap (see Steps 2 and 3).
44 Open the glove box door.
45 Remove the side vent mounting screws and pry the vent from the instrument panel (see illustration).
46 Installation is the reverse of removal.

Passenger's side lower trim panel

47 Remove the end cap (see Steps 2 and 3).
48 Remove the lower glove box (see Steps through).
49 Remove the lower glove box (see Steps through).
50 Remove the DVD player (see Chapter 12), if equipped.
51 Remove the passenger's side lower trim panel fasteners (see illustrations).
52 Remove the passenger's side vent (see Steps 43 through 45).
53 Using a trim tool pry around the perimeter of the lower trim panel, until all the clips are detached then remove it from the dashboard.
54 Installation is the reverse of removal.

24 Instrument panel – removal and installation

Warning: *Models covered by this manual are equipped with a Supplemental Restraint System (SRS), more commonly known as airbags. Always disable the airbag system before working in the vicinity of any airbag system component to avoid the possibility of accidental deployment of the airbag, which could cause personal injury (see Chapter 12).*

1 Disconnect the cable from the negative battery terminal (see Chapter 5).

Note: *This is a difficult procedure for thehome*

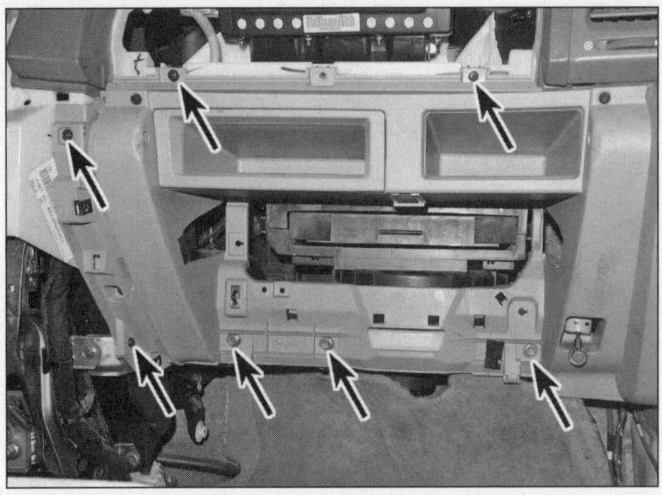

23.51b. . . and the front of the panel

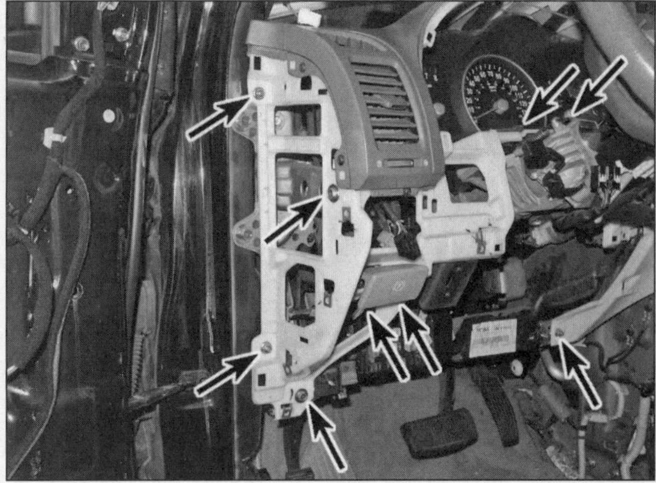

24.4a Driver's side fastener locations for the instrument panel

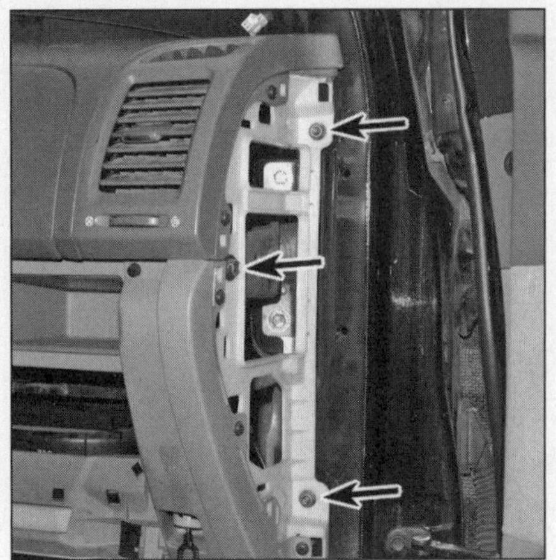

24.4b Passenger's side fastener locations for the instrument panel

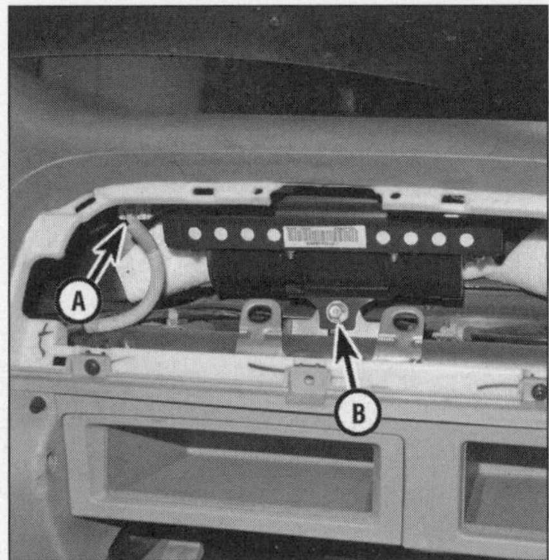

24.5 Disconnect the passenger's side air bag electrical connector (A) then remove the mounting bolt (B)

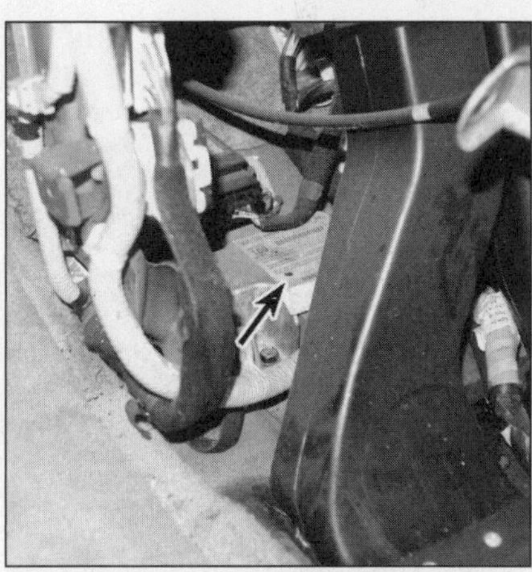

24.9 Location of the supplemental restraint system control module (SRSCM)

mechanic. There are many hidden fasteners, difficult angles to work in and many electrical connectors to tag and disconnect/connect. We recommend that this procedure be done only by an experienced do-it-yourselfer.

Note: *During removal of the instrument panel, make careful notes of how each piece comes off, where it fits in relation to other pieces and what holds it in place. If you note how each part is installed before removing it, getting the instrument panel back together again will be much easier.*

Note: *The instrument panel is mounted to the instrument panel cross bar, the instrument panel must be removed from the cross bar to access all the instrument panel cross bar fasteners.*

2 Remove the following parts:

a) *Steering wheel and column as a unit (see Chapter 10)*
b) *All the dashboard trim panels and the glove boxes (see Section 23)*
c) *Air conditioning and heater control assembly (see Chapter 3)*
d) *Instrument cluster, radio, instrument panel speakers and DVD player, if equpped (see Chapter 12)*
e) *Front seats (though not absolutely necessary, removing both front seats allows more room to work and eliminates the possibility of the occurrence of damage to the seats during this procedure)*
f) *Center floor console (see Section 27)*
g) *Shifter knob and disconnect the shift cable (see Chapter 7).*

Instrument panel

3 Disconnect the wiring harnesses at each A-pillar.

4 Remove the retaining bolts and nuts from the front and sides of the instrument panel (see illustrations).

Note: There are approximately 20 fasteners used to hold the instrument panel to the instrument panel cross bar.

5 Remove the passenger's side air bag electrical connector then the air bag to cross bar mounting bolt (see illustration).

6 With an assistant helping you, carefully separate the instrument panel from the cross bar then remove the instrument panel from the vehicle.

7 Installation is the reverse of removal.

Instrument panel cross bar

8 Remove the instrument panel (see Steps 1 through 6).

9 Disconnect the electrical connectors to the supplemental restraint system control module (SRSCM) (see illustration).

10 Disconnect the A/C and heating wiring harness electrical connector.

11 Remove the bolts that secure the A/C and heating housing to the bottom of the cross bar.

12 Disconnect the antenna harness, main vehicle harnesses, remove the ground wire and separate the data link connector from the instrument panel.

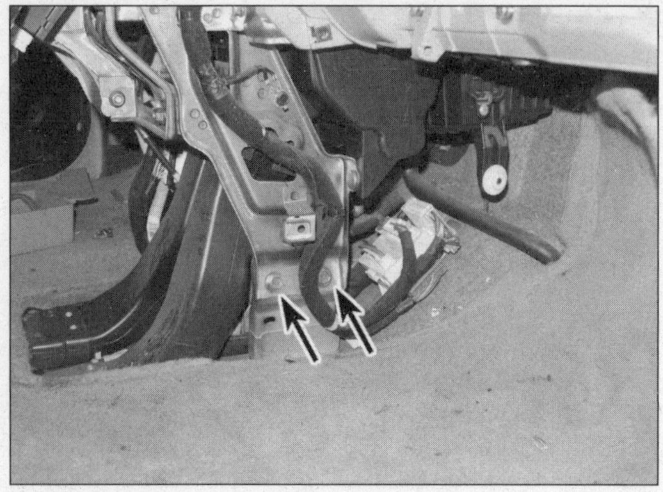
24.14 Location of the cross bar, lower center mounting bolts - right side shown left side similar

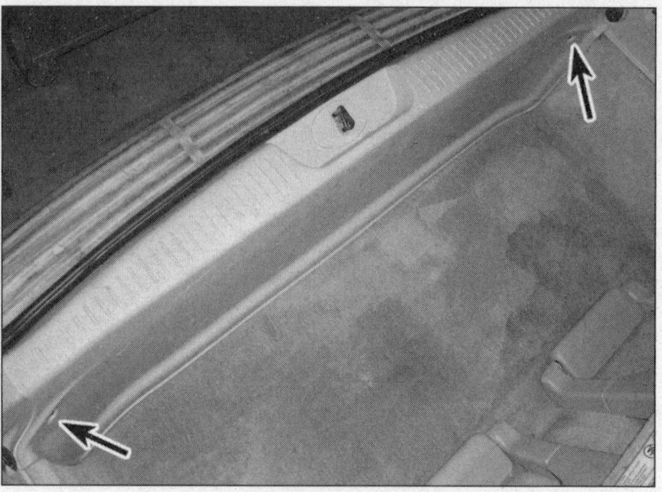
25.5a Remove the threshold mounting screws. . .

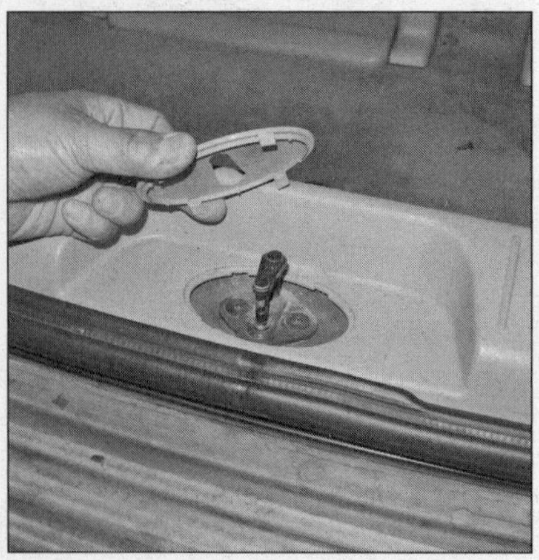
25.5b. . . then remove the striker cover. . .

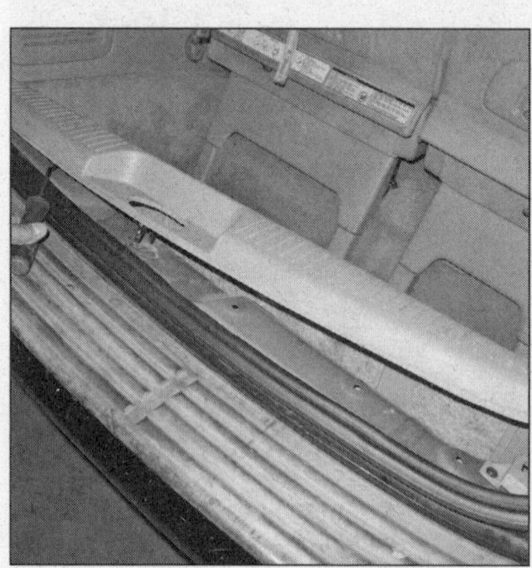
25.5c. . . then pry loose and remove the threshold from the rear of the vehicle

25.5d Unscrew the rear fasteners

25.5e Open the sliding door and pry up the threshold. . .

13 Remove the hood release cable handle (see Section 8).

Note: *There are approximately 18 fasteners used to hold the cross bar to the body.*

14 Remove the instrument panel cross bar mounting bolts and nuts along the front and center (see illustration) of the cross bar.

15 Remove the instrument panel cross bar bolts from each end of the instrument panel.

Note: *There are approximately 18 fasteners used to hold the cross bar to the body.*

Caution: *The cross bar is heavy and once the remaining bolts are removed can fall, have an assistant support the cross bar. You'll also need an assistant's help when installing the cross bar mounting bolts.*

16 With an assistant helping you, remove the instrument panel from the vehicle.

17 Installation is the reverse of removal.

25 Rear trim panels - removal and installation

1 Disconnect the cable from the negative battery terminal (see Chapter 5).

2 Remove the second and, if equipped, the third rear seat (see Section 26).

3 If equipped with a fire extinguisher, remove the cover from the driver's side quarter panel, then remove the fire extinguisher from the mounting bracket. Remove the mounting bracket bolts and bracket.

4 Remove the plastic plugs from the trim panel that is being removed. Use a flat bladed screwdriver.

5 Separate the trim panels from the body. Remove all mounting screws with a screwdriver and release the mounting clips (see illustrations). Disconnect any wire connectors from accessory power outlets, if so equipped.

25.5f. . . until the clips are released, then remove the threshold

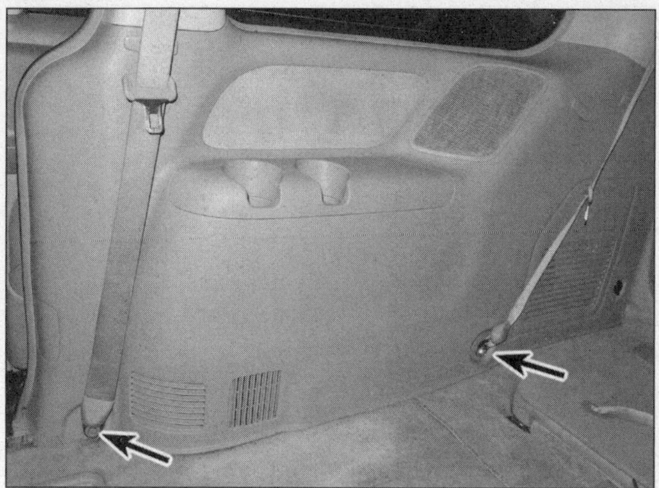

25.5g Remove the seat belt anchors

25.5h Pry the end panel out of the quarter trim panel, then disconnect side airbag connector

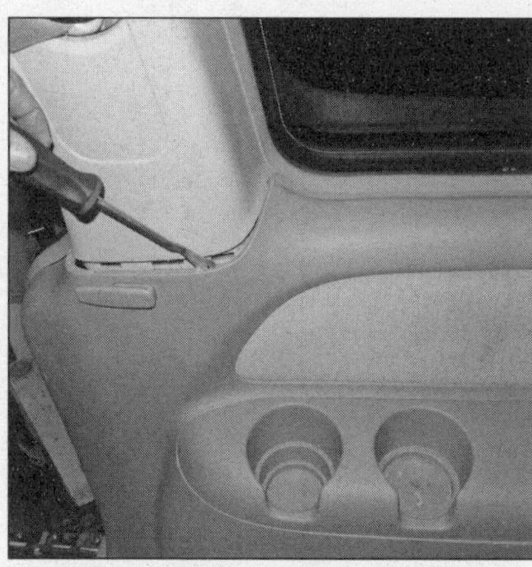

25.5i Pry the front of the quarter panel. . .

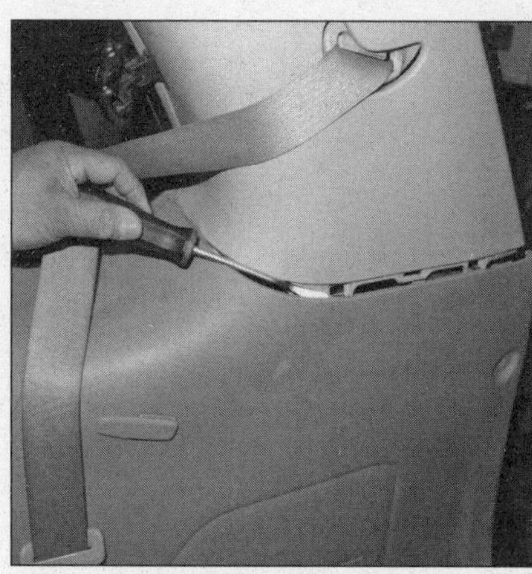

25.5j. . . then the rear of the panel until all the clips are disengaged

25.5k Disconnect the electrical connector to the power outlet, if equipped

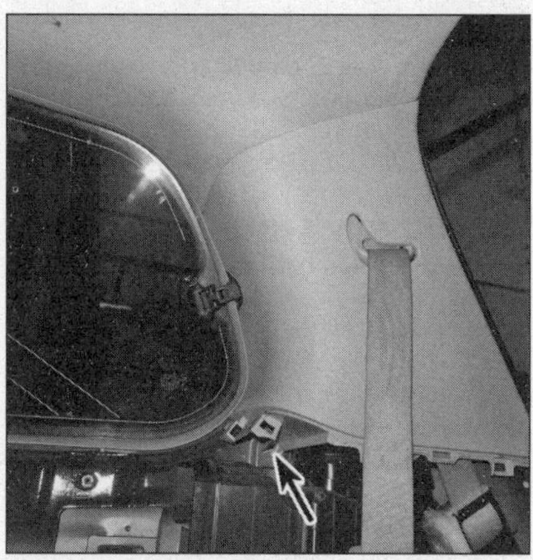

25.5l Remove the D-pillar trim screw. . .

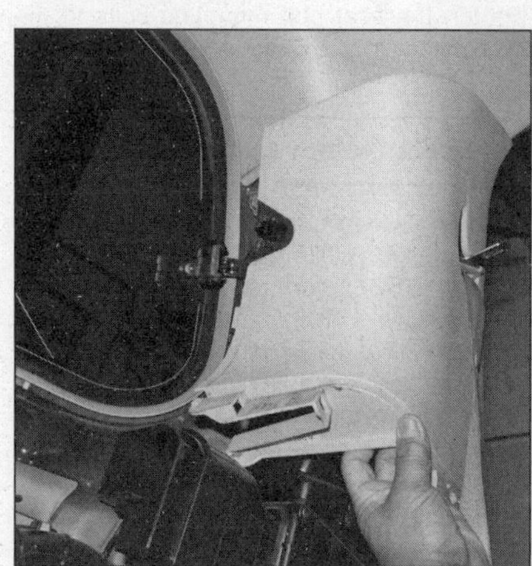

25.5m. . . then remove the trim panel

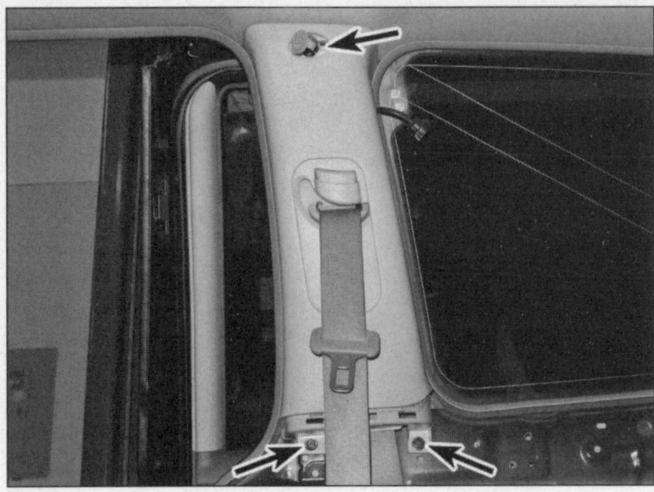

25.5n Remove the C-pillar trim fasteners. . .

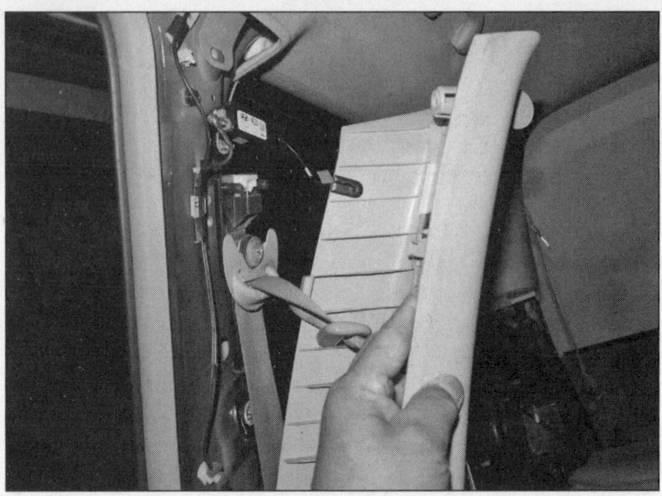

25.5o. . . and carefully pry out the trim panel

26.3a Remove the front. . .

26.3b. . . and rear bolts

6 Installation is the reverse of removal. Tighten the seat belt mounting bolts to the torque listed in this Chapter's Specifications.

26 Seats - removal and installation

Warning: *Models covered by this manual are equipped with a Supplemental Restraint System (SRS), more commonly known as airbags. Always disable the airbag system before working in the vicinity of any airbag system component to avoid the possibility of accidental deployment of the airbag, which could cause personal injury (see Chapter 12).*

1 Disconnect the cable from the negative battery terminal (see Chapter 5).

Front seat

2 Pry off any plastic covers to access the seat tracks and their mounting bolts. Keep them in order, as they are not identical.

3 Remove the retaining bolts (see illustrations).

4 Tilt the seat upward to access the underside, disconnect any electrical connectors, and lift the seat from the vehicle.

5 Installation is the reverse of removal.

Second row seats

6 Fold the seat back down.

7 Lift the release handle on the lower side of the seat and lift the rear of the seat.

8 Pull the release bar at the bottom of the seat and release the seat from its attachments. Remove the seat from the vehicle.

9 Installation is the reverse of removal.

Third row seats

10 Open the liftgate and remove the third row seat fastener trim covers from the rear of the seats (see illustrations).

11 Remove the mounting bolts from the rear of the seat.

12 Lift the seat up at a slight angle to disengage the front of the seat from the lock bar and remove the seat from the vehicle.

13 Installation is the reverse of removal.

27 Center floor console - removal and installation

Warning: *Models covered by this manual are equipped with a Supplemental Restraint System (SRS), more commonly known as airbags. Always disable the airbag system before working in the vicinity of any airbag system component to avoid the possibility of accidental deployment of the airbag, which could cause personal injury (see Chapter 12).*

1 Disconnect the cable from the negative battery terminal (see Chapter 5).

2 Move the front seats all the way to the rear.

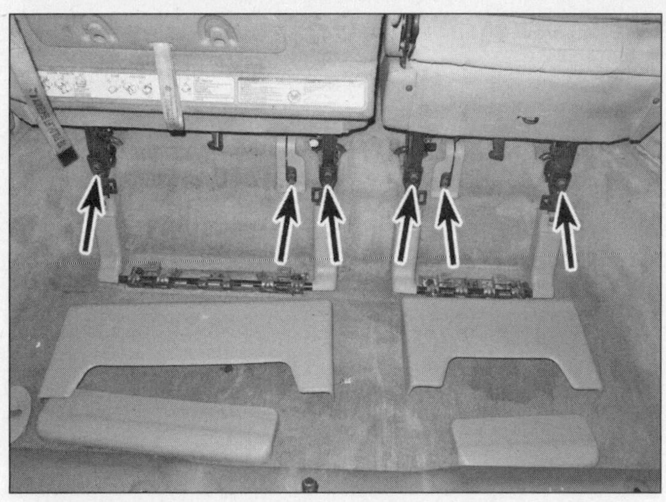

26.10 Remove the seat mounting bolts and remove the seats

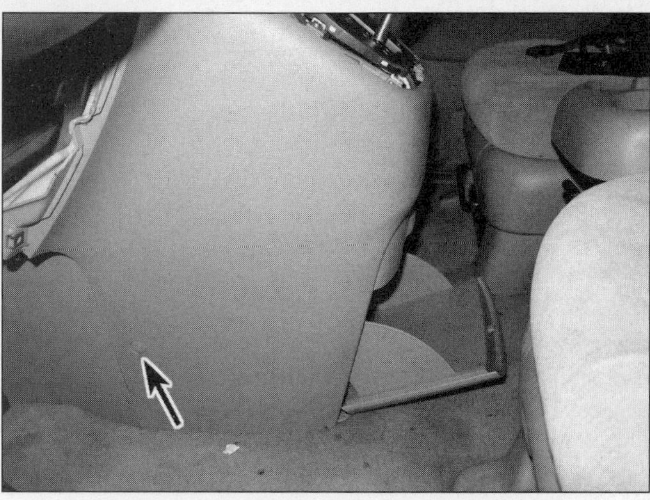

27.4a Remove the plastic fasteners from each side. . .

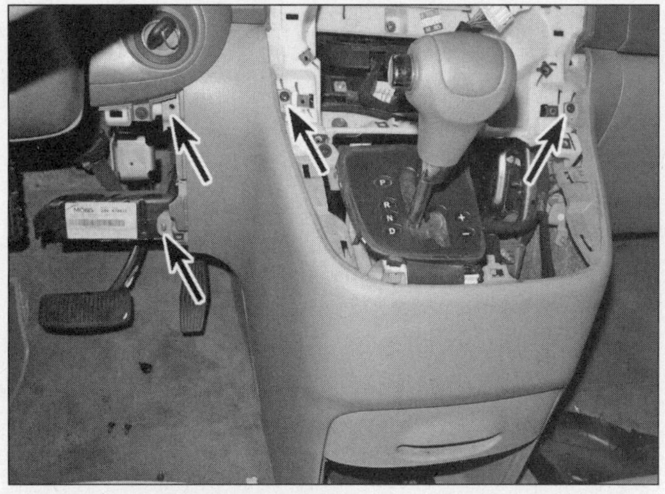

27.4b. . . remove the mounting screws form the left side and the top. . .

27.4c. . . then remove the screws from the right side

3 Remove the lower center console trim panel, the knee bolster and the lower glove box (see Section 23).

4 Remove the center floor console fasteners (see illustrations).

5 Using a trim tool pry out the console lower trim panels to disengage the clips and remove the panels (see illustration).

6 Remove the console back then remove it from the vehicle.

7 Installation is the reverse of removal.

28 Power liftgate motor assembly - removal and installation

1 Disconnect the cable from the negative battery terminal (see Chapter 5).

2 Remove the rear seats (see Section 26).

3 Remove the rear trim panels (see Section 25).

4 Open the liftgate and support the liftgate in the open position then remove the clip from the lift arm at the liftgate and separate the arm from the ball stud.

5 Disconnect the electrical connector to the motor assembly.

6 Remove the motor assembly mounting bolts, then remove the liftgate motor assembly from the vehicle.

7 Installation is the reverse of removal.

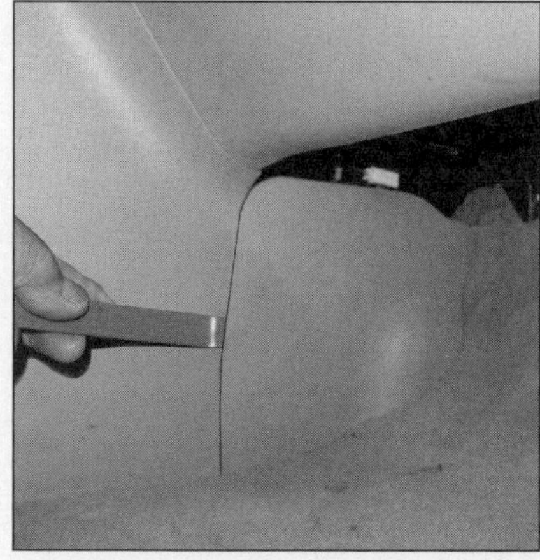

27.5 Pry the console lower trim panels out from each side

Notes

Chapter 12
Chassis electrical system

Contents

	Section
Airbag system - general information and precautions	25
Antenna - replacement	13
Bulb replacement	19
Circuit breakers - general information	4
Cruise control system - description	21
Daytime Running Lights (DRL) - general information	24
Electrical connectors - general information	6
Electrical troubleshooting - general information	2
Fuses and fusible links - general information	3
General information	1
Headlight bulb - replacement	17
Headlight housing - replacement	16
Headlights - adjustment	18
Horn - replacement	20
Ignition switch housing, key lock cylinder and ignition switch removal and installation	8
Instrument cluster - removal and installation	9
Instrument panel switches - replacement	10
Multi-function switches - replacement	7
Power door lock and keyless entry system - description and check	23
Power sliding door and power rear hatch - description and operation	14
Power window system - descripton and check	22
Radio, navigation, speakers and DVD player removal and installation	12
Rear window defogger - check and repair	15
Relays - general information and testing	5
Wiper motor - replacement	11
Wiring diagrams - general information	26

1 General information

The electrical system is a 12-volt, negative ground type. Power for the lights and all electrical accessories is supplied by a lead/acid-type battery that is charged by the alternator.

This Chapter covers repair and service procedures for the various electrical components not associated with the engine. Information on the battery, alternator, ignition system and starter motor can be found in Chapter 5.

It should be noted that when portions of the electrical system are serviced, the negative cable should be disconnected from the battery to prevent electrical shorts and/or fires.

2 Electrical troubleshooting - general information

Refer to illustrations 2.5a, 2.5b, 2.6 and 2.9

A typical electrical circuit consists of an electrical component, any switches, relays, motors, fuses, fusible links or circuit breakers related to that component and the wiring and connectors that link the component to both the battery and the chassis. To help you pinpoint an electrical circuit problem, wiring diagrams are included at the end of this Chapter.

Before tackling any troublesome electrical circuit, first study the appropriate wiring diagrams to get a complete understanding of what makes up that individual circuit. Trouble spots, for instance, can often be narrowed down by noting if other components related to the circuit are operating properly. If several components or circuits fail at one time, chances are the problem is in a fuse or ground connection, because several circuits are often routed through the same fuse and ground connections.

Electrical problems usually stem from simple causes, such as loose or corroded connections, a blown fuse, a melted fusible link or a failed relay. Visually inspect the condition of all fuses, wires and connections in a problem circuit before troubleshooting the circuit.

If test equipment and instruments are going to be utilized, use the diagrams to plan ahead of time where you will make the necessary connections in order to accurately pinpoint the trouble spot.

The basic tools needed for electrical troubleshooting include a circuit tester or voltmeter (a 12-volt bulb with a set of test leads can also be used), a continuity tester, which includes a bulb, battery and set of test leads, and a jumper wire, preferably with a circuit breaker incorporated, which can be used to bypass electrical components **(see illustrations)**. Before attempting to locate a problem with test instruments, use the wiring diagram(s) to decide where to make the connections.

Voltage checks

Voltage checks should be performed if a circuit is not functioning properly. Connect one lead of a circuit tester to either the negative battery terminal or a known good ground. Connect the other lead to a connector in the circuit being tested, preferably nearest to the battery or fuse **(see illustration)**. If the bulb of the tester lights, voltage is present, which means that the part of the circuit between the connector and the battery is problem free. Continue checking the rest of the circuit in the same fashion. When you reach a point at which no voltage is present, the problem lies between that point and the last test point with voltage. Most of the time the problem can be traced to a loose connection. **Note:** *Keep in mind that some circuits receive voltage only when the ignition key is in the Accessory or Run position.*

Finding a short

One method of finding shorts in a circuit is to remove the fuse and connect a test light or voltmeter in place of the fuse terminals. There should be no voltage present in the circuit. Move the wiring harness from side-to-side while watching the test light. If the bulb goes on, there is a short to ground somewhere in that area, probably where the insulation has rubbed through. The same test can be performed on each component in the circuit, even a switch.

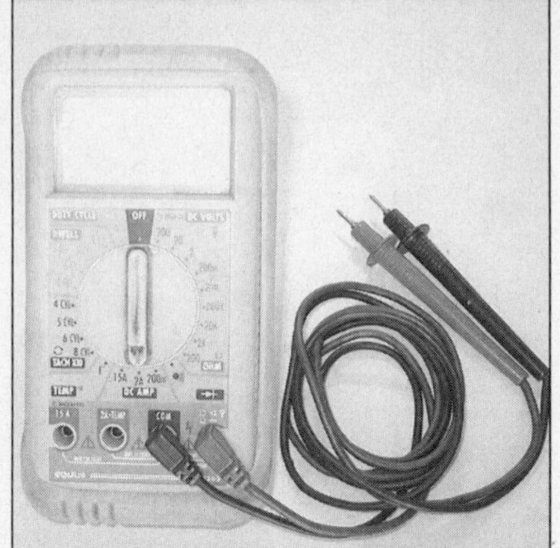

2.5a The most useful tool for electrical troubleshooting is a digital multimeter that can check volts, amps, and test continuity

2.5b A test light is a very handy tool for checking voltage

Ground check

Perform a ground test to check whether a component is properly grounded. Disconnect the battery and connect one lead of a continuity tester or multimeter (set to the ohms scale), to a known good ground. Connect the other lead to the wire or ground connection being tested. If the resistance is low (less than 5 ohms), the ground is good. If the bulb on a self-powered test light does not go on, the ground is not good.

Continuity check

A continuity check is done to determine if there are any breaks in a circuit - if it is passing electricity properly. With the circuit off (no power in the circuit), a self-powered continuity tester or multimeter can be used to check the circuit. Connect the test leads to both ends of the circuit (or to the power end and a good ground), and if the test light comes on the circuit is passing current properly **(see illustration)**. If the resistance is low (less than 5 ohms), there is continuity; if the reading is 10,000 ohms or higher, there is a break somewhere in the circuit. The same procedure can be used to test a switch, by connecting the continuity tester to the switch terminals. With the switch turned On, the test light should come on (or low resistance should be indicated on a meter).

Finding an open circuit

When diagnosing for possible open circuits, it is often difficult to locate them by sight because the connectors hide oxidation or terminal misalignment. Merely wiggling a connector on a sensor or in the wiring harness may correct the open circuit condition. Remember this when an open circuit is indicated when troubleshooting a circuit. Intermittent problems may also be caused by oxidized

2.6 In use, a basic test light's lead is clipped to a known good ground, then the pointed probe can test connectors, wires or electrical sockets - if the bulb lights, the part being tested has battery voltage

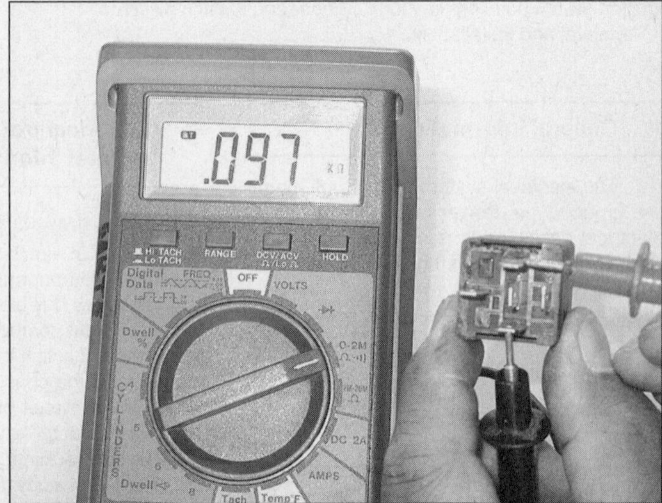

2.9 With a multimeter set to the ohms scale, resistance can be checked across two terminals - when checking for continuity, a low reading indicates continuity, a high reading indicates lack of continuity

3.1 Typical engine comparment fuse/relay box location

3.2 Location of the interior fuse box - 2005 and earlier models

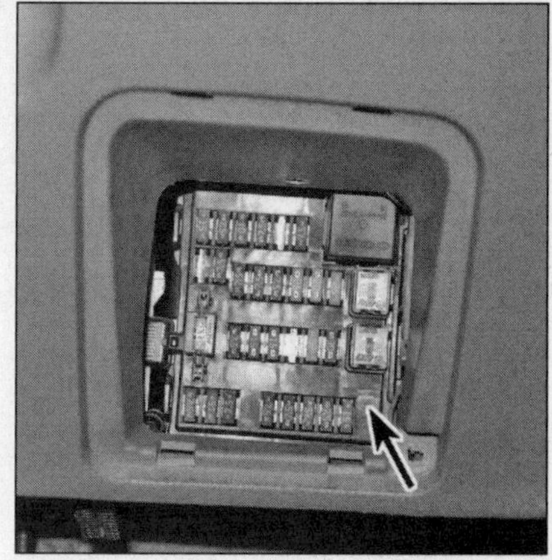

3.4 Location of the interior fuse box

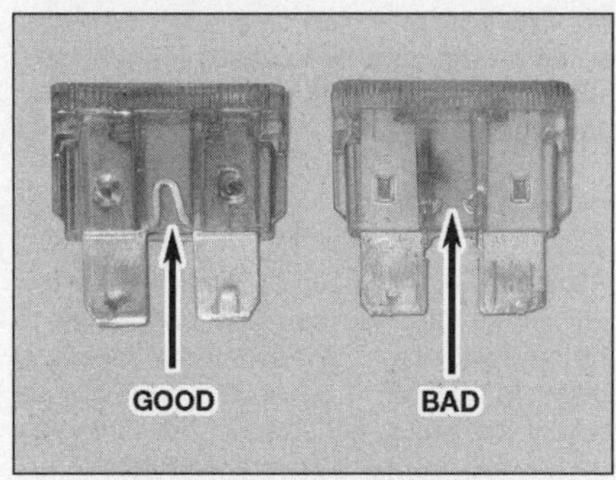

3.10 When a fuse blows, the element between the terminals melts

or loose connections.

Electrical troubleshooting is simple if you keep in mind that all electrical circuits are basically electricity running from the battery, through the wires, switches, relays, fuses and fusible links to each electrical component (light bulb, motor, etc.) and to ground, from which it is passed back to the battery. Any electrical problem is an interruption in the flow of electricity to and from the battery.

3 Fuses and fusible links - general information

Fuses

1 The electrical circuits of the vehicle are protected by a combination of fuses, circuit breakers and fusible links. With the vast number of electrical systems in today's cars there are multiple fuse and relay panels incorporated into them. When you are looking for a certain fuse don't assume it is in just one place. Check your owner's manual for fuse location and description. Also, there are wiring diagrams in this section that will also show where and what each of those fuses are connected to. The main fuse/relay panel is in the engine compartment (see illustration). Each of the fuses is designed to protect a specific circuit, and the various circuits are identified on the fuse panel legend.

Note: *The fuse box has taken on a lot more responsibilities than in the past, and there is more than one location for fuses and various relays. Small micro-processors and even some internal relays and circuits are incorporated into the box that are not serviceable. Replacing the fuse box is the only option. In some instances, when replacing a fuse box, there may be some programming needed to be performed in order for the car to start or operate certain systems.*

2005 and earlier model fuse box locations

2 Passenger compartment fuse box is located on the driver's side left kick panel area (see illustration).

3 Engine compartment fuse box is located under the hood on the driver's side behind the battery.

2006 and later model fuse box locations

4 Passenger compartment fuse box is located on the driver's side knee bolster panel (see illustration).

5 FAM (Front Area Module) is located under the hood on the driver's side left front corner.

6 RAM (Rear Area Module) is located in the rear section on the driver's side quarter panel area. (Open rear hatch or trunk to gain access.)

7 IPM (Instrument Panel Module) is located below the driver's area.

8 ICM (Integrated Circuit Module) is located in the center of the dash near the driver's side.

9 Relay Box is located in the lower right front section of the center dash area.

Note: *Several sizes and types of fuses are employed in the different fuse blocks. There are small, medium and large sizes of the same amperage value. Some are a blade type fuse while others may be bolted in place. In some cases the fuse may need to be removed with a fuse removing tool (usually provided for in the fuse box) or with an appropriate alternative tool.*

10 If an electrical component fails, always check the fuse first. The best way to check most fuses is with a test light. Check for power at the exposed terminal tips of each fuse. If power is present at one side of the fuse but not the other, the fuse is blown. A blown fuse can also be identified by visually inspecting it (see illustration).

Note: *Be sure to replace blown fuses with the correct type. Fuses (of the same physical size) of different ratings may be physically interchangeable, but only fuses of the proper rating should be used. Replacing a fuse with one of a higher or lower value than specified is not recommended. Each electrical circuit needs a specific amount of protection. The amperage value of each fuse is molded into the top of the fuse body.*

Note: *If the replacement fuse immediately fails, don't replace it again until the cause of the problem is isolated and corrected. In most cases, this will be a short circuit in the wiring caused by a broken or deteriorated wire.*

Fusible links

11 Some circuits are protected by fusible links. The links are used in circuits that are not ordinarily fused, such as the high-current side of the charging or starting circuits. Conventional inline fusible links, such as those used in the starter cable, are characterized by a bulge in the cable. Newer cartridge-type fusible links, which are similar in appearance to a large cartridge-type fuse, are located in the engine compartment fuse and relay box (see illustration 3.1). After disconnecting the cable from the negative battery terminal, simply remove the fusible link and replace it with a unit of the same amperage.

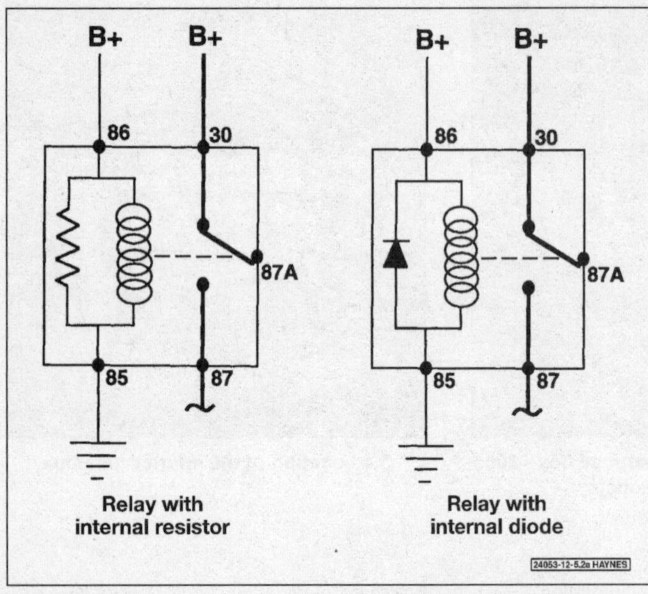

5.2a Typical ISO relay designs, terminal numbering and circuit connections

5.2b Most relays are marked on the outside to easily identify the control circuit and power circuit - this one is of the four-terminal type

4 Circuit breakers - general information

1 Circuit breakers protect certain circuits, such as the power windows or heated seats. Depending on the vehicle's accessories, there may be one or two circuit breakers, located in the fuse/relay box in the engine compartment.

2 Because the circuit breakers reset automatically, an electrical overload in a circuit breaker-protected system will cause the circuit to fail momentarily, then come back on. If the circuit does not come back on, check it immediately.

3 For a basic check, pull the circuit breaker up out of its socket on the fuse panel, but just far enough to probe with a voltmeter. The breaker should still contact the sockets. With the voltmeter negative lead on a good chassis ground, touch each end prong of the circuit breaker with the positive meter probe. There should be battery voltage at each end. If there is battery voltage only at one end, the circuit breaker must be replaced.

4 Some circuit breakers must be reset manually.

5 Relays - general information and testing

General information

1 Several electrical accessories in the vehicle, such as the fuel injection system, horns, starter, and fog lamps use relays to transmit the electrical signal to the component. Relays use a low-current circuit (the control circuit) to open and close a high-current circuit (the power circuit). If the relay is defective, that component will not operate properly. Most relays are mounted in the engine compartment and interior fuse/relay boxes. If a faulty relay is suspected, it can be removed and tested using the procedure below or by a dealer service department or a repair shop. Defective relays must be replaced as a unit.

Testing

2 Most of the relays used in these vehicles are of a type often called ISO relays, which refers to the International Standards Organization. The terminals of ISO relays are numbered to indicate their usual circuit connections and functions. There are two basic layouts of terminals on the relays used in these vehicles (see illustrations).

3 Refer to the wiring diagram for the circuit to determine the proper connections for the relay you're testing. If you can't determine the correct connection from the wiring diagrams, however, you may be able to determine the test connections from the information that follows.

4 Two of the terminals are the relay control circuit and connect to the relay coil. The other relay terminals are the power circuit. When the relay is energized, the coil creates a magnetic field that closes the larger contacts of the power circuit to provide power to the circuit loads.

5 Terminals 85 and 86 are normally the control circuit. If the relay contains a diode, terminal 86 must be connected to battery positive (B+) voltage and terminal 85 to ground. If the relay contains a resistor, terminals 85 and 86 can be connected in either direction with respect to B+ and ground.

6 Terminal 30 is normally connected to the battery voltage (B+) source for the circuit loads. Terminal 87 is connected to the ground side of the circuit, either directly or through a load. If the relay has several alternate terminals for load or ground connections, they usually are numbered 87A, 87B, 87C, and so on.

7 Use an ohmmeter to check continuity through the relay control coil.

Connect the meter according to the polarity shown in the illustration for one check, then reverse the ohmmeter leads and check continuity in the other direction.

If the relay contains a resistor, resistance should be indicated on the meter, and should be the same value with the ohmmeter in either direction.

If the relay contains a diode, resistance should be higher with the ohmmeter in the forward polarity direction than with the meter leads reversed.

If the ohmmeter shows infinite resistance in both directions, replace the relay.

8 Remove the relay from the vehicle and use the ohmmeter to check for continuity between the relay power circuit terminals. There should be no continuity between terminal 30 and 87 with the relay de-energized.

9 Connect a fused jumper wire to terminal 86 and the positive battery terminal. Connect another jumper wire between terminal 85 and ground. When the connections are made, the relay should click.

10 With the jumper wires connected, check for continuity between the power circuit terminals. Now, there should be continuity between terminals 30 and 87.

11 If the relay fails any of the above tests, replace it.

6 Electrical connectors - general information

1 Most electrical connections on these vehicles are made with multiwire plastic connectors. The mating halves of many connectors are secured with locking clips molded into the plastic connector shells. The mating halves of some large connectors, such as some of those under the instrument panel, are held together by a bolt through the center of the connector.

2 To separate a connector with locking clips, use a small screwdriver to pry the clips apart carefully, then separate the connector halves. Pull only on the shell, never pull on the wiring harness, as you may damage the individual wires and terminals inside the connectors. Look at the connector closely before trying to separate the halves. Often the locking clips are engaged in a way that is not immediately clear. Additionally, many connectors have more than one set of clips.

3 Each pair of connector terminals has a male half and a female half. When you look at the end view of a connector in a diagram, be sure to understand whether the view shows the harness side or the component side of the connector. Connector halves are mirror images of each other, and a terminal shown on the right side end-view of one half will be on the left side end-view of the other half.

4 It is often necessary to take circuit voltage measurements with a connector connected. Whenever possible, carefully insert a small straight pin (not your meter probe) into the rear of the connector shell to contact the terminal inside, then clip your meter lead to the pin. This kind of connection is called "backprobing." When inserting a test probe into a terminal, be careful not to distort the terminal opening. Doing so can lead to a poor connection and corrosion at that terminal later. Using the small straight pin instead of a meter probe results in less chance of deforming the terminal connector.

Electrical connectors

Most electrical connectors have a single release tab that you depress to release the connector

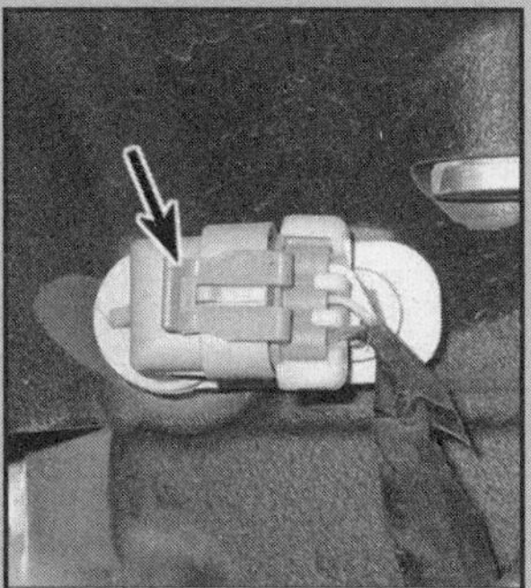

Some electrical connectors have a retaining tab which must be pried up to free the connector

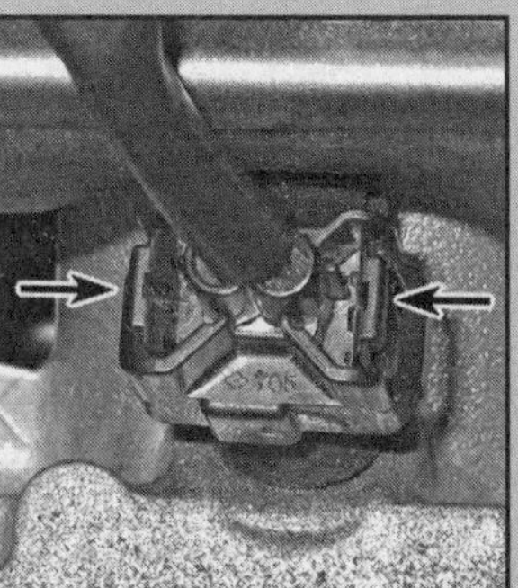

Some connectors have two release tabs that you must squeeze to release the connector

Some connectors use wire retainers that you squeeze to release the connector

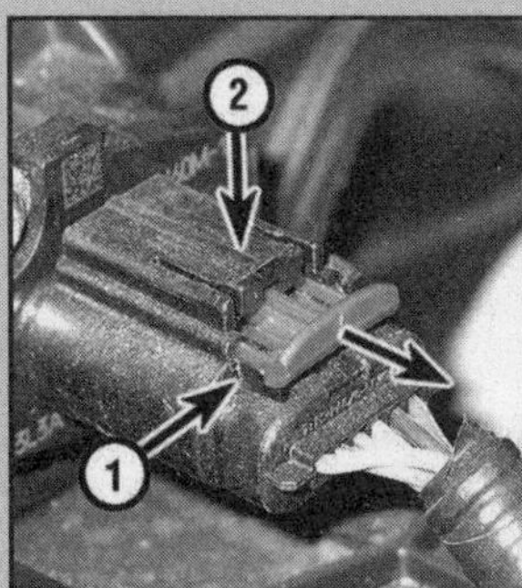

Critical connectors often employ a sliding lock (1) that you must pull out before you can depress the release tab (2)

Here's another sliding-lock style connector, with the lock (1) and the release tab (2) on the side of the connector

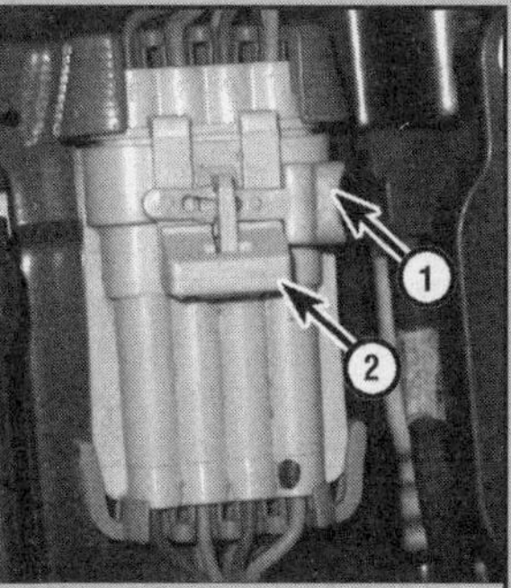

On some connectors the lock (1) must be pulled out to the side and removed before you can lift the release tab (2)

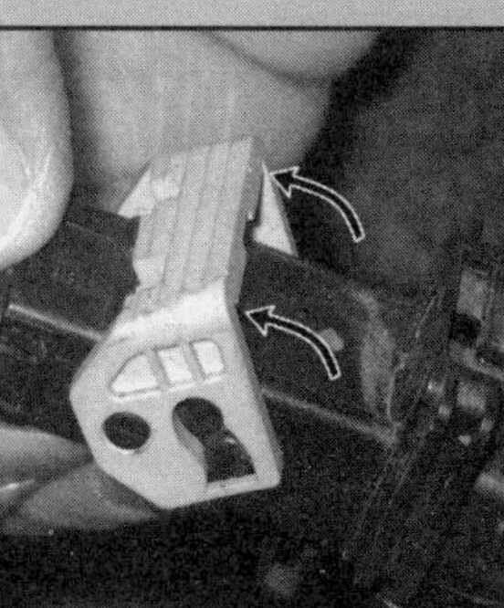

Some critical connectors, like the multi-pin connectors at the Powertrain Control Module employ pivoting locks that must be flipped open

7.9a Depress the tab while removing the headlight switch. . .

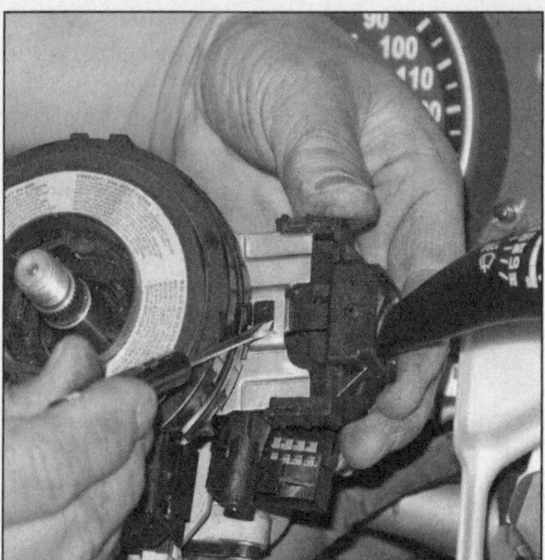

7.9b. . . or the windshield wiper switch

8.3 Drill into the bolts off that secure the ignition switch housing, then use a screw extractor to unscrew the shanks

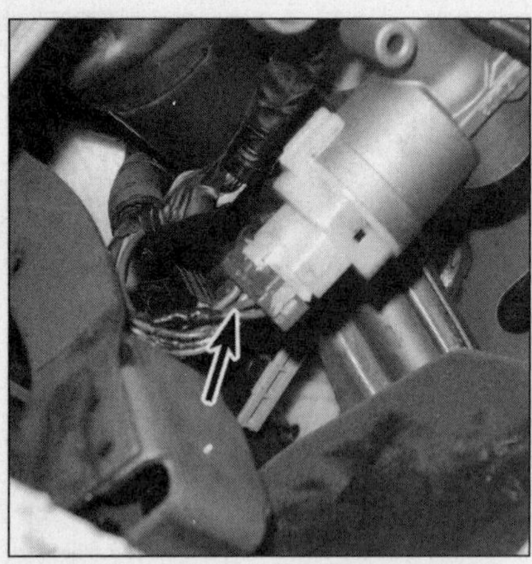

8.12 Disconnect the electrical connector to the ignition switch

7 Multi-function switches - replacement

Warning: *The models covered by this manual are equipped with Supplemental Restraint Systems (SRS), more commonly known as airbags. Always disable the airbag system before working in the vicinity of any airbag system components to avoid the possibility of accidental deployment of the airbags, which could cause personal injury (see Section 25).*

2005 and earlier models

1 Disconnect the cable from the negative terminal of the battery (see Chapter 5).

2 Remove the steering wheel and airbag clockspring (see Chapter 10).

Warning: *Do not turn or rotate the clockspring after removing it. There is a limited amount of turns in each direction. For safety purposes do not turn steering column shaft after steering wheel is removed. Tape the center of the clockspring to its outside section so it can't rotate.*

3 Remove the steering column covers (see Chapter 11).

4 Disconnect the electrical connector from the back side of the multi-function switch.

5 Remove the screws securing the multi-function switch to the steering column and then pull the switch off of the steering column shaft.

6 Installation is the reverse of removal.

2006 and later models

7 Disconnect the cable from the negative terminal of the battery (see Chapter 5).

8 Remove the upper and lower steering column covers (see Chapter 11).

9 Depress the headlight switch retaining tab, while pulling the switch away from the steering column (see illustrations).

10 Installation is the reverse of removal.

8 Ignition switch housing, key lock cylinder and ignition switch - removal and installation

Warning: *The models covered by this manual are equipped with Supplemental Restraint Systems (SRS), more commonly known as airbags. Always disable the airbag system before working in the vicinity of any airbag system components to avoid the possibility of accidental deployment of the airbags, which could cause personal injury (see Section 25).*

Ignition switch housing

1 Disconnect the cable from the negative terminal of the battery (see Chapter 5).

2 Remove the steering column upper and lower covers (see Chapter 11).

3 Use a chisel to cut slots into the shear-head bolts that secure the ignition switch housing to the steering column shaft, or drill a hole into each bolt and use a screw extractor to remove the bolts (see illustration).

4 Remove the bolts, disconnect the electrical connections and remove the ignition switch housing.

5 A new replacement ignition housing will come with new shear-head bolts. Align the new ignition switch housing in its proper position and tighten the two supplied bolts until the heads break off.

6 The remainder of the installation is the reverse of removal.

Key lock cylinder

7 With the key in place, insert a small round tool into the release pin of the ignition switch housing. Rotate the key from On to OFF while depressing the pin and pull the key lock from the housing. (Release the pin when you feel it start to bind on the rotating part of the key lock.)

8 To replace the key lock, simply slide the replacement key lock into the housing and rotate it from OFF to ON. This will lock the retaining pin back into place.

Ignition switch

9 Disconnect the cable from the negative terminal of the battery (see Chapter 5).

10 Remove the knee bolster from below the steering wheel (see Chapter 11).

11 Remove the instrument cluster trim panel (see Chapter 11).

12 Disconnect the electrical connector to the ignition switch electrical unit (see illustration).

13 Remove the small screw securing the ignition switch to the housing and remove the switch.

14 Installation is the reverse of removal.

9 Instrument cluster - removal and installation

Warning: *The models covered by this manual are equipped with Supplemental Restraint Systems (SRS), more commonly known as airbags. Always disable the airbag system before working in the vicinity of any airbag*

9.3 Instrument cluster mounting screw locations

9.4 Disconnect the electrical connector to the back of the instrument cluster

10.3 The instrument dimmer control, door light are in a panel that can be pushed out of the driver's knee bolster from behind

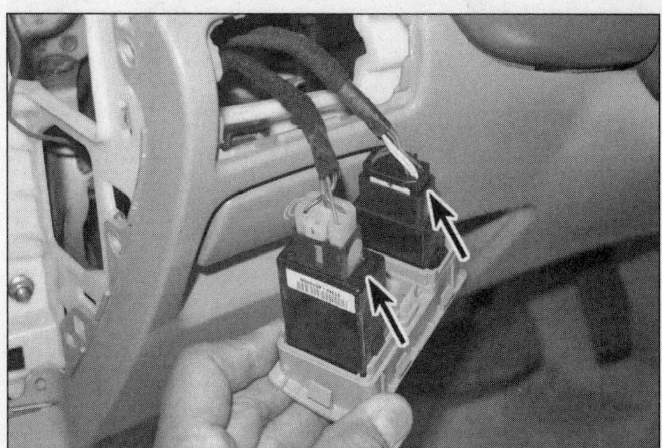

10.4 Disconnect the electrical connector(s) to the switch(s)

system components to avoid the possibility of accidental deployment of the airbags, which could cause personal injury (see Section 25).

1 Disconnect the cable from the negative terminal of the battery (see Chapter 5).

2 Remove the instrument cluster trim panel (see Chapter 11).

3 Remove the four screws securing the instrument cluster (see illustration).

4 Pull the instrument cluster out far enough to disconnect the electrical connector and remove the cluster (see illustration).

5 Installation is the reverse of removal.

10 Instrument panel switches - replacement

Warning: *The models covered by this manual are equipped with Supplemental Restraint Systems (SRS), more commonly known as airbags. Always disable the airbag system before working in the vicinity of any airbag system component to avoid the possibility of accidental deployment of the airbag(s), which could cause personal injury (see Section 25).*

1 Disconnect the cable from the negative battery terminal (see Chapter 5).

Instrument brightness control and door light switch

2 Remove the instrument panel end cap panel (see Chapter 11).

3 Carefully push the panel out from the rear of the instrument panel with a suitable trim panel tool (see illustration).

4 To replace the switches, disconnect the electrical connector and remove the switch from the switch panel (see illustration).

5 Installation is the reverse of removal.

Rear window defogger switch, seat heater switches and traction control switch

6 Remove the center trim panel (see Chapter 11).

7 Remove the center side trim/ vent panels (see Chapter 11).

8 Remove the switch assembly mounting screws and

9 Remove the switch panel retaining screws (see illustration), then pull the panel out of the instrument panel.

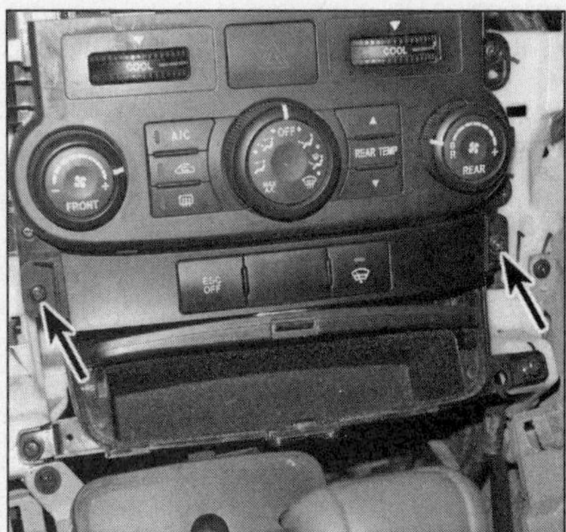

10.9 Remove the switch panel retaining screws

10.10 Disconnect each electrical connector to the switches

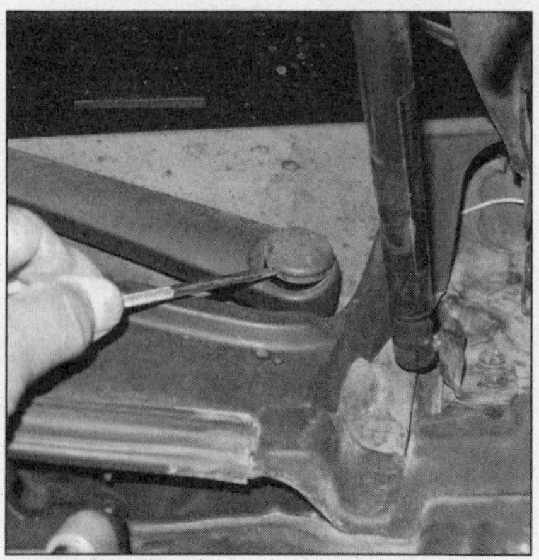
11.6 Remove the caps and unscrew the wiper arm mounting nuts. . .

11.7 Mark the positions of the arms so they can be correctly installed

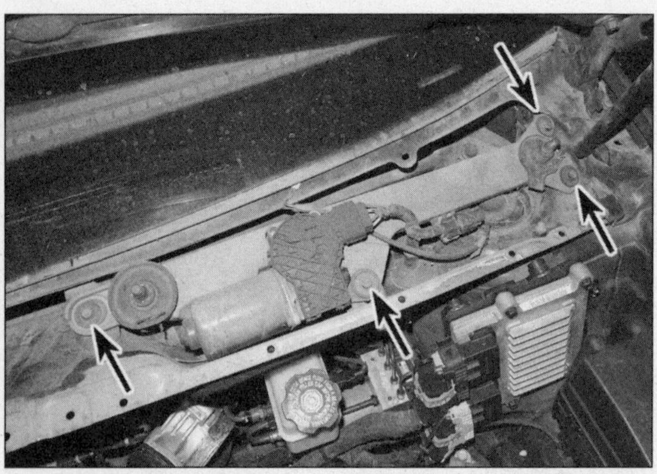
11.10 The windshield wiper assembly mounitng bolt locattions - remove them after disconnecting the wiring, then lift the entire unit out of the cowl

11.11 Pry the link from the crank arm; the crank arm can then be removed from the motor shaft if required

10 Disconnect the electrical connector(s) to the switch(s) and from the backside of the panel (see illustration) then unclip the switch(s) from the panel and remove the switch(s)

Hazard warning light switch

Note: *The hazard switch is incorporated in to the center of the air conditioning heater control unit.*

11 Remove the air conditioning heater control unit (see Chapter 3).

12 Push the switch out from the back side of the control unit.

13 Installation is the reverse of removal.

11 Wiper motor - replacement

Windshield wiper motor

2005 and earlier models

1 Disconnect the cable from the negative terminal of the battery (see Chapter 5).

2 Wiper motor is located in the right-rear corner of the engine compartment. Remove the bolts securing the motor assembly to the firewall.

3 Pull the motor out far enough to gain access to the wiper linkage arm.

4 Rotate the wiper arms far enough to expose the linkage arm. Remove the arm from the linkage assembly by applying pressure with a forked tool to pop the linkage arm ball from the socket.

Note: *Do not remove the nut from the wiper motor shaft that secures the linkage arm to it. This comes with the replacement motor.*

Note: *The ball and socket will have to be pressed back together. Use a large pair of pliers for this purpose.*

5 Installation is the reverse of removal.

2006 and later models

6 Remove the wiper arm mounting nuts (see illustration).

7 Mark the position of each wiper arm to its shaft, then remove the arms (see illustration).

8 Remove the plastic cowl cover (see Chapter 11).

9 Disconnect the electrical connector from the wiper motor.

10 Remove the wiper motor and link assembly mounting bolts (see illustration), thenremove the wiper motor and link assembly from the cowl area.

11 Use a screwdriver to pry the linkage rod from the crank arm pivot of the wiper motor (see illustration).

12 Remove the crank arm nut, mark the relationship of the crank arm to the motor shaft and remove the crank arm from the shaft.

13 Remove the wiper motor mounting bolts and separate the motor from the link rod assembly.

14 Installation is the reverse of removal.

Rear wiper motor

15 Disconnect the cable from the negative terminal of the battery (see Chapter 5).

16 Remove the cap that covers up the wiper arm retaining nut and nut (see illustration).

17 Mark the position of the wiper arm in

11.16 Remove the cap then the wiper arm retaining nut

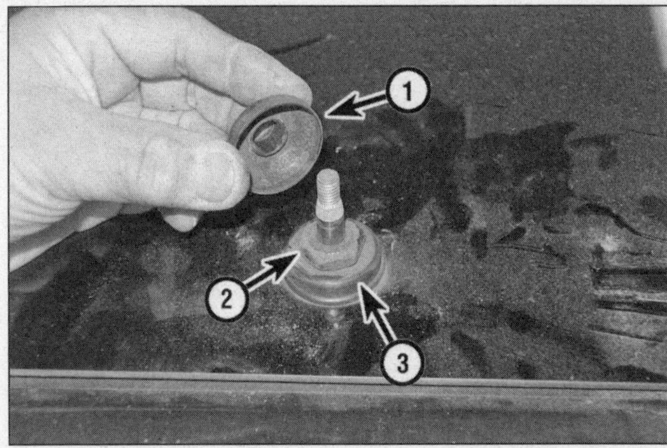

11.19 Remove the wiper motor-to-liftgate nut

1 *Motor mounting nut cover*
2 *Motor mounting nut*
3 *Grommet*

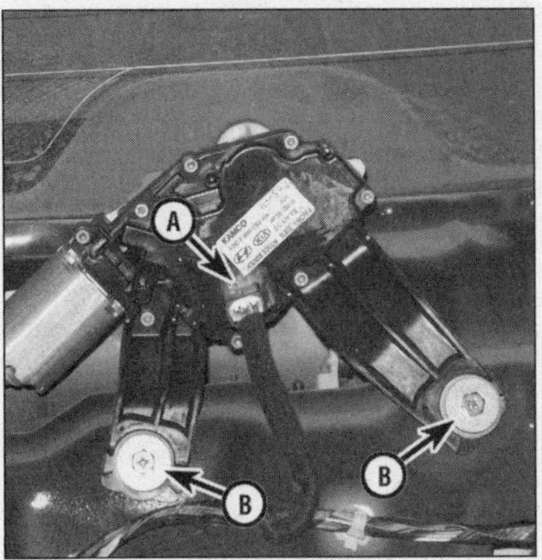

11.22a Disconnect the rear wiper motor electrical connector (A) then remove the mounting bolts (B). . .

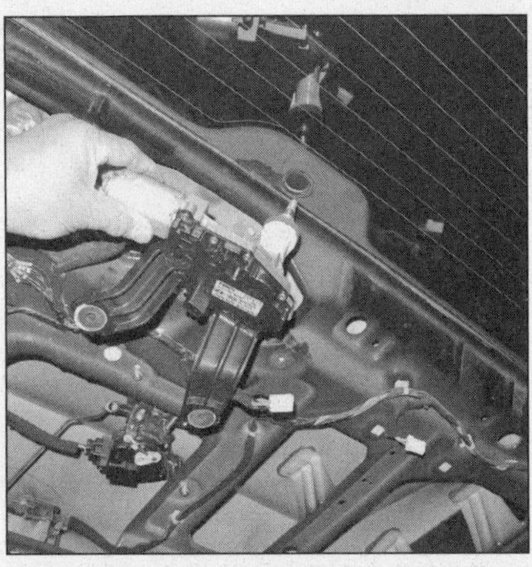

11.22b. . . and lower the motor from the liftgate

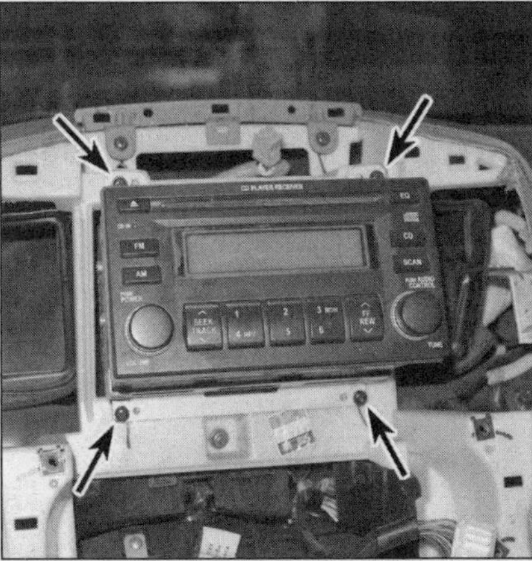

12.4 Location of the radio mounting screws

relation to the wiper motor shaft.

18 Remove the arm from the shaft. If the wiper arm is difficult to remove from the shaft splines, use a small two-jaw puller to detach the arm.

19 Remove the wiper motor-to-liftgate retaining nut cover and nut (see illustration).

20 Remove the liftgate trim panel (see Chapter 11).

21 Disconnect the electrical connector from the rear wiper motor.

22 Remove the rear wiper motor mounting bolts and remove the motor (see illustrations).

23 Installation is the reverse of removal.

12 Radio, navigation, speakers and DVD player - removal and installation

Warning: *The models covered by this manual are equipped with Supplemental Restraint Systems (SRS), more commonly known as airbags. Always disable the airbag system before working in the vicinity of any airbag system components to avoid the possibility of accidental deployment of the airbags, which could cause personal injury (see Section 25).*

1 Disconnect the cable from the negative terminal of the battery (see Chapter 5).

Radio

2 Remove the center trim panel, center console panel and both center vent assemblies (see Chapter 11).

3 Remove the heater/air conditioner control assembly (see Chapter 3).

4 Remove the radio mounting screws (see illustration), then pull the radio out of the instrument panel.

5 Disconnect the electrical connectors and the antenna lead from the backside of the radio (see illustration) and remove the radio.

6 Installation is the reverse of removal.

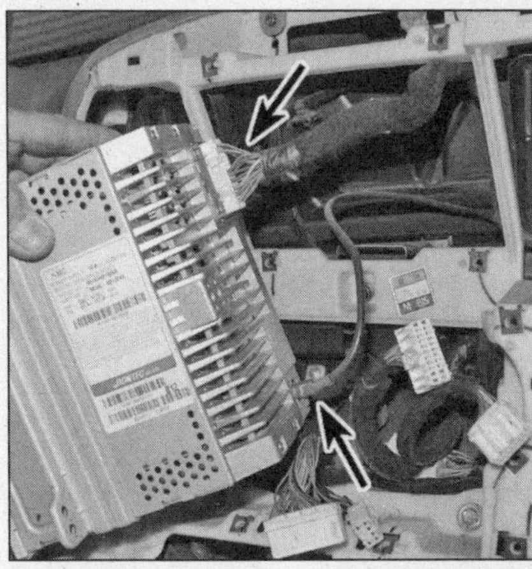

12.5 Disconnect the electrical connector and antenna cable at the back of the radio

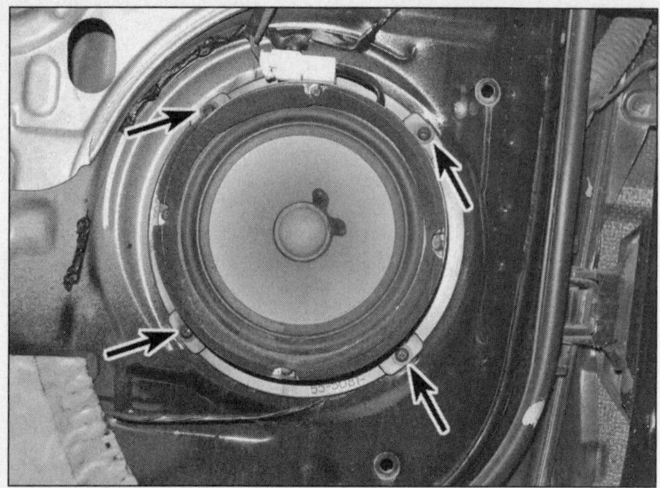

12.13 To detach a front door speaker from the door, remove these four mounting screws

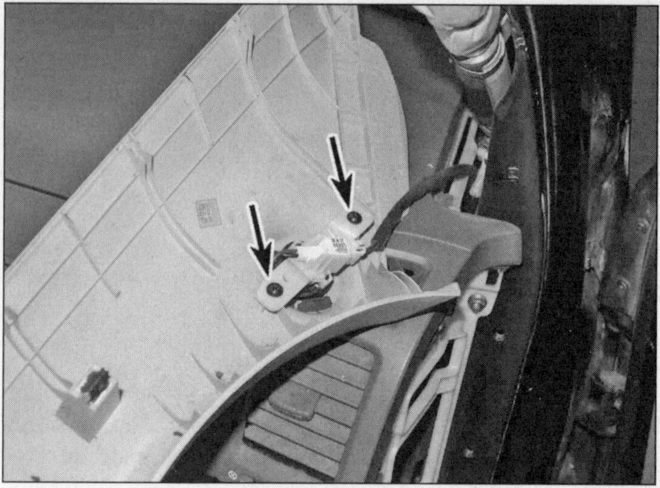

12.17 To detach a speaker from the instrument panel, remove these screws and pull the speaker out of the A-pillar panel

12.22 Lift the speaker from the bracket then disconnect the electrical connector

Navigation unit

7 Remove the center trim panel, center console panel and both center vent assemblies (see Chapter 11).

8 Remove the heater/air conditioner control assembly (see Chapter 3).

9 Remove the navigation unit retaining screws, then pull the unit out of the instrument panel.

10 Disconnect the electrical connectors from the backside of the unit and remove the navigation unit.

11 Installation is the reverse of removal.

Speakers

Front door speakers

12 Remove the front door trim panel (see Chapter 11).

13 Remove the speaker mounting screws (see illustration).

14 Pull out the speaker, disconnect the electrical connector from the speaker and remove the speaker.

15 Installation is the reverse of removal.

Tweeter speakers

16 Remove the A-pillar trim (see Chapter 11).

17 Remove the speaker mounting screws (see illustration).

18 Pull out the speaker, disconnect the electrical connector and remove the speaker.

19 Installation is the reverse of removal.

Quarter-panel speakers and woofer speaker

20 Remove the rear seats and the quarter trim panel armrest/trim bolster (see Chapter 11).

21 Remove the four speaker retaining screws.

22 Pull out the speaker, disconnect the electrical connector and remove the speaker (see illustration).

23 Installation is the reverse of removal.

Center front speaker

24 Remove the center trim facia panel (see Chapter 11).

25 Remove the two screws securing the speaker, then disconnect the electrical connector from the speaker and remove it.

26 Installation is the reverse of removal.

DVD player

27 Open the glove box door, then carefully pry out the trim around the DVD player.

28 Remove the DVD player mounting screws. Pull the player out of the instrument panel far enough to disconnect the electrical connectors and remove the player.

29 Installation is the reverse of removal.

13 Antenna - replacement

Warning: *The models covered by this manual are equipped with Supplemental Restraint Systems (SRS), more commonly known as airbags. Always disable the airbag system before working in the vicinity of any airbag system components to avoid the possibility of accidental deployment of the airbags, which could cause personal injury (see Section 25).*

2005 and earlier models

1 The vehicles covered by this manual are equipped with a wire grid-type antenna attached to the rear window glass. If there's a problem with it, you can repair the antenna grid the same way that you'd repair the rear window defogger grid (see Section 15).

2006 and later models

2 Remove the three clips on the rear of the headliner.

3 Pull down the rear section of the headliner just enough to gain working room between the headliner and the roof.

4 Remove the retaining nut and clips, then remove antenna.

5 Installation is the reverse of removal.

14 Power sliding door and power rear hatch - description and operation

1 The power sliding door and power rear hatch are an electro-mechanical unit that provides easy access to the interior by means of the door handles, interior switches, or keyless transmitter. The door is designed to operate electrically in both directions with a pinch protection feature as well. There are a series of

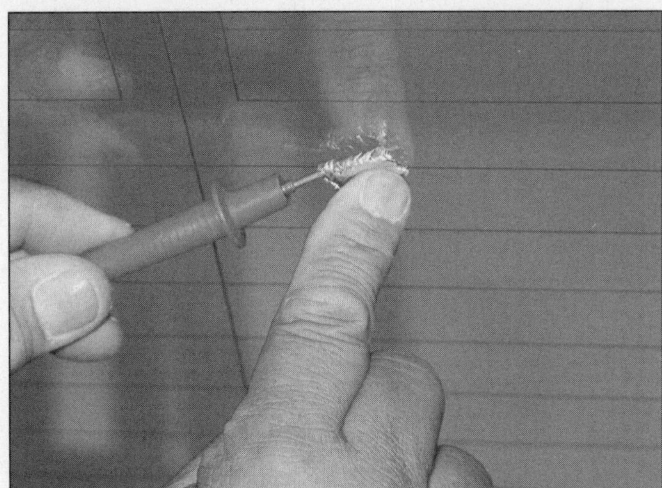

15.4 When measuring the voltage at the rear window defogger grid, wrap a piece of aluminum foil around the positive probe of the voltmeter and press the foil against the wire with your finger

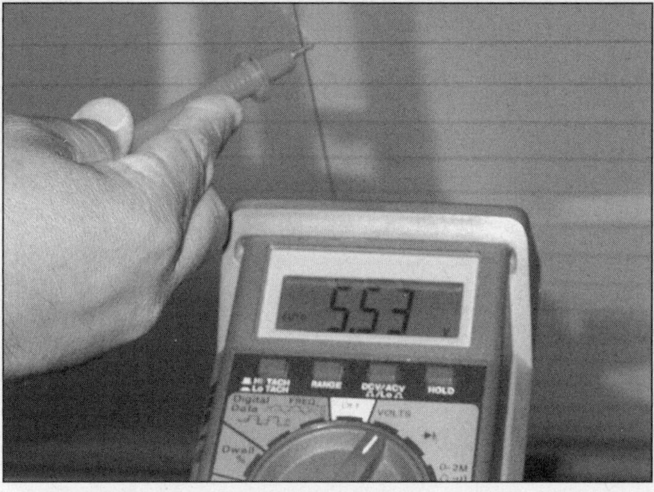

15.5 To determine if a heating element has broken, check the voltage at the center of each element. If the voltage is 5 or 6-volts, the element is unbroken; if the voltage is 10 or 12-volts, the element is broken between the center and the ground side; if there is no voltage, the element is broken between the center and the positive side

cables, optical sensors, electric drive motors, and switches that make this all possible. Determining a fault in these systems requires the proper diagnostic scanners and expertise of a professional technician. No repair or diagnostics is provided in this manual due to the complexity of these systems. See your local dealer or qualified independent repair facility for any repair work needed.

15.7 To find the break, touch the voltmeter negative lead to the defogger ground terminal, place the voltmeter positive lead with the foil strip against the heating element at the positive terminal end and slide it toward the negative terminal end. The point at which the voltmeter reading changes abruptly is the point at which the element is broken

15 Rear window defogger - check and repair

1 The rear window defogger consists of a number of horizontal elements baked onto the glass surface.

2 Small breaks in the element can be repaired without removing the rear window.

Check

3 Turn the ignition switch and defogger system switches to the ON position. Using a voltmeter, place the positive probe against the defogger grid positive terminal and the negative probe against the ground terminal. If battery voltage is not indicated, check the fuse, defogger switch and related wiring. If voltage is indicated, but all or part of the defogger doesn't heat, proceed with the following tests.

4 When measuring voltage during these tests, wrap a piece of aluminum foil around the tip of the voltmeter positive probe and press the foil against the heating element with your finger (see illustration). Place the negative probe on the defogger grid ground terminal.

5 Check the voltage at the center of each heating element (see illustration). If the voltage is 5 or 6-volts, the element is okay (there is no break). If there is not voltage, the element is broken between the center of the element and the positive end. If the voltage is 10 to 12 volts the element is broken between the center of the element and ground. Check each heating element.

6 Connect the negative lead to a good body ground. The reading should stay the same. If it doesn't, the ground connection is bad.

7 To find the break, place the voltmeter negative probe against the defogger ground terminal. Place the voltmeter positive probe with the foil strip against the heating element at the positive terminal end and slide it toward the negative terminal end. The point at which the voltmeter deflects from several volts to zero is the point at which the heating element is broken (see illustration).

Repair

8 Repair the break in the element using a repair kit specifically recommended for this purpose, available at most auto parts stores. Included in this kit is plastic conductive epoxy.

9 Prior to repairing a break, turn off the system and allow it to cool for a few minutes.

10 Lightly buff the element area with fine steel wool, then clean it thoroughly with rubbing alcohol.

11 Use masking tape to mask off the area being repaired.

12 Thoroughly mix the epoxy, following the instructions provided with the repair kit.

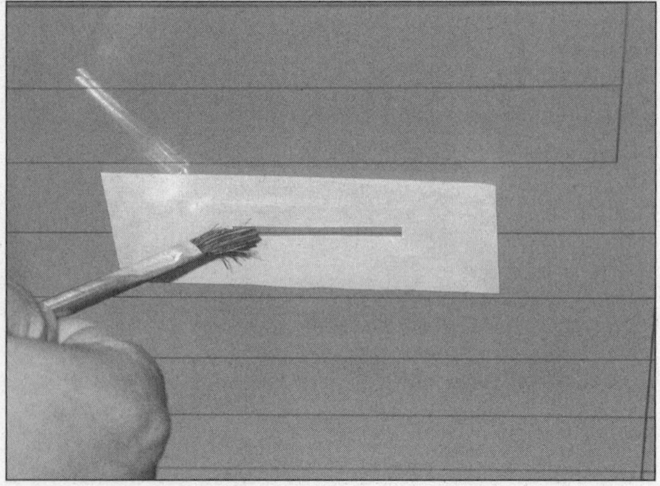
15.13 To use a defogger repair kit, apply masking tape to the inside of the window at the damaged area, then brush on the special conductive coating

16.3 Headlamp housing mounting screw locations

16.4 Disconnect the electrical connectors to the headlamp housing and bulbs

17.3 Unscrew the cover from the rear of the headlight housing

13 Apply the epoxy material to the slit in the masking tape, overlapping the undamaged area about 3/4-inch on either end (see illustration).

14 Allow the repair to cure for 24 hours before removing the tape and using the system.

16 Headlight housing - replacement

Warning: *These vehicles are equipped with halogen gas-filled headlight bulbs, which are under pressure and may shatter if the surface is damaged or the bulb is dropped. Wear eye protection and handle the bulbs carefully, grasping only the base whenever possible. Do not touch the surface of the bulb with your fingers because the oil from your skin could cause it to overheat and fail prematurely. If you do touch the bulb surface, clean it with rubbing alcohol.*

1 Disconnect the cable from the negative battery terminal (see Chapter 5).

2 Remove the radiator support trim panel (see Chapter 11).

3 Remove the headlight housing mounting screws (see illustration).

4 Pull the headlight housing forward enough to disconnect the electrical connectors from the housing (see illustration).

5 Installation is the reverse of removal.

17 Headlight bulb - replacement

Warning: *Halogen bulbs are gas-filled and under pressure and might shatter if the surface is scratched or the bulb is dropped. Wear eye protection and handle the bulbs carefully, grasping only the base whenever possible. Don't touch the surface of the bulb with your fingers because the oil from your skin could cause it to overheat and fail prematurely. If you do touch the bulb surface, clean it with rubbing alcohol.*

1 Disconnect the cable from the negative battery terminal (see Chapter 5).

2 Remove the headlamp assembly (see Section 16).

3 Remove the bulb cover from the rear of the housing (see illustration).

4 Release the retaining spring, disconnect the electrical connector and pull out the old bulb (see illustration).

5 Without touching the bulb glass with your bare fingers insert the new bulb into the headlight housing and attach the bulb retaining spring.

Caution: *Don't touch the surface of the bulb with your fingers because the oil from your skin could cause it to overheat and fail prematurely. If you accidentally touch the bulb surface, clean it with rubbing alcohol.*

6 Installation is the reverse of removal.

17.4 Unlatch the spring-loaded wire retainer for the bulb

18.1 Use a long Phillips screwdriver (A) engaged with the teeth of the adjuster (B) to adjust up-and-down movement

18 Headlights - adjustment

Warning: *The headlights must be aimedcorrectly. If adjusted incorrectly, they could temporarily blind the driver of an oncoming vehicle and cause an accident or seriously reduce your ability to see the road. The headlights should be checked for proper aim every 12 months and any time a new headlight is installed or front-end bodywork is performed. The following procedure is only an interim step to provide temporary adjustment until the headlights can be adjusted by a properly equipped shop.*

1 The headlight adjustment screw, accessed through the radiator support cover (see illustration), controls up-and-down movement.

2 There are several methods of adjusting the headlights. The simplest method requires a blank wall 25 feet in front of the vehicle and a level floor (see illustration).

3 Position masking tape on the wall in reference to the vehicle centerline and the centerlines of both headlights.

4 Measure the height of the headlight reference marks (in the centers of the headlight lenses) from the ground. Position a horizontal tape line on the wall at the same height as the headlight reference marks.

Note: *It may be easier to position the tape on the wall with the vehicle parked only a few inches away.*

5 Adjustment should be made with the vehicle sitting level, the gas tank half-full and no unusually heavy load in the vehicle.

6 Turn on the low beams. Turn the adjusting screw to position the high intensity zone so it is two inches below the horizontal line.

7 Have the headlights adjusted by a dealer service department at the earliest opportunity.

19 Bulb replacement

Bulb removal

Exterior light bulbs

Front park and turn signal bulbs

1 Remove the headlight housing (see Section 16).

2 Rotate the park and turn signal bulb socket counterclockwise (see illustration) and

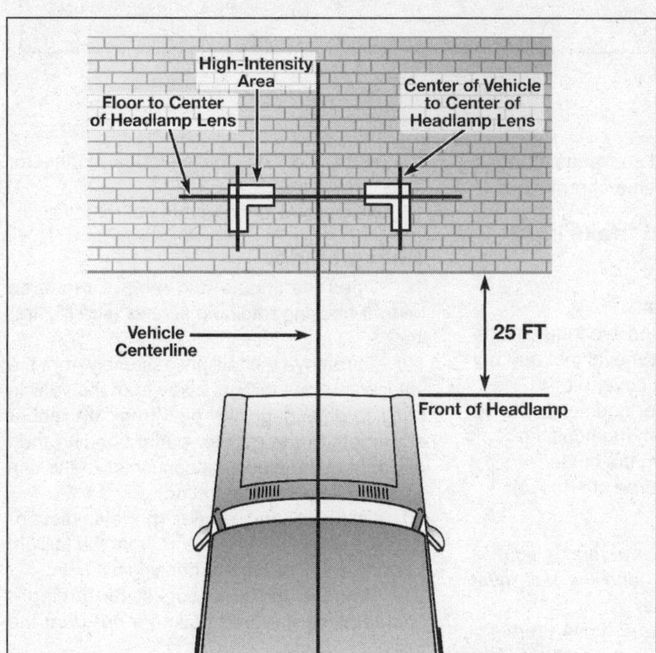

18.2 Headlight adjustment details

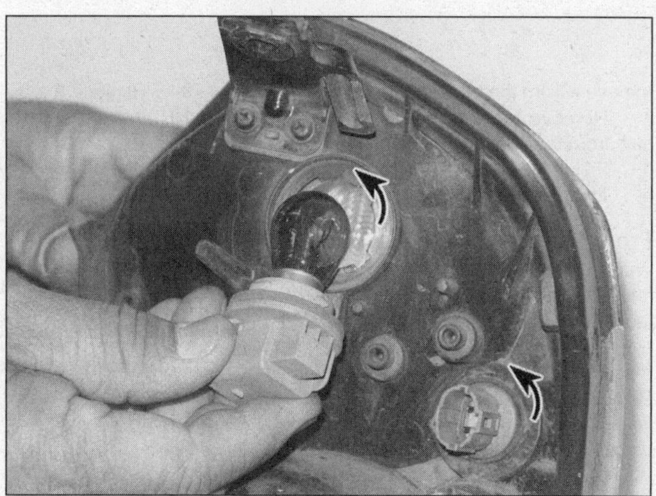

19.2 Rotate the bulb holders counterclockwise to remove them

Bulb removal

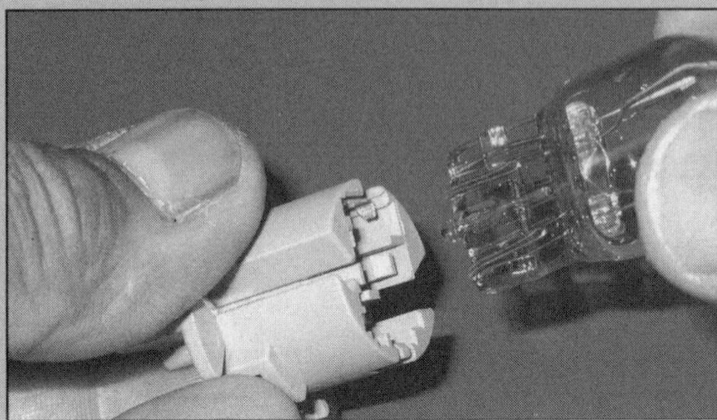

To remove many modern exterior bulbs from their holders, simply pull them out

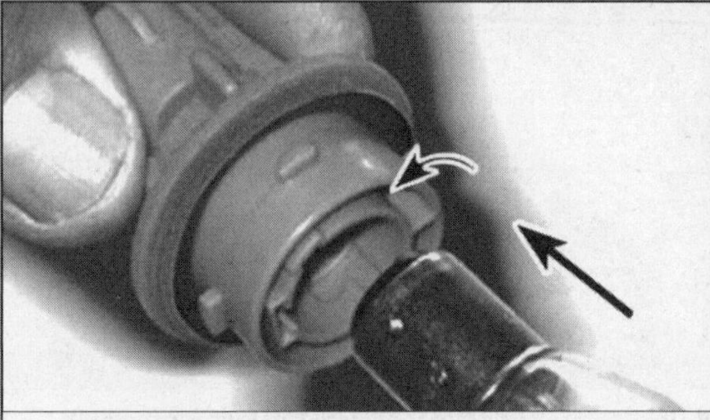

On bulbs with a cylindrical base ("bayonet" bulbs), the socket is spring-loaded; a pair of small posts on the side of the base hold the bulb in place against spring pressure. To remove this type of bulb, push it into the holder, rotate it 1/4-turn counterclockwise, then pull it out

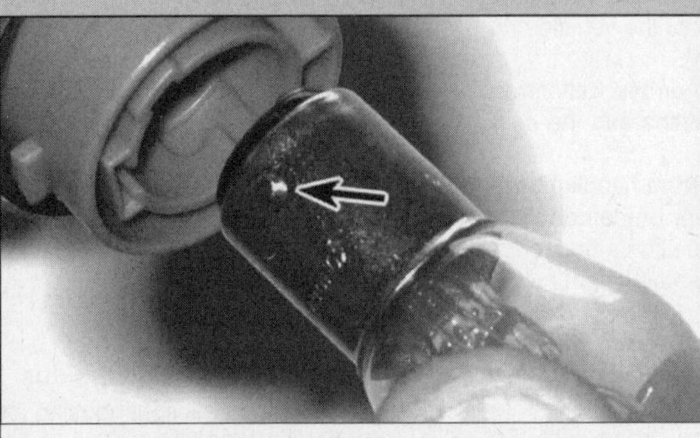

If a bayonet bulb has dual filaments, the posts are staggered, so the bulb can only be installed one way

To remove most overhead interior light bulbs, simply unclip them

remove it from the headlight housing.

3 Remove the front park and turn signal bulb from the socket.

4 Install the new bulb in the socket.

5 Installation is the reverse of removal.

Front fog light bulbs

Warning: *Halogen bulbs are gas-filled and under pressure and might shatter if the surface is scratched or the bulb is dropped. Wear eye protection and handle the bulbs carefully, grasping only the base whenever possible. Don't touch the surface of the bulb with your fingers because the oil from your skin could cause it to overheat and fail prematurely. If you do touch the bulb surface, clean it with rubbing alcohol.*

6 Raise the front of the vehicle and place it securely on jackstands.

7 Disconnect the bulb electrical connector.

8 Rotate the bulb socket counterclockwise and pull it out of the fog light housing.

9 Replace the bulb and socket as a unit.

10 Installation is the reverse of removal.

Center high-mounted brake light bulb

2005 and earlier models

11 Open the lift gate and working on the inside, use a plastic trim removal tool and pry the high-mount brake light cover off.

12 Rotate the bulb holder counterclockwise and remove the holder from the housing.

13 Remove the bulb from the holder.

14 Installation is the reverse of removal.

2006 and later models

Note: *On these models, the brake light is equipped with LED lights, and the unit must be replaced as an assembly.*

15 Open the lift gate and remove the high-mounted brake light housing screws (see illustration).

16 Lift the high-mounted brake light housing out and disconnect the electrical connector (see illustration).

17 Installation is the reverse of removal.

Taillight bulbs

18 Open the liftgate and remove the three taillight housing retaining screws (see illustration).

19 To remove the taillight assembly from the vehicle, pull the taillight away from the vehicle body to disengage the pins from the rubber grommets in the quarter-panel opening then disconnect the electrical connector to the taillight housing (see illustration).

20 On 2005 and earlier models, disconnect the electrical connectors from the taillight sockets and remove the housing.

21 Remove the bulb socket by turning it counterclockwise and pulling it out from the taillight housing.

22 Remove the bulb from the socket.

23 Installation is the reverse of removal.

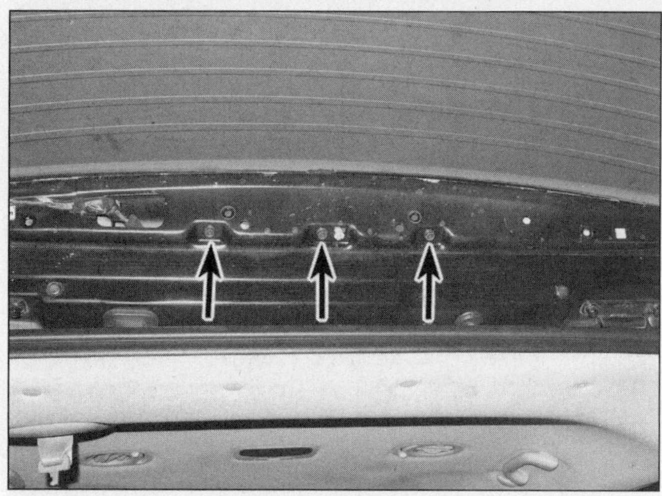

19.15 Remove the fasteners securing the high-mount brake light from the lift gate

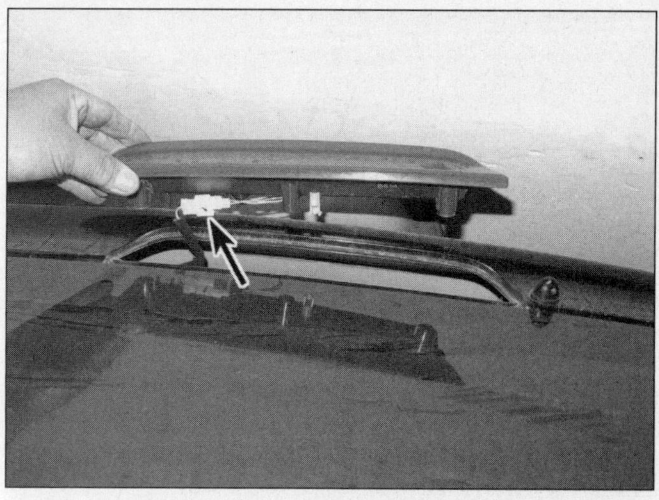

19.16 Disconnect the electrical connector from the assembly

19.18 Remove the taillight housing fasteners

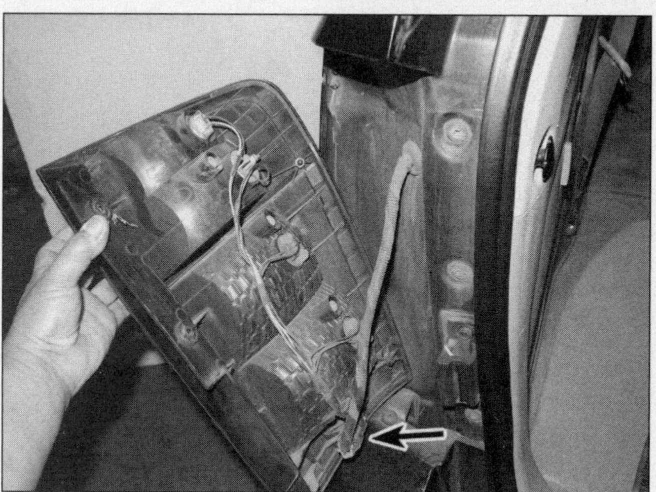

19.19 Disconnect the harness connector to the tailight housing

License plate light bulbs

24 Open the liftgate.

25 Remove the license plate light lens cover screw(s) with a small screw driver (see illustration).

26 On 2005 and earlier models, remove the bulb socket by turning it counterclockwise and pulling it out from the license plate lens housing.

27 All models, pull the bulb from the socket.

28 Installation is the reverse of removal.

Interior lights

Instrument cluster illumination bulbs

29 The instrument cluster LED lamps are an integral part of the cluster, and not separately serviceable. If the lamps stop working, the cluster must be replaced (see Section 9).

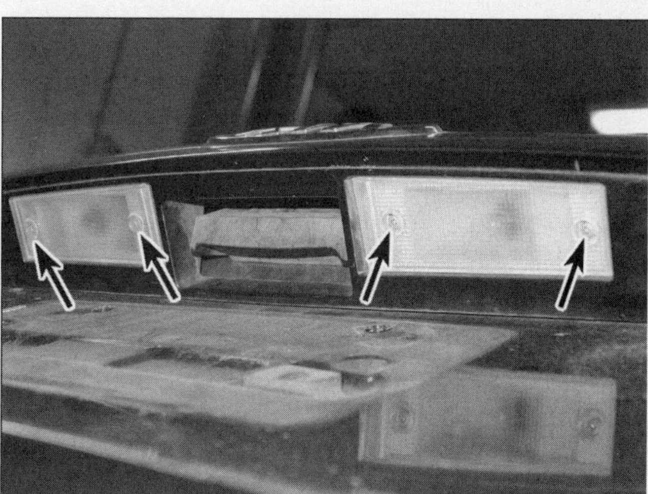

19.25 License plate light lens cover screw locations

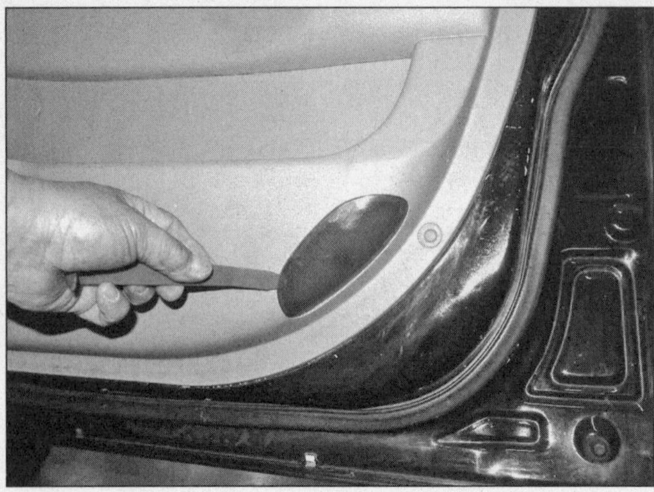

19.30 Pry the light lens from the door panel

19.33 Pry at the top of the cargo light to remove the lens

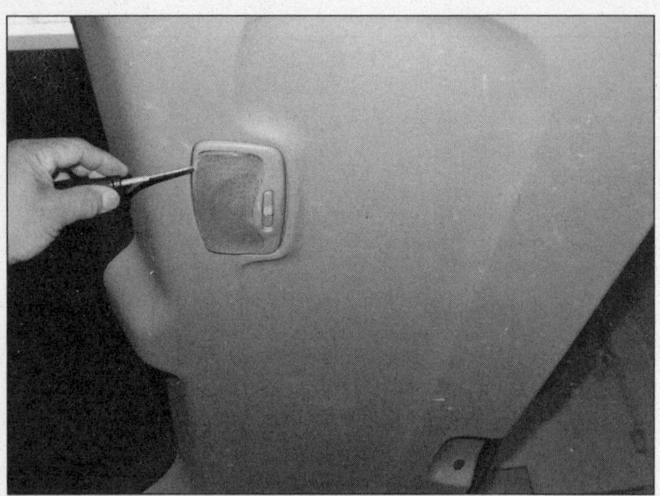

19.36 Pry at the top of the liftgate light to remove the lens

20.3 Remove the fastener securing the horn (right side shown, left side similar)

Courtesy light

30 Using a small flat tip screwdriver or panel removal tool, pry the courtesy light lens from the door trim panel (see illustration).

31 Disconnect the electrical connector from the courtesy light.

32 Installation is the reverse of removal.

Dome/cargo light

33 Using a trim panel removal tool or a screwdriver, pry off the dome/cargo light lens (see illustration).

34 Remove the bulb from the dome/cargo light assembly.

35 Installation is the reverse of removal.

Liftgate light bulb

36 Using a flat-bladed tool, pry the liftgate light lens from the liftgate trim panel (see illustration).

37 Remove the liftgate light bulb.

38 Installation is the reverse of removal.

Overhead console reading lights

39 Pry the lens cover off with a small flat tipped screwdriver.

40 Remove bulb.

41 Installation is the reverse of removal.

Vanity light

42 Remove the lens cover with a small flat tipped screwdriver.

43 Remove bulb.

44 Installation is the reverse of removal.

20 Horn - replacement

Warning: *The models covered by this manual are equipped with Supplemental Restraint Systems (SRS), more commonly known as airbags. Always disable the airbag system before working in the vicinity of any airbag system components to avoid the possibility of accidental deployment of the airbags, which could cause personal injury (see Section 25).*

Note: *The horns are located behind the front grille area. One on the left side and one on the right side.*

1 Remove the radiator support cover (see Chapter 11 Section 8).

2 Disconnect the electrical connector from the horn.

3 Remove the horn mounting fastener and the horn assembly (see illustration).

4 Installation is the reverse of removal.

21 Cruise control system - description

2005 and earlier models

1 The cruise control system maintains vehicle speed with a Cruise Control Module (CCM), which is connected by cable from the accelerator pedal to the CCM and a second cable from the CCM to the throttle body. The system consists of the cruise control module, brake switch, control switches, cable and Vehicle Speed Sensor (VSS). Some features of the system require special testers and diagnostic procedures that are beyond the scope of this manual. Listed below are some general procedures that may be used to locate common problems.

2 Locate and check the fuse (see Section 3).

3 Check the brake light switch (see Chapter 9).

4 Visually inspect the control cable between the cruise control module and the throttle body for free movement, replace if necessary.

5 Test drive the vehicle to determine if the cruise control is now working. If it isn't, take it to a dealer for further diagnosis.

2006 and later models

6 The cruise control system maintains vehicle speed with the Powertrain Control Module (PCM), throttle actuator control motor, brake switch, control switches and associated wiring. There is no mechanical connection, such as a vacuum servo or cable. Some features of the system require special testers and diagnostic procedures that are beyond the scope of the home mechanic. Listed below are some general procedures that may be used to locate common problems.

7 Check the fuses (see Section 3).

8 The Brake Pedal Position (BPP) switch (or brake light switch) deactivates the cruise control system. Have an assistant press the brake pedal while you check the brake light operation. If the brake lights do not operate properly, correct the problem and retest the cruise control.

9 Check the wiring between the PCM and throttle actuator motor for opens or shorts and repair as necessary.

10 The cruise control system uses information from the PCM, including the Vehicle Speed Sensor (VSS), which is located in the transmission or transfer case.

11 Test drive the vehicle to determine if the cruise control is now working. If it isn't, take it to a dealer service department or other qualified repair shop for further diagnosis.

22 Power window system - description and check

Note: *These models are equipped with several different modules that control the functions of the power windows as well as other systems in the car. These control modules allow simple and accurate troubleshooting, but only with a professional-grade scan tool. Have vehicle diagnosed by a dealership service department or other qualified automotive repair facility.*

Power window diagnostics

Note: *These procedures are general in nature, so if you can't find the problem using them, take the vehicle to a dealer service department or other properly equipped repair facility.*

1 The power window system operates electric motors, mounted in the doors, which lower and raise the windows. The system consists of the control switches, the motors, regulators, glass mechanisms, the Body Control Module (BCM) and associated wiring.

2 The power windows can be lowered and raised from the master control switch by the driver or by remote switches located at the individual windows. Each window has a separate motor that is reversible. The position of the control switch determines the polarity and therefore the direction of operation.

3 The circuit is protected by a fuse and a circuit breaker. Each motor is also equipped with an internal circuit breaker; this prevents one stuck window from disabling the whole system.

4 The power window system will only operate when the ignition switch is ON, and for a period of time after the ignition key has been turned Off (unless one of the doors is opened). In addition, many models have a window lockout switch at the master control switch which, when activated, disables the switches at the rear windows and, sometimes, the switch at the passenger's window also. Always check these items before troubleshooting a window problem.

5 If the power windows won't operate, always check the fuse and circuit breaker first.

6 If only the rear windows are inoperative, or if the windows only operate from the master control switch, check the rear window lockout switch for continuity in the unlocked position. Replace it if it doesn't have continuity.

7 Check the wiring between the switches and fuse panel for continuity. Repair the wiring, if necessary.

8 If only one window is inoperative from the master control switch, try the other control switch at the window.

Note: *This doesn't apply to the driver's door window.*

9 If the same window works from one switch, but not the other, check the switch for continuity.

10 If the switch tests OK, check for a short or open in the circuit between the affected switch and the window motor.

11 If one window is inoperative from both switches, remove the switch panel from the affected door. Check for voltage at the switch and at the motor (refer to Chapter 11 for door panel removal) while the switch is operated.

12 If voltage is reaching the motor, disconnect the glass from the regulator (see Chapter 11). Move the window up and down by hand while checking for binding and damage. Also check for binding and damage to the regulator. If the regulator is not damaged and the window moves up and down smoothly, replace the motor. If there's binding or damage, lubricate, repair or replace parts, as necessary.

13 If voltage isn't reaching the motor, check the wiring in the circuit for continuity between the switches and the body control module, and between the body control module and the motors. You'll need to consult the wiring diagram at the end of this Chapter. If the circuit is equipped with a relay, check that the relay is grounded properly and receiving voltage.

14 Test the windows after you are done to confirm proper repairs.

23 Power door lock and keyless entry system - description and check

Note: *These models are equipped with several different modules that control the functions of the door locks as well as other systems in the car. These control modules allow simple and accurate troubleshooting, but only with a professional-grade scan tool. Have vehicle diagnosed by a dealership service department or other qualified automotive repair facility.*

Door lock diagnostics

Note: *These procedures are general in nature, so if you can't find the problem using them, take the vehicle to a dealer service department or other properly equipped repair facility.*

1 The power door lock system operates the door lock actuators mounted in each door. The system consists of the switches, actuators, BCM and associated wiring. Diagnosis can usually be limited to simple checks of the wiring connections and actuators for minor faults that can be easily repaired.

2 Power door lock systems are operated by bi-directional solenoids located in the doors. The lock switches have two operating positions: Lock and Unlock. These switches send a signal to the BCM, which in turn sends a signal to the door lock solenoids.

3 If you are unable to locate the trouble using the following general steps, consult your dealer service department.

4 Always check the circuit protection first. Some vehicles use a combination of circuit breakers and fuses. Refer to the wiring diagrams at the end of this Chapter.

5 Check for voltage at the switches. If no voltage is present, check the wiring between the fuse panel and the switches for shorts and opens.

6 If voltage is present, test the switch for continuity. Replace it if there's not continuity in both switch positions. To remove the switch, use a flat-bladed trim tool to pry out the door/window switch assembly (see Chapter 11).

7 If the switch has continuity, check the wiring between the switch and door lock solenoid.

8 If all but one lock solenoids operate, remove the trim panel from the affected door (see Chapter 11) and check for voltage at the solenoid while the lock switch is operated. One of the wires should have voltage in the Lock position; the other should have voltage in the Unlock position.

9 If the inoperative solenoid is receiving voltage, replace the solenoid.

10 If the inoperative solenoid isn't receiving voltage, check for an open or short in the wire between the lock solenoid and the relay.

11 On the models covered by this manual, power door lock system communication goes through the Body Control Module (BCM). If the above tests do not pinpoint a problem, take the vehicle to a dealer or qualified shop with the proper scan tool to retrieve trouble codes from the BCM.

Keyless entry system

12 The keyless entry system consists of a remote control transmitter that sends a coded infrared signal to a receiver, which then operates the door lock system.

13 Replace the battery when the transmitter doesn't operate the locks at a distance of ten feet. Normal range should be about 30 feet.

Key remote control battery replacement

14 Use the tip of the emergency key, a plastic trim tool or coin to carefully separate the case halves.

15 Remove the battery, making sure to note the direction the battery faces.

16 Snap the case halves together.

Transmitter programming

17 Programming replacement transmitters requires the use of a specialized scan tool. Take the vehicle and the transmitter(s) to a dealer service department or other qualified repair shop equipped with the necessary tool to have the transmitter(s) programmed to the vehicle.

24 Daytime Running Lights (DRL) - general information

1 The Daytime Running Lights (DRL) system, which is required on new Canadian models and an option on models made for the United States, illuminates the headlights when the engine is running. The DRL system supplies reduced power to the headlights so they won't be too bright for daytime use, which also prolongs headlight life. The DRL system is an integral part of the IPM.

25 Airbag system - general information and precautions

General information

1 All models are equipped with a frontal-impact airbag system, which is referred to as the Supplemental Restraint System (SRS). The SRS is designed to protect the driver and the front seat passenger from serious injury in the event of a head-on or frontal collision. The SRS is controlled by the Occupant Restraint Controller (ORC), also referred to as the Airbag Control Module (ACM), which is mounted in the center of the vehicle, on the floor transmission tunnel, below the center of the instrument panel. The SRS uses an array of airbags to protect the front-seat occupants (and on models equipped with side curtain airbags, the rear seat passengers too): the driver's airbag in the steering wheel; the passenger airbag, which is located on the right side of the instrument panel, beneath the instrument panel top pad and above the glove box; and, on models so equipped, the side curtain airbags, which are located above the side windows, in the outer edges of the headliner, between the A- and D-pillars. The SRS is activated by a pair of front impact sensors located on the front of the frame, just behind the bumper attachments. Other important components in the SRS include the clockspring, a wind-up coil that delivers battery voltage to the steering wheel airbag, and the AIRBAG readiness light on the instrument cluster.

2 In addition to the airbags, seat belt pretensioners are incorporated into the front seat belt retractor mechanisms. These are pyrotechnic (explosive) devices which retract the seat belts up to four inches when the airbag system is activated.

Driver airbag

3 The airbag inflator module contains a housing incorporating the cushion (airbag) and inflator unit, mounted in the center of the steering wheel. The inflator assembly is mounted on the back of the housing over a hole through which gas is expelled, inflating the bag almost instantaneously when an electrical signal is sent from the system. The clockspring assembly on the steering column under the steering wheel carries this signal to the module. The clockspring assembly can transmit an electrical signal regardless of steering wheel position. The igniter in the airbag converts the electrical signal to heat and ignites the powder, which inflates the bag.

4 In the event of a frontal collision serious enough to trigger SRS deployment, the knee blocker airbag inflates toward the driver's knees to help protect them and to help put the driver in the optimal position for deployment of the driver's airbag. The knee blocker airbag deploys in about 50 milliseconds.

Passenger airbag

5 The airbag is mounted in the right end of the instrument panel, beneath the instrument panel top pad and above the glove box. It consists of an inflator containing an igniter, a bag assembly, a reaction housing and a trim cover. The passenger airbag is considerably larger than the steering wheel-mounted unit and is supported by the steel reaction housing. The trim cover is textured and painted to match the instrument panel and has a molded seam that splits when the bag inflates.

6 Unlike the inflatable airbag knee blocker on the driver's side, the passenger knee blocker is simply a structural reinforcement that's an integral part of the glove box. But it does the same thing as the driver's inflatable knee blocker: it offers a degree of protection for the passenger's knees in a frontal impact and it positions the passenger for deployment of the passenger airbag.

Side-impact window airbags

7 Optional side-impact window airbags protect vehicle occupants in the event of a side impact. The side-impact window airbags are located above the windows, between the A- and D-pillars. If you're not sure whether your vehicle is equipped with side-impact window airbags, look for the words "SRS AIRBAG" imprinted on a small identification trim button located above the B-and C-pillars.

8 Vehicles equipped with side-impact window airbags use six side-impact sensors, three on the left side of the vehicle and three more on the right side. The front row side-impact sensors are located inside the B-pillars, above the front seatbelt retractors. The second-row side-impact sensors are located in the sliding door track openings, just ahead of the C-pillars. The third-row sensors are located behind the quarter-trim panels, between the C- and D-pillars, above the rear wheelwells.

Occupant Restraint Controller (ORC) or Airbag Control Module (ACM)

9 The ORC or ACM supplies current to the SRS in the event of a collision, even if battery power is cut off. The ORC/ACM checks the SRS every time the vehicle is started, and indicates that it is doing so by turning on the AIRBAG readiness light. If the SRS is operating properly, the ORC/ACM turns off the AIRBAG readiness light. If it detects a fault in the system, the AIRBAG readiness light will remain on. If this condition occurs, take the vehicle to your dealer immediately for service.

Disarming the system and other precautions

Warning: *Failure to follow these precautions could result in accidental deployment of the airbag and personal injury.*

10 Whenever you are working in the vicinity of the driver airbag in the steering wheel or any of the other airbags on your vehicle, DISARM THE SYSTEM. To disarm the system:

a) Point the wheels straight ahead and turn the ignition key to the LOCK position.

b) Disconnect the cable from the negative battery terminal. Isolate the cable terminal so it won't accidentally contact the battery post.

c) Wait at least two minutes for the back-up power supply to be depleted. Back-up power is supplied by a capacitor that takes about two minutes to fully discharge. During this two-minute interval, the SRS is still capable of deploying.

11 Whenever handling an airbag, always keep the airbag opening (the trim side) pointed away from your body. Never place the airbag on a bench or other surface with the airbag opening facing the surface. Always place the airbag module in a safe location with the airbag opening facing up.

12 Never measure the resistance of any SRS component. An ohmmeter has a built-in battery supply that could accidentally deploy the airbag.

13 Never dispose of a live airbag. Return it to a dealer service department or other qualified repair shop for safe deployment and disposal.

Component removal and installation

Driver airbag and clockspring

14 Refer to Chapter 10, Steering wheel - removal and installation, for the driver's side airbag module and clockspring removal and installation procedures.

26 Wiring diagrams - general information

1 Since it isn't possible to include all wiring diagrams for every year covered by this manual, the following diagrams are those that are typical and most commonly needed.

2 Prior to troubleshooting any circuits, check the fuse and circuit breakers (if equipped) to make sure they're in good condition. Make sure the battery is properly charged and check the cable connections (see Chapter 1.

3 When checking a circuit, make sure that all connectors are clean, with no broken or loose terminals. When unplugging a connector, do not pull on the wires. Pull only on the connector housings.

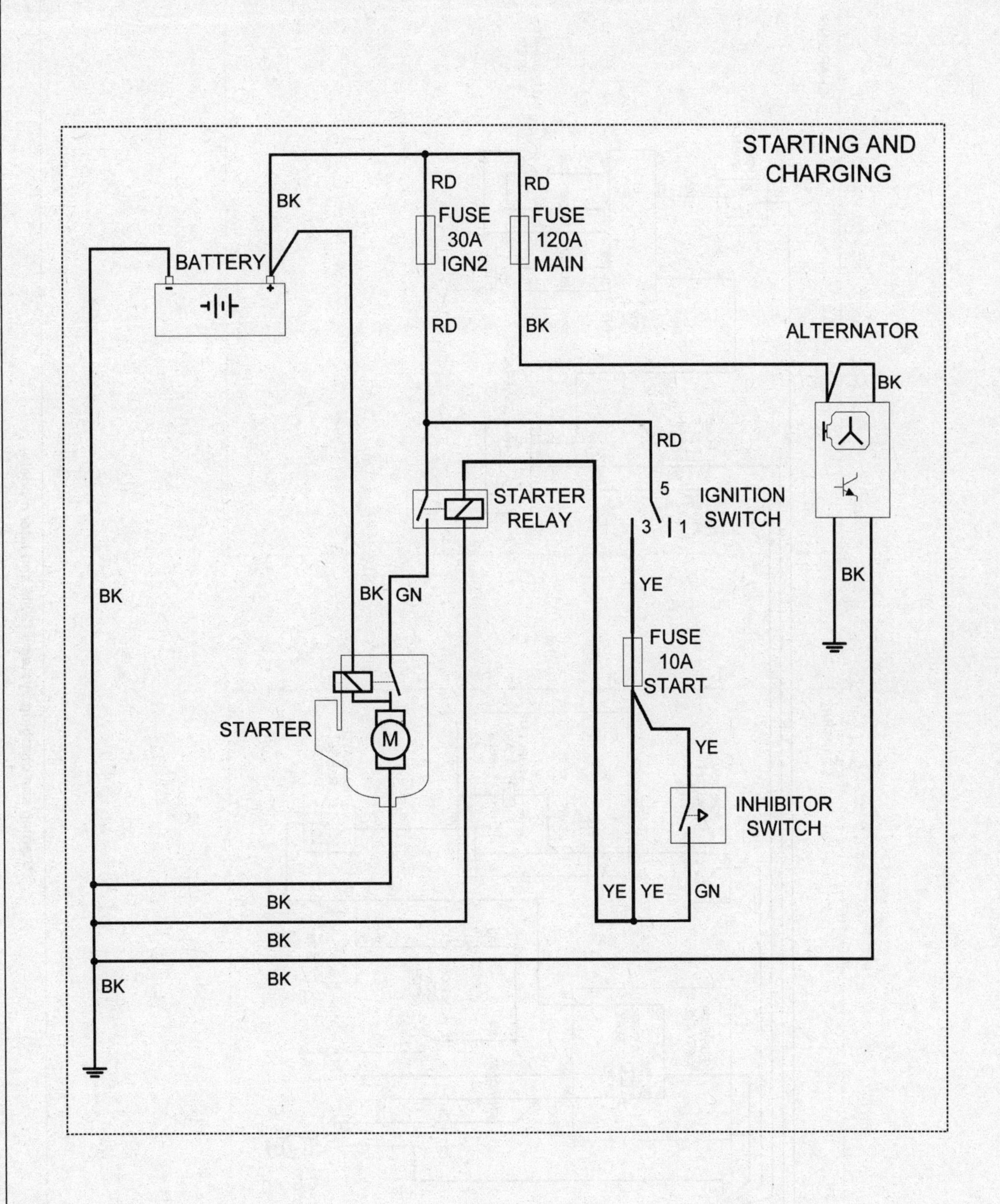

Starting and charging systems (2005 and earlier models)

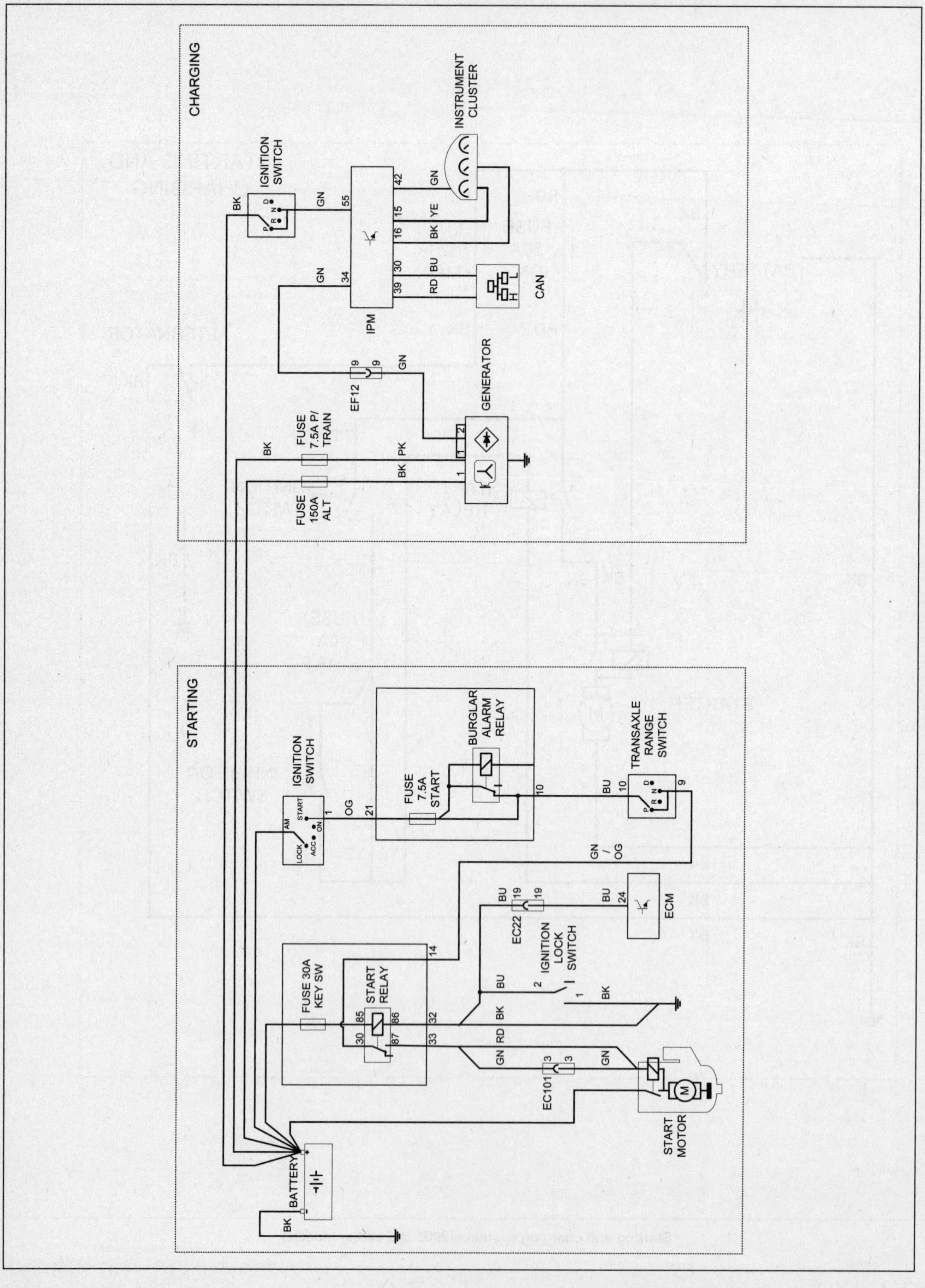

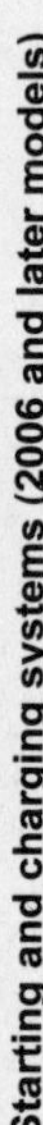

Starting and charging systems (2006 and later models)

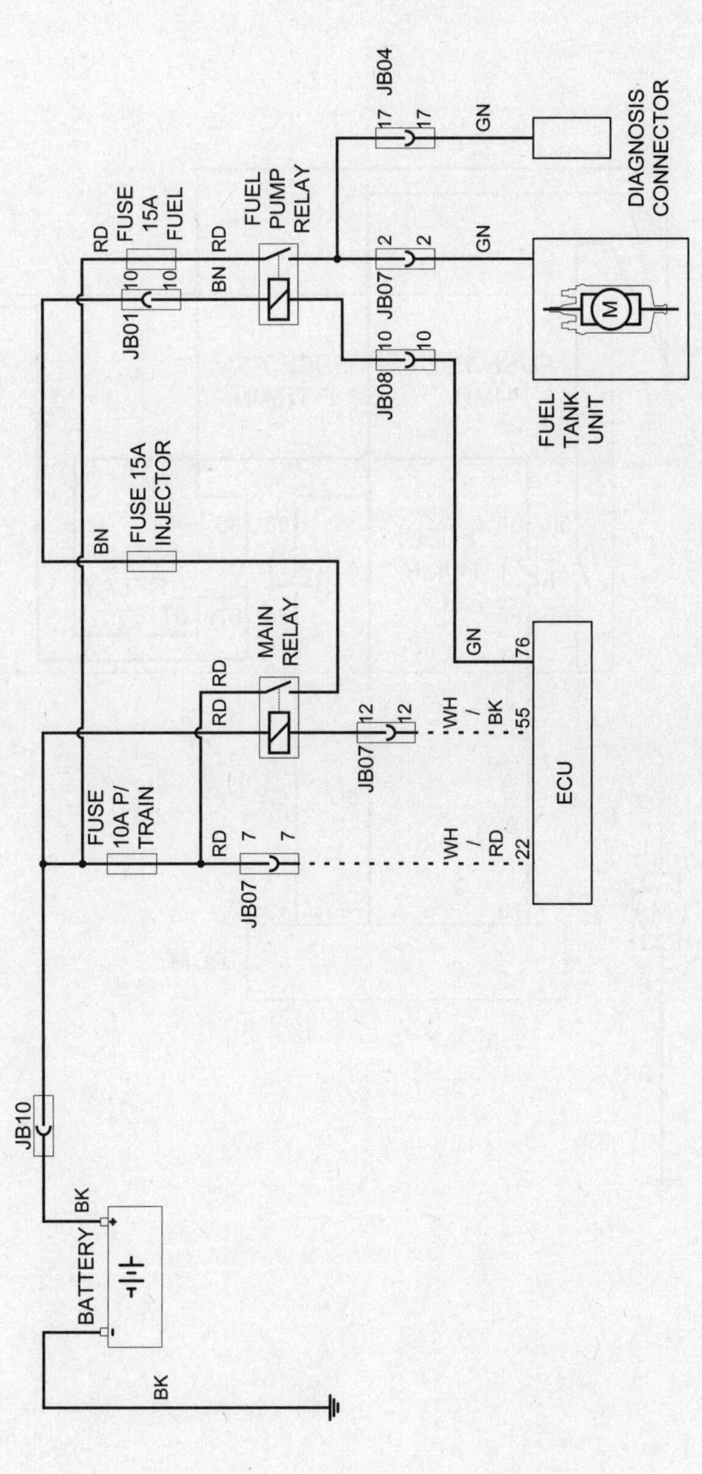

Fuel pump system (2005 and earlier models)

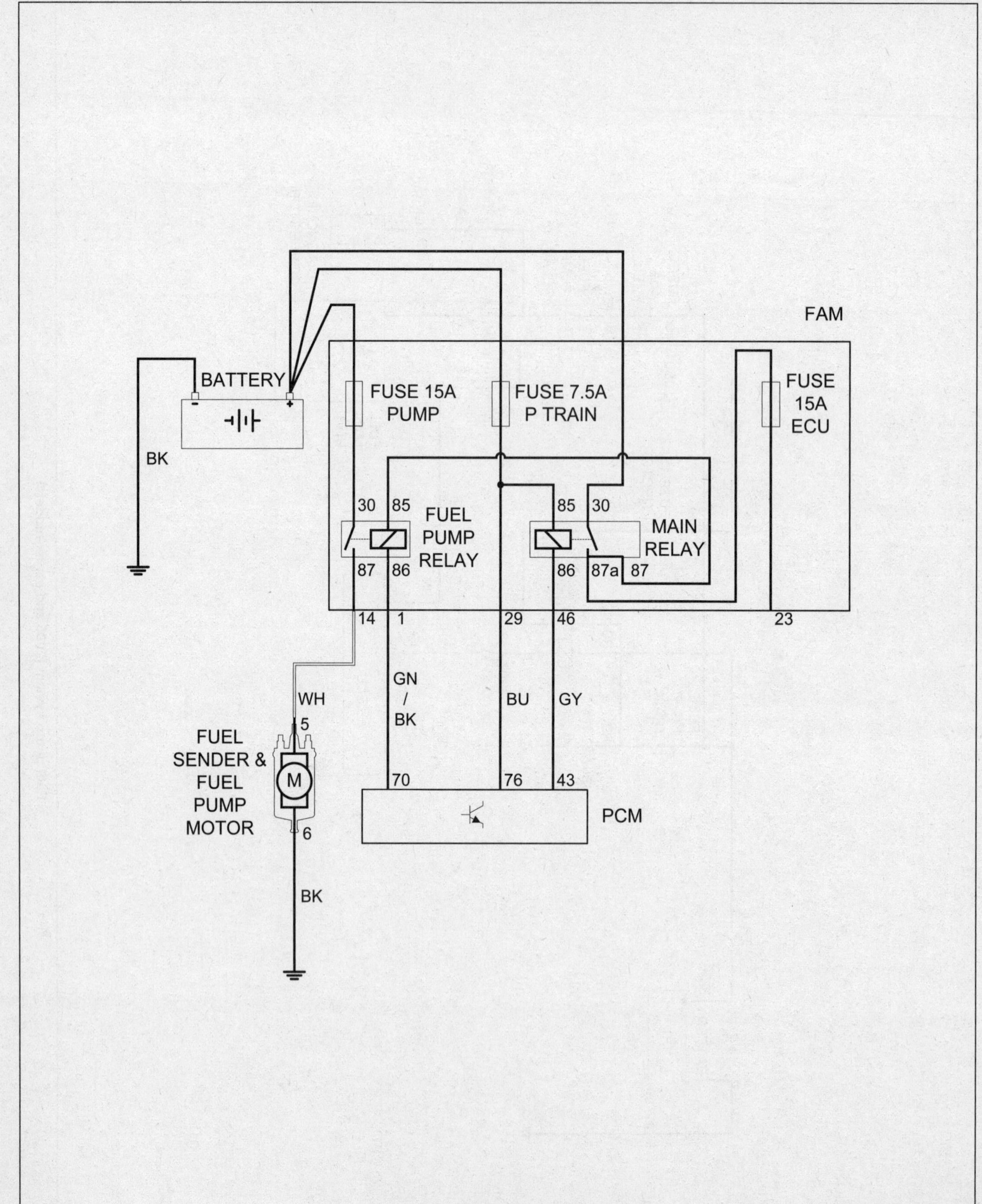

Fuel pump system (2006 and later models)

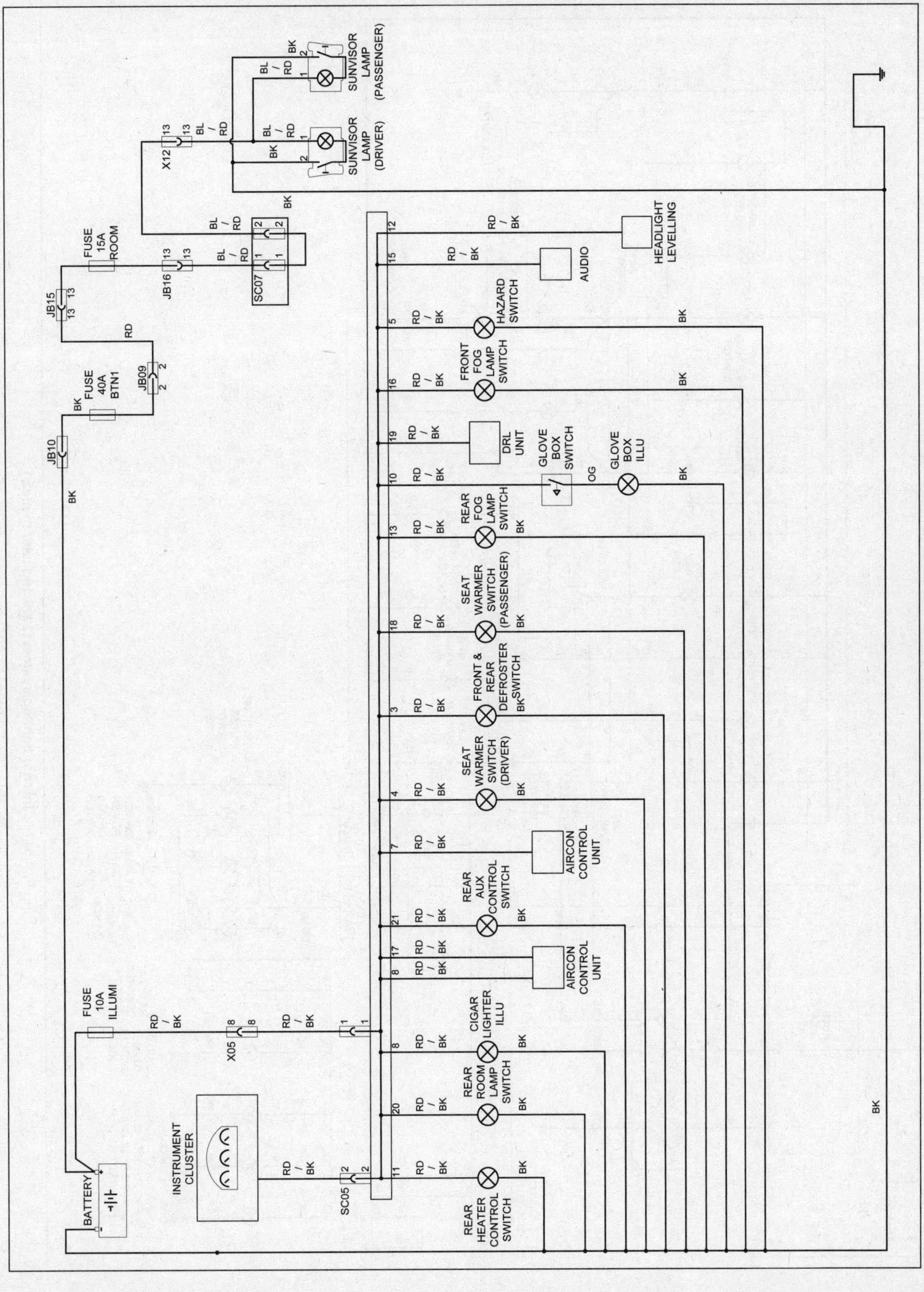

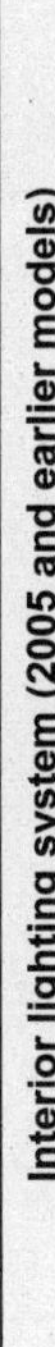

Interior lighting system (2005 and earlier models)

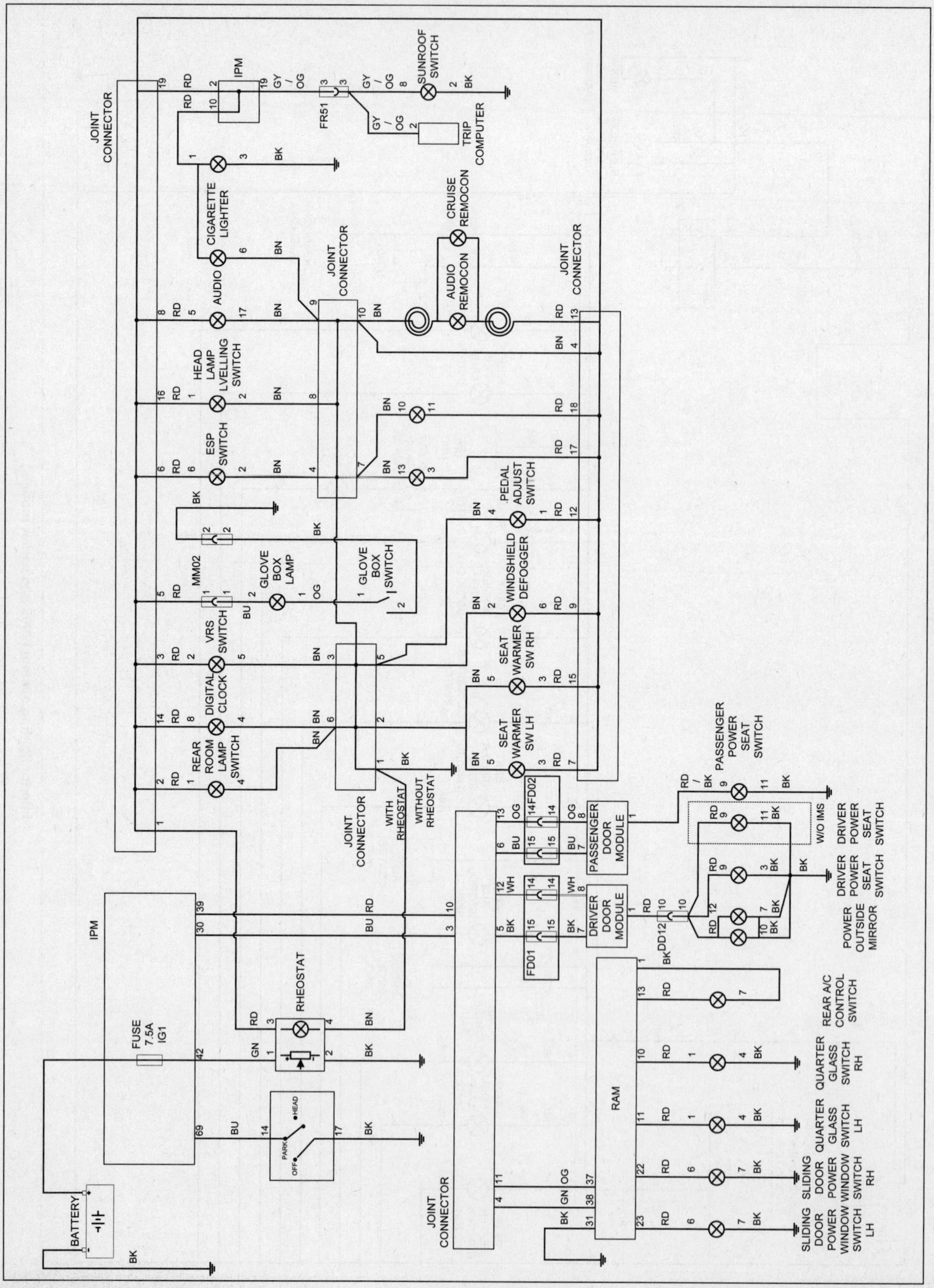

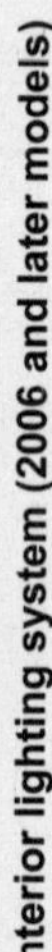

Interior lighting system (2006 and later models)

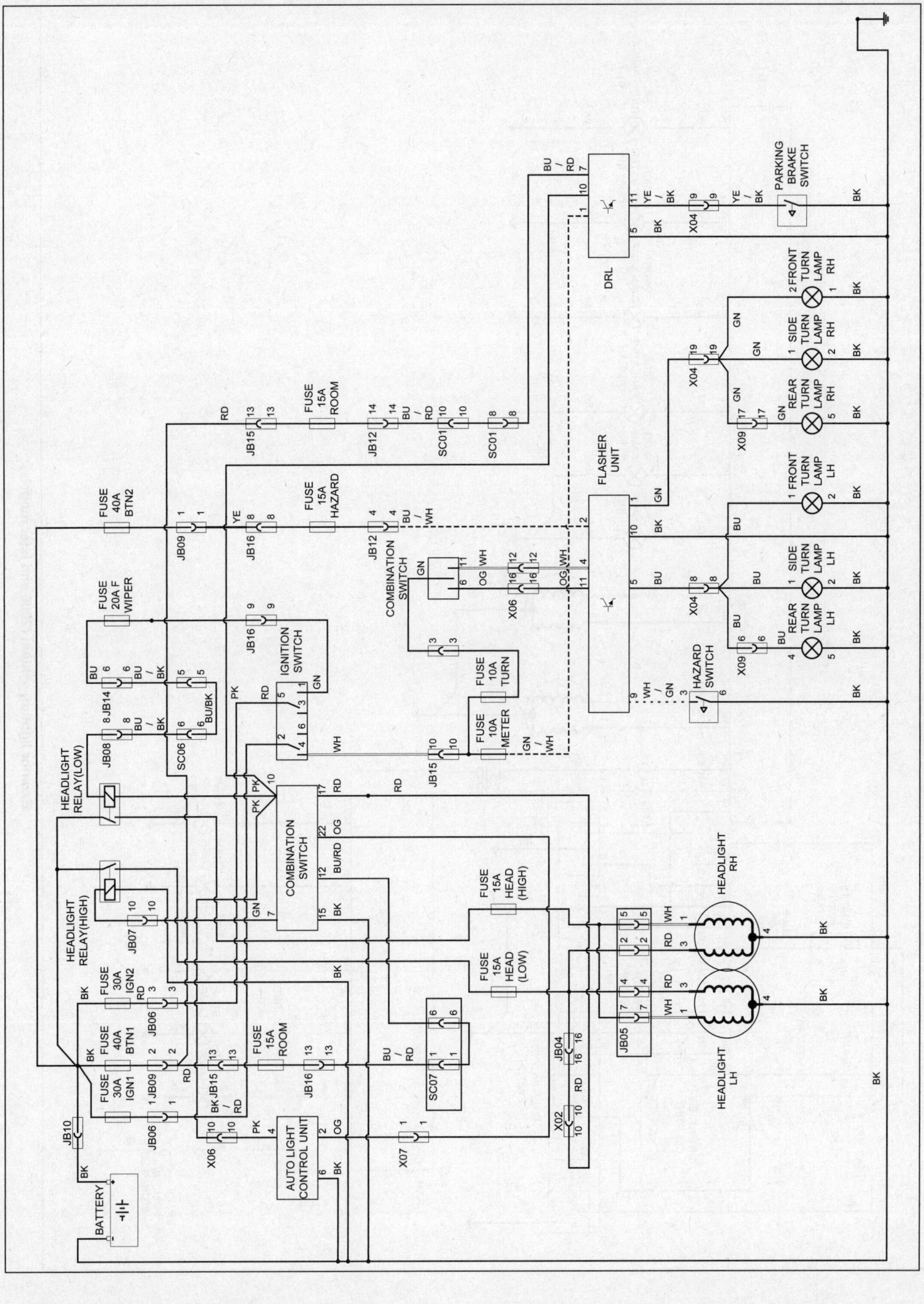

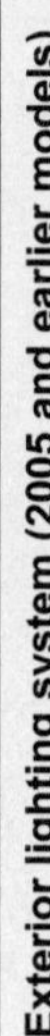

Exterior lighting system (2005 and earlier models)

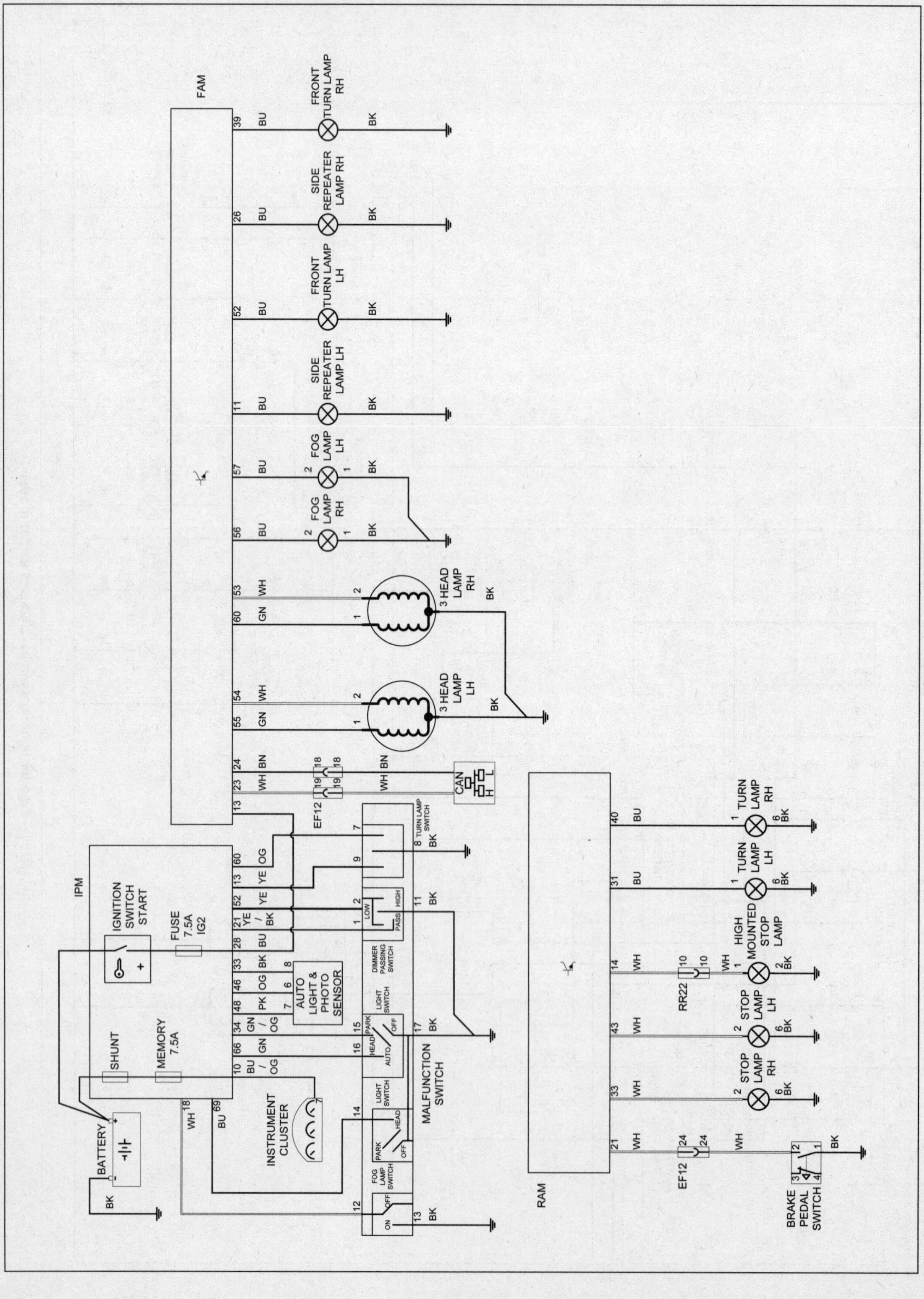

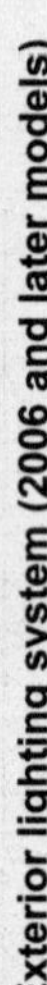

Exterior lighting system (2006 and later models)

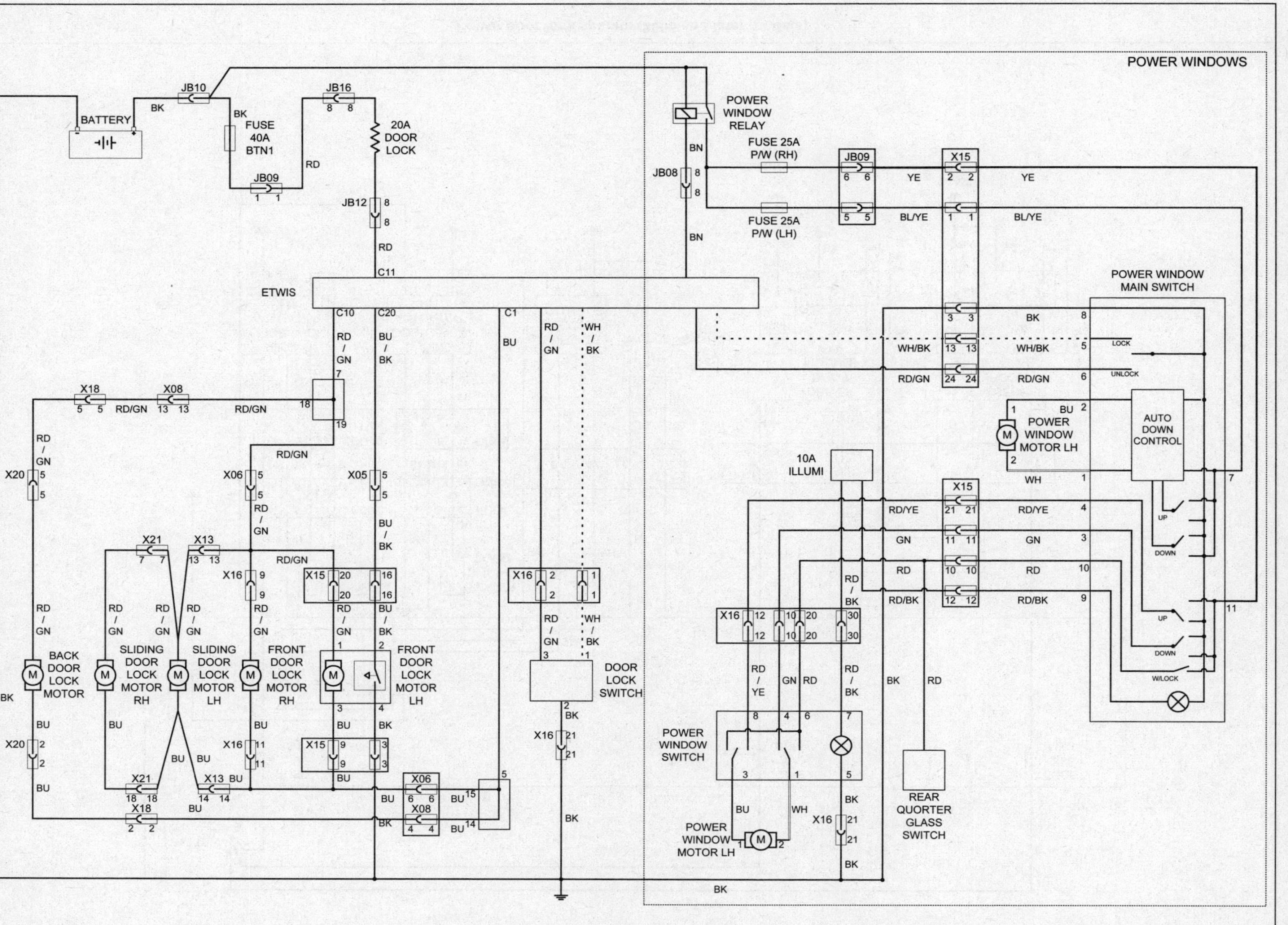

Power door lock and power window systems (2005 and earlier models)

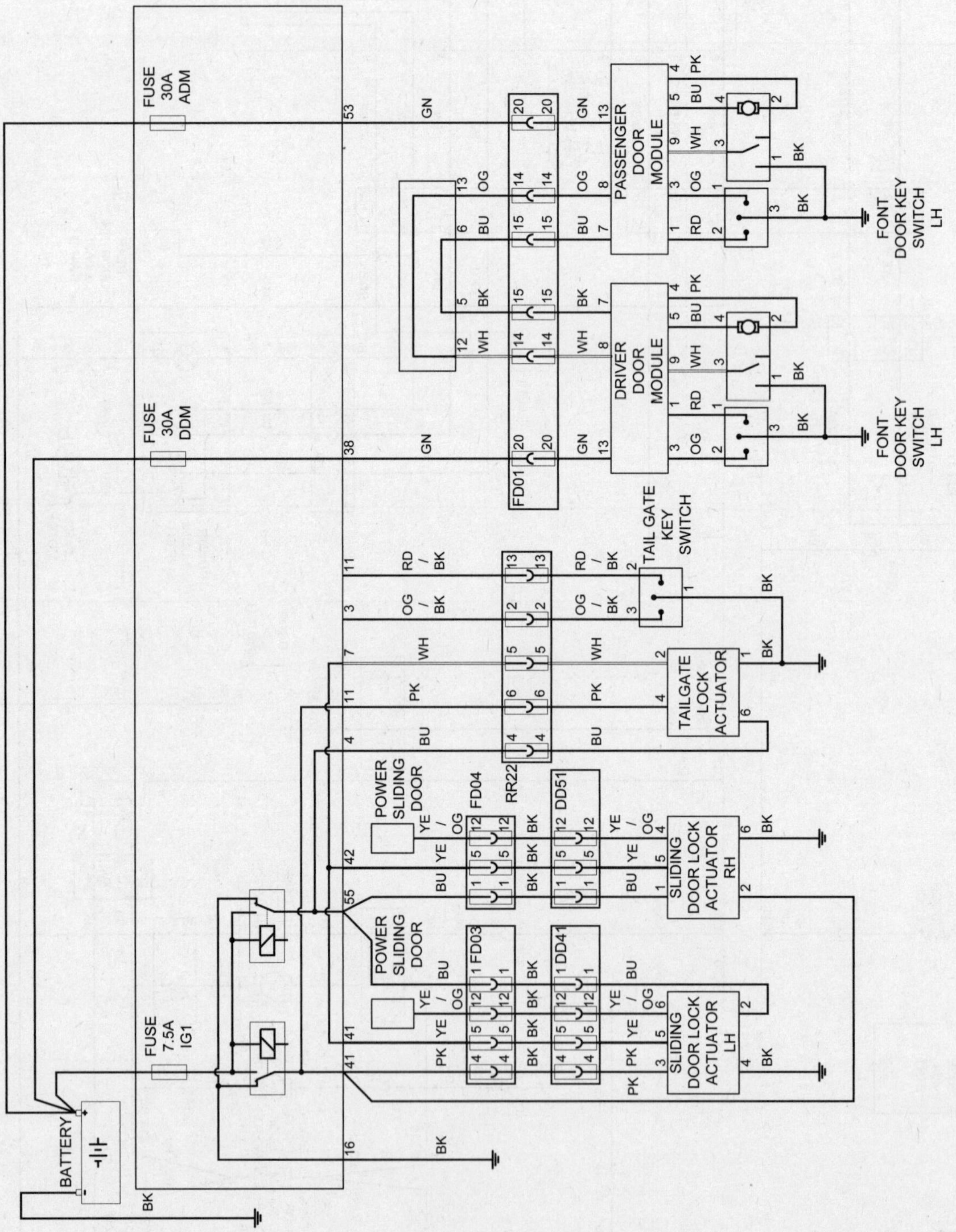

Power door lock system (2006 and later models)

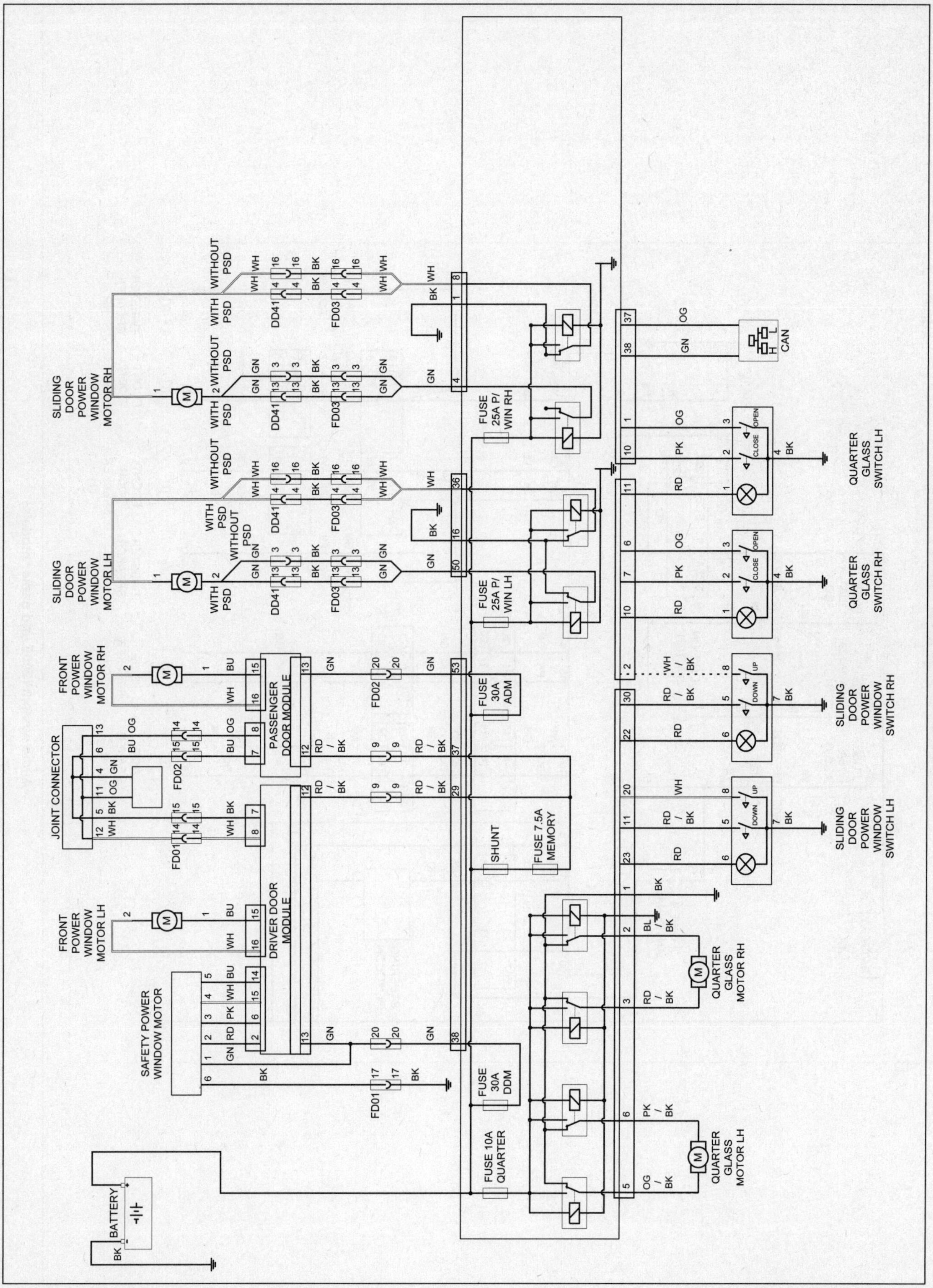

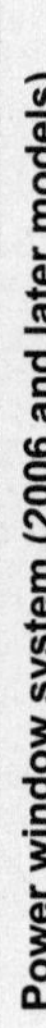

Power window system (2006 and later models)

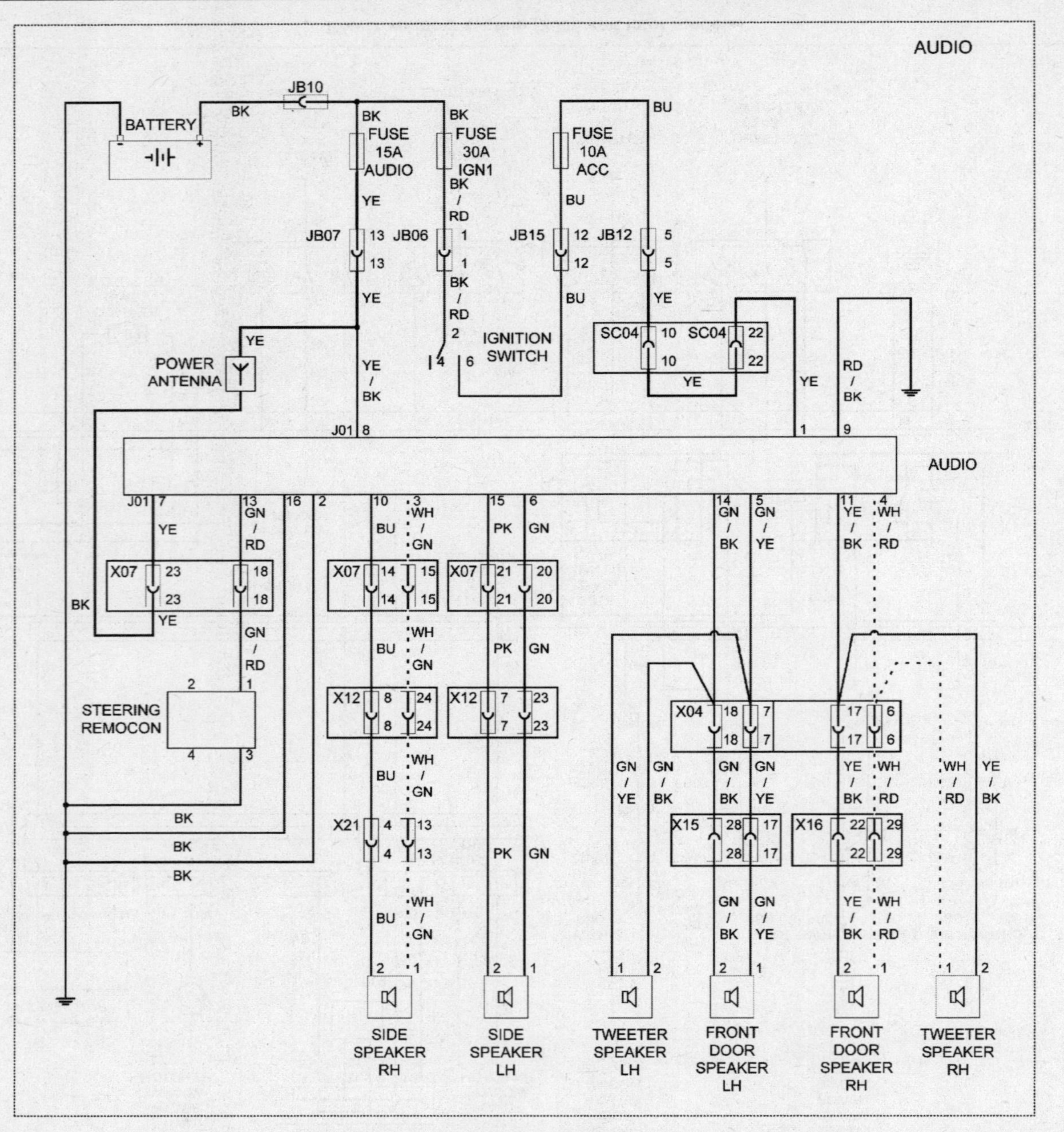

Audio system (2005 and earlier models)

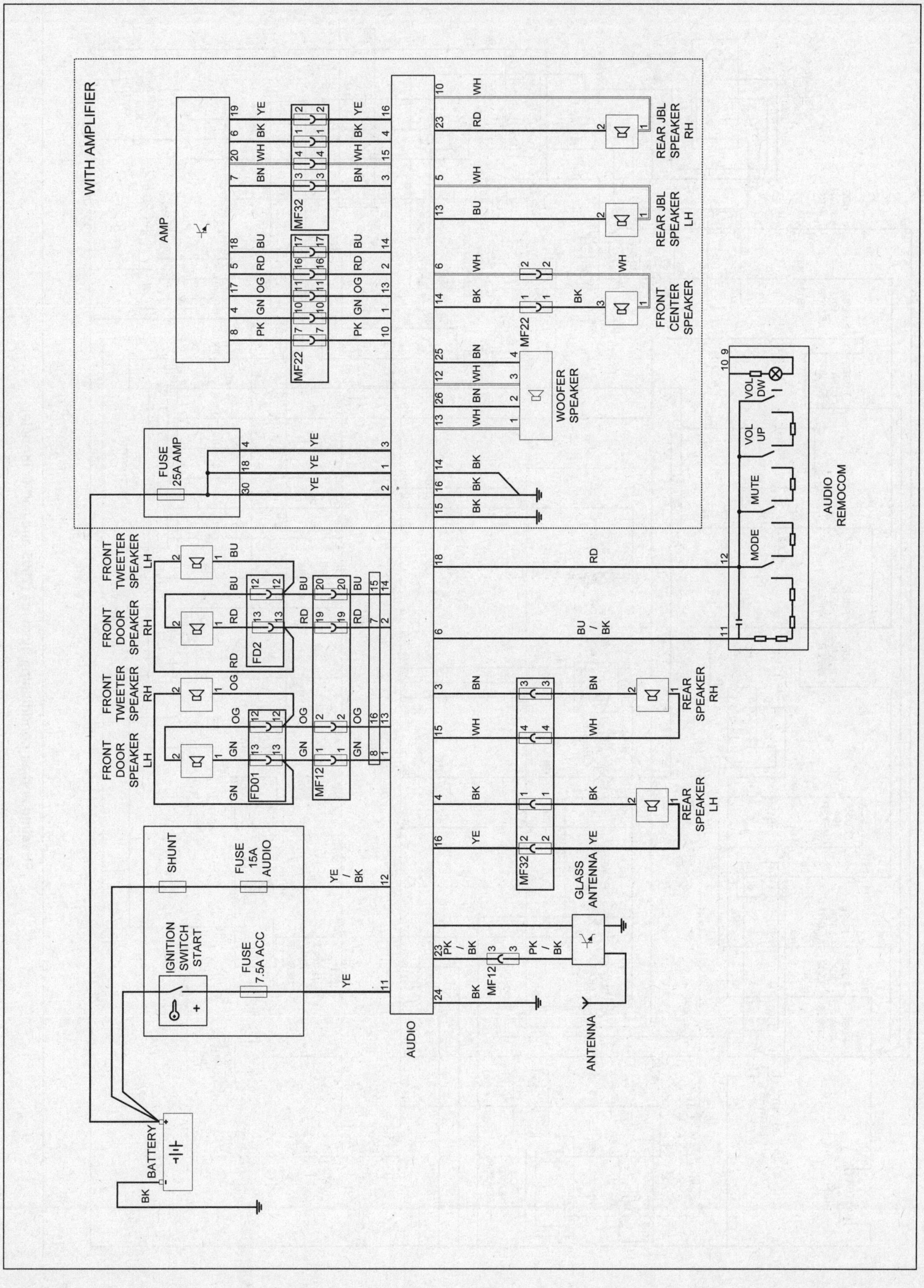

Audio system (2006 and later models)

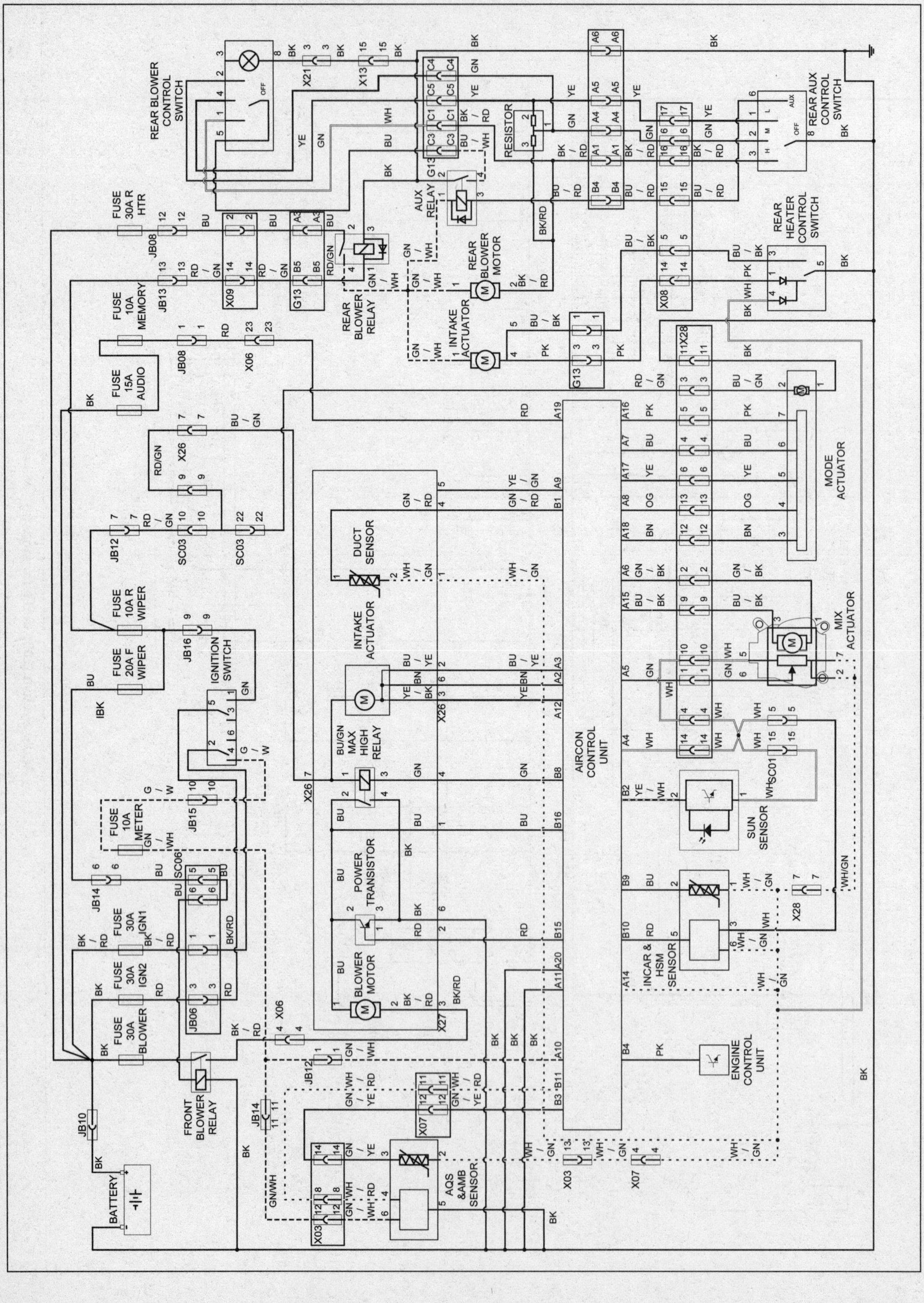

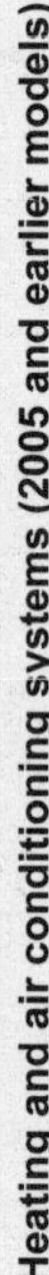

Heating and air conditioning systems (2005 and earlier models)

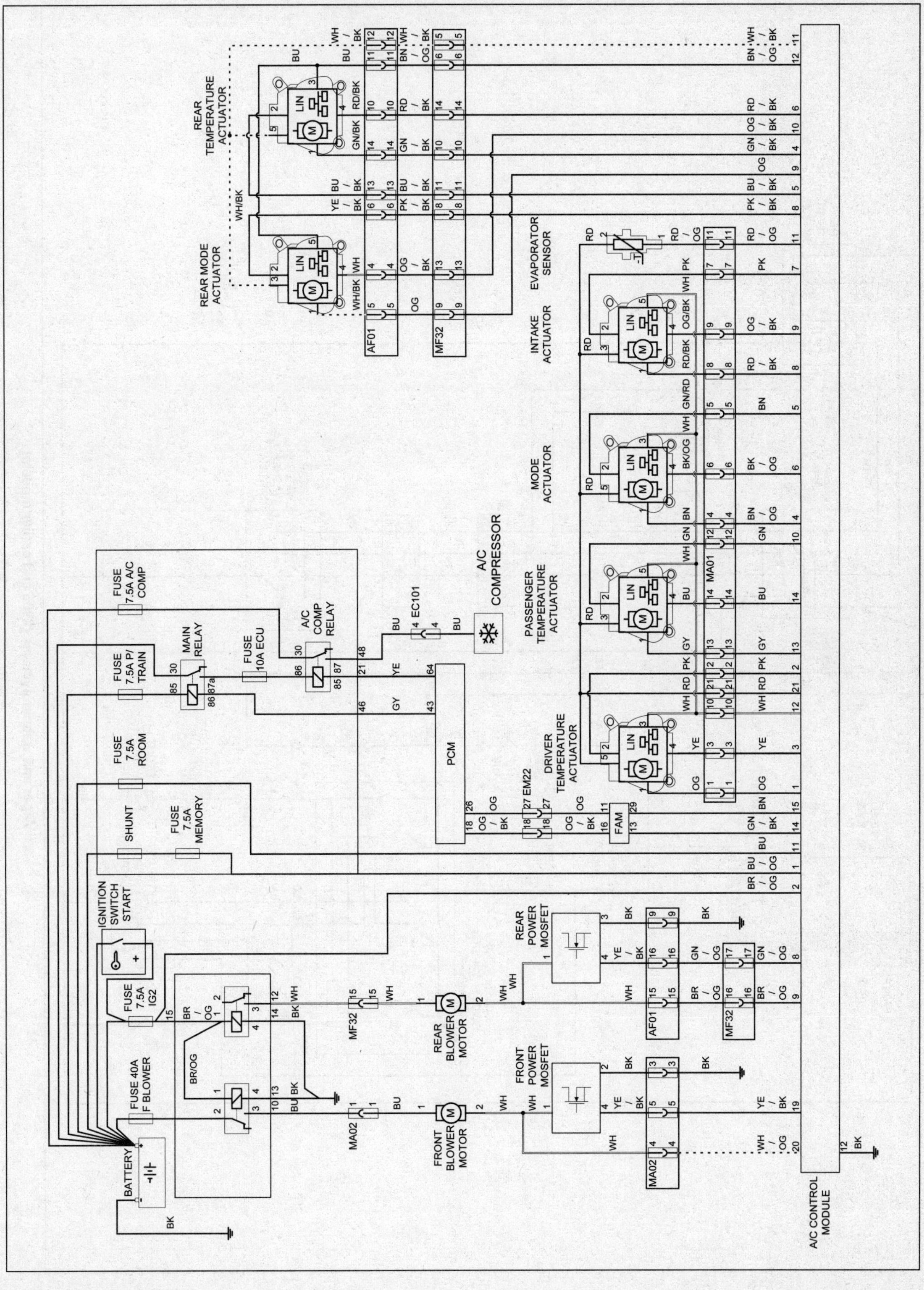

Heating and air conditioning systems (2006 and later models)

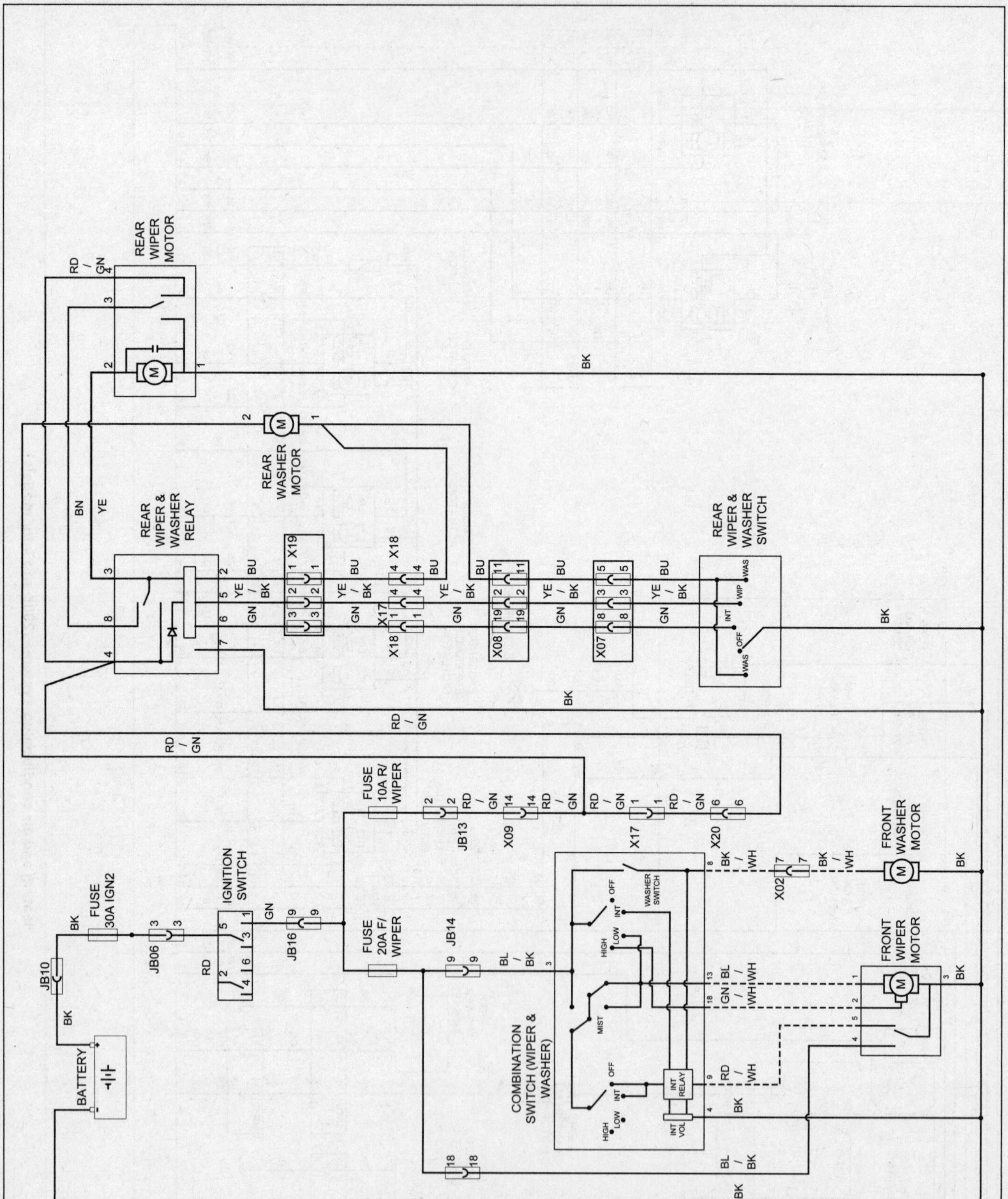

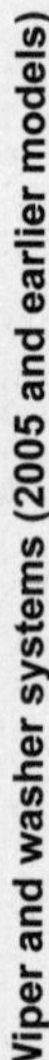

Wiper and washer systems (2005 and earlier models)

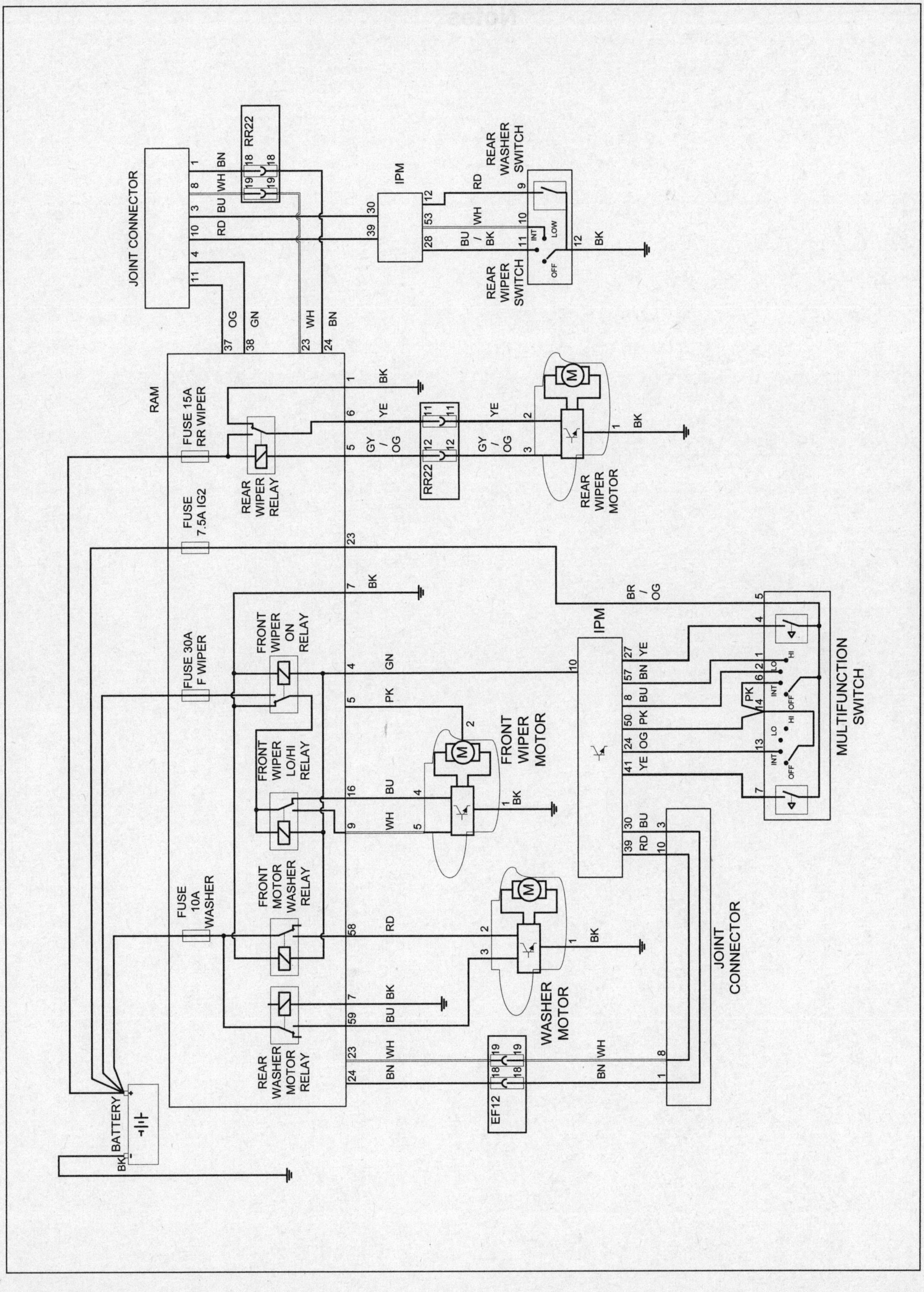

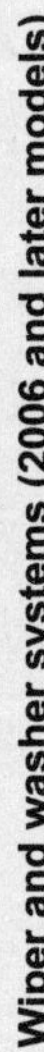

Wiper and washer systems (2006 and later models)

Notes

Index

A

About this manual, 0-5
Accelerator Pedal Position (APP) sensor – replacement, 6-17
Air conditioning
And heating system - check and maintenance, 3-4
Compressor - removal and installation, 3-11
Condenser - removal and installation, 3-12
Receiver-drier - removal and installation, 3-12
Air filter check and replacement, 1-18
Air filter housing - removal and installation, 4-6
Airbag System – general information and precautions, 12-18
Alternator - removal and installation, 5-5
Antenna – replacement, 12-10
Anti-lock Brake System (ABS) - general information, 9-6
Automatic transaxle, 7-1
Automatic transaxle - removal and installation, 7-5
Automatic transaxle overhaul - general information, 7-6
Brake Transmission Shift Interlock (BTSI) system - description, check and replacement, 7-4
Diagnosis - general, 7-2
Driveaxle oil seals - replacement, 7-2
General information, 7-2
Shift cable - removal and installation, 7-3
Shift lever - replacement, 7-3
Transaxle oil cooler - removal and installation, 7-5
Automotive chemicals and lubricants, 0-18

B

Balljoints – replacement, 10-10
Battery - disconnection, 5-4
Battery and battery tray – removal and installation, 5-4
Battery cables - replacement, 5-5
Battery check, maintenance and charging, 1-15
Blower motor resistor/power module and blower motor assembly - replacement, 3-9
Body, 11-1
Body repair - major damage, 11-3
Body repair - minor damage, 11-2
Bumper covers - removal and installation, 11-8
Center floor console - removal and installation, 11-30
Cowl cover - removal and installation, 11-10
Dashboard trim panels - removal and installation, 11-23
Door - removal and installation, 11-14
Door module, latch, lock and handle - removal and installation, 11-16
Door trim panels - removal and installation, 11-11
Door window glass - removal and installation, 11-20
Fastener and trim removal, 11-5
Front fender - removal and installation, 11-9
General information, 11-1
Hood - removal, installation and adjustment, 11-6
Hood and liftgate struts - replacement, 11-15
Hood latch and cable - removal and installation, 11-7
Instrument panel - removal and installation, 11-26
Mirrors - removal and installation, 11-22
Overhead console - removal and installation, 11-22
Power liftgate motor assembly - removal and installation, 11-31
Quarter window glass - removal and installation, 11-21
Radiator grille - removal and installation, 11-8
Rear trim panels - removal and installation, 11-28
Repair minor paint scratches, 11-2
Seats - removal and installation, 11-30
Steering column covers - removal and installation, 11-23
Upholstery, carpets and vinyl trim - maintenance, 11-5
Window glass regulators - removal and installation, 11-21
Booster battery (jump) starting, 0-17
Brake fluid change, 1-23
Brake system check, 1-18
Brake Transmission Shift Interlock (BTSI) system - description, check and replacement, 7-4

Brakes, 9-1
Anti-lock Brake System (ABS) - general information, 9-6
Brake disc - inspection, removal and installation, 9-10
Brake hoses and lines - inspection and replacement, 9-13
Brake light switch - removal, installation and adjustment, 9-19
Brake pedal - adjustment, 9-20
Brake system - bleeding, 9-13
Disc brake caliper - removal and installation, 9-9
Disc brake pads - replacement, 9-7
Drum brake shoes - replacement, 9-11
General information, 9-2
Master cylinder - removal and installation, 9-12
Parking brake - adjustment, 9-19
Parking brake shoes - inspection and replacement, 9-16
Power brake booster - check, replacement and adjustment, 9-14
Troubleshooting, 9-2
Wheel cylinder - removal and installation, 9-12
Bulb replacement, 12-13
Bumper covers - removal and installation, 11-8
Buying parts, 0-9

C

Cabin air filter replacement, 1-21
Camshaft Position (CMP) sensor - replacement, 6-17
Camshafts and valvetrain - removal, inspection, installation and valve adjustment, 2A-10
Catalytic converters - replacement, 6-24
Center floor console - removal and installation, 11-30
Chassis electrical system, 12-1
Airbag System – general information and precautions, 12-18
Antenna – replacement, 12-10
Bulb replacement, 12-13
Circuit breakers – general information, 12-14
Cruise control system - description, 12-21
Daytime Running Lights (DRL) – general information, 12-18
Electrical connectors - general information, 12-5
Electrical troubleshooting - general information, 12-2
Fuses and fusible links - general information, 12-3
General information, 12-1
Headlight bulb - replacement, 12-12
Headlight housing - replacement, 12-12
Headlights - adjustment, 12-13
Horn - replacement, 12-16
Ignition switch housing, key lock cylinder and ignition switch removal and installation, 12-6
Instrument cluster - removal and installation, 12-6
Instrument panel switches - replacement, 12-7
Multi-function switches - replacement, 12-6
Power door lock and keyless entry system – description and check, 12-17
Power sliding door and power rear hatch - description and operation, 12-10
Power window system - description and check, 12-21
Radio, navigation, speakers and DVD player removal and installation, 12-9
Rear window defogger - check and repair, 12-11
Relays - general information and testing, 12-4
Wiper motor - replacement, 12-8
Wiring Diagrams – general information, 12-20
Circuit breakers – general information, 12-14
Coil springs (rear) - removal and installation, 10-11
Control arm and tension arm - removal, inspection and installation, 10-9
Conversion factors, 0-19
Coolant reservoir - removal and installation, 3-7
Cooling system check, 1-17
Cooling system servicing, 1-24
Cooling, heating and air conditioning systems, 3-1
Air conditioning and heating system - check and maintenance, 3-4
Air conditioning compressor - removal and installation, 3-11
Air conditioning condenser - removal and installation, 3-12
Air conditioning receiver-drier - removal and installation, 3-12
Blower motor resistor/power module and blower motor assembly - replacement, 3-9
Coolant reservoir - removal and installation, 3-7
Engine cooling fan - replacement, 3-7
Expansion valve - removal and installation, 3-13
General information, 3-2
Heater/air conditioner control assembly - removal and installation, 3-11
Heater core - replacement, 3-10
Radiator - removal and installation, 3-7
Rear heating and air conditioning housing - removal and installation , 3-13
Thermostat - replacement, 3-6
Troubleshooting, 3-2
Water pump - replacement, 3-8
Cowl cover - removal and installation, 11-10
Crankshaft - removal and installation, 2B-12
Crankshaft Position (CKP) sensor - replacement, 6-18

Crankshaft pulley/vibration damper - removal and installation, 2A-13
Cruise control system - description, 12-21
CVVT Oil Control Valve (OCV) - replacement, 6-21
CVVT Oil Temperature Sensor (OTS) - replacement, 6-21
Cylinder compression check, 2B-3
Cylinder heads - removal, inspection and installation, 2A-12

D

Dashboard trim panels - removal and installation, 11-23
Daytime Running Lights (DRL) – general information, 12-18
Diagnosis - general, 7-2
Disc brake caliper - removal and installation, 9-9
Disc brake pads - replacement, 9-7
Door
Module, latch, lock and handle - removal and installation, 11-16
Removal and installation, 11-14
Trim panels - removal and installation, 11-11
Window glass - removal and installation, 11-20
Driveaxle oil seals - replacement, 7-2
Driveaxles, 8-1
Driveaxle boot replacement, 8-2
Driveaxles - general information and inspection, 8-1
Driveaxle - removal and installation, 8-2
Drivebelt check, adjustment and replacement, 1-21
Driveplate - removal and installation, 2A-15
Drum brake shoes - replacement, 9-11

E

Electrical connectors - general information, 12-5
Electrical troubleshooting - general information, 12-2
Emissions and engine control systems, 6-1
Accelerator Pedal Position (APP) sensor – replacement, 6-17
Camshaft Position (CMP) sensor - replacement, 6-17
Catalytic converters - replacement, 6-24
Crankshaft Position (CKP) sensor - replacement, 6-18
CVVT Oil Control Valve (OCV) - replacement, 6-21
CVVT Oil Temperature Sensor (OTS) - replacement, 6-21
Engine Coolant Temperature (ECT) sensor - replacement, 6-18
Evaporative emissions control (EVAP) system - component replacement, 6-24
Fuel tank pressure sensor - replacement, 6-20
General information, 6-1
Knock sensor - replacement, 6-18
Manifold Absolute Pressure (MAP) sensor - replacement, 6-18
Mass Air Flow/Intake Air Temperature (MAF/IAT), Barometric Pressure/Intake Air Temperature (BARO/IAT)sensors - replacement, 6-19
Obtaining and clearing Diagnostic Trouble Codes (DTCs), 6-4
On Board Diagnosis (OBD) system, 6-4
Oxygen sensors - general information and replacement, 6-19
Positive Crankcase Ventilation (PCV) valve - replacement, 6-25
Powertrain Control Module ((PCM) - replacement, 6-23
Throttle Position (TP) sensor - replacement and adjustment, 6-20
Transmission Range (TR) sensor - removal, installation and adjustment, 6-22
Transmission speed sensors - replacement, 6-23
Variable Charge Motion Actuator - replacement, 6-22
Variable Intake Solenoid (VIS) control valve – replacement, 6-22
Engine - removal and installation, 2B-6
Engine Coolant Temperature (ECT) sensor - replacement, 6-18
Engine cooling fan - replacement, 3-7
Engine electrical systems, 5-1
Alternator - removal and installation, 5-5
Battery - disconnection, 5-4
Battery and battery tray – removal and installation, 5-4
Battery cables - replacement, 5-5
General information and precautions, 5-2
Ignition coils - replacement, 5-5
Starter motor - removal and installation, 5-6
Troubleshooting, 5-2
Engine - general overhaul procedures, 2B-1
Crankshaft - removal and installation, 2B-12
Cylinder compression check, 2B-3
Engine - removal and installation, 2B-6
Engine overhaul - disassembly sequence, 2B-7
Engine overhaul - reassembly sequence, 2B-14
Engine rebuilding alternatives, 2B-5
Engine removal - methods and precautions, 2B-5
General information, 2B-2
Initial start-up and break-in after overhaul, 2B-15
Oil pressure check, 2B-3
Pistons and connecting rods - removal and installation, 2B-7
Vacuum gauge diagnostic checks, 2B-4

Engine, in-vehicle repair procedures
V6 engines
Camshafts and valvetrain - removal, inspection, installation and valve adjustment, 2A-10
Crankshaft pulley/vibration damper - removal and installation, 2A-13
Cylinder heads - removal, inspection and installation, 2A-12
Driveplate - removal and installation, 2A-15
Exhaust manifold/catalytic converter assemblies – removal and installation, 2A-6
General information, 2A-4
Intake manifold - removal and installation, 2A-5
Oil pans - removal and installation, 2A-13
Oil pump - removal, inspection and installation, 2A-14
Oil seals - replacement, 2A-9
Powertrain mounts - check and replacement, 2A-16
Rear main oil seal - replacement, 2A-16
Repair operations possible with the engine in the vehicle, 2A-4
Timing belt and sprockets (2005 and earlier models) - removal, inspection and installation, 2A-8
Timing chain and sprockets (2006 and later models) - removal, inspection and installation, 2A-7
Top Dead Center (TDC) for number one piston - locating, 2A-4
Valve covers - removal and installation, 2A-4
Engine oil and filter change, 1-12
Engine overhaul - disassembly sequence, 2B-7
Engine overhaul - reassembly sequence, 2B-14
Engine rebuilding alternatives, 2B-5
Engine removal - methods and precautions, 2B-5
Evaporative emissions control (EVAP) system - component replacement, 6-24
Exhaust manifold/catalytic converter assemblies – removal and installation, 2A-6
Exhaust system check, 1-20
Exhaust system servicing - general information, 4-4
Expansion valve - removal and installation, 3-13

F

Fastener and trim removal, 11-5
Fluid level checks, 1-8
Fraction/decimal/millimeter equivalents, 0-20
Front fender - removal and installation, 11-9
Fuel and exhaust systems, 4-1
Air filter housing - removal and installation, 4-6
Exhaust system servicing - general information, 4-4
Fuel lines and fitting - general information and disconnection, 4-4
Fuel pressure - check, 4-3
Fuel pressure regulator - replacement, 4-8
Fuel pressure relief procedure, 4-3
Fuel pump/fuel level sending unit - removal and installation, 4-4
Fuel pump module - component replacement, 4-6
Fuel rail and injectors - removal and installation, 4-7
Fuel tank - removal and installation, 4-6
Fuel tank pressure sensor - replacement, 4-8
General information, 4-2
Throttle body - removal and installation, 4-7
Troubleshooting, 4-2
Fuel system check, 1-21
Fuses and fusible links - general information, 12-3

H

Headlight bulb - replacement, 12-12
Headlight housing - replacement, 12-12
Headlights - adjustment, 12-13
Heater core - replacement, 3-10
Heater/air conditioner control assembly - removal and installation, 3-11
Hood - removal, installation and adjustment, 11-6
Hood and liftgate struts - replacement, 11-15
Hood latch and cable - removal and installation, 11-7
Horn - replacement, 12-16
Hub and bearing assembly - removal and installation,
Front, 10-10
Rear, 10-14

I

Ignition coils - replacement, 5-5
Ignition switch housing, key lock cylinder and ignition switch removal and installation, 12-6
Initial start-up and break-in after overhaul, 2B-15
Instrument cluster - removal and installation, 12-6
Instrument panel - removal and installation, 11-26
Instrument panel switches - replacement, 12-7
Intake manifold - removal and installation, 2A-5
Introduction, 0-5

J

Jacking and towing, 0-16

K

Knock sensor - replacement, 6-18

M

Maintenance schedule, 1-6
Maintenance techniques, tools and working facilities, 0-9
Manifold Absolute Pressure (MAP) sensor - replacement, 6-18
Mass Air Flow/Intake Air Temperature (MAF/IAT), Barometric Pressure/Intake Air Temperature (BARO/IAT) sensors - replacement, 6-19
Master cylinder - removal and installation, 9-12
Mirrors - removal and installation, 11-22
Multi-function switches - replacement, 12-6

O

Obtaining and clearing Diagnostic Trouble Codes (DTCs), 6-4
Oil pans - removal and installation, 2A-13
Oil pressure check, 2B-3
Oil pump - removal, inspection and installation, 2A-14
Oil seals - replacement, 2A-9
On Board Diagnosis (OBD) system, 6-4
Overhead console - removal and installation, 11-22
Oxygen sensors - general information and replacement, 6-19

P

Parking brake - adjustment, 9-19
Parking brake shoes - inspection and replacement, 9-16
Pistons and connecting rods - removal and installation, 2B-7
Positive Crankcase Ventilation (PCV) valve
  Check and replacement, 1-23
  Replacement, 6-25
Power brake booster - check, replacement and adjustment, 9-14
Power door lock and keyless entry system – description and check, 12-17
Power liftgate motor assembly - removal and installation, 11-31
Power sliding door and power rear hatch - description and operation, 12-10
Power steering pump - removal and installation, 10-18
Power steering system - bleeding, 10-19
Power window system - description and check, 12-21
Powertrain Control Module (PCM) - replacement, 6-23
Powertrain mounts - check and replacement, 2A-16

Q

Quarter window glass - removal and installation, 11-21

R

Radiator - removal and installation, 3-7
Radiator grille - removal and installation, 11-8
Radio, navigation, speakers and DVD player removal and installation, 12-9
Rear heating and air conditioning housing - removal and installation, 3-13
Rear main oil seal - replacement, 2A-16
Rear trim panels - removal and installation, 11-28
Rear window defogger - check and repair, 12-11
Recall information, 0-7
Relays - general information and testing, 12-4
Repair minor paint scratches, 11-2
Repair operations possible with the engine in the vehicle, 2A-4

S

Safety first!, 0-21
Seat belt check, 1-16
Seats - removal and installation, 11-30
Shift cable - removal and installation, 7-3
Shift lever - replacement, 7-3
Shock absorbers (rear) - removal and installation, 10-12
Spark plug check and replacement, 1-24
Spark plug wire check and replacement, 1-26
Stabilizer bar, bushings and links - removal and installation,
  Front, 10-6
  Rear, 10-11
Stabilizer bar, bushings and links - removal and installation, 10-11

Starter motor - removal and installation, 5-6
Steering
Column - removal and installation, 10-18
Column covers - removal and installation, 11-23
Gear - removal and installation, 10-17
Knuckle - removal and installation, 10-11
Wheel - removal and installation, 10-16
Steering, suspension and driveaxle boot check, 1-19
Strut assembly (front) - removal, inspection and installation, 10-7
Strut/coil spring assembly - replacement, 10-7
Subframe - removal and installation, 10-15
Suspension and steering systems, 10-1
Balljoints – replacement, 10-10
Coil springs (rear) - removal and installation, 10-11
Control arm and tension arm - removal, inspection and installation, 10-9
General information, 10-6
Hub and bearing assembly (front) - removal and installation, 10-10
Hub and bearing assembly (rear) - removal and installation, 10-14
Power steering pump - removal and installation, 10-18
Power steering system - bleeding, 10-19
Shock absorbers (rear) - removal and installation, 10-12
Stabilizer bar, bushings and links (front) - removal and installation, 10-6
Stabilizer bar, bushings and links (rear) - removal and installation, 10-11
Steering column - removal and installation, 10-18
Steering gear - removal and installation, 10-17
Steering knuckle - removal and installation, 10-11
Steering wheel - removal and installation, 10-16
Strut assembly (front) - removal, inspection and installation, 10-7
Strut/coil spring assembly - replacement, 10-7
Subframe - removal and installation, 10-15
Suspension arms and rear axle beam (rear) removal and installation, 10-12
Tie-rod ends - removal and installation, 10-17
Wheel alignment - general information, 10-19
Wheels and tires - general information, 10-19

T

Thermostat - replacement, 3-6
Throttle body - removal and installation, 4-7
Throttle Position (TP) sensor - replacement and adjustment, 6-20
Tie-rod ends - removal and installation, 10-17
Timing belt and sprockets (2005 and earlier models) - removal, inspection and installation, 2A-8
Timing chain and sprockets (2006 and later models) - removal, inspection and installation, 2A-7
Tire and tire pressure checks, 1-11
Tire rotation, 1-16
Top Dead Center (TDC) for number one piston - locating, 2A-4
Transaxle oil cooler - removal and installation, 7-5
Transmission Range (TR) sensor - removal, installation and adjustment, 6-22
Transmission speed sensors - replacement, 6-23
Troubleshooting, 0-22
Tune-up and routine maintenance, 1-1
Air filter check and replacement, 1-18
Automatic transaxle fluid change, 1-26
Battery check, maintenance and charging, 1-15
Brake fluid change, 1-23
Brake system check, 1-18
Cabin air filter replacement, 1-21
Cooling system check, 1-17
Cooling system servicing, 1-24
Drivebelt check, adjustment and replacement, 1-21
Engine oil and filter change, 1-12
Exhaust system check, 1-20
Fluid level checks, 1-8
Fuel system check, 1-21
Introduction, 1-7
Maintenance schedule, 1-6
Positive Crankcase Ventilation (PCV) valve check and replacement, 1-23
Seat belt check, 1-16
Spark plug check and replacement, 1-24
Spark plug wire check and replacement, 1-26
Steering, suspension and driveaxle boot check, 1-19
Tire and tire pressure checks, 1-11
Tire rotation, 1-16
Tune-up general information, 1-7
Underhood hose check and replacement, 1-17
Windshield/rear wiper blade inspection and replacement, 1-14
Tune-up general information, 1-7

U

Underhood hose check and replacement, 1-17
Upholstery, carpets and vinyl trim - maintenance, 11-5

V

V6 engines, 2A-1
Camshafts and valvetrain - removal, inspection, installation and valve adjustment, 2A-10
Crankshaft pulley/vibration damper - removal and installation, 2A-13
Cylinder heads - removal, inspection and installation, 2A-12
Driveplate - removal and installation, 2A-15
Exhaust manifold/catalytic converter assemblies – removal and installation, 2A-6
General information, 2A-4
Intake manifold - removal and installation, 2A-5
Oil pans - removal and installation, 2A-13
Oil pump - removal, inspection and installation, 2A-14
Oil seals - replacement, 2A-9
Powertrain mounts - check and replacement, 2A-16
Rear main oil seal - replacement, 2A-16
Repair operations possible with the engine in the vehicle, 2A-4
Timing belt and sprockets (2005 and earlier models) - removal, inspection and installation, 2A-8
Timing chain and sprockets (2006 and later models) - removal, inspection and installation, 2A-7
Top Dead Center (TDC) for number one piston - locating, 2A-4
Valve covers - removal and installation, 2A-4
Vacuum gauge diagnostic checks, 2B-4
Variable Charge Motion Actuator - replacement, 6-22
Variable Intake Solenoid (VIS) control valve – replacement, 6-22
Vehicle identification numbers, 0-6

W

Water pump - replacement, 3-8
Wheel alignment - general information, 10-19
Wheel cylinder - removal and installation, 9-12
Wheels and tires - general information, 10-19
Window glass regulators - removal and installation, 11-21
Windshield/rear wiper blade inspection and replacement, 1-14
Wiper motor - replacement, 12-8
Wiring Diagrams – general information, 12-20

Notes

Haynes Automotive Manuals

NOTE: If you do not see a listing for your vehicle, consult your local Haynes dealer for the latest product information.

ACURA

12020 **Integra** '86 thru '89 **& Legend** '86 thru '90
12021 **Integra** '90 thru '93 **& Legend** '91 thru '95
Integra '94 thru '00 - *see HONDA Civic (42025)*
MDX '01 thru '07 - *see HONDA Pilot (42037)*
12050 **Acura TL** all models '99 thru '08

AMC

Jeep CJ - *see JEEP (50020)*
14020 **Mid-size models** '70 thru '83
14025 **(Renault) Alliance & Encore** '83 thru '87

AUDI

15020 **4000** all models '80 thru '87
15025 **5000** all models '77 thru '83
15026 **5000** all models '84 thru '88
Audi A4 '96 thru '01 - *see VW Passat (96023)*
15030 **Audi A4** '02 thru '08

AUSTIN-HEALEY

Sprite - *see MG Midget (66015)*

BMW

18020 **3/5 Series** '82 thru '92
18021 **3-Series** incl. Z3 models '92 thru '98
18022 **3-Series** incl. Z4 models '99 thru '05
18023 **3-Series** '06 thru '10
18025 **320i all 4 cyl models** '75 thru '83
18050 **1500 thru 2002** except Turbo '59 thru '77

BUICK

19010 **Buick Century** '97 thru '05
Century (front-wheel drive) - *see GM (38005)*
19020 **Buick, Oldsmobile & Pontiac Full-size (Front-wheel drive)** '85 thru '05
Buick Electra, LeSabre and Park Avenue; **Oldsmobile** Delta 88 Royale, Ninety Eight and Regency; **Pontiac** Bonneville
19025 **Buick, Oldsmobile & Pontiac Full-size (Rear wheel drive)** '70 thru '90
Buick Estate, Electra, LeSabre, Limited, **Oldsmobile** Custom Cruiser, Delta 88, Ninety-eight, **Pontiac** Bonneville, Catalina, Grandville, Parisienne
19030 **Mid-size Regal & Century** all rear-drive models with V6, V8 and Turbo '74 thru '87
Regal - *see GENERAL MOTORS (38010)*
Riviera - *see GENERAL MOTORS (38030)*
Roadmaster - *see CHEVROLET (24046)*
Skyhawk - *see GENERAL MOTORS (38015)*
Skylark - *see GM (38020, 38025)*
Somerset - *see GENERAL MOTORS (38025)*

CADILLAC

21015 **CTS & CTS-V** '03 thru '12
21030 **Cadillac Rear Wheel Drive** '70 thru '93
Cimarron - *see GENERAL MOTORS (38015)*
DeVille - *see GM (38031 & 38032)*
Eldorado - *see GM (38030 & 38031)*
Fleetwood - *see GM (38031)*
Seville - *see GM (38030, 38031 & 38032)*

CHEVROLET

10305 **Chevrolet Engine Overhaul Manual**
24010 **Astro & GMC Safari Mini-vans** '85 thru '05
24015 **Camaro V8** all models '70 thru '81
24016 **Camaro** all models '82 thru '92
24017 **Camaro & Firebird** '93 thru '02
Cavalier - *see GENERAL MOTORS (38016)*
Celebrity - *see GENERAL MOTORS (38005)*
24020 **Chevelle, Malibu & El Camino** '69 thru '87
24024 **Chevette & Pontiac T1000** '76 thru '87
Citation - *see GENERAL MOTORS (38020)*
24027 **Colorado & GMC Canyon** '04 thru '10
24032 **Corsica/Beretta** all models '87 thru '96
24040 **Corvette** all V8 models '68 thru '82
24041 **Corvette** all models '84 thru '96
24045 **Full-size Sedans** Caprice, Impala, Biscayne, Bel Air & Wagons '69 thru '90
24046 **Impala SS & Caprice and Buick Roadmaster** '91 thru '96
Impala '00 thru '05 - *see LUMINA (24048)*
24047 **Impala & Monte Carlo** all models '06 thru '11
Lumina '90 thru '94 - *see GM (38010)*
24048 **Lumina & Monte Carlo** '95 thru '05
Lumina APV - *see GM (38035)*
24050 **Luv Pick-up** all 2WD & 4WD '72 thru '82
Malibu '97 thru '00 - *see GM (38026)*
24055 **Monte Carlo** all models '70 thru '88
Monte Carlo '95 thru '01 - *see LUMINA (24048)*
24059 **Nova** all V8 models '69 thru '79
24060 **Nova and Geo Prizm** '85 thru '92
24064 **Pick-ups** '67 thru '87 - Chevrolet & GMC
24065 **Pick-ups** '88 thru '98 - Chevrolet & GMC
24066 **Pick-ups** '99 thru '06 - Chevrolet & GMC
24067 **Chevrolet Silverado & GMC Sierra** '07 thru '12
24070 **S-10 & S-15 Pick-ups** '82 thru '93, **Blazer & Jimmy** '83 thru '94,
24071 **S-10 & Sonoma Pick-ups** '94 thru '04, including **Blazer, Jimmy & Hombre**
24072 **Chevrolet TrailBlazer, GMC Envoy & Oldsmobile Bravada** '02 thru '09
24075 **Sprint** '85 thru '88 **& Geo Metro** '89 thru '01
24080 **Vans - Chevrolet & GMC** '68 thru '96
24081 **Chevrolet Express & GMC Savana** Full-size Vans '96 thru '10

CHRYSLER

10310 **Chrysler Engine Overhaul Manual**
25015 **Chrysler Cirrus, Dodge Stratus, Plymouth Breeze** '95 thru '00
25020 **Full-size Front-Wheel Drive** '88 thru '93
K-Cars - *see DODGE Aries (30008)*
Laser - *see DODGE Daytona (30030)*
25025 **Chrysler LHS, Concorde, New Yorker, Dodge** Intrepid, **Eagle** Vision, '93 thru '97
25026 **Chrysler LHS, Concorde, 300M, Dodge** Intrepid, '98 thru '04
25027 **Chrysler 300, Dodge Charger & Magnum** '05 thru '09
25030 **Chrysler & Plymouth Mid-size** front wheel drive '82 thru '95
Rear-wheel Drive - *see Dodge (30050)*
25035 **PT Cruiser** all models '01 thru '10
25040 **Chrysler** Sebring '95 thru '06, **Dodge** Stratus '01 thru '06, **Dodge** Avenger '95 thru '00

DATSUN

28005 **200SX** all models '80 thru '83
28007 **B-210** all models '73 thru '78
28009 **210** all models '79 thru '82
28012 **240Z, 260Z & 280Z** Coupe '70 thru '78
28014 **280ZX** Coupe & 2+2 '79 thru '83
300ZX - *see NISSAN (72010)*
28018 **510 & PL521 Pick-up** '68 thru '73
28020 **510** all models '78 thru '81
28022 **620 Series Pick-up** all models '73 thru '79
720 Series Pick-up - *see NISSAN (72030)*
28025 **810/Maxima** all gasoline models '77 thru '84

DODGE

400 & 600 - *see CHRYSLER (25030)*
30008 **Aries & Plymouth Reliant** '81 thru '89
30010 **Caravan & Plymouth Voyager** '84 thru '95
30011 **Caravan & Plymouth Voyager** '96 thru '02
30012 **Challenger/Plymouth Saporro** '78 thru '83
30013 **Caravan, Chrysler Voyager, Town & Country** '03 thru '07
30016 **Colt & Plymouth Champ** '78 thru '87
30020 **Dakota Pick-ups** all models '87 thru '96
30021 **Durango** '98 & '99, **Dakota** '97 thru '99
30022 **Durango** '00 thru '03 **Dakota** '00 thru '04
30023 **Durango** '04 thru '09, **Dakota** '05 thru '11
30025 **Dart, Demon, Plymouth Barracuda, Duster & Valiant** 6 cyl models '67 thru '76
30030 **Daytona & Chrysler Laser** '84 thru '89
Intrepid - *see CHRYSLER (25025, 25026)*
30034 **Neon** all models '95 thru '99
30035 **Omni & Plymouth Horizon** '78 thru '90
30036 **Dodge and Plymouth Neon** '00 thru '05
30040 **Pick-ups** all full-size models '74 thru '93
30041 **Pick-ups** all full-size models '94 thru '01
30042 **Pick-ups** full-size models '02 thru '08
30045 **Ram 50/D50 Pick-ups & Raider and Plymouth Arrow Pick-ups** '79 thru '93
30050 **Dodge/Plymouth/Chrysler** RWD '71 thru '89
30055 **Shadow & Plymouth Sundance** '87 thru '94
30060 **Spirit & Plymouth Acclaim** '89 thru '95
30065 **Vans - Dodge & Plymouth** '71 thru '03

EAGLE

Talon - *see MITSUBISHI (68030, 68031)*
Vision - *see CHRYSLER (25025)*

FIAT

34010 **124 Sport Coupe & Spider** '68 thru '78
34025 **X1/9** all models '74 thru '80

FORD

10320 **Ford Engine Overhaul Manual**
10355 **Ford Automatic Transmission Overhaul**
11500 **Mustang '64-1/2 thru '70 Restoration Guide**
36004 **Aerostar Mini-vans** all models '86 thru '97
36006 **Contour & Mercury Mystique** '95 thru '00
36008 **Courier Pick-up** all models '72 thru '82
36012 **Crown Victoria & Mercury Grand Marquis** '88 thru '10
36016 **Escort/Mercury Lynx** all models '81 thru '90
36020 **Escort/Mercury Tracer** '91 thru '02
36022 **Escape & Mazda Tribute** '01 thru '11
36024 **Explorer & Mazda Navajo** '91 thru '01
36025 **Explorer/Mercury Mountaineer** '02 thru '10
36028 **Fairmont & Mercury Zephyr** '78 thru '83
36030 **Festiva & Aspire** '88 thru '97
36032 **Fiesta** all models '77 thru '80
36034 **Focus** all models '00 thru '11
36036 **Ford & Mercury Full-size** '75 thru '87
36044 **Ford & Mercury Mid-size** '75 thru '86
36045 **Fusion & Mercury Milan** '06 thru '10
36048 **Mustang V8** all models '64-1/2 thru '73
36049 **Mustang II** 4 cyl, V6 & V8 models '74 thru '78
36050 **Mustang & Mercury Capri** '79 thru '93
36051 **Mustang** all models '94 thru '04
36052 **Mustang** '05 thru '10
36054 **Pick-ups & Bronco** '73 thru '79
36058 **Pick-ups & Bronco** '80 thru '96
36059 **F-150 & Expedition** '97 thru '09, **F-250** '97 thru '99 **& Lincoln Navigator** '98 thru '09
36060 **Super Duty Pick-ups, Excursion** '99 thru '10
36061 **F-150** full-size '04 thru '10
36062 **Pinto & Mercury Bobcat** '75 thru '80
36066 **Probe** all models '89 thru '92
Probe '93 thru '97 - *see MAZDA 626 (61042)*
36070 **Ranger/Bronco II** gasoline models '83 thru '92
36071 **Ranger** '93 thru '10 & **Mazda Pick-ups** '94 thru '09
36074 **Taurus & Mercury Sable** '86 thru '95
36075 **Taurus & Mercury Sable** '96 thru '05
36078 **Tempo & Mercury Topaz** '84 thru '94
36082 **Thunderbird/Mercury Cougar** '83 thru '88
36086 **Thunderbird/Mercury Cougar** '89 thru '97
36090 **Vans** all V8 Econoline models '69 thru '91
36094 **Vans** full size '92 thru '10
36097 **Windstar Mini-van** '95 thru '07

GENERAL MOTORS

10360 **GM Automatic Transmission Overhaul**
38005 **Buick Century, Chevrolet Celebrity, Oldsmobile Cutlass Ciera & Pontiac 6000** all models '82 thru '96
38010 **Buick Regal, Chevrolet Lumina, Oldsmobile Cutlass Supreme & Pontiac Grand Prix** (FWD) '88 thru '07
38015 **Buick Skyhawk, Cadillac Cimarron, Chevrolet Cavalier, Oldsmobile Firenza & Pontiac J-2000 & Sunbird** '82 thru '94
38016 **Chevrolet Cavalier & Pontiac Sunfire** '95 thru '05
38017 **Chevrolet Cobalt & Pontiac G5** '05 thru '11
38020 **Buick Skylark, Chevrolet Citation, Olds Omega, Pontiac Phoenix** '80 thru '85
38025 **Buick Skylark & Somerset, Oldsmobile Achieva & Calais and Pontiac Grand Am** all models '85 thru '98
38026 **Chevrolet Malibu, Olds Alero & Cutlass, Pontiac Grand Am** '97 thru '03
38027 **Chevrolet Malibu** '04 thru '10
38030 **Cadillac Eldorado, Seville, Oldsmobile Toronado, Buick Riviera** '71 thru '85
38031 **Cadillac Eldorado & Seville, DeVille, Fleetwood & Olds Toronado, Buick Riviera** '86 thru '93
38032 **Cadillac DeVille** '94 thru '05 & **Seville** '92 thru '04 **Cadillac DTS** '06 thru '10
38035 **Chevrolet Lumina APV, Olds Silhouette & Pontiac Trans Sport** all models '90 thru '96
38036 **Chevrolet Venture, Olds Silhouette, Pontiac Trans Sport & Montana** '97 thru '05
General Motors Full-size Rear-wheel Drive - *see BUICK (19025)*
38040 **Chevrolet Equinox** '05 thru '09 **Pontiac Torrent** '06 thru '09
38070 **Chevrolet HHR** '06 thru '11

GEO

Metro - *see CHEVROLET Sprint (24075)*
Prizm - *'85 thru '92 see CHEVY (24060), '93 thru '02 see TOYOTA Corolla (92036)*
40030 **Storm** all models '90 thru '93
Tracker - *see SUZUKI Samurai (90010)*

GMC

Vans & Pick-ups - *see CHEVROLET*

HONDA

42010 **Accord CVCC** all models '76 thru '83
42011 **Accord** all models '84 thru '89
42012 **Accord** all models '90 thru '93
42013 **Accord** all models '94 thru '97
42014 **Accord** all models '98 thru '02
42015 **Accord** '03 thru '07
42020 **Civic 1200** all models '73 thru '79
42021 **Civic 1300 & 1500 CVCC** '80 thru '83
42022 **Civic 1500 CVCC** all models '75 thru '79

(Continued on other side)

Haynes Automotive Manuals (continued)

NOTE: If you do not see a listing for your vehicle, consult your local Haynes dealer for the latest product information.

42023 **Civic** all models '84 thru '91
42024 **Civic & del Sol** '92 thru '95
42025 **Civic** '96 thru '00, **CR-V** '97 thru '01, **Acura Integra** '94 thru '00
42026 **Civic** '01 thru '10, **CR-V** '02 thru '09
42035 **Odyssey** all models '99 thru '10
Passport - *see ISUZU Rodeo (47017)*
42037 **Honda Pilot** '03 thru '07, **Acura MDX** '01 thru '07
42040 **Prelude CVCC** all models '79 thru '89

HYUNDAI

43010 **Elantra** all models '96 thru '10
43015 **Excel & Accent** all models '86 thru '09
43050 **Santa Fe** all models '01 thru '06
43055 **Sonata** all models '99 thru '08

INFINITI

G35 '03 thru '08 - *see NISSAN 350Z (72011)*

ISUZU

Hombre - *see CHEVROLET S-10 (24071)*
47017 **Rodeo, Amigo & Honda Passport** '89 thru '02
47020 **Trooper & Pick-up** '81 thru '93

JAGUAR

49010 **XJ6** all 6 cyl models '68 thru '86
49011 **XJ6** all models '88 thru '94
49015 **XJ12 & XJS** all 12 cyl models '72 thru '85

JEEP

50010 **Cherokee, Comanche & Wagoneer Limited** all models '84 thru '01
50020 **CJ** all models '49 thru '86
50025 **Grand Cherokee** all models '93 thru '04
50026 **Grand Cherokee** '05 thru '09
50029 **Grand Wagoneer & Pick-up** '72 thru '91 Grand Wagoneer '84 thru '91, Cherokee & Wagoneer '72 thru '83, Pick-up '72 thru '88
50030 **Wrangler** all models '87 thru '11
50035 **Liberty** '02 thru '07

KIA

54050 **Optima** '01 thru '10
54070 **Sephia** '94 thru '01, **Spectra** '00 thru '09, **Sportage** '05 thru '10

LEXUS

ES 300/330 - *see TOYOTA Camry (92007) (92008)*
RX 330 - *see TOYOTA Highlander (92095)*

LINCOLN

Navigator - *see FORD Pick-up (36059)*
59010 **Rear-Wheel Drive** all models '70 thru '10

MAZDA

61010 **GLC Hatchback (rear-wheel drive)** '77 thru '83
61011 **GLC (front-wheel drive)** '81 thru '85
61012 **Mazda3** '04 thru '11
61015 **323 & Protogé** '90 thru '03
61016 **MX-5 Miata** '90 thru '09
61020 **MPV** all models '89 thru '98
Navajo - *see Ford Explorer (36024)*
61030 **Pick-ups** '72 thru '93
Pick-ups '94 thru '00 - *see Ford Ranger (36071)*
61035 **RX-7** all models '79 thru '85
61036 **RX-7** all models '86 thru '91
61040 **626** (rear-wheel drive) all models '79 thru '82
61041 **626/MX-6 (front-wheel drive)** '83 thru '92
61042 **626, MX-6/Ford Probe** '93 thru '02
61043 **Mazda6** '03 thru '11

MERCEDES-BENZ

63012 **123 Series Diesel** '76 thru '85
63015 **190 Series** four-cyl gas models, '84 thru '88
63020 **230/250/280** 6 cyl sohc models '68 thru '72
63025 **280 123 Series** gasoline models '77 thru '81
63030 **350 & 450** all models '71 thru '80
63040 **C-Class:** C230/C240/C280/C320/C350 '01 thru '07

MERCURY

64200 **Villager & Nissan Quest** '93 thru '01
All other titles, see FORD Listing.

MG

66010 **MGB** Roadster & GT Coupe '62 thru '80
66015 **MG Midget, Austin Healey Sprite** '58 thru '80

MINI

67020 **Mini** '02 thru '11

MITSUBISHI

68020 **Cordia, Tredia, Galant, Precis & Mirage** '83 thru '93
68030 **Eclipse, Eagle Talon & Ply. Laser** '90 thru '94
68031 **Eclipse** '95 thru '05, **Eagle Talon** '95 thru '98
68035 **Galant** '94 thru '10
68040 **Pick-up** '83 thru '96 & **Montero** '83 thru '93

NISSAN

72010 **300ZX** all models including Turbo '84 thru '89
72011 **350Z & Infiniti G35** all models '03 thru '08
72015 **Altima** all models '93 thru '06
72016 **Altima** '07 thru '10
72020 **Maxima** all models '85 thru '92
72021 **Maxima** all models '93 thru '04
72025 **Murano** '03 thru '10
72030 **Pick-ups** '80 thru '97 **Pathfinder** '87 thru '95
72031 **Frontier Pick-up, Xterra, Pathfinder** '96 thru '04
72032 **Frontier & Xterra** '05 thru '11
72040 **Pulsar** all models '83 thru '86
Quest - *see MERCURY Villager (64200)*
72050 **Sentra** all models '82 thru '94
72051 **Sentra & 200SX** all models '95 thru '06
72060 **Stanza** all models '82 thru '90
72070 **Titan pick-ups** '04 thru '10 **Armada** '05 thru '10

OLDSMOBILE

73015 **Cutlass** V6 & V8 gas models '74 thru '88
For other OLDSMOBILE titles, see BUICK, CHEVROLET or GENERAL MOTORS listing.

PLYMOUTH

For PLYMOUTH titles, see DODGE listing.

PONTIAC

79008 **Fiero** all models '84 thru '88
79018 **Firebird** V8 models except Turbo '70 thru '81
79019 **Firebird** all models '82 thru '92
79025 **G6** all models '05 thru '09
79040 **Mid-size Rear-wheel Drive** '70 thru '87
Vibe '03 thru '11 - *see TOYOTA Matrix (92060)*
For other PONTIAC titles, see BUICK, CHEVROLET or GENERAL MOTORS listing.

PORSCHE

80020 **911** except Turbo & Carrera 4 '65 thru '89
80025 **914** all 4 cyl models '69 thru '76
80030 **924** all models including Turbo '76 thru '82
80035 **944** all models including Turbo '83 thru '89

RENAULT

Alliance & Encore - *see AMC (14020)*

SAAB

84010 **900** all models including Turbo '79 thru '88

SATURN

87010 **Saturn** all S-series models '91 thru '02
87011 **Saturn Ion** '03 thru '07
87020 **Saturn** all L-series models '00 thru '04
87040 **Saturn VUE** '02 thru '07

SUBARU

89002 **1100, 1300, 1400 & 1600** '71 thru '79
89003 **1600 & 1800** 2WD & 4WD '80 thru '94
89100 **Legacy** all models '90 thru '99
89101 **Legacy & Forester** '00 thru '06

SUZUKI

90010 **Samurai/Sidekick & Geo Tracker** '86 thru '01

TOYOTA

92005 **Camry** all models '83 thru '91
92006 **Camry** all models '92 thru '96
92007 **Camry, Avalon, Solara, Lexus ES 300** '97 thru '01
92008 **Toyota Camry, Avalon and Solara and Lexus ES 300/330** all models '02 thru '06
92009 **Camry** '07 thru '11
92015 **Celica Rear Wheel Drive** '71 thru '85
92020 **Celica Front Wheel Drive** '86 thru '99
92025 **Celica Supra** all models '79 thru '92
92030 **Corolla** all models '75 thru '79
92032 **Corolla** all rear wheel drive models '80 thru '87
92035 **Corolla** all front wheel drive models '84 thru '92
92036 **Corolla & Geo Prizm** '93 thru '02
92037 **Corolla** models '03 thru '11
92040 **Corolla Tercel** all models '80 thru '82
92045 **Corona** all models '74 thru '82
92050 **Cressida** all models '78 thru '82
92055 **Land Cruiser** FJ40, 43, 45, 55 '68 thru '82
92056 **Land Cruiser** FJ60, 62, 80, FZJ80 '80 thru '96
92060 **Matrix & Pontiac Vibe** '03 thru '11
92065 **MR2** all models '85 thru '87
92070 **Pick-up** all models '69 thru '78
92075 **Pick-up** all models '79 thru '95
92076 **Tacoma, 4Runner, & T100** '93 thru '04
92077 **Tacoma** all models '05 thru '09
92078 **Tundra** '00 thru '06 & **Sequoia** '01 thru '07
92079 **4Runner** all models '03 thru '09
92080 **Previa** all models '91 thru '95
92081 **Prius** all models '01 thru '08
92082 **RAV4** all models '96 thru '10
92085 **Tercel** all models '87 thru '94
92090 **Sienna** all models '98 thru '09
92095 **Highlander & Lexus RX-330** '99 thru '07

TRIUMPH

94007 **Spitfire** all models '62 thru '81
94010 **TR7** all models '75 thru '81

VW

96008 **Beetle & Karmann Ghia** '54 thru '79
96009 **New Beetle** '98 thru '11
96016 **Rabbit, Jetta, Scirocco & Pick-up** gas models '75 thru '92 & Convertible '80 thru '92
96017 **Golf, GTI & Jetta** '93 thru '98, **Cabrio** '95 thru '02
96018 **Golf, GTI, Jetta** '99 thru '05
96019 **Jetta, Rabbit, GTI & Golf** '05 thru '11
96020 **Rabbit, Jetta & Pick-up** diesel '77 thru '84
96023 **Passat** '98 thru '05, **Audi A4** '96 thru '01
96030 **Transporter 1600** all models '68 thru '79
96035 **Transporter 1700, 1800 & 2000** '72 thru '79
96040 **Type 3 1500 & 1600** all models '63 thru '73
96045 **Vanagon** all air-cooled models '80 thru '83

VOLVO

97010 **120, 130 Series & 1800 Sports** '61 thru '73
97015 **140 Series** all models '66 thru '74
97020 **240 Series** all models '76 thru '93
97040 **740 & 760 Series** all models '82 thru '88
97050 **850 Series** all models '93 thru '97

TECHBOOK MANUALS

10205 **Automotive Computer Codes**
10206 **OBD-II & Electronic Engine Management**
10210 **Automotive Emissions Control Manual**
10215 **Fuel Injection Manual** '78 thru '85
10220 **Fuel Injection Manual** '86 thru '99
10225 **Holley Carburetor Manual**
10230 **Rochester Carburetor Manual**
10240 **Weber/Zenith/Stromberg/SU Carburetors**
10305 **Chevrolet Engine Overhaul Manual**
10310 **Chrysler Engine Overhaul Manual**
10320 **Ford Engine Overhaul Manual**
10330 **GM and Ford Diesel Engine Repair Manual**
10333 **Engine Performance Manual**
10340 **Small Engine Repair Manual,** 5 HP & Less
10341 **Small Engine Repair Manual,** 5.5 - 20 HP
10345 **Suspension, Steering & Driveline Manual**
10355 **Ford Automatic Transmission Overhaul**
10360 **GM Automatic Transmission Overhaul**
10405 **Automotive Body Repair & Painting**
10410 **Automotive Brake Manual**
10411 **Automotive Anti-lock Brake (ABS) Systems**
10415 **Automotive Detaiing Manual**
10420 **Automotive Electrical Manual**
10425 **Automotive Heating & Air Conditioning**
10430 **Automotive Reference Manual & Dictionary**
10435 **Automotive Tools Manual**
10440 **Used Car Buying Guide**
10445 **Welding Manual**
10450 **ATV Basics**
10452 **Scooters 50cc to 250cc**

SPANISH MANUALS

98903 **Reparación de Carrocería & Pintura**
98904 **Manual de Carburador Modelos Holley & Rochester**
98905 **Códigos Automotrices de la Computadora**
98906 **OBD-II & Sistemas de Control Electrónico del Motor**
98910 **Frenos Automotriz**
98913 **Electricidad Automotriz**
98915 **Inyección de Combustible** '86 al '99
99040 **Chevrolet & GMC Camionetas** '67 al '87
99041 **Chevrolet & GMC Camionetas** '88 al '98
99042 **Chevrolet & GMC Camionetas Cerradas** '68 al '95
99043 **Chevrolet/GMC Camionetas** '94 al '04
99048 **Chevrolet/GMC Camionetas** '99 al '06
99055 **Dodge Caravan & Plymouth Voyager** '84 al '95
99075 **Ford Camionetas y Bronco** '80 al '94
99076 **Ford F-150** '97 al '09
99077 **Ford Camionetas Cerradas** '69 al '91
99088 **Ford Modelos de Tamaño Mediano** '75 al '86
99089 **Ford Camionetas Ranger** '93 al '10
99091 **Ford Taurus & Mercury Sable** '86 al '95
99095 **GM Modelos de Tamaño Grande** '70 al '90
99100 **GM Modelos de Tamaño Mediano** '70 al '88
99106 **Jeep Cherokee, Wagoneer & Comanche** '84 al '00
99110 **Nissan Camioneta** '80 al '96, **Pathfinder** '87 al '95
99118 **Nissan Sentra** '82 al '94
99125 **Toyota Camionetas y 4Runner** '79 al '95

Over 100 Haynes motorcycle manuals also available

7-12